FODOR'S

SCANDINAVIA 1985

Area Editors: AKE GILLE, SVERRE HAMMER, KRISTIN HELGA, ELMER MIKKELSEN, SYLVIE NICKELS
Editorial Contributors: ANDREW BROWN, JAN CHILWELL, ANDREW HERITAGE, SUSAN PRITCHARD, MARGARET SINCLAIR, PAUL STRATHERN
Editor: THOMAS CUSSANS
Executive Editor: RICHARD MOORE
Editorial Associate: LISA MARRONGELLI
Illustrations: ELIZABETH HAINES
Maps and Plans: SWANSTON GRAPHICS, BRYAN WOODFIELD

FODOR'S TRAVEL GUIDES
New York

Copyright © 1984 by FODOR'S TRAVEL GUIDES
ISBN 0-679-01149-8
ISBN 0-340-36258-8 (Hodder & Stoughton edition)
No part of this book may be reproduced in any form without permission in writing from the publisher.

All the following Guides are current (most of them also in the Hodder and Stoughton British edition).

FODOR'S COUNTRY AND AREA TITLES:

AUSTRALIA, NEW ZEALAND AND SOUTH PACIFIC
AUSTRIA
BELGIUM AND LUXEMBOURG
BERMUDA
BRAZIL
CANADA
CANADA'S MARITIME PROVINCES
CARIBBEAN AND BAHAMAS
CENTRAL AMERICA
EASTERN EUROPE
EGYPT
EUROPE
FRANCE
GERMANY
GREAT BRITAIN
GREECE
HOLLAND
INDIA, NEPAL, AND SRI LANKA
IRELAND
ISRAEL
ITALY
JAPAN
JORDAN AND HOLY LAND
KOREA
MEXICO
NORTH AFRICA
PEOPLE'S REPUBLIC OF CHINA
PORTUGAL
SCANDINAVIA
SCOTLAND
SOUTH AMERICA
SOUTHEAST ASIA
SOVIET UNION
SPAIN
SWITZERLAND
TURKEY
YUGOSLAVIA

CITY GUIDES:

AMSTERDAM
BEIJING, GUANGZHOU, SHANGHAI
BOSTON
CHICAGO
DALLAS AND FORT WORTH
GREATER MIAMI
HONG KONG
HOUSTON
LISBON
LONDON
LOS ANGELES
MADRID
MEXICO CITY AND ACAPULCO
MUNICH
NEW ORLEANS
NEW YORK CITY
PARIS
ROME
SAN DIEGO
SAN FRANCISCO
STOCKHOLM, COPENHAGEN, OSLO, HELSINKI, AND REYKJAVIK
TOKYO
TORONTO
VIENNA
WASHINGTON, D.C.

FODOR'S BUDGET SERIES:

BUDGET BRITAIN
BUDGET CANADA
BUDGET CARIBBEAN
BUDGET EUROPE
BUDGET FRANCE
BUDGET GERMANY
BUDGET HAWAII
BUDGET ITALY
BUDGET JAPAN
BUDGET LONDON
BUDGET MEXICO
BUDGET SCANDINAVIA
BUDGET SPAIN
BUDGET TRAVEL IN AMERICA

USA GUIDES:

ALASKA
CALIFORNIA
CAPE COD
COLORADO
FAR WEST
FLORIDA
HAWAII
NEW ENGLAND
PACIFIC NORTH COAST
PENNSYLVANIA
SOUTH
TEXAS
USA (in one volume)

GOOD TIME TRAVEL GUIDES:

ACAPULCO
MONTREAL
OAHU
SAN FRANCISCO

MANUFACTURED IN THE UNITED STATES OF AMERICA
10 9 8 7 6 5 4 3 2 1

CONTENTS

FOREWORD — viii

PLANNING YOUR TRIP — 1
  Sources of Information 1; Package Tours or Independent Travel? 1; Travel Agents 2; Tour Operators 2; When to Go 3; Time 4; What to Pack 4; Taking Money Abroad 4; Passports 5; Health and Insurance 6; Student and Youth Travel 7; Hints for Handicapped Travelers 7.
  Getting to Scandinavia: From the U.S. by Air 8; From the U.S. by Boat 10; From the U.K. by Air 10; From the U.K. by Train 10; (*Chart of Ferry Routes* 11); From the U.K. by Bus 13; From the U.K. by Car 13.
  Getting Around Scandinavia: By Air 14; By Train 14; By Ferry 15; By Car 16.
  Conversion Tables 17; Customs on Returning Home 18.

AN INTRODUCTION TO SCANDINAVIA—Variety within Harmony — *Sylvie Nickels* — 20

SCANDINAVIAN HISTORY—Prosperity Out of Conflict — 30
  Map of Viking Conquests 33
  Map of Swedish Empire 37
  Map of Growth of Modern Scandinavian States 43

SCANDINAVIAN CULTURE—A Subtle Taste for Living — *Andrew Brown* — 44

FOOD AND DRINK—How to Skal and Survive — 52

DENMARK

Map of Denmark 60

FACTS AT YOUR FINGERTIPS — 61

PRELUDE TO DENMARK—The Virtues of Sanity — 68

COPENHAGEN—Scandinavia's Fun Capital — 73
  Map of Copenhagen 76–7

ZEALAND AND ITS ISLANDS—Holiday Haunts and History — 98

THE CENTRAL ISLANDS—Funen, the Garden of Denmark — 110

JUTLAND—Birds, Beaches and Runic Stones — 118

ISLE OF BORNHOLM—The Baltic Hideaway — 136

CONTENTS
FINLAND

Map of Finland 144

FACTS AT YOUR FINGERTIPS — 145

PRELUDE TO FINLAND—Scandinavia's Rich Secret — 152

HELSINKI—Broad Avenues and Bright Prospects — 157
Map of Helsinki 160–1

THE SOUTH COAST AND ISLANDS—The Gateway for Finnish Culture — 173

THE CENTRAL PROVINCES—Way of Poets and Pioneers — 181

OSTROBOTHNIA—Rural Plains and Forested Ravines — 195

FINNISH LAPLAND—Adventure Among Forest Wilds — 203

ICELAND

Map of Iceland 214

FACTS AT YOUR FINGERTIPS — 215

PRELUDE TO ICELAND—Land of Ice and Fire — 221

EXPLORING ICELAND—Volcanos, Hot Springs and Glaciers — 226
Map of Reykjavik 227

NORWAY

Map of Norway 244

FACTS AT YOUR FINGERTIPS — 245

PRELUDE TO NORWAY—Something New Under the Midnight Sun — 253

OSLO—The Countryside Capital — 258
Map of Oslo 262–3

THE OSLO FJORD DISTRICT—Vikings, Whalers and Twisting Valleys — 280

TELEMARK AND THE SOUTH COAST—A Land Fit for Heroes — 287

THE FJORD COUNTRY—Wonders and Waterfalls — 300

CENTRAL MOUNTAINS, EASTERN VALLEYS—Cradle of Liberty—Home of Giants — 318

BERGEN, CAPITAL OF WEST LAND—City of Quays and Grieg — 327

CONTENTS

ANCIENT TRONDHEIM AND DISTRICT—Stronghold of Crown and Church 339

WAY TO THE NORTH—Folklore, Finnmark and the Midnight Sun 347

SWEDEN

Map of Sweden 362

FACTS AT YOUR FINGERTIPS 363

PRELUDE TO SWEDEN—Dolls' Houses in the Wilderness 370

STOCKHOLM—Open Nature and City Planning 376
Map of Stockholm 380–1

STOCKHOLM ENVIRONS AND GOTLAND—The Capital as an Excursion Center 401

SWEDEN'S SOUTHLAND—Breadbasket, Battlefield and Summer Playground 408

GOTHENBURG AND THE WEST COAST—Gateway to Northern Europe 424

LAND OF LAKES AND FOLKLORE—Home of the Goths 435

NORRLAND AND LAPLAND—Europe's Last Wilderness 452

INDEX 465

Europe And
Don't Miss

Now you can sail the legendary QE2 to or from Europe—and fly the other way, free! That means you can begin or end your European vacation with five unforgettable days and nights on the last of the great superliners. And get a free British Airways economy-class ticket between London and most major U.S. cities.

For only $499 extra per person, you can fly a specially reserved British Airways Concorde between London and New York, Miami or Washington, D.C.

Only the QE2 offers four top restaurants and five lively nightspots. A glittering disco, a glamorous casino and a 20,000-bottle wine cellar. The famed "Golden Door Spa at Sea,"® with yoga and aerobic dance, a gym and jogging deck, saunas, swimming pools and Jacuzzi® Whirlpool Baths.

- Wide choice of crossings between England and New York, some calling on Boston, Philadelphia or Port Everglades, as well.
- Cunard's choice European tours—varying in length, attractively priced, either escorted or independent—all include a QE2 crossing.
- 20 percent discount at Cunard hotels—including London's fabulous Ritz—and at Inter-Continental Hotels throughout Europe.
- Enchanting QE2 and Vistafjord European cruises, which may be combined with a crossing.

For all the facts, including any requirements or restrictions, contact your travel agent or Cunard, Dept. F84, P.O. Box 999, Farmingdale, NY 11737; (212) 661-7777.

CUNARD

Certain restrictions apply to free airfare and Concorde programs.
All programs are subject to change. See your travel agent.

FOREWORD

Scandinavia is an unusual part of Europe. It is a small group of nations, with interdependent histories, many elements of society and background in common, and yet each fiercely proud of its own national identity; a sort of mini United Nations. It is also a region which offers perhaps the widest variety of holiday opportunities in Europe, ranging from the sophistication of such capitals as Copenhagen and Stockholm, through the calm serenity of clear, ice-blue waters, unpopulated forests and unspoiled countryside to the adventure of the far northern tracts of the Arctic Circle. All this with the genuine friendliness and hospitality of the people themselves into the bargain.

But perhaps "bargain" is not quite the right word. If Scandinavia does have a drawback as a vacation destination, it is that it is unquestionably an expensive region. This in itself can be taken as a compliment to the industriousness and consequent prosperity of the Scandinavians. Their countries are among the most affluent in the world, and living standards, and therefore of course the cost of living, are correspondingly high. Moreover, the Scandinavians all enjoy remarkably comprehensive welfare benefits, and this in turn—admirable though it is—pushes up the cost of living still further by dint of very much higher-than-average taxes on almost all services and goods.

But all need not be gloom. The particular pleasures of Scandinavia are nearly all—with the exception of her capital cities—to be found in the great outdoors. The opportunities for openair holidays—farm vacations (raised to a fine art here), riding, camping, fishing, sailing, canoeing—are absolutely second to none; and all, by their very nature, are of course essentially inexpensive. Moreover, the very industriousness that has raised Scandinavia to her present lofty place on the world's pecking order, also ensures that all these activities are excellently-organized and superbly-run.

There are other plus marks too. Scandinavia is easy to reach and easy to travel around in. The quality of hotels, even those in the depths of the country, is almost always high. For those who do want to spend time in one or more of the capital cities—and there are compelling reasons for doing so—ttherre are a whole host of travel bargains, museum entry cards and inexpensive hotel and restaurant deals. And of course, the cities themselves, as well as being among Europe's most orderly, are uniformly elegant, urbane and charming. And wherever you go in Scandinavia, there is the added bonus of knowing that English will not only be spoken—it will be spoken excellently, no small relief when you consider the tortuosities of Finnish. All in all, it's hard to think of reasons not to go.

* * * *

We are indebted once again to the Directors of the Scandinavian National Tourist Offices in London for their generous cooperation; specifically to Boris Taimitarha of the Finnish Tourist Board and to Phyllis Chapman; to Barbro Hunter of the Swedish National Tourist Office; to Bent

FOREWORD

Nielson of the Danish Tourist Board; to Knut Sjøvorr of the Norwegian Tourist Board; and to Johann Sigurdsson of the Icelandic Tourist Information Bureau.

We would especially like to acknowledge the hard work and helpful interest of our team of Area Editors, Sylvie Nickels, Elmer Mikkelsen, Ake Gille, Sverre M. Hammer and Kristin Helga, without whom this edition would not have been possible.

* * * *

All prices quoted in this guide are based on those available to us at the time of writing, mid-1984. Given the unpredictability of such inconstants like rates of inflation and exchange rates, it is inevitable that changes will have taken place by the time this book becomes available. We trust, therefore, that you will take prices quoted as indicators only, and will double-check to be sure of the latest figures.

Similarly, be sure to check all opening times of museums and galleries on the spot. We have found that such times are liable to change with no notice at all, due to staff illness, strikes, fires, Acts of God, and a hundred other reasons, and you could easily make a trip only to find a locked door.

Errors are bound to creep into any guide. When a hotel closes or a restaurant produces an inferior meal, you may question our recommendation. Let us know, and we will investigate the establishment and the complaint. We welcome your letters, which will help us pinpoint trouble spots.

Our addressess are:

In the US: Fodor's Travel Guides, 2 Park Ave., New York, N.Y. 10016.

In the UK: Fodor's Travel Guides, 9–10 Market Place, London W.1.

National Travel Club

Over 75 Years of Service To Our members

You Are Cordially Invited To Join!

Membership brings you 14 money-saving benefits and services INCLUDING a subscription to TRAVEL-HOLIDAY magazine AND $35,000 travel accident insurance coverage ($50,000 IMMEDIATELY with an initial 2-year membership) for ALL your travels ANYWHERE in the world and for the ENTIRE TERM of your membership. You enroll JUST ONCE (at incredibly low annual dues) — No monthly payments to make or bother about.

NO OTHER TRAVEL CLUB GIVES YOU SO MUCH FOR SO LITTLE

Over a HALF MILLION members consider these benefits indispensable:

- $35,000 Travel Accident Insurance ($50,000 on renewal; Immediately with initial 2-year membership
- Subscription to TRAVEL-HOLIDAY magazine
- Travel Information Service
- Book Discounts (25% savings)
- Routing Service
- Travel Digest Evaluation Program
- Avis & National Car Rental Discounts
- Mediguide Service
- Discount travel film Library
- Mail Forwarding Service
- Discount Pharmaceutical Service
- Discount Film Processing
- Car/Puter-Discount Auto Pricing & Buying Service
- Membership Card & Club Emblems

Accident insurance provided by Nationwide Insurance Company, Columbus, Ohio.

National Travel Club

Travel Building, Floral Park, N.Y. 11001

Please enroll me as a member for the term indicated:
- ☐ 1 Year **($35,000** travel accident insurance) $12.00
- ☐ 2 Years **($50,000** travel accident insurance) $23.00
- ☐ **I enclose remittance**

Charge to my ☐ Mastercard ☐ Visa
☐ Diner's ☐ American Express

Acct. # _____ Exp. Date _____

Name _____
(Signature if charging)
Address _____

City _____ State _____ Zip _____

FG-1

PLANNING YOUR TRIP

SOURCES OF INFORMATION. The major sources of information for anyone planning a vacation in Scandinavia are the National Tourist Offices of the five Scandinavian countries. They will be able to supply information on all aspects of travel to and around Scandinavia—from which type of vacation is best suited to your needs and purse to the best and most economical ways of getting to Scandinavia, as well as information on hotels, restaurants, excursions, museums, travel discounts and so on. They produce copious amounts of information, much of it free and all of it useful. Anyone planning a vacation in Scandinavia would be well advised to make the National Tourist Offices their starting point.

In the U.S., all five Scandinavian countries operate from one principal office in New York, though the Danish Tourist Board also have an office in San Francisco. In the U.K., each country has its own office.

Their addresses are:

In the U.S.: *Scandinavian National Tourist Office,* 75 Rockefeller Plaza, New York, N.Y. 10019 (212–582 2802).

Danish Tourist Board, 8929 Wilshire Blvd., Beverly Hills, CA 90211 (213–854 1549).

In the U.K: *Danish Tourist Board,* 169–173 Regent St., London W.1 (01–734 2637). *Finnish Tourist Board,* 66–68 Haymarket, London S.W.1 (01–839 4048). *Iceland Tourist Information Bureau,* 73 Grosvenor St., London W.1 (01–499 9971). *Norwegian Tourist Board,* 20 Pall Mall, London S.W.1 (01–839 6255). *Swedish National Tourist Office,* 3 Cork St., London W.1 (01–437 5816).

In addition, within Scandinavia each country has a network of highly efficient local tourist offices (some open summer only) which can supply specific information on where to stay and eat, what's on and where, local travel discounts and sightseeing trips. We give addresses and telephone numbers of all the major local offices at the beginning of every *Practical Information* section.

PACKAGE TOURS OR INDEPENDENT TRAVEL? The best and most economical way to visit Scandinavia, especially from the States and Canada, is on a package tour. The number and variety of these is immense and most offer excellent value for money. The principal advantage of any package tour is that the two single most expensive components of any vacation—getting there and accommodations—will generally be very competitively priced and will be arranged for you.

At the same time, most packages offer considerable flexibility. You can, for example, buy an all-inclusive, pre-paid package, which gives you flight, accommodations, meals and excursions—all at a fixed price—leaving only incidental expenditure (drinks, shopping, mail etc.) for you to pay for during your trip. For those making a first visit and unsure of where to visit or how to get around, this is frequently an excellent introduction to a country. Many, however, might find this type of trip too stifling or regimented. There is also the drawback that you might find your fellow packagees—from whom there is no escape—dull, though of course at the same time you might get on fine.

Alternatively, therefore, there are packages which give you flight and accommodations only, with optional pre-paid meals and excursions. To a large extent, this sort of semi-independent package gives you the best of both worlds. Accordingly, it tends to be the most popular.

Other options available include fly-drive, which is particularly suitable for those who want the maximum independence, though here costs tend to be steeper, or a rail-air combination. Similarly, special interest packages, again offering varying degrees of flexibility and independence, are also available. Popular themes include sailing, bird-watching, castle touring, painting, photography, art tours, gourmet tours, sporting activities of all kinds, farm vacations, and much else besides.

However, if you do plump for a package, be very sure to find out in advance exactly what is included in the price and how much you will have to pay for once in Scandinavia. For example, how many meals are included? How tied to the tour are you? If it is a bus tour, do you have to stay with the tour city by city or can you leave and rejoin it at will? If you have a car, is the rate included in the package or is there an additional fee per mile? Is the car exactly what you want? Airconditioning is certainly unnecessary at any time of year in Scandinavia, and there is a substantial difference between the charge for standard and automatic shifts. Can you drive a standard? What is the tour operator's responsibility for getting you home on time?

In other words, be absolutely certain you know what you are paying for, *and read the fine print very carefully.*

Independent travel, on the other hand, has the great advantage of allowing you to do precisely as you please, but it also has the drawback of almost always being more expensive than a comparable package tour. That is not to say it can't be better value for money. For instance, while dinner and meals on a package tour may generally be very inexpensive, this is normally because the tour operator has struck a cut-price rate with your hotel or restaurant. Accordingly, you will tend to get cut-price food and service, while anyone traveling on their own will almost certainly get both better food and better service. Is this better value for money? Possibly, but individual preference is clearly the dominant factor in choosing any vacation and it is up to you to decide.

TRAVEL AGENTS. Regardless of whether you plan to visit Scandinavia independently or take a package, it is advisable to consult a reputable travel agent. If you are only after an inexpensive flight, at the very least he will be able to guide you through the impenetrable maze of trans-Atlantic air fares. But if you want to buy a complete package, or even have an entire itinerary devised (which will prove expensive) he will be able to recommend the most appropriate for your particular needs. He will also be able to arrange insurance and passports. A good travel agent can save you time, money and a good deal of inconvenience, and is an invaluable extra source of information.

If you are in any doubt which agent to contact, consult the American Society of Travel Agents, 711 Fifth Ave., New York, N.Y. 10022, or the British Association of Travel Agents, 53 Newman St., London W.1. Both will point you in the right direction.

TOUR OPERATORS. Full details of the many operators offering trips to Scandinavia are available from the Scandinavia National Tourist Office, Scandinavian airlines (SAS) and of course your travel agent. But such is the range of tours and vacations on offer from both North America and the U.K., that a summary of some of the more typical should provide you with a handy pointer to availability. Bear in mind, however, that the few we list here are only the tip of the iceberg and that many, many more are available. All details quoted below are for 1984 only—check latest information with your travel agent.

From the U.S.: A package offering you both considerable independence and covering the extremes of budget and deluxe living is *Bennett's* "Wonderful Copenhagen," a one-week fly-drive vacation that includes air fare, car rental and hotel accommodations in the basic price. This, however, can vary considerably. Car rentals, for example, can run from $95 to $550, and there is a similar range in hotel prices. For those who want maximum independence, this package is also available without hotel accommodations, allowing you to book your own hotels as you go. *Bennett* also run a 15-day "Scandinavian Vikinglands" tour taking in Oslo, Stockholm and Copenhagen and including a short fjord cruise. Accommodations are all in first-class hotels and cost is about $950 per person excluding airfare.

PLANNING YOUR TRIP

A similar 15-day tour is *Four Winds'* "Scandinavian Highlights," a bus tour that also takes in two overnight cruises and a scenic mountain rail trip from Oslo to Flåm. Accommodations are all first-class and cost is around $1,500 per person excluding air fare. For those in search of more rugged landscapes but who don't want to have to sacrifice creature comforts, *Four Winds* also have a 21-day "Iceland and North Cape" tour. Five days are spent in Iceland and the Oslo–Flåm rail trip is also included. Cost is around $2,700. Another excellent introduction to the high latitudes of Scandinavia, especially for those with salt in their veins, is *Linblad's* 15-day North Cape cruise; cost varies from $1,200 to $2,300 depending on your class of cabin. There is also an optional eight-day land excursion for an additional $850.

From the U.K: One of the major operators offering holidays in Scandinavia is *Longship Holidays,* who have a wide range of vacations in Sweden, Norway and Finland. These cover the entire spectrum, from camping in Lappland to cruising round the Norwegian fjords. The emphasis is generally on the great outdoors and on family holidays, with cabin and farm vacations high on their list. The *Norwegian State Railways Travel Bureau* offer an equally impressive range of vacations in the four main Scandinavian countries, though the bulk of their tours are Norwegian based. Unlike Longship, however, they also have city tours, of varying lengths, most in deluxe or first-class hotels. Those after a little more in the way of culture could do worse than head in the direction of *Heritage Travel,* who for £405 inclusive offer a five-day escorted tour in and around Copenhagen taking in all the major museums and sites and staying in first-class hotels.

Finally, for vacations in Iceland, contact *Icelandair* who are able to supply information on camping, fishing, fly-drive, city and safari vacations in Scandinavia's Atlantic outpost.

WHEN TO GO. By far and away the best time to visit any of the Scandinavian countries is in the summer. The Scandinavian winter is not only very long and very cold, with shorter and shorter days the further north you go (and correspondingly lower and lower temperatures), but almost all the major tourist facilities—museums, sightseeing excursions, ferries, even many museums—are scaled right down or in some cases, the Tivoli Gardens in Copenhagen, for example, closed completely. More to the point, however, is the fact that most of the real fun is to be had in Scandinavia takes place outdoors, and with the exception of winter sports, of which more in a moment, there is very little you are liable to want to do, or will even be able to do, outside during the Scandinavian winter. That said, however, clear, crisp and sunny days are by no means uncommon in the winter, and though short they can be delightful.

Nonetheless, it is from mid-May to mid-September that Scandinavia is at its best. Summer temperatures are surprisingly high—certainly comparable to Maine or Vermont, for example—while the sea is generally much warmer than you might expect, largely as a result of the Gulf Stream and the shallowness of the Baltic. At the same time, however, prices are also at their highest during the peak summer period. You may accordingly consider visiting in April or late September, but bear in mind that the weather can be unpredictable.

For devotees of the midnight sun, Norway, Sweden and Finland are the countries to visit. Both Iceland and Denmark are to the south of the Arctic Circle—in the case of Iceland only just—so in neither country is there any time when the sun never sets, though in the height of summer there is always a certain luminosity in the night sky, even at midnight. But in the far north of Scandinavia —Norway's North Cape or Utsjoki in Finland for example—the sun does not sink below the horizon from the second week in May until the last week in July. (At the same time of course, during the corresponding period in the winter, the sun never rises.)

The winter sports season lasts from mid-December to mid-April, though neither Denmark, principally as a result of its almost total absence of mountains, or Iceland, warmed by the Gulf Stream, can offer much in the way of winter sports. Both Sweden and Finland have well developed winter resorts, offering cross-country skiing, skating and curling, though little in the way of Alpine, or

SCANDINAVIA

downhill, skiing. Norway, while it has equally good facilities for all forms of Nordic skiing, also has some good downhill skiing. Winter sports facilities are now generally good throughout these three countries, but bear in mind that the winter weather here is not always equally accommodating.

TIME. Iceland operates on Greenwich Mean Time, which is five hours ahead of Eastern Standard Time, while Denmark, Norway and Sweden are all one hour ahead of Greenwich Mean Time and six hours ahead of Eastern Standard Time. Finland is two hours ahead of Greenwich Mean Time and seven hours ahead of Eastern Standard Time.

WHAT TO PACK. The golden rule is to travel light; generally, try not to take more than you can carry yourself. Not only are porters more or less wholly extinct in Europe these days (where you can find them they're very expensive anyway), the less luggage you take the easier checking in and out of hotels becomes, similarly airports (increasingly the number one nightmare of all modern travel) become much easier to get through and, if you only take one piece of luggage, the less risk there is of your luggage being lost en route, and, in theory anyway, the less time you need to wait for it to appear when you get off the plane. It's an excellent idea also to make sure that your luggage is sturdy; there's no worse way to start or finish your vacation than by discovering that your clothes are generously distributing themselves along a station platform or, even worse, have already scattered themselves around the hold of a 747. It can also be a good idea to pack the bulk of your things in one large bag and put everything you need for overnight, or for two or three nights, in a smaller one, to obviate packing and repacking at brief stops.

Bear in mind that on trans-Atlantic flights there is, in any case, a size limit to the amount of luggage you may take with you. Charges for excess baggage are high. On most flights you may check in no more than two pieces of luggage, neither more than 62 inches overall (that is, height plus length plus width) and both together no more than 106 inches. Hand baggage is restricted to one piece no more than 65 inches overall.

Having said all this, however, don't forget to leave room for shopping. Though at the same time remember that almost all Scandinavian stores can have goods sent directly to your home.

Clothes. Informality is the key word throughout Scandinavia, even in relatively more upright and old fashioned Norway. So at even the smartest restaurants or at the theater—and this applies to the opera and ballet as well—you are not likely to have to dress up. Those few restaurants that do expect men to wear a tie will always lend you one if necessary. Thus normal summer clothes, with a generous sprinkling of sports clothes, will happily suffice, but also take along sweaters and stout shoes if you are going into the mountains. And don't forget a light topcoat or raincoat. The summer weather is generally fine, but rain is by no means uncommon. If you are going to Scandinavia in the winter, it will be very cold, so take along plenty of warm clothing. Be prepared to shed it once indoors, however; Scandinavian central heating is nothing if not efficient.

Finally, mosquitoes, especially in the far north, can be a real nuisance from the end of June to early August. Take some repellent with you.

TAKING MONEY ABROAD. Traveler's checks are still the standard and best way to safeguard your travel funds; and you will usually get a better exchange rate in Europe for traveler's checks than for cash. In the U.S., Bank of America, First National City Bank and Republic Bank of Dallas issue checks only in U.S. dollars; Thomas Cook issues checks in U.S., British and Australian currencies; Barclays Bank in dollars and pounds; and American Express in U.S., Canadian, French, German, British, Swiss and Japanese currencies. Your choice of branch will depend on several factors. American Express checks are widely known, Bank of America has some 28,000 correspondents

PLANNING YOUR TRIP

throughout the world, Thomas Cook about 20,000. The best-known British checks are Cook's and those of Barclays, Lloyds, Midland and National Westminster banks.

Britons holding a Eurocheque Encashment card can cash checks in Europe for up to £75 a day at any bank participating in the Eurocheque scheme. Ordinary British cheque cards, which before 1983 automatically allowed the holder to cash cheques in Europe, are no longer valid.

Details of currency within each Scandinavian country, changing money and exchange rates are given at the beginning of the *Facts at Your Fingertips* for each country later in this guide.

Credit Cards. Most major credit cards are generally, but by no means universally, accepted in larger Scandinavian hotels, restaurants and shops. Accordingly, you would be well advised to check carefully which cards *are* accepted, particularly in hotels and restaurants, before checking in or ordering a meal.

Our hotel and restaurant listings in the *Practical Information* sections at the end of every chapter give details of each of the four major cards—American Express, Diner's Club, MasterCard (incorporating Access and EuroCard) and Visa, which are listed under the abbreviations AE, DC, MC and V—accepted in each hotel and restaurant we carry. But as we say, double check. As a general rule, you will find that Visa is the most commonly accepted.

PASSPORTS. Americans. All U.S. citizens require a valid passport to enter any Scandinavian country. Visas are not required. If you do not have a passport, apply in person at U.S. Passport Agency Offices, local county courthouses or selected Post Offices. If you have a passport not more than eight years old you may apply by mail; otherwise you will need:

—Proof of citizenship, such as a birth certificate.

—Two identical photographs, in either black and white or color, on non-glossy paper and taken within the past six months.

—$35 for the passport itself plus a $7 processing fee if you are applying in person (no processing fee when applying by mail) for those 18 years and older, or if you are under 18, $20 for the passport plus a $7 processing fee if you are applying in person (again, no extra fee when applying by mail).

—Proof of identity such as a driver's license, previous passport, any governmental ID card, or a copy of an income tax return.

Adult passports are valid for 10 years, others for five years; they are not renewable. Allow four to six weeks for your application to be processed, but in an emergency, Passport Agency offices can have a passport readied within 24–48 hours, and even the postal authorities can indicate "Rush" when necessary.

If you expect to travel extensively, request a 48- or 96-page passport rather than the usual 24-page one. There is no extra charge. When you receive your passport, write down its number, date and place of issue separately; if it is later lost or stolen, notify either the nearest American Consul or the Passport Office, Department of State, Washington DC 20524, as well as the local police.

Canadians. Canadian citizens should apply in person at regional passport offices and Post Offices, or by mail to Passport Office, 200 DuPortage, 6th. Floor, Place du Center, Hull, Quebec K1A 0G3. A $20 fee, two photographs and evidence of citizenship are required. Canadian passports are valid for five years and are non-renewable.

Britons. You should apply for passports on special forms obtainable from main post offices or a travel agent. The application should be sent or taken to the Passport Office according to residential area (as indicated on the guidance form) or lodged with them through a travel agent. It is best to apply for the passport 4–5 weeks before it is required, although in some cases it will be issued sooner. The regional Passport Offices are located in London, Liverpool, Peterborough, Glasgow and Newport. The application must be countersigned by your bank manager or by a solicitor, barrister, doctor, clergyman or justice of the peace who knows you personally. You will need two full-face photos. The fee is £15; passport valid for 10 years.

British Visitor's Passport. This simplified form of passport has advantages for the once-in-a-while tourist to most European countries, including Scandinavia.

SCANDINAVIA

Valid for one year and not renewable, it costs £7.50. Application may be made at main post offices in England, Scotland and Wales, and in Northern Ireland at the Passport Office in Belfast. Birth certificate or medical card for identification and two passport photographs are required—no other formalities.

HEALTH AND INSURANCE. The different varieties of travel insurance cover everything from health and accident costs, to lost baggage and trip cancelation. Sometimes they can all be obtained with one blanket policy; other times they overlap with existing coverage you might have for health and/or home; still other times it is best to buy policies that are tailored to very specific needs. Insurance is available from many sources, however, and many travelers unwittingly end up with redundant coverage. Before purchasing separate travel insurance of any kind, be sure to check your regular policies carefully.

Generally, it is best to take care of your insurance needs before embarking on your trip. You'll pay more for less coverage—and have less chance to read the fine print—if you wait until the last minute and make your purchases from, say, an airport vending machine or insurance company counter. If you have a regular insurance agent, he or she is the person to consult first.

Flight insurance, which is often included in the price of the ticket when the fare is paid via American Express, Visa or certain other major credit cards, is also often included in package policies providing accident coverage as well. These policies are available from most tour operators and insurance companies. But while it is a good idea to have health and accident insurance when traveling, be careful not to spend money to duplicate coverage you may already have ... or to neglect some eventuality which could end up costing a small fortune.

For example, basic Blue Cross-Blue Shield policies do cover health costs incurred while traveling. They will not, however, cover the cost of emergency transportation, which can often add up to several thousand dollars. Emergency transportation *is* covered, in part at least, by many major medical policies such as those underwritten by Prudential, Metropolitan and New York Life. Again, we can't urge you too strongly that in order to be sure you are getting the coverage you need, check any policy carefully before buying. And bear in mind also that most insurance issued specifically for travel will not cover pre-existing conditions, such as a heart condition.

Several organizations offer coverage designed to supplement existing health insurance and to help defray costs not covered by many standard policies, such as emergency transportation. Some of the more prominent are:

NEAR, (Nationwide Emergency Ambulance Return). Rates range from $70 a person for 1–8 days, to $360 for a year (800–654 6700).

Carefree Travel Insurance, c/o ARM Coverage Inc., 9 East 37th. St., New York, N.Y. 10016, offers medical evacuation throughout Europe arranged by Assistance of Paris (212–683 2622). Carefree coverage is available from many travel agents.

International SOS Assistance Inc. has fees from $14 a person for seven days, to $175 for a year (800–523 8930).

IAMAT (International Association for Medical Assistance to Travelers), 736 Center St., Lewiston, N.Y. 14092 (716–754 4883) in the U.S.; or 123 Edward St., Suite 275, Toronto, Ontario MSGIE2 in Canada.

Europ Assistance Ltd. offers unlimited help to its members. There are two plans: one for travelers using tours or making their own trip arrangements, the second for motorists taking their cars abroad. Multilingual personnel staff a 24-hour, 7-days-a-week telephone service which brings the aid of a network of medical and other advisors to assist in any emergency. Special medical insurance is part of the plan. Write to Europ Assistance Ltd., 252 High St., Croydon, Surrey CRO INF, for details. The scheme is only available to residents of Britain. Highly recommended.

The British Insurance Association, Aldermary House, Queen St., London E.C.4 (01–248 4477), will give comprehensive advice on all aspects of vacation travel insurance from the U.K.

Another frequent inconvenience to travelers is the loss of baggage. It is possible, though often a complicated affair, to insure your luggage against loss

PLANNING YOUR TRIP

through theft or negligence. Insurance companies are reluctant to sell such coverage alone, however, since it is often a losing proposition for them. Instead, this type of coverage is usually included as part of a package that also covers accidents or health. Should you lose your luggage or some other personal possession, it is essential to report it to the local police immediately. Without documentation of such a report, your insurance company might be very stingy. Also, before buying baggage insurance, check your homeowner's policy. Some such policies offer "off-premises theft" coverage, including the loss of luggage while traveling.

Trip cancellation coverage is especially important to travelers on APEX or charter flights. Should you be unable to continue your trip during your vacation, you may be stuck having to buy a new one-way fare home, plus paying for the charter you're not using. You can guard against this with "trip cancellation insurance." Most of these policies will also cover last minute cancellations.

STUDENT AND YOUTH TRAVEL. All student travelers should obtain an *International Student Identity Card*, which is generally needed to get student discounts, youth rail passes, and Intra-European Student Charter Flights. Apply to *Council On International Educational Exchange*, 205 East 42 St., New York, N.Y. 10017 (212–661 1414); or 312 Sutter St., San Francisco, CA 94108. Canadian students should apply to the *Association of Student Councils*, 44 St. George St., Toronto, Ontario M5S QE4 (416–979 2604).

The following organizations can also be helpful in finding student flights, educational opportunities and other information. Most deal with international student travel generally, but those listed cover Scandinavia.

American Youth Hostels, 1332 I St. NW, Washington DC 20005 (202–783 6161). Members are eligible to use the worldwide network of youth hostels. The organization publishes an extensive directory on same.

Council on International Educational Exchange (CIEE), 205 East 42 St., New York, N.Y. 10017 (212–661 1414); and 312 Sutter St., San Francisco, CA 94108, provides information on summer study, work/travel programs and travel services for college and high school students, and a free Charter Flights Guide booklet. Their *Whole World Handbook* ($6.95 plus $1 postage) is the best listing of both work and study possibilities.

Institute of International Education, 809 United Nations Plaza, New York, N.Y. 10017 (212–883 8200) is primarily concerned with study opportunities and administers scholarships and fellowships for international study and training. The New York office has a counseling service and library; satellite offices are located in Chicago, Denver, Houston, San Francisco and Washington. They also produce *Vacation Study Abroad*, an annually-revised guide to over 900 courses offered by both foreign and American colleges and universities, and *U.S. College-Sponsored Programs Abroad*, which gives details on foreign study programs run by American schools and for academic credit. These publications are $9.95 each, including first class postage and handling.

Also worth contacting is *Educational Travel Center*, 438 North Frances, Madison, WI 53703 (608–256 5551).

Specific information on rail and other discounts is listed in the *Facts at Your Fingertips* sections for each Scandinavian country.

HINTS FOR HANDICAPPED TRAVELERS. Facilities for the handicapped in Scandinavia are generally good, if somewhat variable. Most of the major tourist offices produce information detailing facilities. The Danish Tourist Board have an *Access in Denmark—A Tourist Guide for the Disabled* booklet; alternatively, write *Bolig-, Motor- og Hjaelpemiddeludvalget* (Committee for Housing, Transportation and Technical Aids), Hans Knudsens Plads 1A, DK-1200 Copenhagen. The Norwegian Tourist Board produce a *Travel Guide for the Disabled*, available only from the Tourist Board in Oslo (H Heyerdahlsgate 1, Oslo 1, Norway), and a leaflet detailing all hotels with facilities for handicapped visitors.

SCANDINAVIA

In Sweden, the Tourist Board plan to publish a brand new guide for 1985 giving comprehensive information on all aspects of travel for the disabled. The Finnish Tourist Board, however, produce no specific information for the handicapped, though their *Finland Handbook* gives details of those hotels with facilities for the handicapped.

Otherwise, the major sources of information are: *Access to the World: A Travel Guide for the Handicapped,* by Louise Weiss, an outstanding book covering all aspects of travel for anyone with health or medical problems; it features extensive listings and suggestions on everything from availability of special diets to wheelchair accessibility. Order from *Facts On File,* 460 Park Ave. South, New York, N.Y. 10003 ($14.95). *Rehabilitation International U.S.A.,* 1123 Broadway, New York, N.Y. 11242, publish an *International Directory of Access Guides,* a listing of publications describing access facilities in specific countries and cities. The *Moss Rehabilitation Hospital,* 12th St. and Tabor Rd., Philadelphia, PA 19141, gives information on facilities for the handicapped in many countries and also provides toll-free numbers of airlines with special lines for the hearing impaired; they can also provide listings of tour operators who arrange vacations for the handicapped. But for a complete list of tour operators, write to the *Society for the Advancement of Travel for the Handicapped,* 26 Court St., Brooklyn, N.Y. 11242.

In the U.K., contact *Mobility International,* 43 Dorset St., London W.1; the *National Society for Mentally Handicapped Children,* 117 Golden Lane, London E.C.1; the *Across Trust,* Crown House, Morden, Surrey (they have an amazing series of "Jumbulances," huge articulated ambulances, staffed by volunteer doctors and nurses, that can whisk even the most seriously handicapped across Europe in comfort and safety). But the main source in Britain for all advice on handicapped travel is *The Royal Association for Disability and Rehabilitation,* (RADAR), 25 Mortimer St., London W.1.

GETTING TO SCANDINAVIA FROM THE U.S. By air. Flights from major departure points in the U.S. and Canada to the Scandinavian capitals, and some other major Scandinavian cities, are frequent and generally easy to arrange. And, given the perpetual battle for customers among airlines flying the Atlantic, even to relatively less important destinations such as Scandinavia, fares are generally inexpensive. We give details of sample fares and of the principal carriers operating from North America to Scandinavia below.

However, be warned that though fares may be low and flights numerous, long-distance flying today is no bed of roses. Lines and delays at ever-more-crowded airports, perfunctory in-flight service and shrinking leg-room on board a giant jet with some 400 other people, followed by interminable waits for your luggage when you arrive, are the clearest possible signals that the glamor of air travel—if it ever existed—is very much a thing of the past.

Unfortunately, these problems are compounded when flying to Europe by the fact that most flights from the States are scheduled to arrive first thing in the morning. Not only are you in for a night's discomfort on the plane, but you arrive at the start of a new day to be greeted by the confusion (some would say chaos) of a modern airport. To make life even more difficult for the weary traveler, many hotels will not allow you to check in before noon or even 1 P.M. giving you as much as six hours with nothing to do and nowhere to go.

There are a number of steps you can take, however, in order to lessen the traumas of long-distance flying. The first and possibly most important of all is to harbor no illusions about the supposed luxury. If you approach your flight knowing that you are going to be cooped up for a long time and will have to face delays and discomforts of all kinds, the odds are that you will get through it without doing terrible things to your blood pressure or being disillusioned—but there's no point expecting comfort, good service and efficiency because you won't get them.

The right attitude is half the battle, but there are a number of other practical points to follow. Wear comfortable, loose-fitting clothes and take off your shoes. Try to sleep as much as possible, especially on night flights; this can very often mean not watching the movie (they are invariably dull anyway) as it will

PLANNING YOUR TRIP

probably be shown during the only period when meals are not being served and you can sleep. If you have difficulty sleeping, or think you might, take along a light sedative and try to get a window seat in order to avoid being woken up to let the person next to you get to the toilet or being bashed by people walking down the aisle. Above all, avoid alcohol, or at least drink only a little. The dry air of a pressurized airplane causes rapid dehydration, exaggerating the effects of drink and jet lag. Similarly, drink as much water as possible. Finally, once you arrive, try to take things easily for a day or so. In the excitement of being in a new place, especially for the first time, you can very often not realize how tired you are and optimistically set out sightseeing, only to come down to earth with a bump. Whatever you do, don't have any business meetings for at least 24 hours after arriving.

Fares. With air fares in a constant state of flux, the best advice for anyone planning to fly to Scandinavia independently (rather than as part of a package tour, in which case your flight will have been arranged for you) is to check with a travel agent and let him make your reservations for you. Nonetheless, there are a number of points to bear in mind.

The best bet is to buy either an Apex or Super Apex ticket. First Class, Business and even the misleadingly-named Economy, though giving maximum flexibility on flying dates and cancellations, as well as permitting stop overs, are extremely expensive. Apex and Super Apex, by contrast, are reasonably priced and offer the all-important security of fixed return dates (all Apex tickets are round trip). In addition, you get exactly the same service as flying Economy. However, there are a number of restrictions: you must book, and pay for, your ticket 21 days or more in advance; you can stay in Scandinavia no less than and no longer than a stated period (usually six days and six months); if you miss your flight, you forfeit the fare. But from the point of view of price and convenience, these tickets certainly represent the best value for money.

If your plans are sufficiently flexible and tighter budgeting is important, you can sometimes benefit from the last-minute bargains offered by tour operators otherwise unable to fill their plane or quota of seats. A number of brokers specializing in these discount sales have sprung up who can book seats of this type. All charge an annual membership fee, usually around $35–45.

Among them are: *Stand-Buys Ltd.,* P.O. Box 10291, Chicago, IL 60610 (800–621 5839; in Illinois call 800–972 5858); *Moments Notice,* 40 East 49th St., New York, N.Y. 10017 (212–486 0503); *Discount Travel Intl.,* 7563 Haverford Ave., Philadelphia, PA 19151 (215–878 8282); and *Worldwide Discount Travel Club,* 1674 Meridian Ave., Miami Beach, FL 33139 (305–895 2082).

Charter flights are also available to Scandinavia, though their number has decreased in recent years. Again, a travel agent will be able to recommend the most reliable. You might also consider, though this too should be done via a travel agent, buying a package tour to Scandinavia but using only the plane ticket. As packagers are able to get substantial discounts on fares through block booking seats, the price of the total package can sometimes be less than an ordinary air fare alone.

Typical fares as of mid-1984 for New York to Copenhagen were: $1,700 First Class, one way (year round); $703 Business Class, one way (year round); $395 to $900 Apex or Super Apex, roundtrip (fares varying according to season); Charter fares are about the same, or possible slightly lower than Apex.

Please note that these fares will certainly change either before or during 1985.

The principal airlines serving Scandinavia from the U.S. (generally flying via New York) are:

SAS, 138–02 Queens Blvd., Jamaica, N.Y. 11435 (212–657 2575). *Finnair,* 580 Fifth Ave., New York, N.Y. 10036 (212–689 9300). *Icelandair,* 630 Fifth Ave., New York, N.Y. 10111 (212–572 9300). *Northwest Orient,* International Airport, Minneapolis/St. Paul, MN 55111 (612–726 2111). *Air Florida,* P.O. Box 592337, AMF, Miami, FL 33159 (800–327 2971). (Operates out of Miami Airport, FL).

From Canada, *Air Canada,* Place Air Canada, Montreal, Quebec H2Z 1X5 (514–879 7000) operate regular flights out of Toronto and Montreal to Copenhagen.

SCANDINAVIA

GETTING TO SCANDINAVIA FROM THE U.S. By boat. There are very few direct sailings from either the U.S. or Canada to Scandinavia on passenger or cruise ships, though *Royal Viking,* One Embarcadero Center, San Francisco, CA 94111, do have a handful of sailings from New York scheduled for 1985. Prices, however, are high. Sailing time is around five or six days.

Alternatively, some freighter lines have a limited number of cabins for paying passengers to Scandinavia, though you may find you will have to up wait for up to a year for a berth. However, for details, contact one of the following agents: *Air Marine Travel Service,* 501 Madison Ave., New York, N.Y. 10022, publisher of the *Trip Log Quick Reference Freighter Guide;* or *Pearl's Freighter Tips,* 175 Great Neck Rd., Great Neck, N.Y. 11021.

GETTING TO SCANDINAVIA FROM THE U.K. By air. All the Scandinavian capitals are well served by regular flights from the U.K., principally from London's Heathrow and Gatwick airports, but there are also flights from a limited number of other U.K. airports. The greatest frequency of flights is to Copenhagen—some seven daily—but there are at least four flights a day to both Oslo and Stockholm. Helsinki has only two flights daily, while Reykjavik has only one flight daily, though *Finnair* also operate flights from Glasgow three times a week with connections from London. *British Airways* and *SAS* are the principal carriers to all other Scandinavian destinations.

Fares. European air fares are high, disproportionately so in many cases, and unfortunately flights to Scandinavia are no exception. The cheapest Scandinavian destination is Oslo, with Super Apex fares starting at about £125; Apex fares to Copenhagen and Stockholm start at around £130, while to Helsinki and Reykjavik Super Apex starts at around £200. All these fares, however, are the cheapest on offer from the scheduled carriers and you may in any case find that by summer 1985 some or all of them will have increased.

Accordingly, it is well worth searching out the bucket shop ads in the Sunday papers and magazines such as *Time Out* and *Business Traveler* (the latter an excellent source of information on budget fares). Bucket shops—some more reliable than others, so don't hand over all your money until you have the ticket—offer tickets at rates significantly below the so-called official ones, and can often prove very good value. But they do often operate at rather short notice and so may not be suitable for anyone hoping to book their flight some time in advance.

GETTING TO SCANDINAVIA FROM THE U.K. By train. If you are in a hurry, go by air! The Scandinavian countries, with the exception of Denmark, are relatively isolated from the U.K. and the rail/ferry trek can occupy up to two full days. Approximate journey times from London are: Copenhagen 24 hours, Stockholm 30 hours, Oslo 34 hours, Helsinki 46 hours.

This having been said, getting to Scandinavia by train and ferry is great fun! The classic route is from London (Liverpool Street) to Harwich by rail, then by ferry to the Hook of Holland. From the Hook of Holland you go by train on to Hamburg, then by way of the Vogelfluglinie and the Puttgarden to the Rødby train ferry to the Danish capital, Copenhagen. From Copenhagen the routes fan out to the other Nordic countries.

You can travel on to Helsingør for the train ferry to Helsingborg in Sweden and then on to Stockholm. From Helsingborg you can also go direct by train to Oslo, though the Norwegian capital can also be reached direct by ferry from Copenhagen. From Stockholm there are ferry services to Helsinki. Incidentally, it is possible to travel by train from Stockholm to Helsinki—but more of this mini-marathon later!

To Denmark. The "Nord West Express" is a useful service, with a morning departure (day 1) from London, giving a daytime crossing of the North Sea to Holland. The main train leaves the Hook in the early evening (5 P.M.) and then runs overnight to arrive in Copenhagen just after 8 the following morning (day 2). Second-class couchettes are available from the Hook to Copenhagen and

PLANNING YOUR TRIP

FERRY SERVICES SUITABLE FOR TRAVEL TO SCANDINAVIA FROM BRITAIN

	Services operate	Sailings per week	D.F.D.S.	SEALINK	SEALINK JETFOIL	FRED OLSEN	OLAU
NEWCASTLE							
—ESBJERG	Jun-Sep	2	●				
—BERGEN	May-Sep	2	●				
—GOTHENBURG	May-Sep	2	●				
HARWICH							
—ESBJERG	All Year	Daily	◆				
—HAMBURG	=	3-4	◆				
—HOOK OF HOLLAND	=	Daily		◆			
—GOTHENBURG	=	2-3	●				
—KRISTIANSAND	Jun-Aug	1				◆	
SHEERNESS							
—VLISSINGEN	All Year	Daily					●
DOVER							
—OSTEND	All Year	Daily		◆	◆		

Note: It is essential to check the dates of Operation of each service.
● Recommended for Rail travellers – easy rail/ship interchange.
◆ Through trains for Copenhagen operate from Ostend and the Hook of Holland. (Reservation is essential.)

● Only really suitable for car-borne travellers. Several of the Operators provide bus services between the local railway stations and the port terminal buildings. They are only suitable for passengers with light luggage.

12 SCANDINAVIA

there are also ordinary seats. Alternatively use the "Holland-Scandinavia Express." This departs from London (Liverpool Street) in the evening (7.40) and the North Sea crossing is made overnight. Departure from the Hook is at 7.10 A.M. on day 2 and Copenhagen is reached at 7.30 P.M. The great advantage of this service is that it gives you a more comfortable overnight crossing on the ferry. You also travel over the beautiful Vogelgluglinie with its spectacular Fehmarn bridge and enjoy the Puttgarden to Rødby crossing all in daylight. One note: at Puttgarden the whole train goes on board the ship so there's no need to change.

There are also other rail routes to Copenhagen involving much shorter train journeys if you don't like the idea of the long overland haul. *DFDS* ferries for example operate from Harwich and Newcastle to Esbjerg in Jutland (See ferry chart). (There are connecting rail services from London to Harwich and from Esbjerg to Copenhagen by the aptly named "Englanderen"). On this route, by leaving London in the early afternoon of day 1 you will be in Copenhagen at 7.15 P.M. the following day.

Alternatively, if you wish to minimize the sea crossing make use of the Jetfoil service *(Sealink)* from Dover to Oostende and there join the "Nord Express" for the overnight run to Copenhagen. This train has the advantage of having first- and second-class sleeping cars as well as couchettes. Reservation is obligatory on this service.

To Sweden. For travel to Sweden read the section on getting to Denmark; this explains the initial part of the journey. The "Nord-West Express" during the summer has through carriages from the Hook of Holland to Stockholm and this makes things very simple! The train re-starts from Copenhagen at 8.20 A.M. (day 2 from London) and pulls into Stockholm at 4.50 P.M. The train carries a restaurant car from Hässleholm to Stockholm.

The "Holland-Scandinavia Express" doesn't have any through coaches for Stockholm, but there is a conveniently timed connecting service which leaves Copenhagen at 8.35 P.M. and runs overnight to the Swedish capital, arriving there at 7.05 the following morning (day 3 from London). A light refreshment service is available throughout the run from Copenhagen. The train has first- and second-class sleeping cars, and second-class couchettes only, no day carriages. For less comfortable overnight travel use the later departure from Copenhagen at 11.35 P.M.

Alternatively you can reach Stockholm by using the *DFDS* service from Harwich to the port of Gothenberg and then continue by train across Sweden. The ferry service runs on three days a week and the sea crossing takes a little over 24 hours. *British Rail* run a boat service from Liverpool Street Station to Harwich and from Gothenberg to Stockholm. DFDS also run a bus but it's quicker by rail. Leave London day 1 and arrive Stockholm very late on day 2. On this route schedules vary from sailing to sailing so check carefully with *DFDS.*

To Norway. For rail travel to Norway first read the sections on getting to Denmark. The "Nord-West Express" reaches Copenhagen in good time (8.10 A.M.) to catch a through train to Oslo. This departs at 9.35 and runs via the Helsingør–Helsingborg ferry and Gothenberg. Oslo is reached at 7.30 P.M.—day 3 from London. There is also a good (summer only) overnight service from Copenhagen to Oslo which dovetails nicely into the "Holland-Scandinavia Express." This train leaves at 8.35 P.M. and gets you into Oslo just before 7 in the morning (day 3 from London). It has first-class sleepers and second-class couchettes as well as ordinary day coaches.

To Finland. First of all read the section on rail travel to Denmark and Sweden using the "Nord West Express," or the 8.35 P.M. overnight sleeping car train connecting with the "Holland-Scandinavia Express." This will have taken you as far as Stockholm. Rail travelers have three choices for onward travel to Helsinki. First, one can abandon the rails and sail by one of the suberb *Silja Line* ferries direct to Helsinki. There is one sailing a day leaving Stockholm at 6 P.M. and berthing in the Finnish capital at 9 the next morning. The sailing is very conveniently timed for passengers using the "Nord-West Express" as this arrives in Stockholm at 4.50 P.M. allowing ample time to transfer to the ferry terminal at Värtan. Secondly, there is the sea/rail route via Turku. There are two sailings a day on this route, with the morning departure 8.15 reaching

PLANNING YOUR TRIP

Turku at 8.10 P.M. where there is a connecting train at 8.30 to Helsinki arriving at 11.20 P.M. The overnight sailing leaves at 8.45 with the connecting train leaving Turku at 8.30 the following morning and arriving in Helsinki just after 11.30. Thirdly, for the real railway/travel buff there is the overland "all rail" route taking you up around the head of the Gulf of Bothnia to Helsinki via Haparanda/Tornio (change to Finnish broad gauge) and then down the other side. This mini-marathon will take the best part of three days to complete.

Finally less dedicated rail travelers (or their families!) may prefer to use the long sea crossing to Helsinki from Travemunde in north Germany. This is operated by the *Finnjet-Line*. First of all travel to Hamburg by rail, from where there is a bus connection to the ferry terminal at Skaninavienkai.

GETTING TO SCANDINAVIA FROM THE U.K. By bus. There are few bus services serving Scandinavia from the U.K. The only regular operators are *Grey Green* who, in conjunction with the Swedish company *GDG*, have three buses weekly to Malmö (37 hours), Gothenburg (41 hours) and Stockholm (47 hours). Fares are relatively high—around £70 one way—especially when compared with the bargain rail fares (Inter-Rail, EurailPass etc.) available. Check with *Grey Green Coaches*, 53 Stamford Hill, London N.16 (01-800 8010) for details.

GETTING TO SCANDINAVIA FROM THE U.K. By car. This can be a delightful journey, especially if you enjoy sea trips, as many of the ships sailing to Scandinavian ports are really mini-liners. Alternatively, if you wish to keep the sea crossings to a minimum, use one of the shorter North Sea or English Channel crossings and then drive up through Holland and Germany to Denmark and the rest of Scandinavia. However, remember that all this takes time, and you should carefully consider one of the numerous fly-drive packages, either with or without hotel accommodations.

To Denmark. This is the easiest of the Scandinavian countries to get to, with one region—Jutland—being a part of mainland Europe. The capital, Copenhagen, is situated on the island of Zealand. There are two direct ferry services to Denmark from the U.K., both run by *DFDS*. The crossing time from Harwich to Esbjerg is around 19 hours. Fares are relatively high, for a car, driver and passenger allow £120 each way (including couchette). Demand is particularly heavy during the summer, especially at weekends, so book well in advance.

DFDS—under the banner of *Longship Holidays*—also offer a wide range of inclusive arrangements, including go-as-you-please holidays which are excellent value for money. It is well worth checking them out.

If you drive through Holland and Germany to Denmark it's no problem either, as the train ferries from Puttgarden to Rødby carry cars as well. Coupled with the excellent roads in north Germany and Denmark itself, this means that things couldn't be easier for the motorist.

To Sweden. There are two direct ferry services to Sweden from the U.K., both operated by *DFDS* and both running to Gothenberg (see ferry chart). One, from Harwich, is thrice weekly and takes 24 hours. The second is a twice weekly sailing from Newcastle and runs summer only; this takes slightly longer. In 1985, fares should work out at around £125 one way for a car, driver and one passenger.

If you decide to drive up through Germany there are several ferry services to Sweden. A *Stena Line* ferry makes the crossing from Kiel to Gothenberg daily, contact *DFDS* for details. *TT Saga Line* have two services daily from Travemünde to Trelleborg on the southernmost tip of Sweden. On this route *Olau Line* offer a special low fare when combined with their service from Sheerness to Vlissingen. The crossing takes seven hours.

If you want to drive north through Denmark before crossing over to Sweden, this too is easily done. *DFDS* run a ferry shuttle from Dragør (just south of Copenhagen) to Limhamn outside Malmø. Further north there is another shuttle from Helsingör to Helsingborg, again run by *DFDS*. The most northerly crossing is from Frederikshavn (in Jutland) to Gothenberg. Many of these crossings can be booked in advance through *DFDS,* 199 Regent St., London W.1 (01–265 0821).

To Norway. There are two direct routes to Norway, both summer only. One is from Harwich to Kristiansand and operated by *Fred Olsen Lines;* the second is from Newcastle to Bergen by *DFDS* (see ferry chart). For both book well in advance. Fare, for car plus driver and passenger, is around £110 one way (including couchette). Alternatively you can travel via Denmark, driving north through Jutland and then taking the ferry from Hirstals to Kristiansand, or from Frederikshavn to Oslo. *DFDS* offer a 50% discount on this latter route if the passage is booked at the same time as their crossing to Esbjerg in Denmark from Harwich/Newcastle.

To Finland. There are no direct ferry services to Finland from the U.K. The least complicated route is to use one of the convenient North Sea crossings and then to sail direct to Helsinki from Travemünde on the Baltic coast of Germany by the *Finnjet-Line.* Alternatively, drive to Stockholm (see section on Sweden) and then use one of the shorter sea crossings to Helsinki/Turku. Both *Viking* and *Silja* lines sail to these two ports from Stockholm.

To Iceland—By sea. The journey to Iceland is frankly rather complicated and difficult, not least because it is necessary to sail via the Shetland Islands and the Faroes. For the first part of the journey use one of the thrice weekly *P & O* sailings from Aberdeen to Lerwick. From Lerwick there is a weekly sailing by the *Smyril Line* to Torshavn in the Faroe Islands and from there on to Seydisfjordur in Iceland.

The *Smyril Line* services are marketed by *P & O;* details from *P & O Ferries Ltd,* PO Box 5, Jamieson's Quay, Aberdeen.

GETTING AROUND SCANDINAVIA. The following section gives general travel facts for the whole of Scandinavia. For specific and more detailed information on traveling within individual Scandinavian countries, see *Facts at Your Fingertips* for each country.

BY AIR. SAS and Finnair operate an extensive air network between all the major Scandinavian cities, as well as flying to many more remote points within the region. Services between the capitals are the most frequent and journey times are short; no more than 90 minutes between Oslo and Helsinki, for example, the two Scandinavian capitals most widely separated. Between Oslo, Copenhagen and Stockholm, journey times are around one hour.

BY TRAIN. Rail travel in Scandinavia is to be recommended, not only for the comfort of the majority of the rolling stock, but also its cleanliness and general efficiency of the systems. Speeds may not always match those in France or Germany, but the majority of the routes are scenic or have considerable interest. Fares are based on a sliding scale, the farther you travel the cheaper per kilometer it gets.

Iceland is the only Scandinavian country that is without any rail system at all. The problems created by the nature of its terrain and severe climate make the building of railroads impossible.

Discount tickets. As well as the discount tickets available in each Scandinavian country (see the relevant *Facts at Your Fingertips* sections for details), the following rail discount tickets are good for the whole of Scandinavia.

Eurailpass. Visitors from outside Europe should take advantage of the Eurailpass which covers all the European railways (except Britain) including Denmark, Sweden, Norway and Finland. The Eurailpass is first-class only and can be bought for periods of 15 days ($260), 21 days ($330), 1 month ($410), 2 months ($560) and 3 months ($680). The card is excellent value especially if you intend to tour widely. You might also consider adding on a Scandinavian Bonus Pass to obtain reduced rates at first-class hotels (see below) for $17 (1984 price). Younger travelers (under 26) should purchase the Eurail Youth pass—second-

PLANNING YOUR TRIP

class only—for either 1 month ($290) or 2 months ($370). *Note:* these prices may increase after January 1985.

Nordturist Ticket. For Europeans the best bargain for getting around the whole of Scandinavia is the Nordturist ticket (note: this ticket is also promoted as the *Scanrail* card). The Nordturist gives unlimited travel in Denmark, Sweden, Norway and Finland for 21 days for $160 or £100 (mid-1984 figure). First-class is 50% extra but is well worth it as trains can get very full with Inter-Railers (see below) in the peak summer months. Included with the Nordturist ticket is the *Scandinavian Bonus Pass.* This gives discounts of up to 40% for accommodations in over 95 first-class hotels throughout the region. Details and bookings from *Norwegian State Railways Travel Bureau,* Norway House, 21–24 Cockspur St., London S.W.1.

Inter-Rail Card. Youthful travelers (under 26) should consider the Inter-Rail Card which gives the freedom of Europe for one month for £115 (1984 price), especially as this will cover large parts of the rail journey to Scandinavia (and also half fare in the country of purchase and on Sealink cross channel routes). There are close associations between Inter-Rail and the Youth Hostel Association giving inexpensive accommodations when you arrive. Details from *YHA,* 14, Southampton St., London W.C.2.

Rail Europ Senior Card. More elderly travelers who hold a Senior Citizens Railcard can buy an add-on Rail Europ Senior Card which gives discounts of up to 50% on rail travel throughout Scandinavia. There is also an *Inter-Rail Senior Card* (equivalent to the Inter-Rail Card) but this is not obtainable in Britain, though it can be bought elsewhere in Europe and is very good value for money.

BY FERRY. The major boat routes within Scandinavia are operated by car-carrying (as well as passenger) ferries. Services between Sweden and Finland run from Stockholm or nearby ports to Helsinki, Turku and Mariehamm (Åland); Kapellskär (near Stockholm) to Mariehamn and Naantali; also Skellefteå–Pietarsaari, Umeå–Vaasa and Sundsvall–Vaasa.

There are daily sailings between Copenhagen and Oslo. From Jutland in Denmark it is possible to cross directly into Norway and Sweden. Various companies operate from North Jutland to Norway, namely from Frederikshavn to Oslo, Frederikshavn–Larvik, Hanstholm–Arendal, Hanstholm–Kristiansand, and Hirtshals to Kristiansand. From Copenhagen to Sweden only passenger ferries (hydrofoils) leave the city center, but car ferries connect Dragør outside Copenhagen with Limhamn in the south of Sweden. The Elsinore (Helsingør)–Helsingborg route with frequent departures takes both cars and passengers and is the shortest connection available. Other car ferries provide regular services between Denmark and Sweden, running from Grenå to Varberg or Helsingborg and from Frederikshavn to Gothenburg.

DFDS operates between Copenhagen and Oslo and the Faroe Islands. *Smyril* links the Faroes, Bergen (Norway) and Hanstholm (Denmark) with Iceland and Scotland during the summer.

Tours. The most famous of Scandinavian coastal voyages is the 11-day trip from Bergen via North Cape to Kirkenes and return, leaving Bergen daily. A similar round-Iceland voyage takes about a week.

In Norway summer cruises along the fabulous coastline to North Cape and even to Spitsbergen are offered by *Chandris, Cunard, North Star Line, Norwegian American Line* and *Royal Viking Line.* The Telemark Canal, a famous inland waterway, runs from Skien on the Oslo fjord to Dalen among the mountains of Telemark. Also during the summer, the world's oldest paddle steamer, the *Skibladner,* plods its way from Eidsvoll to Lillehammer on Lake Mjøsa, the largest lake in Norway.

In Finland you can cruise for up to a week—over some 700 miles—on Europe's largest lake area, the Saimaa lake region, eating and sleeping on board. There are also interesting trips across the Gulf of Finland from Helsinki to Tallinn in Estonia (visa essential).

In Sweden, there is the delightful trip on the Göta Canal from Gothenburg to Stockholm, through the country's lovely Lake District. The trip takes 3 days and there are several sailings weekly.

Hydrofoils. There are frequent daily services between Copenhagen and Malmö (35-minute crossing). There is also a hydrofoil service on the Finnish lake of Päijänne.

Hydrofoil boats are widely used in Norway. Stavanger, Haugesund and Bergen on the west coast are linked by hydrofoil services, as are the Ryfylke fjords from Stavanger, the Hardangerfjord from Bergen. Speed boat services, too, from Bergen to the Sognefjord and Nordfjord areas.

BY CAR. Scandinavia is an excellent area to visit by car, not least because its great size and small population mean that many very beautiful areas are easily accessible in a car. However, though roads in Denmark and most of southern Norway, Sweden and Finland are generally very good, in more remote regions they can be both narrow and twisting, and badly surfaced. Even the affluent Scandinavians have not yet found a way of protecting their roads from the destructive effects of their long and bitter winters.

Iceland's roads, on the other hand, are almost all poor. The only stretch of highway is between Keflavik and Reykjavik and is a toll road. Roads on the outskirts of towns are surfaced, but elsewhere they consist of scraped lava, occasionally disappearing altogether when a riverbed changes course, though there is usually a crossing place. In consequence, though distances are not very great, journeys by road can be slow.

Regulations. You drive on the *right* in all Scandinavian countries. In Denmark, the town speed limit is 37 m.p.h. (60 km.p.h.), in other Scandinavian towns, 31 m.p.h. (50 km.p.h.), except in Iceland, where it is 27 m.p.h. (45 km.p.h.). Denmark has a general limit of 50 m.p.h. (80 km.p.h.), but 60 m.p.h. (100 km.p.h.) on motorways. (Maximum speed for trailers on motorways is 70 km.p.h.) In Iceland, the general limit is 45 m.p.h. (70 km.p.h.), in Norway 50 m.p.h. (80 km.p.h.), in Sweden 56 m.p.h. (90 km.p.h.) and in Finland 50 m.p.h. (80 km.p.h.) in non built-up areas.

As the liquor regulations might lead you to suspect, Scandinavians are strict about drinking. When it comes to driving a car, they are absolutely inflexible. If you are involved in an accident, a blood test is taken as a matter of course, and if you have had more than a mild whisky and soda, you will spend up to three weeks in jail. No exceptions are made for anyone, so you'd better take a taxi if you've been out on the town. In Sweden, incorrectly parked cars are towed away and dipped headlights used all day.

Documents. For Denmark, Norway, Sweden, and Finland, you need only your national driving license. In Sweden, unless your driving license is issued in English, French, Dutch, Italian, Spanish or German, you must produce a special certificate confirming the authenticity and validity of the license, written in Swedish, English or French. For Iceland, an international license is necessary. Internationally valid third-party insurance (Green Card) is not required but is recommended.

Maps. The Scandinavian touring and automobile clubs will supply you with maps and itineraries. All publish excellent touring books and have branch offices in the larger towns in addition to the following headquarters.

Denmark: *De Forenede Danske Motorejere* (FDM), Blegdamsvej 124, in Copenhagen. The official Geodaetisk Institut maps, available in most bookshops, are among the world's best.

Finland: *The Automobile and Touring Club,* Kansakoulunkatu 10, Helsinki. Excellent maps of Finland on various scales are published by that country's Map Service of the National Board of Survey. They can be obtained from main bookshops in Finland or from the Map Service shop at Eteläesplanadi 10, Helsinki 13.

Iceland: excellent maps are available from the Iceland tourist bureau.

Norway: *Kongelig Norsk Automobilklub* (KNA), Parkveien 68, and *Norges Automobil-Forbund,* Storgate 2, both in Oslo.

PLANNING YOUR TRIP

Sweden: *Kungliga Automobil Klubben* (KAK), and *Motormännens Riksförbund* (M), Sturegatan 32, in Stockholm.

Car hire. All leading car hire firms offer self-drive cars throughout Scandinavia ranging from Volkswagens to Land-Rovers. Chauffeur-driven cars are also available.

Addresses are given in the *Practical Information* after each chapter. Package fly-drive arrangements with unlimited mileage are also available offering flexibility and advantageous rates.

In Sweden there is a low-price go-as-you-please rental check which can only be bought outside the country. Low rental rates are also offered as part of rail and air packages.

In Iceland, Land-Rovers and minibuses are especially suitable; they cost more and must be booked well in advance. Rental rates are higher than elsewhere here and a sales tax of 20% does nothing to help, but fly-drive arrangements bring costs down.

CONVERSION TABLES. One of the most confusing experiences for many motorists is their first encounter with the metric system. The following quick conversion table may help to speed you on your way.

Kilometers into Miles. This simple chart will help you to convert to both miles and kilometers. If you want to convert from miles into kilometers read from the center column to the right, if from kilometers into miles, from the center column to the left. Example: 5 miles = 8.5 kilometers, 5 kilometers = 3.1 miles.

Miles		Kilometers	Miles		Kilometers
0.6	1	1.6	37.3	60	96.6
1.2	2	3.2	43.5	70	112.3
1.9	3	4.8	49.7	80	128.7
2.5	4	6.3	55.9	90	144.8
3.1	5	8.0	62.1	100	160.9
3.7	6	9.6	124.3	200	321.9
4.3	7	11.3	186.4	300	482.8
5.0	8	12.9	248.5	400	643.7
5.6	9	14.5	310.7	500	804.7
6.2	10	16.1	372.8	600	965.6
12.4	20	32.2	434.9	700	1,126.5
18.6	30	48.3	497.1	800	1,287.5
24.8	40	64.4	559.2	900	1,448.4
31.0	50	80.5	621.4	1,000	1,609.3

Motor fuel. Imperial gallon is approximately 4½ liters; a U.S. gallon about 3¾ liters.

Liters	Imp. gals.	U.S. gals.
1	0.22	0.26
5	1.10	1.32
10	2.20	2.64
20	4.40	5.28
40	8.80	10.56
100	22.01	26.42

Tire pressure. Measured in kilograms per square centimeter instead of pounds per square inch; the ratio is approximately 14.2 lbs. to 1 kg.

Lbs per sq. in.	Kg per sq. cm	Lbs per sq. in.	Kg per sq. cm
20	1.406	26	1.828
22	1.547	28	1.969
24	1.687	30	2.109

SCANDINAVIA

CUSTOMS ON RETURNING HOME. If you propose to take on your holiday any *foreign-made* articles, such as cameras, binoculars, expensive timepieces and the like, it is wise to put with your travel documents the receipt from the retailer or some other evidence that the item was bought in your home country. If you bought the article on a previous holiday abroad and have already paid duty on it, carry with you the receipt for this. Otherwise, on returning home, you may be charged duty (for British residents, Value Added Tax as well). In other words, unless you can prove prior possession, foreign-made articles are dutiable *each time* they enter the U.S. The details below are correct as we go to press. It would be wise to check in case of change.

American residents who are out of the U.S.A. at least 48 hours and have claimed no exemption during the previous 30 days are entitled to bring in duty-free up to $400 worth of bona fide gifts or items for their own personal use. Do not think that *already used* will exempt an item. If you buy clothing abroad and wear it during your travels it will nonetheless be dutiable when you reenter the U.S.

The $400 duty free allowance is based on the full fair *retail* value of the goods (previously, the customs' estimation was on the wholesale value). You must now list the items purchased and *they must accompany you when you return.* So keep all receipts handy with the detailed list, and pack the goods together in one case. The $50 mailed gift-scheme (see below) is also based on the retail value. Every member of a family is entitled to this same exemption, regardless of age, and their exemptions can be pooled. Infants and children get the same exemptions as adults, except for alcoholic beverages and tobacco. Beyond the first $400 worth of goods, inspectors now assess a flat 10% duty on the next $1,000 worth; above $1,400 duties vary according to the kind of merchandise.

One quart of alcoholic beverages and up to 100 cigars (non-Cuban!) may be included in the exemption if you are 21 years of age or older. There is no limitation on the number of cigarettes you bring in for your personal use, regardless of age. Alcoholic beverages in excess of one quart are subject to customs duty and internal revenue tax. Approximate rates are (1/5 gallon); brandy or liquor, $2–$3; champagne, 90¢; wine, 15¢. The importation must not be in violation of the laws of the state of arrival. Furthermore, your tobacco and alcohol may be reported to the authorities in your own home state, to be taxed by them.

Only one bottle of certain perfumes that are trademarked in the United States (Lanvin, Chanel, etc.) may be brought in unless you can completely obliterate the trademark on the bottle, or get written permission from the manufacturer to bring more. Other perfumes are limited by weight or value. The specialized Paris houses will give you the complete list.

Foreign visitors to the U.S. (nonresidents), and U.S. military personnel returning from duty abroad should inquire separately about regulations and exemptions pertaining to them.

American rates of customs duty may change, so it is best to check the regulations with the nearest American Embassy during your visit. There are special Customs advisors at the U.S. embassies in London, Paris, Rome and Bonn and at the Consulate in Frankfurt. In general, of course, narcotics, pornography, seditious materials, and dangerous articles (fireworks, poisons, switchblades) are forbidden in the U.S.

You do not have to pay duty on art objects or antiques, provided they are over 100 years old. Remember this and ask the dealer who sells you that Sheffield plate or that 17th-century Dutch landscape for a certificate establishing its age. But when you buy, remember also that some countries regulate the removal of cultural properties and works of art.

Gifts which cost less than $50 may be mailed to friends or relatives at home, but not more than one per day (of receipt) to any one addressee. Mark the package: Unsolicited Gift—value less than $50. These gifts must not include perfumes costing more than $1, tobacco or liquor; however, they do not count as part of your $400 exemption.

Do not bring home foreign meats, fruits, plants, soil, or other agricultural items when you return to the United States. To do so will delay you at the port of entry. It is illegal to bring in foreign agricultural items without permission,

PLANNING YOUR TRIP 19

because they can spread destructive plant or animal pests and diseases. For more information, read the pamphlet "Customs Hints", or write to: "Quarantines", Department of Agriculture, Federal Center Bldg., Hyattsville, Maryland 20782, and ask for Program Aid No. 1083, entitled "Traveler's Tips on Bringing Food, Plant and Animal Products into the United States."

Procedures for customs and immigration have been greatly simplified recently. Customs declaration forms are distributed on your plane or ship before you arrive. If your purchases are worth no more than $400 you fill out only the identification portions of the form and make an oral declaration when you pass the inspector. If you have over $400 worth you must make a written declaration. Under the Citizens Bypass Program, American citizens can show their passports to the customs inspector and eliminate the separate inspection by an immigration officer.

Canadian residents may, in addition to personal effects, bring in the following duty free: a maximum of 50 cigars, 200 cigarettes, 2 pounds of tobacco and 40 ounces of liquor, provided these are declared in writing to customs on arrival and accompany the traveler in hand or checked-through baggage. These are included in the basic exemption of $300 a year or $100 per quarter. Personal gifts should be mailed as "Unsolicited Gift—Value Under $40." Canadian customs regulations are strictly enforced; you are recommended to check what your allowances are and to make sure you have kept receipts for whatever you have bought abroad. For details ask for the Canada Customs brochure, *I Declare*.

British residents face two levels of duty free allowance entering the U.K.; one, for goods bought outside the EEC or for goods bought in a duty free shop within the EEC; two, for goods bought in an EEC country but not in a duty free shop.

In the first category you may import duty free: 200 cigarettes or 100 cigarillos or 50 cigars or 250 grammes of tobacco (*Note* if you live outside Europe, these allowances are doubled); plus one liter of alcoholic drinks over 22% vol. (38.8% proof) or two liters of alcoholic drinks not over 22% vol. or fortified or sparkling wine; plus two liters of still table wine; plus 50 grammes of perfume; plus nine fluid ounces of toilet water; plus other goods to the value of £28.

In the second category you may import duty free: 300 cigarettes or 150 cigarillos or 75 cigars or 400 grammes of tobacco; plus 1½ liters of alcoholic drinks over 22% vol. (38.8% proof) or three liters of alcoholic drinks not over 22% vol. or fortified or sparkling wine; plus four liters of still table wine; plus 75 grammes of perfume; plus 13 fluid ounces of toilet water; plus other goods to the value of £120 (*Note* though it is not classified as an alcoholic drink by EEC countries for Customs' purposes and is thus considered part of the "other goods" allowance, you may not import more than 50 liters of beer).

In addition, no animals or pets of any kind may be brought into the U.K. The penalties for doing so are severe and are strictly enforced; there are *no* exceptions. Similarly, fresh meats, plants and vegetables, controlled drugs and firearms and ammunition may not be brought into the U.K. There are no restrictions on the import or export of British and foreign currencies.

Anyone planning to stay in the U.K. for more than six months should contact H.M. Customs and Excise, Kent House, Upper Ground, London S.E.1 (tel. 01-928 0533) for further information.

AN INTRODUCTION TO SCANDINAVIA

Variety within Harmony

by
SYLVIE NICKELS

Space—vast quantities of it—is one of the first qualities you're likely to associate with Scandinavia. Between them, the five Scandinavian nations cover an area of some 500,000 square miles, give or take a few (and that doesn't include the huge and largely autonomous Danish territory of Greenland). You could fit the U.K. five times into that, or Texas twice, and still have acreage to spare. What's more, all this is shared out among some 20 million souls—rather less than three Londons or New Yorks. So if plenty of elbow room makes you feel nervous, you had better keep away!

If you have any pre-conceived ideas that one Scandinavian country is much like another, you can also begin by forgetting these. Of course, they all share a broadly similar cultural background, have strong historical and economic ties, and enjoy many similarities in political and social structure. But that said, the individual components of the Scandinavian scene are just that—highly individual. The special qualities of each are no more comparable than are the tidy, well-husbanded land-

AN INTRODUCTION TO SCANDINAVIA

scapes and long sandy beaches of Denmark with the wild tawny fjords and fells of Norway; which in turn are quite different to the huge lake-and-forestscapes that so characterize Sweden and Finland, and the bizarre volcanic majesty of much of Iceland.

So, space and magnificent scenery are among the great (and free) trump cards of the region. To these you can add several natural phenomena which, in European terms, are unique to Scandinavia: long golden summer evenings stretching right into next day's dawn as you travel into the northern latitudes of the midnight sun; and, in winter, the rippling veils of the Northern Lights that weave magical curtains across the sky. The fall colors, too, have a special brilliance as you progress northwards, and spring, though relatively late, banishes the long winter with a welcome speed and vigor.

With so much unadulterated nature around, you won't find it too surprising that in large areas people—and all the paraphernalia that goes with them—can be rather thin on the ground. In fact, their numbers work out more or less in direct ratio to their latitude; from relatively (but only relatively) crowded little Denmark to the almost (but only almost) empty far north of Lapland up there beyond the Arctic Circle. Which brings us to another Scandinavian certainty, one that may at first sight seem somewhat paradoxical given the harsh climate: wherever there are people, there are good living conditions. These nordic folk learned long ago how to make themselves at home in conditions that range from the temperately comfortable to the downright inhospitable. The result is that, however remote a community may be, you can expect it to have all the amenities that the traveler of the 1980s is likely to need. They won't be lacking in finesse either. The Scandinavians like things to be not only practical, but aesthetic as well.

Transports of Delight

As far as you, the visitor, is concerned, the combination of human and natural history has tailor-made these countries for three particular types of holiday. The first is touring. Though you won't find historical monuments and art treasures in such multiplicity as in some other parts of Europe, there is nevertheless an enormous amount to see: prehistoric and Viking burial grounds, runic stones, Viking ships, medieval wooden or stone churches, Hanseatic merchants' houses, Renaissance castles and manors, the occasional Gothic cathedral, the graciously neo-Classical 19th-century buildings of Stockholm and Helsinki, and a great deal of spectacular modern architecture, to name but some of the region's specialties.

With the exception of Denmark and the more urban areas of Norway, Sweden and Finland, however, the serious culture vulture may need to cover quite a lot of territory to get his fill, though most of it is, happily, very travel-worthy terrritory, well serviced by varied means of communication. Outside urban areas, roads are blessedly uncrowded, in addition to being well maintained—if occasionally bumpy—and, if you haven't a car, you can fall back on northern Europe's finest public transport systems—air, rail, bus, ferry, lake steamer, hydrofoil —often interlinked to meet the needs of widely differing terrain.

For those intent on seeing as much as possible, there are good transport bargains to be investigated. Some depend on your age—both ends of the age-scale benefit, but the minimums and maximums vary from country to country, as do the types of transport to which they apply. Others depend on the composition of your group—families with one child or more get good concessions on air and rail throughout much of the region. Yet others depend on nothing more than careful advance planning, as in the case of the Scanrailpass and the comparable facilities that give unlimited rail travel in individual countries for fixed periods, such as the Finnrail Pass, or Sweden's very advantageous low-price card. But check these *before* you arrive in Scandinavia, and remember that many of them are also marketed as part of reasonably priced packages from your home country.

Hand-in-hand with flexible travel facilities go flexible accommodation systems. A variety of "hotel check" schemes—hotel vouchers essentially—operate in each of the countries, except Iceland, the greatest choice being in Sweden. Some, such as Scandic hotel checks, extend across borders and are valid in specified hotels in Sweden, Norway and Denmark. The Danes also have an attractive scheme concentrating on the *kro* or country inn, nearly all in rural settings, most of them family run and many contained in fine old half-timbered buildings of considerable vintage. Similarly, summer hotels are a feature of all five countries. These act as student accommodation during the rest of the year, offer good value for money and are often enthusiastically run by the students themselves.

Catering to the Self

There are ways, though, of getting to even closer grips with the way of life of your chosen country; and this brings us to the second type of vacation in which Scandinavia excels: self-catering. One of its most popular forms is the farm vacation, which the Danes in particular have developed to a fine art. Usually these vacations are on a half- or full-board basis, but in most cases the great attraction is that you will be staying on a working farm with the option of participating in the way of life of a working family. The potential benefits hardly need stressing, especially if you have youngsters in tow. The rural settings are likely to be idyllic, if remote, so it's an advantage to have your own transport.

But if you want to savor the northern summer as only the Scandinavians know how, you should give serious thought to that quite indispensable feature of their way of life: the summer cottage. It probably isn't too much of an exaggeration to say that most families in all five nations own, rent, borrow or otherwise have access to four walls and a roof somewhere in the great beyond of the countryside. It can be anything from a simple shack to a minor mansion, but is likely to be somewhere in between with an almost guaranteed tranquillity—except perhaps on a few popular coastal stretches of Denmark and Sweden—on some lake, river or sea shore.

To such havens, families will retire for the entire summer, working members joining them at every opportunity, spending their time swimming, fishing, boating, walking in woods or over hills and fells, or simply watching the ever changing interplay of light and color as reflections are flung from water to sky and back again, or the surrealistic sunsets that linger far into the nordic night. You, the visitor, would do well to follow suit.

AN INTRODUCTION TO SCANDINAVIA

The best-equipped (and most expensive) summer cottages usually form part of a holiday village, often featuring a restaurant, shop, some sports facilities and perhaps entertainment. Centers of this kind tend to reach a higher degree of sophistication in Denmark and Sweden than in Norway and Finland (you won't find them in Iceland), and it is this type of holiday property that is mainly marketed overseas. Rentals for individually sited cottages, for which there are many agencies in Scandinavia, can be very much lower—even downright cheap if you are content to "get back to nature" as so many Scandinavians are (whatever they like to say)—which, at its most basic, may mean drawing water from a well, hewing your own firewood or accepting the sufficiency of an outdoor privy. Whatever the standard, though, the setting will certainly be memorable.

Nature, Naturally

So we come to the third and final type of holiday for which these lands are especially well suited: holidays in which the emphasis is, quite simply, on nature itself and the various ways of savoring it to the full. The most obvious way is on foot; Scandinavia, after all, is the home of orienteering. But never fear—you won't need to go armed with a compass. Marked trails cater for those whose energies are geared only to a short stroll through fragrant pinewoods along a lake shore all the way up to those more rugged types whose idea of fun is many days back-packing through terrain as isolated as any that Europe can offer. Punctuating the latter, overnight shelter is available in strategically-sited wilderness refuges or well-equipped hostels and mountain cabins. In Norway they have taken things a stage further with a unique system of mountain huts where basic essentials (blankets, food, fuel, etc.) can be purchsed or hired on a self-service basis, offering a welcome economy in muscle power. Not to be outdone, the Danes, whose greatest claim to a mountain touches the sky at around 500 feet in Jutland, have evolved their own specialty: organized "marches" or, better, rambles of various duration, one of the most popular being along the old Military Road, a historic track through Jutland. Hundreds of people take part in these but, of course, the trails are available at any time if you're not the gregarious type.

Cycling is another activity that the Danes have got well organized, though the lack of hills does give them a substantial headstart. Packages include a detailed itinerary, accommodations of various grades and, of course, the bike itself, though you can also bring your own, transported free on most North Sea ferries. Similar packages have spread to Sweden and, to a lesser extent, Norway and Finland. In Iceland, the sturdy little horses directly descended from Viking-era ancestry are rather better adapted to the rugged terrain.

With so many lakes and so much sea around, messing about in boats is an activity more or less built-in to the Scandinavian summer scene. You'll find that a rowing boat comes almost, as it were, as part of the furniture with a lot of self-catering accommodation, and there will be something that floats available, either free or at nominal cost, at many hotels and most campsites. The Finns and Swedes are great canoeists, with a whole range of rallies weaving across the blue and green landscapes. On one Swedish river, you can even build your own log raft for a leisurely float of several days, borne by the current at a mile per hour. Sailing is immensely popular—after all, some of the most famous windjammers from the great era of sail were built and had their home ports in Baltic waters, and a number of them are now museum ships. Today, the vessels may be more modest, but the flutter of sails is pretty well a constant feature of any coastal scene and the spectacle provided by the major regattas that punctuate the Danish calendar especially are sights to remember. Chartering a yacht isn't quite so easy (the best chances are in Denmark and Sweden), but if you want to get a good grounding in what every budding yachtsman ought to know, a number of sailing schools are ready to oblige.

The Scandinavians are also inveterate swimmers. Don't be put off by the latitudes. Water temperatures won't, of course, match those of the Mediterranean, but in summer you'll find them surprisingly acceptable and, at worst, refreshing! The best sands are on the west coast of Denmark's Jutland, where they're so firm and extensive that you can drive a car along them for miles on end; other good sands are on the west coast of Finland. Almost anywhere else, whether by lake or sea, the bathing is off rocks, usually long, smooth shoulders of granite comfortably shaped for soaking in the sun, which happens to be another favorite occupation in these parts.

If you get the opportunity to take a sauna bath—and you almost certainly will—you'll never have a better one, especially if you are in Finland, the home of the sauna, where for many people, it is still almost as intrinsic a part of life as eating and sleeping. A true country sauna poised on lake- or sea-shore bears little resemblance to its urbanized descendant, even less to most exported versions. For the Finn, the sauna is a social as well as a cleansing experience—for some almost a spiritual one, too; and when you relax afterwards looking out across quiet waters under the huge northern sky, you may begin to understand why. The Icelanders have their own specialty: an abundance of natural warm water piped from the bowels of the earth into swimming pools in which you can bathe in the openair even in the depths of winter.

And this brings us to that entirely different part of the Scandinavian scene: the Nordic winter. Skiing as a sport was born in Norway: to be precise in the village of Morgedal, in the province of Telemark. As far as large numbers of Norwegians, Swedes and Finns are concerned, skiing was—and for some still is—an essential part of everyday life for several months of the year. For most, however, the element of necessity has been entirely removed, though does not prevent them from donning their skis at any excuse, or even without one, for it's a quite common sight to see city dwellers skiing to work across their parks. Though there are quite a few resorts, many of them well-known, offering good downhill facilities, especially in Norway, those accustomed to the more vertical type of skiing will find things a bit different here. The terrain varies enormously from the considerable mountains of Norway to the smooth treeless slopes of the northern Swedish and Finnish fells, and the great white expanses of lowland lake-and-forestscapes. But generally speaking, the Scandinavian preference remains for cross-country skiing—or the other extreme of hurling themselves into the void from the top of a sky-scraping ski jump. In both, their successes in Olympic and World Championship events speak for themselves.

Of Nansen and Nobel

Maybe these preferences reflect certain traits of the northern temperament, so what of the Scandinavians themselves? There is little argument that the extrovert Danes are the easiest to get to know. Norwegians and Finns have a self-sufficiency and reserve which you might even interpret as indifference, though you'd be quite wrong; you may have to make the first move, but the results will probably be overwhelming. In between are the Swedes, a little more solemn, still a bit sensitive about their long neutrality and material well-being, but responsive to a friendly interest in their affairs.

That said, they all share common characteristics, most of them rooted in the pioneer spirit which has led them to develop one of the highest standards of living anywhere, despite a predominantly harsh climate. One is a fine, dry sense of humor allied to an endearing ability to laugh at themselves. Another is more paradoxical, for the very pioneer spirit which has produced some exceptional explorers, from Viking times onwards, is matched by a rare compassion and concern for the more wretched affairs of the world. Thus 20th century Scandinavia has been in the vanguard in helping the under-privileged and in striving to inject peace into a humanity sometimes seemingly bent upon self-destruction.

Just one example is the Norwegian, Fridtjof Nansen, who achieved majestic feats of human endurance as an Arctic explorer and then, with equal single-mindedness, applied his energies to the seemingly intractable problems of the world at the League of Nations, concerning himself especially with the agonies of the world's refugees. In 1923, he won the cherished Peace Prize instituted by yet another Scandinavian, Alfred Bernhard Nobel, the Swedish inventor of dynamite. Since those days, international forums seeking disarmament accords have regularly taken place on Scandinavian soil, while young Scandinavians participate in peace-keeping forces and medical missions in various troubled parts of the globe.

Design as Art

We've already established that the Scandinavians know how to make themselves comfortable under almost any circumstance. But they are also very insistent that things should be beautiful as well as practical. Scandinavian architects have established reputations that are worldwide, Scandinavian designers regularly carry off prizes at international contests. And this is probably largely because the "average" citizen cares to a degree that is rare elsewhere about the design and craftsmanship that has gone into the bowl which decorates his table, the ceramics or glass from which he eats and drinks, the textiles that hang at his windows, even the pots and pans he cooks in or the tools with which he will further endeavour to improve the quality of life. This intrinsic preference for the aesthetic, and the talents with which to satisfy it, have visible repercussions on the holiday scene. A less obvious, but nonetheless pleasing side effect is the number of crafts centers or studios to be stumbled upon, often in the most unexpected backwoods areas, where talented artists—many of them escapees from city life—

are producing beautiful items in wood, ceramics, textiles, precious or semi-precious metals and stones, either for practical use or pure adornment.

When it comes to the fine arts, interestingly (and with a few obvious exceptions), the Scandinavians are more successful as sculptors than as painters, though there are probably proportionately more of both than in most other parts of the world. Openair art exhibitions are a strong feature of the Scandinavian summer, some of them so remotely tucked away among the woods and lakes that you wonder how anyone ever gets to hear of them, let alone make the effort to go there. But they do. They're also prolific writers and avid readers not only of their own literature, but everyone else's too. To a degree you'll probably find shaming, they will almost certainly know more about you than you know about them.

Markets and Midsummer Madness

Openair exhibitions are only one small aspect of the al fresco activities that characterize the long days of the Scandinavian summer. Most symbolic of all is the great festival common to the whole region which celebrates Midsummer, usually at the weekend closest to the longest day. Focal points of the festivities are the huge bonfires lit on Midsummer's Eve pretty well everywhere; except, that is, in Sweden and western Finland where these are replaced by decorated maypoles. Music and dancing is the order of the day—or rather night, for few people will see their beds on this occasion.

During the light summer evenings, openair theaters take over when most regular theaters are closed for the season. Street entertainment is particularly popular, especially in the cities and towns of Denmark and Sweden. The main ones will probably attract a few protest marches, too, with the Scandinavian young passionately recording their assent or (more likely) dissent on issues ranging from local laws to distant wars. Sporting activities confined for so many months of the year to indoor sports complexes are smartly transferred to the great outdoors. This sporting exodus to the great outdoors is by no means confined solely to more obviously athletic pursuits. One of the sights of Sweden's urban parks are the openair chess games, played with giant-size chessmen and great solemnity to the accompaniment of murmured advice from the audience of enthusiasts which invariably gathers round.

The openair museum, reconstructing the living conditions and way-of-life long past, was born in Scandinavia: in Stockholm, to be precise, where you can visit the original Skansen whose name has been adopted by a proliferation of "skansens" the world over. And, of course, there are openair markets filling the squares and narrow streets of many of the pretty provincial towns and, incidentally, providing a good hunting ground for less expensive handicrafts. In fact in larger cities, some of these markets flourish year-round, and there's nothing that quite matches the atmosphere of a mid-winter market with be-furred and heavily-booted stall holders stamping their feet in the snow, the sun low on the horizon.

Festivals of a more cultural nature—of all kinds and at all levels—now pack the Scandinavian summer calendar. Some cover just about every cultural activity you can think of, others are more specialized,

AN INTRODUCTION TO SCANDINAVIA

ranging from jazz to chamber or organ music and folklore to historic pageantry. The top events attract top international performers from the world of theater, ballet, opera and music; among the leading festivals are those at Bergen, Helsinki and Århus. But if you've made opera your scene, you want to head for the gorgeous Rococo theater of Drottningholm, Stockholm, or the splendid medieval castle that provides the setting for the Savonlinna Opera Festival in Finland. For lovers of jazz, the choice includes Copenhagen, Molde in Norway, Pori in Finland, while the Roskilde Festival in Denmark tops the lot in northern Europe for a feast of rock, jazz and folk music. Allegorical plays are a specialty of Dalarna province in Sweden; the Swedish island of Gotland focuses on a moving mystery pageant; the Danes of southern Jutland have a nostalgia for medieval times with tilting at the ring tournaments; and their compatriots in Frederikssund grow beards (or at least the men do!) and recreate the life and times of the Vikings at their annual Viking Festival.

Some events will never make the international calendar and are just pure fun, like the Sleepyhead Day of Naantali in Finland when, if you're a late riser, you might just qualify for being thrown into the sea! Folkloric custom and culture are strong favorites, whether as part of an organized festival (Kaustinen in Finland, Skagen in Denmark) or perpetuating such deep-rooted traditions as church boat processions, again in Dalarna where this was once the only way of traveling to worship, or the peasant-style weddings of western Norway.

With a bit of careful planning, you could fill the months from late spring to early fall moving from one event to another. For the rest of the year, the theater, opera and concert season takes over in the towns and cities, and out in the country districts workaday activities, geared to the rhythm of the seasons, provide some of the most colorful events of all. Up around the Arctic Circle and beyond, for example, the reindeer round-ups of northern Norway, Sweden and Finland provide a memorably boisterous scene of whirling lassos and thundering hooves, strongly reminiscent of the Wild West, yet muted by deep-freeze temperatures and a thick blanket of snow. And still way beyond the Arctic Circle, thousands of fishermen in hundreds of vessels converge during the early months of the year on the icy seas around Norway's spectacular Lofoten Islands for the annual harvest of the Lofotens Fisheries. This scene of extraordinary activity, which depends on nothing more or less than the life cycle of the cod, goes back to the Middle Ages, and such is its importance that the whole procedure comes under the jurisdiction of its own special Fisheries "government."

Of the People . . .

But what of the broader canvas of the Scandinavian social and political scene? Certainly, the flame of democracy burns steadily here and with historic continuity. Here the world's first parliament saw the light of day (in Iceland around A.D. 930). Here originated the post of Ombudsman to investigate complaints against government departments (in Sweden in 1809). Here the first women in Europe—the second in the world—won the franchise (in Finland in 1906). And here the first woman ever was freely elected as head of state (presently, the President of Iceland). Yet traditions die hard and few Scandinavians have any inclination to tamper with their aristocratic and royal heritage where it exists. Three of the countries can produce a royal family apiece, two of them a plethora of counts and barons.

That said, the Scandinavian royals are as much "of the people" as you are likely to find anywhere, as you'll discover when you brush elbows with the Swedish king in a Stockholm theater lobby, or meet the Danish royal family cycling along a rural lane, or learn that the Norwegian Crown Prince underwent all the same hardships of a military winter exercise as his contemporaries. The fact of the matter is that these monarchs provide the stabilizing influence, above and beyond political considerations, and the continuity so necessary to the continued well-being of the countries. It's probably no exaggeration to say that if the monarchy were abolished in any of the three countries where it exists, the king would be a strong contender for president!

Politically, the emphasis is on moderation. If you are accustomed to a two-party system, you may find the number of parties from which Scandinavian electors need to choose their representatives a little excessive (11 in Norway, for example, and nine in Finland), and it's true that coalitions are often a necessary by-product. In parts of the region, too, the Communist party is rather more in evidence than most of us are used to, though its steady decline is equally apparent, its position in Finland (one of its former strongholds) having dropped from a close second in 1945 to a lagging fourth in 1983. It is also important to realise that Scandinavia's brand of Eurocommunism has moved some distance from the Soviet variety with which it is often in conflict.

But for the most part, it's the Social Democrats—broadly comparable to the Democrats—who constitute the overall political makeup of Scandinavia, at the expense of such other major groups as the the Center, Conservative and Liberal parties.

Economy and Enterprise

In any survey of the contemporary Scandinavian scene, the question arises sooner or later, on what have the Scandinavians based their current considerable prosperity? Fortuitously, most of the natural features that contribute so much to their countries' attractions can be translated one way or another into hard cash. Thus, timber, fish, iron and steel, dairy farming, hydro-electric energy, shipping and, in more recent years, oil, all constitute a major part of the region's economy, along with their by-products and the specialized equipment with which to process them. But in modern times, overspecialization has revealed its own hazards, as became evident to the Finns once dangerously dependent on timber and paper exports, and Icelanders whose economy was almost entirely based on fishing.

But like the rest of us, the Scandinavians have recognized the vital need to diversify and are now applying their special talents to a much broader range of goods. The latest in electronic equipment and medical supplies, complex machinery of all kinds, fashions and furniture, sports equipment and household appliances, all swell the selection of items that now appear on their order books. To such exports an all-important addition can be made, albeit an invisible one: know-how. All over the world, you'll come across Scandinavians bringing their expertise to the development of new enterprise, whether it's a tractor factory in Brazil, a telex-data installation in Saudi Arabia, a smelting furnace in India, a paper mill in Canada, or a hotel in the Balkans.

You could almost call it a new Viking era.

SCANDINAVIAN HISTORY

Prosperity Out of Conflict

Scandinavia today presents a picture of harmonious unity: five countries, linked by a common culture, geography and history, politically and technologically sophisticated, at peace with themselves and the world. There are, to be sure, differences between them. Finland, for example, has a language that owes nothing to the other Scandinavian tongues. Norway, Sweden and Denmark are monarchies, Finland and Iceland are republics. Denmark is the only Scandinavian member of the EEC, the Common Market. Sweden and Finland have long been politically non-aligned, Norway, Denmark and Iceland are all active members of NATO. But what unites Scandinavia is ultimately of greater significance than what divides her, and it is difficult to think of any other grouping of countries in the modern world more happily or naturally united.

But it was not always so. Her present enviable prosperity and stability are a striking tribute to the new maturity of once rival and warring lands, with little more than a common tongue—Finland excepted—and their harsh climate and isolation on the northern fringes of Europe to unite them.

Bog People and Berserkers

More than anything else, it is the fact of her isolation that provides the key note of much early Scandinavian history. With the exception of Denmark and parts of southern Sweden, Scandinavia is a vast and frequently inhospitable land, underpopulated even today; a land of endless forests and mountain fastnesses, laced by rivers and lakes and buffeted by the long northern winter. This combination of remoteness and vast scale long conspired to ensure that she remained in the backwaters of early European history.

Not surprisingly, Scandinavia's earliest inhabitants seem naturally to have gravitated towards its most fertile and temperate regions. Though relics dating back six or seven thousand years—in particular primitive skis—have been found in the empty wastes of Finland and northern Sweden, it was in the south of Scandinavia, in present day Denmark and southern Sweden, that the first sizeable settlements existed. There is considerable evidence to suggest that by the Bronze Age (c. 1500 B.C.–500 B.C.) the early Scandinavians had become successful farmers and hunters, skilled also at pottery and weaving. A number of Scandinavian museums—the Nordic Museum in Stockholm pre-eminently—contain sizeable collections of jewelry, pottery and other artefacts from burial mounds which attest to the relative sophistication of these early inhabitants. Remarkably, two of the men themselves, pickled by the peat bogs in which they were buried, have also been found. The severed heads of these grisly remains—Graubolle man and Tollund man—are today on view, for those with strong stomachs, at the Århus and Silkeborg museums in Denmark.

Yet despite this evidence of a not inconsiderable population, Scandinavia remained isolated from the main centers of Europe. Even the Romans baulked at her trackless forests and vast unpopulated expanses, no doubt discouraged also by her brutal winters, and the northernmost limits of their empire stopped far to the south of the Scandinavian lands. Nonetheless, it seems clear that merchants from the south were happy to barter with the mysterious northern tribes. The pieces of amber that could be picked up on Denmark's beaches were particularly prized by the Romans, who traded ivory, silver and gold for them. Roman coins have even been found in remote and rugged Iceland—*Ultima Thule* indeed.

By about A.D. 700 much of coastal southern Scandinavia had been settled, though vast areas of the interior remained uninhabited. Interestingly, though perhaps not surprisingly, the most densely populated areas, at the heart of the most important agricultural lands and strategically placed for trade, were subsequently to grow into modern Scandinavia's capitals. But in addition, Trondheim, on the northwest coast of Norway, also developed as an important center.

As well as being successful hunters and farmers, the Scandinavians also traded extensively. The Swedes, for example, controlled the fur trade between north and south Scandinavia, while the Norwegians of the Atlantic coast had trade links with both southern Sweden and Denmark and the Frisian islands on the west coast of Germany. However, the inhospitable interior meant that most trade was dependent on sea travel, and it is evident that despite their primitive navigational know-how the early Scandinavians were skilled shipwrights and routinely undertook long and arduous sea voyages. At the same time, increasingly persistent warring between rival tribes also made the possession of sea-going vessels necessary.

Around A.D. 800 something very strange happened to these somewhat primitive hunters and farmers, relegated to the outer fringes of Europe. Without warning, and for reasons that still remain the subject of speculation, they exploded onto the European scene, sallying forth from Scandinavia in their long ships and wreaking havoc—pillaging, looting and terrorizing—over the length and breadth of Europe. The Vikings had arrived. "From the fury of the Norsemen, Good Lord deliver us," was to become a deeply-felt and oft-uttered prayer in many parts of Europe.

Whatever the reasons for the sudden appearance of the Vikings—whether economic pressure created by population increases in their homelands, changes in the climate, or just a simple-minded taste for a wandering life of excitement and exploration (the ultimate test of Viking manhood was to enter battle bare-chested or "berserk")—one thing is clear. The Vikings were successful because the disintegration of the Roman empire had created a power vacuum in Europe, leaving the continent weak and disordered, a prey to any who chanced upon her. Thus the Vikings remorselessly swept through Europe, as though a cannon loaded with grapeshot had been suddenly fired.

Swedes thrust southeastwards across the Baltic, founding Russia some say (*rus* means Swede), and reaching the Black Sea by means of the Dnieper river, and Persia by the Volga river and Caspian sea. In Constantinople they enrolled as Varangian (or Viking) guards, elite bodyguards to the Byzantine emperor. The Norwegians sailed west and north, overtaking Orkney and Shetland, which remained Scandinavian until 1468 when they were mortgaged to the Scottish crown. Step by step, they then bridged the Atlantic, reaching the Faroes (850), Iceland (874), Greenland (984) and finally Vinland—North America—(1000). The Atlantic leap itself was achieved in just two generations. Eric the Red left Norway to farm in Iceland, and then moved on to found the Greenland colony. It was his son, Leif, who discovered America.

The Norwegians also swept down the west coast of Britain, to the Isle of Man, the Lake District and Ireland. The Danes meanwhile landed in eastern England, establishing York as their major center. In the south of England, the Danish king Canute eventually reigned (1016–1035) over a combined English, Danish and Norwegian domain. At the same time Northern France became Normandy, the land of the northmen, soon to emerge as an independent country and, under Duke William, to begin the conquest of Britain in 1066.

The Coming of Christianity

Though the impact of the Vikings was great, the Viking age itself was relatively short lived, lasting from about 800 to 1050. Perhaps its very vividness was such as to ensure that it exhausted itself quickly. At all events, by the middle of the 11th century, the Viking period was rapidly being superceded by a new and much more stable economic and political order that was to last right up to the Renaissance. And at the heart

SCANDINAVIAN HISTORY

of this new medieval society was Christianity, slowly but inevitably dispersing the seemingly endless night of the Dark Ages.

The Vikings themselves yielded to the forces of the "pale Galilean." Some indeed appeared positively to welcome the new religion and proved themselves enthusiastic converts and, later, missionaries, happy to despatch those whose interest was more tepid to the Viking Valhalla. Nonetheless, the old beliefs and religions of the Vikings lingered on— their Gods Tyr, Wodon, Thor and Frey are still with us, disguised as Tuesday, Wednesday, Thursday and Friday. For a time, Christianity fused with the Viking religions to create curious hybrids, nowhere better illustrated than by the 12th-century stave churches of Norway, a number of which have survived to the present day at Fantoft, Borgund and Lom. These tall, pagoda-like structures, whose tiered wooden roofs rise delicately skywards, are always surmounted by a cross, but on their eaves and along the door jambs dragons and other pagan symbols are carved. Even today there are clear traces of the old Scandinavian religions in the far north among the Lapps and in Finnmark.

But Christianity proved itself an irresistable force and by 1300 had established itself throughout Scandinavia. Sweden even produced a saint, Bridget, born in 1303. She subsequently moved to Rome where she wrote a series of widely influential mystic *Revelations* and founded an order of nuns, the Bridgettines.

The Middle Ages

For all that Christianity underpinned Scandinavian society in the Middle Ages, Scandinavian history in this period nonetheless presents a confused picture of suceeding dynasties, recalcitrant nobles and scheming bishops. And for much of the period, that is until the beginning of the 17th century, Scandinavia remained essentially remote from developments on the wider European stage, a minor player in an increasingly important game. Even Denmark, for example, long the most developed and prosperous of the Scandinavian countries, largely by virtue of its proximity to the European mainland, was reduced to bit part status, falling under the sway of the Hanseatic League, the predatory merchants of Hamburg and Lübeck in north Germany who negotiated for themselves lucrative trading monopolies among the hapless Scandinavians. The Hansa quays in Bergen, Norway, have survived as potent evidence of Hanseatic power.

At the same time that Scandinavia was groaning under the Hanseatic yoke in the 13th and 14th centuries, another catastrophe struck in the form of the Black Death. Norway alone lost a third of her population between 1349 and 1350. Essential reading for an idea of the impact of the Black Death on the infant Scandinavian states is Sigrid Undset's sprawling novel *Kristin Lavransdatter*.

Literature of another sort was actually being produced during this period, in Iceland, by the aristocratic and cultured Snorri Sturlson (1179–1241). He it was who committed to writing the achievements and adventures of the Viking age, and celebrated early Iceland's turmoil and warring, in the Sagas and Eddas, the greatest monuments of early Scandinavian literature and an invaluable treasure house of historic myths and tales. Ironically perhaps, he did so at a moment when not only had the Vikings all but faded from the scene but when Iceland itself, until the 13th century a considerable political force in Scandinavian affairs and a proudly independent land—it is Iceland's happy boast that she is the site of the oldest republic north of the Alps—was fast fading herself, a decline continued in 1264 when Iceland succumbed to Norwegian rule, as had Greenland three years earlier.

However, this period of Norwegian expansion in the 13th century was to prove brief and, the Hanseatic League notwithstanding, by the 14th century it was Denmark that had emerged as the dominant voice in Scandinavian affairs, consolidating her hold on the whole of the region in 1389 in the shape of the Kalmar Union by which Sweden, Finland and Norway were united under Danish rule. The Kalmar Union, which lasted until 1521, was essentially the work of the remarkable Queen Margrethe of Denmark. She was, however, Regent only and in 1397 handed the reigns of power to her incompetent nephew, Eric of Pomerania. The combination of his maladministration and the greed of his henchmen was more than sufficient to cause a seemingly endless series of revolts among his subject peoples, especially in Sweden. The Danish rulers that followed Eric were hardly less inept, but nonetheless the Union struggled precariously through the 15th century. By the end of the century, following the ascendency of the energetic and authoritarian Christian II of Denmark, it appeared set for greater things, however. Determined to stamp out dissent among the Swedes once and for all, in 1520 Christian initiated a massacre of the leading members of the so-called Freedom Party in Stockholm. But his efforts were to prove entirely counter-productive, and only sparked greater demands for Swedish independence. This the Swedes were dramatically and violently to achieve, principally under the imaginative and forceful leadership of Gustavus Vasa. Capitalizing on a popular uprising in the province of Dalecarlia, Gustavus fanned the flame of revolt and by 1523 had established himself as undisputed ruler of a newly-independent and aggressive Sweden. Thus the stage was set for Sweden's greatest moment of glory and expansion.

The Reformation and Sweden's Rise

The Sweden now ruled by the indomitable Gustavus Vasa was still an essentially impoverished and downtrodden land following almost two centuries of Danish domination. Similarly, though the Danes had been ousted from Sweden, their military intentions toward her were by no means exhausted and they remained in control of parts of southern Sweden, a permanent threat to Gustavus. Thus much of Gustavus's reign was characterized by an urgent need to consolidate Sweden's independence from Denmark and to build up trade as rapidly as possible in order to finance his increasingly ambitious military goals.

In this, Gustavus shrewdly and pragmatically took advantage of the slow spread of the Reformation into Scandinavia. Like his contemporary Henry VIII in England, Gustavus, guided largely by political rather than spiritual considerations, took advantage of the split with Rome to support and eventually to establish as the new national church the Reformed—that is, the Protestant—religion. Simultaneously, he systematically confiscated much of the considerable wealth of the old Catholic church in Sweden, using it to finance his armies.

As Sweden grew in strength, in the process ridding herself of the remaining monopolies enjoyed by the waning Hanseatic League, so Gustavus began to interest himself more and more in foreign affairs. And it was under Gustavus that for the first time since the Vikings a Scandinavian country began to enjoy influence and status on the wider European stage. An alliance with Francis I of France against the future emperor of the Holy Roman Empire, Charles V, represented only the first stirrings of Sweden's ambitions toward, and influence over, the affairs of the Holy Roman Empire on the European mainland.

The Reformation enjoyed equal success in the rest of Scandinavia, spreading throughout the joint kingdom of Denmark and Norway and into Swedish controlled Finland, and finally to Iceland. To some extent, the Reformed Church acted as a new focus of nationalism for the Danes, still smarting from their defeat at the hands of Gustavus Vasa. Sweden's position by the end of the 16th century was still somewhat precarious. Her only outlet to the North Sea, for example, was a narrow strip at the mouth of the Göta river between hostile Denmark and Norway, and her ambitions in the Baltic were permanently under threat from Russia and Poland as well as Denmark herself. Moreover, by the beginning of the 17th century Denmark had acquired a new ruler in Christian IV (1588–1648) whose dynamism and ambition were formidable. As well as being an indefatigable builder—Copenhagen's fairy-tale summer palace of Rosenborg and the Borsen (Stock Exchange) with its barley-sugar-twist spire both owe their existence to the energetic Christian; similarly, he rebuilt Oslo, moving it nearer to its present location and renaming it Christiania in the process—Christian made strident efforts to regain the dominance Denmark had enjoyed during the heyday of the Kalmar Union. Denmark still controlled all shipping passing through the narrow sound between Copenhagen and southern Sweden—the Sound of Sounds, as it came to be known, and the principal link between the Baltic and the North Sea. Similarly, her maritime prowess in the Baltic remained impressive.

Under Christian the Danes embarked on an extended series of military campaigns against the Swedes. However, while the Danes were fortunate to have so outstanding a ruler in Christian, the Swedes were even more blessed. And in Gustavus II Adolphus, the Lion of the North who roared his way to the throne in 1611, they found themselves a ruler of outstanding military abilities, more than the equal of even one as apparently awesome as Christian IV.

Under Gustavus, Sweden swept confidently into the 17th century and her age of greatness, during which she defeated the Danes, driving them out of southern Sweden, and turned the Baltic into what was to amount to her own private preserve. In addition, the brilliant military campaigns waged by Gustavus were to ensure Sweden a decisive role in the complex entanglements of the Thirty Years War (1618–1648), in which the Catholic forces of the Holy Roman Empire, ruled by the Habsburgs, grappled brutally and somewhat pointlessly with the Protestant forces of northern Europe, represented principally by Sweden. By 1632, in fact, the Swedes under Gustavus had swept through the whole of present day Germany and were poised to take Austria, the heart of the Holy Roman Empire, when Gustavus was killed at the battle of Lutzen in 1632. The Swedes were victorious at Lutzen, but the death of their charismatic general and king broke the momentum of

SCANDINAVIAN HISTORY

The Swedish Empire, 1523 to 1721
- Sweden in the reign of Gustavus Vasa (1523-60)
- Swedish gains, 1561-1645
- Swedish gains, 1645-58
- greatest extent of Swedish Empire, 1658
- fortress
- 1617 dates refer to Swedish acquisition

their campaign, and the battle was to mark the high point of the European adventures.

Gustavus Adolphus was succeded by his young daughter, the enigmatic and ambivalent Christina. In the early part of her reign, however, when Christina was still a child, the country was governed by a Council headed by the able statesman Axel Oxenstierna. Though Sweden under Oxenstierna remained a major military influence in the Thirty Years War, which, as it neared its climax, was to turn Germany into one vast and chaotic battlefield, Oxenstierna himself turned his attentions increasingly towards developments in the Baltic, seeking to establish Sweden as the pre-eminent power there. In this, as in other matters of foreign policy, Christina played no very significant role once she had come of age. Though a woman of striking intelligence (but of less-than-lovely appearance), Christina devoted herself almost exclusively to establishing luxury, elegance and learning in her court. Her reckless extravagance and neglect of matters of state, despite the warnings of Oxenstierna, were eventually to prove her undoing and in 1654 she was forced to abdicate. Her disgrace in the eyes of her countrymen, who by now she affected to despise for their ignorance and crudity, was compounded by her subsequent conversion to Catholicism in Paris. She thereafter settled in Rome, living in the same house that St. Bridget had used, where she died in 1689.

However, the combined efforts of Oxenstierna and Christina's successors Charles X Gustavus and Charles XI Gustavus were equal to the task of ensuring that Sweden's dominant role in Scandinavia and the Baltic was continued. Indeed it was under Charles X in the Danish-Swedish war of 1657–60 that Sweden eventually reclaimed the remaining Danish territories in southern Sweden, confining Denmark once and for all to the areas west of the Sound.

By the end of the 17th century Sweden was again ruled by a man of outstanding military ability, the romantic soldier-king Charles XII Gustavus. He needed to be, too, for in 1700 Sweden was attacked simultaneously by the combined armies of Poland, Denmark and Russia. Despite the overwhelming numerical superiority of his enemies, Charles achieved a remarkable victory over the Russians at Narva in 1700, which effectively destroyed the enemy alliance. He subsequently marched on Moscow but was defeated—as much by the Russian winter as by the Russian army—at Poltava in 1709. Charles sought refuge in Turkey from where, extraordinarily, he continued to rule over distant Sweden. By now, however, Sweden faced an even larger alliance, made up of Russia, Poland, Denmark, Britain and two of the north German states, Hanover and Prussia. Hopelessly outnumbered, Charles then attempted to disrupt the alliance between Russia and Britain, to which end he returned, incognito, to Scandinavia in 1718. In the middle of these clandestine negotiations, Charles was mysteriously murdered in Norway, ending all hope of disrupting the powerful forces ranged against him. The Swedes were forced to capitulate.

Much of Sweden's Baltic empire was ceded to the Russians, including large parts of Finland, and by 1721 the once indomitable Swedes found that their empire had all but vanished leaving the way clear for the Russians, who soon after emerged as the dominant power in the Baltic.

Rococo and Revolution

Though Sweden remained the dominant power in the 18th century among the Scandinavian nations, the period as a whole witnessed the gradual decline of Scandinavian influence. For example, while Denmark continued to enjoy considerable maritime prestige, she was also to fall increasingly under the influence of Prussia in northern Germany, a trend that continued into the 19th century. Similarly, Norway and Finland, the one still ruled by Denmark, the other partitioned between Sweden and Russia, remained obscure and generally insignificant lands. And Sweden herself was forced to watch the gradual erosion of what remained of her Baltic empire.

Nonetheless, it was in Sweden that the most interesting developments occurred, especially during the reign of Gustavus III, who came to the throne in 1771. He was responsible both for a radical reshaping of Swedish government—a vital early step in the development of democracy in Sweden—and for a great upsurge in the importance of Swedish arts. His marvelous palace at Drottningholm, just outside Stockholm, with its delightful Rococo theater, is eloquent proof of the artistic revolution that occurred under this most enlightened of Swedish kings. The period also saw Sweden step into the intellectual and scientific limelight. Carl von Linée—we know him as Linnaeus—was the leading botanist of his day, whose revolutionary *Systems of Nature* pioneered the same essential system of classification for plants as that used today. Gustavus—a great admirer of all things French—also founded the Swedish Academy, modeled on its famous French cousin.

But in 1792 Gustavus was assassinated, a victim of the violent political opposition his far-reaching reforms had stirred up among the Swedish aristocracy. Yet to some extent even his death amounted to little more than a sideshow, for by the end of the 18th century, internal events in Scandinavia were being more and more overshadowed by the turmoil engulfing Europe as a whole following the French Revolution. As Napoleon and his revolutionary armies marched across the Continent, the Scandinavians found themselves inexorably drawn into the greater European conflict, with consequences that were to influence decisively the further development of Scandinavian history.

Thus in 1801, for example, Nelson attacked Copenhagen to prevent Napopleon obtaining the Danish navy for his intended invasion of Britain. Six years later, Wellington bombarded the capital again and seized the fleet himself. Similarly, Sweden under Gustavus IV Adolphus, having declared herself for Britain largely on the strength of her trading links, was attacked by the Russians in 1807 following a recent alliance forged between Napoleon and Russia. The Swedish–Russian conflict was in fact to have a number of very important consequences. Not only did Sweden lose her remaining Finnish territories to the Russians, she also found herself with a new, and very unexpected ruler. This was one of Napoleon's marshalls, one Bernadotte, who, with the active collusion of Napoleon (who saw Bernadotte as a swift means of obtaining control over Sweden), was elected king of Sweden in 1809. However, the French emperor's hopes were quickly dashed when Bernadotte revealed himself as both profoundly opposed to Napoleon's scheming and shrewd in the extreme. At the Congress of Vienna in

1815, which settled the fate of post-Napoleonic Europe, Bernadotte was able to obtain considerable compensation for the loss of Sweden's Finnish lands, and even more spectacularly confirmed the transfer of Norway, which had been ruled by Denmark since the 14th century, from Denmark to Sweden. Denmark meanwhile was left only with the politically and economically insignificant North Atlantic islands of Iceland, Greenland and the Faroes.

Industrialization and Independence

More than the political map of Scandinavia was changed by the events of the first decades of the 19th century, however. By about 1820, it was evident that Scandinavia was economically crippled, unable to keep pace with the ever more rapid developments of the Industrial Revolution or to exploit the growing opportunities for trade created by the opening of new markets outside Europe by the leading European nations, among whom the Scandinavians emphatically no longer numbered.

The 19th century was in fact a generally dismal time for the Scandinavians. Lacking the capital to develop their own modern industries, their trade was gradually taken over by foreign concerns, causing a decline in home markets that made only all the more remote the likelihood of the industrialization that by 1850 had become long overdue. Simultaneously, Scandinavian agriculture also declined, giving rise to wide-spread rural poverty which in turn led to massive emigration, particularly to America. This reached a peak between 1880 and the turn of the century.

But bankruptcy was in some senses the mother of Scandinavian invention, and from the middle years of the 19th century, a slow industrialization spread throughout the region. Such breakthroughs as Ørsted's in electro-magnetism helped the Nordic lands, lavishly endowed with water for electricity, to industrialize efficiently. Nobel's invention of dynamite changed the nature of war and mining. Similar inventive genius assisted in the growth of Danish dairying, Norwegian nitrates and Swedish ball-bearing factories. Developments in steamships helped found an expanding Norwegian merchant navy for fishing, world trade and, at home, provided the coastal services from Bergen to Kirkenes and back, forerunner of today's Coastal Express. Railways opened up vast interior tracts and serviced mines in Sweden and Finland, while canals bypassed the Baltic, linking Stockholm with Gothenburg through the great lakes. The Danes established Esbjerg in 1868 especially for trade with Britain, while the United Steamship Company was created two years earlier to link the nation's scattered areas, and is still with us as DFDS.

Scandinavians, with their small populations, were also among the first to realize the importance of an educated, fully participatory majority. Here the chief figure was the Dane Gruntvig (1783–1872), whose deep reading in the Sagas, widely-based religious views, boundless energy and patriotism led him to create the highly influential Folk High School movement. These schools, somewhat misnamed in English, offered "Education for Life"—culture, history and poetry, moral and practical subjects and economics for all.

SCANDINAVIAN HISTORY

While the latter half of the 19th century saw a slow rise in prosperity in Scandinavia and the political foundation of the modern Scandinavian states, it also saw the only serious foreign entanglement to befall Scandinavia since the end of the Napoleonic wars. This occurred on Denmark's southern border with Prussia in Germany, long a source of friction between Danes and Germans. By the 1860s, the Prussians, guided by their wily Chancellor Bismarck, had begun to cast covetous eyes on Denmark's border provinces, the acquisition of which they saw as the first step in the unification of Germany under Prussia. When war came in 1864 the military might of the Prussians was rapidly decisive and Denmark, having lost Norway only 50 years earlier, now found herself stripped of one sixth of her remaining lands. That the Danish monarchy survived such a crushing national humiliation spoke volumes for its stability and popularity. (Denmark's southern provinces were eventually restored to her in 1920).

The latter part of the 19th century was also marked by the growing spread of democratic and nationalistic ideals, culminating in 1905 with the dissolution of the joint kingdom of Sweden and Norway and the granting of full independence to Norway. Finland's independence from Russia in 1917, however, was achieved at much greater cost. All the Scandinavian nations had managed to remain neutral in World War I (though all, especially Norway, suffered considerable disruption of their trade). The Finns were thus well placed to take advantage of the Russian Revolution in 1917, which plunged an already war-torn Russia into terrible chaos, and declare themselves independent. Though the new Russian regime under Lenin soon recognized this independent Finland, a large body of opinion in Finland did not and civil war broke out; the "whites" favoring independence, the "reds" continued union with Russia, or the Soviet Union as it had now become. The whites were quickly victorious, however, and in 1920 the borders of modern Finland were established.

The Modern States

The Scandinavian nations continued on their peaceful course until the late '30s, all by now determinedly neutral and essentially removed from the growing tensions in Europe caused by the rapid rise of Nazism and the Soviet Union. But in 1939, despite their professed neutrality, the Finns were invaded by the Soviet Union, with whom they had signed a pact of non-agression in 1932. Remarkably, Finland resisted the vast but disorganized Soviet army for over 100 days before capitulating in March 1940. Under the terms of the subsequent peace treaty the Finns were obliged to cede large parts of their eastern lands to Russia.

This, however, was only the beginning of Scandinavia's troubles. As in World War I, all the Scandinavian nations attempted to remain neutral following the outbreak of World War II. The Swedes alone succeeded in doing so. Both Norway and Denmark were invaded by Nazi Germany in April 1940, while Iceland was occupied by Britain and, later, by the Americans who used it as a vital staging post for ferrying men and supplies across the Atlantic. Finland, meanwhile, then sided with the Nazis; not, as they are quick to point out, for any ideological reasons but because they saw the Nazi invasion of Russia in 1941 as an ideal opportunity to regain the territories lost in 1940. In this they were singularly unsuccessful, and ended the war by fighting the Russians *and* the Germans. Though non-combatants, the Danes and, even more particularly, the Norwegians, had suffered almost equally grave destruction by the end of the war. To some extent the very effectiveness of the Resistance movements both spawned was responsible, provoking the occupying Nazis into terrible acts of reprisal.

By 1945 Norway, Denmark and Finland were all seriously weakened, the Finns in addition having lost again to the Russians all the territory they had regained following their initial invasion with the Germans. Even neutral Sweden ended the war with severe economic problems caused by the disruption of her trade and the expense of the rapid armaments program she had been forced into in order to maintain her neutrality.

Thus it is really only in the immediate post-war period that Scandinavia has grown into the plenty and excellence that so distinguishes her today. Politically, the major developments of this period were the granting of full independence to Iceland in 1944, followed by the granting of full autonomy to Greenland in 1979. 1956 saw the formation of the Nordic Council, a loose grouping of all the Scandinavian states designed to further co-operation and development. Still a thriving organization today, it expresses eloquently the new and happy unity of this much-troubled region.

Yet even in today's affluent society—and Scandinavia seems to have weathered the recessions of the '70s and early '80s better than most—there are many reminders that the Scandinavia of the past, the vast and trackless land that even the Romans failed to penetrate, lingers on, a permanent reminder of an ancient people. In the far north Eskimos still hunt seal and polar bear where best they can be found, and Lapps still wander in search of fresh pastures for their reindeer. They may have walkie-talkies and central heating, but their lives are otherwise little changed from those of their ancestors two thousand years ago.

SCANDINAVIAN HISTORY

The Rise of the Modern States

- national borders
- areas which have changed hands since 1815

ICELAND
granted home rule by Denmark 1874
1918 Sovereign state, in personal union with Denmark
Independent republic 1944
Reykjavik

Arctic Ocean

PECHENGA (Petsamo)
1920 to Finland
1944 to USSR

1944 to USSR

Arctic Circle

Norwegian Sea

USSR

SWEDEN

Trondheim

FINLAND
Swedish to 1809
1809-1917 to Russia
Independent 1917

NORWAY
Independent 1905

united 1814-1905

Tammerfors

1944 to USSR

Gulf of Bothnia

Bergen

Christiania (renamed Oslo 1925)

Åbo Helsinki Lake Ladoga

Stavanger

Uppsala

Vyborg

Stockholm

Leningrad (St. Petersburg)

Gulf of Finland

Åland Is.
1809 to Russia
1921 to Finland, neutralized

ESTONIA
Swedish, to Russia from 1721

Gotland
1645 to Sweden

DENMARK

Esbjerg Malmö

Copenhagen

Baltic Sea

LIVONIA
Swedish, to Russia from 1721

USSR

Tønder

Bornholm
1660 to Denmark

LITHUANIA
Swedish, to Russia from 1721

Flensburg

Kiel Rügen I.

PRUSSIA

SCHLESWIG-HOLSTEIN
1866 to Prussia
1920 north divided by plebiscite between Denmark and Germany

Stettin

SWEDISH POMERANIA
1815 to Prussia

POLAND

N

W GERMANY | E GERMANY

SCANDINAVIAN CULTURE

A Subtle Taste for Living

by
ANDREW BROWN

Andrew Brown is an Englishman who has lived in Sweden for the last eight years, with his Swedish wife. He has traveled widely in Scandinavia as a journalist and is a regular contributor to many English papers and magazines, notably the London Spectator.

The chief modern cultural product of Scandinavia is children's stories. Though one expects "Scandinavian Culture" to be a quite exceptionally gloomy affair; it is really quite hard work to find the gloomy bits nowadays. And even harder to take them seriously once you have.

But almost everyone has read Scandinavian children's stories with pleasure: Hans Christian Andersen, Astrid Lindgren, Tove Jansson (the inventor of Moomintroll)—even the Norwegians have produced the delightful stories of "Old Mrs Pepperpot"; and all these sell in vast quantities throughout the world. They deserve to, too. It is a considerable compliment to Scandinavian culture in its broadest sense that children's literature flourishes here as it does. Good children's books are not less important or easier to write than good books of any sort, and most of us can far more easily remember the books that we read as children than the books we read last week.

Nonetheless, it is surprising that so little that is worth the attention of grown-ups should nowadays be produced in Scandinavia, when one considers that writers, musicians, sculptors and architects as good as any in the world were flourishing here as recently as 50 years ago. This is a point to which I will return; for the moment, it's worth concentrating on what is good now.

The Idyll of Spring

Scandinavian children's books are for the most part idyllic: they are set in small, isolated communities in the country. Very little machinery is involved: and when it appears it is always quaint and unimportant. What really matters is the weather. Astrid Lindgren and Tove Jansson, for example, are both extraordinarily sensual writers, in the pristine sense of the world. "Sensual" on a book-jacket nowadays is merely a code-word for "steamy," as if all skin were good for were the transmission of sexual excitement. But children's skin is good for a great deal more than that, and both Astrid Lindgren and Tove Jansson write as if they can still feel the exhilaration that each fresh summer brings to your skin: cool water; the thin, refreshing scent of wild-flowers borne incongruously on warm air; the smell of mushrooms poking through pine-needles after rain.

Perhaps all these things are the gift of winter: for four months a year there are no smells and no sounds in the Scandinavian forests at all. Only when the snow melts and the earth warms do the smells return, and then the migratory birds start singing. Everything drips, trickles or gurgles for a fortnight. You can walk for hours in the woods just listening to the noises snow makes when it melts. Each one seems to promise deliverance, and, sure enough, when all the snow has gone, you feel as if you were stepping onto some undiscovered, paradisal planet after several million years in suspended animation in a very old and creaky spaceship.

This sort of overwhelming change is something denied to the adult inhabitants of more temperate places, but childhood anywhere is full of times like that: and by close concentration on the seasons Tove Jansson and Astrid Lindgren can perfectly reproduce the child's sensation of exhilarating uncertainty. Tove Jansson's "Moomintroll" books tend in fact to be named for the seasons; in Astrid Lindgren the weather is less prominent than the adventures of the hero or heroine, but without it almost all the emotional color would be lost, and you would be left with a comic-strip.

But these books are set in a hermetically sealed world. It is not sealed off from adults. On the contrary, the books allow us to rediscover our own childhoods; but it is sealed off from the present as tightly as, say, P.G.Wodehouse's world is. In the "Moomintroll" books, the characters are not even clothed in human form. A Filijonk or a Hemulen are both far more accurately described human types than you will find in most "serious" adult novels, but they are both animals about six inches high, living in hidden valleys along the Baltic coast of Finland. Astrid Lindgren's families live in a rural Sweden that has now quite vanished:

even the food they eat is never nowadays cooked because it's too much trouble.

Meetings in the Potato Patch

Yet as soon as one comes to the present, it seems that Scandinavian literature has wholly lost its power. Leaving aside Ingmar Bergman's film scripts, hardly anything has been written in any Scandinavian language of any real quality since about 1950. This is all the more extraordinary because of the great importance Scandinavians attach to culture. They read more books and newspapers than anyone else in the world: their libraries are flexible, imaginative, and rich; their museums are marvelous; culture is even news, so that a new book or play will be announced and discussed on the primetime television news. And it's all rubbish. The student of modern Scandinavian fiction can weep tears of pure joy if he encounters even competence, let alone interest or quality. This has at least one reassuring feature for the traveler: you need not feel you are missing anything because you are unable to read Scandinavian languages. What hasn't been translated isn't worth it (except for some poetry that couldn't be translated anyway).

Yet the reasons for the current cultural drought in Scandinavia are worth examining, if only because what came before was so very good indeed. It is difficult to believe that a region which produced Selma Lagerlöf, Ibsen, Knut Hamsun, Strindberg, and Hjalmar Söderberg, to mention only the writers, should have so thoroughly collapsed in the following generations.

The first reason was Adolf Hitler. With Stalin's help, he completely destroyed the German cultural hegemony in Central Europe: and it was from there that Scandinavian culture had traditionally been influenced. Stockholm, Helsinki, and Oslo were all largely built by German architects; German was the first foreign language of any educated Scandinavian; and in a longer perspective, German traders and missionaries had done much of the work of civilizing and Christianizing Sweden, Denmark, and Finland. After 1945, all this was gone. The Germans had invaded both Denmark and Norway; the Finns had troubles of their own, and the Swedes were extremely anxious to prove that they had had nothing to do with the losing side in the war that had just ended.

Into the vacuum created by the disappearance of the once-dominant German influence, poured Anglo-American culture, and this, for a variety of reasons, had an almost wholly corrupting effect on the native product. The two elements just haven't blended, instead they've curdled, like badly-made mayonnaise, so that the biggest-selling author in Sweden at the moment writes (quite good) copies of Kerouac, 30 years after the thing was first done. Others, more in fashion, copy Latin American authors, and so on.

But the second, and perhaps most important reason, is the importance that Scandinavians allow to culture. They devote to their own efforts an attention that would shame a population six or seven times their size. All this attention must have something to feed on, so a great many books get published that would never have seen the outside of a publisher's rubbish basket in most countries.

Gradually—or not so gradually—the average standard sinks, until only the most exceptional writers could hope to be published in a foreign country, but these too are corrupted by the great Scandinavian culture hunger.

Imagine the feelings of the reviewer who spends his time, week after week, writing things like, "X's new novel deals with sexual frustration and religious mania in Lapland at the turn of a century. Signhild, a farmer's daughter, is courted by Thorbjörn, an itinerant pedlar. But soon the dark influence of Edgar, an evangelist preacher, makes itself felt. Edgar and Thorbjörn confront each other in the market at Gnarp. Thorbjörn drowns himself. Edgar rapes Signhild, to symbolize the triumph of religious repression, but in the process her back is broken on a nearby cartwheel. Their child has many problems."

I should add that this plot is quite genuine, and such a book really has been published. I have even attempted to read another novel by X. In chapter one the characters stood around exchanging significant silences in a frozen potato patch. In chapter two they were doing the same thing a month later in the same potato patch. I cannot really comment on the following chapters.

Anyway, there you are, reviewing this sort of thing week after week, and fighting off the mounting temptation to follow Thorbjörn's example and drown yourself, when you come across a book that is both literate and interesting, if not very remarkable. Naturally, you over-praise it grotesquely: in order to show off your learning, you compare it with foreign models; and the poor author believes you. Why shouldn't he? No one else is likely to read his book and tell him otherwise; and so another promising young author is ruined.

Only Finland is free of this sort of thing, saved by the innate flamboyance of the Finnish character. And the Finnish author Henrik Tikkannen, many of whose books have been translated into English, is one of the real delights of modern Scandinavian writing.

A Chronicle of Need

What came before 1950 will not enrich your experience of modern, Americanized Scandinavia, but it is well worth reading anyway. The plays of Ibsen and Strindberg should really be seen rather than read: which means that they should be seen before you travel, since they are seldom performed in English in Scandinavia, for obvious reasons. But the novels of Selma Lagerlöf, Hjalmar Söderberg, and Knut Hamsun can be read with pleasure and profit anywhere. They are three very different writers, and the differences between them make plain the difficulty of discussing "Scandinavian Culture." Quite apart from the fact that Hamsun wrote in Norwegian, and the other two in Swedish—this hardly matters in translation—the tones they adapt could hardly be further apart. What they do have in common is that they all wrote about the same sort of carefully stratified society, where you might not like your place but you knew it well. There, if you like, was a common Scandinavian culture.

Quality is always extraordinary, so perhaps one should regard Selma Lagerlöf as the strangest author of the three; but Knut Hamsun is the one who least resembles any other author (with the possible exception of the early George Rowell, which is odd, for Hamsun died a Nazi).

The book that made his name was *Hunger,* published in 1892. The title is not to be taken metaphorically: the book is a study of the effects of starvation on a young author in Oslo over a period of three months. It is, when you think of it, a subject so obvious that it is astonishing that no-one else before or since has dealt with it. Orwell tried to in his early work, but there was always a flavor of pity in Orwell's work: the sense that this was happening to other people too. Hamsun is truer to life in that his hero is intensely selfish: you cannot imagine Orwell's narrator in *Down and Out in London and Paris* fighting over a garbage can, yet this is the sort of thing that really hungry people do.

A mere chronicle of need would not be terribly interesting: what gives *Hunger* its peculiar power is the sense of personal outrage. Appetite eats at the narrator like a cancer. "Erst kommt das Fressen, dann die Moral," wrote Brecht, (First you must pig yourself; then think of morality). With Hamsun you can see it happening. And just as the narrator's own body rebels against him, demanding food when he would rather consider morality, so he rebels against the social organism surrounding him. The society of Hamsun's day was still extremely formal: you will find traces of this in modern Finland, but nowhere else in Scandinavia nowadays. The pressures of good, or respectable behavior are as great as the demands of hunger, and together they grind at the narrator like the jaws of a pike.

A little of this crushing movement tends to be lost in translation, for a technical reason that must also be borne in mind when reading Selma Lagerlöf: Swedes, and Scandinavians generally, swear religiously, rather than sexually, as Anglo-Saxons do. So when characters in these books go around exclaiming: "The Devil!", as they are prone to do, this should be understood as something a great deal ruder and more shocking in English. It is anything but quaint in the original.

Tale against Saga

Geographically speaking, the nearest great novelist to Hamsun was Selma Lagerlöf, whose stories are set in Värmland, a hilly, forested, and exceptionally beautiful province of Sweden along the southern edge of the border with Norway. Värmland remains an untamed place to this day: the last thriving family of wild wolves in Sweden lives on elk and sheep in the forests there now. It is the sort of place where children walked seven or eight miles to school every day through the forests, with their coats turned inside out as a charm against trolls. The towns and settlements are isolated and hierarchical places, almost like ships in the unfriendly wilderness. The likeness is deliberate, since from this unpromising countryside, Lagerlöf was able to extract much the same lessons as Joseph Conrad drew from the Far East. Both writers are concerned with courage more than anything: not the histrionic, mannered courage of Hemingway, where the hero can always expect an opportunity to be brave, even if no one (except five million readers) is watching him, but the more difficult exercise of bravery when there seems no reason or opportunity for it. Gösta Berling, the alcoholic priest in *Gösta Berling's Saga,* has much in common with Lord Jim. I can see them together drinking in a bar in Penang, though they would not need to say much to each other. Berling, a priest and an educated man, was at least as strange to his parishioners as "Tuan Jim" was to his Malay tribesmen.

The likeness between Selma Lagerlöf and Conrad should not be driven too far. Lagerlöf has a much less involuted style, for one thing; then there is a difference in the time their stories cover: Gösta Berling's Saga as against *A Tale of the Islands*. Selma Lagerlöf's characters have children, which Conrad's seldom do, and this gives a quite different significance to their actions.

Conrad, too, had a political understanding and interest that you would not find in any Scandinavian (or native English) writer: only someone born in Central Europe could have written *Under Western Eyes*. But the comparison is still worth making, if only because it may suggest just how good Selma Lagerlöf can be.

An Urban Miniaturist

Hjalmar Söderberg is an altogether more delicate writer; almost a miniaturist. He is the most urban and civilized of the three: equable, detatched, and clear. His effects are gained by exact concentration on small things, like a masterless dog wandering loose in the streets. All through the story in which the dog appears, its master has been a brutal boor, cowing and beating the animal whenever he gets the chance. The narrator is refined and disdainful as he watches this. Then the master dies, unmourned and the dog runs howling through the streets all night, not because he was happy with his treatment, but because any master is better than none at all: nothing could be more terrible than to be a dog for whom no one cares. If one considers the English writer who could have written such a story without sentimentality, it becomes clear that Kipling or Jack London would have made it a story about the dog, about suffering and loyalty, and living up to your alloted fate. Graham Greene would have made it a story about the boorish master— in fact this situation does appear in one of his short stories, set on the Mexican border. Söderberg makes it a story about the narrator, or you and I, who so dislike the squalor of other people's lives. The dog's ridiculous and humiliating longing is no more incongruous or avoidable than any of our aspirations; and they are just as likely to be arbitrarily crushed as the dog's was.

This sounds a very "Scandinavian" plot. It doesn't read like that at all. Söderberg's style is far too poised for melodrama or vulgarity. You don't notice the barb until it cannot be extracted, just as the beautiful color of the blood in a Renaissance painting disguises the fact that its subject is a crucifixion.

Another point in Söderberg's favour is that he wrote short stories, which make ideal reading on journeys. Perhaps *A Masterless Dog* would be a little overpowering in an airport departure lounge, which makes most people feel like that anyway; but even the best-planned journeys involve a certain amount of waiting in pointless places, and a volume of Söderberg's short stories makes a splendid charm against such horrors.

Visual Delights

There are of course other Scandinavian authors worth reading than the five I have discussed, but those you will have to discover for yourself. It's easy enough when once you've started, but the difficulty is beginning. All that a guide book can achieve is to point out things that are known to be good, without pretending to give a comprehensive coverage. Besides, few visitors will spend more than a month in Scandinavia, and there's a limit to what anyone can read in a month.

Language forms another limiting factor. The rhythms of Scandinavian languages are sufficiently strong to make the accurate translation of poetry into English extremely difficult. Similarly, the language barrier cuts one off from the theater. Swedish and Finnish drama is very good indeed: the production and the acting can be as good as anything you could see in London or New York. And the theater—and films—give great scope to the Swedish talent for collective belief.

Fortunately, there are theatrical experiences that are not dependent on language. Both opera and ballet thrive in Scandinavia. The best—and most expensive—performances, are to be seen in Copenhagen. You must book in advance for them, but it is well worth doing so. The Swedish equivalent would be the little theater at Drottningholm, a perfectly restored 18th-century Court theater, set in a palace on an island just outside Stockholm. This is where Ingmar Bergman's production of *The Magic Flute* was filmed, and it's hard to think of a more perfect setting for Mozart than Drottningholm. It is another place that can be difficult to get into because it seats so few people, but if you have any feeling for the theater at all, it is worth making very strenuous efforts to get to Drottningholm.

Finland presents a more difficult case. This is not because it is an uncultured country—on the contrary, the arts are in a better condition there than anywhere else in Scandinavia. But the Finns *will* speak Finnish, which makes their culture difficult of access. What is the point of knowing that there are five good theaters in Helsinki when you cannot understand a word that is said in any of them?

But there is hope for the traveler in music and architecture. Musically—obviously—there is Sibelius, though other Finnish composers well repay attention. There is also a considerable tradition of Russian music in Finland, and this can take unexpected forms. The Finnish equivalent of the Drottningholm theater—in as much as it is the perfect marriage of what you see with what you hear—is a high mass sung in the Russian Orthodox cathedral in Helsinki.

But in addition, the old town of Helsinki is itself a considerable aesthetic experience. Whether it is "Scandinavian" is another matter—it was built by German architects for a Russian Tsar: but it would be worth traveling to see even if it had been built on the moon by Martian trilobites. Those looking for a specifically Finnish cultural experience should try for the annual Arts Festival at Jyväskylä in the forests of Central Finland. The town of Jyväskylä is perhaps the best showplace for modern Finnish architecture, while the festival itself is famous, among other things, for the performance of that traditional Finnish music—jazz.

The Richest Scandinavians

The point behind these observations is a serious one: there is no longer any such thing as a specifically Scandinavian high culture. Such experiences are available, and I have tried to suggest some. But they are not greatly different from things you can find elsewhere in Europe. Yet if culture is taken in its broadest sense—as all organized human activities that tend to make life more worth living—then there does exist a specifically Scandinavian culture, and one which is very enjoyable. That is why children's books are important: they suggest the sort of areas where Scandinavian culture should be sought.

It is a cliché that the culture of any society tends to reflect the interests and concerns of the most powerful groups in the society, but it is an instructive cliché; and, by comparison with the rest of the world, it is women and children who are the most powerful and the richest Scandinavians. In consequence, you will find what the Scandinavians do best in the sort of places where women and children spend their money. The effort that in other countries is devoted to the arts is in Scandinavia used to make homes. What flourishes here is not so much culture as taste, and Scandinavian taste is easily acquired. Anything woven, sewn, or crotcheted that can be used to brighten up a home will be done beautifully in Scandinavia. Glass, tableware, even the most humble piece of kitchen equipment, all show a perfect balance between form and function. Such things may not seem terribly important, but they do make a tremendous difference to one's day-to-day mood, and they are the things that Scandinavians make excellently.

It is significant that the most popular museum in Scandinavia is the openair adjunct of the Anthropological Museum at Skansen in Stockholm. What Skansen commemorates is the lives and homes of ordinary people through the ages. Whole houses from all over Sweden have been moved and rebuilt there, so that visitors can peek around and see how other people made their homes. This is the culture that the Scandinavians really care about, and there is more to be seen in the Anthropological Museum itself.

Here—in a neat touch—you can buy the patterns to weave or sew the clothes you see; while tucked away in the basement are the exhibitions about the the Lapps. They are really another story, stemming from a quite different tradition, but their artefacts are the strangest and most beautiful to be found in all Scandinavia.

FOOD AND DRINK

How to Skål and Survive

Although the Viking custom of drinking toasts out of somebody else's skull went out of fashion quite some time ago, it's only fair to warn you, as a visitor to Scandinavia, that you're still in danger of losing your head. But the threat to the visitor is more subtle these days, as you'll discover when you first slide your feet under a Scandinavian table.

When Do We Eat?

The first thing which will puzzle you as you edge uncertainly towards the *spisesal* (dining room) is the question of mealtimes. Breakfast, of course, is a natural, and is consumed sometime between the early morning bath and a glance at the newspaper. But now the difficulty begins. The next meal of the day defies definition. Some Anglo-Saxons are tempted to call it dinner, counting the sandwiches and glass of milk that many businessmen eat at their desks around noon as lunch. There are even those who stick by this theory doggedly, refusing to notice that the clatter of silverware against china, which starts up around 4.30 P.M. and becomes deafening towards 6.00 P.M. has completely disappeared, in Norway at least, by the dinner hour. The Scandinavians, being practical people, avoid the dispute by calling it *middag*. We

FOOD AND DRINK

advise you to do the same, thereby working for peace in a troubled world.

Instead of sowing discord, the Scandinavians are interested merely in making maximum use of the long and bright summer evenings. Accordingly, families sit down to the main meal of the day as soon as father comes home from work, somewhere towards the tag end of the afternoon. The great advantage of this arrangement is that, once *middag* is over, everyone is free for the rest of the day. If you come hotfoot from South Dakota or South Kensington with a hatful of introductions to near relations or business acquaintances, you can turn this custom into a game. Don't refuse three or four dinner invitations you received for the same day. Just fix a different hour for each.

While you have your napkin unfolded and are wondering who's going to eat all that food, we should urge you to save some room for *aftens* or supper, the final meal of the day, not counting incidental snacks. This may be no more than cakes and coffee or it may consist of no less than a complete cold buffet, depending on the circumstances and whether or not your eyes have the socially-accepted glaze. No one is looked down upon for starting this as early as 7.00 P.M. although, at a formal party, it might well not appear until midnight.

With this overall timetable in mind, let's get down to particular dishes. The typically Scandinavian breakfast is more varied than the typical English or American one. The larger hotels, accustomed to catering to visitors from abroad, will be able to offer you bacon and eggs, though this honorable combination is not indigenous to the Scandinavian ménage. Instead, eggs, cheese, cold meats, herrings in a number of guises, jams, and fruit are all likely to make their appearance, in addition to less usual items such as cereals, porridge, hot meatballs, and salad. These you'll discover together with a great variety of bread, many kinds rarely found in other countries. One of them, *Knekkebrød*, is of the hard, unleavened type which you've undoubtedly seen elsewhere under the proprietary name of Ry King. Unless you specify otherwise, your egg will normally be served soft-boiled and still in its shell.

By the time you've tried everything, chances are you'll have a solid foundation which will carry you through to mid-afternoon. But if you find your fancy gradually turning towards thoughts of food around about noon, you have a number of choices. In most of the bigger cities there are sidewalk stands displaying signs reading *Pølser* or *Varm Korv*. At these you will be able to buy hot dogs, often wrapped in what looks like a pancake instead of a roll. They are smaller than what you're used to, and you will probably agree that they taste better.

If all you want is something cool, look for another kind of sidewalk stand, marked *Is* or *Glass*. The name has nothing to do with the verb "to be" or with windowpanes, but informs you that here you can have ice cream. The Finns, incidentally, call it *jäätelö*.

The Mysterious Open Sandwich

Failing both of these (and still assuming you're interested), make for the nearest restaurant. If you see the word *smørbrød*, you're in luck, for this is Scandinavia's most typical dish. The word means simply, "butter-bread," but there's nothing simple about it, as you'll discover when the waiter hands you a menu listing dozens of varieties.

Smørbrød is the rich uncle of its English or American nephew, the sandwich. Unlike the anonymous sort of thing served at garden parties or railway stations, it is a single-decker, and presents its offering naked and unashamed. Lobster, smoked salmon, prawns, shrimps, smoked herrings, all appropriately and artistically garnished, cold turkey, chicken, roast beef, pork, a host of sausages, cheeses, eggs, and salads, all tastefully and appetizingly arranged. Variously called *smörgås* by the Swedes and *voileipä* by the Finns, three of them taken with a cool lager are generally considered an excellent lunch, whether or not you abandon all caution and succumb to a piece of pastry for dessert. Hot food is available too, if you are still hungry.

Wherever you may be in Scandinavia, the sea is never far off, and this is a good thing to remember when you sit down to *middag*. Perhaps because the fish served in restaurants and hotels is invariably fresh, the Scandinavians are all great fish-eaters. Whatever the reason, their seafood dishes are justly renowned for their variety and excellence. Lobster, salmon, and trout are great favorites, but you will also have your choice of cured herrings, crayfish, crab, oysters, shrimps, prawns, hake, eel, and other seaborne morsels. Boiled cod may sound unromantic, yet you'll find it transformed when served *à la Scandinave* with melted butter and parsley. In the summer the Swedes and Finns indulge in traditional crayfish weeks when you can go on eating these succulent little creatures until your conscience begins to bother you. In Denmark you'll compare the Limfjord oysters to the best that Baltimore or Colchester has to offer.

Then there are a number of fish dishes which only the bolder spirits are advised to try. The first of these is *rakørret*, which is trout that, like Keats' wine, has "lain long years in the deep-delved earth." There is actually much more to the preparation of this highly odiferous *spécialité de la maison* than burying it in the backyard, but it is undoubtedly an acquired taste. Next comes *surströmming*, another form of man's inhumanity to fish, except that this time it's a herring who suffers. As the name sugests, the taste is distinctly sour; that is, if you get that far. The third of our "don'ts" for cautious gourmets is *lutefisk*, which is codfish steeped in a lye of potash. The finished product has the consistency of frog spawn and a taste which can only be experienced and not described. The Norwegians who eat this "delicacy" anesthetize themselves with such copious drams of *akvavit* one might suspect that the *lutefisk* is only an excuse.

While we are on the subject of dishes which should be approached circumspectly, we may as well complete the story with a mention of *geitost* or goat's cheese, which has the hue of scrubbing soap or milk chocolate and the texture of plastic wood. Give it a try anyhow; you'll be called on for your own opinion sooner or later. And if you are too disappointed, all the Scandinavian countries produce excellent imitations of such well-known favorites as Roquefort, Camembert, Gruyère, and even England's Stilton. Danish Blue is another local variety with which no cheese-lover could possibly quarrel.

Scandinavian cooks use margarine or butter for their cooking, and not oil as the Latins do. Game and roasts are usually served with a cream sauce which is delicious. In some cases, sour cream is used, and

FOOD AND DRINK

ryper (a variety of grouse or ptarmigan) prepared with this sauce and accompanied by cranberry jam is a rare treat.

By now you are doubtless wondering what has happened to the renowned Swedish *smörgåsbord*. It's doing fine, thank you. But let me first explain to the uninitiated that the *smörgåsbord* (called *voileipäpöytä* by the Finns) is a very special *hors d'oeuvre*, offering the diner a stupendous number of small dishes, each more calculated than the last to whet his appetite and make him forget all rash resolutions to respect his waistline. The beauty of this institution is that it contains no *pièce de résistance* to dominate the table. You roam at will like the honey bee, savoring here a morsel of smoked eel, there a little lobster, and roving through the delicacies of the animal kingdom, with regular rounds of *akvavit* and beer to give you fresh incentive. These days, the *smörgåsbord* is seldom the prelude to a four-course dinner in private homes, but some restaurants feature it as a specialty, maybe on a certain day in the week.

Desserts do not run to the English or American pattern. Neither the English pudding nor the American ice cream desserts are as prevalent as soufflés, large, tiered cream cakes, and berries in season. Strawberries reach the table somewhere around the end of June and manage to survive for a commendable number of weeks. Later on in the year, Finland, Norway and Sweden offer a delicious wild berry which is hardly known elsewhere, the cloudberry, called *suomuurain* or *lakka* in Finnish, *hjortron* in Sweden, and *multer* in Norway. In appearance rather like an overgrown unripe raspberry, it has a delicate aroma which is unique. Incidentally, the Finns make a delicious liqueur from the juice of this berry.

Speaking of liquid refreshments, we should note that the Scandinavians are coffee-drinkers rather than tea-drinkers, and they make their coffee good and strong, in the best Continental tradition. In Denmark and Norway, coffee is somewhat expensive, and families who drink a lot have to make up for it with some sort of substitute. This trend has, of course, resulted in an increase in tea-drinking, but on the whole the Scandinavians have not yet acquired the English touch. So be sure to emphasize that you want your tea strong. Don't expect to find that the cult of tea has made the Scandinavians tea-conscious. The buttered toast, crumpets and muffins of Belgravia have no afternoon counterpart in Bergen or Bornholm. Instead, look for a restaurant-type of place with the sign *"Konditori"* over the door. The waitress will bring cakes to your table along with tea, coffee, milk or a soft drink. You'll be hard put to choose among the several delicious varieties.

Skål

Scandinavia's local brand of firewater is known as *akvavit*, and a glass of this is known in Denmark, Sweden and Finland as *snaps*, whereas the Norwegians call it a *dram*. Served at the beginning of the main meal of the day—at the *hors d'oeuvre* stage, or occasionally with the first course—it is invariably taken with a beer chaser. *Akvavit* emphatically is not a drink for the tyro toper and you'll find it takes a little practice to attain proficiency in the local ritual of gulping it down without falling off your chair. The mysteries of the *skål* or toast, apart from regional variations, are too complicated to explain here, but you won't go far wrong if you stick to the following procedure.

First, at the start of any meal, wait for someone to give the signal. At a formal party, the host, after clearing his throat ominously or belaboring the nearest piece of china or crystal with a soup spoon, will seize his glass and launch into a *velkommen til bords* speech. All this means is "welcome to the table" and you may even find it a gracious gesture of hospitality. Anyhow, the crucial thing is to listen intently for the word *skål*. This is your cue. Seizing your own glass, you hold it firmly in a position of tantalizing proximity to your parched lips, though preferably far enough away from your nose to avoid asphyxiation. Then you nod your head north, south, east, and west as you echo "*skål.*" Now, and not a moment sooner, your *akvavit* starts its downward journey. This is the supreme test. As all hell breaks loose somewhere in your gullet, you may be tempted to reach convulsively for the beaker of cool beer that beckons by your plate. Not so the trained snapser. He returns his glass to its original position just south of his chin, nods blandly to the four points of the compass while simulating an air of complete indifference to the fires consuming within, and then sends a mouthful of malt brew in pursuit of the *akvavit*.

When the urge to wet your whistle descends on you, don't try a surreptitious drink on your own, but pick up your glass boldly, fix a fellow diner with a purposeful stare, pronounce the word "*skål,*" and proceed as above. Anyone is fair game for this except your hostess; after all, someone has to keep track of the time. Apart from achieving a drink, you will undoubtedly have won the undying gratitude of your friend across the table, who was almost certainly contemplating a similar move. Remember that husbands are expected to *skål* their wives, who, if slighted, are entitled to collect a pair of stockings by way of damages.

Although there are so many striking points of similarity between the food and drink of each of the Scandinavian countries, it is surprising that in a few unimportant details, which only indirectly affect the table, there should be some startling discrepancies. For example, one may say without any risk of offending the Swedes and the Danes, that the Finns and Norwegians make infinitely better dessert and eating chocolate. On the other hand, the Danish Aalborg akvavit and the Swedish Norrland akvavit can be said to be the best of its kind—but the Norwegians have gone one step further by producing their *linje akevitt,* which is stored in huge sherry vats of American white oak, and then sent on Norwegian cargo liners to Australia and back. It is said that the rolling of the ship, combined with the change of climate when crossing the Equator—the "Linje"—adds an unusual flavor to the "scalplifter." Lager beer in Scandinavia is of top quality, whether you drink Danish Carlsberg or Tuborg or Norwegian Ringnes or Schou, all of which are exported around the world.

There is, unfortunately, one more essential piece of advice to impart while on the subject of liquor in Scandinavia—namely, that it is very expensive. The Danes get away quite lightly in this respect, but in all the other Scandinavian countries, alcohol, especially the imported variety, is very, very pricey. And just to add insult to injury, you'll also discover that the Scandinavians, like the British, have strict and inflexi-

FOOD AND DRINK

ble licensing hours, outside which it is not possible to buy so much as the humblest glass of beer. Don't say you haven't been warned.

A Final Word

You will find that the Scandinavians have elevated the culinary arts to a high place among the graces which add flavor to life. Wherever you dine you will discover that the serving is on a par with the cuisine. Helpings are generous, dishes and drinks which are supposed to be hot really are hot, and iced drinks never arrive in a semitepid state. This is only natural where hospitality is regarded as one of the supreme virtues.

After finishing a meal in Scandinavia, it is a time-honored custom for the hostess to stand near the door of the dining room. The guests, one by one, shake her hand on their way into the living room and pronounce the words, *"takk for maten."* Badly translated, this means "thank you for the food." A phrase well-worn by usage, perhaps, but nonetheless welcome from those who have dined well in congenial company.

DENMARK

60   **DENMARK**

FACTS AT YOUR FINGERTIPS

DENMARK—FACTS AT YOUR FINGERTIPS

NATIONAL TOURIST OFFICE. In the U.S.: Danish Tourist Board, 75 Rockefeller Plaza, New York, N.Y. 10019 (212–582 2802); Wilshire Boulevard 8929, Beverly Hills, CA 90211 (213–659 9494).

In Canada: Danish Tourist Board, P.O. Box 115, Station "N," Toronto, Ontario M8V 3S4 (416–823 9620).

In the U.K.: Danish Tourist Board, 196–173 Regent St., London W.1 (01–734 2637).

Within Denmark, there are some 172 local tourist offices, all of which can supply information on their own areas and can also make reservations for you in local hotels, boarding houses and the like. Not all are open all year, but those that are display the international "i" sign. We list all the major Danish tourist offices at the beginning of each *Practical Information* section.

CURRENCY. The unit of currency in Denmark is the *krone*, written as Dkr. It is divided into 100 *øre*, but as the smallest coin is 5 øre, all prices are rounded up to the nearest 5 øre.

The rate of exchange at the time of writing (mid-1984) was 9.49 Dkr. to the U.S. dollar and 13.76 Dkr. to the pound sterling. However, these rates will certainly change both before and during 1984, so be sure to keep a careful check on them while planning and during your trip.

COSTS IN DENMARK. Like all the Scandinavian countries, Denmark has a high standard of living and costs are correspondingly high. At the same time, however, while it cannot easily be considered a budget destination, Denmark is definitely less expensive to visit than either Norway or Sweden, for example. Similarly, a favorable exchange rate and reasonably low rate of inflation have also helped keep costs manageable. Nonetheless, certain items, especially alchohol, are very expensive, and it is as well to keep a watchful eye on your budget.

A typical day in Copenhagen might cost two people:

Hotel (Moderate) with bath or shower and breakfast	Dkr.	500
Lunch, in Moderate restaurant, no beer or wine		135
Dinner, in Moderate restaurant, with bottle of wine		270
Transportation, 2 buses, 1 taxi		105
	Dkr.	1,010

Sample costs. A cinema seat for one, Dkr. 30; visit to a museum or castle, Dkr. 10 (but may be more, though many are open free of charge); bottle of beer in a restaurant, Dkr. 12; house wine, by the glass in a cafe, Dkr. 10 to 15, by the bottle in a restaurant, Dkr. 80; a coke, Dkr. 7; taxi ride in Copenhagen, Dkr. 12 plus Dkr. 6.75 per kilometer; bus ride in Copenhagen, Dkr. 6.

SEASONAL EVENTS. Almost all Denmark's special events take place in the summer. However, their number and excellence more than compensate for the scarcity of winter events. The Danish Tourist Board produces a comprehensive list of events in Denmark twice a year, but among the more famous and popular are the following.

DENMARK

April, or at any rate the end of April, marks the end of the long northern winter, and the Danes celebrate in suitable fashion. Meanwhile the Numus Festival in Århus at the end of the month is one of the biggest festival of contemporary music in Europe.

May 1 traditionally sees the opening of the Tivoli Gardens in Copenhagen, while toward the end of the month the Copenhagen Carnival sees thousands of Copenhageners dancing through the streets in fancy dress. The "Wonderful Copenhagen" marathon is also at the end of the month, now in its sixth year.

June sees the summer under way with a vengeance. A number of important cultural events, some lasting to the end of the summer, take place now. Among them are the Egeskov Summer Festival Matinees, held every Sunday to the end of August at Egeskov Castle in Funen. The 16th International Organ Festival, lasting through to September and held at Søro church, consists of a series of concerts on Wednesdays featuring a wide range of works, both old and new. The Copenhagen Municipal Summer Entertainment also starts in June and lasts till September. At locations throughout the city, music, theater, dance, drama and the like is presented every day. Mid-June also sees the Zealand sailing race, the world's largest yacht race with upwards of 2,000 competitors. The end of the month also sees the Frederikssund Viking plays; audience participation and traditional feasts set the tone.

July has more Viking plays, this time at Jels in south Jutland. The Copenhagen Summer Festival also gets under way in July, and lasts until the middle of August; young Danish singers and musicians perform at Charlottenborg's Grand Hall and in the Christianborg chapel. Among numerous music festivals, the Roskilde and Copenhagen Jazz Festivals are the two most important; the former presenting music of all types, the latter concentrating on jazz, naturally. Meanwhile, over in Bornholm, in the middle of the month there's another music festival, this presenting music from all ages in churches throughout the island every Wednesday and Monday.

August kicks off in fine style with the Hans Christian Andersen Festival at Funen; local children perform one of the master's fairy tales in the open air. A rather more upmarket festival is that at Lerchenborg Castle in Kalunborg where classical and contemporary music is performed. The month ends with jazz, at the Tønder Jazz and Folk Festival in south Jutland.

September sees the country's most important cultural event, the Århus Festival Week at the very beginning of the month. Ballet, theater, opera, jazz, classical and folk music, street parties and sports abound.

LANGUAGE. English speaking visitors will have very few language difficulties in Denmark. Nearly all younger Danes speak excellent English, while most older people are almost equally fluent. In fact in larger cities, you'll have a job finding people who don't speak English. And you can rest assured that in hotels, restaurants, tourist offices, museums, bars and so on, English will practically be as common as Danish.

CUSTOMS. There are three levels of duty-free allowance for people entering Denmark. Anyone coming from outside Europe may import duty-free: 400 cigarettes or 100 cigars or 500 grams of tobacco; plus, ¾ of a liter of spirits and 2 liters of wine and 2 liters of alcoholic beverage up to 22°; plus, 55 grams of perfume and ¼ liter of toilet water; plus, other goods up to the value of Dkr. 1,400.

Entering Denmark from an EEC country you may import duty-free: 300 cigarettes or 75 cigars or 400 grams of tobacco; plus, 1½ liters of spirits and 3 liters of wine and 3 liters of alcoholic beverage up to 22°; plus, 75 grams of perfume and 0.375 liters of toilet water; plus, other goods up to the value of Dkr. 1,400.

Entering Denmark from a non-EEC European country you may import duty-free: 200 cigarettes or 50 cigars or 250 grams of tobacco; plus, ¾ of a liter of spirits and 2 liters of wine and 2 liters of alcoholic beverage up to 20°; plus, 50 grams of perfume and ¼ of a liter of toilet water; plus, other goods up to the value of Dkr. 300.

Import allowances for tobacco and alcohol are only for those aged 17 or over.

You may also import and export any amount of foreign currency, provided you declare it on arrival. You may also export any amount of Danish krone, provided you can prove they were legally imported or obtained by converting declared foreign currency.

HOTELS. Danish hotels are the equal of those anywhere in Scandinavia, or anywhere else in Europe come to that. Indeed, standards are very high throughout the country, and, with the exception of certain rather seedy city hotels which are best avoided, even the smallest and most modest hotels will be clean, comfortable and welcoming. We give prices below, but bear in mind that for the most part high season prices (generally early-May to late-September) are quite a bit higher than in the rest of the year. As a rule, breakfast and taxes are always included in the price, but be sure to check before booking that this is the case.

A good budget bet in towns are the Mission Hotels, where clean, low-priced rooms are very much the norm. They are somewhat puritanical establishments, however, and liquor tends to be rather frowned on. Nevertheless, they are very good value for families. Away from cities, Denmark is studded with *kros*, traditional country inns, often a little lacking in mod cons, but more than compensating by way of atmosphere and good value. To help cut costs even further, you can buy nightly vouchers for these inns at Dkr. 160 for two people in a double room. There's a small surcharge for single occupancy, but the price otherwise includes breakfast, and there's also a refund for every night in an inn with no private bath. The vouchers are particularly good value for motorists, not least as you make reservations as you go along, and so can be as flexible as you like. Vouchers are available from travel agents; alternatively, contact *Dansk Kroferie*, Horsens Tourist Office, Kongensgade 25, DK-8700 Horsens.

All local tourist offices will be able to help with finding places to stay and making reservations.

Prices. We have divided all the hotels we list into four categories—Deluxe (L), Expensive (E), Moderate (M) and Inexpensive (I). These grades are determined solely by price.

Two people in a double room can expect to pay (prices in Dkr.)

	Copenhagen	Elsewhere
Deluxe	850 and up	—
Expensive	700—850	500 and up
Moderate	500—700	350—500
Inexpensive	300—500	200—350

All prices are inclusive of service and taxes

SELF-CATERING. If you want to spend more than a few days in the countryside, you might consider one of Denmark's country vacations. Summer chalets rent for a minimum of one week and it is important to book early as they are very popular. Peak season prices: Dkr. 1,125–3,000 per week. A good substitute for these chalets are the *Danish Country Holidays*. You have two choices:

1. *Farmhouse Holiday* with full or half board. Guests have rooms in the farmhouse (sometimes with separate facilities) and usually eat at the same table as the host family. Prices are Dkr. 130 per person per day on a half board basis

and Dkr. 150 per person per day on a full board basis. Available all the year round (reductions for children under 12). Minimum stay 3–5 days, usually one week.

2. *Carefree Country Holidays* where guests stay in a detached cottage or in an apartment on a self-catering basis. You are supposed to bring your own linen and bedclothes. Prices are Dkr. 850–1,150 per week in the peak season with reductions for off-season stays.

Minimum stay for this program is 7 days. These holidays are especially recommended for families with children.

The Danish Tourist Board are keen to promote holiday packages which emphasize active, outdoor family vacations in rural areas, and there are many variations on the basic Carefree Country Holiday scheme. It should not be difficult to find the one that suits you. We suggest careful research into the options on offer, especially with regard to the nature and quality of accommodations provided (baths or showers, full- or half-board, self-catering, reductions for children, etc.) in order to avoid unexpected disappointments. It is worth remembering that local tourist offices will probably be able to furnish you with more detailed pamphlets and information, and will be happy to make your reservations for you. A list of their addresses is available from the Danish Tourist Board.

CAMPING. Denmark has more than 500 approved camp sites, about 70 of which are open all year round. All are rated from one to three stars. You can be sure that those with three stars will be of very high quality, with many facilities, but even the more lowly sites will be well-maintained and clean. Lists of all sites are available from the Danish Tourist Board and from local tourist offices. Note, however, that camping is not permitted outside official sites without the landowner's permission.

An International Camping Carnet or Danish camping pass—available at any campsite and valid one year—is required to stay at any camp. Passes cost Dkr. 21.

YOUTH HOSTELS. There are 90 Youth Hostels in Denmark, all comfortable, clean and well-run. Hostels are open to all, regardless of age, but you must have an International Youth Hostels Association card. These are available from the Youth Hostels Association in the U.S., Canada and U.K., but you can also buy them at any hostel. Family rooms (for families *only*) with four beds are available at most hostels. A small supplement in addition to the normal nightly fee of Dkr. 30 to 40 is charged for these, and only families with children under 18 may use them.

The Danish Tourist Board produces a list of all Youth Hostels. This is also available from *Danmarks Vandrerhjem,* Vesterbrogade 39, DK-1620, Copenhagen V.

RESTAURANTS. Though a little on the expensive side, for the most part Danish restaurants are excellent. The Danes take their food very seriously, and you'll find that even the most humble meal will be carefully prepared and served, so you need feel no qualms about eating in more modest establishments. But of course, if you do splurge, you can be very sure it will be well worth it.

Many Danish restaurants, even the most expensive, also offer fixed price menus, so always check the menu displayed in the window. But in addition, look out for the *DanMenu* sign. Around 600 restaurants have joined this scheme whereby you get a two-course meal, either lunch or dinner, for Dkr. 60 per person including service. This price has been fixed until April 30 1985, but should not increase too greatly thereafter. Another good budget bet are the restaurants at rail stations. This may not sound too tempting a prospect, but in

FACTS AT YOUR FINGERTIPS

fact you can be sure of very good value. Similarly, you'll find that many department stores and supermarkets have good cafeterias.

Be sure also to try one—or more!—of Denmark's famous sandwiches. You can buy packaged sandwiches more or less anywhere in towns and cities. Some can be huge meals in themselves, but even the most extravagant will not cost you more than about Dkr. 35. Alternatively, you can also buy a packet of three or four sandwiches for around Dkr. 25 to 35. Many country inns cater for guests who bring their own sandwiches. These usually have a notice saying *Madkurve kan medbringen* or *Medbragt mad kan spises her.* All you have to do is order a bottle of beer and ask for "service." You will then be provided, without charge, with a plate, knife, fork, pepper and salt. If you also order coffee you will be doubly welcome.

Fast food chains are also to be found everywhere in Denmark these days. All the familiar names from home are here.

Finally, note that the Danes tend to eat early. Lunch is around noon and dinner around 6. (This also has the added bonus of allowing the Dane to have a snack around 9 or 10 P.M.). But at the same time, restaurants also stay open pretty late, so there is no need to do as the Danes do.

Prices. We have divided the restaurants in our listings into three categories—Expensive (E), Moderate (M) and Inexpensive (I). These grades are determined solely by price.

Prices, per person, excluding drinks (in Dkr.)

Expensive	130 and up
Moderate	80—105
Inexpensive	45—80

All prices quoted here and in restaurants include service.

FOOD AND DRINK. As we say, the Danes take their food seriously. And nowhere is this more obviously demonstrated than by the "Cold Table," or *smørrebrød,* most usually found at lunchtimes. This consists of an enormous table groaning with an assortment of fish and cold meat or fowl. These may be boiled, pickled, fried, or roasted. The Danish way of coping with these is to take a piece of bread and delicately pile on the fish or meat together with pickles and relishes of various kinds. The result is *smørrebrød.* Don't charge into the fray too recklessly, because a hot dish usually follows if you are taking the set lunch.

Many restaurants offer a lengthy list of *smørrebrød* and you just check your choice. (The fresh shrimp, salmon, varied species of herring, roast beef with onions topped by a fried egg, are all specialties to be recommended.) There are columns for rye bread *(rugbrød)* and wheat bread *(franskbrød).* Three per person is par. If you don't find a particular restaurant's list offered to you with the daily menu, just ask for it.

There are 50 or more varieties of Danish beer made by as many breweries, and the best known come from Carlsberg and Tuborg. Most popular is Pilsner, a light beer, but there is also Lager, a darker beer. ("Lager" in Britain is called "Pilsner" in Denmark.) Each of these varieties has a stronger brother. The strong brother of Pilsner is "Gold Export", and the strong brother of Lager has several names, depending on the brewery that makes it. Among the popular Danish-made spirits and liqueurs are Cloc Liqueur, Cherry Heering, and the cherry wine *Kijafa.*

The national drink of Scandinavia is popularly called *snaps,* the famous Aalborg Aquavit. This is neither an aperitif, a cocktail nor a liqueur, but is meant to be drunk with food, preferably with a beer chaser. Some claim they drink it for the good of their tummies. *Snaps* at room temperature tastes vile, which is why it is served icy cold and should never be sipped or left to get warm. Knock it back and damn the consequences. Remember that snaps goes with cold food, particularly herrings and cheese, not hot.

DENMARK

TIPPING. Following the introduction of a 22% value added tax some years back, tipping, except for *very* special service, is categorically *not* expected in hotels, restaurants, taxis, bars, etc. All prices are fully inclusive.

MAIL. Buy stamps at post offices—all clearly marked—or from shops selling postcards. Postal rates for airmail letters to the U.S. are Dkr. 4.20, to the U.K Dkr. 2.70; postcards to the U.S. are Dkr. 3.30, to the U.K. Dkr. 2.70. These prices may change in 1985.

CLOSING TIMES. Banks are open from 9.30 to 4, Saturdays closed (6 P.M. on Thursdays). You can also exchange money outside normal closing hours at Copenhagen's Central Station and at Kastrup Airport. Shops usually operate from 9 to 5.30, staying open Fridays until 7 or 8, closing Sat. at 1 or 2 P.M. Supermarkets at Central Station and the Airport open until midnight.

Most post offices are open from 10 to 5, but the one at Copenhagen's Central Railway Station is open from 9 to 9 P.M., except on Sun., when it is open from 10 to 4.

GETTING AROUND DENMARK. By air. Though a small country, Denmark has good internal air services, most operated by SAS. There are flights from Copenhagen to Århus, Aalborg, Billund, Esbjerg, Karup, Skrydstrup, Sønderborg and Thisted, all in Jutland, and to Odense in Funen and to Rønne on the island of Bornholm. 50 minutes is the maximum flying time; must flights are much shorter, however.

By train. Denmark has an excellent rail network. Trains are fast, reliable and clean. Long distance services (by Danish standards, that is; no journey is more than five hours long) are all fast Inter City trains—shown as IC in timetables—or *Lyntog*—shown as L in timetables and meaning, literally, Lightning Train. Both have first- and second-class carriages, and most have either refreshment or dining cars. All trains between Zealand and Funen—this is known as the "Great Belt" route—require reservations. Reservations are not required for any other trains, however.

There are a variety of excellent discount tickets available for Denmark. Family tickets, valid only for a minimum of three people traveling together, give reductions of between 20 and 50%. Similarly, *Mini-Group* tickets, available to groups of at least two adults, one child under five and one other child, give discounts of between 20% and 50%. For both, discounts vary depending on when you travel and the number in your group. Otherwise, children under four are carried free; up to 12, they travel for half fare.

65 Tickets, for those over 65, are also excellent value. With these, a round-trip ticket is available for the cost of the one-way fare. However, there are restrictions on weekend travel, so check carefully before making your journey.

In addition to these exclusively Danish discounts, the *Nordturist* (or Scanrail card), the *Inter-Rail* card, the *Eurailpass* and *Eurail Youthpass, Rail Europ Senior Card* and the *Inter-Rail Senior Card* are all valid within Denmark. See "Getting Around Scandinavia by Rail" in *Planning Your Trip* for further details.

By car. Denmark's small size, charming countryside and excellent roads make it an ideal country for touring by car. Bridges connect many of the islands and all are toll-free. Similarly, ferries on inland routes are generally free, while on inter-island routes fares are moderate.

There is a general speed limit of 60 km.p.h. (37 m.p.h.) within towns; outside towns, the limit is 80 km.p.h. (50 m.p.h.) and 100 km.p.h. (60 m.p.h.) on motorways. Towing a trailer, you may never exceed 70 km.p.h. (45 m.p.h.) on motorways. Seat belts are compulsory for drivers and front seat passengers.

FACTS AT YOUR FINGERTIPS

In every town with time-limited parking restrictions you are required to use a parking disc unless you're parked at a meter. You can get a parking disc at FDM, banks, tourist offices, police stations and some shops. Place the pointer on the time of arrival in the right front window of your car and beware of exceeding the time allowance (or of parking your car illegally) as the police do come by and have cars towed away. A circular blue sign with red rim and cross means no stopping at all. Parking on country highways and motorways is prohibited.

A selection of car hire firms is given under "Useful Addresses" in *Practical Information* sections.

By bike. Denmark, like Holland, is one of those countries every cyclist dreams of: the people are friendly, the country pretty, there are lots of places to stop for the night and, above all, it is almost entirely flat. Rental bikes are widely available (the Danish Tourist Board or any local tourist office can supply lists of where to rent bikes), and in addition a growing number of tour operators are offering inclusive cycling holidays in Denmark. These are in no sense "conducted" tours, but hotels, inns or youth hostels are all arranged for you. All you have to do is pedal.

The Danish awareness of the pleasures and advantages of cycling extend to their towns and cities too. Almost every town of consequence has well-marked bike routes, from which motorized traffic is expressly banned.

By ferry. Ferry services in Denmark are generally excellent. Between Copenhagen and Rønne on the island of Bornholm there are two or more ferries daily in summer; one daily (at night) in winter. There are also good ferry links between Denmark and southern Sweden and to Norway.

The Danish Tourist Board produces an excellent booklet called *Denmark—Car Ferries,* giving comprehensive details of the multitude of car ferries connecting the various islands, as well as listing all international ferries serving Denmark.

By bus. Bus services are closely interlinked with Denmark's excellent train network and the Danish State Railways' annual timetable also details all bus services. In some more remote parts of the country, buses are often the only means of public transport.

PRELUDE TO DENMARK

The Virtues of Sanity

by
ANDREW BROWN

Denmark is a fat man's country; comfortable, cosy, and fertile. The Danes make all other Europeans seem either poor or neurotic, or both.

Perhaps the secret of this enviable state is that Denmark is a small country. Few people live in any of the Scandinavian countries: the largest and most populous—Sweden—has a population of only nine million, though it is 1,000 miles long. Denmark has a population of only five million, but what really distinguishes it from the other Scandinavian countries is that it has no wilderness. The rest of Scandinavia is beautiful because it seems that no one could live there. Denmark is beautiful because it has obviously been inhabited, and changed by people, for thousands of years. There is hardly an inch of Denmark that is not part of a farm, a house, or a garden. There are few hills, and no mountains. The visitor's first—and wholly accurate—impression is of almost indecent prosperity.

Farming, trade, and fishing had made the Danes rich long before modern industry. Admittedly the government went bankrupt in 1814, something that not even South American countries do nowadays, but this was largely a result of the Napoleonic Wars. The signal to which Admiral Nelson turned his famous blind eye was one that ordered him to stop shelling the Danish fleet to bits in Copenhagen harbor. He continued until the job was done. Though this action was subsequently dignified as "The Battle of Copenhagen," it was not a very glorious chapter in British history. You can find the scars if you look hard enough, but no one walking around Copenhagen today would suppose that anything very terrible had ever happened to the city. Poverty and misfortune have left few traces on the city, whereas the evidence of successive ages of prosperity has been lovingly preserved. Public buildings in other countries tend to be ostentatious, proclaiming the power and wealth of the people who built them. The public buildings of Copenhagen boast only of the solid comforts that their owners could afford. They are not awe-inspiring: the only emotion they arouse is envy for the people who can look at them every day.

Scandinavia's Best Joke

History is a misleading guide to the other Scandinavian countries because they have had so little of it for so long, and then changed so rapidly in the last 100 years. In 1885 two of them did not even exist: Finland was a Russian province and Norway was a part of Sweden. But history is a misleading guide to Denmark because the country has had so much of it. 100 years ago it was very poor. Now it is very rich. But this has happened to the Danes before. Everything has happened to the Danes before. They have had empires and lost them. For the last 200 years, their role in the world has been largely to provide target practice for aggressive neighbors (though they did manage to stay out of World War I). What this experience seems to have taught the Danes is that you should not take seriously anything you cannot eat.

This is just as well, since the Danes are not good at taking things seriously. They will do it if they have to—they dealt very well with a German occupation in World War II—but the effort does not really suit their character. The philosopher Kierkegaard tried it in the 19th century with unhappy results—he invented existentialism. Danish politicians have tried it, and the result of that was Mogens Glistrup, the best joke ever to come out of Scandinavia.

Glistrup was a very successful tax lawyer in the '60s. The field was a profitable one because Denmark has the most comprehensive Welfare State, and had then the highest taxes, of anywhere in the world. Though it is Sweden that is famous in America for socialism, the Danes can actually get far more goodies from the state than the Swedes can. They just think less about it: or they did, until Glistrup came along. By 1972, Glistrup was a recognized authority on tax law. He had graduated from University with the highest marks ever attained by a legal student, and had only just failed to be appointed as Denmark's first professor of tax law. So he was a natural choice to give a talk on nationwide television on the consequences of the budget for 1972. This was not an exciting subject, however important, and Glistrup's script duly fell to the occasion. In fact, it was so boring that the producer begged him to think of something even slightly more interesting to say.

Glistrup replied that the only really interesting thing about income tax was that a clever man need pay none at all. Of course, it would have been grossly irresponsible to allow him to say as much on television, but the producer was a Dane, and it was more interesting than taking the budget seriously, so Glistrup went right ahead and said it. There he was, on nationwide television, a fat man with an even fatter man inside him struggling to get out, explaining that everyone could beat the system, if only their tax lawyer was good enough.

The Ministry of Finance disagreed. Glistrup's office and home were raided, and the investigators settled down to the long job of discovering how he did it, and what he could be charged with. Glistrup responded by forming a political party, dedicated to the total abolition of income tax. The government's books would be balanced by such reforms as replacing the Armed Forces with a tape recorder in the Ministry of Defence that would repeat to curious visitors the message "We surrender," in Russian.

This programme won 20% of the votes in the first election the party contested. Overnight, Glistrup became the leader of the second-largest party in Denmark. Unfortunately, he remained a crook. The Danes could have tolerated this, though their politicians could not; but it slowly became apparent that, though Glistrup took nothing else seriously, he did believe in himself, and this was intolerable. In 1983 he was returned to parliament from a prison cell, where he was serving a four year sentence for Gross Tax Fraud. Going to prison was for him the equivalent of death for a rock star—an admittedly drastic, but very effective way of prolonging a career that would otherwise have come to an end.

On Being Balanced

The moral of the Glistrup story is not that the Danes detest income tax, but that they will not stand for pomposity. Balance, not moderation, is the Danish virtue. The National Anthem should really consist of a recording of a fat man chuckling at the world after a very good meal indeed. The Danes are an extremely stable people, but the price they pay for this is a rather low center of gravity—in the stomach perhaps, or some inches lower.

There is a children's toy, a sort of egg-shaped doll, heavily weighted on the bottom, so that however you tip it over it will always come back to an upright position. The Danes are a lot like that.

They can recover from anything: in World War II they fought less than anyone when the Germans invaded them, yet they developed an effective resistance movement. When the Nazis ordered that all Jews should wear a yellow star, the King set an example to his people by himself appearing the next day in a yellow star. It was a brilliantly Danish solution: if everyone in the country pretended to be a Jew, there was really not very much that the Germans could do about it; meanwhile almost all the real Jews were smuggled across the Sound to neutral Sweden.

But, just as typically, this was a counterpunch. Left to themselves, the Danes would have left everyone else alone. The finest monument to Danish foreign policy this century is, fittingly enough, in Copenhagen, where the world's first specialized hospital for the rehabilitation of torture victims has been set up. It's a very simple and very necessary idea. Only the Danes of all the Scandinavians, are sufficiently rich, practical, and thoughtful to have done anything about it.

Everyday Excellence

Given the Danish center of gravity, it should not be surprising that Danish food is so very good. Nonetheless, it is surprising, if only because all of it is good. In the rest of Scandinavia you can eat well, but you must make an effort to do so. In Denmark you must make an effort to eat badly: it is characteristic that the Danes should have raised the sandwich to an art-form. Everywhere else in the world, it is an everyday and unromantic food, but it is in the perfection of everything that is everyday and unromantic that the Danes excell. This may not sound exciting, but it is very enjoyable.

None of this sounds very "Scandinavian"; nor is it. If the Swedes can believe in anything, the Danes find great difficulty—until they are disturbed—in supposing that anything is worth believing in. They are as realistic as the Finns, but quite without the Finnish habit of drama. The only thing about the Danes that corresponds to the Scandinavian stereotype is their attitude to sex. They rather enjoy it.

Nor do they mind other people enjoying it, each in his or her own way, provided that no one who does not want to gets hurt. So Copenhagen has become the pornographic capital of Europe. This need not bother the visitor—all the unsavory things happen in a very small portion of the city, and you can walk for hours through the more beautiful parts of Copenhagen without seeing or suspecting anything untoward. But it is worth a warning, since the cheapest hotels in the city are clustered on the fringes of the red light area. It would be a pity if the unprepared visitor were to take one look, get a frightful shock, and then run screaming into the night—in either direction.

The Danes do not really approve of this sort of thing; but the paradigm of all Danish pleasures is eating, which is not an activity about which one can moralize, so they tend not to moralize about anything else. I suppose that the final Danish comment on commercial sex has been made by the evening paper that runs columns and columns of ads from willing girls and boys, who display all the persistence of an aardvaark in their efforts to get to the front of the alphabet, and so attract the casual reader. Yet these advertisements are sandwiched undramatically between the flats for sale and the used cars.

The Danes enjoy drink in much the same way. It is not cheap but it is very freely available. This means that if you see a drunk in Denmark, you can be almost certain that he is a Swede. It is another example of the Danish capacity for balance. Not that Denmark is a statically perfect place. The Danish press is the liveliest and best in Scandinavia largely because it has so much bad news—or so many good stories—to report. Such things happen all over Scandinavia; only the Danes can whole-heartedly regard them as amusing.

And this is really the point of going to Denmark. There is, of course, a great deal to see and do, but what one remembers most of all is the way the Danes live together. In an unspectacular way, they have addressed themselves to the task of making life more comfortable and amusing; and they have had great success. The rest of Scandinavia is attractive because it is exotic; Denmark may seem exotic, but what you remember afterwards is how well the Danes do the things that everybody has to do. It is a very civilized country indeed.

COPENHAGEN

Scandinavia's Fun Capital

The center of Danish fun is Copenhagen, biggest and happiest of the Scandinavian capitals and by almost unanimous agreement one of the liveliest cities of Europe. More than a million Danes, a quarter of the country's population, live and let live here. The city, on the island of Zealand, is just as flat as the sea that embraces it, as flat as the rest of Denmark, which averages only 98 feet above sea level. (This is why every second inhabitant has a bicycle.)

When is the best time to come? "Even in winter," wrote one Scottish editor, "Copenhagen is an ideal summer resort." A Danish journalist was more objective about his own country. "Denmark was never intended to be inhabited in winter," wrote he. So much for the ambiguous nature of reality. On the subject there is no argument: Denmark is lovely in summer, fall and spring. In winter, well, let's just say that while Copenhagen is as welcoming as ever, it can be a little chilly.

By May, however, Denmark has escaped from the bonds of the long Nordic winter, a fact neatly underlined by the opening of the world-famous Tivoli Gardens on May 1. Celebratory candles flicker in the windows of every home too, in commemoration of Denmark's liberation on May 4, 1945, while the next day there are celebrations in every Danish town from southern Jutland to the far reaches of Bornholm. The circus comes to Copenhagen, too, in May; the amusement park, Bakken, opens in the Klampenborg Forest in April, and Denmark begins to rock like the yachts between Helsingør (Elsinore) and Copenhagen, warming up for that water carnival known as "Round Zealand" in late June—the world's biggest yacht race (1,600 participants last year). The Royal Danish Ballet end their season, and June comes to a climax on 23 June with Midsummer's Eve, a night of outdoor dancing, singing, feasting, bonfires and fireworks, transforming the whole nation into one big carnival. Try to celebrate this night along the Sound. You'll never forget the unreal summer twilight, streaked with rockets edged with a thousand fires along the shores of the Kattegat, as though Sweden and Denmark were both aflame.

With the end of June, everyone enjoys the long, sunflooded days and short balmy nights in Denmark. Make your reservations early; the Danes will do the rest.

The Lie of the Land

Many visitors find it odd that Denmark's capital should be on the extreme eastern edge of one of the country's larger islands, only a few miles from Sweden. But the reason is simple. Historically, Copenhagen was the capital not only of Denmark in its modern form, but also of Norway and southern Sweden and other Baltic territories. As a well-sheltered port with immediate access to the high seas—large ships still sail from the city center—Copenhagen in days gone by was an ideally situated capital.

Being on the coast, Copenhagen is a cleaner capital than most. Though it lacks a background of mountains to set it off, viewpoints from which it can be admired, hills to which its houses can cling, and though much of it has had to be rebuilt, Copenhagen remains a charming city.

Exploring Copenhagen

If you suggest to someone that, although Copenhagen has a history stretching back to the 11th century, the city really doesn't look very old, you are likely to get the reply, "Considering it's been bashed about by the Swedes a few times, ravaged by a number of fires and bombarded by the British, that's hardly surprising." Strategically located on the Sound connecting the Baltic with the Kattegat and the North Sea, Copenhagen was just a small village ceaselessly harassed by Wendian pirates until the middle of the 12th century. But in 1167 Bishop Absalon, warrior and politician as well as priest, like many contemporary clerics, decided to protect the infant village by building a castle on the small central island known as Slotsholmen, today the very heart of the old city.

Shortly thereafter the town adopted the name of Køpmannaehafn (Merchants' Haven), and proceeded to grow apace within its protecting walls. In the 15th century, the king came to live in Copenhagen and a university was started. Increasing in both size and importance little by little, the prosperous city entered upon a great period of expansion with the accession of King Christian IV (1588–1648) to the throne. This man of extraordinary energy was possessed with a passion for building. Whenever he could take time off from waging wars, he started some new project, and even today so many of his works remain that

COPENHAGEN

whenever there's a question about who erected what, Christian gets the credit. Rosenborg Slot (Rosenborg Castle), the Runde Tårn (the Round Tower) and the Børsen (Stock Exchange) with its exotic dragon spire, were all built by him. He also gave the town an arsenal and a naval dock, and put up the "Nyboder," or rows of small houses which are still inhabited by naval personnel and pensioners.

In 1659, when the Swedish King Carl Gustaf tried to put an end to the continual Dano-Swedish wars by the simple strategy of conquering Denmark outright, Copenhagen found itself in a difficult situation. The town was besieged and everyone, including Frederik III, the then king, took a hand at defending it. After attempting to take the city by storm, the Swedes were routed and driven back to their own shores. This same Frederik thereupon built the Kastellet (Citadel) near Langelinie, which served the reverse of its intended function in 1940 when the Germans initiated their occupation of Denmark by capturing the old fortifications.

Back in 1728 and 1795, fires swept Copenhagen and destroyed vast portions of it. The devastation had scarcely been repaired when a British fleet twice bombarded the city during the Napoleonic Wars in 1801 and 1807. Fortunately the palaces survived—Amalienborg, Christiansborg and Rosenborg—and the vacant sites undoubtedly provided opportunities for rebuilding that might not otherwise have been undertaken. After the Napoleonic Wars, Denmark enjoyed relative peace and Copenhagen expanded far beyond the ramparts and water fortifications. Industries such as brewing, shipbuilding and manufacturing hardware became immensely profitable, and the city grew from a population of 130,000 in 1850 to its present size of well over a million inhabitants, suburbs included.

Strolls About Town

With this partial introduction to the Copenhagen scene, the time has come to sally forth into the bewildering jumble of winding streets, unexpected canals and multitudinous buildings which are the distinguishing features of the Danish capital. The average visitor from abroad, as he steps out of the Central Station into the warm sun of a summer morning, is likely to be a bit baffled at the start. As we've already pointed out, there is a serious scarcity of distinguishing landmarks by which the new arrival can easily chart his course through this intricate city. While it's true that Copenhagen a few years back seemed to be largely a collection of charmingly distinctive spires, there are now so many tall modern buildings that you can no longer see them. And to top it off, about the time you are at last getting yourself oriented, you are so unnerved by the sudden appearance of a platoon of bicyclists bearing down upon you that all idea of where you are or where you intended to go is just as precipitously driven from your head. Watch out too for the special bicycle lanes; the Danes take their cycling seriously and most major roads have bicycle lanes on either side.

Any attempt to plot out some interesting tours for the person bent on discovering the "real" Copenhagen is fraught with danger. Assuming that you master your fear of two-wheeled traffic and have provided yourself with a suitable map, it's more than possible that you'll start off in the wrong direction and be so captivated by what you see that

76   **DENMARK**

COPENHAGEN

COPENHAGEN

1. Amalienborg Palace
2. Borsen (Stock Exchange)
3. Central Post Office
4. Central Station and Air Terminal
5. Charlottenborg Palace
6. Christiansborg Palace
7. Vor Frelser's Kirke
8. Frihedsmuseet (World War II Museum)
9. Vor Frue Kirke (Cathedral)
10. Geologish Museum (Museum of Geology)
11. Glyptoteket
12. Hirschsprung Collection
13. Holmen's Kirke
14. Kongelige Bibliotek (Royal Library)
15. Kongelige Teater (Royal Theater)
16. Kunstindustrimuseet (Museum of Decorative Arts)
17. Lille Havfrue (Mermaid)
18. Marmorkirken
19. Nationakmuseet (National Museum)
20. Osterport Station
21. Rådhus (Town Hall)
22. Regensum
23. Rosenborg
24. Runde Taarn (Round Tower)
25. Statens Museum for Kunst (Royal Museum of Fine Arts)
26. Thorvaldsen Museum
27. Tøjhusetmuseet (Arsenal Museum)
28. Tourist Information Office
29. University
- Pedestrian Streets (Strøget)

you won't detect your error until you've gone several blocks out of your way. Don't be alarmed, however—before you've had a chance to get the points of the compass properly unscrambled, it's more than likely that a friendly Dane will stop and politely offer to show you the way.

So let's plunge in and start at the Rådhus Pladsen, or Town Hall Square. Dominating the square is the Town Hall itself, an immense and impressive redbrick building surmounted by a tall tower. It was completed in 1905. High above the main entrance is the figure of Bishop Absalon, founder of the city. Inside you see first the World Clock invented and built by Jens Olsen. They you come to a large hall surrounded by a balcony, which is used for official functions. Here there are marble busts of Hans Christian Andersen, poet, playwright and writer of the famous stories for children, of Bertel Thorvaldsen, the noted sculptor, and of Martin Nyrop, the building's architect.

Above, on the first floor, are the council chamber and the municipal reception room. You can climb up the 105-meter (350-foot) tower, but only on one of the official guided tours. From its top there are fine views of the city and the surrounding countryside.

As you emerge from the Town Hall, a turn to your left would take you up Vesterbrogade, and in a moment you would come to the main entrance of the famous Tivoli Gardens. Just down from here, on Hans Christian Andersens Boulevard, is the city tourist office. Hardly anyone comes to Denmark without first having heard of the Tivoli Gardens. These date back to 1843, when Georg Carstensen, Danish architect and man of letters, persuaded Christian VIII to let him lay out an amusement park on the site of Copenhagen's old fortifications. "If only people are allowed to amuse themselves," he argued, "they will forget to talk politics." Within a few months Tivoli, patterned after London's now long-extinct Vauxhall Gardens, was a reality. In 1951 the wheel turned a full circle when the Festival of Britain organizers used Tivoli as a model for the Festival Gardens in London's Battersea Park. During its short season from May to September, Tivoli welcomes an average of 4 million visitors.

Whatever you happen to be doing in Tivoli, on a Saturday or Sunday you will enjoy the appearance of the Tivoli Guard. This is a group of toytown soldiers (age limit 17) dressed in the style of the Queen's Guard, who march through the Gardens to the music of their own band.

On certain nights, the Gardens close with a magnificent display of fireworks. As rockets fly to meet the moon and colorful set pieces vie with the electric brilliance of the Chinese Pagoda, the illuminated fountain, and the fairy-like lights among the trees, you will begin to appreciate something of what Tivoli means to the Danes.

At the southern end of the Gardens, again on Hans Christian Andersens Boulevard, is the Glyptotek. It is a rather fanciful neo-Classical building, but contains an excellent collection of French sculpture, with fine pieces by Degas, Gauguin, and other Impressionists. There is also an outstanding collection of Egyptian works, including a famous statue of a hippopotamus, and much Greek and Roman statuary, all well-displayed. A gift to the municipality from Carl Jacobsen, founder of the Carlsberg breweries, the museum is maintained by the Carlsberg Foundation, which has done much to further cultural and scientific activities in Denmark. The winter garden outside contains Kai Nielsen's *Water-*

mother sculpture, serenely watching the 14 marble babies who tumble over her.

Back again on Vesterbrogade, you'll find the SAS building, one of the city's few skyscrapers. It also contains the Royal Hotel. Opposite is the Central Station, and in the same building, though the entrance is on Bernstorffs Gade, is the Air Terminal. There is an obelisk in front of the station commemorating the freeing of the Danish peasants from the feudal yoke in 1788. Just beyond, in the black Vesterport building, is Den Permanente, The House of Danish Design, where the best of modern Danish arts and crafts are displayed and sold. Ten minutes' walk from here along Vesterbrogade brings you to the Bymuseum, the City Museum. Outside is a model of medieval Copenhagen, while inside are exhibits depicting the city's history. Absalonsgade, a little street running down one side of the Museum, is due to be returned to its 19th-century appearance, with old sidewalks, gaslights and, of course, no cars.

Up Strøget to Slotsholmen and Christianshavn

The next part of our exploration of the city, again using Rådhus Pladsen as a jumping-off point, takes us to the "Strøget," a series of narrow streets running eastwards from Rådhus Pladsen. The principal street here is Frederiksberggade, a pedestrian-only shopping street that more than any other in Copenhagen is the city's answer to Fifth Avenue or Bond Street. Not far along Frederiksberggade, we come to a double square, the northern half of which is called Gammeltorv and the southern, Nytorv. The most interesting thing about these twin squares is the splendid fountain in the middle of the former. On April 16, the Queen's birthday, children are brought here to see the "golden apples dance." These golden apples are gilded metal balls which "dance" on the jets of water.

Looking to the right from the Nytorv half of this square, you may be able to see a spot of water to the south. A few steps in this direction bring you to Rådhusstraede and then to Frederiksholms Canal, where you'll find the entrance to one of Copenhagen's most fascinating places, the National Museum, built in the 1740s for Crown Prince Frederik, who later became King Frederik V. Inside you can see the world's finest collection of Stone Age tools and runic stones dating from the Viking period. Note particularly the beautiful Hindsgavl Dagger, fashioned and used several thousand years before the birth of Christ. You can also get some idea of Viking camp life, the ships with which they traveled all over the world, and their unusual burial mounds in which it was the custom to put a jug of liquor beside the body of the deceased to assure him happiness in heaven.

One of the featured exhibits in the Historical Music section is a number of Bronze Age *lur*, unusual musical instruments between four and six feet in length, which were popular 3,000 years ago; 36 lurs or fragments have thus far been found in peat bogs all over Denmark. The museum offers for sale interesting silver and bronze replicas of certain of the exhibits.

Directly across the bridge from the National Museum is the Christiansborg Slot, seat of the Folketing, or Danish parliament, and the Supreme Court. It's an imposing building that dominates the little island—Slotsholmen, the very heart of the city—on which it and the National Museum stand. And appropriately, this is where Bishop Absalon built his first fortress in 1167. Its ruins can be visited under the present building, which is the sixth on this site. From 1441 until the fire of 1794 Christiansborg was used as a royal residence.

On the same island with the palace are clustered a number of other important buildings. Set in an idyllic garden is Det Kongelige Bibliotek, the Royal Library, with Denmark's largest collection of books, newspapers, incunabula and manuscripts, including the earliest records of Viking expeditions to America and Greenland. On one side of the library is Tøjhuset, Copenhagen's arms museum, with outstanding displays of uniforms, weapons, and armor, in an arched hall nearly 180 meters (200 yards) long.

On the other side of the library is the low, red-brick Børsen, former Stock Exchange. This fine example of Renaissance architecture is claimed to be the oldest stock exchange in the world still used for its original purpose, though the main part of the business has now been moved to other premises. The Børsen stands in tribute to the skill and originality of Christian IV. Indeed, it is said that he lent a hand in the twisting of the tails of the four dragons that form its spire. The spire, as unusual as it is beautiful, is certainly the most distinctive feature of the Børsen, but the entire structure—with its myriad gables, tiny windows and steep copper-clad roofs—is very fine and one of the city's greatest architectural treasures.

Still on Slotsholmen and on the island side of Christiansborg Slot, we come to the Thorvaldsen Museum. Here the great sculptor is buried, surrounded by the originals or casts of all his works. Beyond and to the north of this museum we recross the canal over Højbro, or High Bridge.

To the left is a delightful row of houses bordering the northern edge of Slotsholmen. The quays in front of them were for long Copenhagen's fish market, and a sadly much-diminished market is still held here regularly. The fishy theme is reflected too by the presence of two excellent and long-established fish restaurants hard by the site of the market.

Let's stand in the middle of Højbro for a moment and look back down the canal to the right. Just across from Børsen is Holmens Kirke, where two of Denmark's greatest naval heroes are entombed. One is Niels Juel, the man who shredded the Swedish fleet at Køge in 1677, and the other is the almost legendary Tordenskjold, who defeated Charles XII of Sweden during the Great Northern War. At the far end of the canal you see Knippelsbro, the big drawbridge leading to the island of Christianshavn. That green and gold spire with the curious spiral staircase winding around it is part of Vor Frelsers Kirke (Our Saviour's Church). After a look inside, you'll find that the excellent view from the tower is well worth the climb.

Christianshavn is one of the oldest quarters of Copenhagen. Though somewhat dilapidated now, and haunt of more than its fair share of low-life types, the area has retained some of its Left Bank charm, not least along the canals that thread through it where old houses lean out over houseboats and yachts. Row boats are available for hire; particularly attractive on a moonlit night.

The Runde Tårn and the University

Alternatively, head north from Højbro along Købmagergade. Continue past the equestrian statue of Bishop Absalon and the charming brick Nikolaj Kirke (actually part restaurant and exhibition center today, but still one of the principal landmarks of the city, not least for its towering spire). Cross over the Strøget and continue north. A couple of hundred meters up on the right you'll come to the Runde Tårn, the Round Tower, which Christian IV built as an observatory, not as part of the church to which it is attached, though this, with a handsome interior, is well worth a visit. If you are energetic, you can climb to the top of the Runde Tårn up the internal spiral ramp. Peter the Great of Russia, so the story goes, drove up in a horse-drawn carriage. Not being an emperor, you will have to walk. If you prefer mental to physical exercise, try solving the Hebrew and Latin rebus printed in letters of gold outside the tower. Translated it means: "Lord, make the King's, Christian the Fourth's, heart faithful and just."

Perhaps this is the place for a few more words about Denmark's amazing warrior-architect-scholar-king. Vitally alive to every new idea, Christian IV was much more than a builder. During his busy life he found time to revolutionize farming, reform the administration of his Norwegian kingdom, create seven new chairs of learning at the University and start trading companies to exploit the fabled riches of the East and discover a Northwest Passage. Even when he went for a walk, he would pull a ruler out of his pocket and check the workmanship of local masons and carpenters.

Across the road from the Runde Tårn is the Regensen, since 1628 a residential college for university students. It is worth pushing aside the heavy door and taking a quick look at the courtyard. The old lime tree there celebrates its birthday with a private May lunch, after which the students "shake hands" with a pair of gloves hung up in its branches.

From the Regensen, continue along Krystalgade to the University and, on Nørregade, the Vor Frue Kirke, the Church of Our Lady. The University celebrated its 500th anniversary in 1979, but the bulk of its buildings, including the main university, dates from the period of Copenhagen's great expansion in the 19th century. The growth of the University has lately been such, however, that many departments have had to be moved to more spacious quarters outside the city center.

The Vor Frue Kirke has been Copenhagen's cathedral since 1924. Bishop Absalon is believed to have built a chapel here in the early-13th century. Ravaged by fire in 1728 and hit during Nelson's bombardment in 1807, it was rebuilt in stern neo-Classical style in the early-19th century. The entire structure was extensively restored between 1977 and 1979. Bronze statues of Moses and David flank the entrance, and Thorvaldsen's marble sculptures of Christ and the Apostles can be seen inside. The ruins of the first church (1320) can now be seen in the basement, and a small historical collection has been opened on the first floor. On coming out take a turn to the left down Nørregade and, before you know it, you are back at the twin squares of Gammeltorv and Nytorv, our first stop.

Kongens Nytorv to Langelinie

Thus far we have described a large circle in the older part of town. The trip we are about to start upon will take us pretty much in a straight line. It begins at Kongens Nytorv, which lies at the opposite end of Strøget from Rådhus Pladsen. Strøget, you will recall, is the series of streets with different names that comprise Copenhagen's principal shopping district. The better stores are at the end from which we are about to set out.

In the center of Kongens Nytorv is a mounted statue of Christian V. Near the end of June every year, newly matriculated students arrive here in horse-drawn wagonettes and dance around the silent figure of the king. The southern side of the square is flanked by the Kongelige Theater, featuring ballet and opera as well as classical drama. Next door stands the Theater's annex, popularly called the "Starling Box". The Dutch Baroque building of Charlottenborg, which has housed the Danish Academy of Fine Arts since 1754, is also in Kongens Nytorv.

The stretch of water you see running up to Kongens Nytorv is the Nyhavn Canal. Picturesque 18th-century buildings, mostly containing sailors' cafés, crowd along both sides. A veritable fleet of old-time sailing ships normally lines the quays along Nyhavn, and on one side the *Fyrskib XVII,* a stout old lightship dating from 1893, permanently moored, is seeing out her days as a floating museum. The far end of Nyhavn is the departure point for the hydrofoil to Malmö in Sweden, while beyond, the passenger ships from England and the Baltic dock.

Our path, however, is down Bredgade, a wide street leading north from Kongens Nytorv, to the first turning to the right, Sankt Annae Plads, then the next left into Amaliengade.

Before you stands an imposing colonnade. Although it looks like stone, it is actually made of wood—if you don't believe us, try tapping it. When you've gone through the arches, the square you are in contains the four residences that comprise Amalienborg Palace. The one immediately to the right is used by Queen Margrethe and her family, the following (facing you on the right) is occupied by dowager Queen Ingrid. During the fall and winter, when the Queen lives in Copenhagen, the guards, complete with bearskins and headed by their band, march through the city from the barracks adjoining Rosenborg Slot every day, to relieve the Amalienborg sentries at noon. Colorful, too, is the sight of a royal coach with its scarlet-coated drivers giving the team some brisk trotting exercise through the busy streets.

Turning left out of the palace square we come back to Bredgade. Directly in front of us broods the Marmorkirken, the Marble Church, a somewhat topheavy building with an enormous dome several sizes too large for it. Its ponderous Baroque exterior contrasts a little painfully with the delicate facades of the Amalienborg Palace. Perched around the outside are 16 statues of various religious leaders from Moses to Luther, and below them stand other sculptures of outstanding Danish ministers and bishops. The building was completed in 1894, after having lain in ruins since 1770.

We turn right into Bredgade and continue past the three brilliantly-gilded onion domes of the Russian Church before arriving in front of the Museum of Decorative Arts, the Kunstindustrimuseet, a fine Rococo building that was originally a royal hospital. Today, it contains an excellent collection of artefacts—ceramics, silverware and Flemish tapestries—from the Middle Ages to the present day, as well as a collection of musical instruments.

A few steps more take us up to Esplanaden, where there is a small museum, the Frihedsmuseet, documenting the heroic efforts of the Danish resistance in World War II. Close by, you will see the Gefion Fountain. Powerfully and dramatically this commemorates the legend of the goddess Gefion, who was promised as much of Sweden as she could plough around in one day. Changing her four sons into oxen, she carved out the island of Zealand. Perhaps there may be an element of truth in the story, for if you look at a map of Sweden you'll see that Lake Vänern is much the same size and shape as Zealand itself.

The park in front of us, alongside Esplanaden, is graced by the English Church standing at its entrance. In the center, surrounded by two rings of moats, is the Kastellet, or Citadel. It dates from the late-17th century when it was begun by Frederik III. Much work, renovating and expanding it, was also carried out in the 18th century, by which time it was the principal fortress of the city. The grounds are open to the public. Stretching straight ahead of us is the Langelinie Promenade, where foreign navies moor their ships, and all of Copenhagen meets on Sunday afternoon. About halfway along it, the Little Mermaid of Hans Andersen's famous fairy story perches on a rock by the water's edge and gazes wistfully across the harbor.

Jewels, Flowers and Old Masters

The last of our three excursions begins in Kongens Have, the King's Gardens, where little children play around the statue of Hans Christian Andersen. Our objective is the Renaissance-style Rosenborg Slot, now a museum containing not only a breathtaking display of all the Danish crown jewels but also a fine collection of furniture, together with the personal effects of Danish kings from the time of Christian IV, including that monarch's precious pearl-studded saddle.

Just opposite the palace are some 25 acres of botanical gardens, as well as an observatory and mineralogical museum. Across the street from the north end of these gardens we come to Statens Museum for Kunst, the national art gallery, whose liveried doorkeeper sports buckle shoes and a cocked hat on chilly days. An imposing late neo-Classical facade hides an excellently modernized interior, with a good, though cramped cafeteria. The collections, however, with few exceptions, are frankly dull, consisting mainly of second-rate Old Masters and endless rooms of 19th-century Danish pictures. However, the contemporary works should at least provide some light relief. There is also a better than average collection of works by Matisse. Behind the main building is the Hirschsprung Collection, containing more Danish 19th-century works.

We have now been through most of the better-known parts of the heart of Copenhagen, but it would be an error to forget that the real heart of any city is the living one. The red-coated postmen, the bear-skinned, not over-military-looking Royal Guard, the spirited Tivoli Guard, the cyclists, the Nyhavn rowdies and drunks, the little fat man who delivers the milk all week and then blossoms out as a racehorse owner on Sundays, Queen Margrethe: all these are the real sights of Copenhagen.

Short Excursions Out of Town

When the sun is shining, whether there is spring in the air or snow on the ground, and the Copenhagener wants a few hours in the country the chances are he will go to Dyrehaven, the Deer Park near Klampenborg. Here nearly 2,000 of these timid, graceful animals wander about at complete ease. A golf course, a summer fun-fair (open mid-April to late August) and several all-year-round restaurants occupy the rest of the 3,500 acres of forest, paths and ponds that make up this lovely park. Near the entrance to the park is the Bellevue bathing beach. Farther along the seaside drive from the capital to Elsinore (Helsingør) are a host of luxurious villas and charming places to stop. Also near Elsinore is Denmark's only casino, the Marienlyst Hotel.

Even closer to Copenhagen than Klampenborg is the fashionable suburb of Charlottenlund. It is a lovely walk from the S-station to Strandvejen where the Akvarium is. Across the road is the beach, popular though less fashionable than the one at Bellevue, and nearby are the picturesque Chalottenlund Fortress and an unofficial, though good, campsite for foreigners only.

Starting from either Lyngby or Holte, you can go for a walk in the woods close by, or else stroll around lakes Lyngbysø and the much larger Furesø. At Lyngby, near Sorgenfri station, you'll find the open-air museum known as Frilandsmuseet. In a park covering 40 acres is a collection of reconstructed old Danish farms, several windmills, and country houses moved here from the other parts of Denmark and southern Sweden. The houses are furnished and equipped with the implements and utensils of the period and place they represent.

The Hareskov woods can be reached from Svanemøllen station (train B). From Hareskov you may ramble through the forest to Fiskebaek and have lunch there. Afterwards you might vary your return journey by riding the motorboat to Lyngby or Holte station.

A shorter trip which many enjoy is to Dragør on the island of Amager. This quaint old fishing village, where geese still roam in the crooked streets, has a charm of its very own. The oldest house contains a museum of furniture, costumes, drawings, and model ships. Its chimney is twisted to prevent the Devil finding his way through. The museum in Store Magleby, an old, half-timbered farmhouse, displays Amager furniture, dresses, and needlework.

Another haunt you might enjoy, as much for the trip out as for what you find at your destination, is to Grundtvigs Kirke. Consecrated in 1940 and built in a style based on the typical Danish village church, this building, with its organ-like façade stands in memory of the poet, clergyman and founder of the Folk High School, whose name it bears.

PRACTICAL INFORMATION FOR COPENHAGEN

GETTING TO TOWN FROM THE AIRPORT. There is a frequent bus service from Copenhagen's Kastrup Airport to the Central Station. Buy your ticket (16 Dkr.) on the bus. Buses also run to the airport from the station. The bus calls at the Hotel Scandinavia. Ordinary buses are cheaper: routes 32, 32H for Rådhus Pladsen, route 9 for Kongens Nytorv and Østerport, route 38E for Valby Station.

Taxis are expensive, costing around 75 Dkr.

TOURIST INFORMATION. The Tourist Information Office, run by the Danish Tourist Board, is at H.C. Andersens Blvd. 22 (11 13 25). Summer opening hours are: May through June, Mon. to Sat. 9–6; July through Aug., Mon. to Sat. 9–8; Sept., Mon. to Sat. 9–6; Sun. and public holidays 9–1.

For students and young people "Use it" *(Huset)* at Magstraede 14 (15 65 18), has useful information and an accommodations service. Open daily, 10–5; 15 June to 15 Sept., daily 10–8.

USEFUL ADDRESSES. Embassies. *British Embassy*, Kastelsvej 36–40 (26 46 00). *Canadian Embassy*, Kristen Bernikowsgade 1 (12 22 99). *U.S. Embassy*, Dag Hammarskiölds Allé 24 (42 31 44).

Travel Agents. *American Express*, Dagmarhus, Amagertov 18 (12 23 01). *Wagons-Lits/Cooks*, Vesterbrogade 2 (14 27 47). *Spies Rejsebureau*, Nyropsgade 41 (12 35 00). *Viking Nordturist*, Ørsteds vej 70. *Tjaereborg Rejser*, Rådhus Pladsen 75 (11 41 00). *Dansk Vandrelaug*, 7 Kultorvet. *Bennett*, Rådhus Pladsen 45 (12 78 78).

Car-Hire. *Avis*, Kampmannsgade 1 (15 22 99). *Hertz*, Hammerichsgade 1 (12 77 00). *Pitzner*, Trommesalen 4 (11 12 34). All have offices at the airport. *Share-a-Car*, Studiestraede 61 (12 06 43), is cheaper and also hires out campers and tents.

TELEPHONE CODE. The telephone code for Copenhagen is 01. To call any number in this chapter, unless otherwise specified, this prefix must be used. Within the city, no prefix is required.

HOTELS. Hotels in Denmark's capital are numerous and range from the luxurious down to the very plain and modest side-street hotel. During the season (May through Oct.) it is advisable to book your room well in advance, either directly or through your local travel agent. If you happen to come without a reservation, go to the "Room Service" at Kastrup Airport or at the Central Station. Young people may go to "Use It" *(Huset)*, Magstraede 14 (15 65 18), where there is also a noticeboard indicating room availability outside opening hours.

The accommodations service at the Central Station is at Kiosk P and it is open daily to personal callers from 1 May to 15 Sept., 9 A.M. to midnight (off-season hours are shorter). Telephone inquiries can be made on 12 28 80, Mon. to Fri. 9–5. The postal address is *Hotelbooking Copenhagen*, Hovedbanegården, DK-1570 Copenhagen V.

During the off-season (Nov. to Apr.) many hotels, especially the new ones, lower their rates considerably. It is therefore advisable when reserving to have the prices confirmed. Hotels designated (BE) charge for breakfast. The budget hotel area is near the Central Station, around Colbjørnsengade/Helgolandsgade, and best among the cheaper establishments are the so-called Mission Hotels (unlicensed).

Deluxe

D'Angleterre. Kongens Nytorv 34 (12 00 95). 246 beds. Ranks first among the Copenhagen hotels. Aristocratic, spacious, with excellent food and service. Its sidewalk terrace is a permanent fixture during the tourist season. Bar, restaurant with music, beauty salon, barber shop. (BE). AE, DC, MC, V.

Kong Frederik. Vester Voldgade 23–27 (12 59 02). 210 beds. Comfortable rooms, fine restaurant, English-type bar. AE, DC, MC, V.

Royal. Hammerichsgade 1 (14 14 12). 500 beds, all rooms with bath. This modern hotel has the best of Danish architecture, art and furniture. Every comfort. Sauna, restaurant, bar. (BE). AE, DC, MC, V.

Scandinavia. Amager Blvd. 70 (11 23 34). 1,100 beds. Enormous tower block mid-way between the airport and the city facing the old city moats. Pool, sauna. (BE). AE, DC, MC, V.

Sheraton Copenhagen. Vester Søgade 6 (14 35 35). 846 beds, 34 suites, all rooms with T.V. Sauna. (BE). AE, DC, MC, V.

Expensive

Copenhagen Admiral. Toldbodgade 24 (11 82 82). 815 beds. Massive 18th-century granary whose imposing exterior disguises considerable interior comforts; sturdy wooden beams throughout harmonize with ultra-modern decor. Located between the southern end of Nyhavn facing the passenger ship terminal and the Amalienborg Palace. Sauna, restaurant and nightclub. DC, MC, V.

Imperial. Vester Farimagsgade 9 (12 80 00). 331 beds, all rooms with bath. Centrally located, pleasant decoration and furniture. Openair restaurant famed for good food, cafeteria. AE, DC, MC, V.

"3 Falke" (Three Falcons). Falkoner Allé 9 (19 80 01). 286 beds. In the Frederiksberg section; the name describes the municipal arms. Good bus connections and parking facilities. AE, DC, MC, V.

71 Nyhavn (11 85 85). A former storehouse at this address, converted to hotel. 123 beds, all rooms with bath. AE, DC, MC, V.

Moderate

Alexandria. H.C. Andersens Blvd. 8 (14 22 00). 116 beds. Close to the Rådhus Pladsen, the center of the capital. Quiet and modest. Restaurant. AE, DC, MC, V.

Ascot. Studiestraede 57 (12 60 00). 95 beds, all rooms with bath; also 13 apartments with 1 to 5 beds. Centrally located. AE, DC, MC, V.

Astoria. Banegårdspladsen 4 (14 14 19). 155 beds, most rooms with bath. Near Tivoli and the Central Station. AE, DC, MC, V.

Bel Air. Løjtegardsvej 99 (51 30 33). 430 beds, all rooms with shower or bath. Near airport; Bus 34 to Copenhagen in 25 min. Restaurant, bar, sauna. DC, MC, V.

Codan. Skt. Annae Plads 21 (13 34 00). 243 beds, all rooms with bath. Ground-floor and roof restaurants, sauna. (BE). AE, DC, MC, V.

Danhotel. Kastrup Airport (51 14 00). 511 beds, all rooms with bath, some with T.V. Bus 32 or 32H to city takes about 30 mins. DC, MC, V.

Esso Motor Hotel. Kettevej 4 (49 82 22). 321 beds. Indoor pool, sauna. At Hvidovre, western Copenhagen. (BE). DC, MC, V.

Excelsior. Colbjørnsengade 4 (24 50 85). Basic, near Central Station. AE, DC, MC, V.

Gentofte. Gentoftegade 29 (68 09 11). 126 beds, all rooms with shower and toilet. Quiet, on the outskirts. Bus 24 to Nørreport (25 min.) or train A. DC, MC, V.

Marina (02 89 17 11). At Vedbaek, north of Copenhagen. 208 rooms, all with bath. Also has 31 apartments of 2 to 6 beds, bath and kitchen. Music, ping-pong, billiards, sauna. Near beach and station, or buses 188, 27 and 1 via Klampenborg. MC, V.

Neptun. Skt. Annae Plads 18 (13 89 00). 90 beds, all rooms with bath or shower, attractively furnished. Also has 2 apartments with 4 beds at 2,000 Dkr. per week. AE, DC, MC, V.

Park. Jarmers Plads 3 (13 30 00). 114 beds. Central. (BE). AE, DC, MC, V.
Østerport. Oslo Plads 5 (11 22 66). 136 beds, some rooms with bath. Bar, music; very fine restaurant with French and Danish specialties. AE, DC, MC, V.
SAS Globetrotter. Engvej 171 (55 14 33). Near Kastrup Airport. 265 beds. Modern, with restaurant, bar and cafeteria, bowling and sauna. Bus 9 to the Børsen takes 15 min. DC, MC, V.
Savoy. Vesterbrogade 34 (31 40 73). 138 beds. Older. AE, DC, MC, V.
Viking. Bredgade 65 (12 45 50). 159 beds. Large rooms, but few with private bath. Well managed. AE, DC, MC, V.
Vestersøhus. Vestersøgade 58 (11 38 70). 87 beds. Good for long stays. AE, DC, MC, V.
Weber. Vesterbrogade 11 (31 14 32). 138 beds, some rooms without baths. Central. DC, MC, V.

Inexpensive

Amager. Amagerbrogade 29 (54 40 08). 48 beds. On the way to the airport, but still central. MC, V.
Carlton. Halmtorvet 14 (21 25 51). 99 beds, in various room categories. Away from the main streets, but in the "naughty" district. AE, DC, MC, V.
City. Peder Skrams Gade 24 (13 06 66). 162 beds. Near the harbor and Det Kongelige Teater. Well furnished, but no rooms with private bath. DC, MC, V.
Comfort. Løngangsstraede 27 (12 65 70). Large former mission hotel. DC.
Dragør Faergegård. Dragør (53 05 00). 40 beds. In idyllic fishing resort south of town, near beach and airport. Buses 30 and 33 to Rådhus Pladsen take 40 min. (BE). DC, MC, V.
Esplanaden. Bredgade 78 (13 21 75). 92 beds, very few rooms with private bath. Centrally located near Langelinie and Kastellet. Fine bus and train connections. No credit cards.
Skovriderkroen. Strandvejen 235 (62 63 40). 48 beds. Lovely location near beach; bus no. 1 to town in about 35 min. Music, garden, good food. (BE). DC, MC, V.
West. Westend 11 (24 27 61). 41 beds. Simple, few facilities. (BE). DC.

Mission Hotels

Ansgar. Colbjørnsensgade 29 (21 21 96). DC, MC, V.
Hebron. Holgolandsgade 4 (31 69 06). MC, V.
Nebo. Istedgade 6 (21 12 17).
Westend. Helgolandsgade 3.

Youth Hostels

Copenhagen Hostel. Sjaellandsbroen 55 (52 29 08). 448 beds in 2- and 4-bed rooms. Open all year, 3 miles from center, bus 37 from Holmens Bro near Holmens Kirke.
Københavns Vandrerhejm. Herbergsvejen 8 (28 97 15). 336 beds. 2 miles from city.

Camping

Absalon Camping. Korsdalsvej, Rødovre (41 06 00). West of Copenhagen.
Strandmøllen. DK-2942 Skodsborg (02 80 38 83). North of Copenhagen.

HOW TO GET AROUND. By bus and train. Copenhagen and its environs are well served by an extensive bus network and an electrified local railroad system, the "S" trains, as well as harbor ferries. The whole area is divided into zones which are the basis for the fare structure with facilities for transfer at no extra charge on routes within the zone and in some adjacent zones. Tickets are 6 Dkr. per zone (valid for two zones). Free transfers on bus and train inside an area comprising Helsingør, Roskilde, Køge and Copenhagen. Stamp cards

(9 trips per card, each trip valid for a minimum of three zones) can save money. If you start by train, you must cancel the card (but not full-rate tickets) in the yellow machine at platform entrances.

Best value of all is the *Copenhagen Card,* a tourist ticket valid for one, two or three days at 60, 110 and 150 Dkr. respectively. It gives unlimited travel by rail and bus in Copenhagen and North Zealand, plus free admission to 36 sights including Tivoli. Available from rail stations, the Tourist Information Office, hotels and travel agents.

By taxi. Taxis are expensive but all are metered. The basic charge is 12 Dkr. plus 6.75 Dkr. per kilometer (including waiting time at traffic lights, etc.). Tipping is optional and rarely expected. Cabs available for hire have the *Fri* sign. They may be hired at taxi stands, en route, or by telephone on 35 35 35.

By bicycle. Bicycles may be hired for about 20 Dkr. per day, deposit 50 Dkr., from *Danwheel-Rent a bike,* Colbjørnsensgade 3 (21 22 27); *Rent a Bicycle, Jet-Cycles,* Istedgade 71 (23 17 60); *Københavns Cyclebørs-Velonia,* Gothersgade 157–159 (14 07 17); and from Helsingør, Hillerød, Klampenborg and Lyngby rail stations, Apr. through Oct., tel. 14 17 01.

By horse-drawn cab. For romantics there are horse-drawn cabs in the famous Deer Park (Dyrehaven), and in the city center. Expensive.

TOURS. From May to October there are various bus tours around the city and beyond. Here we outline the tours of Copenhagen: for further details and tickets contact tourist information offices, travel agents and some hotels. All sightseeing buses depart from Lur Blower Column on Rådhus Pladsen. Although tickets may be purchased from the guide at the point of departure, to be sure of a seat buy them in advance.

The "City Tour," lasting one and a half hours, takes in the highlights of the city. It runs once or twice daily from 15 May to 15 Sept. If the Carlsberg or Tuborg breweries are visited too, the tour lasts two and a half hours.

The "Grand Tour of Copenhagen" covers all the major sights, with stops at the Gefion Fountain, den Lille Havfrue (the Little Mermaid) and Grundtvigs Kirke. It lasts two and a half hours, and runs twice daily, Apr. through Oct.; in winter, once a weekday, twice on Sun.

The "Royal Tour of Copenhagen" covers Christiansborg Slot with the Royal Reception Rooms, Rosenborg Slot (crown jewels), passes by other royal buildings, and ends at Amalienborg Slot. It takes two and three quarter hours and is available May through Sept., daily except Mon.

The "City and Harbor Tour" starts by coach and includes a harbor tour of the charming canals of Christianshavn. Duration is two and a half hours and it takes place from 1 May to 15 Sept. three times a day.

The "Industrial Art Tour" includes visits to a porcelain factory (either Bing & Grøndahl or Royal Copenhagen Porcelain), the Kunstindustrimuseet (Museum of Decorative and Applied Arts), and Den Permanente, the Danish design center. This tour lasts two and a half hours and runs from 15 May to 15 Sept., every Thurs.

"An Afternoon of History and Romance" includes a visit to an old village in a Copenhagen suburb, a river cruise, the Frilandsmuseet (Open Air Museum) and the Dyrehaven (Royal Deer Park). Coffee and Danish pastry is included in the price. This tour lasts four hours and runs 15 June to 31 Aug., every Sat.

The "Midsummer Night Tour" takes you to Bakken amusement park, Marienlyst Hotel in Helsingør with folk dancing and a casino, ending up at a Copenhagen restaurant where you can meet Danes over a glass of beer. Duration is five hours, and the tour takes place Tues. and Fri. from 19 June to 19 Aug.

To join a motor boat tour (with or without guide) go to Gammel Strand or Kongens Nytorv. The boats also stop at Den Lille Havfrue and some go to Christianshavn. A fine way to experience Copenhagen and wonderfully refreshing on a hot summer's day.

There are guided walking tours, lasting two hours, with various starting points and routes, July through Aug. Consult the Copenhagen dailies or ask for information at the Tourist Information Office.

COPENHAGEN

Guided tours of the Carlsberg Brewery, Ny Carlsbergvej 140, are on Mon. to Fri. at 9, 11 and 2.30. The Tuborg Brewery, Strandvejen 54 (buses 1 and 21) may be visited Mon. to Fri. at any time between 8.30 and 2.30.

MUSEUMS. Copenhagen is a fine city to stimulate a sense of history and it certainly has its fair share of museums and art galleries. We list here the major museums plus a few smaller ones of special interest, together with opening times. Note that off-season opening hours tend to be shorter, and that most museums close on Monday.

Although admission to many museums is free it could pay you to invest in a *Copenhagen Card*, a tourist ticket giving unlimited bus and rail travel in Copenhagen plus free admission to 36 sights including Tivoli. Valid for one, two or three days at 60, 110 or 150 Dkr. respectively, it can be bought from rail stations, the Tourist Information Office, hotels and travel agents.

Davids Samling (C.L. David Collection). Kronprinsessegade 30. Medieval Islamic pottery, European decorative art from 18th cent. Open all year, Tues. to Sun. 1–4; closed Mon. Adm. free.

Frihedsmuseet (Liberty Museum). Esplanaden. Exhibits detailing the efforts of the Danish Resistance in World War II. Open May through Sept., Tues. to Sat. 10–4, Sun. 10–5; closed Mon. Adm. free.

Fyrskib XVII. Nyhavn 10. Lightship dating from 1895. Open all year, Mon. to Fri. 9–2; closed Sat. and Sun. Adm. 2 Dkr.

Geologisk Museum (Geological Museum). Øster Voldgade 5–7. Open all year, Tues. to Sat. 1–4, Sun. 10–12; closed Mon. Adm. free.

Glyptotek. Dantes Plads. Egyptian, Greek, Etruscan and Roman collections, 19th-cent. French and Danish art. Open May through Aug., Tues. to Sun. 10–4; closed Mon. Sept. through Apr., Tues. to Sat. 12–3, Sun. 10–4, closed Mon. Adm. 12 Dkr., Wed. and Sun. free.

Den Hirschsprungske Samling (Hirschsprung Collection). Stockholmsgade 20. 19th-cent. Danish art. Open all year, Wed. to Sun. 1–4; closed Mon. and Tues. Also open Wed. eve. 7–10, Oct. through Apr. Adm. free.

Jagt- og Skovbrugsmuseet (Hunting and Forestry Museum). Hørsholm. Train to Holte then bus to Hørsholm, or bus 84 or faster 75E (weekdays only). Open Mar. through Nov., Tues. to Sun. 10–4. Closed Mon. Adm. 5 Dkr.

Kobenhavns Bymuseum (Copenhagen City Museum). Vesterbrogade 59. Guild relics, costumes, paintings and engravings illustrating the history and appearance of the capital through the ages. Also Søren Kierkegaard reliquae. Open May through Oct., Tues. to Sun. 10–4; closed Mon. Nov. through Apr., Tues. to Sun. 1–4; all year, Tues. 7 P.M.–9 P.M. Adm. free.

Kunstindustrimuseet (Museum of Decorative and Applied Arts). Bredgade 68. Collections from Middle Ages to present. Open all year, Tues. to Sun. 1–4; closed Mon. Adm. free except Sun., July and Aug., 7 Dkr.

Nationalmuseet (National Museum). Frederiksholms Kanal 12. Exhibits illustrate Danish civilization from Stone Age to recent times; also, ethnographical and coin collections. The Prehistoric and Greenland collections are outstanding. Opening times of the different sections are complex, but most sections are open Sun. 10–4, some Tues. to Sun. 10–4, and others 1–4. Closed Mon. Adm. free.

Ordrupgårdsamlingen (Ordrupgård Collections). Vilvordevej 110, Charlottenlund. 19th-cent. French paintings, especially Impressionists. Bus 160 from Klampenborg or Lyngby S-stations. Open all year, Tues. to Sun. 1–5; Wed. 7 P.M.–10 P.M.; closed Mon. Adm. 5 Dkr.

Statens Museum for Kunst (National Gallery). Sølvgade. Danish and European paintings, including Matisse collection. Open all year, Tues. to Sun. 10–5; closed Mon. Adm. free.

Teaterhistorisk Museum (Theater Museum). Christiansborg Ridebane 18. Open June through Sept., Wed., Fri. and Sun. 2–4. Adm. 5 Dkr.

Thorvaldsens Museum. Slotsholmen. Works by Danish sculptor (1770–1844). Open May through Sept., daily 10–4. Adm. free.

Tøjhusmuseet (Royal Arsenal Museum). Tøjhusgade 3. Open May through Sept., Tues. to Sat. 1–4; Sun. 10–4; closed Mon. Adm. free.

Zoologisk Museum (Zoological Museum). Universitetskparken 15. Open May through Sept., daily 10–5. Adm. free.

TIVOLI GARDENS. This world-famous amusement park is open daily from May 1 to mid-September, 10 A.M. (amusements all in operation by 2.30 P.M.) to midnight. It covers an area of 850,000 square feet. In May, amusements are cheaper, and on some Wednesdays children get free afternoon tickets for a few amusements. **Concert Hall:** Not only does Tivoli lie in the heart of Copenhagen, but during the summer months it is the city's musical center as well. Symphony concerts are given every evening at 7.30 and 9 (sometimes free). Also free daily "proms".

Pantomime Theater ("Peacock Building" to left of main entrance). Performances every evening except Sun., pantomimes 7.45, ballets 9.45. Pantomime came to Denmark from Italy via France and England about 150 years ago. This is the only place in the world where traditional pantomime is still performed.

Open-air Stage (in middle of gardens). International variety acts every evening at 7 and 10.30, weekends 5, 7, and 10.

Amusements. In the farthest righthand corner of the gardens ("The Fun Corner") and in "The Alley" behind the scenic railway; open from 2 or 4 until midnight.

Variety Theater Glassalen has a varied program with Danish revues during the summer.

Tivoli Boy Guards. Parade every Sat. and Sun., 6.30 and 8.30.

Fireworks. Weds. and Sats. at 11.45 P.M. on lake and open-air stage. Sun., stage fireworks at 11.15 P.M.

Restaurants. Eating places of all categories; open daily 9 A.M.-midnight. *Divan I* and *Divan II* are noteworthy but by no means inexpensive. Of greater gastronomic interest but no cheaper is *Belle Terrasse.* Over beer and sausages at *Ferry Inn (Faergekroen)* you can join in the folk singing. Also *Perlen, Balkonen, Grøften* and *Nimb.*

Dancing. Every night from 10-midnight at *Taverna.*

Jazz, Folk. *Slukefter* and *Vise Vers Huset.*

PARKS AND ZOOS. In the **Botanisk Have** (Botanical Gardens) you can enjoy Danish wild flowers. There is a *Kaktushus* (open Sat. and Sun. 1–3) and a *Palmehus,* 130 Gothersgade, open daily, June through Aug. 8.30–6. Adm. free.

Danmarks Akvarium is at Charlottenlund. Take the S-train and walk, or bus 1 or 27. The largest aquarium in Europe, it is open Mar. through Oct., daily 10–6. Adm. 16 Dkr., children 8 Dkr. The **Zoologisk Have** (Zoo) is at 32 Roskildevej. Founded in 1859, it is the largest and oldest zoo in Scandinavia. Open daily 9–5, winter 9–4. Adm. 22 Dkr., children 8 Dkr.

The **Dyrehaven** (Deer Park) is near Klampenborg and can be reached by S-train or bus 27. At Hellerup is the World War II Resistance memorial park, **Mindeparken Ryvangen,** reached by S-train or bus 21, and open 10 A.M. to sunset.

HISTORIC BUILDINGS AND SITES. Devastated over the centuries by war and fire, Copenhagen has been re-built many times. Its surviving genuine Renaissance buildings are therefore especially worthy of attention; however architects of later centuries also put up exceedingly handsome buildings. You may wish to take a trip out of town to see rather more homely historic buildings at Sorgenfri and Dragør.

Amalienborg (Amalienborg Palace). Four identical mansions (1740–50) creating a delightful Rococo square. One is Queen Margrethe's residence. Changing of the Guard at noon; famous equestrian statue in the center.

COPENHAGEN

Børsen (Stock Exchange). Slotsholmen. Built by King Christian IV around 1640. Fine Dutch Renaissance building with remarkable dragon-tail spire. Still in use.

Christiansborg Slot (Christiansborg Palace). Slotsholmen. State apartments, knights' hall, palace ruins. Open all year, daily 10–4, but closed Sat. Sept. through May. Adm. 5 Dkr. Frequent guided tours in English June through Aug., daily except Mon., 11 Dkr.

Dragør. Amager. Seaside village settled by Dutch immigrants. Museum open May through Sept., Tues. to Fri., 2–5; Sat. and Sun. 12–6. Closed Mon. Adm. 3 Dkr. Bus 30 or 33 from Rådhus Pladsen.

Folketing (Parliament). Christiansborg Slot. Open June to Sept., Sun. to Fri. 10–4. Closed Sat. Guided tours also Sun. year-round on the hour. Adm. free.

Frilandsmuseet (Openair Museum). Sorgenfri. Original old Scandinavian buildings in natural surroundings. Bus 84, or S-train CC (weekdays only) or A. Open mid-Apr. through Sept., Tues. to Sun. 10–5; closed Mon.; Oct. to Apr., Sun. only. Adm. 5 Dkr.

Grundtvigs Kirke. På Bjerget. Village-style church. Bus 10, 16, 19, 43. Open Mon. to Sat 9–4.45; Sun. 12–4. Adm. free.

Holmens Kirke. Holmens Kanal. Royal chapel and naval church, built 1619. Open 15 May to 15 Sept., Mon. to Sat. 9–2. Closed Sun. Adm. free.

Kastellet (Citadel). At Langelinie. 17th-cent. fortifications. Open year-round daily 6 A.M. to sunset. Adm. free.

Det Kongelige Bibliotek (Royal Library). Christians Brygge 8. Enter from Christiansborg courtyard. National Library of Denmark, topical exhibitions, exquisite gardens. Open all year Mon. to Sat. 9–7. Closed Sun. Adm. free.

Rådhuset (Town Hall). Open Mon. to Fri. 10–3. Guided tours 1 P.M., Sat. 10. A.M. Rådhustårnet (tower) tours Mon. to Fri. 11 and 2, Sat. 11; 2 Dkr.

Rosenborg Slot (Rosenborg Castle). Oster Voldgade 4a. Built by Christian IV, 1606–17. Open daily June through Aug. 10–3; May and Sept. 11–3. Adm. 15 Dkr.

Runde Tårn (Round Tower). Købmagergade. Christian IV's observatory, built 1642. Open daily June through Aug. 10–5; Apr., May, Sept., Oct., Mon. to Sat. 10–5, Sun. 12–4. Adm. 5 Dkr.

Vor Frelsers Kirke (Our Saviour's Church). Skt. Annaegade. Baroque church (1682). Open Mon. to Sat. 10–4, Sun. 12–4. Adm. free. Tower with external stair, 4 Dkr.

SPORTS. Copenhagen is a paradise for active sports people. The Tourist Information Office and Idraettens Hus (02–45 55 55) are good sources of information. **Jogging** may be practised in the parks and woods, and there is a fitness-testing course at Brøndbyskoven. For information on **squash** courts and rackets for hire at *Svanemøllehallen* (20 77 01) **Tennis** clubs that allow visitors to become temporary members are: *B.93*, next to Østerbro Stadium; *H.I.K.*, Hartmannsvej 37, Hellerup; *K.B.*, Peter Bangsvej and Pile Allé. In winter **skating** is mainly an outdoor sport; but there are some indoor rinks at Østerbro Stadium and in Hvidovre, and there is skating on Peblingesø. **Riding horses** may be hired at the Dyrehaven (Deer Park), Klampenborg.

Swimming. The nearest sandy beach is at Charlottenlund. More popular is the artificial beach a little further north at Bellevue. Go to Klampenborg by S-train C or bus 27 (from Hellerup). Beaches free. Swimming pools, open during the summer are: Gladsaxe Bad, Vandtårnsvej 55, Søborg; Vestbad, Nykaer 26, Rødovre; Bellahøj Friluftsbad, Bellahøjvej; Bavnehøj Friluftsbad, Enghavevej 90; Emdrup Friluftsbad, Bredelandsvej and Sundby Friluftsbad, Sundbyvestervej. South of Dragør (bus 30 or 33) are low meadows alongside the beach, with shallow water (the cleanest near Copenhagen); ideal for children. A 5-mile man-made beach is now open to the public at Køge Bugt Strandpark, south of Copenhagen. It is fine, sandy and clean. Bus 121 from Valby Station, or by S-train A to Ishøj or Hundige station and from there by the beach bus (season only) direct to the beach.

Sailing is popular in Copenhagen, and the waters are ideally suited to it. Visitors can obtain assistance through the big clubs, especially the *Royal Danish*

Yacht Club (14 87 87) and the *Copenhagen Amateur Sailing Club*, Klubhuset Svanemøllehavnen (20 71 72). Sailing boats and motor boats can be hired from *Maritim Camping* at Jyllinge (02–38 83 58) or *Danish Boat Charter*, Strandvejen 327, Klampenborg (63 08 00).

Golf. You have four choices in the vicinity of the capital. The 18-hole *Copenhagen Golf Club* is at Eremitagesletten in the Klampenborg Deer Park, 35 min. by car or train from Copenhagen. The 18-hole course at the *Rungsted Golfklub* is 30 minutes by car or train from Copenhagen. There is an 18-hole course at *Helsingør Golfklub*, Gl. Hellebaekvej, and an 18-hole course at *Hillerød Golfklub*, Ny Hammersholt, 40 minutes from Copenhagen. Near Copenhagen there are further golf clubs at Kokkedal, Birkerød, Søllerød/Holte. Ask for the special golf pamphlet at the Tourist Information Office.

Horseracing is accompanied by totalizator betting in Copenhagen. Flat racing takes place between the latter part of Apr. and mid-Dec. at the Klampenborg Race Course. Bus 27 or S-train C to Klampenborg, then bus 160 or bus 176 from station. Trotting events are held year-round, Sun. and Wed., at Charlottenlund Race Course; S-train C or bus 1 to Charlottenlund. **Cycle races** take place on the Ordrup track at Charlottenlund, usually Mon. and Tues. **Soccer** is played at the Idraetsparken at Østerbro or Valby, Sun. afternoons or evenings, except July.

MUSIC, MOVIES AND THEATERS. Copenhagen is without doubt the liveliest city in Scandinavia. In fact, planning an evening out is always rather a perplexing process because there are so many possibilities. *Copenhagen This Week* may help you. It is a free publication obtainable from hotels, travel agencies, etc.

Movies. You have nearly 50 choices to consider before you even leave your hotel room. A high proportion of films are American and British, and except for children's films, soundtracks are in their original languages with Danish subtitles. Performances begin at fixed hours and seats are usually reserved. No need to tip. No smoking in cinemas.

Theaters and Concerts. Copenhagen's theaters play in Danish almost exclusively. One exception is the *Mermaid Theater*, Ny Vestergade 7, where all performances are in English. *Det Kongelige Teater* (Royal Theater), Kongens Nytorv, offers opera and outstanding ballet in addition to plays. Since tickets are normally in great demand you should ask your travel agent or the hotel porter to secure reservations for you up to a week before. During the summer months it is worth remembering that some theaters feature revues and ballet by international companies.

Det Kongelige Kapel, the Royal Theater's orchestra, and the Radio Symphony Orchestra are outstanding, and are often directed by well-known foreign conductors. Famous soloists give recitals from time to time, which are listed in *Copenhagen This Week*. Most concert tickets (except for Tivoli) are sold at *Wilhelm Hansen* (15 54 57) and *ARTE* (10 16 22).

SHOPPING. Copenhagen is something of a shopper's paradise. Prices are high, but then so is the quality. At the same time, many shops offer tax free shopping—look for the sign; it's always prominently displayed. Note, however, that you can claim back tax only when your total purchases from any one shop exceed 1,700 Dkr.

The first place to head for on any shopping expedition in Copenhagen are the Strøget, the pedestrians-only streets—all lined with shops—that lace the heart of the old town.

Design. Near the Central Station at *Den Permanente* (The Permanent Exhibition of Danish Arts and Crafts, which also sells exhibits) there is a purposeful selection of the finest handwork from all over the country.

A store where you'll find a beautiful and large display of Scandinavian design, plus the best of handicrafts from other countries is *Illum*, Østergade 52, the local Harrods. There are over 70 departments, including porcelain, the best names in Danish and Scandinavian furniture, fabrics and Finnish Rya rugs; a tax-free

COPENHAGEN

shipping service, two restaurants, a hairdresser, and credit cards are accepted. A shopper's delight.

Illums Bolighus, Amagertorv 10 (not to be confused with the above store), is *the* Center of Modern Scandinavian Design. If you are interested in some of the most attractive and yet practical things that are being marketed today, this is the spot to visit.

The furniture of Fritz Hansen is well known throughout the world, but you may also have heard the name of Finn Juhl, several of whose chairs have been purchased by the New York Museum of Modern Art. Jens Thuesen and Niels Vodder are also tops.

Ikea, Mårkaervej, Tåstrup (bus 119 from the station), is a huge furniture store with own, often cheaper, designs. *Brugsmøbler,* Albertslund off Highway A1 (bus 123), have specially designed quality furniture at moderate prices.

Silver. You will, of course, be interested to see the home of *Georg Jensen Silver* at Østergade 40. Here you will find the largest collection of Jensen hollowware in the world. Browse among his extensive offerings of gold and silver jewelry and study his permanent exhibit of tables laid with many of the famous patterns in sterling silver and stainless steel.

Danish design achieves beauty by classic lines and graceful forms, and centuries of sensitive craftsmanship are reflected in every piece of contemporary silver. *Hans Hansen* at Amagertorv 16 features stunning flat ware, cigarette boxes, and such.

Peter Hertz, Købmagergade 34, is one of the oldest silversmiths in town and makes most of his pieces to order. He specializes in marvelous place settings and delicate jewelry.

But moderns must first visit *A. Michelsen,* Bredgade 11—their prize-winning cigarette container and silver pitcher, their graceful tubecluster candelabra and the enameled anniversary and enameled Christmas spoons designed each year, are all collectors' items.

A bit further along Bredgade, at number 17, is *A. Dragsted,* whose jewelry and tableware are favorites with the Royal Court.

Porcelain and Glass. The *Royal Copenhagen Porcelain Manufactory* (actually a shop on the original factory site) at Amagertorv 6 might be your next stop. If it is blue anniversary plate or beautiful brown and blue figurines with their fine underglaze you desire, your best bet may be in some antique shop in Kompagnistraede, which runs parallel with Strøgetstraede.

Bing & Grøndahl porcelain is next door and ranks equally high in quality and design. *Rosenthal,* Frederiksberggade 21 has a choice of porcelain and glassware primarily by Scandinavian artists such as Bjørn Wiinblad and Tapio Wirkkala. *Skandinavisk Glas,* Ny Østergade 1 has excellent designs, too.

Holmegaard glassware is on display at Østergade 15, offering everything in Danish design from snaps klukflaske to beautiful opalescent vases. A permanent glass exhibition/museum has been opened.

Arts and Crafts. At Ny Østergade 11 is the *Bjørn Wiinblad House,* with a sales display of the artist's own products.

For native crafts, see *Håndarbejdets Fremme,* Vimmelskaftet 38, which has embroideries, handprinted fabrics, and gleeful trinkets in impeccable taste. Every article is handmade; patterns and materials are also sold.

Clara Waever at Østergade 42 features special embroidery, lace, and linen.

Elling, at Bredgade 24, features materials of fanciful design together with bright printed pieces amusing for a child's room.

In the 1785 Potter's House at Overgaden oven Vandet 10, *P. Brøste* displays modern Danish and foreign arts and crafts.

Hanne Hansen, a fine quality shop at Fiolstraede 19, and *Form & Farve,* Nicolaj Plads 3.

At Bredgade 47, the captivating wooden toys, bowls, and plates of *Kay Bojesen* are on display.

Department Stores. *Magasin du Nord,* a huge, modern department store at Kongens Nytorv is the biggest of its kind in Denmark, with particularly good buys in silver, ceramics, and furs.

Illum, Østergade 52, see above, under *Design.*

Daells Varehus, Nørregade 12, is a smaller store, but offers good quality at extremely reasonable prices. Cash only sales.

RESTAURANTS. Copenhagen has scores of excellent restaurants, though practically all the city's hotels also have first-class eating places. Prices are high, however, for the most part, so always be sure to check the menu, which by law must be displayed outside, before going in. However, a number of restaurants, even the more expensive, offer good-value fixed-price menus, usually of three courses. In addition, look out for restaurants displaying *Dan-Menu* sign, where a two-course meal—either lunch or dinner—will cost 60 Dkr. (This price will be held until April 30 1985; thereafter, a small increase can be expected). Service is always included in all bills and tipping is not expected.

Further budget bets are the many foreign restaurants—Chinese, Greek, Italian, etc.—that have appeared in recent years. You'll also find all the familiar fast food chains here.

Many foreign restaurants—Chinese, Greek, Italian, etc.—have opened in recent years. There are many pizzerias, particularly in the old city, and American-style burgers are sold all over town at **Burger King, McDonalds** and elsewhere. There are cafeterias in the **Magasin, Anva, S & E** and **Favør** department stores, which close half an hour before the shop.

Expensive

Baghuset. Gothersgade 13 (12 32 61). In the rear, specializes in charcoal-grilled steaks and fish served in 200-year-old former backstage store. Small, nautical, nice bar. Book ahead. Closed Sun. and for lunch. AE, DC, MC, V.

Bourgogne. Donningens Tvaergade 2 (12 03 17). Lovely old-fashioned basement restaurant. Good fish dishes. Closed Sun. AE, MC, V.

La Cocotte. Vester Farimagsgade 33 (14 04 07). The Hotel Richmond restaurant serves French cuisine and new Danish cuisine in its cosy corners with slate tables and old rustic furniture. Closed Sun. AE, MC, V.

Egoisten. Hovedvagtsgade 2 (12 79 71). Modern bar-restaurant hard by the Hotel d'Angleterre; lacking in atmosphere, but the excellent food, with service to match, more than compensate. Definitely sophisticated. Closed Sat. and Sun. AE, DC, MC, V.

Hos Jan Hurtigkarl. Dronningens Tvaergade 43 (15 05 54). This restaurant is considered to serve the best food in Copenhagen; as French as anywhere outside France itself. Value for money. Closed Sun. and for lunch. AE, DC, MC, V.

Kong Frederik Hotel. Vester Voldgade 25–27 (12 59 02). Modern international cuisine; charming outdoor dining. AE, DC, MC, V.

Kong Hans. Vingårdsstraede 6 (11 68 68). Haute cuisine served in 13th-century surroundings, or in the Oyster Bar. Changing menu according to seasonal dishes. Small, best to reserve. Closed July. AE, DC, MC, V.

Krogs Fiskerestaurant. Gammel Strand 38 (15 99 15). Serves up its fruits of the sea in plusher—and more expensive—surrounding. Try, for example, the *Tout de Paris.* Closed Sun. AE, DC, MC, V.

Langelinie Pavillionen. Langelinie (12 12 14). In the Royal Yacht Club. Excellent for lunches, teas, dinners; magnificent view of the harbor. Evening music and dancing. AE, DC, MC, V.

Pakhuskaelderen. Hotel Nyhavn 71 (11 85 85 or 11 32 32). Grill restaurant in former storehouse basement. AE, DC, MC, V.

Sct. Gertruds Kloster. Hauser Plads 32 (14 66 30). Enjoy a candlelit dinner with more than 50 specialties on the menu, excellent wines, and all in medieval surroundings. Closed for lunch. AE, DC, MC, V.

Viking Carver. Rådhus Pladsen 57 (14 40 50). In Palace Hotel; convenient, serves better-than-average meals; and prides itself on fine service. AE, DC, MC, V.

Moderate

Bee Cee Cafe. Østergade 24 (15 02 77). Lunch restaurant in the beautiful restored Pistolstraede; an architectural experience. Entrance from Strøget. The restaurant itself is in a basement with modern decor and good food. Open to 8 P.M. Closed Sun. AE, DC, MC, V.

Bøf og Ost. Gråbrødretorv 13 (11 99 11). French rural-inn style; on popular square off Strøget. Closed Sun.

COPENHAGEN

Cheval Blanc. Mikkel Bryggersgade 6 (11 51 57). Unpretentious, cozy inn with fixed menu and varying "weekly offers." Reasonable prices. Closed Sun. DC, MC, V.

Copenhagen Corner. Rådhus Pladsen (14 45 45). Opened in 1979, this restaurant serves good food in attractive surroundings. The menu always includes a "today's special"—which means that the price is low.

Glyptoteket. Stormgade 35 (14 63 20). Across the street from the museum of the same name, revives weary art-lovers with excellent cooking. AE, DC, MC, V.

La Guitarra. Grønnegade 33 (15 15 65). Cheerful and atmospheric Italian restaurant with good food and service; located off the Strøget behind Kongens Nytorv. Open 4 P.M. to midnight. Closed Mon. AE, MC, V.

Heering. Pilestraede 19 (15 22 40). Friendly, attractively-decorated café and restaurant, with Danish specialties. Closed on Sat., and Sun. lunch. AE, DC, MC, V.

Nikolaj. Nikolaj Plads 24 (15 50 28). In former Nikolaj Kirke. Danish food at its best; plus delightful local-style decor.

Østerport. Oslo Plads 5 (11 22 66). Hotel restaurant. Decor matches excellent Danish and French cuisine. Cold table is excellent. AE, DC, MC, V.

Queens Pub. Vestervoldgade 25–27 (12 59 02). At Hotel Kong Frederik. English pub-style food and drink. AE, DC, MC, V.

Streckers Restaurant. Kompagnistraede 20 (11 72 94). Also called Beefy's Brother. Highly recommended. In basement and not very impressive from outside, but inside, a pleasant surprise with delicious food. Closed Sun.

Tivolihallen. Vester Voldgade 91 (11 01 60). Basement inn, dating from 1850; especially good for lunch, but open for dinner too (closes 8 P.M.). Closed Sat. and Sun.

Victor's. Ny Østergade 8 (13 36 13). *The* place to go. Restaurant with French-style menu, bar and café. MC, V.

Inexpensive

Bad København. Studiestraede 63 (11 52 72). Homemade buffet in this lunch restaurant attached to a public bath. Closed Sat. and Sun.

Cafe Lindevang. P.G. Ramms Allé 4 (34 38 34). Public and cozy lunch restaurant at Frederiksberg (also hot food). Enormous dishes. Closed Sat. and Sun.

DSB Bistro & Grill. Central Station (14 12 32). Quick restaurant with reasonably priced breakfast, lunch and dinner mainly for the busy traveler, children welcome. AE, DC, MC, V.

Els. Store Strandstraede 3 (14 13 41). Near Nyhavn. Founded in first half of 19th century, with mainly original interior. Danish lunch, closed Sat. and Sun. Best book.

Familiehaverne. Pile Alle 10–18 (16 11 33 or 30 92 57). Traditional outdoor restaurants, open May to 15 Sept. Near the Zoo. Favorite with families. DC.

Gyllen. Nørre Voldgade 2 (12 78 95). Unpretentious lunch restaurant near Rådhus Pladsen. Plain, but very good. Closed Sun. MC, V.

Havfruen. Nyhavn 39 (11 11 38). In sailors' quarter.

Hos Karl Kik (Slotskaelderen). Fortunstraede 4 (11 15 37). Lunch restaurant now run by third generation of Kik family. Specializes in smørrebrød. Closed Sun.

Parnas. Lille Kongensgade 16 (11 49 10). Where artists meet over music and Danish food. AE, DC, MC, V.

Tokanten. Vandkunsten 1 (12 73 09). Caters primarily for families. Very popular with all ages. Large menu for children. DC, MC, V.

Vista. Vesterbrogade 40 (24 67 10). Cheap restaurant with self-service.

Vivaldi. Torvegade 49–51 (57 75 10). Italian spot in the heart of Christianshavn; large and atmospheric. Handy lunch spot of exploring Christianshavn.

DENMARK

NIGHTLIFE. Still feeling strong? We have a long way to go before we have exhausted all the city has to offer. All-night membership clubs are now things of the past. About 35 restaurants are permitted to stay open until 5 A.M. (ask your hotel porter or see the newspaper). For shows, see the *Ekstrabladet* newspaper advertisements. For the young, many discos have been opened in recent years. Bohemians in general might like to make their way to the district around Nikolaj Kirke, locally known as "The Minefield." Here are dozens of small music and dance spots, and a beer is the price of admission. If you want to see the kind of scenes Hogarth painted, visit the sailors' dives of Nyhavn. These places are mostly male but not likely to prove dangerous if you go with someone else, are a "good mixer," and stay reasonably sober. If you are reluctant to go home, the first morning restaurants open around 5 A.M. to serve you a nice early breakfast and another drink.

The nightspots listed below are moderate to expensive and usually have an admittance fee.

CLUBS AND DISCOS

Alexandra Rock Theater. Nørregade. Across from cathedral. Live music, one of the hottest places in town, selective admittance.

Annabel's. Lille Kongensgade 16, just off Kongens Nytorv. Disco. 10 P.M.–5 A.M.

Bristol–8 Days a Week. Strøget, near Rådhus Pladsen. Fascinating dance spot for the young.

Cafe Royal. Opposite Christiansborg. Known as "Lauritz Betjent," its inner room is a favorite place for those-in-the-know.

Club Ambassadeur. Rådhuspladsen 57. Disco. 9 P.M.–3 A.M., Fri. and Sat. to 5 A.M. Closed Sun. and Mon.

Compass Club. Amager Blvd. 70. In Scandinavia Hotel. Disco. Thurs., Fri. and Sat. only, 10 P.M.–5 A.M.

Daddy's. Axeltorv 5. Disco. 10 P.M.–4 or 5 A.M.

Hong Kong. Nyhavn 7. Entrance through the gate across the courtyard. Popular dance restaurant. 5 P.M.–1 A.M.

Københavnerkroen. Bernstoffsgade 3. Soloists, entertainment and a public of all ages. No hot food. 9 or 9.30 P.M.–2 or 4 A.M. Closed Sun.

Lorry Landsbyen. Allegade 7–9. Roofed beer garden restaurant with revues and jazz concerts.

Montmartre. Nørregade 41. One of the most famous jazz spots in Europe. 8 P.M.–1 A.M., Fri. and Sat. to 5 A.M. Closed Sun. and Mon.

Musikcaféen. Magstraede 14. Folk singers and jazzbands, dancing. 9 P.M.–1 A.M. Closed Sun.

Penthouse Club. Sheraton Hotel, Vester Søgade 6. Disco. 10 P.M.–5 A.M.

Vin Og Ølgod. Skindergade 45. German beerhouse atmosphere with singing and dancing. 8 P.M.–2 A.M. Closed Sun.

Vognporten. Magstraede 14. Jazzbands, dancing. 8 P.M.–2 A.M.

Waterloo Night Club. 7 Gammel Kongevej. Popular dance restaurant.

BARS

D'Angleterre. Kongens Nytorv 34. Hotel bar.

Hviids Vinstue. Kongens Nytorv 19. Otherwise known as "Smoky Joe's," has an English pub atmosphere. 10 A.M.–1 A.M. Closed Sun. in summer.

Imperial. Vester Farimagsgade 9. Hotel Bar.

Kakadu Bar. Colbjørnsensgade 6 (near Central Station). Mostly singles. 10 P.M.–5 A.M.

Ole Nezers Pianobar. Løngangsstraede 39 (near Rådhus Plads). Host plays the piano and his wife is a well-known singer. 10—5, Sat. to 3.

Palace. Rådhus Pladsen 57. Hotel bar.

Queen's Pub. Kong Frederik Hotel, Vester Volgade 25–7. Popular imitation of an English pub.

Richmond. Vester Farimagsgade 33. Hotel bar.

Royal. Hammerichsgade 1. Hotel Bar.

Sorgenfri. Brolaeggerstraede 8 (11 58 80). Tiny basement haunt off Nytorv; reputedly the oldest bar in the city. Can get very crowded, but a must for those who enjoy smoky conviviality and atmosphere by the gallon.

Wonder Bar. Studiestraede 69. Mostly singles.

ZEALAND AND ITS ISLANDS

Holiday Haunts and History

Next to Copenhagen, Zealand (Danish, Sjaelland) is the part of Denmark that is seen by more visitors than any other. Even so, most visitors see only part of Zealand, a very small part. They miss not only the very beautiful island of Møn but also the interesting and lovely Odsherred region. The classic tour—up the coast of the Sound to Helsingør (Elsinore) and Hamlet's castle (Kronborg Slot), down to Fredensborg Slot, on to Frederiksborg Slot and back to Copenhagen—covers no more than a corner of the rolling and often beautiful country which is Zealand.

Helsingør

Helsingør is one of Denmark's oldest towns. Yet it did not achieve any importance until 1429, when Eric decided to impose "sound dues" on all vessels entering or leaving the Baltic. Now it is the Danes who have to pay dues when they cross from one part of their country to the other across the Great Belt on the State Railway ferries. There have been plans of bridges here and a tunnel from Helsingør to Sweden, but they've been put off for the time being.

"Hamlet's town," or "the pleasant corner in Scandinavia," has a rich tradition of trade and shipping. The romantic center of the city, with the many idyllic little houses goes back to about 1574 when the monumental Kronborg Slot was built.

Erected between 1574 and 1582 by Frederik II, the Renaissance Kronborg Slot is a must. Visit the central yard first and then take a walk on the inner and outer ramparts. The visitable parts of the castle include a 60-meter (200-foot) long banqueting hall, a commercial and maritime museum, dungeons and casemates where the sleeping Ogier will awake and fill every Dane with his spirit when Denmark is in danger. The chapel interior is luxurious, and people are still married there. There is a long tradition of performances of *Hamlet* in the courtyard, including many by famous interpreters of the role over the years, both English and from other countries.

Marienlyst Slot was built in 1587 as a summer house for Kronborg, and was later used by Queen Juliane Marie. It was rebuilt in 1760 and French-style gardens were added. It is now a city museum and is used for ceremonial occasions.

The Karmeliterklosteret and Sct. Mariae Kirke were both founded in 1430 and are among the foremost examples of Danish medieval architecture. Although still partly inhabited, both the former chapter hall and refectory can be visited. Skt. Olai Kirke has been a cathedral since 1961; building was started about 1200 and not completed until 1559. Fragments of the original 13th-century building are still to be seen on the north side.

Danmarks Tekniske Museum contains noteworthy old technical products made in Denmark, for example the 1886 Hammel car. In the Øresundsakvariet are displayed Sound fauna as seen in ten different localities, with emphasis on sea-anemones and crustaceans.

Two summer events in Helsingør are the marching of the girls' guard through the town every Friday, and the annual festival of church music held in late August and early September.

North Zealand

Around Helsingør is a string of quiet seaside resorts with pleasant, sandy beaches inviting you to linger for a day, or longer. On summer Sundays, a veteran railroad goes to Gilleleje instead of the normal "railbus." Vedbaek, Humlebaek (with the fine Louisiana art gallery) and Snekkersten are to the south; Hellebaek and Hornbaek are to the north; and Sweden (Helsingborg) is to the east, with ferries every 20 minutes.

One example of a vacation village is Tisvildeleje. In winter a fishing village, in summer there is an enormous expansion in population. People walk through its only main road with its low, one-story houses, either to the coast and beach behind the dunes, or back to their summer cottages. Or they walk to the funny "railbus" which will take them back to Hillerød and Copenhagen. Other people will throng at the packed parking lot and walk from their cars down to the beach or into the hilly woodland. Some go fishing, others go to the Troldeskoven (Troll Forest), a part of the wood with twisted, mysterious pines—if you do the same, you might possibly meet some figures who are clearly *not* trolls; there is a naturist bathing beach nearby. One could instead go inward to Tisvilde or Tibirke and enjoy the village atmosphere.

For the tourist the towns of Hillerød and Fredensborg, only six miles apart, form a unit of the classic tour of north Zealand. South of Hillerød, there's the charming village of Søllerød with its medieval church, terraced yard and thatched-roofed inn. North of Hillerød a belt of fishing-villages are now completely changed into summer bathing resorts. In Hillerød itself is the Nordsjaellandsk Folkemuseum in a 200-year-old smallholding, and there is the fine Renaissance palace, Frederiksborg Slot.

Frederiksborg Slot was built between 1600 and 1620 by Christian IV on his birthplace. This king erected several other architectural gems, but for Frederiksborg he chose the beautiful site between the wide lake on one side and a double moat on the other. After a fire in 1859 the castle was restored with money from the founder of the Carlsberg brewery. Today it is the Nationalhistorisk Museum, with fine furniture, paintings, other art treasures. The Chapel is famed for its interior and a Compenius organ dating from 1610, still in use. Before the fire the castle was a royal summer residence, and Danish kings were crowned here—today they are not crowned at all.

Palace Park is French-style, with views to the castle. The Bath (a country seat) is still sometimes in use for royal hunting lunches.

AEbelholt, six km. (four miles) west, is a monastery with ruins dating from 1175.

Fredensborg is known for its palace and its inn. The palace, Fredensborg Slot, was built in 1721–3. It is still a royal palace, the Queen's residence in spring and fall. With its 420 rooms grouped around the Dome Hall it is an exquisite setting for royal parties, and also contains some valuable paintings. The park, which runs down to a lake, Esrum Sø, is one of the most beautiful in Europe. The Marble Garden is the royal family's private garden. There are Italian Baroque sculptures and a rose garden.

West of Copenhagen

Selsø Herregårdsmuseum, at Skibby between Frederikssund and Roskilde, has been uninhabited since 1829 and is now being restored as a museum by an enthusiastic journalist. You will find a 400-year-old Baroque banqueting hall and Louis XVI tapestries. West of Roskilde is Odsherred with the main towns Holbaek and Nykøbing. The central part of Holbaek grew up around a 14th-century Blackfriars' convent and the museum is in a late 17th-century building. Surroundings include Tuse Kirke with frescos dating from 1450 picturing the childhood of Jesus. Southwest of Holbaek is a miniature Frederiksborg, Løvenborg Slot, erected behind protecting moats in about 1634 (no admission). Tveje Merløse Kirke south of the town is extraordinary in its architecture, being an example of an early medieval church. It has a restored ceiling and the western end still contains the gallery for the master and mistress.

Nykøbing is the main town in a popular holiday resort area. The western part of this coastal area has a ferry connection with Ebeltoft.

Near the road from Nykøbing to Kalundborg is Dragsholm Slot, built in the 13th century by the Roskilde bishop as a fortress. After the Reformation, the castle was used as a state prison; one of the "guests" was the Earl of Bothwell, who died here in 1578 and is buried in

Fårevejle Church. Today the castle serves hotel guests in its restored buildings.

To the west in the bottom of a narrow fjord is Kalundborg, basis for ferries to Samsø and Jutland. Until 1658 the city was strongly fortified, but since its castle was destroyed that year, the strange church is the only unruined part of the fortification. Vor Frue Kirke (Our Lady's Church), circa 1170, has a groundplan shaped like a Grecian cross. With its five towers and Eastern European patterns it serves—together with the radio masts—as a landmark. There are old thatched houses, especially in Praestegade and Adelgade, where Lindegården houses the local museum which occupies over 15 rooms, partly Rococo, and has a fine collection of local costumes.

Nearby is Røsnaes, with dolmens, windmill, cliffs and lighthouse. The Rococo Lerchenberg Slot at Asnaes is situated in a marvelous French-style park with rose garden, English-style lawns and summer concerts.

From Lerchenborg, go south to Slagelse; five km. (three miles) west from town you will find Trelleborg, a Viking fortress which is nearly 1,000 years old. Actually there are two forts, one much larger than the other, each with a huge circular rampart and a moat. The remains of some 30 barracks survive, and one has been reconstructed to show the peculiar, slightly curving shape given to the walls of these 30-meter (100-foot) long buildings. The site layout is thought to have been influenced by Byzantine models. Slagelse is on the main road between Korsør and Copenhagen.

Returning to Copenhagen along the main road you will pass the towns of Sorø, Ringsted and Roskilde. Sorø has an old Cistercian abbey dating from the second half of the 12th century. Today it is dominated by the abbey church and its academy serves as a public school. Sorø Kirke is Denmark's largest abbey church, with the tomb of Bishop Absalon, the founder of Copenhagen, behind the altar. Three kings are buried here and so are two well-known Danish poets, Ludvig Holberg and B. S. Ingemann. The latter rests outside the abbey in the churchyard. Sorø Akademi, from 1586 a school, and from 1623 an academy, was destroyed by fire in 1813 and rebuilt 14 years later. Visitors are admitted only during the school's summer holiday.

The Susåen (Suså river) nearby is good for canoeing, and the hilly woodland around the Tystrup-Bavelse-søerne (lakes) are pleasant, as is the walk round Sorø Sø, the lake, from the Academy. At Bjernede, near Sorø, is Zealand's only round church, an early brick-built church dating from about 1170.

Ringsted was an important medieval town, and is today a commercial town of 28,000 inhabitants. The Romanesque Sankt Bendts Kirke (St. Benedict's Church) was originally a Benedictine abbey, and was the first church in Scandinavia to be built of brick. It was built by King Valdemar 1160–70 as a monument over his father, Knud Lavard, who had been murdered in 1131. The Roman Church rewarded him by canonizing Knud Lavard, who is the only Danish saint. During the next 200 years the church served as the royal sepulchral chapel.

Roskilde, with 50,000 inhabitants, is Zealand's second largest town. It was a royal residence as early as the 10th century. In the Middle Ages the town was the most important spiritual center in northern Europe, with 12 parish churches and eight large convents and charitable institutions apart from the cathedral. The first railroad in Denmark, linking Copenhagen and Roskilde, was opened in 1847. In 1972 Roskilde University was founded.

Roskilde Domkirke (Roskilde Cathedral) was erected by Bishop Absalon about 1170 on the site of a wooden church 200 years older. It is a most important medieval building, where the Romanesque and Gothic styles intermingle. Various porches and chapels have been added or extended from time to time in the prevailing architectural style, so that the result is a longitudinal section of Danish building history. The chapels have been added to serve as royal tombs, today numbering 38, the most recent burial being that of King Frederick IX in 1972. There is also an interesting 500-year-old clock and a pillar on which several royal personages, including Peter the Great and the Duke of Windsor, have marked their heights.

In 1962 five Viking ships were found in Roskilde Fjord and excavated. They had been sunk in the 11th century to form a barrier against enemy ships sailing towards Roskilde. In the Vikingeskibshallen, the museum built near where the ships were discovered, you can see the ships as well as exhibitions and films tracing their history and restoration.

Take a cruise on the Fjord on the veteran ship Skjelskør, visit nearby Ledreborg manor, or the Lejre Forsøgscenter—a working historical-archeological museum and research center at the Iron Age village of Herthadalen.

South through Køge to the Cliffs of Møn

Interesting towns in southern Zealand, if you pass near them, are Køge, Naestved, and Vordingborg. Køge boasts more ancient half-timbered houses than any other town in Zealand. The oldest, dated 1527, is at Kirkestraede 20. There are also the smithy at Kirkestraede 13, the mayor's house to Brogade 16, the weaver's house on the square, and, in particular, Vestergadegården (Vestergade 16) which is richly carved and has an overhanging first floor.

Køge Bay is the site of two great naval battles between Danes and Swedes. The Danish national anthem refers to the earlier of these two (1677) in its first line, "King Christian stood by the lofty mast," although some sources claim the King observed the engagement from the tower of Køge's Skt. Nikolai Kirke. Whatever the facts of the matter may be, this tower did provide a convenient place for hanging pirates.

In the Køge district are a number of fine castles: Gisselfeld, a stunning two-storied Renaissance edifice moated all round, with a beautiful park; Rococo Bregentved with copper spires and magnificent gardens; Gjorslev, built in 1400 by the Bishop of Roskilde, in the shape of a cross crowned by a tower in the center; Vallø and Vemmetofte, impressive castles, founded as homes for unmarried ladies of rank.

Near Rødvig are the chalk cliffs called Stevns Klint, which are striking, though not as impressive as the ones at Møn, nearly three times higher. The Højerup Kirke on Stevns Klint, however, has rather a pathetic air about it. Built around 1250, the church found its foundation being undermined by the sea and, so the story goes, moved itself an inch inland every Christmas. Unfortunately this retreat was far too cautious, because first the cemetery and then the choir toppled into the

ZEALAND AND ITS ISLANDS

sea. In recent years the church has been restored and the cliffs below it bolstered with masonry to prevent further damage.

Naestved also has a number of half-timbered houses. Boderne is a medieval suite of houses, one of them a museum of arts and crafts. Apostelgården in Riddergade dates from about 1500, and is noteworthy for the figures of Christ and the Twelve Apostles carved under its eaves. There are more old houses in Kompagnistraede, as well as the impressive Gothic church of Skt. Peder, which has a fresco depicting King Valdemar Atterdag and Queen Helvig. Also of interest is the 15th-century Helligåndshuset (House of the Holy Ghost) containing a museum with regional collections. A mile outside of town, there's Herlufsholm Manor, once an abbey, with a 13th-century chapel. Holmegårds Glasvaerk (glassworks) makes an interesting visit, while regional handicrafts can be seen in the museum at Stenboderne.

On a small island just south of Naestved is the beautifully furnished castle of Gavnø, privately-owned but open to visitors. The delightful garden has modern sculptures in wood and stone. There is a flower show here in May.

The best Zealand canoe trip (85 km. or 52 miles up the Suså river) starts in Naestved and takes you through the most beautiful part of this island. There are many resting spaces, and canoes with life-jackets can be hired.

Vordinborg, Zealand's most southerly town, is splendidly situated on the Great Stream or Storstrøm, the strait separating Zealand from Falster. Here are the ruins of King Valdemar Atterdag's castle, the place where he died in 1182. Besides an outer wall nearly one km. (½ mile) long, there is the Gåsetårnet (Goose Tower), 26 meters (115 feet) tall (if you include the Golden Goose on top) from which there is a view over to Falster and Møn. Around the castle are extensive grounds, now a botanical garden.

From Vordingborg a three-km. (two-mile) long bridge runs to the island of Falster, whose rich soil is used to grow most of Denmark's sugar beet. Nykøbing is the principal town, with excellent hotels and the Czarens Hus, House of the Czar, an 18th-century half-timbered structure where Peter the Great stayed in 1716. Another bridge connects with the island of Lolland. There are good sandy beaches about 10 km. (six miles) away.

Lolland's main attractions are the towns of Maribo and Nysted, the latter known for Ålholm Slot, an old "robbers' castle" dating from the 12th century. Once a royal dwelling, today especially known for the nearby automobile museum with vintage and veteran cars owned by the Ålholm baron. The cars date from 1896 to 1930 and there are about 250 of them. A steam train dating from 1850 crosses the castle park and takes the visitors down to the Baltic. Maribo, in the middle of the island, is dominated by the 15th-century Domkirke (Cathedral), originally a Bridgettine abbey. Ruins of the convent are still to be seen. The open-air museum has a farmhouse representing the original regional dwelling. On summer weekends a veteran railway will take passengers to Bandholm on the northern coast over the lands of Knuthenborg Manor. The Knuthenborg Safari Park contains game, botanical sights, a monkey jungle and other safari animals. There is also a children's zoo. You can drive through the park, but take care to keep the windows closed unless you want to be visited by a baboon.

From Stubbekøbing on Falster, a short ferry crossing takes you to Bogø, with a dam connected with Møn near Fanefjord. Its white 13th-century church has an overwhelming number of frescos.

A few miles east of Stege, the main town, with its 15th-century gate, is the church of Keldby. This 13th-century church contains a lot of frescos, too, painted between 1275 and 1480. Even the royal wedding of King Valdemar and Queen Helvig in 1340 is pictured here. The third frescoed church is at Elmelunde further east. The nave here dates from about 1075.

The east coast of Møn displays 75-million-year-old chalk cliffs, Mons Klint, towering 120 meters (400 feet) above the sea, a great natural sight, seen from the top or the bottom. The charming 18th-century Liselund Slot with its English-style park and pavilions is nearby.

On your way back to Zealand you can make a detour to Nyord, a dammed island with many 250-year-old unspoiled farmhouses. Cars are not allowed in the hamlet, so you should walk there. Via Stege you reach the main road and the bridge to Zealand.

PRACTICAL INFORMATION FOR ZEALAND

TOURIST INFORMATION. The main towns of Zealand and its islands have tourist information (Dantourist) offices: **Helsingør,** Havnepladsen 3 (02–21 13 33). **Hillerød,** Torvet 1 (02–26 28 52). **Kalundborg,** Volden 12 (03–51 09 15). **Køge,** Vestergade 1 (03–65 58 00). **Maribo,** Torvet 1A (03–88 04 96). **Nykøbing (Falster),** Østergade 2 (03–85 13 03). **Ringsted,** Sct. Bendtsgade 10 (03–61 34 00). **Roskilde,** Fondenx Bro 3 (02–35 27 00). **Sorø,** Rolighed 5C (03–63 02 69). **Stege (Møn),** Storegade 5 (03–81 44 11).

TELEPHONE CODES. We have given telephone codes for all the towns and villages in the hotel and restaurant lists that follow. These codes need only be used when calling from outside the town or village concerned.

HOTELS AND RESTAURANTS. The roads running north and south from Copenhagen pass through seaside resorts and small villages, so you can expect accommodations to range in price and comfort accordingly. Remember that the peak season at the seaside places runs from 15 June to 20 August, elsewhere from 1 May to 30 September. During other months, ask for off-season rates. The local tourist offices will help you with booking.

ALBERTSLUND (Tåstrup). *Motel Wittrup* (M), (02–64 95 51). 104 beds, 48 rooms with shower. Near Copenhagen. (BE). AE, DC, MC, V.

FREDENSBORG. *Store Kro* (E), (02–28 00 47). 49 rooms, all with bath. Near castle. As comfortable as any hotel in Denmark and food is unrivaled. Many rooms have terrace. DC, MC, V.

GLOSTRUP. *Glostrup Park Hotel* (E), (02–96 00 38). 100 beds, all rooms with bath. Near Copenhagen. AE, DC, MC, V.

GREVE STRAND. *Canteen* (I), (02–90 11 30). 20 beds. Motel between Copenhagen and Køge. (BE). DC, MC, V.

ZEALAND AND ITS ISLANDS

HELSINGØR. *Marienlyst* (E), (02-21 18 01). 398 beds, all rooms with bath. Private beach, sauna, roulette, indoor salt pool. Fashionable, with music and dance. There are also 63 apartments, each sleeping 4-6 people, with kitchenette and bath. AE, DC, MC, V. *Meulenborg* (M), (02-21 52 20). 50 beds; annex. Open mid-May through Sept. Old manor house in extensive grounds with pool, fish ponds and sea fishing. *Missionshotellet* (M), (02-21 05 91). 65 beds. *Skandia* (M), (02-21 09 02). 90 beds. MC, V.

HOLBAEK. *Strandparken* (M), (03-43 06 16). 52 beds, all rooms with bath. In park. DC, MC, V.

HORNBAEK. *Trouville* (E), (02-20 22 00). 81 beds, all rooms with bath. Near beach; pool, sauna, fishing, sailing, music, garden. AE, DC, MC, V.

JYDERUP. *Bromølle Kro* (M), (03-55 00 90). 6½ km. (four miles) south off Roskilde-Kalundborg road, Denmark's oldest inn (1198), in beautiful surroundings, opposite children's amusements. A former host supplemented his income by murdering his sleeping guests, but this hobby isn't practised any longer. (BE). AE, DC, MC, V. *Snertinge Kro* (M), (03-46 80 35). Five km. (three miles) north. Typical Danish country inn (BE).

KARREBAEKSMINDE. Restaurant. *De hvide Svaner* (E). Old thatched-roofed buildings, first-class food.

KØGE. *Hvide Hus* (E), (03-65 36 90). 224 beds. Sauna. AE, DC, MC, V. *Centralhotellet* (I), (03-65 06 96). 24 beds (BE).
Restaurant. *Casino* (M), (03-65 01 75). Good food.

KORSØR. *Klarskovgård* (M), (03-57 23 22). 172 beds, all rooms with shower. *Tårnborgkroen* (I), (03-57 10 69). 23 beds, 5 doubles with shower. (BE). MC, V.

MARIBO (Lolland). *Hvide Hus* (M), (03-88 10 11). 130 beds. Modern, with sauna and pool. AE, DC, MC, V.
Restaurant. *Bang's Have* (E). In lovely surroundings, fine for meals on outings. Music Sat. all year round. DC.

MENSTRUP. *Menstrup Kro* (M), (03-74 30 03). 70 beds. Renovated country inn, near beach, homemade country food. AE, DC, MC, V.

MOGENSTRUP. *Mogenstrup Kro* (M), (03-76 11 30). 85 beds. Cozy country inn, renovated. AE, DC, MC, V.

MULLERUP HAVN. Between Kalundborg and Slagelse. *Skipperkroen* (M), (03-55 81 95). Accommodations in 10 cottages with 6 beds each, bath and kitchen. Inn has unusual interior. AE, DC, MC, V.

NAESTVED. *Vinhuset* (M), (03-72 08 07). 65 beds. Very pleasant, nightclub. AE, DC, MC, V. *Axelhus* (I), (03-72 06 00). 30 beds, no rooms with private bath. Spacious (BE).

NYKØBING (Falster). *Baltic* (M), (03-85 30 66). 130 beds, pleasant. DC, MC, V. *Liselund* (I), (03-85 15 66). 50-bed motel.

NYKØBING (Sjaelland). *Hotel du Vest* (M), (03-41 12 38). DC. *Klintekroen* (M), (03-42 11 91). 24 beds, all rooms with bath. (BE). DC.

Restaurant. *Den gyldene Hane* (I), Sjaellands Odde (03-42 63 86). On road to Ebeltoft ferry. Almost entirely fish dishes. Fresh food. Also hotel (18 beds) (BE). DC, MC, V.

RINGSTED. *Casino* (M), (03-61 08 00). 20 beds. Try their "stage-coach luncheon." *Postgården* (I), (03-61 35 15). 24 beds. Old, but modernized. DC, MC, V.
Restaurants. *Apotekergården.* Exclusive, good food. AE, DC, MC, V. *Møllekroen.* Good food. DC, MC, V.

RØNNEDE. *Axelved* (I), (03-71 14 01). 18 beds. Motel near town. (BE).

ROSKILDE. *Motel B.P.* (M), (02-35 43 85). 58 beds in modern rooms, some (I). AE, DC, MC, V. *Prindsen* (M), (02-35 80 10). 70 beds. DC, MC, V. *Risø* (M), (02-35 68 00). 40 beds, all rooms with bath. AE, DC, MC, V.
Restaurant. *Prindsen* hotel (M), charming, shrimp a specialty. MC, V.

SLAGELSE. *Hotel E2* (M), (03-53 03 22). 98 beds, all rooms with bath. AE, DC, MC, V.
Restaurants. *Centrum; Helene,* DC, MC, V; *Postholderen,* for lunch.

SØLLERØD. Restaurant. *Søllerød Kro.* Old thatched inn with rustic furniture.

SORØ. *Postgaarden* (M), (03-63 22 22). 44 beds, 9 rooms with bath or shower. AE, DC, MC, V.

STEGE (Møn). *Hunosøgård* (I), (03-81 20 30). At Møns Klint (cliffs). 56 beds. Lounge with open fireplace; good cooking; free fishing. Open Apr.–Oct. *Stege Bugt* (I), (03-81 54 54). 51 beds. DC, MC, V.

TISVILDELEJE. *Helenkilde* (I), (02-30 70 01). Inexpensive summer pension with full board.

VORDINGBORG. *Gl. Masnedøgård Holiday Center* (M), (03-77 00 63). Open all year. *Kong Valdemar* (M), (03-77 00 95). 150 beds. Music, dance, garden. AE, MC, V.

Youth Hostels

There are youth hostels in the following towns and villages: Helsingør, Fakse, Frederiksvaerk, Korsør, Maribo, Naestved, Nakskov, Nykøbing Falster, Ringsted, Roskilde, Sakskøbing, Slagelse, Store Heddinge, Vordingbord.

Camping

Camping sites are to be found near all towns, and often on or near beaches. Tourist Information Offices will tell you where they are, or just follow international wigwam signs.

HOW TO GET AROUND. By bus and train. Buses and trains link Copenhagen with all important points in Zealand: to Helsingør in 50 min., Hillerød 40 min., Roskilde 20 min., and Køge 1 hour. Special sightseeing tickets for the DSB (Danish State Railways) comprise day return ticket from Copenhagen Central Station and admission charge. Included in this scheme are the Knuthenborg Safari Park on Lolland, Ålholm Slot og Automobil Museum on Lolland, the Louisiana museum of modern art in Humlebaek, Roskilde with Domkirke

ZEALAND AND ITS ISLANDS

and Vikingeskibshallen, Helsingør for a steam train ride, or there is a two-day round trip to Helsingør and Sweden (no admission charges included).

The *Copenhagen Card* can also offer an excellent deal as it gives unlimited travel on buses and trains in Copenhagen and North Zealand—west beyond Roskilde and south as far as Køge, plus admission to many sights. Valid for one, two or three days, at 60, 110 and 150 Dkr. respectively, it can be bought at rail stations, travel agents, tourist information offices and some hotels.

Travel by bus and train without the benefit of a tourist card of some kind can be expensive as there is no discount on round-trip tickets: they cost twice the one-way fare. Bus tickets are usually purchased on the bus, and train tickets at a rail station, or on the train if the station happens to be closed.

By car. For those who are driving, here is a suggested two-day itinerary for Zealand:

First day: Depart Copenhagen–Helsingør–Fredensborg–Hillerød–Frederiksvaerk–Hundested–Rørvig–Nykøbing Sjaelland–Fårevejle–Snertinge/Jyderup–Kalundborg/Ruds Vedby–Slagelse/Trelleborg–Skaelskør–Naestved. Distance, 272 km. (170 miles).

Second day: Naestved–Vordingborg–(Møn)–Praestø–Fakse Ladeplads–Vemmetofte–Rødvig–(Stevns Klint)–Store Heddinge–Køge–Roskilde–return Copenhagen. Distance, 195 km. (122 miles).

By bicycle. Cycling is popular in Denmark and many roads have cycle tracks. Motor traffic uses chiefly motorways, leaving older roads safer for cyclists. Local tourist information offices will either hire bikes out or refer you to a dealer who does. Cycles may also be hired from the following rail stations: Klampenborg, Helsingør, Hillerød, Lyngby, Nykøbing Falster, and the hire charge is 20 Dkr. per day, plus a 50 Dkr. deposit.

TOURS. Here we give details of three bus tours of Zealand which start from Copenhagen. The Tourist Information Office and some hotels will be able to supply you with further information. The "Vikingland Tour" takes you to Roskilde with its splendid cathedral, lunch at an inn (not included in fare), a 4,000-year-old passage grave, a typical Danish farm, and the Vikingeskibhallen at Roskilde to see the 1,000-year-old Viking ships. This tour takes six hours and is available Sun. and Wed., 15 May to 15 Sept. Off-season, but not in Dec. or Jan., it's on Fri.

The "Castle Tour of North Zealand—Hamlet Tour" takes you through the beautiful countryside north of Copenhagen to Kronborg Slot at Helsingør, i.e. Hamlet's castle at Elsinore. You will visit the royal residence of Fredensborg Slot as well as Frederiksborg Slot at Hillerød. This tour takes seven hours and is available Tues., Thurs., Sat. and Sun., May through Oct. Off-season, it's on Sat. and Sun. in Apr.; and Wed. and Sun., Nov. through Mar.

The "Afternoon Hamlet Tour" is a shorter version of the above. It takes five hours and is available daily, May through Sept.; and Tues., Wed., Thurs. and Fri. in Apr.

PLACES TO VISIT. Zealand offers not only a feast of ancient churches, splendid castles and stately homes set in lovely parks, but also some important museums—for technology, automobiles, archeology, and trading and maritime history. Remember that the Copenhagen Card may be used in North Zealand (see *How to Get Around*). Here we list places to visit described in the chapter on Zealand together with opening times and admission charges.

FREDENSBORG. Fredensborg Slot (Fredensborg Palace). Open July only, daily 1–5. Guided tours every 30 min. Park open all year.

FREDERIKSSUND. Selsø Herregårdsmuseum (Selsø Manor), Skibby. Bus 318 from Frederikssund. Open May through mid-June, Sat. 1–4, Sun. 11–4; mid-June to beg. Aug., daily 11–5; mid-Aug. to beg. Sept., Sat. and Sun. 1–4 Adm. 15 Dkr.

DENMARK

HELSINGØR. Danmarks Tekniske Museum (Danish Technical Museum). Nordre Strandvej section open all year, daily 10–5; Old Rømersvej section open all year, Mon. to Fri. 10–4, Sat. and Sun. 10–5. Adm. 12 Dkr. each section, 14 Dkr. both sections.

Karmeliterklosteret og Sct. Mariae Kirke (Carmelite Monastery and St. Mary's Church). Church open all year, 1–4. Guided monastery tours from 15 May to 15 Sept., daily at 11, 2 and 3. 2 P.M. tour is year-round. Adm. 15 Dkr.

Kronborg Slot (Kronborg Castle). Also **Handels- og Søfartsmuseet** (Danish Maritime Museum). Both open May through Sept., daily 10–5; Apr. and Oct., daily 11–4; Nov. through Mar., daily 11–3. Adm. 8 Dkr. each; 12 Dkr. both.

Marienlyst Slot (Marienlyst Castle). Open June through Aug., daily 12–5; May and Sept., Wed., Fri., Sat. and Sun. 1–3, gardens all day.

Skt. Olai Kirke (St. Olai's Church). Open Apr. through Sept., daily 10–5; Oct. through Mar., daily 10–3.

Øresundsakvariet (Øresund Aquarium). Open mid-May through Aug., daily 1–5; rest of year, Sat. and Sun. only, 1–5.

HILLERØD. AEbelholt Kloster (AEbelholt Monastery). Bus from Hillerød, 5½ km. (3½ miles). Open May through Aug., Tues. to Sun. 10–4; Sept., Tues. to Sun. 1–4; closed Mon.

Frederiksborg Slot (Frederiksborg Castle). Home of **Nationalhistorisk Museum** (National Historical Museum). Museum and chapel open Apr., daily 11–4; May through Sept., daily 10–5; Oct. daily 10–4; Nov. through March, daily 11–3. Adm. 15 Dkr.

Nordsjaellandsk Folkemuseum (North Zealand Folk Museum). Open June through Aug., Tues. to Sun. 2–5; closed Mon.

HUMLEBAEK. Louisiana. Modern Art Museum in park. Open all year, daily 10–5. Adm. 18 Dkr; times and charges for special exhibitions vary.

KALUNDBORG. Lerchenberg Slot (Lerchenberg Castle). At Asnaes. Open mid-June to mid-Aug., Mon. to Thurs. and Sat. 11–5, Sun. 10–6; closed Fri.

KØGE. Bregentved Slot (Bregentved Castle). Gardens open Wed., Sat., Sun. and public holidays 9–8.

Gisselfeld Slot (Gisselfeld Castle). Park open daily 10–4, 5 or 6.30, depending on season; weekends only in winter.

Gjorslev Slot (Gjorslev Castle). Free admission to park.

Vallø Slot (Vallø Castle). Park open daily.

MARIBO (Lolland). **Knuthenborg Manor and Safari Park.** At Bandholm. Open May through Sept., 9–6.

MØN. Liselund (Liselund Manor). Open May through Oct. Conducted tours Mon. to Sat. at 10.30, 11, 1.30 and 2; Sun. and public holidays also at 4 and 4.30. Park open all year.

NAESTVED. Gavnø Slot (Gavnø Castle). Open May through Sept., daily 10–4 or 10–5.

Holmegårds Glasvaerk (Holmegård Glassworks). Open Mon.-Fri. 9–1.30; summer season also Sat. and Sun 11–3.

Herlufsholm (Herlufsholm Manor). Chapel open May through Oct., daily 11–5; winter, daily 11–1.

NYSTED (Lolland). **Ålholm Slot og Automobil Museum** (Ålholm Castle and Automobile Museum). Museum open summer, daily 10–6; castle open summer, daily 11–6. Park open all year.

ZEALAND AND ITS ISLANDS

RINGSTED. Sankt Bendts Kirke (St. Benedict's Church). Open year round 10–12 and in summer also 1–5. Adm. free. Concerts held June through Aug., on Tues. afternoons and Wed. evenings.

ROSKILDE. Domkirke (Cathedral). Open Apr. through Sept., Mon. to Sat. 9–5.45; Oct. through Mar., Mon to Sat. 10–3.45, Sun. 12.30–3.45. Adm. (unless a service is in progress) 3 Dkr.

Ledreborg (Ledreborg Manor). Open June, daily 11–5; June and Aug., Sun. 11–5.

Lejre Forsøgscenter (Historical-archeological research center). At Lejre. Train or bus. Open May through Sept., daily 10–5. Adm. 26 Dkr.

Vikingeskibshallen (Viking Ship Museum). At Havnen. Open Apr. through Oct., daily 9–5; June through Aug., daily 9–6; Nov. through Mar., daily 10–4. Adm. 12 Dkr.

SORØ. Sorø Kirke (Sorø abbey church). Open May through Sept., Mon. to Sat. 10–5, Sun. 2–5.

THE CENTRAL ISLANDS

Funen, the Garden of Denmark

Funen (Fyn), like many a Dane, is rather rotund. Not only does it contain some of the country's richest agricultural land, but most of Denmark's fruit grows here as well.

Its capital is Odense, and, despite its inland location, is the nation's fourth largest port by virtue of a ship canal. Next in importance is beautifully situated Svendborg, a busy seaside town and jumping-off place to the smaller islands in the south. Southern Funen has more lovely old castles and manor houses to the square mile than perhaps anywhere else in Europe.

Exploring the Central Islands

Your first acquaintance with Funen might be Nyborg, the terminal for train ferries from Zealand. Newcastle, as its name is in translation, grew up around the castle, which was built in 1179 as a guard against Wendish pirates; its central position in the Danish kingdom led to its use as the meeting place of the Danehof, an early parliament. The first Danish constitution, the Great Charter, was granted here by Erik Glipping in 1282. Ten years later the town got a charter, too, and today it has about 18,000 inhabitants. Contrasting with the medieval castle, where plays are performed on the ramparts, are the most modern hotels on Funen.

THE CENTRAL ISLANDS

North of Nyborg is Kerteminde, but make a stopover at Ladby. Here, in an air-conditioned underground burial mound, are preserved the remains of the Ladbyskibet, a 1,100-year-old Viking ship, 22 meters (72 feet) long and 2.7 meters (nine feet) wide. In it was interred a Viking chief together with his arms, his most valuable treasures, four hunting dogs, and 11 horses. Kerteminde itself is Funen's most important fishing town, and a picturesque summer resort with old half-timbered buildings in Langegade. Nearby are Viby, an unspoiled hamlet, and Munkebo, which underwent a sudden expansion when the Lindø shipyard was started in the 1950s. Today, this small village 16 km. (10 miles) from Odense, has one of the greatest shipyards in the world.

The two largest towns on the island, Odense and Svendborg, are equally suited as a center for exploring the Danish "butter hole." Odense, a port since 987 although 22 km. (14 miles) from the sea, is the third largest Danish city and above all is known as the birthplace of Hans Christian Andersen, who spent the first 14 years of his life here. The Odense river, where his mother did her laundrywork, runs through Funen Village to the harbor at the narrow fjord leading to the sea.

Museums and Sights

Hans Andersen's probable birthplace is today a museum—H.C. Andersens Hus—containing his personal belongings, sketches, works and silhouettes, and letters from Dickens and Jenny Lind.

Hans Andersen's Barndomshjem, childhood home, has been described by the writer in *The Story of My Life*. From his second to his 14th year he lived with his parents, the cobbler and the washerwoman in the flat to the right.

Skt. Knuds Kirke (St. Canute's Cathedral) is Gothic, erected in the 13th century on the site of St. Alban's Church, where King Canute was killed and later canonized. Today he is enshrined here. Two royal tombs are those of King Hans and King Christian II, with their queens. See also Claus Berg's golden 16th-century altarpiece. The font dates from 1660.

Den fynske Landsby (Funen Village), two miles south, is an open-air museum of 22 Funen country buildings including a water mill and open-air theater with Andersen plays for the children in summer. Return to town along the river (boats, path).

Mønterstraede is a museum street where four houses dating from 1547 to 1646 show the town culture and life of those days. The Stiftsmuseet has a local prehistoric collection (especially Iron Age) and collection of Funen art, e.g. Jens Juel. The DSB Jernbanemuseum displays the State Railway collections: two royal wagons and a Newcastle steam engine from 1869.

Other places of interest are: Skt. Hans Kirke, dating partly from the 13th century; old houses in Overgade; the Zoo; Tivoli; town hall and the university (built 1966). There are also river cruises.

At Nørre Lyndelse, 13 km. (eight miles) south, is the native home of Carl Nielsen, the best-known Danish composer, who recalled his home in *My Childhood in Funen*.

Svendborg and the Southern Isles

To the south is Svendborg and the bordering island of Tåsinge, both beautifully situated on the sea. Svendborg, second largest Funen town, got its town charter in the 13th century. Today it is devoted to industry, commerce and navigation and is ideal for stopovers because of good beaches and "unexplored" surrounding isles. The islands of Tåsinge and Langeland are connected by bridges to Svendborg. The other islands are reached by ship only. Among them, visit AErø and if time allows, Hjortø.

While in Svendborg, visit the Skt. Nikolai Kirke, devoted to the sailors' patron, a Romanesque basilica prior to 1200. Restored 1892, it has frescos in the arches. Anne Hvide's Gård is the regional museum in the oldest preserved building, dating from 1560, with medieval material, ship models and local collections. The Zoologisk Museum has a complete collection of Danish mammals, birds and eggs.

Thurø is connected by a dam to Funen at the Christiansminde woods. Thurø is an orchard with 1,600 inhabitants and used to be the home of some Danish painters and poets who were inspired by its doll-like village and sailors.

Tåsinge, south of Svendborg, has 5,000 inhabitants. Here and in Svendborg was the setting of Elvira Madigan's romance, and the movie was made on location here. (The tombs are at Landet churchyard). Visit Bregninge Church which has magnificent views of the Funen archipelago from its tower, and the nearby skipper's home with ship models and mementos of Elvira Madigan. Troense is one of the best preserved Danish villages, with a row of half-timbered houses. The former school is a museum of shipping, which used to be the living of the islanders. Nearby Valdemarsslot dates from around 1640 and is now a naval museum with much sumptuous furnishing.

Langeland, largest in the archipelago, is connected by bridge and dam to Tåsinge. The main town is Rudkøbing, where H. C. Ørsted, the discoverer of electromagnetism, was born. Today it is dominated by merchants' estates. In Brogade and Østergade are many preserved old houses. South of the town are Ristinge and Bagenkop with good beaches, and ferry to Kiel in Germany. North of Rudkøbing are the 13th-century Tranekaer Slot and Egeløkke, a manor which was once the living of Bishop Grundtvig, founder of the Danish Folk High School movement in the 19th century. The northernmost village is Lohals (ferry to Korsør). As a whole Langeland is rich in relics of the past, and you can always find a beach.

AErø has two towns, Marstal and AErøskøbing. Had it not been because of its competitor, Marstal would have been famous. Today its museum houses a collection of model ships, and the church interior and small shipyards tell a story of bygone grandeur one or two centuries ago. The town has ferry connection with Rudkøbing. However, the smaller, AErøskøbing has the most to offer the tourist. Even the sparrows sleep in its 17th and 18th-century streets with 36 protected houses. As in Ebeltoft you will find an isolated community, today revived because of tourism. However, you can still see its post office dating from 1749, its wooden pumps and cook house, although the latter serves today's requirements better as a public toilet! Also see the

Dukkehuset (Dolls' House) and the unique collection of bottle ships (750 models), plus Gunnar Hammerichs Hus with its old furniture. The attractive church dates from 1756 and has an interesting pulpit with carvings of dubious ladies with fig leaves. The town is still lit by gaslight at night.

When leaving, you can take ferries to Mommark (Als), Fåborg or Svendborg (Funen) or Rudkøbing.

Southern Funen

Along the lanes around Svendborg you find numerous picturesque spots, but one you must visit is Egeskov. The castle here is the best-preserved island castle in Europe. Its name comes from the oak forest which was felled around 1524 to form 30 years later the piles on which was built an impregnable Renaissance castle. It is still impregnable to tourists, but its five gardens and the museum of vintage cars and aircraft can be visited. You are now about halfway between Nyborg and Fåborg, both of which should be seen. On the road to Nyborg is Holckenhavn Manor dating from 1580, where Cortifz Ulfeldt, the most notorious traitor in Danish history, lived with his wife Leonora Christiana, daughter of King Christian IV.

On the road from Egeskov to Fåborg is Brahetrolleborg, a Cistercian abbey dating from 1172. After the Reformation it was crown property, but became a baronial seat in 1668. It was here that Johan Ludvig Reventlow let the peasants burn a wooden horse symbolizing his release of them.

Other interesting châteaux are the somber, moated Broholm; the lovely Renaissance-style Rygård; Hesselagergård, built in 1538 with walls more than six feet thick and encircled by a moat; Glorup, a manor house from 1580, rebuilt in Baroque style in the 18th century; Lykkesholm, Hellerup, Ravnholt, and Ørbaeklunde.

Fåborg was a privileged town in the 13th century but damaged by a fire in 1728, which, however, spared many old houses that can still be seen in Vestergade and Holkegade. Moreover, one of five medieval gates survives, and so does the belfry, all that remains of the Skt. Nikolai Kirke, to which it once belonged. The museum contains the best collection of Funen painters, a private donation, also works by Kai Nielsen, the sculptor who did the controversial Ymerbrønden ("Ymer Well") in the market square. Just east of town is the 600-year-old Kaleko Møllegård, a water mill, now a museum. There are ferry crossings to either Avernakø, which has 120 inhabitants (especially recommended at Shrovetide and Whitsuntide), or to Lyø (200 inhabitants). This will show you idyllic landscapes and Lyø Village. There is another ferry to Gelting near Flensburg, and the main road leads west to the Bøjden ferry for Fynshav, on Als. On the way one passes the round church at Horne, the only one of its kind in Funen. With walls two meters (seven feet) thick it served both as church and fortress, but today only the core of the building remains. North of Fåborg is a former manor house, now the Hotel Stensgård. Between Fåborg and Assens to the northwest lie the Svanninge Bakker, hills known jokingly as the Funen Alps.

The western coast of Funen offers less of interest than the rest of the island. Assens has a church of minor note and a 17th-century house which was the home of Peter Willemoes. At the age of 18, this Danish hero commanded a battery during the bombardment of Copenhagen with such distinction that Lord Nelson complimented him personally. Middelfart claims to have the only suspension bridge in Denmark, built in 1970, and is worth a stop if only for its Folk Museum, housed in Henning Friisers Hus at Brogade 6. Just outside town is Galsklint, a memorial park in honor of British pilots shot down during World War II.

PRACTICAL INFORMATION FOR THE CENTRAL ISLANDS

TOURIST INFORMATION. The main towns of Funen and the other central islands have tourist information (Dantourist) offices: **AErøskøbing**, Torvet (09-52 13 00). **Fåborg**, Havnegade 2 (09-61 07 07). **Kerteminde**, Strandgade 5A (09-32 11 21). **Middelfart**, Havnegade 10 (09-41 17 88). **Nyborg**, Torvet 9 (09-31 02 80). **Odense**, Rådhuset (Town Hall) (09-12 75 20). **Svendborg**, Møllergade 20 (09-21 09 80).

TELEPHONE CODES. We have given the Central Island telephone code for all the towns and villages in the hotel and restaurant lists that follow. This code need only be used when calling from outside the Central Islands.

HOTELS AND RESTAURANTS. Odense makes an excellent base for exploring Funen and the other islands. In general, hotels maintain the same rates throughout the year, although some may offer reductions during the off-season (Oct. through Apr.) and it is always as well to inquire. By joint arrangement you can stay in one Funen inn and take half-pension in another of about 20 choices (min. two days, 230 Dkr.). You can also buy an "inn check" for 160 Dkr. covering one night's stay and breakfast. The meal coupons are also on sale separately from *Dantourist* in Svendborg.

AERØSKØBING (AErø). *AErø* (I), (09-52 10 03). 66 beds, some rooms with bath; also six 2-4-bed apartments. The best. Half-timbered house, good country-style food, sauna. *Motel Damgården* (I), Borgnaes (09-52 16 56). Former farm. *Phønix* (I), (09-52 12 20).

ASSENS. *Ebberup Kro* (I), (09-74 11 11). 22 beds. Four miles east; country-style inn; fishing possibilities. DC, MC, V. *Lillebaelt* (I), (09-71 10 28). Some rooms with bath. *Marcussens* (I), (09-71 10 89). Some rooms with bath. DC, MC, V. *Phønix* (I), (09-71 10 18). No private facilities.

FÅBORG. *Falsled Kro* (E), (09-68 11 11). 11 rooms. Near Stensgård, charming country inn, with French food and wines; superb, expensive food; also English pub. (BE). DC, MC, V. *Fåborg Fjord* (M), (09-61 10 10). 90 beds. Recent. AE, DC, MC, V. *Klinten* (M), (09-61 38 00). 120 apartments with 6 beds, bath and kitchen. Sauna, pools, weekly rentals. (BE). MC, V. *Steensgård* (M), (09-61 94 90). Former manor house. MC, V.

THE CENTRAL ISLANDS

KERTEMINDE. *Tornøes* (I), (09-32 16 05). 25 beds. Garden; venison in season. DC.
Restaurant. *Munkebo Kro* (M), (09-97 40 30). By main highway. Famous for fried eel. Also has 6 rooms, all with bath. DC, MC, V.

MARSTAL (AErø). *AErø* (I), (09-53 19 00). 68 beds, 25 rooms with bath or shower. Renovated. There are also 5 cottages. AE, DC, MC, V.

MIDDELFART. *Byggecentrums Kursuscenter* (M), (09-41 14 41). Close to Hindsgavl Manor with lovely park. MC, V. *Grimmerhus* (I), Kongebrovej 42 (09-41 03 99). 20 beds, no private bath or comfort. Beautifully situated; closed around Christmas. (BE).

NYBORG. *Hesselet* (E), (09-31 30 29). 92 beds, all rooms with bath. On beach, close to 18-hole golf course. Sauna and pool. (BE). AE, DC, MC, V. *Nyborg Strand* (M), (09-31 31 31). 400 beds, some rooms with bath. On beach, close to 18-hole golf course. Offers keep-fit holidays. AE, DC, MC, V. *Øksendrup Kro & Motel* (M), a few miles south. 30 beds (BE).
Restaurant. *Danehofkroen* serves good value tourist menu.

ODENSE. *Frederik VI* (E), (09-94 13 13). 92 beds, some (M) rooms. Suburban, with garden. *Grand* (E), (09-11 71 71). 235 beds, 113 rooms with bath. Ask for new rooms. One of Denmark's best, and with fine cuisine, bar. AE, DC, MC, V. *Hotel H.C. Andersen* (E), (09-14 78 00). In new concert house. 296 beds, all rooms with bath. DC, MC, V. *Windsor* (E), (09-12 06 52). 109 beds. Restored, with modern rooms. AE, DC, MC, V. *Brasilia/Blommenslyst Kro* (M), (09-96 70 12). 100 beds, all rooms with bath. Motel in park 8 km. (five miles) west. *Munkeris* (M), (09-15 90 41). 91 beds, all rooms with shower. Recent motel. DC. *Odense* (M), (09-11 42 13). 82 beds in attractive rooms with shower. Motel in converted farmhouse, garden in former fruit orchard, delightful. AE, DC, MC, V. *Mørkenborg Kro* (I) (09-83 10 51). 30 beds. On beautiful site 11 miles northwest. Has antiques and children's playground. DC.
Restaurants. *Skoven* (E), in Hunderup Forest, excellent. AE, MC, V. *Under Lindetraet* (E), vis-à-vis Andersen's house. Excellent. MC, V. *Franck-A* (M). Moderately-priced meals served in differently-styled interiors. MC, V. *Den gamle Kro* (M). Lovely timbered inn with charming atmosphere and long list of specialties. AE, MC, V. *Den grimme AElling* (M), steak house. MC, V. *Sortebro Kro* (I), in Funen Village, for simple fare. MC, V.

RUDKØBING (Langeland). *Skandinavien* (I), (09-51 14 95). 15 beds, all rooms with shower. T.V. room. (BE). DC.
Restaurant. *Spodsbjerg Kro og Badehotel* (I), (09-50 10 64). Also 35 beds.

SVENDBORG. *Svendborg* (M), (09-21 17 00). 100 beds, all rooms with bath. Music and dance. AE, DC, MC, V. *AErø* (I), (09-21 07 60). 18 beds, no private bath. Older. Restaurant with aeronautical, marine and sailors' rooms. DC, MC, V. *3 Roser* (I), (09-21 64 26). 256 beds, all rooms with bath. Also weekly 4-5 bed apartments with kitchen. Modern motel. Free golf and pool. (BE). AE, DC, MC, V. *Stella Maris* (I), (09-21 38 91). 28 beds, 13 rooms with bath. Mission hotel. Garden. (BE).
Restaurants. *Røde Mølle*, Hvidkilde. In former water mill; venison a specialty. *Svendborg*, hotel restaurant with dancing.

TRANEKAER (Langeland). *Tranekjaer Gjaestgivergård* (I), (09-59 12 04). 32 beds. Terrace. Restaurant with raftered ceiling and open hearths; venison a specialty in season.

TROENSE (Tåsinge). *Troense* (M), (09-22 54 12). 64 beds in new rooms overlooking the Sound. Free golf course nearby. DC, MC, V.

DENMARK

Youth Hostels

There are youth hostels in the following towns and villages: Årup, Assens, Fåborg, Kerteminde (new), Marstal (AErø), Odense, Ringe, Rudkøbing (Langeland), Svendborg.

Camping

Camping sites are dotted along the coast around Funen and its islands, and are also to be found in beautiful locations inland. Tourist Information Offices will tell you where they are, or just follow the international wigwam signs.

HOW TO GET AROUND. Funen is linked to Jutland by the Little Belt Bridges (at Middelfart) and ferries (Fynshav–Bøjden); to Zealand by ferry (Nyborg–Korsør and Halsskov–Knudshoved); to the island of Langeland via the Tåsinge brige; and to AEro by ferry. Its main town of Odense may be reached from Copenhagen in three hours by "L" train, or more quickly by air.

By bus and train. All important towns on the island of Funen are served by local trains and buses. Trains serve the Nyborg–Odense–Middelfart route and the Odense–Svendborg route. All other local transport is by bus, as it is on the small islands. Go to the "rutebilstation" (coach station) in towns that are big enough to have one; otherwise consult timetables displayed at bus stops.

Bus tickets are usually purchased on the bus, and train tickets at a rail station, or on the train if the station happens to be closed. There is no discount on return tickets: they cost twice the one-way fare. One-day tourist tickets are available in Odense.

By car. Apart from the east–west motorway across Funen, this is very charming motoring country, with winding but wide roads. A detailed regional map is essential if you plan to explore the smaller byways. To avoid delay book ahead for the car on the ferry between Funen and Zealand. *Dantourist* in Svendborg offers several package tours including Funen in the itinerary: for example, a seven-day "Castle Tour" at 2,450 Dkr. per person including overnight stay and half board at hotels with private bath.

By bicycle. With short distances everywhere, the central islands are made for cycling. Local tourist offices will be pleased to suggest itineraries through the most characteristic scenery. Cycles are for hire in AErøskøbing, Assens, Fåborg, Kerteminde, Marstal (AErø), Middelfart, Nyborg, Odense, Ringe, and Svendborg.

TOURS. Tours for motorists are mentioned above. Those without their own transport may like to know about two opportunities to visit Odense, the main town, from Copenhagen. Firstly, the "Hans Christian Andersen Tour" takes you by coach from Copenhagen to Odense to see Andersen's birthplace and museum. The tour last 11 hours, and runs every Sun., 15 May to 15 Sept. Further details from tourist information office and some hotels in Copenhagen.

Secondly, Odense, with Andersen's house and two other museums, is included in the DSB (Danish State Railways) special sightseeing ticket scheme. This ticket includes day return by train from Copenhagen Central Station and admission charges.

PLACES TO VISIT. FÅBORG. Brahetrolleborg Slot (Brahetrolleborg Castle). Park open daily, 9–5.

Egeskov Slot (Egeskov Castle). N.E. of Fåborg. Vintage car and aircraft museum open Easter to Oct., 10–5; June to Aug., 9–6. Park open all year.

THE CENTRAL ISLANDS

NYBORG. Glorup (Glorup Manor). Park open Thurs., Sat. and Sun., 9–6.
Holckenhavn (Holckenhavn Manor). Park open daily 9–4. Chapel open by appointment.
Nyborg Slot (Nyborg Castle). Open June through Aug., daily 10–5; Mar. through May and Sept. through Nov., Tues. to Sun. 10–3, closed Mon.

ODENSE. H.C. Andersens Barndomshjem (childhood home), Munkemøllestraede 3. Usually open June through Aug., daily 10–5.
H.C. Andersens Hus (Hans Andersen Museum), Hans Jensensstraede 39–43. Generally open June through Aug., daily 9–7. Best check.
DSB Jernbanemuseum (Danish Railways Museum), Dannebrogsgade. Open May through Sept., daily 10–4; Oct. through Apr., Sun. only, 10–3.
Den fynske Landsby (Funen Village). Open Apr. through Oct., daily 9 to dusk; Nov. through Mar., Sun. and public holidays only.
Møntergården, Monterstraede. Open all year, daily 10–4.
Skt. Knuds Kirke (St. Canute's Cathedral). Open May through Aug., Mon. to Sat. 10–5, Sun. 11.30–12.30; Sept. through Apr., Mon. to Sat. 10–4.

SVENDBORG. Anne Hvide's Gård (regional museum), Fruestraede 3. Open May through Oct., daily 10–4; winter, daily 1–4.
Skt. Nikolae Kirke (St. Nicholas's Church). Open daily except during services.
Zoologisk Museum (Zoological Museum), Dronningemaen 30. Open Apr. through Sept., daily 9–5; winter, daily 10–4.

JUTLAND

Birds, Beaches and Runic Stones

The peninsula of Jutland (Jylland) is the only part of Denmark that is attached to the continent of Europe. Its southern boundary is the frontier with Germany. A tenth of the peninsula consists of moors and sand dunes, the latter being almost entirely along the west coast. The other nine-tenths are devoted to agriculture and, to a much lesser extent, to forestry. Jutland's west, or North Sea, coast has but one deep-water port, Esbjerg, though fishing harbors have been developed in recent years at Hirtshals and Hvide Sande. Apart from Esbjerg, the main fishing ports are still Skagen and Frederikshavn in the extreme northeast of Jutland. The geography of the eastern side is quite unlike that of the western. Along the shore facing Funen are deep, well-wooded fjords running miles inland.

Exploring Jutland

The region of Jutland bordering Germany is one that has been fought over a number of times. When bricks replaced mud and wood as Denmark's chief building material one of the first uses made of them by the Danes was the construction of the Dannevirke wall across the neck of Jutland to keep the Germans out. Today the people try to invite them into Denmark instead, tempting them with nature, open beaches and signboards with German texts. However, the population is mixed,

JUTLAND

and the provinces of Schleswig (Slesvig in Danish) and Holstein (Holsten) caused many feuds and wars between Denmark and Germany. A plebiscite in 1920 established the present boundary, and today the inhabitants on either side of the border cooperate or compete in such plans as an extra North Sea dike or in making Danish cultural arrangements south of the border. But still some administrative features indicate that this southernmost area has a history of its own.

Traveling north along the east coast, you first meet the island of Als, with Sønderborg, separated by the Sound. On the way you pass Gråsten Slot, rebuilt after a fire in 1757 and since then much restored. Today it serves as summer residence for the Queen's Mother, Queen Ingrid. Just before Als is Dybbøl Mølle, perhaps the most revered spot in Denmark and today a national symbol that has been re-erected three times. It is the focal point in a memorial park to the wars in 1848 and 1864. Sønderborg Slot is still intact in spite of the wars; parts of it date back to the 12th century, and it is now a museum. If time allows, the rest of Als is also worth a visit. It bears the mark of the Danfoss factories and of "riding at the ring" festivities in Sønderborg (four days, starting the second Saturday in July).

Back on the mainland again, the road is set for Åbenrå, an ancient town that has suffered from fire and bombardment through the ages. Take a walk through Slotsgade and Vaegterpladsen towards the 15th-century Brundlund Slot, a private residence not open to the public, but there is a good view of it from the road. North of Åbenrå you meet Knivsbjerg, the tallest South Jutland hill, which served as a German rallying point and was blown up by the Danes during the German occupation. Haderslev is dominated by the Domkirke (cathedral, dating back to about 1265 and later rebuilt). Christiansfeld was founded on 1 April 1773, by Moravian Brethren, who found here a refuge; their observances were similar to those of the Danish church, but with music and handicrafts playing a leading part. The settlement is still special and was awarded a European medal in 1975 for its intact atmosphere. Also visit their church and churchyard, the Gudsageren (Field of God), with female burials to the right, male burials to the left.

Our next stop is the medium-sized modern town of Kolding, dominated by the Koldinghus ruin, once a 13th-century royal residence surrounded by a moat. The castle and its chapel were burnt down by Spanish troops in 1808. From 1892 onwards the rooms have gradually been restored and house a historical museum in the castle tower. Kolding's other main attraction is Den Geografiske Have (Geographical Garden) where you can see about 2,000 different species of plants from all over the world arranged according to their habitat.

Fredericia is an important railroad junction, trains from Funen and all parts of Jutland meeting here. Before that, it was an important, though not pleasant fortress, the inhabitants being either soldiers or religious fugitives who were granted religious liberty. The ramparts are well preserved and the central part of town has straight, crossing streets, giving unobstructed fields of fire. Take a walk on the ramparts, which are five km. (three miles) long. On 6 July 1849 they withstood the assault of the Slesvig army, and on 5 July every year there is a flower pilgrimage to the soldiers' graves, followed the next day by a trooping parade and procession in the uniforms of 1849.

But don't forget the western coast of this region. From Kolding the road will take you back to the frontier district and the old community of Tønder (founded 1243). This town is known for its exquisite lace. There is a modern art museum (Sønderjyllands Kunstmuseum), but the collections of the old museum, Tønder Museum—lace, Dutch tiles, furniture, silver and faience—might well interest you more. There are many attractive houses and doorways, especially in Østergade, Vestergade and Uldgade. Kristkirken (Christchurch) is richly decorated. Though built in 1591 much of the contents are from an earlier church —a black marble font dates from 1350, the pews and the pulpit from about 1586. Also notice the handcarved epitaphs dating from 1586 to 1695, and the lectern of 1623 with 18 handcarved biblical scenes. The marshes nearby are unique in Denmark in that dikes protect this region against the periodic floods which formerly caused tremendous damage; even so, the town had to be evacuated as recently as 1976 because of the threat of flooding. Now Danish and German authorities have agreed to build an extra dike. Many couples from abroad know Tønder as a continental Las Vegas or Gretna Green because liberal Danish laws have allowed them to marry here.

Five km. (three miles) to the west nestles the lovely, thatch-roofed village of Møgeltønder. Its cobbled main street, bordered by old lime trees and 17th-century Frisian houses, is considered the most beautiful village street in Northern Europe. Here, in a 17-acre park, is the 18th-century Baroque Schackenborg manor house. The ownership will pass over to Prince Joakim, younger son of Queen Margrethe, when he comes of age. The 12th-century village church, part of the estate, has 16th-century frescos, a Gothic altar-piece sculpted by Flemish artists, an arch dating back to 1240, and an outstanding 13th-century wooden Madonna and Child. The Baroque organ (1679) is the oldest church organ still in use in Denmark.

Not far away is the remarkable village of Rudbøl. The Danish-German frontier runs right through its center, though the dividing line is no more substantial than a few metal discs set among the Dutch bricks with which the street is paved. Rudbøl's inn has achieved a certain amount of fame. The building stands in Denmark, but the front entrance is in Germany.

Trip to the Past

The town of Ribe has changed little since the Middle Ages, and its narrow winding streets, its venerable houses and the cathedral have made it a fascinating attraction for visitors from abroad and Danes alike. The 800-year-old Ribe Domkirke is one of Scandinavia's finest churches, built of Danish brick and stones brought from the Rhineland. The main tower of the cathedral was raised some seven centuries ago by citizens who were as concerned with the defense of their city as with the salvation of their souls. Don't miss the "Cat Head Door" on the south side. According to legend this was provided for the exclusive use of the devil.

The market place features the old inn known as Weis' Stue. In the parlor are panels with biblical pictures and a 400-year-old clock. A carved cupboard is dated 1500, and a candelabrum 1599. Hospitality is the rule of the house.

Many half-timbered houses can be seen in Sønderportsgade, Puggårdsgade and Sortebrødregade, many of them dating from the 16th century. Ribe's smallest building huddles at Klostergade 72. Other points of interest are the Sct. Catharinae Kirke and Kloster (Church of St. Catharine and the Black Friars Abbey), both dating from the mid-13th century. The abbey is the best-preserved and most beautiful monastery in Denmark, except for the one at Helsingør. On Slotsbanken you can view all that remains of the huge 12th-century stronghold of Riberhus. Skibbroen is the oldest Danish port. On the quay stands the Floodwave Column, whose marks show the water levels of previous floods—the top level mark is the 1634 flood, which also hit the cathedral. Only the weak dikes prevented two new floods in 1976, when the entire coastal region down to Germany was threatened by a sea a mere 12 yards below the dike top.

In days past, every town was free to set its own legislation, and the legend goes that a mother watching her son being hanged in another Jutland town cried out: "Oh, my boy, thank heaven you were not tried at Ribe." However, female criminals were treated with more consideration in Ribe. The town's legal code declared that a thief of the weaker sex should not be hanged—she was to "be buried alive, because she is a woman."

In 1973 traces of the original Ribe were found north of the river, and these excavations have brought to light coins dating from *c.* 700, proving that the town is the oldest in Denmark.

Esbjerg and the Western Islands

In Esbjerg we have a town that, for a change, is not old. It is, in fact, one of Denmark's youngest and is often the first impression of Denmark for Britons arriving by ship. A hundred years ago only 20 people lived here, now there are over 79,000. Apart from being Denmark's main gateway for imports and exports and an important fishing port, it is West Jutland's cultural and school center with folk high school, conservatory and museum. Being the only deep-water port on the west coast of Jutland, the town is also the home of several hundred fishing cutters, and you might visit the yards where they are built. Also interesting is the trip to the fish auction halls, but be sure to get there early if you are to see anything.

Fanø is the northernmost of the three Danish tidal area islands, reached by a 20-minute ferry crossing from Esbjerg. The islanders were known as sea-faring people, and a shipbuilding industry arose about 1760. The first half of the 19th century was a successful time, and the fleet was the second largest, after Copenhagen. The islands still have lots of reminders from this time, goods brought home from Holland and other countries. But since 1850 bathing guests have been the main source of income, Fanø offers some 16 km. (10 miles) of sandy beach. The island has but two main roads, one crosswise and one lengthwise between Nordby (north) and Sønderho (south). Though the minor of those two Sønderho (350 inhabitants) has most to offer in remaining skippers' houses dating from about 1800; 47 of them are protected. The national costume is unchanged and still in use, at least on Sønderhoday (late July).

South of Fanø is the islet of Mandø. To reach it you have to go by the postal van which will carry you along the road at low tide. 125 people live here, they have their own church dating from 1727 and an inn (apply ahead if you want a room). Bird lovers would find this islet a paradise.

Rømø is the largest and southernmost of the islands, access is over a causeway 13 km. (eight miles) long, and the only main road is supplemented at low tide by the five km. (three miles) broad beach which is also used by automobiles. 800 people live here. A few of the farmhouses of the whaling captains from the old sea-faring times remain and one (dated 1744) at Toftum is a museum, the Nationalmuseets Kommandørgård. Nearby is Denmark's smallest school (1784). Rømø church, Sct. Clement Kirke, was a seamen's church. It has wrought-iron hat pegs above each pew and whaling captains are buried in the churchyard beneath interesting gravestones.

Holiday Haunts on the Jutland Coast

Northwest of Esbjerg stretches the promontory known as Blåvandshuk. From here it is possible to drive for miles through wonderful scenery behind the sea and dunes. After Graerup Strand you motor along some 24 km. (15 miles) of sand before reaching Henne Strand. Continuing in your vehicle with the sea on one side and the lagoon on the other, you reach the old fishing village of Hvide Sande, strategically placed between Ringkøbing Fjord and the North Sea, with a canal and locks. At the northern end of the lagoon you arrive at the North Sea resort of Søndervig.

Skipping about 80 km. (50 miles) of dunes and beach, we stop at Bovbjerg, just beyond Lemvig on the western end of the Limfjord. Here, cliffs 42 meters (140 feet) high tower above the ocean. Until breakwaters were built here in 1909 the sea had cut its way nearly 200 meters (700 feet) in less than a century.

If your time is limited and you are not yet tired of sea and sand, you may continue further up north to Thyborøn on the western mouth of the Limfjord and continue on its northern side. However, another longer route inland will offer you more variation and other landscapes and scenery.

From Bovbjerg we continue to the small towns of Lemvig and Struer. Lemvig is terraced in the hilly landscape, and you arrive and depart along hairpin bends. Dominating Struer are the factories of Bang & Olufsen, known the world over for their radio and television products. After Struer and Vinderup is Sahl Kirke with a magnificent golden altarpiece from about 1200. The gold is, in fact, copper. Not far away is the open air museum at Hjerl Hede, where you'll find several village houses from various regions, one of them dating back to about 1530. At Hjerl Hede is a reconstructed Iron Age house which is occupied in summer. Also visit the magnificent surrounding area around the Flyndersø lake.

Now it is time to go north along the east side of the Limfjord to visit Spøttrup which will give you an impression of a medieval manor, erected about 1500 and now owned by the state and made a museum. Notice the thick walls and the knights' hall and watchmen's gallery.

The adjoining gardens have been reconstructed according to old descriptions of medieval spices and medicinal herbs.

In 1978 a high-level bridge across the Sallingsund gave easier access to the island of Mors in the Limfjord. The bridge runs between the Pain and the Torment (on Mors side), two place-names reminiscent of earlier problems coming to and from the island. The main town is Nykøbing, but the best sights are to be found among the natural sights of Legind Bjerge near the bridge, at Feggeklit, and finally at Hanklit.

We leave Mors across the Vildsund bridge, and via Thisted, where a well-known Danish poet, J. P. Jacobsen, was born. Heading northwest we reach again the North Sea coast at Klitmøller, where the country with its woods and lakes is particularly beautiful. Today it is a favorite summer resort. Off Bulbjerg coast, Denmark lost a major tourist attraction in 1978, when sea undermined the 46-meter (154-foot) high Skarreklit rock. All that now remains is a fast-eroding stump, and only local postcards tell how it once looked. You may make a detour to Frøstrup, where you can find the northernmost European storks in a private garden. Other birds can be studied inland near Bygholm.

Presently we approach a second beach at Blokhus, another popular West Jutland seaside resort, and further up north the somewhat larger Løkken, Lønstrup and Hirtshals (ferries to Norway). North of Tannisby is Råbjerg Mile, a "drifting" dune, now some four km. (2½ miles) inland which, during the past 400–500 years was moved 9 meters (30 feet) east by the west wind every year. This once fruitful area was the setting of some outdoor scenes in Peter Brook's film of *King Lear* and is today a natural dune desert reached on foot only from Kandestederne.

We have now covered so much of Western Jutland that little remains but the very tip of the peninsula where the waters of the North Sea collide with those of the Kattegat at the spit of Skaw. Just south of this point you find Skagen and Old Skagen (Gl. Skagen), popular both among artists and tourists. Many artists and writers have been inspired by the picturesque quality of Skagen and by its wonderful air and light. The local museum has an outstanding collection of paintings of the period 1830–1930 by artists connected with the locality. One of the sights of Skagen is a church tower buried by sand.

Going back south along the east coast we reach Frederikshavn with daily connections to Sweden and Norway. The fishing harbor is one of Denmark's largest. The entire area is popular with holiday-making Danes and is plentifully supplied with summer chalets (some of them for rent) and campsites.

A ferry from Frederikshavn forms the connection to the isle of Laesø, an untouched and unspoiled landscape with rich fauna and 2,600 inhabitants. Byrum's 500 inhabitants live in the biggest town in the middle of the island. If you don't bring your car to Laesø and its beaches, there are bus tours to the various views and the farmhouses with seaweed roofs. On your way you may pass an islander in her national costume richly decorated with forged silver, perhaps the most beautiful in Denmark.

Aalborg

When you reach Aalborg, you have crossed the Limfjord and leave the northern part of Jutland known as Vendsyssel. Aalborg is known for the schnapps produced here, and also the tasty Limfjord oysters which are dredged in the neighborhood. The town is the most important north Jutland town and, together with her twin town north of the fjord, the fourth largest in Denmark. You find charming combinations of new and old, and twisting lanes filled with medieval houses exist side by side with broad modern boulevards. Sights include the magnificent Jens Bangs Stenhus (Jens Bang's stone house), which has a charming wine cellar and restaurant; a 16th-century cathedral, the Budolfi Kirke, dedicated to the English St. Botolph; the early 16th-century Aalborghus and the early 15th-century Helligåndsklosteret (Monastery of the Holy Ghost). Aalborghallen, a colossal modern hall in the middle of town, is a magnificent center for concerts and exhibitions. In 1972 the Nordjyllands Kunstmuseum by the Finnish architect Alvar Aalto with its open-air theater became the home of Danish paintings and sculptures since 1800 and of modern foreign art. East of Aalborg is Denmark's latest university campus, and north of Aalborg and Nørresundby you will find Lindholm Høje, a Viking burial place with 682 graves.

Among the excursions from Aalborg, the one to Himmerland is 160 km. (100 miles). It takes you past the late 16th-century Lindenborg Slot to Lille Vildmose, a 34-square-mile marsh where the rare black stork can still be found. After 43 km. (27 miles) Hadsund is reached and Mariager Fjord crossed. Following the southern bank inland you arrive in rosefilled Mariager, Denmark's smallest market town, and Hobro at the head of the fjord. Near Hobro is Fyrkat, another 1,000-year-old Viking settlement resembling the one at Trelleborg. Today the settlement is reconstructed. North of Hobro, pay a visit to the delightful, hilly Rold Skov (forest) and the Rebild Bakker (Hills) in its northern part.

Every 4th of July thousands of Danes and Danish-Americans gather here to celebrate America's Independence Day. "Old Glory" and "Dannebrog" wave stoutly in the breeze, flanked by the flags of all the 50 states, and important Americans and Danes are invited to take part in speechmaking and other festivities. Since their purchase by Danish-Americans in 1911, these heather-clad hills have been a national park. In it stands the Lincoln Memorial Cabin built of logs from the original 13 states. Also in the neighbourhood are the Tingbaek Kalkminer (limestone workings), with the original models of monuments by two well-known Danish sculptors.

1,400-year-old Viborg

Southeast of Hobro is Viborg, an important medieval town. In 1727 this town claimed to be 1,600 years old, tracing its history back to the crowning of Dan, the first king of Denmark. The road to Viborg leads you past the rambling 16th-century manor house of Tjele, known as the setting of many Danish literary works. It was probably more correct, however, when, in 1950, Viborg celebrated 1,400 years of existence as an assize town, 1,000 years as a trading center, 900 years as a bishopric, 800 as a market and 700 years of civic government. As if this were not enough, legends insist that Canute set out from Viborg to conquer England. On sale locally are reproductions, made as cuff links, of a silver coin minted on Canute's orders and inscribed, *Knud, Englands Konge:* Canute, King of England.

Dominating Viborg is its Domkirke, at one time the largest granite church in the world. Of the original edifice, built in 1130, only the crypt remains. The cathedral was restored and reopened in 1876 after it had been damaged by fire several times. Its wall-paintings, executed between 1901 and 1913, were the work of a team of artists inspired and supervised by Joakim Skovgaard. Another church worth visiting is Søndre Sogns Kirke, an old monastery with a golden altarpiece (1520) and more than 200 paintings dating from the early 18th century.

About eight km. (five miles) south of Viborg you will find some of the loveliest scenery in Denmark. Hald Sø (Hald Lake) and the rustic heatherclad Dollerup Bakker (Dollerup Hills) together form a district where it is possible to walk for hours on end and still discover new delights. This region is also known as the "fisherman's paradise."

From Viborg Highway 16 continues to Randers. However, you are recommended to use the longer tour via Rødkaersbro and Bjerringbro which will offer you a beautiful ride along the Gudenå, Denmark's longest river.

Randers and Djursland

Randers occupies a niche in Danish history because it was here in 1340 that Niels Ebbesen killed the German oppressor, Count Gert the Bald, commander of a German army which had occupied almost all of Jutland. Ebbesen's statue stands in front of the Rådhus (Town Hall). The 15th-century Skt. Mortens Kirke has been extensively restored. The carved wooden pulpit and screen, the exquisite organ, and the saintly figures have all been re-gilded. One of the most interesting buildings in the narrow streets is the Helligåndshuset (House of the Holy Ghost) on Erik Menveds Plads. In the Middle Ages friars from the nearby monastery nursed the sick here. Today it is occupied by the Tourist Association, and on its roof you may notice a cluster of storks' nests. It is considered only a matter of time before the last stork disappears from Denmark forever. Today they are to be found in only a few places in Jutland.

East of Randers lied Djursland, a holiday area which draws people from all over Denmark. Here there are several fine old manor houses, churches, ancient burial places and ruins. Rosenholm Slot, the property of the Rosenkrantz family since its erection in 1560, is an imposing Danish Renaissance structure. Nearer Randers, Gammel Estrup, a grand 17th-century manor house, is now a museum full of rich period furnishings including an alchemist's cellar; and an agricultural museum. About 14 km. (eight miles) southeast of Randers off Highway 10 is the fine Baroque manor of Clausholm, set in a beautiful park with terraces and small cascades. From here, Anna Sophie Reventlow, daughter of the High Chancellor, was abducted by King Frederik IV, who married her morganatically and later made her Queen. To the east of the region is its main town, Grenå, ravaged several times in the 17th century by Swedish troops. Today Swedes still invade the town, but because of the ferry route to Varberg in Sweden. It is also possible to go by ferry to Hundested on Zealand, and there is a ferry to the isle of Anholt 44 km. (27 miles) out in the Kattegat.

A Hidden Gem

Anholt is 22 square kilometers (8½ square miles) of unspoiled nature of a very special kind. You will find here Denmark's only desert, natural beauties, 25 km. (16 miles) of beaches, and three km. (two miles) from the harbor the only town with 160 inhabitants. You can walk here happily for hours, enjoying both the idyllic Anholt Village, the desert consisting of open gravel plains filled with sand, and the viewpoint Sønderbjerg, at 47 meters (157 feet) the highest point on the island. The village has a memorial for Danes who fell against the English in the battle of 1811. To nature-lovers Anholt is a paradise with its many plants and birds. If you cross to the eastern point, Totten, you may be rewarded with the sight of seals.

It is possible to take your car to Anholt, but not necessary since you can drive only to the village. However, since ferry connections are bad, count on an overnight stay in the inn.

Mols and Ebeltoft

Below Djursland stretches the countryside of Mols. The drive to Fuglsø, Agri and Femmøller is magnificent, with rolling hills covered by heather and spruce, sandy roads winding past thatched cottages and peacefully grazing cattle, and dikes everywhere to keep the sea in place. The natives of this region have the reputation of being hillbillies, and an infinite number of stories are told of their simple ways and slow wit.

One place you must be sure to see is Ebeltoft, a miniature town which, like AErøskøbing, belongs to the past. Wandering up and down among the winding, cobbled streets lined with quaint old houses, you will imagine that you have walked out of the present into a fairytale. From Mols or Ebeltoft you are also able to see Århus, situated on a broad bay and surrounded by woods.

Århus, Old and New

Århus is Denmark's second largest town. Its history goes back more than 1,000 years, but it is also a modern city with a bustling seaport.

The copper roof and red brick walls of the 13th-century Århus Domkirke, Scandinavia's longest church, can be seen for many miles around. Inside is the largest, most highly carved and richly colored reredos in Denmark. The pulpit dates from 1588, and the early 18th-century organ is particularly fine. Just as remarkable is the Rådhuset (Town Hall), built between 1938 and 1942. A Danish showpiece, everything about it is impressive; its unusual architecture, its lavish use of glass, its mural-decorated lobby and its immense carpet depicting a stylized map of Århus. Most people either like it or detest it on sight. Behind the Town Hall, and designed not to conflict with it, is the new Musikhuset (Concert House) inaugurated in 1982.

JUTLAND

The best ties with the past are to be found in another church and the openair museum. The Vor Frue Kirke (Our Lady's Church) and Kloster (monastery) in Vestergade is the oldest building in the city. The friars' court and a number of Gothic arches can still be seen. In the chapter hall are medieval frescos. South of the town, at the Moesgård manor, is the Forhistorisk Museum Moesgård, which houses the 2,000-year-old Grauballe Man, discovered in a peat bog, plus rune stones and an ethnographic collection.

The openair museum called Den gamle By ("The Old Town") is a collection of town rather than country houses now brought together in the middle of Århus. Here there are 61 homes, each one furnished and equipped according to its period. With their streets and gardens, their shops and markets, the buildings provide an authentic picture of what life was like in the good old days. The houses are populated every year during the Festival Days in the beginning of September, and you are able to taste bread as it was baked in previous times.

The University, started in 1933 and not yet completed, has a spacious 37-acre campus. From the architectural point of view as well as the academic, it has already won an outstanding place for itself in Scandinavia. A corner of the campus grounds houses the new art museum with Danish art since 1770.

Situated on a central spot, Århus is an ideal base for exploring middle Jutland. Some places have already been described but another tour should be made to the Danish lake district.

The Lake District

Silkeborg is a modern town lying on the banks of the river Gudenå west of Århus. It is situated in the middle of some of the loveliest scenery in Denmark. The town has two museums. The Silkeborg Museum houses on its top floor the Tollund Man, dated at 2,200 years old. The new Silkeborg Kunstmuseum gives pride of place to the works of Asger Jorn, who was born here.

Surrounded by the river and lakes, it is quite natural to leave Silkeborg by water. The river winds through an area of hills covered with woods and heather. You can make the tour by rowboat, canoe, punt, or if you are less energetic by a paddle-steamer built in 1861. A *must* for anyone in this region is the ascent of Denmark's second highest hill, the 147-meter (483 foot) high Himmelbjerget (Sky Mountain). The tower on top, another 24 meters (80 feet), was inaugurated on Constitution Day, 1875, in commemoration of King Frederik VII.

Country roads run north and south of the lakes in the direction of Skanderborg. Off the southern banks near Rye are the few remaining stones of Øm. Founded in 1172 by the Cistercian Order, it was once one of the richest monasteries in that part of the world. After the Reformation Frederik II lived here for a while before having it demolished and the stones carried to Skanderborg to be used in the erection of a new castle. The museum there will show you the culture of that time and bones that had been treated surgically by the monks, and coins.

Samsø

Another day trip from Århus could be to the island of Samsø, but the car ferries leave from Hou, northeast of Horsens. Here, on 44 square miles, you can find a cross-section of Danish landscapes. The flora and fauna differs from that which can be found in the rest of Denmark. The Stavns Fjord is a bird sanctuary with many gulls and wading birds. Samsø also has an "English" country house in the shape of Brattingsborg, built in 1870. Other sights include the Ballebjerg viewpoint and the village of Nordby, one of the most beautiful Danish villages. Don't forget to visit the village pond surrounded by the houses of the former day laborers, today now used as summer dwellings.

Around Vejle

South of Silkeborg you find Vejle, another town with a beautiful position among water and forest-clad hills. To the east a lovely tree-lined fjord stretches to the Kattegat. A motorway bridge is being built here. North of Vejle is Grejsdalen, a mysterious valley which you can also see from the train to Jelling. Jelling is the oldest known royal dwelling. King Gorm lived here more than 1,000 years ago with his queen, and two burial mounds have long been known as the King Mound and the Queen Mound. However, the royal tombs are not under them, but, it seems, in the church itself, rather a strange feature, since they were not Christians. However, on the churchyard you will find "Denmark's Certificate of Baptism," the greater of the two runic stones outside the church. It depicts the oldest figure of Christ in Scandinavia, and the text explains that the stone was erected by King Harald over Gorm, his father, and Thyra, his mother, and that Harald christened the Danes. The event took place in about 960. The minor stone was erected by Gorm as a memorial over his queen.

West of Vejle is the little village of Billund, known because of Legoland, founded by the inventor of the famous Lego construction toy. This amusement park is entirely built of his plastic toy bricks and contains miniature copies of the Amalienborg Palace, an English provincial town, the Mount Rushmore presidents and a Wild West saloon. Plenty of time could be spent here, and when you are tired of playing, go and see the antique doll collection, dating back to 1580. But the sensation here is "Titania's Palace," originally built by Sir Neville Wilkinson, who started its construction in 1907 as a gift for his daughter. Everything is a correct miniature copy of older models, and includes a bathroom basin, given by Queen Mary, who was herself a dolls house aficionado, which is inscribed "From the Queen of England to the Queen of Fairyland." In 1978 it was sold at Christie's in London to Legoland for £135,000 and was put on display there for the first time in 1979.

The last sight in the neighborhood is at Givskud, further along the Jelling road, where you will find a Lion Park (Løveparken), where 40 lions live in open surroundings. There are other species to be found here, for instance baboons and a "savanna" with elephants and camels. There is a mini-farm with animals for children.

PRACTICAL INFORMATION FOR JUTLAND

TOURIST INFORMATION. All the main towns in Jutland have tourist information (Dantourist) offices: **Aalborg,** Østerågade 8 (08–12 60 22). **Århus,** Rådhuset (Town Hall) (06–12 16 00). **Ebeltoft,** Torvet 9–11 (06–34 14 00). **Esbjerg,** Skolegade 33 (05–12 55 99). **Fredericia,** Axeltorv (05–92 13 77). **Frederikshavn,** Brotorvet 1 (08–42 32 66). **Herning,** Bredgade 2 (07–12 44 22). **Hjørring,** Akseltorv 5 (08–92 02 32). **Hobro,** Vestergade 2 (08–52 22 88). **Horsens,** Kongensgade 25 (05–62 31 32). **Kolding,** Helligkorsgade 18 (05–53 21 00). **Løkken,** Vrenstedvej 6 (08–99 10 09). **Lønstrup,** Strandvejen 90 (08–96 02 22). **Nykøbing Mors,** Havnen 4 (07–72 04 88). **Randers,** Erik Menveds Plads 1 (06–42 44 77). **Ribe,** Torvet 3–5 (05–42 15 00). **Ringkøbing,** Torvet (07–32 00 31). **Rømø,** Havnebyvej 30, Tvismark (04–75 51 30). **Samsø,** Langgade 32, Tranebjerg (06–59 14 00). **Silkeborg,** Torvet 9 (06–82 19 11). **Skagen,** Sct. Laurentiivej 8 (08–44 13 77). **Skive,** Østerbro 7 (07–52 32 66). **Saeby,** Krystaltorvet 1 (08–46 15 19). **Sønderborg,** Rådhustorvet 7 (04–42 35 55). **Thisted,** Store Torv 6 (07–92 19 00). **Tønder,** Østergade 2A (04–72 12 20). **Vejle,** Rådhustorvet (05–82 19 55). **Viborg,** Nytorv 5 (06–62 16 17).

TELEPHONE CODES. We have given telephone codes for all the towns and villages in the hotel and restaurant lists that follow. These codes need only be used when calling from outside the town or village concerned.

HOTELS AND RESTAURANTS. Inn vouchers are available from the tourist office at Horsens for the majority of Jutland's inns. They cost around 160 Dkr. per night, including breakfast.

AALBORG. *Hvide Hus* (E), (08–13 84 00). 361 beds, all rooms with bath. Sauna, pool, music in winter periods. AE, DC, MC, V. *Phønix* (E), (08–12 00 11). 280 beds. Traditional, good food, music in winter periods. AE, DC, MC, V. *Central* (M), (08–12 69 33). 113 beds, some rooms with bath. MC, V. *Missionshotellet Ansgar* (M), (08–13 37 33). 86 beds (BE). *Park* (M), 08–12 31 33). 97 beds. AE, DC, MC, V. *Scheelsminde* (M), (08–18 32 33). 90 beds. Motel; park. DC, MC, V.

Restaurants. *Duus Vinkjaelder* (E). Serves wine from centuries-old wine cellars under Jens Bang's house. *Faklen* (E), Jomfru Ane Gade. With a carillon. AE, DC, MC, V. *Jomfru Ane* (E), Jomfru Ane Gade. Pleasant. AE, DC. *Stygge Krumpen* (E). AE, DC, MC, V. *Brix' Gård* (M), C.B. Obels Plads. Nice, good food. DC, MC, V. *Caféen* (M). AE, DC, MC, V. *Fyrtøjet* (M), Jomfru Ane Gade. A pleasant restaurant. AE, DC, MC, V. *Kniv og Gaffel* (M), Maren Turisgade. Nice, good food. DC, MC, V. *Peberkvaernen* (M), at Håbets Gård. Wine bar with plain food. DC, MC, V. *Regensen* (M). Steak house with open grill. AE, DC, MC, V. *Skråen* (M), at Håbets Gård. Jazz and folk place. *Pizzeria Napoli* (I), Borgergade. Good food. DC.

ÅBENRÅ. *Grand* (M), (04–62 26 22). 75 beds, some rooms with bath. Sauna. AE, DC, MC, V. *Hvide Hus* (M), (04–62 47 00). 98 beds. Garden, sauna. AE, DC, MC, V. *Missionshotellet* (I), (04–62 36 12). 30 beds (BE).
Restaurant. *De 3 Makreller.* Quaint cellar restaurant.

ANHOLT. *Anholt Kro* (I).

DENMARK

ÅRHUS. *Atlantic* (E), (06–13 11 11). 186 beds. At the harbor; bar, music, dance. AE, DC, MC, V. *Marselis* (E), (06–14 44 11). 130 beds. Bar. AE, DC, MC, V. *Missionshotellet Ansgar* (M), (06–12 41 22). 233 beds. At station; garden. *Ritz* (M), (06–13 44 44). 92 beds, 63 rooms with bath. Near station; clean and well-kept. AE, DC, MC, V. *Royal* (M), (06–12 00 11). 230 beds. Central. AE, DC, MC, V. *Krags* (I), (06–12 11 27). 25 beds (BE). *La Tour* (I), (06–16 78 88). 90 beds, all rooms with bath. Motel. (BE). AE, DC, MC, V.

Restaurants. *Café Mahler* (E), Vestergade 39. Excellent food; intimate with few tables. AE, DC, MC, V. *De 4 Årstider* (The 4 Seasons) (E), Åboulevarden. Opposite the Magasin department store. French cuisine, excellent food, one of the finest restaurants in Europe. AE, DC, MC, V. *Gammel Åbyhøj* (E), Åbyhøj Bakke Allé 1. Excellent French cuisine. DC, MC, V. *Kellers Gård* (M), Frederiksgade 84. Excellent Danish food. AE, DC. *Klostergården* (M), Børsen. Excellent food. DC. *Tropicana* (M), Ryesgade. Music and floor show. MC, V.

Near town are *Sjette Frederik's Kro,* Risskov, an old inn situated on cliffs above the bay and among woods. At Marselisborg Wood are *Frederikshøj Kro* with excellent cuisine at moderate prices, and *Skovmøllen,* an old half-timbered water mill.

EBELTOFT. *Hvide Hus* (M), (06–34 14 66). 104 beds, rooms with bath and balcony overlooking the bay. Modern; rooftop restaurant, sauna, pool, golf. AE, DC, MC, V. *Molskroen* (M), (06–36 22 00). 46 beds. Near beach in Fenmøller. DC, MC, V.

Restaurants. *Mellem Jyder,* next to old Town Hall; *Den skaeve Kro.*

ESBJERG. *Bangs* (M), (05–12 69 33). 55 beds, 38 rooms with bath. Breakfast only. DC, MC, V. *Bell-Inn* (M), (05–12 01 22). 53 beds. DC. *Britannia* (M), (05–13 01 11). 132 beds, all rooms with bath. Music at weekends. AE, DC, MC, V. *Missionshotellet Ansgar* (M), (05–12 82 44). 90 beds. AE, DC, MC, V. *Palads* (M), (05–12 30 00). 77 rooms, 27 with bath. Cheerful; dancing Fri. and Sat. AE, DC, MC, V.

Restaurants. *Bonbonnieren* (M). Dinner-dancing. DC, MC, V. *Discothèque Blue Heaven,* Skolegade 20. Rather exclusive, with floor show. MC, V. *Discothèque Lord Nelson,* Skolegade 31. For the younger set.

FANØ. *Sønderho Kro* (E), (05–16 40 09). Charming inn with (M) rooms also. AE, DC. *Kongen af Danmark* (M), (05–16 33 33). 96 beds, all rooms with shower. *Krogården* (M), (05–16 20 52). 32 beds (BE). *Vesterhavet* (M), (05–16 32 77). 6-bed apartments with bath and kitchen; weekly rental. Sauna, pool. MC, V. *Golfhotel* (I), (05–16 30 43). 26 beds, private bath. *Kellers Hotel* (I), (05–16 30 88). 36 beds, some with bath.

FREDERICIA. *Landsoldaten* (M), (05–92 15 55). 118 beds. Bar, music. (BE). AE, DC, MC, V. *Peter Ågegården* (I), (05–94 21 00). 16 beds, all rooms with shower. Not central. (BE).

FREDERIKSHAVN. *Jutlandia* (E), (08–42 42 00). 196 beds, all rooms with bath. Music and dance Fri. and Sat. AE, DC, MC, V. *Hoffmanns* (M), (08–42 21 66). 127 beds, 37 rooms with bath. Cozy and well-furnished. DC, MC, V. *Lisboa* (M), (08–42 21 33). 90 beds. Motel; good service. (BE). AE, DC, MC, V.

GRENÅ. *Du Nord* (E), (06–32 25 00). 180 beds; also apartments with 4 beds, bath and kitchen. Garden, pool, music, dance. AE, DC, MC, V.

HADERSLEV. *Haderslev* (M), (04–52 60 10). 66 beds. Motel in park; music and dance Sat. in winter. DC, MC, V. *Syd* (I), (04–53 13 00). 46 beds. Motel. (BE). DC.

JUTLAND

HANTSHOLM. *Hantsholm* (M), (07-96 10 44). 162 beds, most rooms with bath. Unusual cliff setting; sauna, pool, golf, garden. AE, DC, MC, V.

HERNING. *Birkegården* (M), (07-22 15 22). 112 beds. Garden, pool. (BE). AE, DC, MC, V. *Eyde* (M), (07-22 18 00). 163 beds. Bar. AE, DC, MC, V. *Østergaards* (M), (07-12 45 55). 160 beds, all rooms with bath. AE, DC, MC, V. *Missionshotellet* (I), (07-15 54 44). 77 beds. AE, DC.

HIMMELBJERGET. *Landsbykroen* (M), (06-94 37 16). 14 beds. At Nørre Vissing on Skanderborg-A 15 road. Rural surroundings. Possibilities for angling and boat-hire. DC, MC, V. *Gl. Rye Kro* (I), (06-89 80 42). 32 beds in modern wing added to old inn. For anglers. (BE). DC, MC, V.

HORSENS. *Bygholm Parkhotel* (M), (05-62 23 33). 131 beds, 70 rooms with bath. 18th-cent. castle in idyllic park. (BE). AE, DC, MC, V. *Jørgensens* (M), (05-62 16 00). 76 beds, 48 rooms with bath. In baroque mansion, modernized. AE, DC, MC, V. *Missionshotellet* (M), (05-62 18 00). 85 beds, 10 rooms with bath.
Restaurant. *Steak-House Helene.* Spanish-style, dance. DC, MC, V.

HOVBORG. *Hovborg Kro* (M), (05-39 60 33). 54 beds. Lodgings and food in old inn in rural surroundings. Good for anglers. DC, MC, V.

HVIDSTEN. Restaurant. *Hvidsten Kro* (I), (06-47 70 22). Historic old country inn with picturesque interior. Also has 12 beds. (BE).

KARUP. *Centrum* (I), (07-10 12 80). 8 beds. Motel, for anglers (BE). *Karup* (I), (07-10 10 19). 27 beds, 2 with shower. For anglers. DC, MC, V.

KOLDING. *Kolding* (M), (05-52 50 00). 70 beds, 20 rooms with bath. Bistro, discothèque. AE, DC, MC, V. *Saxildhus* (M), (05-52 12 00). 138 beds, some rooms with bath and balcony. An outstanding hostelry, near castle, bar, music. AE, DC, MC, V. *Tre Roser* (M), (05-53 21 22). 61 beds, all rooms with bath. Motel which also has 4-bed apartments with kitchenette (weekly rentals). Pool, sauna, garden, park. (BE). AE, DC, MC, V.
Restaurant. *Krybi-i-Ly* (M), (05-56 25 55). At Taulov on Kolding-Middelfart highway overlooking Kolding Fjord. Also has 50 beds. DC, MC, V.

LAESØ. *Carlsen's Hotel* (I), Vesterø Havn (08-49 94 15). 20 beds. At ferry berth; restaurant.
Restaurant. *Bakken,* at Byrum.

NYMINDEGAB. *Nymindegab Kro* (M), (05-28 82 11). 63 beds, 12 rooms with bath. Magnificent scenery, overlooking Ringkøbing Fjord. Excellent food; sauna, garden, fishing. Also has 5-bed apartments with kitchen (weekly rentals). (BE). DC.

ØSLØS. *Bygholm Holiday Center* (I), (07-99 31 39). 20 beds. Also motel apartments of 4 or 6 beds and shower. In sanctuary between Thisted and Fjerritslev on the Limfjorden. Pool, sauna, riding, fishing, own beach, cafeteria; camping.

RANDERS. *Kongens Ege* (M), (06-43 03 00). 170 beds, all rooms with bath. Nightclub. AE, DC, MC, V. *Randers* (M), (06-42 34 22). 140 beds, all rooms with bath. One of Denmark's best: attractive décor, personalized service, delicious food. AE, DC, MC, V.
Restaurant. *Nummer 1.* Old-style pub with garden, music. AE, DC, MC, V.

RIBE. *Dagmar* (M), (05–42 00 33). 78 beds, 20 rooms with bath. Atmospheric 16th-cent. building, fine antiques. (BE). AE, DC, MC, V. *Sønderjylland* (I), (05–42 04 66). 21 beds. *Weis' Stue* (I), (05–42 07 00). 9 beds, no room with private bath. In a protected 16th-cent. house; interior has the oldest cupboard in Denmark and Dutch tiles (this inn has been copied by an enthusiastic hotel owner in Maine). (BE).

RINGKØBING. *Fjordgården* (M), (07–32 14 00). 111 beds, all rooms with bath. Music on summer evenings, bar, garden, sauna. AE, DC, MC, V. *Ferienhotel Søndervig* (I), (07–33 92 00). 44 beds, all rooms with bath. Also 84 apartments.

ROLD SKOV. *Rold Storko* (M), Rebild, (08–37 51 00). 92 beds, 53 rooms with bath. Sauna, pool, garden, angling, hunting. DC.

SAEBY. *Viking* (M), (08–46 17 00). Modern facilities. AE, DC, MC, V. *Åhøj* (I). 17 beds. Pension, no private facilities. *Oda* (I), (08–46 12 49). 10 beds. Motel, open Apr. to 15 Sept. (BE). *Voerså Kro* (I), (08–46 00 06). 12 rooms. 16 km. (10 miles) south, in picturesque surroundings. Inn with folk dancing in summer in garden; music, occasional dancing. Cozy tap room. (BE).

SAMSØ. *Sølyst* (I), (06–59 16 59). 24 beds, all 12 rooms with bath. Sauna, indoor pool, garden.

SILKEBORG. *Dania* (M), (06–82 01 11). 80 beds, 35 rooms with bath. Bar, music. AE, DC, MC, V. *Impala* (M), (06–82 03 00). 79 beds, 41 rooms with bath. Fine view, color T.V., indoor pool, sauna, garden, music Sat. (BE). AE, DC, MC, V.
Restaurants. *Dania* has restaurant, bar and bodega. *La Strada,* on market square, dancing Sat. AE, DC, MC, V.

SKAGEN. *Brøndums* (E), (08–44 15 55). 67 beds, 14 rooms with bath. Attractive building with garden and music, near beach. Danish "cold table" and fish specialties in restaurant. (BE). AE, MC, V. *Skagen* (E), (08–44 22 33). 82 beds, all rooms with bath. Pool, garden. *Klithotellerne* (M), Gammel Skagen (08–44 13 22). 47 apartments with bath and kitchen.
Restaurants. *De to Have* (The Two Seas), on the spit of Skaw. Summer restaurant. *Fiskerestauranten,* opposite the fishermen's houses, fish market and boat moorings. All kinds of fish served in traditional atmosphere.

SKANDERBORG. *Skanderborghus* (M), (06–52 09 55). 82 beds, nearly all rooms with bath. Modern, magnificent lakeside location out of town, with sauna and garden. (BE). MC, V.

SØNDERBORG. *City* (M), (04–42 16 26). 20–30 beds, most rooms with bath. AE, DC, MC, V. *Alssund* (I), (04–42 30 70). 54 beds, some rooms with bath. *Ansgar* (I), (04–42 24 72). Mission hotel with 90 beds, some rooms with bath. DC, MC, V. *Arnkilhus* (I), (04–42 23 36). 20–30 beds, some rooms with bath. *Dybbøl Banke* (I), (04–42 34 11). 30 beds, some rooms with bath. DC, MC, V. *Garni* (I), (04–42 34 33). 10 rooms with bath. *Lido* (I), (04–42 13 30). 20–30 beds. *Park* (I), (04–42 13 30). 20–30 beds, some rooms with bath.

THISTED. *Aalborg* (I), (07–92 35 66). 48 beds, some rooms with bath. Near swimming pool. AE, DC, MC, V.

TØNDER. *Tønderhus* (M), (04–72 22 22). 58 beds, 31 rooms with bath. DC, MC, V. *Hostrups* (I), (04–72 21 29). 39 beds. *Romantic* (I), (04–72 21 08). 70 beds, some rooms with bath. (BE). DC, MC, V.

JUTLAND

VEJLE. *Munkebjerg* (E), (05-82 75 00). 234 beds. Magnificently located on a fjord 6½ km (4 miles) east. Pool, sauna, music, garden, bar. AE, DC, MC, V. *Australia* (M), (05-82 43 11). 150 beds, all rooms with bath. Bar. AE, DC, MC, V. *Hedegården* (M), (05-82 08 33). 72 beds, all rooms with bath. Modern motel 3 km. (2 miles) from center. AE, DC, MC, V. *Grand* (I), (05-82 94 00). 63 rooms with bath. Bar. AE, DC, MC, V. *Grejsdalens* (I), (05-85 30 04). Small with limited facilities, but beautifully situated.

Restaurants. *Flamingo, Grand Bistro, Granddisco* and *Moulin Rouge* have dancing.

VIBORG. *Missionshotellet* (M), (06-62 37 00). 73 beds, many rooms with bath. Modernized, garden. AE, DC, MC, V. *Kongenshus* (I), (07-54 81 25). 19 beds. Motel. *Søndersø* (I), (06-61 02 22). 80 beds. Motel in park, garni. MC, DC, V.

Restaurants. *Salonen,* with concerts and dancing. Closed Mon. MC, V.

Between Viborg and Århus, *Kongensbro Kro* (I), (06-87 01 77), serves simple, typically Danish dishes and has 26 attractive rooms for overnight guests; good fishing and the Gjern automobile museum nearby. AE, DC, MC, V.

Youth Hostels

There are youth hostels at the following places: Åbenrå, Aalborg, Blokhus, Brande, Århus, Bedsted (Thy), Bryrup, Ebeltoft, Esbjerg, Farsø, Fredericia, Frederikshavn, Gram, Grenå, Grindsted, Haderslev, Hals, Henne Strand, Herning, Hirstshals, Hjørring, Hobro, Holstebro, Horsens, Hvide Sande, Højer, Juelsminde, Kolding, Kruså, Løgumkloster, Laesø, Nykøbing Mors, Oksbøl, Randers, Ribe, Ringkøbing, Roslev, Ry, Rødding, Rømø (Havneby), Rønde, Skagen, Skanderborg, Skørping, Struer, Saeby, Sønderborg, Thisted, Tinglev, Samsø (Tranebjerg), Tønder, Varde, Vejle, Viborg.

Camping

Camp sites are signposted by the international wigwam sign.

HOW TO GET AROUND. By plane. There are direct flights from Copenhagen to Århus, Billund, Aalborg, Karup, Sønderborg, Skrydstrup, Thisted and Esbjerg.

By boat. From Copenhagen a good way to northern Jutland is by comfortable and frequent car and passenger ferries from Kalundborg to Århus or to Juelsminde, Hundested to Grenå, and, shortest, Sjaellands Odde to Ebeltoft. Cars are carried on all these services.

By train. There are "L" and "IC" train services from Copenhagen to the main towns, taking 5-6 hours, and trains connect all important points on the peninsula. The DSB (Danish State Railways) special sightseeing ticket scheme —comprising return fare from Copenhagen Central Station and admission charges—will take you to Legoland in Billund.

By bus. Jutland is covered by a network of buses, most of them run by the DSB (Danish State Railways). As elsewhere in Denmark, bus fares are high, with no reductions on return fares, so it may be worth asking about discount passes ("rabatkort"). In Århus tickets cost 7 Dkr., more than in Copenhagen, but with a discount pass they can cost 5.50 Dkr. Århus also has one-day tourist tickets, valid for a sightseeing tour plus free bus rides in and around the city.

By car. It is advisable to book ahead for ferry crossings, especially in summer. Especially busy are the Kalundborg-Århus crossing (state run), and Sjaellands Odde-Ebeltoft and Grenå-Hundested (privately run). Consult an FDM office or the pamphlet "Car Ferries" on timetables, prices and booking. Bookings for the state routes can be made at any major rail station 2 months ahead.

Jutland differs from the rest of Denmark in having more open country, and long, lonely stretches of road with little traffic.

DENMARK

By bicycle. Bicycles are available for hire in every sizeable town. Tourist offices either hire out bikes themselves or will refer you to dealers who do so. They will also suggest tours.

PLACES TO VISIT. We give here the opening times of recommended places to visit, details of which you will find in the chapter. For further information consult local tourist information offices. Note that churches and cathedrals are usually open daily except during services.

AALBORG. Aalborghus (Aalborg Castle). Parts (e.g. dungeon) open in summer, Mon. to Fri. 8–4.
Budolfi Kirke (St. Botolph's Cathedral). Open daily except during services.
Helligåndsklosteret (Monastery of the Holy Ghost). Guided tours from mid-June to end of Aug., Mon. to Fri. at 2 and 3.
Nordjyllands Kunstmuseum (North Jutland Museum of Art). Open July and Aug., daily 10–5; Sept. through June, Tues. to Sun. 10–5, closed Mon.

ÅRHUS. Forhistorisk Museum Moesgård (Museum of Prehistory at Moesgård Manor). Open May through to mid-Sept., daily 10–5; mid-Sept. through Apr., Tues. to Sun., 10–5, closed Mon.
Den gamle By ("The Old Town" open-air museum). Open Apr., daily 10–4; May through Sept., daily 10–5; Oct., daily 10–4; Nov. through Mar., daily 11–3.

BILLUND. Legoland. Open 1 May to mid-June, daily 10–8; mid-June to mid-Aug., daily 10–9; mid-Aug. to mid-Sept., daily 10–8.

GIVSKUD. Løveparken (Lion Park). Open May to mid-June, daily 10–4.30; mid-June to mid-Aug., daily 10–6; mid-Aug. through Sept., daily 10–4.30.

HJERL HEDE. Hjerl Hede (open-air museum). Open Apr. through Oct., daily 9–5. Demonstrations of old crafts: July, daily 1.30–5. Open weekends in Dec., 10–5 for old-time Christmas preparations.

HOBRO. Lincoln Log Cabin (Lincoln Memorial Cabin). In the Rebild Bakker (Rebild Hills). Open May to mid-June, daily 10–5; mid-June to mid-Aug., daily 9–6; last two weeks of Aug., daily 10–5; Apr., Sept. and Oct., Sat., Sun. and bank holidays 10–5.
Tingbaek Kalkminer (Tingbaek Limestone Workings). Opening times as for Lincoln Log Cabin.

KOLDING. Den Geografiske Have (Geographical Garden). Open June and Aug., daily 9–7; July, daily 9–8; Sept. through May, daily 10–6.
Koldinghus. Open May through Sept., Mon. to Sat. 10–5, Sun. 12–3; Oct. through Apr., daily 12–3.

RANDERS. Clausholm. Open Easter to 15 May, Sat., Sun. and bank holidays 10–12 and 2–5.30; 15 May to 15 Sept., daily 10–12 and 2–5.30; 16 Sept. to last Sun. in Oct., Sat., Sun. and bank holidays 10–12 and 2–5.30. Park open all year, daily 9–6.
Gammel Estrup. Open May through Oct., daily 10–5.
Rosenholm Slot. Manor, park and gardens open mid-June through Aug., daily 10–5.

RIBE. Ribe Domkirke (Ribe Cathedral). Open in summer, Mon. to Sat. 10–6, closed Sun. morning; winter, Mon. to Sat. 10–12, closed Sun. No admittance during services.

JUTLAND

Sct. Catharinae Kirke og Kloster (Church of St. Catharine and the Black Friars Abbey). Open May through Sept., daily 10–12 and 2–5; Oct. through Apr., daily 10–12 and 2–4.

RØMØ. Nationalmuseets Kommandorgård (island museum), Toftum. Open May through Sept., daily 10–6; Oct., 10–3.

SAMSØ. Brattingsborg. Park open June through Sept., Tues. and Fri. 10–4.

SILKEBORG. Silkeborg Kunstmuseum (art museum). Open Apr. through Oct., Tues. to Sun. 10–5, closed Mon.; Nov. through Mar., Tues. to Fri. 12–4, Sat. and Sun. 10–4.
Silkeborg Museum. Open mid-Apr. to mid-Oct., daily 10–12 and 1–5; mid-Oct. to mid-Apr., Wed., Sat. and Sun. 10–12 and 2–4.

SKAGEN. Skagen Museum. Open Apr. through Oct., daily 10–5 or 10–6; Nov. through Mar., Sat. and Sun. 11–3.

SKANDERBORG. Øm Kloster (Øm Monastery). Open Apr., Tues. to Sun. 9–4, closed Mon.; May through Aug., Tues. to Sun., 9–6, closed Mon.; 1 Sept. to 21 Oct., Tues. to Sun. 9–4, closed Mon.

SØNDERBORG. Dybbøl Mølle (Dybbøl Mill). Open Apr. through June, daily 1–4; July, daily 10–5; Aug. through Oct., daily 1–4.
Gråsten Slot (Gråsten Castle). Except when castle is occupied, chapel is open Apr. through Sept., daily 10–12 and 2–5; and park is open all year from 7 to sunset.
Sønderborg Slot (Sønderborg Castle). Open May through Sept., daily 10–5; Oct. through Apr., 1–4.

SPØTTRUP. Spøttrup. Open Apr., Sun. and bank holidays, 11–5; May through Aug., daily 10–6; Oct., during school fall holidays, 10–5.

TØNDER. Sønderjyllands Kunstmuseum (South Jutland Museum of Modern Art). Open May through Oct., daily 10–5; Nov. through Apr., Tues. to Sun. 1–5, closed Mon.
Tønder Museum. Open May through Oct., daily 10–5; Nov. through Apr., Tues. to Sun., 1–5, closed Mon.

SPORTS Water sports are understandably popular here. There are over 320 km. (200 miles) of continuous sand beach on the west coast; good bathing can also be had on the eastern side. You can drive on the beach from Løkken to Blokhus as well as the 18-km. (11-mile) stretch of Fanø's coastline. The best known resorts include Skagen, Hirtshals, Løkken, Blokhus, Ålbek, Saeby, Aså, and Hals; Århus and Grenå also have fine beaches.

There's excellent **sailing** on the waters of the East Jutland fjords and the Limfjord, and **fishing** for salmon trout in the West Jutland streams. The river Guden, Denmark's longest, offers wonderful possibilities for a week's **canoeing** or **kayaking** tour from Tørring to Randers.

Aalborg, Århus, Brønderslev, Ebeltoft, Esbjerg, Fanø, Vesterhavsbad, Frederikshavn, Herning, Hobro, Holstebro, Horsens, Kolding, Randers, Silkeborg, Skagen, Skive, Skjern, Vejle and Viborg all have **golf** courses.

There are excellent opportunities for **jogging** in forests and along beaches.

ISLE OF BORNHOLM

The Baltic Hideaway

Far from the rest of Denmark, in the Baltic between Sweden and Poland, is an island 225 miles square. Since 1658, when Jens Kofoed's islanders threw out Swedish troops, the Bornholmers' Danish nationality and feelings have never been doubted. The 150 km. (93 miles) of coastline change from cliffs and rocks to skerries and dunes of the world's finest sand. The flora and fauna is special, too, and here you'll find Almindingen, the third largest forest in Denmark. Bornholm is the only place in Denmark where towns were built on sloping rocks and the independent farmers never settled in villages. There are many special trades connected with a "Bornholmer," hence the word designates an islander, a grandfather clock—or a smoked herring. Today fortified round churches and ruins still bear witness to times not so idyllic.

Exploring Bornholm

You may wonder how so many natural sights could have been put together as on Bornholm. It seems as if the "splendid isolation" also has concentrated and isolated a lot of nature that was not allowed to spread to the rest of Denmark. So even if you have seen other parts of Denmark you will be surprised here.

Rønne

The main city if Rønne, port for ships to Copenhagen, Sweden and Germany (the latter service is rather erratic). When arriving by ship you will be fascinated by the half-timbered tower which appears before you disembark, but the church is young, from 1915–18, and the real half timber is to be found in the streets behind the church. The majority of those houses were built around 1800, though some go back as far as late 17th century. Notice that nearly all houses have but one story, a fact that has given the city a large extension. The most beautiful of the houses is Erichsen's Farm in Laksegade where Holger Drachmann, the poet, and Dr. Zahrtmann, the Bornholm painter, lived.

An interesting museum, the Forsvarsmuseum, Defense Museum, is at Kastellet in Rønne. On the last Thursday in the month, from April to December, the Rønne Day gives rise to much activity and, among other amenities, free horse-carriage rides are given in the old town.

Jons Kapel and Hammershus

Let us start our island excursions with a visit to the northwest corner. The bicycle is a very popular means of transportation, although many people also travel by car. We pass through Hasle, well suited for discovery walks, and continue to Jons Kapel on the coast. Before reaching it you may make detours to the coast to see tiny Helligpeder and Teglkås.

According to legend, Brother Jon, the monk, lived in a cave on the steep cliff. He gave his sermons from the rock, which since then has borne the name Jons Kapel (Jon's Chapel). He must have had strong legs and lungs, since he lived on a rock 40 meters (130 feet) high and preached from the 22-meter (72-foot) high Pulpit rock.

Jons Kapel is halfway between Hasle and the marvellous ruins of the Hammershus Slot. The castle was built about 1255 as a fortress on a strategic spot. The stronghold was in use until 1743, but before that time its importance had decreased. It was occupied by Swedish troops in 1648, but Jens Kofoed, the Bornholm hero, killed its governor and the castle was given back to Denmark. The remaining ruins were protected in 1822, the biggest in North Europe.

At Borrelyng young children would enjoy a visit to the small zoo where there are animals roaming free in a natural environment.

Fashionable Allinge and Sandvig

The dominating Hammerknude with a good view from the lighthouse stands as the northern protection of Bornholm against the sea and enemy ships of earlier days. It also protects the twin towns of Sandvig and Allinge, together with the fashionable district of Bornholm. Here you find most of the hotels, but also several low half-timbered houses, especially in Allinge. In spite of the modern signs of civilization one of the characteristic Bornholm smokehouse chimneys still dominates the town. Also from these towns you can walk along the coast. Tejn and Sandkås further down the north coast are other popular beach resorts.

A Round Church

But, for a change, go inland to Olsker. Its church will serve as your introduction to the four round churches of Bornholm. They were all erected about 1150, and with their shape and thick walls they served a double purpose as both physical and spiritual protection of the poor souls who were often attacked by pirates or enemy armies. The church was defended from the third story. The church at Olsker is the smallest but tallest of the round churches.

Rø and its Neighborhood

Our next stop is at Rø between Helligdomsklipperne and Rø Plantage (plantation). If you choose the Helligdomsklipperne on the coast you will meet a famous rock formation towering up to 22 meters (72 feet) above sea level and filled with crevices, caves and rock columns. It is one of the great natural sights of Bornholm, and in summer it is also possible to see it from the sea. You may then realize why it got its name, which may be translated as the Sanctuary or Sacred Thing.

Rø Plantage is a natural sight of quite another kind. Here as you walk in heather, among trees or on stones, you may meet the black woodpecker or deer. Scenery that you won't forget soon surrounds the artificial lake.

Østerlars and Gudhjem

From Rø we go inland once more, now heading for the greatest of the round churches at Østerlars. This church seems to be the most imposing of all because of the strong buttresses. The structure is the same as we saw at Olsker, only this one is better adorned, and better suited for defense purposes. The nave diameter is about 16 meters (18 yards).

You will probably understand why generations of painters have visited Gudhjem, whether you see it from the top of the Bokul Klippeknude (cliff) or from the narrow roads looping down the terraces to the charming little village. The small, well-kept houses have to a great extent been carved out of the rock, and two little harbors and the smokehouses give evidence of the main occupation, at least outside the tourist season.

A Riviera Tour and a Prize Town

Ever been to the Riviera? If so, compare the Bornholm counterpart along the coast road from Gudhjem to Salene on the Svaneke road. Shortly after leaving the coast a path leads from the Hotel Randkløveskår down to the coast. A little inland you find the Randkløveskår, a narrow gorge between tall rock formations, later dividing into two clefts. Now refreshed we continue along the main road to Svaneke.

In 1975 the Council of Europe awarded a gold medal for the "consistent preservation of the historical character of the typical little port" to the easternmost Danish provincial town, Svaneke. So here you will

BORNHOLM

meet mostly 18th- or 19th-century houses. The harbor was cut into the rock, and steep streets and houses on high plinths show the difficulties of constructing this original fishing-hamlet in the Middle Ages. Two different mills are its landmarks. But it seems that conditions were not so harsh as one might believe, because you find here vines, figs and mulberries.

Inland, between Svaneke and Nexø, you find a peculiar landscape known as the Paradisbakkerne (Paradise Hills). A beautiful view will meet you among the valleys full of rocks, woodland and forest lakes. The best "entrance" to this area is from Klinteby west of Nexø. Map and route descriptions for this area have been worked out to secure the best enjoyment from your visit, where you can only move on foot. Marked tours take 1, 2 or 3 hours respectively.

Sand, Dunes and Beaches

The Bornholm coast, from Nexø to Boderne on the south coast, is the area almost entirely devoted to bathing and water sports, although you will also find beaches on other parts of the coast. Some people even bathe from the rocks. The water is shallow and thus also suited for the children. At Dueodde you find dunes 14 meters (45 feet) high and miles upon miles of beach with the most fine-grained sand in the world. Here is also the 44-meter (145 feet) tall lighthouse with a marvelous view from its top.

Central Bornholm

Let us conclude our visit to the Bornholm landscapes with a glance at the central part. It is dominated by one town, Åkirkeby, and the third largest Danish forest, the Almindingen. Åkirkeby is the oldest town on the island with a municipal charter from 1346 and in the Middle Ages a spiritual center as well. You can see that when visiting the Å Kirke, Bornholm's largest church, built in the second half of the 13th century. Both walls and tower are well suited for defense purposes, but the church is not round. The church furniture here is worth studying. The altarpiece and pulpit are Dutch Renaissance from about 1600; there is also one of the best examples of a Scandinavian Romanesque font, of the same age as the church. Eleven arcaded panels depict scenes from the life of Christ, and they are explained with more than 500 runic letters also cut into the sandstone. More runes are to be found on stones in the porch.

The Almindingen is one of the most varied Danish forests, with trees, rocks, lakes and ponds. You find here the Rytterknaegten, Bornholm's highest "mountain" (156 meters or 516 feet!) with the Kongeminde tower, even now, it seems, too low to come above the treetops of this vast area. Near the Rytterknaegten you can take a walk in the Echo Valley (Ekkodalen) with walls 22 meters (72 feet) over you.

The forest is only 16 km. (10 miles) from our starting point, Rønne. On your way back you may make detours to the round churches at Nylars (between Åkirkeby and Rønne) and Nyker northeast of Rønne. The one at Nylars is the best preserved and most decorated of the four Bornholm round churches.

Christiansø

Before leaving Bornholm, you should make a point of crossing to the idyllic island of Christiansø (Christian's Island), the largest of the group of islets that includes Frederiksø, Graesholm, and other smaller rock formations. Originally a bastion, only the towers "Storetårn" and "Lilletårn" remain of the fort, which was started in 1684 and dismantled in 1855. The barracks, street and the gardens, for which the earth was transported in boats, have a distinctive atmosphere of their own. Not only was the foundation of the bastion an architectural achievement, but the flora is also something special, with vines and Southern European plants that are watered only by rain water from the basins. There is no ground water on the island.

Although no longer used as a fortification, all the islets come under the Ministry of Defense, and the 118 inhabitants pay no local taxes. Graesholm is an inaccessible bird sanctuary. It is the only place in Denmark where the razorbill and guillemot breed.

PRACTICAL INFORMATION FOR BORNHOLM

TOURIST INFORMATION. The main tourist information (Dantourist) offices are at **Allinge**, Hammershuvej 2 (03-98 00 01) and **Rønne**, Havnen (03-95 08 10). There are offices also at: **Åkirkeby, Gudhjem, Hasle, Nexø, Svaneke** and **Tejn**. For activity holidays and all types of bookings: *Bornholms Kongresbureau*, Snellemark 13, DK-300 Rønne (03-95 12 11).

TELEPHONE CODES. We have given the Bornholm telephone code for all the towns and villages in the hotel and restaurant lists that follow. This code need only be used when calling from outside Bornholm.

HOTELS AND RESTAURANTS. Bornholm has long been a favorite summer holiday resort of Danes and tourists alike. Recent hotel development has provided plenty of modern accommodations, primarily in Rønne and the coastal resorts. As well as the hotels listed, some of which have apartments, Bornholm offers quite a number of small holiday homes for renting, many of which are well built and equipped. The tourist offices at Åkirkeby, Allinge, Nexø, Rønne and Svaneke handle bookings.

There are youth hostels at Gudhjem, Hasle, Neksø (Dueodde), Rønne, Sandvig-Allinge, and Svaneke, and about 20 camping sites are dotted along the coast, with one inland at Åkirkeby.

And, of course—as elsewhere in Denmark—you can eat well practically anywhere.

ÅKIRKEBY. *Kanns* (I), (03-97 40 12). 42 beds, all with bath. Garden. (BE).

ALLINGE. *AEblehaven* (M), (03-98 12 22). 280 beds in 70 apartments with kitchen (weekly rentals). Pool, sauna. *Abildgård* (I), at Sandkås (03-98 09 55). 250 beds, all rooms with shower. Half-board terms, small apartments with fridge, no cooking. Tennis, garden, sauna, pool, solarium. MC, V.

BORNHOLM

Restaurant. *Grotten.* At Sandkås. Dance restaurant, with an underground disco set in the rocks.

GUDHJEM. *Ellebaek* (I), (03–98 51 00). 46 beds, pension only; garden. *Helligdommen* (I), (03–98 40 20). 41 beds, most rooms with bath. (BE). AE, DC, MC, V. *Thern's* (I), (03–98 50 99). 95 beds; garden.
Restaurant. *Bokulhus.* On top of Bokul rock; fish specialties.

HASLE. *Herold* (I), (03–96 40 24). 40 beds, 14 rooms with bath; harbor view.

NEXØ (Neksø). *Balka Søbad* (M), (03–99 22 25). 320 beds, all pension only. Tennis, garden, sauna, pool. AE. *Balka Strand* (M), (03–99 21 50). 70 beds. Music, dance, garden, pool. *Bornholm* (M), (03–98 83 83). 27 beds. On Dueodde beach. Garden, heated pool. Also 4–5 bed apartments with kitchen (weekly rentals). *Linds Pension* (I), (03–98 80 80). 32 beds; limited facilities.
Restaurant. *De tre Søstre* (The Three Sisters) E, (03–99 33 93). An excellent place, with fish specialties (from split cod to lobster) and entertainment in summer; in winter a bodega only. AE, DC, MC, V.

RØNNE. *Badehotel Ryttergården* (E), (03–95 19 13). 224 beds, all rooms with bath. Near beach, with pool and riding. Also 35 4–5 bed apartments for weekly rental. *Fredensborg* (E), (03–95 44 44). 128 beds, all rooms with bath and balcony. Faces the sea, with beach, sauna. Also 12 apartments. AE, DC, MC, V. *Griffen* (E), (03–95 51 11). 284 beds, all rooms with shower. Sauna, tennis, restaurant with local dishes; newish, near airport. AE, DC, MC, V. *Missionshotellet* (M), (03–95 03 86). 210 beds, 110 rooms with bath. Sauna, pool. In town center but charming. AE, DC, MC, V.
Restaurants. *De fem Ståuerna,* exclusive fish and steak restaurant in Hotel Fredensborg. AE, DC, MC, V. *Rådhuskroen,* old half-timbered house in town center. Excellent smørrebrød, also a few rooms. DC, MC, V.

SANDVIG. *Hammersø* (M), (03–98 03 64). 90 beds, 49 rooms with bath; pension. Summer hotel, near beach. Garden, pool. *Strandslot* (M), (03–98 03 15). 110 beds, nearly all rooms with shower; pension. Summer hotel, with garden. *Strandhotellet* (I), (03–98 03 14). 80 beds, 20 rooms with shower. Summer hotel, on the beach, with garden; refurnished with modern décor.
Restaurant. *Burgundia.* Fish restaurant.

SVANEKE. *Siemsens Gård* (E), (03–99 61 49). 90 beds, 42 rooms with shower. Open May to Nov. Garden, sauna. *Østersøen* (M), (03–99 60 20). 35 beds, 5 rooms with shower. Garden. *Nansens Gård* (I), (03–99 61 70). 14 beds, pension, minimum seven days. Sauna. Limited facilities, but art lovers will find this hotel interesting if they don't mind sharing a bathroom with other guests. Open mid-June to mid-Sept.
Restaurant. *Louisekroen,* Bølshavn. Well prepared food served in stylish atmosphere. DC, MC, V.

HOW TO GET AROUND. By bus. There is no railway on Bornholm, but there is a good bus network. A BAT-kort (discount pass) offers considerable savings on bus fares, and one-day tourist tickets are also available.
By car. There is a car ferry from Ystad in Sweden, but it's more practical to hire one on Bornholm. Several dealers hire out cars. Danish speed limits apply, of course, and good braking will be useful on Bornholm's steep stretches of road. Bornholm's landscape is very unlike the rest of Denmark: rock and cliff dominate every view.
By bicycle. Cycles may be hired in Allinge, Gudhjem, Hasle, Pedersker near Åkirkeby, Rønne and Svaneke. There are splendid cycling routes along the coast, but be sure to check your brakes before setting out.

DENMARK

By boat. The island of Christiansø can be reached by boat year-round from Svaneke, and mid-May to mid-Sept. from Allinge and Gudhjem.

PLACES TO VISIT. ÅKIRKEBY. Å Kirke. One of the island's few churches that *isn't* round. Dates from the 13th century, and retains its original font. The altarpiece and pulpit are Dutch (16th-century). Open late-June through mid-Aug. 9–12, 2–5. Key available from verger rest of year.

ALLINGE-SANDVIG. Hammershus. Castle ruins, built originally in about 1250 by archbishop Jakob Erlandsen on high cliff overlooking the sea; the largest ruined castle in northern Europe. Open all year.

BORRELYNG. Zoo, 3 km. south of Allinge. Animals roam free through beautiful grounds. Open May through Sept., 9–6.

NYKER. Ny Kirke, 10 km. (6 miles) northeast of Rønne. The smallest round church on the island. Note especially the column with original late-Gothic frescos. Open late-May through mid-Sept., 8–7.

NYLARS. Nylars Kirke. 10 km. (6 miles) southeast of Rønne. Large round church with attractive 14th-century frescos. Open late-May through mid-Sept., 10–5.

OLSKER. Ols Kirke, 5 km. south of Allinge. The most elevated round church on the island, 113 meters (350 ft.) above sea level; is believed to date from the late-12th century. Also has Renaissance pulpit. Key available from priest.

ØSTERLARS. Østerlars Kirke, 10 km. (6 miles) south of Gudhjem. The largest of the island's many round churches, dating probably from the 12th century. Hollow column in the nave contains the font; another is decorated with frescos that are believed to date from the 14th century. Open mid-May through late-Oct, 9–5. Closed Sun.

RØNNE. Forsvarsmuseum (Defense Museum). In the castle, and charts the military struggles of the island, principally against the Swedes. Open July and Aug., Mon. to Fri. 1–4; June and Sept., Tues., Thurs. and Sat. 1–4. Closed Sun.

SPORTS. Swimming is excellent—from flat rocks, from the sandy beach that stretches for miles on the south coast, and from sizeable sandy beaches to the west. It is possible to bathe in the sea until late September. There are good swimming pools at Gudhjem, Rønne and Sandvig. Instruction is available in **windsurfing:** short courses at about 300 Dkr.; courses leading to a certificate at about 800 Dkr.

Sailing and **fishing** for salmon in the waters offshore attract the deep-sea sportsman, and there's free trout fishing south of Rønne off "Stampen."

Bornholm also has a **golf** course at Åkirkeby.

SHOPPING. Ceramics are manufactured in Rønne and may be bought directly from *Michael Andersen, L. Hjorth, Joghus and Søholm. Gaveboden* at Allinge sells ceramics, glass and trinkets, and there are *Keramikstå-uan* shops for ceramics and stoneware at Gudhjem, Nexø and Snogebaek. In Svaneke, three shops are worth noting: *Waldorff* for stoneware, *I Stalden* for textiles and ceramics, and *Staugård* for stoneware, paintings and ceramics. Local folk art may be bought from *Alkemisterne* at Snogebaek, and smoked fish from Espersen harbor at Rønne.

FINLAND

FINLAND

FACTS AT YOUR FINGERTIPS

FINLAND—FACTS AT YOUR FINGERTIPS

NATIONAL TOURIST OFFICE. In the U.S.: 75 Rockefeller Plaza, New York, N.Y. 10019 (212–582 2802).

In the U.K.: 66–68 Haymarket, London S.W.1 (01–839 4048).

The mailing address for the Finnish Tourist Board's head office in Finland is P.O. Box 53, 00251 Helsinki 52. The Helsinki Tourist Office and most travel agencies in Helsinki can supply personal callers with information on most aspects of travel in Finland. In addition, every town and resort has a tourist office (often identified by the international "i" sign), and usually one or more travel agencies *(matkatoimisto)*. We list all the major Finnish tourist offices at the beginning of each *Practical Information* section.

CURRENCY. The unit of Finnish currency is the *markka* (Fmk) divided into 100 *penniä* (singular *penni*). The rate of exchange at press time (mid-1984) was 5.60 Fmk to the U.S. dollar and 8.20 Fmk to the pound sterling.

You can change money or travelers' checks in banks and exchange bureaux (see *Closing Times*); most hotels will also change money, though the rate is likely to be less favorable.

COSTS IN FINLAND. The standard of living in Finland is high and so are prices, though by mid-1984 inflation was running at a reasonably low level. You can keep costs down very substantially by following the suggestions given in the following pages, but don't expect to get very far on a shoestring.

A typical day in Helsinki might cost two people:

Hotel (Moderate) with bath and breakfast	220 Fmk
Lunch, in Moderate restaurant, no beer or wine	66
Dinner, in Moderate restaurant, with beer	110
Transportation (2 buses, 1 taxi)	40
	436 Fmk

Sample costs. A cinema seat for one, 20–30 Fmk; visit to a museum or castle, 1–5 Fmk; coffee, 2 Fmk; beer (per bottle), 6.05 Fmk; house wine, by the carafe (¼ liter) in a Moderate restaurant, 20 Fmk, by the bottle, 48 Fmk; coke, 2–5 Fmk; a moderate taxi ride in Helsinki, 21 Fmk, elsewhere, 18 Fmk; an average bus ride in Helsinki, 4.60 Fmk, elsewhere, 3.50–4.00 Fmk.

SEASONAL EVENTS. The summer season lasts from mid-May to mid-September, reaching its peak in July, but note that some facilities, such as lake traffic, only operate from June through August. This is also the period of the summer "Finland Festivals," are featuring major cultural events. The skiing season begins in January in the southern parts of the country and lasts until the end of April in the north.

A free calendar of events is published every year by the Finnish Tourist Board. The following are the major ones.

January 1 is the signal for New Year celebrations throughout the country.

FINLAND

March sees the Lahti Games, Finland's premier winter sports event, in the early part of the month. Toward the end of the month the Lady Day Festival is held at Enontekiö in Lapland, a gathering of the Lapps with traditional dress being worn, and reindeer driving and lassoo-throwing competitions among the celebrations. The end of March also sees the Ounasvaara Winter Games, an international winter sports event at Rovaniemi on the Arctic Circle.

April 30 is Vapunaatto, May Day eve, a nation-wide celebration that combines Labor Day and student festivities into one emphatic welcome to the Spring. Many never see their beds this night.

May 1 is Vappu or May Day itself, when the celebrations are continued from the previous night. Students and workers also have their own processions.

June has a whole host of activities. Lasting from June all the way to September is the Pradznik Festival, a traditional Orthodox church and folk festival, centered mainly on eastern Finland. The most important event is held in Ilomantsi in mid-July.

Two events at the beginning of the month are the Vaasa Summer, a puppet theater festival, and the Kuopio Dance and Music Festival, with performances ranging from classical ballet to modern dance. In the second week of June the Ilmajoki Music Fesitval takes place, with performances of all kinds of music, including openair Finnish folk opera. The Naantali Music Festival, in the third week of the month, has mainly classical music.

Midsummer Eve, or Juhannusaatto, sees nation-wide celebrations on the weekend closest to the 24th, with festivities around immense bonfires, or, in western Finland, maypoles. At the very end of the month and stretching into July the Jyväskyla Arts Festival is held, with varied cultural events on a different theme every year.

July sees the Savonlinna Opera Festival, three weeks of international performances in the splendid setting of medieval Olavinlinna castle; but there are also many song and orchestral events in various other locations around the country.

The middle of the month has the Pori Jazz Festival, an international event with openair concerts and street events. Also starting in the middle of the month and lasting through to the end of July is the Kuhmo Chamber Music Festival, two weeks of chamber music featuring Finnish and international musicians.

The third week of July sees the Kaustinen Folk Music Festival, when over 1,000 performers participate in dozens of concerts. The very end of the month sees Sleepyhead Day in Naantali and Hanko, when the laziest person in town is thrown into the sea; it's a day-long fun event.

August is the time of the Lahti International Organ Week; the main venue is the beautiful Church of the Cross. The middle of the month sees the Turku Music Festival, a week-long celebration of all types of music, and the Tampere Theater Summer. The main venue is the splendid openair Pyynikki Theater, with its revolving auditorium.

Finally, the end of the month sees the Helsinki Festival, two weeks of cultural events of all kinds.

NATIONAL HOLIDAYS. January 1 (New Year); January 12 (Epiphany); April 5, 7, 8 (Easter); April 30–May 1 (Labor Day); May 16 (Ascension); May 25–26 (Whitsun); June 21–22 (Midsummer); November 2 (All Saints); December 6 (Independence Day); December 24–26 (Christmas).

LANGUAGE. Finnish and Swedish are both Finland's official languages, but Swedish is the mother tongue of only 6.3% of the population. Finnish belongs to an entirely different language group (Finno-Ugrian) from Swedish and the other Nordic languages. It's melodic, logical, easy to pronounce but very difficult to learn (it has 14 grammatical cases). Fortunately, English is widely spoken throughout the tourist industry and by many in the young to

FACTS AT YOUR FINGERTIPS

middle age groups. Older people tend to know German better. It's worth learning some basic phrases in Finnish for the surprised pleasure it will give!

CUSTOMS. Residents of non-European countries may bring duty-free into Finland 400 cigarettes or 500 grams of tobacco products; plus, for persons aged 20 or over, 2 liters of beer and 2 liters of other mild alcoholic beverage (those aged 18 or 19 may bring in 2 liters of beer and 1 liter of other mild alcoholic beverage); plus, non-commercial goods to the value of 500 Fmk.

For residents of European countries, the same duty-free allowances are valid with the exception that only 200 cigarettes or 250 grams of other tobacco products may be imported.

There is no limit to the amount of foreign currency that may be imported or exported, but no more than 10,000 Fmk may be exported.

HOTELS. There is no official grading system for Finnish hotels. Nonetheless, basic standards are very high. Nearly all hotels, except some in the lower price ranges, have baths or showers in all or most rooms. Similarly, many hotels also have restaurants, and in the more expensive there will usually be music or dancing on some or all evenings. A number also offer roulette, though as the maximum stake is 5 Fmk you can't expect to win a fortune. Any other special amenities, such as night clubs or sports facilities are indicated in our hotel listings.

For inexpensive accommodations, Finland also boasts a number of summer hotels, most common in larger towns and cities. These usually modern and excellent-value hotels act as student accommodations for the rest of the year, and some are run by students themselves. The lowest-priced accommodations of all are boarding houses *(matkustajakoti)*.

Motorists especially will find the Finn Check scheme useful. The scheme operates from June 1 to August 31 and gives discounts in around 160 hotels throughout the country. You may buy as many of the checks as you want—they operate really as a series of vouchers—and each check costs 110 Fmk per night, per person, inclusive of breakfast. In the most expensive hotels, an additional 50 Fmk will be charged, in less expensive hotels the check also covers the cost of a self-service lunch. Only your first night can be reserved in advance, but reservations for subsequent nights can be made free of charge from any hotel participating in the scheme. Details from travel agents and the Finnish Tourist Board.

Prices. We have divided all the hotels we list into four categories—Deluxe (L), Expensive (E), Moderate (M) and Inexpensive (I). These grades are determined solely by price.

Two people in a double room can expect to pay (prices in Fmk)

	Helsinki	Elsewhere
Deluxe	450—600	400—500
Expensive	300—450	250—400
Moderate	200—300	150—250
Inexpensive	120—200	90—150

These prices include breakfast and a 15% service charge. Some hotels also include a free morning sauna and swim.

SELF-CATERING. In summer, most Finnish families disappear to their summer cottages, usually tucked away in the forests by some lake, sea or river shore, or on an island. Visitors can follow suit by renting a summer cottage, either in a holiday village or in a more remote location. In many holiday villages, sports facilities are provided and in most cases a sauna and use of a boat

FINLAND

are available free or for a small charge. The range of weekly rentals is from 400–2,500 Fmk, average 700–1,200 Fmk.

A main booking center for the whole country is *Lomarengas,* Museokatu 3, 00100 Helsinki 10 (90–441 346).

FARM VACATIONS. A free booklet, *Farm Holidays in Finland,* is issued by the Finnish Tourist Board. These increasingly popular accommodations give you an opportunity to participate in rural family life. They are usually available on half- or full-board basis, and include a sauna.

A central booking office for the whole country is *Suomen 4H-liitto,* Bulevardi 28, 00120 Helsinki 12 (90–645 133).

CAMPING. The best way to enjoy Finland's wealth of lake-and-forest scenery is to get out into it. There are camping sites near most cities and throughout the countryside, open to all from May or June to August or September. About 350 camp sites classified into three grades have been established by various organizations in Finland and, as the Finn has an eye for beauty, most of them have choice locations on the shore or lake, river or sea. In about 200 of these, caravans can be linked to the electric current (220 V.) Only a few sites have facilities for filling and changing gas bottles, which can be done at most service stations and hardware stores. Outside these sites camping is not generally allowed without the landowner's permission. It is also of the utmost importance in this forest-bound land to take the greatest possible care with regard to fire.

Camping is handled by the *Finnish Travel Association's Camping Department,* Mikonkatu 25, 00100 Helsinki 10 (90–170 868). A system of Finncamping Checks is sold as part of a package arrangement through some travel agencies. Otherwise the charge is usually in the 18–45 Fmk range per family (two adults, two children, a car and tent or caravan). And though services vary, the charge normally includes facilities for cooking, washing, and dish washing. At some sites, those not holding an international camping pass (FICC) must have a national camping card costing 5 Fmk.

A free list of camp sites is available from the Finnish Tourist Board, and most of them are marked on the excellent *Suomen Tiekartta* (Finnish Road Map) and *Autolijan Tiekartta* (Motorist's Road Map), both available from bookshops or the *Automobile and Touring Club* in Helsinki.

YOUTH HOSTELS. There are about 150 hostels, graded in four categories, throughout the country. They range from small farms or manor houses to empty schools, many offering "family rooms." There are no age restrictions and all are also open to motorists. Coffee and refreshments are available at most of them, and there are usually cooking facilities. Many have boats or bicycles for hire. Overnight charges range from 20–49 Fmk per night. Sleeping bags may not be used, but sheets can be hired at an additional charge.

Further details from the *Finnish Youth Hostels Association,* Yrjönkatu 38 B 15, 00100 Helsinki 10 (90–694 0377). A free list of hostels is available from the Finnish Tourist Board.

RESTAURANTS. The choice of eating places in Finland, in main towns and cities at any rate, is varied both in style and price. Away from larger centers, the best restaurants are likely to be in hotels. Considering Finland's high standard of living and consequent reputation for priceyness, meal costs are generally reasonable, especially if you stick to the *table d'hôte,* or suggested menus, served in many hotels and restaurants, though usually only between certain fixed times. This is usually fairly early, especially in more moderately-priced places. You'll find that food is always attractively served.

FACTS AT YOUR FINGERTIPS

The Finnish Tourist Board promotes a special Finland Menu. This comes in various price categories and is available at some 200 restaurants and cafes throughout the country, and often features national dishes. A full list of all restaurants participating in the scheme is available from the Finnish Tourist Board. In addition, the Tourist Board also produces a *Lappi à la Carte* leaflet listing gourmet routes in Finnish Lappland, again with the emphasis on traditional dishes.

Fast food is readily available in cities, especially Helsinki. Similarly, English-type "pubs," with inexpensive food have become popular.

Prices. We have divided the restaurants in our listings into three categories— Expensive (E), Moderate (M) and Inexpensive (I). These grades are determined solely by price.

Prices, per person, excluding drinks (in Fmk)

	Helsinki	Elsewhere
Expensive	60—100	40—60
Moderate	40—60	30—50
Inexpensive	28—40	18—30

These prices are for *table d'hôte* menus; for *à la carte* dishes expect to pay approximately twice as much. In addition, a 14% service charge is added to all meal checks. On Friday evenings and at weekends and on public holidays *and* the day before, this rises to 15%.

FOOD AND DRINK. The cold table (*voileipäpoytä* in Finnish) is as varied and attractive here as elsewhere in Scandinavia. Other national specialties include *poronkieltä* (reindeer tongue with lemon sauce), *poronkäristys* (reindeer casserole, particularly good in Lapland), *hiilillä paistettua silakkaa* (Baltic herring grilled over charcoal), *kalakukko* (fish and pork baked in a rye flour crust, specialty of Kuopio), *lihapullia* (meat balls with a tasty sauce), and *uunijuustoa* (oven cheese). If you happen to be around from about the end of July to early September, don't miss a crayfish party—when the Finns don bibs and tuck into boiled crayfish, flavored with dill and washed down with fiery *akvavit* far into the white nights. Desserts are good and rich, and to digest them they provide some delicate liqueurs, *Lakka* (cloudberry) and *Mesimarja* (Arctic bramble).

Be warned that imported spirits are very expensive, those bottled in Finland merely expensive! Wines are relatively reasonably priced, especially if bottled in Finland.

Licensing laws are quite liberal. Beer is served from 9 A.M. onwards and other liquor from noon until the restaurant closes. Beer is now also sold in supermarkets, many cafés and a number of otherwise unlicensed premises. Otherwise ALKO, the Finnish State Alcohol Monopoly, have many shops where you can buy all kinds of alcoholic drinks. But note the strict laws (see *By Car*) governing drinking and driving.

At the other end of the scale, drinking water is safe everywhere, and the excellent coffee is drunk in great quantities, black or with cream.

TIPPING. A general guide line is that you should tip for good service, but that tipping is not otherwise taken for granted. The service charges mentioned under *Hotels* and *Restaurants* (see above) are sufficient, though a few extra coins are usually left. There's an obligatory cloakroom fee to hotel or restaurant doormen—usually 3 Fmk. Taxi drivers, theater ushers, washroom attendants, barbers and beauty salon attendants are not normally tipped.

FINLAND

MAIL. Post offices are marked *Posti* and mailing boxes are yellow, normally fixed to a wall. Postage stamps can also be bought in most hotels, many kiosks, tobacconists and some book shops.

Postal rates for airmail letters are 1.70 Fmk to the U.K., 2.20 Fmk to the U.S.; postcards airmail 1.50 Fmk to the U.K., 1.70 Fmk to U.S.

TELEPHONES. Public booths are well distributed. The procedure is to lift the receiver, insert the money and dial; the money is returned if you are not connected. If you're checking a number in the telephone directory, remember that the Finnish letters "å," "ä" and "ö" come at the end of the alphabet.

CLOSING TIMES. Shops are usually open from 9 to 6 Monday to Friday, 9 to 2 on Saturdays; they may close an hour earlier in summer. In Helsinki, department stores also stay open until 8 P.M. on Monday and Friday. Additionally, in the subway by Helsinki rail station, shops of all kinds operate until 10 P.M., including Sunday. On national holidays, all shops are closed and on the eve of national holidays they observe Saturday times.

Banks open 9.30 to 4 Monday to Friday, closed on Saturdays. Longer hours apply in international airports, harbors, main rail stations and certain exchange bureaux in main cities.

SPORTS. The Finnish landscapes seem tailor made for a number of outdoor activities, all of which have a very large following among the Finns themselves. The best areas for individual sports are outlined in the regional chapters, but some principal addresses for information are as follows. The Finnish Equestrian Federation, Finnish Golf Union, Finnish Yachting Association, Finnish Motor Boat Association and Finnish Canoe Association are all at Topeliuksenkatu 41 A, 00250 Helsinki 25. Flotilla sailing is arranged through the Nautic Center, Karhusaari 02100 Espoo 10, near Helsinki.

GETTING AROUND FINLAND. If you can work out your detailed itinerary in advance, you can buy a tourist ticket, valid 2 months, combining travel by train, lake boat, bus and plane, offering savings of about 10%.

By air. Finland has an elaborate service of internal flights operated by *Finnair*. Helsinki is connected with most Finnish towns and there are also cross-country flights linking several of these. Fares are among the lowest in Europe, with special rates for family groups, children, pensioners (over-65s), and weekend discounts. In addition, the *Finnair Holiday Ticket* ($240) offers unlimited travel on domestic routes for a maximum of 15 days to any non-resident of Finland.

By train. Finland's extensive rail system reaches all main centers of the country. The network stops short a little north of the Arctic Circle. Standards of comfort and cleanliness are high. Most trains have first and second class; a few have second class only. A *Finnrail Pass* gives unlimited travel for 8, 15 or 22 days; sample cost for 15 days is 470 Fmk second class, 705 Fmk first class (no reductions for children). Seat tickets (7 Fmk) are recommended and, on special fast trains (12 Fmk), are obligatory. Round trip tickets cost slightly less than double one way ones. Reductions apply to groups of a minimum of three persons.

Car-carrying trains operate from Helsinki, Turku or Tampere to Rovaniemi; also from Helsinki to Oulu, Kajaani and Kemi.

Finland is also a partner in the following international schemes: *EurailPass* (first class only, unlimited travel); *Eurail Youth Pass* (second class only, unlimited travel for under-26s); *Nordturist* (unlimited travel for 21 days throughout Scandinavia); *Inter Rail Ticket* (for under-26s); *Inter Rail S Ticket* (for men over

FACTS AT YOUR FINGERTIPS 151

65, women over 60). See "Getting Around Scandinavia" in *Planning Your Trip* for further details.

By bus. Bus travel plays a leading role in Finland with an extensive network, linked in many cases to the rail system. In the far north and in parts of the east, it is the only means of public transport. Costs are lower than by rail. There is an additional charge (4 Fmk) for express services. Reductions apply to children, family groups and to over-65s holding a special *65 Card* costing 5 Fmk and available from bus stations in Finland.

By car. An extensive road-building programme has resulted in a good network of asphalted main roads throughout much of the country. In the south, four-lane motorways grow a little annually. Other major roads have a surface of oil and sand. Where the old dirt roads still remain, as in many parts of the far north and remoter areas, the gravel is often bound with clay and dustlaying chemicals, thus making the surface even and hard; but when it rains these roads can be somewhat slippery, dirty and smelly. In winter all main roads are kept open for traffic and the going is usually good. During the spring thaw (April-early June, according to latitude), some roads are at times impassable or very difficult to negotiate; look out for the road sign *"kelirikko"* which warns you of bad conditions. Another warning sign, with appropriate drawing, concerns elk (moose) and reindeer; take heed for collision with up to 600 kg. of elk is no joke. They are especially active at dusk.

Speed limits are 60, 80, 100 or 120 km per hour, according to the classification of the road and traffic density, and the limit applicable is indicated by signs. If it is not, the basic speed limit is 50 km.p.h. in built-up areas, 80 km.p.h. in the countryside, or, on motorways, 120 km.p.h.

At intersections, cars coming from the right have priority. The rights of pedestrians on pedestrian crossings must be rigorously observed. The use of seat belts is now compulsory. *Important:* the laws regarding drinking and driving are very strict. If you exceed the exact limit of .5 milligrams of alcohol in the blood, the penalty is nearly always imprisonment or a heavy fine.

Super gasoline costs 3.54–3.68 Fmk per liter. There is a good network of service stations and repair garages, but it is wise to keep topped up if you are in less populated regions or taking minor roads in wilderness areas.

The address of the *Automobile and Touring Club of Finland* is Kansakoulukatu 10, 00100 Helsinki 10 (90–694 0022).

A selection of car hire firms is given under "Useful Addresses" in *Practical Information* sections.

By bike. Cycling has become very popular, and planned routes are now arranged in many areas through local tourist offices. Cycles can be hired in most tourist centers.

By boats/cruises. Modern comfortable ferries link Helsinki and Turku with the Åland islands; both cities also have a network of small ferries serving island communities within their orbit.

Lake steamers and motorships, with restaurants on board, ply the inland waterways. Increasingly, trips are organized as cruises, ranging from a few hours or a weekend to several days, but there is still a number of regular schedules (see Regional Chapters) which you can join or leave at will. A pilotage scheme is available on several lake routes, taking care of the transfer of the motorist's car between terminals at reasonable charges. In addition, boat services operate to the Saimaa Canal from Lappeenranta.

On foot. Almost the whole of Finland is ideal hiking country, and in many areas there are marked trails with refuge huts for overnights. Remember that many of these areas are remote and wild, especially in the north and east, and it is always essential to be properly equipped, to heed local advice, and tell your hotel or friends where you are heading and how long you intend to be away. A free booklet *Hiking Routes* is issued by the Finnish Tourist Board.

PRELUDE TO FINLAND

Scandinavia's Rich Secret

by
ANDREW BROWN

Finland is the toughest of the Scandinavian countries. It is tough in both sense of the word: resilient and difficult. For foreigners it is difficult: Finland is the only European country that had a common border with Russia in 1939 and yet remains independent today. It is also the only country in the world to have fought Communist Russia to a standstill—in the Winter War of 1939-40; and though the Finns lost the "Continuation War" of 1941-44, when they fought alongside the Germans against the Russians, Finland survived even this loss. The Russians annexed a great deal of territory; installed a governor, and extracted very heavy reparations from their defeated foes. But they did not absorb all Finland. The governor went home after three years to die of cirrhosis; the refugees from the ceded territories were settled; the reparations were duly paid. Finland survived and prospers.

But such a history leaves scars: the Finns are nowadays both fiercely patriotic, and quite free of aggressive nationalism. They are not proud of their wars, though they are proud of the way in which they have subsequently learned to live in peace with Russia. They remain resilient, and very difficult for foreigners to understand. The language is part of this difficulty. Finnish is partially comprehensible to Estonians, and related to the Lapp languages. It is also very distantly related to Hungarian. But it is quite unrelated to the other Scandinavian languages. Nor would the Finns have things otherwise. They think of their language as far more flexible and expressive than either Swedish or English—and most Finns speak both these languages.

Flamboyant Savagery

Language is not the only thing that sets Finland apart from the rest of Scandinavia. Helsinki is probably the least Americanized city in capitalist Europe. The other Scandinavian capitals all have their natures partially concealed by modern buildings. Helsinki remains as it was, and very beautiful. Everything *works* with Scandinavian efficiency, but it all *looks* central European. There is a flamboyant savagery about the Finns quite alien to the rest of Scandinavia: a Finnish writer was once approached by a broke colleague for a loan.

"I can't," he said, "I'm broke myself." And to prove his point, he took from his wallet his last hundred Finnmark bill, tore it into shreds, dumped them in the ashtray—this happened in a pub, of course—and set light to them. This is the sort of behavior one would expect from a Polish or Hungarian nobleman between the wars, not from a phlegmatic Scandinavian. But then, the Finns are anything but phlegmatic. If they seem to accept their appalling history calmly, this is not indifference, but tough-mindedness. They could say with Bishop Burnett that "Things are as they are. They will be as they will be. Why, then, should we wish to be deceived?"

This tough-mindedness sets them apart from practically everyone else in the world; but even if Finland is not like anywhere else—and that is one reason why it is worth visiting—you can at least partly prepare yourself for it by imagining a Central European country that has been shifted 500 miles north into Scandinavia.

The countryside is Scandinavian: smallholdings set among the lakes and forests of the interior, and along the coast the marvellous Baltic archipelagoes. It is a tourist cliché to speak of the lakes and forests of Finland, just as one cannot mention Lapland without talking about the Midnight Sun. But in fact these things do not reward the traveller. They are indeed beautiful, and entirely overwhelming, but once you have seen them that is that; they are not stimulating in themselves. Unless you have business in the forest, or beneath the midnight sun, you will very rapidly get bored. You get nothing for free in Finland, and if you wish to be interested in the wilderness, then you must bring your own interests to it. If you can do that, then you will be repaid handsomely. The fisherman, the hunter, and the botanist will all find their heart's desire in the Finnish wilderness.

Life and Death on the Lakes

The Finnish smallholder must have all these skills and more. It is through this sort of pioneer farming that the Scandinavian element has impressed itself upon Finnish culture. Even well within modern times, times in Finland were very difficult, and the memories of extreme poverty remain potent. A sense of being crushed by unending, almost fruitless toil is perhaps the proper explanation of "Scandinavian gloom." It is an emotion that has little to do with long winter nights—then at least you can rest—and a great deal to do with constant physical fatigue. Even now there are stories where the darkness of the forest seems to douse and choke the clear aseptic brightness of modern life.

Consider the life and death of Lauri Rapala. He was born in 1907, in great poverty. His father was unknown, so he was given the surname of Rapala—the name of the village where he was born. After a spell as a lumberjack, he set up as a freshwater fisherman, using nets and standing lines in the lakes of the interior. It was not a profitable life. For 21 years he lived with his wife—and, eventually, seven children—in a one-room cabin the size of a modern Finnish living-room, with only one bed. So as not to waste time while rowing between his nets, he whittled small fish out of spruce bark, stuck hooks in them, and towed them behind the boat while he rowed. These "wobblers" caught a great many fish, and Rapala started to make a little extra money by selling them.

Then the war came. He spent five years on the Russian Front, and survived. He returned to his old way of life: fishing all day, and in the evenings whittling his "wobblers." He had posted some to Finnish friends in America, where they began to sell. The hobby had become a business, and then an enormous success. By 1964, Lauri Rapala had set up a factory, and was selling 800,000 a year. He was rich, though still generous, and he could move his family to new houses. And then, one night in 1965, his youngest son drowned in one of the lakes where the original wobblers had been tested. The circle was closed: the lakes that had first kept the Rapala family alive, and then made them rich had claimed their price. After the accident, Lauri Rapal set out to drink himself to death. It took him nine years: he was a strong man. He is buried beside his drowned son. The business flourishes still.

It is a very Finnish story: one of toughness, and almost unimaginable resilience; hard work, success, and finally vodka. But anyone who thinks it shows an unreasonable gloominess, should consider what vast reserves of courage and cheerfulness Lauri Rapala must have had to get as far as he got.

Neighbors and Colonizers

In the plain of Western Finland, along the Baltic Coast, another Scandinavian influence is felt. These are the Swedish-speaking regions. The Swedes and Finns have had a long and complicated relationship, that somewhat resembles that between England and Ireland. The parallels cannot be drawn too far, but they are nonetheless illuminating. They help one also to understand the relationship between Finland and Russia. The frontier that Stalin drew in 1940 is almost exactly the same as the frontier that Peter the Great drew up when Finland was still a Swedish colony in 1721.

In the beginning, the Swedes were military colonizers. The Finnish-speaking tribesmen of the interior traded in valuable furs, and the Swedes wished both to control this trade, and to profit from the valuable fishing in the gulf of Bothnia. These were the days before there were any Russians. The word "Russian" itself comes from the name that Swedish Vikings foraging eastwards gave themselves—"Rus."

Then the Swedes settled, like the Normans in Ireland. They formed the land-owning, aristocratic classes, divided by languages from the peasantry that worked for them. And, just as in Ireland, it was among the these settlers, absorbed in the country yet still remote from the indigenous population, that nationalism first became an articulate political force. As early as the 14th century, the Swedish ruling class in Finland were championing Finnish interests against central authority.

The differences start in the 16th century, with the Reformation. The Finns did not retain a separate religion to their conquerors, as the Irish did, and this homogeneity of religion helped to preserve the separate languages. When the Swedes and Finns adopted Protestantism, the Bible was translated into Finnish, and this was to prove crucially important. Finnish nationalism in modern times is based on the Finnish language, and without a Finnish Bible, it is questionable whether the language would have survived, any more than Gaelic for example has. Nor have the Finns fought the Swedes as the Irish fought the English. But the two countries have had a long, intimate, and fertile connection, and the Swedish-Finns, like the Anglo-Irish, have made contributions to literature and the arts quite out of proportion to their numbers, which are tiny.

Architecture and Alcohol

Culture returns us to the Central European, German influence. This is apparent to the visitor in two ways. The first is the astonishing beauty of Finnish buildings. Architecture is an art in Finland, with a power comparable to that of any other art form, and it is taken very seriously. The results do not much resemble anything anywhere else in the world. All one can say about Finnish taste is that it owes nothing to anyone else's ideas of what is beautiful. When it works, it enlarges our ideas of what can be beautiful—and what more can any art achieve? Even when it fails, it both expresses and transmits strong, clear emotions. There is a building in Helsinki that appears to be modelled on the artist's worst hangover: life-sized, or slightly larger, rendered in grey and brown knobbly concrete. No one could call it beautiful, but it is one of the most eloquent buildings you could ever hope to see.

The German influence, too, is apparent in the formality of Finnish manners. Flowers for the hostess at a dinner party; little formal speeches of thanks; a certain reserve symbolized by the use of a formal and an informal pronoun for "you":—socially Finland remains a very old-fashioned place. This stress on formality and reserve may seem odd when practically the first thing any visitor to Finland will notice are the drunks. Finland without alcohol is as difficult to imagine as Finland without winter, yet even in his cups a Finn retains a certain style.

"Nowadays," you may be told, "we make it a point of honor to remain upright until the dinner is over." But even if a Finn is going to get so drunk that he passes out nose first into the soup, he will still dress up to do so. Such a gesture has no value if it is made in a T-shirt. Statistics will tell you that the Finns do not drink all that much. The French, for example, drink far more alcohol every year, but they do so as an accompaniment to other things. There is nothing absent-minded about a Finnish drunk. Nothing could be further from Finnish practice than the American working lunch, where you get just drunk enough to prevent yourself from doing any serious work for the rest of the day, but not so drunk as to make social life impossible, or even difficult. If a Finn has decided to drink, he will keep at it for as long as is humanly possible, and then perhaps for a couple of bottles longer. It is, if you like, another example of Finnish tough-mindedness, of a capacity to grasp the essentials of any situation, and to cling to this insight no matter what the cost may be.

This digression on alcohol should not be allowed to obscure the fact that Finland is a very civilized country. History and geography have forced the Finns to face some of the nastiest aspects of human life. They have faced them with great courage and a certain elegance. Just as their proximity to Russia sharpens their appreciation of the value of their own freedom, so the ghastliness of Finnish history has reinforced their appreciation of the arts of peace. There are five theaters in Helsinki, a city of scarcely half-a-million people which also contains the largest and best bookshop in Scandinavia.

Denmark may be more comfortable, and Norway may be more beautiful. Sweden is richer, and easier for the visitor to appreciate. But Finland is the strangest and the most civilized of all the Scandinavian countries, as well as the toughest. It is quite unique; and when you have peeled off all that is Scandinavian, and all that is Central European, there remains a quality that is as rich and secret as the language. You would have to live there for years to discover quite what the secret is—and when you had discovered it, you would probably find it incommunicable.

HELSINKI

Broad Avenues and Bright Prospects

Helsinki (Helsingfors to the Swedish-speaking minority) is very much a city of the sea, sprawling over peninsulas, curving round bays and spilling out across islands that are linked by bridges, causeways or even by boat to the central hub. This hub fills a chunky peninsula where, somehow, without overcrowding, are to be found the single-chamber Parliament, or Eduskuntatalo, the leading technical and educational institutes, art galleries, theaters, museums, business houses, the great Olympic Stadium (scene of the 1952 Olympic Games and 1983 World Athletics Championships), much outstandingly good architecture, the head offices of every big industrial enterprise—in fact all that constitutes the legislative, cultural, scientific, commercial and economic life of the country. And still there is space left for airy parks and broad streets.

Helsinki owes its origin to the chance whims of two monarchs, and its development has largely been the result of a series of accidents. Some 400 years ago King Gustav Vasa of Sweden ordered the citizens of four Finnish towns—Porvoo (Borgå), Tammisaari (Ekenäs), Rauma and Ulvila (Ulfsby)—to leave their homes and proceed to a place on the rapids of the river Vantaa. There they were to build a new town to attract the trade of the Estonian city of Tallinn, thus challenging the power of the Hanseatic League. Like many another city of this period, Helsinki's growth was interrupted by wars, plagues and fires. Not until

1809, when Finland became an autonomous Grand Duchy of Russia, was Helsinki really able to start developing; then three years later, it became the capital of Finland, primarily because the Czar found Turku (Åbo) was too far away from Russia and too close for comfort to Sweden to remain the capital of his newly-acquired territory.

The first of the accidents which stimulated the new capital's growth was the Great Fire in Turku. So much of the latter city was gutted that the University was moved bodily to Helsinki, which at once became the cultural as well as the political center of the country. In 1808, thanks to chance again, another Great Fire played a part in the young city's future. This time it was Helsinki that burned, allowing the German-born architect, Carl Ludvig Engel, an opportunity to plan the rebuilding of the city practically house by house and stone by stone. It is to Engel and to his partner, Ehrenström, that Finland must be grateful for her beautiful capital.

Around the Senate Square which Engel designed stand the Thomiokirkko or Cathedral, the University and the State Council Building—a group built in one of the purest styles European architecture can boast. Perhaps it was Engel's inspiration, but from his day Finland has always had good architects. Two of them, Eliel Saarinen and Alvar Aalto, became world famous. You can hardly walk down any street in Helsinki without seeing splendid examples of the work of modern architects whose fame is already spreading beyond the frontiers of Finland, such as Heikki and Kaija Sirén, Rewell, Ervi, Petäjä, Pietilä, Penttilä.

Under the protective shadows of the island fortress of Suomenlinna (Sveaborg), Helsinki developed rapidly during the 19th century. The lovely park-strewn suburb of Töölö, and the island residential districts of Lauttasaari, and Kulosaari came into being quite recently. Still newer suburbs grew up in the post-World War II period, and the city continues to expand, as indeed it must, for like most capitals, it has not enough accommodation for all who wish to live there.

Exploring Helsinki

From the visitor's point of view, Helsinki has the virtue of compactness. Once you have oriented yourself and found out where you are on the city map, it will be difficult to get lost. The piers where ships from abroad dock, the railway station and, to a lesser extent, the air terminal, are all in the center of the city. So, however you come, you can start wandering around on foot at once.

It's an idea to begin by finding a good viewpoint from which to make your first survey of the city—such as the top of the Olympic Stadium Tower, the hill of Tähtitorninmäki, or comfortably installed in a top floor bar or restaurant as in the Torni, Hesperia, Inter-Continental, Palace or Vaakuna hotels. Probably the first buildings you will notice are the Cathedral and the railway station, both in the center of the town, together with the House of Parliament and the Stadium Tower. The great broad street running from the center of town through the city and out to the main Turku road is Mannerheimintie, or Mannerheimvägen. (*Tie* in Finnish, and *vägen* in Swedish, mean street or road.) Along this broad avenue, named after Finland's great hero Marshal Mannerheim, you'll be able to pick out the Post Office, the House of

HELSINKI

Parliament, the National Museum (Suomen Kansallismuseo), the fine new Concert and Congress Center of Finlandia Hall, and the Olympic Stadium.

Another simple introduction to the city is to take the No. 3T or 3B tram which describes a figure of eight through the city, bringing you back to where you started. No. 3T has a commentary in several languages in summer (see "Tours" in the *Practical Information*). After that, as good a way as any of planning your sightseeing is to start in the middle and work outwards. In point of fact, by far the greatest number of interesting sights are contained in the central part of the city, branching out from the Market Square (or Kauppatori).

The Helsinki Tourist Office have prepared a series of walking tours with maps, which you'll also find very helpful. Their premises are near the Market Square down by the South Harbor, a few hundred meters from some of the passenger quays. The colorful openair market flourishes each morning, ending around 1 P.M. and reopening in summer from 3–8, when the emphasis is more on arts and crafts. Grouped around the striking statue of Havis Amanda, by Ville Vallgren, are the flower sellers, and the fruit stalls with their mountains of strawberries, raspberries, blueberries, red currants and red whortleberries. You may even be fortunate enough to find the special cloudberry, *suomuurain,* which grows mostly north of the Arctic Circle and is ripened by the Midnight Sun. Fish are sold at the very edge of the harbor, straight from the boats in which they were caught earlier in the morning and so fresh they are still alive and flipping. Meat and dairy produce is sold in the covered market, just beyond the fish stalls.

Havis Amanda, incidentally, the beautiful lady loved by all Helsinkiites, is a center of *vapunaatto* (May Day Eve) revelry. She is crowned again and again on this festive night with the white caps of students who wade through the protective moat surrounding her and climb up to embrace her. Another statue of interest is the stone monument commemorating the time in 1833 when Nicolas I and his consort Feodorovna visited Finland. Known as the Empress Stone, it stands just opposite the quay used by the small boats which head out to the islands of the harbor archipelago. Follow the west side of the harbor southwards, past the arrival quay for ships from Sweden, Germany and Denmark and you come to the pleasant park and district of Kaivopuisto, where most of the embassies are to be found. On the shore, here and elsewhere, you will see small wooden structures from which some Helsinki housewives follow an old tradition of scrubbing their carpets in the sea (or lake, as the case may be).

Leading out of the Market Square are Pohjoisesplanadi and Eteläesplanadi (North and South Esplanades), with gardens running up the middle. Compositely known as Esplanadi, it is a dangerous thoroughfare at four every afternoon when car owners race up the street on their way home from the office. In an hour, peace reigns and Esplanadi becomes a favorite promenade. Lovers of porcelain, fashion and crafts will find here some of the display rooms of Finland's top firms.

Along the edge of the Market Square facing the sea stands the President's Palace, with a sentry in field grey patrolling the entrance. Near it you can see the City Hall and various administrative buildings, and behind it towers Helsinki's most famous landmark, the Cathedral. A few steps in the direction of this impressive church bring you to the

FINLAND

HELSINKI 161

HELSINKI

1. Air Terminal
2. Ateneumin Taidemuseo
3. Bus Station
4. City Hall
5. City Theater
6. Eduskuntatalo (Parliament)
7. Findlandia Hall
8. Finnish Design Center
9. Helsingin Kaupunginmuseo
10. House of Nobility
11. Kauppatori (Market Square)
12. Linnanmäki Amusement Park; Peacock Theater; Swimming Stadium
13. Main Post Office
14. Mannerheim-museo
15. National Opera Theater
16. National Theater
17. Olympic Stadium
18. Presidential Palace
19. Railway Station
20. Rowing Stadium; Operetta Theater
21. Suomen Kansallismuseo
22. Swedish Theater
23. Temppeliaukion Kirkko
24. Tourist Information Office
25. Tuomiokirkko
26. University
27. Uspenskin Kathedraali
F. Ferry

Senate Square, where facing you is Walter Runeberg's statue of Alexander II of Russia, the enlightened despot who was so well disposed to Finland.

Opposite the Cathedral a lively new shopping center adds a new dimension to this gracious but rather quiet district. Most of the streets leading off the Senate Square contain government and administrative offices. Snellmaninkatu is named after J. V. Snellman, whose statue stands in front of the Bank of Finland. Known as the awakener of the Finnish national spirit, he was instrumental in persuading the Russian overlords to accept the idea of a separate Finnish currency and officially recognizing the Finnish language. Nearby is the House of the Estates, site of Finland's Parliament during the Russian era, and now occupied by several scientific societies.

Snellmaninkatu leads into the district of the town known as Kruununhaka, a sleepy residential quarter built around the northern harbor, from which regular boats cross to the island of Korkeasaari on which lies Helsinki's zoo.

The Senate Square and Baron Mannerheim

But return to the Senate Square. With your back to the Cathedral and its enormous cupola, look left, and you will see the gleaming "onions" of the Orthodox Uspenski Cathedral towering high above the rocky island of Katajanokka. Connected to the mainland by a bridge, this district houses the customs administration and other port offices.

On January 28, 1951, the great Marshal Baron Carl Gustaf Mannerheim, died in Switzerland. He was flown back to his native land and lay in state in the Cathedral for three days before his state funeral. The citizens of Finland were allowed to pay their last respects to him while he lay there in the dim vastness of this lovely church. Young war widows, children, officers and soldiers, who had fought in Finland's wars against Russia under Mannerheim's leadership, filed past in their thousands, and the only sound was one of weeping. Never in Finland's history has there been such an expression of national feeling.

But let us leave the Senate Square and the "Whitehall district" of Finland, which, quite appropriately, is rather sleepy and slow. Let's take a stroll up Aleksanterinkatu, the main shopping center of Helsinki. At its top end, where it runs into Mannerheimintie, is Stockmann's, Finland's largest department store. At this corner is the famous statue of the Three Smiths by Felix Nylund, a common rendezvous for people who have to meet somewhere in town. Near the center of town, off Esplanadi, is the permanent Finnish Design Center at Kasarmikatu 19, where there is a changing display of the best in Finnish industrial art. Goods displayed here can be bought in Helsinki's departmental stores.

Where Mannerheimintie meets Esplanadi stands the Swedish Theater where plays are given in the Swedish language. To reach its Finnish-language rival, the older National Theater, you must turn around and go back down Aleksanterinkatu to the first street on your left, which leads into the huge square in front of the railway station, which is also the hub of the city's impressive new metro network. Here, however, the National Theater is overshadowed by the massive station itself, designed by Eliel Saarinen. Although he became an American citizen during the war, Saarinen's last wish was to be buried in his native country. His ashes were flown to Finland in 1950 and interred in the grounds of the beautiful home he built for himself along the shore of lovely Lake Hvitträsk.

Right opposite the Railway Station is the City Center, a complex of shops, restaurants, cafés, with underground passageway of shops leading to the railway station. Also on the opposite side of the Railway Square and facing the National Theater is the Art Museum of the Ateneum (Ateneum in Taidemuseo), which houses specimens of the works of Finland's greatest painters. The paintings of Gallen-Kallela, Hugo Simberg, Albert Edelfelt, Eero Järnefelt, and Magnus Enckell are known far beyond the borders of Finland and are well worth a visit. You'll also find some sculptures by the world-famous Wäinö Aaltonen.

Just behind the railway station stands the Main Post Office. Opposite is Sokos House which contains a large hotel and restaurant, plus numerous business offices and shops. Nearby is one of Helsinki's latest shopping precincts, Kaivopiha, an attractive oasis linked to the railway station, with an entrance from Mannerheimintie.

The Post Office marks one boundary of the "downtown" part of the capital. From here, following Mannerheimintie, let us go northwards toward Töölö. A stone's throw from where we stand takes us to the House of Parliament, the impressive structure in red granite which seems so striking because of the ample space around it. No rows of flats and business houses crowd in here. The Parliament building looks solid and, if you go inside you will agree that it is solid, built to withstand storms of debate within and criticism from without. It is lavishly and beautifully decorated inside, even to the special caucus room reserved exclusively for the score or more of lady representatives. Finland's 200 members of Parliament are elected by proportional representation.

National Museum and Olympic Stadium

A short distance west of Mannerheimintie in Tempeliaukio is the Temppeliaukion church, one of Europe's most unusual modern churches, built into the living rock. Designed by the brothers Timo and Tuomo Suomalainen, it is also used as a concert hall. Returning to Mannerheimintie, just a few hundred meters from the House of Parliament is an odd-looking edifice with a tower which gives it a church-like appearance. This is the National Museum, which houses a large collection of ethnographical exhibits illustrating Finland's history. This area, round the shores of Töölönlahti Bay, is the site of the big new city plan designed by Alvar Aalto. Part of this is Finlandia Hall, the Concert and Congress Center, designed by him, which opened in 1971, close to the shore of the bay and not far from the National Museum. The Intercontinental Hotel is nearby, while the ultramodern City Theater, designed by Timo Pentilä, is across the bay.

Further along Mannerheimintie, not half an hour's walk from the railway station and but ten minutes by tram, rises the imposing tower of the Olympic Stadium. One of the finest views of Helsinki can be obtained from the top of this tower. Further north still and to the east of Mannerheimintie, less than two miles from the city center, is Helsinki's fine new International Fair Center, which opened in 1975. Exhibition halls, a restaurant, cafeteria and well-planned open spaces make it a showplace of its kind.

The street leading off at right angles from Mannerheimintie, Helsinginkatu, leads to the beautiful Botanical Gardens and the Water Tower, from which there is a fine view. Nearby is Helsinki's Tivoli, or permanent amusement park, called Linnanmäki, offering top-class entertainment of universal family appeal. Continuing along this street we come to the "East End" of Helsinki where there is little to see except proof of the fact that Helsinki has indeed no slums.

If you return to Mannerheimintie and cross the street, you will find yourself in the hospital center of the capital. Actually, it is still Töölö, the biggest residential district, but in this little section are concentrated most of the city's biggest and newest hospitals.

Although it may seem a startling suggestion, you next ought to go and see the Hietaniemi Cemetery. When you get there, you will realize why it is a favorite rendezvous for a promenade, for it is a beautiful place. Marshal Mannerheim is buried in the military section. It is a custom to place candles on each grave on Christmas Eve, a moving sight.

Another place well worth visiting is Arabia. This is one of the largest pottery factories in Europe and can be visited by appointment. Although the Arabia plant is some distance out of town, a tram service runs practically to the gate.

Helsinki's Islands

A number of Helsinki's most interesting sights are on islands, a major one being the fortress of Suomenlinna. In fact, this covers a series of interlinked islands, and the entire Finnish army assisted in its construction, which began in 1748. Under the protection of this fortification, Helsinki first began to develop and flourish. Once called the Gibraltar of the North, it was indeed impregnable, never having been taken by assault. Twice, however, it was surrendered without a fight, first to the Russians in the war of 1808–1809, and then during Finland's war of independence when the German Baltic Division, assisted by the Finnish Civic Guard, captured the city of Helsinki. During the Crimean War a combined British and French fleet bombarded the fortress and the fires caused by the cannonade convinced the army that the fortress could not withstand modern artillery fire.

Yet Suomenlinna is more than an ancient military monument with several museums; its parks and gardens are lovely, especially in the spring. One of the forts near the historic King's Gate has an outstanding restaurant. Bearing the historic name of Walhalla, it has been changed as little as possible. This group of islands is currently being developed into an all-purpose center for cultural and leisure activities. It includes the new and expanding Nordic Arts Center, focussing on exhibitions and the promotion and exchange of ideas on Scandinavian art.

Seurasaari, an island linked by bridge to the mainland, is another good spot to visit. It houses a delightful open-air museum which brings together houses, ranging from simple huts with turf roofs to lovely wooden villas furnished with original furniture, transported from various parts of the country. The President's residence is nearby.

Yet another island, Korekeasaari, houses Helsinki's zoo, reached by ferry from the North Harbor or by foot bridge from Mustikkamaa. The

HELSINKI

latter is the home of Helsinki's Summer Theater and is also an island, but accessible by road bridge. Close to Korkeasaari, the islet of Hylkysaari is the setting for the recently opened National Maritime Museum. Still more islands in this sea-girt city feature such amenities as bathing beaches, restaurants, yacht clubs.

Environs

A trip round some of Helsinki's suburbs will give you a fine idea of that special Finnish talent for creating imaginative residential districts in harmony with nature. These provide the theme for some sightseeing tours, but if you want to explore independently, head for Tapiola Garden City, situated in the forests and close to the sea, to the west of town.

PRACTICAL INFORMATION FOR HELSINKI

GETTING TO TOWN FROM THE AIRPORT. A frequent bus service links Seutula Airport with the air terminal (Hotel Intercontinental, Töölönkatu 21) in the city center. Journey time is 30 minutes, cost 10 Fmk. Check-in takes place at the airport.

TOURIST INFORMATION. Free publications such as *Helsinki This Week* and *Helsinki Today* are good sources of information on what's on and where. The City Tourist Office is at Pohjoisesplanadi 19 (169 3757).
Helsinki Card. This entitles you to free entry to about 40 museums and other sights, a guided sightseeing tour and unlimited travel on the city's public transport. The cost is 45 Fmk (one day), 60 Fmk (two days), 70 Fmk (three days); under half-price for children. You can buy it from the City Tourist Office, hotels and some travel agencies.

USEFUL ADDRESSES. Embassies. *Canada,* Pohjoisesplanadi 25B (171 141). *U.K.,* Uudenmaankatu 16–20 (12 574). *U.S.A.,* I. Puistotie 14A (171 931).
Car Hire. *Avis,* Fredrikinkatu 36 (6944 400). *Europcar Car Rental,* Mariankatu 24 (661 151). *Finn-Rent,* Hietaniemenkatu 6B (497 161). *Hertz,* Polarpoint, Itälahdenkatu 20 (675 211). *Inter-Rent,* Hitsaajankatu 7 (775 6133).
American Express. Keskuskatu 4B (651 266).
Main Post Office. Mannerheimintie 11 (1951).
Emergency hospital for foreigners. Helsinki University Central Hospital (4711). Information on health care available round the clock on 736 166.
Emergency (police, fire, ambulance) tel. 000.

TELEPHONE CODES. The telephone code for Helsinki is 90. To call any number in this chapter, unless otherwise specified, this prefix must be used. Within the city no prefix is required.

FINLAND

HOTELS. Reservations are highly recommended as the city is busy with conferences and exhibitions when it is not full of tourists. There is a Hotel Booking Service in the railway station for hotel and private accommodations, open mid–May through mid–Sept., Mon. to Fri. 9–9, Sat. 9–7, Sun. 12–7; mid–Sept. through mid–May, Mon. to Fri. 9–6, closed Sat., Sun. Unless otherwise stated, all the hotels listed below are open all the year and have licensed restaurants.

Deluxe

Hesperia. Mannerheimintie 50 (441 311). 285 rooms, pool, night club. A short stroll from center. AE, DC, MC, V.

Inter-Continental. Mannerheimintie 46 (441 331). 468 rooms, pool, nightclub. Perhaps Helsinki's plushest. A short stroll from center. AE, DC, MC, V.

Kalastajatorppa. Kalastajatorpantie 2 (488 011). 235 rooms, pool, tennis, boating, fishing. Glorious seashore situation and linked by underground passage-way with famous nightclub of same name. AE, DC, MC, V.

Marski. Mannerheimintie 10 (641 717). 162 rooms, nightclub. Centrally-located. AE, DC, MC, V.

Presidentti. E. Rautatiekatu 4 (6911). 500 rooms, several restaurants, pool, nightclub, all-night café. Central. AE, DC, MC, V.

Seurahuone. Kaivokatu 12 (170 441). 114 rooms, nightclub, disco, elegant Café Socis. Very central, opposite rail station. AE, DC, MC, V.

Torni. Yrjönkatu 26 (644 611). 158 rooms, several restaurants with different specialties, in high rise block. Central. AE, DC, MC, V.

Vaakuna. Asema-aukio 2 (171 811). 290 rooms. Central location on main railway station square. AE, DC, MC, V.

Expensive

Dipoli. Jämeräntaival (461 811). 213 rooms, most with sea view, sports facilities. In garden suburb of Otaniemi, 9 km. from center. AE, DC, MC, V.

Helsinki. Hallituskatu 12 (171 401). 85 rooms, disco. Very central. AE, DC, MC, V.

Klaus Kurki. Bulevardi 2 (602 322). 75 rooms, central. AE, DC, MC, V.

Korpilampi. (Forest Lake) Lahnus (855 8431). 162 rooms, pool, nightclub, sports facilities, popular for congresses. Lovely forest setting in Espoo, 20 km. northwest of city. AE, DC, MC, V.

Merihotelli. Hakaniemenranta 4 (711 455). 87 rooms, pool, disco. AE, DC, MC, V.

Olympia. L. Brahenkatu 2 (750 801). 100 rooms, disco, pool. AE, DC, MC, V.

Palace. Eteläranta 10 (171 114). 59 rooms. Stunning view over South Harbor. AE, DC, MC, V.

Rantasipi. Near Seutula airport (826 822). 176 rooms. Excellent for transit stop-overs with shuttle service to airport. AE, DC, MC, V.

Tapiola Garden. Tapiontori (461 711). 82 rooms, pool. In the garden suburb of Tapiola. AE, DC, MC, V.

Moderate

Aurora. Helsinginkatu 50 (717 400). 75 rooms, unlicensed restaurant. AE, MC, V.

Dipoli Summer Hotel. Jämeräntaival (461 811). 363 rooms, summer only. AE, DC, MC, V.

Espoo. (523 533). 13 km. (8 miles) from city. 94 rooms, rooftop pool. AE, DC, MC, V.

Finn. Kalevankatu 3B (640 904). 28 rooms, no restaurant.

Haaga. Nuijamiestentie 10 (578 311). Not so central, part of the Hotel and Restaurant College, 40 rooms, pool, tennis. AE, MC, V.

Helka. P. Rautatienkatu 23 (440 581). 101 rooms, unlicensed restaurant. AE, MC, V.

Hospiz. Vuorikatu 17B (170 481). 141 rooms, unlicensed restaurant. AE, MC, V.

Martta. Uudenmaankatu 24 (646 211). 44 rooms, unlicensed cafeteria. AE, MC, V.

Ursula. Paasivuorenkatu 1 (750 311). Not so central, 43 rooms, cafeteria. MC, V.

Inexpensive

Academica. Hietaniemenkatu 14 (440 171). Summer only, 217 rooms, pool, disco, tennis. AE, MC, V.

Kustaa Vaasa. Vaasankatu 10 (765 600). Summer only, 90 rooms. AE, DC, MC, V.

Mercur. Ruusulankatu 5 (407 313). Summer only, 50 rooms. AE, DC, MC, V.

Satakuntatalo. Lapinrinne 1 (694 0311). Summer only, 64 rooms. AE.

Cheapest accommodations are in boarding houses such as **Clairet,** It. Teatterikuja 3 (669 707). **Erottajanpuisto,** Uudenmaankatu 9 (642 169). **Lönnrot,** Lonnrotinkatu 16 (605 590). **Omapohja,** It. Teatterikuja 3 (666 211). **Pensionat Regina,** Puistokatu 9 (656 937).

Camping

Rastila. 13 km. (8 miles) east of city center.

Youth Hostels

Stadionin Retkeilymaja. Olympic Stadium, Pohjoinen Stadionintie 3B (496 071). Open all year.

Academica. Hietaniemenkatu 14 (440 171). Open June through Aug.

HOW TO GET AROUND. By tram/bus. A ride costs 4.60 Fmk (small reduction for ten-ride tickets), allowing transfers within a one-hour period. A tourist ticket valid for 24 hours for unlimited travel costs 24 Fmk from the Helsinki Tourist Office or public transport ticket offices (but not on board the vehicles). But don't forget the Helsinki Card, which gives unlimited travel on all public transport within the city. The 3T tram, with commentary in several languages in summer, follows a figure-eight circuit right around the city center.

By metro. The first section of Helsinki's splendid new subway goes from the main railway station northeast to Itäkeskus, where it links with bus services to the outer suburbs. Same fare and transfer system as tram/bus above.

By taxi. These bear the sign "taksi." Minimum charge is 9.40 Fmk, with a surcharge added after 6 P.M. and at weekends. The fare increases according to the length of journey, amount of luggage and number of passengers. No tips are necessary or expected.

By boat. Regular ferries link the South and North Harbors with island communities, in addition to sightseeing boats throughout summer.

On foot. The Helsinki City Tourist Office have worked out some excellent itineraries, with maps, for exploring various parts of the city on foot.

TOURS. There is a good selection of half– and full–day sightseeing tours of the city, some extending to the suburbs. Sightseeing trips by boat leave from the Market Square (South Harbor) visiting Helsinki's archipelago. Some include a lunch stop ashore.

Further afield is Hvitträsk with its lovely lake and the former studio-home of three leading Finnish architects. Another short excursion is to Ainola, near Järvenpää, the lovely home of Sibelius, now open to the public. The composer is buried in the grounds. Among other trips that can be made in one day, three are especially recommended: Porvoo Borgå, Hanko and Hämeenlinna combined with Aulanko. You can travel to Porvoo by boat in three hours, returning by bus; or go both ways by boat.

Full details of all these trips are available from the tourist office.

FINLAND

MUSEUMS. The opening times given below are for the summer; check for other seasons. Entrance fees are usually 2–5 Fmk; in a few cases admission is free. Don't forget the Helsinki Card which gives free admission to around 40 museums and other sights.

Ateneumin Taidemuseo (Art Museum of the Ateneum). Railway Square. Mainly paintings, sculptures, drawings, etc., by Finnish artists; some foreign and old masters. Open Mon. to Fri. 9–5, Wed. 9–8, Sat. and Sun. 11–5.

Arabian museo (Museum of Arabia). Hämeentie 135. Table ware and ceramic art by this famous Finnish porcelain factory. Open by appointment. By terminal of tram no. 6.

Gallen-Kallelan museo (Gallen-Kallela Museum). Leppävaara, Tarvaspää, reached by no. 4 tram to Munkkiniemi, then pleasant 2 km. walk. The home and works of one of Finland's greatest painters in charming surroundings. Open Tues. to Thurs. 10–8, Fri. to Sun. 10–5.

Helsingin Kaupunginmuseo (Helsinki City Museum). Mannerheimintie, beside Finlandia Hall. Art, furniture, archives illustrating history of city. Open daily 12–4, Thurs. 12–8.

Helsingin kaupungin Taidemuseo (Helsinki City Art Museum). Tamminiementie 6, near Seurasaari. Finnish and French art from 20th century. Open Wed. to Sun. 11–6.30.

Mannerheim-museo (Mannerheim Museum). Kalliolinnantie 14, Kaivopuisto. Home of Marshal Mannerheim, containing his collected trophies. Open Fri. and Sat. 11–3, Sun. 11–4.

Ruiskumestarin talo (Burgher's House). Kristianinkatu 12. Oldest wooden house in Helsinki (1817). Open Sun. to Fri. 12–4, Thurs. 12–8; closed Sat.

Seurasaaren ulkomuseo (Seurasaari Open Air Museum). Seurasaari island. Farm and manor buildings from different parts of the country. Open daily 11.30–5.30, Wed. 11.30–7.

Suomen kansallismuseo (National Museum). Mannerheimintie 34. Three sections: prehistoric, historic, ethnographic. Open 11–4 daily, Tues. also 6–9.

Suomen merimuseo (National Maritime Museum). Hylkysaari island, ferry 10 min. from Market Square (South Harbor). Specialized maritime history museum. Open daily 10–3.

Suomen rakennustaiteen museo (Museum of Finnish Architecture). Kasarmikatu 24. Archives of Finnish architecture, past and present. Open daily 10–4.

Taideteollisuusmuseo (Museum of Applied Arts), Korkeavuorenkatu 23. Development of design. Open Tues. to Fri. 11–5, Sat. and Sun. 11–4.

PARKS AND ZOOS. The *City Conservatories* are in Eläintarha Park, open Mon. to Sat. 12–3, Sun. 11–3. Two central parks are *Tähtitorninmäki* (Observatory Hill) on the west side of the South Harbor and, a little to the south, *Kaivopuisto*—both rather more natural than formal. A beautiful oasis west of the center is the shore-side cemetery of *Hietaniemi;* Marshal Mannerheim is buried here. A little north of this is *Sibelius Park* with its distinctive sculpture by Eila Hiltunen commemorating the great Finnish composer.

Helsinki *zoo* is on the island of Korkeasaari, reached by ferry from the North Harbor, or by foot bridge from Mustikkamaa island which is accessible by road. Open June and July 10–9; shorter hours in other months.

HISTORIC BUILDINGS AND SITES. Eduskuntatalo (Parliament). Mannerheimintie. An imposing granite building, designed by Siren and completed in 1931. Shown to visitors Mon. at 2, Sat. at 11, Sun. at 12 and 1 (except when Parliament meets and holidays). Public admitted to gallery during full session.

Stadionin torni (Olympic Stadium Tower). Eteläinen Stadionintie 3. Offers superb views. Open Mon. to Fri. 9–8, Sat. and Sun. 9–5.

Suomenlinna. Frequent ferry service from South Harbor. Fortifications on series of islands, currently being developed into a multi–purpose center: Nordic

HELSINKI

Arts center, museums, summer restaurants, summer theater, guided tours. Museums open daily 11–5.

Temppeliaukion kirkko (Temppeliaukio church). Lutherinkatu 3. Beautifully carved out of living rock to the plans of Timo and Tuomo Suomalainen. Open Mon. to Sat. 10–9, Sun. 12.30–4, 6–9.

Toumiokirkko (Cathedral). Senaatintori. Fine classical building by Engel dating from the 1830s. Open 9–7, Sun. 12–7.

Uspenskin Kathedraali (Uspenski Cathedral). Kanavankatu 1. Completed in 1868, the most important Orthodox church in Finland. Open Mon. to Fri. 10–4.

Vanhakaupunki (Old Town). Original site of city founded in 1550, reached by tram no. 6.

SPORTS. Golf. There is a good 18–hole course at Talin kartano (Tali Manor), some 7 km. (4 miles) from city center. The tourist office can supply details about green fees and playing conditions.

Saunas. Nearly all hotels have them, but also recommended (and inexpensive) are those attached to swimming halls listed in the leaflet *Helsinki Tourist Information.*

Swimming. The rocky shores and small beaches in and around the city offer plenty of opportunities. Among them are: Uunisaari, an island opposite the residential and diplomatic district of Kaivopuisto; the sandy beach of Hietaranta; the island of Seurasaari (accessible on foot); Mustikkamaa; farther out on the island of Pihlajasaari; Suomenlinna. Also at the Swimming Stadium or at Kumpula openair pool.

Tennis. There are indoor courts at: Tennispalatsi, Ruskeasuo, Yrjönkatu 21B, Kulosaari, Meilahti Sports Park, Töölö Sports House, Tali Tennis Center, Myllypuro Tennis Center. Outdoor courts are at: Kaisaniemi, Kalastajatorppa, Kulosaari, Meilahti Sports Park, Taivallahti.

Winter sports. In winter, you can ski in the heart of the city through the parks (as some Helsinki–ites do on their way to work!), or anywhere in the surrounding countryside. More specifically, Nuuksionpää, northwest of the city by bus, offers good terrain or, further afield, the ridges of Hyvinkää can be reached by bus or train. There is also ice skating at numerous public rinks in Helsinki.

MUSIC, MOVIES AND THEATERS. Music. The *National Opera Theater* at Bulevardi 23–27 offers performances of international and Finnish operas and ballets. Concerts are often held in the magnificent Aalto-designed *Finlandia Hall* on Mannerheimintie. Musical performances are also held in a number of attractive settings in summer, such as organ recitals on Sunday evenings in the Cathedral, concerts in *Temppeliaukion Church* and the *House of Nobility,* and openair concerts of various kinds in several parks.

Movies. You can choose from about 50 movie theaters. All films are shown in their original language with Finnish subtitles.

Theaters. The Finns are enthusiastic theatergoers and, though the main theaters will present most visitors with a language problem, it's well worth attending one of the several openair summer theaters for the atmosphere and setting. The main ones are: *Helsinki Summer Theater* on Mustikkamaa island; *Operetta Theater* at the Rowing Stadium; *Peacock Theater* (variety shows) at Linnanmäki amusement park; *Ryhmäteatteri* on Suomenlinna; *Student Theater,* Seurasaari; *Summer Theater,* Central Park, in the grounds of Laakso riding field; *Töölönranta Summer Theater* at Töölölahti Bay.

SHOPPING. Prices may not be low, but quality is high as is the standard of design of most Finnish products. Items to look out for especially are glass, handwoven textiles, fashion wear, furs, stainless steel, metal and semi-precious jewelry, wooden toys. Hand-made candles in brilliant or subtle shades are charming inexpensive buys, while at the other end of the scale, the Finns produce beautifully designed modern furniture! Note that some shops

FINLAND

offer an export service, dispatching your purchases abroad and thus entitling you to a 16% (food stuffs 5%) deduction of sales tax.

If you haven't much time to shop around, your best bet is to go to the permanent exhibition at the *Finnish Design Center*, Kasarmikatu 19, or one of the big stores. The most famous is *Stockmann's*, founded in 1862, filling a block between Aleksanterinkatu, Mannerheimintie and Keskuskatu; it has an efficient export service.

Two big marketing groups with a nationwide network are SOK with their *Sokos* stores and hypermarkets, and E Marketing with their *Centrum* and *EKA-Market* (cut price) department stores.

The main shopping streets are Pohjoisesplanadi and Aleksanterintie, and the smaller streets off these. Stroll along Pohjoisesplanadi (North Esplanade) and you'll find the showrooms and shops of many major firms such as *Arabia* (ceramics and porcelain), *Nuutajärvi* (glass), *Marimekko* and *Vuokko* (fashions and fabrics), and *Aarikka* (costume jewelry, wooden buttons and other crafts).

For a selection of small shops, go to the Station Tunnel (linking the rail station with the City Center complex opposite), or *Hakaniemi Market Hall*, where 50 shops above the covered food market in Hämeentie offer interesting variety. Several new and attractive shopping precincts include *Kaivopiha*, off Mannerheimintie and linked to the railway station. A smaller one, *Agora*, is off Unioninkatu near the South Harbor, and others are burgeoning.

A "must" is a morning visit to Kauppatori (Market Square) where the lively openair market flourishes, year-round, by the South Harbor, selling fruit, vegetables, fish and household goods. It reopens in the afternoon in summer when the emphasis is on arts and crafts.

Among specialist shops, the following are particularly worth a visit: Jewelry—*Kalevala Koru*, Unioninkatu 25 (especially beautiful traditional Kalevala motifs); *Galerie Björn Weckström*, Unioninkatu 30, or *Lindroos*, Aleksanterinkatu 48 (truly handsome modern jewelry). Furs—*Turkistuottaja* have an auction at Martinkyläntie 40 (in the suburb of Vantaa); *Ali Fur*, Erottaja 1–3; *Polar Turkis*, Yrjönkatu 1; *Fur–Lyx*, Eteläesplanadi 22.

Finally Scandinavia's biggest bookshop is *Akateeminen Kirjakauppa* (Academic Bookstore), Keskuskatu 1.

RESTAURANTS. Helsinki's eating houses cater for every taste and pocket, ranging from the gourmet to the budgeteer in a hurry. All establishments listed below are fully licensed unless otherwise stated.

Expensive

Adlon. Fabianinkatu 14 (664 611). Smart and with floorshow. AE, MC, V.

Bellevue. Rahapajankatu 3 (179 560). Russian style. DC, MC, V.

Fen Kuan. Eerikinkatu 14 (604 077). Oriental cuisine.

Fennia. Mikonkatu 16 (175 433). Floorshow. MC, V.

Havis Amanda. Unioninkatu 23 (666 882). By the South Harbor; two sections of which one specializes in fish. AE, MC, V.

Kaivohuone. (177 881). In attractive location in Kaivopuisto Park looking out to the harbor; floorshow. AE, DC, MC, V.

Kalastajatorppa. (Fisherman's Cottage). Kalastajatorpantie 2 (488 011). A famous showpiece, beautifully situated near the seashore, but bearing little resemblance to the original fisherman's cottage! Floorshow. See also under *Hotels.* AE.

Karl Konig. Mikonkatu 4 (171 271). Subdued, sophisticated setting, below ground. AE, MC, V.

Katajanokka Casino. Laivastokatu 1 (653 401). In fine seashore location. MC, V.

Kulosaari Casino. Hopeasalmenpolku 1 (688 201). Pleasantly placed on island of the same name, but accessible by road. Dancing. AE, DC, MC, V.

Mestaritalli. Toivo Kuulan puisto (498 431). Formerly stables, now an elegant restaurant in a seashore park. Dancing. AE, MC, V.

Motti. Töölöntorinkatu 2 (494 418). Has some unusual items on the menu. AE, DC, MC, V.

HELSINKI

Savoy. Eteläesplanadi 14 (176 571). A favorite lunch place for Finland's tycoons. Designed by Alvar Aalto. DC, MC, V.

Svenska Klubben. Maurinkatu 6 (628 706). Intimate manorial atmosphere in listed historic house by North Harbor. AE, DC, MC, V.

Walhalla. (668 552). On fortress island of Suomenlinna, reached by short ferry journey from South Harbor. You dine in the authentic 18th–century atmosphere of a fortress never taken by storm, in a setting of ancient ramparts and flowering lilac bushes—one of the memorable sights of Helsinki. Summer only.

Moderate

Agora Tea Room. Unioninkatu 30. Especially for tea enthusiasts.

Cafe Socis. In Seurahuone hotel, elegant rendezvous, lunch (M), coffee and cakes (E).

El' Greco. Eteläesplanadi 22 (607 750). Greek food. AE, MC, V.

Esplanadikappeli. (179 242). In the Esplanade near the South Harbor, recently renovated with several sections including openair summer restaurant. MC, V.

Happy Days. Pohjoisesplanadi 2 (624 023). Adjoining Swedish Theater, with several restaurants of various price levels and types. AE, MC, V.

Karelia. Käpylänkuja 1 (799 088). Karelian specialities. MC, V.

Kultainen Orava. Siltasaarenkatu 18 (714 155). Dancing. MC, V.

Parrilla Espanola. Eerikinkatu 4 (603 305). Spanish food. MC, V.

Perho. Mechelininkatu 7 (493 481). Run by the Helsinki Hotel and Restaurant College and recently renovated. Excellent value. AE, MC, V.

Punainen Hattu. Keskuskatu 7 (639 527). Intimate atmosphere. DC, MC, V.

Säkkipilli. Kalevankatu 2 (605 607). Cozy English atmosphere. AE, MC, V.

Troikka. Caloniuksenkatu 3 (445 229). One of a chain of three small eating places, specializing in Russian food.

Tullinpuomi. Mannerheimintie 118 (412 058). Dancing. MC, V.

Välskarin Kellari. Hallituskatu 3 (174 395). Intimate cellar atmosphere in the "Whitehall" of Helsinki. MC, V.

Wanha Manala. Töölönkatu 3 (446 940). Finnish specialities. MC, V.

Wellamo. Vyökatu 9 (663 139). Small, intimate, rustic atmosphere, good food if you like garlic. MC, V.

White Lady. Mannerheimintie 93 (413 562). Elegant. AE, DC, MC, V.

Inexpensive

Carrols. Self-service hamburger restaurants in Mannerheimintie 19, in the City Passage, and in Puotinharju Shopping Center; disposable plates and cups; good value. Unlicensed.

Chez Marius. Mikonkatu 1 (669 697). French cuisine, beer and wine only.

Davy's. Fredrikinkatu 22 (651 939). Good tavern-style pizzeria. Beer and wine only. AE, MC.

Eliel. In the railway staton (177 900). Genuine *art nouveau* style. Self-service. MC.

Groovy. Ruoholahdenkatu 4 (694 5118). Good jazz restaurant. MC.

Kasvisravintola. Korkeavuorenkatu 3. Self-service vegetarian restaurant. Unlicensed.

Kellarikrouvi. P. Makasiininkatu 6 (655 198). Cozy wine cellar atmosphere. AE, DC, MC.

Pizzeria Rivoli. Albertinkatu 38 (643 455). Italian food. DC, MC.

Tuuliviiri. Eteläranta (662 958). Beer and wine only.

Vanhan Kellari. Mannerheimintie 3 (654 646). In cellar of Old Students' House. MC.

Voudin Grilli. Torivoudintie 1. Beer and wine only.

Many modern and attractive cafés (*kahvila* or *baari*), dotted about town, offer refreshments and sometimes hot meals, as well as coffee, cakes, etc. Among several chains of cafés and low-priced restaurants are: **Fazer** and **Go-Inn.**

A selection of English-style pubs includes: **Angleterre** (M), Fredrikinkatu 47 (647 371), AE, MC; **Annan Pub** (M), I. Roobertinkatu 16 (633 316); **Richard's Pub** (M), Rikhardinkatu 4 (667 232); and **St. Urho's Pub** (M), Museokatu 10 (446 940).

NIGHTLIFE. Young people wanting to meet their Finnish counterparts can try one of the following student clubs: Botnia, Museokatu 10; Harald's, Kasarmikatu 40; KY, Pohj. Rautatiekatu 21; Poli, Lönnrotinkatu 29; Tavastia, Urho Kekkosenkatu 4–6; TF-Discotheque, Otakaari 22, Otaniemi.

For family fun, there's Linnanmäki amusement park (summer only), Helsinki's Tivoli with Peacock Theater, side shows, open air dancing, Monorail and jungle train.

See under *Hotels* for establishments with nightclubs and under *Restaurants* for those featuring floor shows and dancing.

THE SOUTH COAST AND ISLANDS

The Gateway for Finnish Culture

Anyone with a weakness for islands will find a magic world of them stretching along Finland's coastline. There, in the Gulf of Finland and the Baltic, over 30,000 islands form a magnificent archipelago. Westward from Turku ride the rugged but fascinating Åland Islands group, forming an autonomous province of their own. Turku, the former capital, was also the main gateway through which cultural influences reached Finland over the centuries. The coastal district of Porvoo, east of Helsinki, is another area stuffed with history and cultural associations.

In this section, where two place names are given for a center, the second is the Swedish one and it indicates that there is a substantial Swedish-speaking element in the population. An exception is the Åland archipelago, where the population is entirely Swedish-speaking and therefore preference has been given to Swedish names.

Exploring the South Coast

Fifty km. (31 miles) east of Helsinki and on the coast lies Porvoo (Borgå), one of the oldest towns in Finland. It was only Helsinki's privileged position, plus the usual run of fires and wars, that kept Porvoo from growing into a great port. The major landmark of Porvoo Cathedral dates from the 15th century and it is famous as the setting for the first meeting of the Finnish Diet, called by Czar Alexander I in 1809, at which he proclaimed Finland an autonomous Grand Duchy. Today it is thought of as a town of poets and painters, for it has been the home of many of Finland's most famous names in the realm of arts and letters; the colorful wooden houses and shady alleys of the old district are enchanting. The greatest of Porvoo's sons was J. L. Runeberg, the national poet, whose home, kept as it was when he lived in it, stands at the corner of Runeberginkatu and Aleksanterinkatu in the new part of town. Also worth seeing are the old Town Hall, now a historical museum, and the Ville Vallgren Museum housed in typical 18th-century buildings.

Loviisa comes next, a rather charming summer resort; a special feature is its open-air theater with revolving auditorium, on a smaller scale to the famous one at Tampere.

Farther east are the two islands of Kotka and Hovinsaari, at the mouth of the Kymi river. Kotka was practically unknown until the naval battles of Ruotsinsalmi fought off its shore in 1789 and 1790 revealed its suitability as a harbor. (There is an open-air museum to the battle on Varissaari (Fort Elisabeth) reached by boat.) The Russians also saw the Kotka area as an excellent place to build frontier fortifications against attacks by land or sea from the west. Work on the fortifications was begun in 1791, and at the same time the fortress of Kyminlinna was built on the northern end of Hovinsaari. In 1855, during the Crimean War, a British naval force bombarded the island, landed on the shore, and fortifications and garrison buildings were destroyed. Ten years later, thriving sawmill industry brought it back to life, and today Kotka is Finland's largest export harbor for timber.

An idyllic haven, an hour away by motor boat, is the island of Kaunisaari, with beautiful beaches of fine sand.

West of Helsinki

Hvitträsk, 28 km. (17 miles) west of Helsinki, was the home of famous Finnish architects Eliel Saarinen, Armas Lindgren and Herman Gesellius. Today it is a museum, with an excellent restaurant attached, beautifully situated above Hvitträsk lake. There are Stone Age traces in the vicinity.

Next comes Tammisaari (Ekenäs). Predominantly Swedish-speaking, Tammisaari has little of historical interest, although like most towns along Finland's south coast, it, too, can produce a cannon ball that was fired at it by the British fleet during the time of the Crimean War. But it is a pretty town, with narrow old streets, and the drive to it from the capital is a pleasant one. The forests here are more of the broad-leaved variety, as opposed to the vast majority of Finland's forests, which are of pine and fir. Tammisaari also goes in for the cultivation of what the foresters term exotic plants and trees, and it is interesting to find oak trees here, some of the very few in Finland. An excursion from Tammisaari is to the ruins of medieval Raasepori (Raseborg) Castle, about 16 km. (10 miles) east.

THE SOUTH COAST AND ISLANDS 175

An hour's drive farther to the west is the popular seaside resort of Hanko (Hangö), with its long stretch of sandy beach. This very popular sailing center was once a major launching point for emigrants to the U.S.A., Canada and Australia.

Turku, the old Capital

Finland's oldest city, founded in the 13th century, and its capital until 1812, Turku is situated on both banks of the Aura river. With a population of 165,000, it is the country's third largest city and is sometimes called "the cradle of Finnish culture". Commercially its great importance lies in the fact that its harbor is the most easily kept open throughout the winter. In fact, the very word, *turku,* means trading post. It is also widely known for its shipyards. It has both Finnish and Swedish Universities, the new buildings of the Finnish one being well worth a visit.

Called Åbo by the Swedish-speaking Finns, Turku is the center of the southwest part of the country, whose land is fertile and winters are milder. With a cathedral over 700 years old, the city is still the seat of the Archbishop of Finland. Although gutted by fire in 1827, the cathedral has been completely restored. In the choir can be seen R. W. Ekman's frescos portraying Bishop Henry (an Englishman) baptizing the heathen Finns, and Mikael Agricola offering the Finnish translation of the New Testament to Gustav Vasa of Sweden.

Where the Aura river flows into the sea stands Turku Castle, the city's second most important historical monument. The oldest part of the fortress was built at the end of the 13th century, whereas the newer part dates back to the 16th century. Once a prison, it has been attractively restored and contains today the Historical Museum, with collections of furniture, portraits, arms and implements covering 400 years.

Among the unusual features of Turku is the Handicraft Museum. A group of wooden houses that survived the 1827 fire, it contains over a score of small shops of that period. The comb-maker, the weaver, and the potter still ply their trades using equipment and techniques that date back a century and a half. In summer, visitors may also try their hand under expert guidance. Notable, too, is the Resurrection Chapel, one of the outstanding creations of modern Finnish architecture. Also well worth visiting in Turku are the Sibelius Museum and the Wäinö Aaltonen Museum, the latter devoted to the works of Finland's great sculptor and additionally featuring changing exhibitions of contemporary art. Both are on the banks of the River Aura as is the striking modern theater.

Besides several old churches erected during the Middle Ages not far outside the city, there is the Ruissalo National Park, located on an island though accessible by road; it has the largest oak woods in the country. There is also a pleasant sandy beach, modern accommodations and good sports facilities.

But one of the greatest attractions in the vicinity of Turku is the beach at the coastal resort of Naantali (Nådendal), where the President of Finland has his summer residence. Finland's oldest known author, Jöns Budde, was a monk in the 15th-century monastery whose chapel now serves as the church. There are water-bus trips on certain summer evenings from Turku to Naantali. Other good excursions from Turku include the Tour of Seven Churches, covering some of the delightful medieval churches of the area.

Åland Islands

From Turku there are air and sea connections to the Åland (Ahvenanmaa) islands, where rural calm combines with fine coastal scenery. In all, there are over 6,500 islands and skerries, a handful of them inhabited by a total population of 23,000. Virtually all of them are Swedish-speaking and the Ålanders are very proud of their largely autonomous status. Nearly half the population lives in the pleasant little capital of Mariehamn (Maarianhamina) which straddles a narrow peninsula, its two harbors linked by the shady main avenues of Norra Esplanadgatan and Storagatan. The Maritime Museum near the main harbor is well worth visiting for the islands have a very long seafaring tradition; nearby is the splendid four-masted barque *Pommern.*

Åland is particularly well organized for cycling and fishing packages, motor tours (you can go island-hopping on the network of car or passenger ferries), farmhouse holidays and self-catering cottages—2,000 of them scattered about the islands. These are marvelous sailing waters though, as yet, only a few yachts are available for rent.

There is much of historic interest for the archipelago has been inhabited since prehistoric times. Some of the medieval stone churches on the islands are particularly well preserved, notably those of Jomala, seven km. (four miles) north of Mariehamn; Finström, 25 km. (16 miles) north; Hammarland, 21 km. (13 miles) northwest; Eckerö, 37 km. (23 miles) northwest; Sund, 25 km. (16 miles) northeast; and Lemland, 13 km. (eight miles) southeast. Also of interest are the scattered ruins of a big naval fortress built by the Russians in the early 19th century and only half completed when it was blasted out of existence by Anglo-French forces during the Crimean War in 1854. These are at Bomarsund, about 35 km. (22 miles) northeast of Mariehamn and, only ten km. (six miles) away, is Kastelholm Castle built by the Swedes in the 14th century, though considerably damaged. The castle is currently being completely restored, a process which will take several years though parts of it, including the museum, can be visited. Very close is the excellent open-air museum of Jan Karlsgården, a collection of farm buildings from the mid-19th century. In the vicinity is a new golf course.

In prehistoric times, the Åland isles were—relatively speaking—heavily populated, as shown by traces of no less than 10,000 settlements, graves and strongholds from antiquity, though they are mostly difficult to find. One of the largest Viking cemeteries is near the 13th century ruins of Lemböte chapel in the parish of Lemland.

PRACTICAL INFORMATION FOR THE SOUTH COAST AND ISLANDS

TOURIST INFORMATION. Hanko. Bulevardi 15 (911 -82 239). **Kotka.** (City) Kirkkokatu 8 (952-11 736). (Region) Keskuskatu 13 (952-13284). **Lohja.** Laurinkatu 37-39 (912-201 217). **Loviisa.** Brandensteinsgatan (915-52 212). **Mariehamn.** Storagatan 18 (928-16 575). **Naantali.** Tullikatu 12 (921-755 391). **Porvoo.** Rauhankatu 20 (915-140 145). **Tammisaari.** Skillnadsgatan 16 (911-14 600). **Turku.** (City) Käsityöläiskatu 4 (921-336 366). (Region) L. Rantakatu 13 (921-517 333).

TELEPHONE CODES. We have given telephone codes for all the towns and villages in the hotel and restaurant lists that follow. These codes need only be used when calling from outside the town or village concerned.

HOTELS AND RESTAURANTS. Unless otherwise stated, all the hotels listed below have all or some rooms with bath or shower, licensed restaurants, and are open all the year.

We have divided the hotels and restaurants in the lists that follow into four categories—Deluxe (L), Expensive (E), Moderate (M) and Inexpensive (I). Where two names are given below for a town or village, the second is the Swedish one and it indicates that there is a substantial Swedish–speaking element in the population.

HANKO (Hangö). Bathing and sailing resort. *Regatta* (E), Merikatu 1 (911-86 491). 32 rooms, near sea. MC, V.
Restaurant. *Casino* (E), Appelgrenintie 10 (911-86 509). Traditional style, summer only. AE, DC, MC, V.
Camping. *Silversand,* mid-June to mid-August.
Youth Hostel. Bulevardi 15 (911-82 239).

KOTKA. Major sea port with nearby bathing. *Kymen Motelli* (E), out of town (952-85 600). 104 rooms, pool. *Seurahuone* (E), Kaivokatu 16 (952-11 090). 100 rooms, disco. AE, DC, MC, V. *Kesti–Karhu* (M), Karjalantie 7 (952-63 466). 20 rooms, sports facilities. *Ruotsinsalmi* (M), Kirkkokatu 14 (952-13 440). 24 rooms. MC, V. *Koskisoppi* (I), Keisarinmajantie 4 (952-25 555). 48 rooms, summer only.
Restaurants. *Kotkan Klubi* (E), Kirkkokatu 2 (952-15 020). MC, V. *Fennia* (M), Kirkkokatu 3 (952-12 566). MC, V. *Meriniemi* (M), Puistola (952-11 945). Summer only. AE, MC, V. *Mesikämmen* (M), Vesivallinaukio 5, Karhula (952-61 091). *Puistogrilli* (I), Ruotsinsalmen katu 12 (952-11 866). Beer and wine only. MC, V.
Camping. *Santalahti,* Mussalo (952-288 060), open June 1 through Aug. 31.
Youth Hostels. *Municipal youth hostel,* Sports Center (952-11 603). *Kärkisaari,* Mussalo (952-24 215).

LOHJA. *Laurinportti* (M), Laurinkatu 1 (912-11 771). 16 rooms.
Camping. *Haikari* (912-24 735), open June 1 through mid-Aug.
Youth Hostel. *Haikari* (912-24 735).

FINLAND

LOVIISA (Lovisa). South coast town. *Skandinavia* (M), Karlskronabulevardi 9–11 (915–531 725). 20 rooms, pool. MC, V. *Zilton* (M), Mariankatu 29 (915–52 191). 10 rooms.

MARIEHAMN (Maarianhamina). Cozy capital of the Åland islands. *Arkipelag* (L–E), Strandgatan 31 (928–14 020). 86 rooms, pools, nightclub disco, the islands' newest and plushest. AE, DC, MC, V. *Adlon* (E), Hamngatan 7 (928–15 300). 54 rooms, pool. AE, MC, V. *Cikada* (E–M), Hamngatan 1 (928–13 333). 60 rooms, unlicensed restaurant, pool. *Park* (E–M), Norra Esplanadgatan 3 (928–14 130). 47 rooms, pool. AE, MC, V. *Passat* (M), modern apartments with kitchen, no restaurant, pool, opposite *Pommern* (M), Norragatan 8 (928–12 140). 45 rooms, cafeteria. AE, MC, V. *Savoy* (M), Ålandsvägen 41 (928–15 400). 45 rooms, unlicensed restaurant, pool. AE, MC, V. *Esplanad* (M–I), Storagatan 5 (928–16 444). 28 rooms, beer and wine only. MC, V.
The islands have many *boarding houses* (M–I) offering half board, and well organized *self-catering accommodations.*
Restaurants. With dancing at several of the hotels and also at the *Sabina* (E), Ålandsvägen 42 (928–11 988). AE, MC, V. The *Galleri* disco is near the Arkipelag hotel.
Camping. *Gröna Udden,* near bathing beach, is the nearest to town. *Möckelö,* on peninsula west of town.

NAANTALI. Attractive small coastal town, near Turku. *Moshulu* (E), Luostarinkatu 20 (921–751 881). 50 rooms, pool, beer and wine only. MC, V. *Naantalin Kylpylä Spa* (E), Kalevanniemi (921–510 300). 92 rooms, pool, sports facilities, near seashore. MC, V. *Kultainen Aurinko* (M), Kalevanniemi (921–752 961). 29 rooms, pool. AE, DC, MC, V.
Restaurants. *Kaivohuone* (E), Nunnakatu 7 (921–751 291). Summer only. MC, V. *Merenrantaravintola* (M), Mannerheiminkatu 2 (921–751 383). Summer only.
Camping. *Kuparivuori,* open June 1 through late Aug.

PORVOO (Borgå). Delightful old coastal town, east of Helsinki. *Haikko Manor Hotel and Congress Center* (L–E), several km. southwest of town in lovely seashore setting (915–153 133). 179 rooms in converted old manor house, superbly furnished, pools, extensive sports facilities, disco, health treatment. AE, DC, MC, V. *Seurahovi* (E), Rauhankatu 27 B (915–149 555). 32 rooms, tennis. AE, MC, V.
Restaurant. *Wanha Laamanni* (E), Vourikatu 17 (915–130 455). 18th-century décor, excellent food. MC, V.
Camping. Kokonniemi, 2 km. (just over one mile) from town center.
Youth Hostel. *Porvoon Retkeilymaja,* Linnankoskenkatu 1–3 (915–130 012).

TAMMISAARI (Ekenäs). Attractive south coast center. *Kongressihotelli* (M), Pohjoinen Rantakatu 1 (911–13 131). 18 rooms, pool, near seashore. AE, MC. *Marine* (M), Kammantekijänkatu (911–13 833). 24 rooms, unlicensed cafeteria, tennis. AE, MC, V. *Gästis* (I), Pitkäkatu 16 (911–11 023). Nine rooms, without bath or shower. AE, MC, V.
Restaurants. *Knipan* (E), Stallörsparken (911–11 169). On the water, summer only. AE. *Gnägget* (M), Stallören (911–13 331). Cozy "stable" atmosphere, beer and wine only. AE. *Svenska Klubben* (M), Bryggerigatan 9 (911–11 296).
Camping. Ormnäs (911–14 434), open late May through late Aug.
Youth Hostel. *Ekenäs Vandrarhem,* Ladugårdsgatan 11 (911–14 434).

TURKU (ÅBO). Major sea port and interesting former capital of Finland. *Hamburger Börs* (L), Kauppiaskatu 6 (921–511 211). 160 rooms, recently renovated, pool, nightclub, popular beer garden. AE, MC, V. *Marina Palace* (L), Linnankatu 32 (921–336 600). 182 rooms, pool, nightclub, attractive riverside location. AE, DC, MC, V. *Maakunta* (E), Humalistonkatu 7 (921–337 337). 166 rooms, disco. AE, DC, MC, V. *Rantasipi Ruissalo* (E), Ruissalo, in lovely park–like setting about 5 km. (three miles) from town (921–306 222). 132 rooms,

THE SOUTH COAST AND ISLANDS

pool, sports facilities including golf. AE, DC, MC, V. *Rantasipi Turku* (E), Pispalantie 7 (921–376 111). 150 rooms, nightclub, pool, tennis. AE, DC, MC, V. *Seurahuone* (E), Humalistonkatu 2 (921–20 681). 63 rooms, disco. AE, DC, MC, V. *Rantasipi Turku Summer Hotel* (M), Pispalantie 7 (921–376 111). 576 rooms, pool, disco, tennis. AE, DC, MC, V. *Turku* (M), Eerikinkatu 30 (921–26 252). 36 rooms. MC, V. *Domus Aboensis* (I), Piispankatu 10 (921–29 470). 76 rooms, unlicensed cafeteria, summer only. AE, MC, V. *Turun Karina* (I), Itäinen Pitkäkatu 30B (921–336 666). 18 rooms, unlicensed cafeteria. *Turisti-Aula* (I), Käsityöläiskatu 11 (921–334 484). 22 rooms without bath.

Restaurants. *Brahen Kellari* (E), Puolalankatu 1 (921–25 400). AE, DC, MC, V. *Pietari* (E), Brahenkatu 1 (921–10 505). MC, V. *Samppalinna* (E), Itäinen Rantakatu (921–11 165). Dancing, summer only. *Le Pirate* (E–M), Läntinen Rantakatu (921–511 443). On a boat in the river, beer and wine only. MC, V. *Hämeenportti* (M), Hämeenkatu 7 (921–15 054). *Jarrita* (M), Martinkatu 1 (921–359 829). Spanish décor and food (also Finnish), intimate atmosphere, beer and wine only. MC, V. *Pinella* (M), Porthanin puisto (921–11 102). Traditional style, good atmosphere, openair section in summer. MC, V. *Pippurimylly* (M), Stålarminkatu 2 (921–359 501). Beer and wine only. MC, V. *Kultainen Hirvi* (I), It. Pitkäkatu 12–14 (921–21 241). Beer and wine only. *Hiivari* (I), Rauhankatu 10 (921–22 511). Beer and wine only. *Tammio* (I), Konstantsankatu 4 (921–390 737). Beer and wine only.

Camping. *Saaronniemi*, Ruissalo, about 5 km. (three miles) from city, open June 1 through Aug. 31.

Youth Hostel. *Turku Youth Hostel*, Linnankatu 39.

HOW TO GET AROUND. By air. Regular flights serve Mariehamn and Turku. **By train.** Apart from the Helsinki–Turku line, train routes in the region are rather devious, so you'd best travel by bus

By bus. Regular schedules link all parts of the region.

By boat. There are regular trips by boat from Helsinki to Porvoo in summer, taking three hours one way.

By bike. Three planned cycling routes of 52, 90 and 118 km. (32, 56 and 73 miles) are available on the mainland; details from the Hanko and Tammisaari Tourist Offices. Individual packaged cycling tours are organized on the Åland Islands by Ålandsresor, Norra Esplanadgatan 1, Mariehamn, tel. 928–12 140.

TOURS. In summer, sightseeing trips by boat are arranged from Hanko, Kotka, Mariehamn, Porvoo and Turku. Bus tours from Mariehamn take in the principal historic sights of the main island. There are daily city tours of Turku in summer, as well as longer tours into the surrounding countryside, such as the Seven Churches Tour visiting some of the beautiful medieval churches of the area.

PLACES TO VISIT. The heavily indented coastline and thousands of islands and skerries, especially in the southwest, offer a great deal that is scenically beautiful. Much of the country's early history is associated with this region, so this is the area richest in historical monuments. The following is a selection of principal sights. Opening times apply to the peak season.

KOTKA. Imperial Czar's Fishing Lodge. By the rapids of Langinkoski, a few km. from town; a favorite spot of Alexander III and his Danish princess Dagmar. Open daily 10–7.

Karhula Glass Museum and Shop. Open daily 12–5.

Vaarisaari Open Air Museum. Fort Elisabeth, Vaarisaari island; commemorating the naval battle of Ruotsinsalmi, 1790. Motor boat connection.

MARIEHAMN. Åland Museum. Stadshusparken, Öhbergsvägen 1; official historical museum of the province. Open 11–4, Tues. also 6–8, closed Mon.

FINLAND

Maritime Museum. Devoted to Åland's rich seafaring history. Open Mon. to Sat. 9–5, Sun. 10–4.

Pommern. Four-masted barque, now museum ship to the great days when Åland's windjammers carried grain from Australia to England. Open daily 9–7.

Major historic monuments on the main island of the Åland archipelago include the fortifications of **Bomarsund**, the fortress of **Kastelholm**, the farm museum of **Jan Karslgården**, and many medieval churches.

NAANTALI. Convent Church of St. Birgitta. Founded in 1443. Open Mon. to Sat. 11–6, Sun. 12–6.

Kultaranta. Summer residence of the President of Finland; the park is open on Fri. 6–8.

PORVOO. Cathedral. Greystone church from 15th century with old frescoes and statue of Alexander I commemorating historic meeting here in 1809. Open Mon. to Sat. 10–6, Sun. 2–5.

Doll Museum. Open daily 11–3.30.

Edelfelt-Vallgren Art Museum. Commemorating two major Finnish artists. Open Tues. to Sat. 11–4, Sun. 12–4; closed Mon.

Historical Museum. In Old Town Hall (1764). Open Tues. to Sat. 11–4, Sun. 12–4; closed Mon.

Runeberg's home. Museum to Finland's national poet. Open Mon. to Sat. 9.30–4, Sun. 10.30–5.

TURKU. Cathedral. Expanded and restored many times since its founding in the 13th century. Open Mon. to Fri. 9–7, Sat. 9–3, Sun. 2.30–4.30.

Handicrafts Museum. A surviving street from the great fire of 1827, with original interiors and crafts displays. Open daily 10–6.

Museum Ship Sigyn. Open Tues. to Fri. and Sun. 10–3, Sat. 10–5; closed Mon.

Pharmacy Museum. Läntinen Rantakatu 13, in an 18th century wooden building. Open daily 10–6.

Resurrection Chapel and Holy Cross Chapel. Skanssinmäki, on the city outskirts; fine examples of modern architecture by Erik Bryggman and Pekka Pitkänen. Open by arrangement.

Sibelius Museum. Piispankatu 17, devoted to the great composer. Open Tues. to Sun. 11–3, Wed. also 7–8; closed Mon.

Turku Castle and Provincial Museum. Major historic sight near the mouth of the river Aura. Open daily 10–6.

Wäinö Aaltonen Museum. Itäinen Rantakatu 38; the works of Finland's great sculptor and others. Open Mon. to Sat. 10–4, Sun. 10–6.

SPORTS. Boating. Rowing boats are available at all centers. Motor and sailing boats can be rented in Kotka, Mariehamn and Turku.

Golf. There is an 18-hole course at Turku, a 9-hole course near the fortress of Kastelhom, Åland.

Riding. Available in Hanko, Kotka, Lohja, Mariehamn, Porvoo, Turku.

Swimming. Boundless opportunities, mainly off smooth granite. There are fine sandy beaches on the island of Kaunisaari, reached in an hour by motor boat from Kotka.

Windsurfing. Facilities in Hanko, Kotka, Lohja, Mariehamn, Turku.

THE CENTRAL PROVINCES

Way of Poets and Pioneers

Romantics sometimes speak of "the land of a thousand lakes," but they don't even come close. Actually there are something like 60,000 of them, comprising in all nearly a tenth of the Finnish countryside. Almost all of the rest of the land is covered with forests. In the midst of all this, the Finns have somehow managed to find space for their cities, homes and farms. Yet though they have built well and solidly, though they have bent the land to their will, Nature is still triumphant. Indeed the magnificent and sometimes wild country Finland possesses is perhaps its most notable attraction. The constant theme of lake and island, forest and ridge may sound potentially monotonous, but the variations are infinite, and the interplay of light and color at different seasons and different times of day provides endless permutations.

Since one of the greatest attractions this nation offers the visitor is the opportunity to come really close to nature, you would be wise to allow a little time to savor the true delight of life outdoors, even if it is just to slip away from your hotel and walk in the forests which will almost certainly be on the doorstep. For the more ambitious, there are plenty of marked trails.

Exploring the Central Provinces

If you only have time for a brief trip into the Finnish countryside, you could do far worse than head for Aulanko. In the middle of a park of great natural beauty, Hotel Aulanko is one of Finland's showpieces. Here you can indulge your athletic whims, wander through the spacious park, or swim in the lake nearby. An observation tower in the grounds provides a magnificent and extensive view.

There are a number of sights to be seen in the vicinity. The town of Hämeenlinna, birthplace of Jean Sibelius, boasts a castle, the oldest part of which probably dates from the crusades which Birger Jarl led into Finland in 1249. Ten km. (six miles) away on the road to Tampere is Hattula Church, built of stone about the year 1250. The few remaining old country churches in Finland are well worth visiting because of their unique interior decoration, dominated by paintings covering the walls and ceilings. Artists of those days had a firm belief in all the horrors of hell fire, and spared no pains in depicting their beliefs with the brush. Hattula Church also has some fine wood carvings.

Even closer to Helsinki is Hyvinkää, with its forested ridges, and one of Finland's most fascinating museums, the Railway Museum which dates back to the 1870s. Among the exhibits are the two Imperial carriages used by the Russian czar.

Tampere, the Weaving Wonderland

Almost every book, pamphlet, brochure, and guide will inform you that Tampere, the country's second largest city, is Finland's Pittsburgh. However, the resemblance begins and ends with the concentrated presence here of industry—the settings are quite incomparable.

From about the year 1,000, this part of Finland was a base from which traders and hunters set out on their expeditions to northern Finland and even to Lapland. But it was not until 1779 that a Swedish king actually founded the town of Tampere. Some 41 years later a Scotsman by the name of James Finlayson came to the infant city and established a factory for spinning cotton. This was perhaps the beginning of "big business" in Finland. The firm of Finlayson exists today and is still one of the country's leading industrial enterprises.

Artful location is the secret of Tampere's many factories. An isthmus little more than a kilometer wide at its narrowest point separates the lakes Näsijärvi and Pyhäjärvi, and at one spot the Tammerkoski Rapids provide an outlet for the waters of one to cascade through to the other. Called the "Mother of Tampere", these rapids provide the power on which the town's livelihood depends. Their natural beauty has been preserved in spite of the factories on either bank, and the well-designed public buildings of the city grouped around them enhance their general effect. Also in the heart of town is Hämeensilta bridge with its four statues by the well-known sculptor Wäinö Aaltonen.

The high ridge of Pyynikki forms a natural park near the center of town, and on its top is an outlook tower commanding a view of the surrounding countryside. Not far away, the even higher, modern observation tower of Näsineula soars above the lake, forest and town, topped by a revolving restaurant. The same building houses the first planetari-

THE CENTRAL PROVINCES

um in Scandinavia and a well-planned aquarium. From these towers you can fully appreciate the truly amazing contrasts between the industry humming at your feet and the quiet lakes stretching out to meet the horizon. At one moment you are in the midst of a busy city, at the next you are confronted with a seeming wilderness. At the foot of this Pyynikki Ridge is the Pyynikki Open Air Theater with its revolving auditorium which can be moved even with a full load of spectators to face any one of the sets, ready prepared by nature.

A number of museums include a pleasantly-situated provincial museum, a good art gallery, the charming Haihara Doll Museum just outside town, and the Lenin Museum (it was in Tampere that Lenin and Stalin first met in 1905). Most of the buildings in Tampere itself, including the cathedral, are comparatively modern. The latter was completed in 1907, but it houses some of the best known masterpieces of Finnish art, including Magnus Enckell's fresco, *The Resurrection,* and two works by Hugo Simberg, *Wounded Angel* and *Garden of Death.* Another modern building is the startling Kaleva Church, which was designed by Reima and Raili Pietilä. Just outside of town, there are one or two fine 15th-century characteristic small stone churches.

The "Poets' Way" boat tour along Lake Näsijärvi, north of Tampere, passes through the agricultural parish of Ruovesi where J. L. Runeberg, Finland's national poet, used to live. At Petoniemi Mansion he collected the material for his famous *Tales of Ensign Stål.* Not far away, artist Akseli Gallen-Kallela built himself a castle-like building in Kalevalan style. Shortly before the boat docks at Virrat you pass through the straits of Visuvesi, a place where many artists and writers today spend their summers. Not far north of Virrat is Ähtäri where Finland's first wildlife park has been established in a beautiful setting, with a holiday village, a good hotel and recreation facilities.

The center of a region considered by some to be even more beautiful than the "Poets' Way," Kangasala, southeast of Tampere, was immortalized in Z. Topelius' poem, *A Summer Day at Kangasala.* (The poem has been set to music and is one of the loveliest of many haunting Finnish songs.) It lies on one of the routes of the Finnish Silver Line, through Lakes Roine and Vanajavesi to Aulanko and Hämeenlinna.

Along the way, the modern water bus passes by Valkeakoski, a town typical of the many Finnish industrial communities which are set in idyllic surroundings. Here a plant of the great United Paper Mills combine provides practically the only livelihood. Here and there across the country, sometimes in the middle of a forest, but always on a waterway, you will find similar towns. Each has a factory and an old church, and around these two poles cluster the mill employees' dwellings. The factory provides recreation grounds, clubhouses, indoor tennis courts and gymnasiums, and supplies fresh vegetables from the firm's greenhouses all through the winter. Other places of interest along the Silver Line route include the Iittala glass factory and museum, and the home and studio of the sculptor Emil Wikström.

Lahti, Gateway to Central Finland

Let's look now at the center of the country, starting with a short trip to the modern town of Lahti. Located at the southern end of one of Finland's largest lake systems, Vesijärvi-Päijänne, this community is now the sixth biggest town in the country, with rapidly expanding industries. Its City Hall was designed by Eliel Saarinen. But there are a number of other notable modern buildings, including the Church of the Cross by Alvar Aalto, and a fine concert hall. The town is also noted for the nearby athletic academy of Vierumäki, possessing an international reputation and an unsurpassed location.

Lahti is better known, however, for winter sports. Good enough, in fact, to have been selected for the 1958 World Ski Championships. In general, Finland is comparatively flat, but running across the country is the very prominent Salpausselkä Ridge formed during the Glacial Age. Where this crosses the town boundaries, it has given its name to winter games which attract thousands of Finns and many foreigners every March.

At the northern end of Lake Päijänne lies Jyväskylä. Known as a cultural center Jyväskylä was the first to establish a secondary school that used Finnish as the language of instruction and now has its own university by Aalto, who also designed the City Theater. This brings up an interesting point. The schools of Finland may conduct their classes in either Finnish or Swedish, both of which share equal status guaranteed by law. Whichever school a child attends, he must learn the second official language of the country in addition to any other foreign tongues, included in the syllabus. Today, English is the most popular, and in many schools, is compulsory. German or French ranks next. Like the inhabitants of all small nations, the unfortunate Finns have to spend a lot of time learning to decline and conjugate. The town has an attractive openair museum and, on the outskirts, the well-equipped sports center of Laajavuori.

Jyväskylä is also an important woodworking center for it is right in the forested heart of Finland. The whole region and Viitasaari to the north has been developed as a holiday area with delightful holiday villages in log-cabin style scattered about the vast, deeply forested and lake-strewn region. The holiday villages offer sports facilities as well— and also a good opportunity to probe deep into Finland's "off-the-beaten-track." Jyväskylä's annual Arts Festival in summer has become a major event, and the town is also important as a starting point for the boat trip down Lake Päijänne, the second largest in Finland. During the early part of the journey south to Lahti, the scenery is wildly beautiful, with forest-covered ridges and completely uninhabited rocky shores. The landscape grows milder and more serene as you travel south, and numerous villas are scattered along the banks or built on the many islands that cup up the lake throughout its 113 km. (70 miles) length. A hydrofoil service covers the same trip in three hours instead of nine, but it is naturally not so tranquil. If you're traveling between Lahti and Jyväskylä by car, the eastern route is the more beautiful and takes you through Sysmä, near which is the delightful Suvi-Pinx open-air art exhibition (summer only) in a beautiful forest setting. It has a restaurant and amusements for children.

Saimaa Lake District

Now that we have explored some of the more interesting parts of central Finland, let's move on eastwards to the region known as the Saimaa Lake system. It is in this area that many of the most beautiful

THE CENTRAL PROVINCES

places in the country are concentrated, and it is here that some of the most interesting pages of Finnish history have been written. It might be a good idea to adopt Savonlinna as your new headquarters. It is an attractive lakeside resort also noted as a watering place and is a terminus of the Saimaa lake steamers. The healing baths are to be found in the Casino Park. The latter is on one of the many islands, all linked by bridges, which, together with a cape jutting out into the lake, constitute the town of Savonlinna. Besides its location and its baths, Savonlinna's outstanding attraction is the fortress of Olavinlinna, Finland's finest medieval castle and one of the best-preserved historical monuments in Scandinavia. Still surrounded by the water that formed such an essential part of its defensive strength centuries ago, it is in the eastern part of the old section of town.

A Danish-born knight built this fortress with the object of providing a bastion for the eastern frontier of the then kingdom of Sweden-Finland to assist in repulsing attacks and invasions from the east. Apart from the important role it played in the wars of those days, Olavinlinna Castle helped to protect and support the Finnish colonists who began to develop the land for several miles around. During the numerous wars of the 18th century it changed hands repeatedly, but it lost its military significance when Finland became a Grand Duchy of Russia.

In recent years the main courtyard has been the setting for operatic and theatrical performances, and an Opera Festival is held here lasting three weeks in July. From mid-June onwards there also occur other events such as the annual Operatic Course, Savonlinna Music Days and a Music Summer Seminar, so the town becomes a veritable musical mecca for a month or so each summer. Arts and crafts are also strongly featured in studios and exhibitions around town in summer, including a special Opexpo near the castle during the festival.

Of special interest, too, is the *Salama,* a steam schooner, built in 1874, shipwrecked in 1898 and raised from the lake in 1971. Very well preserved, she has been turned into a museum showing the history and development of lake traffic, including the fascinating floating timber trains which are still a common summer sight on Saimaa.

Until recently Savonlinna was the central hub of a network of regular lake traffic leaving for and arriving from the four points of the Saimaa compass each morning and evening. Some of these regular schedules have been replaced by sightseeing cruises, but the quaysides of Savonlinna still present a lively scene with the daily to-ing and fro-ing of these venerable vessels.

A short distance from Savonlinna is the famous ridge of Punkaharju; eight km. (five miles) long, it rises between the lakes and at some points is no more than eight meters (25 feet) wide though it manages to accommodate both a road and railway. A leisure and art center has been created in this area. Nearby, Punkaharju's National Hotel, originally built in 1845 as a gamekeeper's lodge by Czar Nicholas I and subsequently enlarged, has been restored as a restful oasis in which to stay or simply enjoy a meal. At Kerimäki, 23 km. (14 miles) east of Savonlinna, is the world's largest wooden church from the 1840s, holding 5,000 people. Both areas offer good and expanding water sports facilities, and some particularly well equipped camp sites and holiday villages.

You can either continue farther to the north, or start your return, still a leisurely one, towards the capital, and in most directions you can still travel by boat. Helsinki-bound, the steamer runs through the Saimaa lake system to Lappeenranta. This is a lively resort and town on the southern shores of Saimaa and, from here, trips are available on the Saimaa Canal, re-opened a few years ago. The canal crosses into the Soviet Union to Viipuri (Viborg), but for the moment this route, which leads eventually to Leningrad via the Gulf of Finland, is not open to non-Scandinavian visitors. The old fortress area of Lappeenranta is of particular interest. A half-hour drive from here is Imatra whose magnificent rapids, tamed and diverted to help power the considerable local industry, are released as a tourist attraction on certain Sundays each summer. Other possibilities from Savonlinna are to take a ship in the opposite direction northwest to Kuopio, or train or bus northeast to Joensuu. These routes pick their way through or beside an amazingly long and immensely intricate system of lakes, canals and narrow channels, all part of the Saimaa network, Finland's (and Europe's) largest lake system.

Joensuu and Koli

Joensuu is the only town of any size in the vast area known as North Karelia. Its chief claim to distinction is a town hall which, like the one at Lahti, was designed by Eliel Saarinen. Our objective, however, is Koli on the western shore of Lake Pielinen (Pielisjärvi), nearly 64 km. (40 miles) due north of Joensuu. By boat, three times a week, the journey takes a leisurely six to seven hours, but you can also go by train to Vuonislahti, on the lake's eastern shore, and take a motorboat across to Koli. Alternatively, there is a bus service from Joensuu to Koli.

As we mentioned earlier, Finland is realtively flat; thus, in comparison with the hills found in most parts of the country, Koli is considered a mountain. This is its great appeal. From the rocky summit of Ukko-Koli more than 300 meters (1,000 feet) up, there are some of the most magnificent views to be found anywhere. There is a recently modernized tourist hotel near the hill top and holiday villages on the lake shore. Much has been done for the visitor to Koli in the way of well-marked footpaths and tracks for the hiker and other facilities. On the Pielisjoki river the canoeing is excellent. But it is for winter sports that this region is particularly noted.

The region to the east of Joensuu is little–known to foreign visitors though of special interest as a traditional stronghold of the Orthodox church. The summer calendar features a number of Pradznik festivals, traditional Orthodox church and folk celebrations, the most important being at Ilomantsi in July.

Kuopio

From Kuopio there are almost daily monastery cruises to the Orthodox convent of Lintula and monastery of Uusi-Valamo, which removed to these remote parts from Lake Ladoga when that region of Karelia was ceded to Russia. Kuopio itself is an interesting town and excellent ski center. It has an Orthodox as well as a Lutheran Cathedral. Housed in a modern building on the outskirts of town is a museum whose

THE CENTRAL PROVINCES

collections from Orthodox Karelia must be unique in the western world. Kuopio's market place is a colorful spot. The slender tower on Puijo hill offers superb views—and a revolving restaurant.

Farther north still, you come into the wilderness landscapes of Kainuu, with Kajaani as the main (and only!) town. It has 17th-century castle ruins and a town hall designed by Engel; but the region's chief claims for attention are its scenery and amenities for outdoor activities —especially for enthusiasts of fishing or canoeing or, in winter, cross-country skiing.

PRACTICAL INFORMATION FOR THE CENTRAL PROVINCES

TOURIST INFORMATION. Hämeenlinna. Raatihuoneenkatu 13 (917–202 388). **Heinola.** Kauppakatu 5 (910–52 683). **Hyvinkää.** Hämeenkatu 3D (914–251 441). **Imatra.** Keskusasema (954–23 333). **Joensuu.** Koskikatu 1 (973–25 111). **Jyväskylä.** (Town) Vapaudenkatu 38 (941–294 083). (Region) Vapaudenkatu 38 (941–10 866). **Kuopio.** (Town) Haapaniemenkatu 17; (971–121 411). (Region) Haapaniemenkatu 17 (971–114 101). **Lahti.** Torikatu 3B (918–182 580). **Lappeenranta.** Bus Station; (953–18 850). **Mikkeli.** (Town) Hallituskatu 3a (955–13 938). (Region) Maaherrankatu 12 (955–365 399). **Savonlinna.** Olavinkatu 35 (957–13 492). **Tampere.** (Town) Aleksis Kiven katu 14 B (931–26 652). (Region) Aleksis Kiven katu 14 B (931–24 488). **Varkaus.** Ahlströminkatu 11 (972–292 383).

TELEPHONE CODES. We have given telephone codes for all the towns and villages in the hotel and restaurant lists that follow. These codes need only be used when calling from outside the town or village concerned.

HOTELS AND RESTAURANTS. Unless otherwise stated, all the hotels listed below have all or some rooms with bath or shower, licensed restaurants, and are open all the year.

HÄMEENLINNA. Sibelius' birthplace and with other cultural associations. *Rantasipi Aulanko* (L), 3 km. (2 miles) from town center (917–29 521). 216 rooms, nightclub, pool, extensive sports facilities. Lovely lake-side location. AE, DC, MC, V. *Cumulus* (E), Raatihuoneenkatu 18 (917–28 811). 57 rooms, pool. AE, MC, V. *Vouti* (E), Raatihuoneenkatu 23 (917–25 928). 41 rooms. AE, DC, MC, V.

Restaurants. *Linnanvouti* (E), Sibeliuksenkatu 3 (917–25 911). MC, V. *Kultainen Orava* (M), Rauhankatu 5 (917–26 411). *Paukero* (M), Ojoistenkatu 2–4 (917–23 111). *Papukaija Pub* (I), Aulangontie 35 (917–24 144). Beer and wine only.

Camping. *Aulanko,* 3 km. (2 miles) from town (917–28 560), open June 1 through late Aug.

Youth Hostels. *Aulangon Heikkila,* 5 km. (3 miles) from town (917–22 605).

HEINOLA. Lakeside town and resort. *Seurahuone* (M), Lampikatu 16 (910–52 061). 25 rooms. AE, MC, V.

Camping. *Heinäsaari* (910–53 083), open June 1 through Aug. 31.
Youth Hostel. *Retkeilymaja,* Opintie 1 (910–52 425).

FINLAND

HYVINKÄÄ. Small town amidst forested ridges. *Rantasipi Hyvinkää* (L), Härkävehmaankatu 4 (914–18 820). 190 rooms, nightclub, pool, sports facilities. Fine location in woods just outside town. AE, DC, MC, V. *Hopealyhty* (E), Hämeenkatu 2–4 (914–12 400). 27 rooms, pool. MC, V.
Restaurants. *Stefan* (E), Hämeenkatu 24–26 (914–11 260). *Teho* (E), Uudenmaankatu, 4–6 (914–19 501). *Kauppakerho* (M), Uudenmaankatu 8–10 (914–11 532). *Eila Airola* (I), Hämeenkatu 13–17 (914–17 093), beer and wine only.
Youth Hostel. *Sveitsin Retkeilymaja,* Sveitsi (914–89 444).

IMATRA. Industrial center with famous rapids. *Imatran Valtionhotelli* (L-E), Torkkelinkatu 2 (954–63 244). 62 rooms, disco, pool. Located by the rapids (only seen in full flood on selected summer Sundays). AE, DC, MC, V. *Kuutostie* (E-M), Korvenkylä (954–28 322). 15 rooms, pool. *Niskahovi* (E-M), Vuoksenniskantie 71 (954–32 644). 48 rooms, beer and wine only. AE, MC, V. *Mansikkala* (I), Rastaankatu 3 (954–22 133). 52 rooms, unlicensed cafeteria, summer only. MC, V.
Camping. *Ukonlinna,* located in the Leisure Center.
Youth Hostels. *Mansikka,* Rastaankatu 3 (954–22 133). *Ukonlinna,* (954–21 270).

JOENSUU. Lake resort and industrial town. *Karelia* (E), Kauppakatu 25 (973–24 391). 36 rooms. AE, MC, V. *Kimmel* (E), Itäranta 1 (973–34 521). 130 rooms, pool, nightclub, disco. AE, MC, V. *Pohjois-Karjala* (E-M), Torikatu 20 (973–27 311). 50 rooms. AE, DC, MC, V. *Viehka* (E), Kauppakatu 32 (973–29 531). 40 rooms. MC, V. *Jeonsuun Elli* (I), Länsikatu 18 (973–259 27). 71 rooms, unlicensed cafeteria, boating. MC, V.
Restaurants. *Shemeikka* (E), Kauppakatu 29 (973–21 358). *Teatteriravintola* (E), Rantakatu 4 (973–22 256). MC, V. *Puikkari* (M), Puronsuunkatu 1 (973–822 136). *Virvatuli* (I), Nurmeksentie 14 (973–822 218), beer and wine only.
Camping. Linnunlahti (973–21 151), open June 1 through Aug. 31.
Youth hostels. *Partiotalon retkeilymaja* (Scout Lodge), Vanamokatu 25 (973–23 381). *Joensuu Youth Hostel,* Länsikatu 15 (973–24 385). *Wiiri,* Suvikatu 19 (973–23 022).

JYVÄSKYLÄ. University and industrial town in heart of lakes and forests. *Rantasipi Laajavuori* (L), Laajavuori (941–251 122). 176 rooms, nightclub, pool, extensive sports facilities. Fine location on outskirts of town. AE, DC, MC, V. *Cumulus* (E), Väinönkatu 5 (941–215 211). 203 rooms, pool. AE, MC. *Jyväshovi* (E), Kauppakatu 35 (941–213 322). 121 rooms, pool. AE, DC, MC, V. *Milton* (M), Asema-aukio (941–213 411). 35 rooms. MC, V. *Rentukka* (M), Taitoniekantie 9 (941–252 211). 136 rooms, disco, summer only. AE, MC, V. *Amis* (I), Sepänkatu 3 (941–12 920). 93 rooms, without bath or shower, unlicensed cafeteria, summer only.
Restaurants. *Katinhäntä* (E), Asemakatu 7 (941–18 115). Intimate, gracious atmosphere. MC, V. *Ilokivi* (M), Keskusairaalantie 2 (941–19 306). *Kantakrouvi* (M), Hannikaisenkatu 27–29 (941–217 198). MC, V. *Mörssäri* (M), Voionmaankatu 32 (941–18 434). *Priimus* (M), Taulumäntie 45 (941–216 711). Good value in hotel and restaurant school. DC, MC, V.
Camping. *Tuomiojärvi* (941–294 086), open June 1 through Aug. 31.
Youth hostels. *Kisakeskus,* Laajavuori (941–294 083). *Pelastakaa Lapset,* Korkeakoskentie 3 (941–241 985).

KAJAANI. Interesting regional capital of Kainuu district. *Kajaani* (E), Leiripolku 2 (986–38 911). 72 rooms, pool. MC, V. *Seurahuone* (E), Kauppakatu 11 (986–23 076). 34 rooms. MC, V. *Valjus* (E), Kauppakatu 20 (986–24 191). 32 rooms, pool. MC, V. *Vanha Välskäri* (E-M), Kauppakatu 21 (986–25 661). 32 rooms. AE, DC, MC, V.
Restaurants. *Kellari-Kievari* (M), Kauppakatu 30 (986–23 003). *Kuukkeli* (M), Leiripolku 2 (986–38 911). *Sampola-Kievari* (I), Lönnrotinkatu 5 (986–22 894), beer and wine only.

THE CENTRAL PROVINCES

Camping. *Onnela,* 1 km. (half a mile) from town (986–22 703), open June 1 through Aug. 31. *Paltaniemi,* 9 km. (6 miles) from town (986–475 140), open June 1 through Aug. 31.

KOLI. Small tourist center in beautiful, hilly lake and forest setting. *Koli* (E), Ylä-Koli (973–672 221). 42 rooms, pool, superb views. AE, MC, V. *Loma-Koli* (M), Loma-Koli (973–672 241). 36 rooms, boating. AE, MC, V.
Camping. *Loma-Koli* (973–672 241), open early June through mid-Aug.

KUOPIO. Lake resort, skiing center and industrial town. *Cumulus* (E), Asemakatu 32 (971–123 555). 134 rooms, pool. AE, MC, V. *Kuopio* (E), Haapaniemenkatu 20 (971–114 522). 24 rooms. MC, V. *Puijonsarvi* (E), Minna Canthin katu 16 (971–123 333). 61 rooms, nightclub. AE, DC, MC, V. *Kalla* (M), Tulliportinkatu 19 (971–123 522). 37 rooms. *Kaupunginhotelli* (M-I), Maaherrankatu 5–7 (971–114 061). 27 rooms, disco. *Savonia Summer Hotel* (M), Sammakkolammentie 2 (971–225 333). 26 rooms, pool, summer only. AE, MC, V. *Tekma* (M), Taivaanpankontie 14 (971–222 925). 60 rooms without bath or shower, beer and wine only, summer only. AE, MC, V. *Hospitsi* (I), Myllykatu 4 (971–114 501). 27 rooms without bath or shower, unlicensed restaurant.
Restaurants. *Peräniemen Kasino* (E), Väinölänniemi (971–114 522), summer only. MC, V. *Puijon Torni* (E) (971–114 841) Revolving restaurant on top of tower on outskirts of town. *Henry's Pub* (M), Kauppakatu 18 (971–122 002). *Kummeli* (M), Puijonkatu 19 (971–127 711). MC, V. *Sampo* (I), Kauppakatu 13 (971–122 998). Fish specialties, shabby but excellent value. *Taverna Traviata* (I), Kauppakatu 40–42 (971–127 646), beer and wine only. MC.
Camping. *Rauhalahti,* 4 km. (6 miles) from town (971–312 802), open mid-May through early Sept. *Taivalharju,* 4 km. (6 miles) from town (971–341 088), open early June through mid-Aug.
Youth hostels. *Jynkkä* (971–312 361). *Tekma Youth Hostel,* Taivaanpankontie 41 (971–222 925).

LAHTI. Lake resort, major ski-ing center and industrial town. *Musta Kissa* (E), Rautatienkatu 21 (918–37 851). 71 rooms, disco. AE, MC, V. *Seurahuone* (E), Aleksanterinkatu 14 (918–25 161). 121 rooms, nightclub, pool, long gastronomic tradition. AE, MC, V. *Tallukka* (E), Tallukantie 1 (918–661 481). 144 rooms, nightclub, pool, sports facilities. *Valtakulma* (E), Rauhankatu 14 (918–47 811). 40 rooms. AE, MC, V. *Jukola* (M), Hämeenkatu 20 (918–27 891). 40 rooms. MC, V. *Messilä* (M), 8 km. (5 miles) from town (918–531 666). 36 rooms, pool, sports facilities. In a charming and peaceful location. AE, MC. *Mukkulan Kartano* (M), 4 km. (just over 2 miles) from town (918–306 554). 14 rooms without bath or shower, sports facilities. In attractive converted old manor in lovely location. MC, V. *Mukkula Summer Hotel* (M), part of the Mukkula complex above (918–306 253). 80 rooms, sports facilities. MC, V. *Kauppahotelli* (I), Rautatienkatu 12 (918–25 146). 28 rooms, old-fashioned but comfortable. MC, V.
Restaurants. *Kommodori* (E), Myllysaari (918–531 272). *Seurahuone* (E)—see *Hotels* above. The food here is notable. *El Toro* (M), Mariankatu 8 (918–25 388). Spanish style and food (also Finnish). MC, V. *Hoijakka* (M), Vesijärvenkatu 18 (918–27 851). *Nelonen* (M),Lahdenkatu 26 (918–48 543). *Takkatupa* (I), Viipurin Valtatie 1 (918–20 413). Beer and wine only. *Tunneli* (I), Kiverionkatu 35 (918–333 710). Beer and wine only.
Camping. *Mukkula,* part of the Mukkula tourist complex 4 km. from town (918–306 554), open June 1 through Aug. 31.
Youth Hostel. Kivikatu 1 (918–26 324).

LAPPEENRANTA. Major lake resort with some industry. *Cumulus* (E), Valtakatu 31 (953–50 870). 95 rooms, pool. MC, V. *Lappee* (E), Brahenkatu 1 (953–50 950). 145 rooms, nightclub, pool. *Lappeenranta Spa* (E), Ainonkatu 17 (953–17 400). 22 rooms, pool, tennis. MC, V. *Lappeenranta* (E-M), Helsingintie 1 (953–14 940). 40 rooms, disco, boating. AE, DC, MC, V. *Viikinkihovi* (E), Valtakatu 41 (953–14 910). 28 rooms, pool. AE. *Karelia-Park* (M), Korpraalin-

kuja 1 (953-15 620). 73 rooms, tennis. MC, V. *Majarest* (I), Mattilantie 1 (953-17 110). 11 rooms, unlicensed cafeteria. *Rotelli* (I),Huhtiniemi, Kuusimäenkatu 18 (953-15 555). 20 rooms, unlicensed restaurant, pool, tennis.
   Restaurants. *Casa Nostra* (E), Kauppakatu 57 (953-18 180). Good Italian food. *Kasino* (E), Ainonkatu 10 (953-10 200). Traditional style, near harbor, summer only. MC, V. *Kolme Lyhtyä* (M), Kauppakatu 27 (953-10 100). *Willimies* (M), Kauppakatu 39 (953-15 011). *Adriano Bar* (I), Kauppakatu 27 (953-13 454), beer and wine only. *Pappilan kahvila* (I), attractive coffee house in the fortress area, with Orthodox music and specialties. *Sirmakka* (I), Valtakatu 31 (953-12 140), beer and wine only.
   Camping. *Huhtiniemi* (953-11 888), open May 15 through Aug. 31.
   Youth Hostels. *Huhtiniemi Camping,* (953-11 888). *Youth Hostel Rotelli,* Huhtiniemi (953-15 555). *Kesä-Loas,* Karankokatu 4 C (953-28 111). *Karelia Park,* Korpraalinkuja 1 (953-15 620).

MIKKELI. Lakeside and industrial town. *Cumulus* (E), Mikonkatu 9 (955-369 222). 115 rooms, pool. MC, V. *Nuijamies* (E-M), Porrassalmenkatu 21 (955-363 111). 40 rooms, disco. AE, MC, V. *Rantasipi Varsavuori* (E), Kirkonvarkaus (955-367 111). 98 rooms, nightclub, pool, sports facilities. AE, DC, MC, V. *Kaleva* (M), Hallituskatu 5 (955-12 041). 34 rooms. AE, MC, V. *Pillinki* (M), Porrassalmenkatu 16 (955-12 233). 13 rooms. *Tekuila* (M), Raviradantie 1 (955-366 542). 69 rooms, unlicensed cafeteria. MC, V.
   Restaurants. *Teatteri Holvi* (E), Savilahdenkatu 11 (955-368 444). MC, V. *Kestikievari* (M), Mikonkatu 6 (955-14 121). *Suur-Savo* (M), Maaherrankatu 13 (955-11 154). *Kahveri* (I), Maaherrankatu 12 (955-13 382), beer and wine only.
   Camping. *Viisulahti Tourist Center* (955-26 181), open all year. *Rauhaniemi* (955-11 416), open June through mid-Aug.

PUNKAHARJU. Ridge and beauty spot near Savonlinna. *Valtionhotelli* (National Hotel) (E) (957-311 761). 29 rooms, sports facilities. In beautifully restored 19th-century building in lovely situation. MC, V.
   Camping. *Kultakivi* (957-315 110), open mid-April through mid-Sept. *Punkaharju Holiday Center,* (957-311 761), open June 1 through early Sept.

SAVONLINNA. Major lake resort with medieval castle. *Casino* (E), Kasinonsaari (957-22 864). 79 rooms, pool, sports facilities, health treatment. MC, V. *Seurahuone* (E-M), Kauppatori 4 (957-22 267). 32 rooms, disco. MC, V. *Tott* (E), Satamakatu 1 (957-22 925). 49 rooms, nightclub, disco, boating, roof terrace restaurant. MC, V. *Kyrönsalmi* (M), Olavinkatu 15 (957-22 901). 46 rooms, unlicensed cafeteria. *Malakias* (M), Pihlajavedenkuja 6 (957-23 383). 220 rooms, unlicensed cafeteria, tennis, summer only. MC, V. *Vuorilinna* (M), Kasinonsaari (957-22 864). 157 rooms, pool, sports facilities, summer only. *Otava* (I), Talvisalonkatu 27 (957-22 481). 7 rooms without bath, no restaurant.
   Restaurants. *Kasino* (E), Kasinonsaari (957-22 864). Turn-of-century style, summer only. *Rauhalinna* (E), Tolvanniemi (957-53 119). Charming turn-of-century castle-like villa, 16 km. (10 miles) from town (4 km. (2 miles) by boat). *Linnantupa* (Castle Tavern) (M), Olavinlinna (957-22 384), in the castle. *Majakka* (M), Satamakatu 11 (957-21 456). Unpretentious, but good food. MC, V. *Hopeasalmi* (I), restaurant ship (957-21 701). In the harbor, beer and wine only. *Musta Pässi* (I), Tulliportinkatu 2 (957-22 228). Beer tavern. MC, V. *Savo* (I) Pilkkakoskenkatu 2 (957-21 222). Tavern style (with sauna!).
   Camping. *Kyrönniemi* (957-21 507), open May through Sept.
   Youth Hostels. *Malakias,* Pihlajavedenkuja 6 (957-23 283).*Mertamalakias VI,* Otavankatu 8 (957-20 685). *Hospits,* Linnankatu 20 (957-22 443).

SOTKAMO. In north central district of Kainuu. *Tulikettu* (E), Hiukanharju, near village (986-62 222). 46 rooms, pool, extensive sports facilities, MC. V. Nearby*Hiukan Retkeilyhotelli* (M), rooms and similar facilities. *Asteli* (M), Vuokatti (986-60 071). A few km. from village in fine wilderness setting. 35 rooms, unlicensed restaurant, pool, extensive sports facilities.

SYSMÄ. Small, inexpensive lake and forest resort. *Ilolan Kartano* (M) (910-797 556). 24 rooms, near lake shore, boating. MC. *Uoti* (M), Keskustie 1 (910-71 351). 8 rooms, disco.

TAMPERE. Finland's second city, major industrial town and lake-side center. *Rosendahl* (L-E), Pyynikintie 13 (931-112 233). 213 rooms, nightclub, pool, sports facilities. AE, DC, MC, V. *Cumulus* (E), Koskikatu 5 (931-35 500). 229 rooms, pool. AE, DC, MC, V. *Grand Hotel Tammer* (E), Satakunnankatu 13 (931-25 380). 90 rooms, nightclub. AE, MC, V. *Jäähovi* (E), Sammonvaltatie 2 (931-559 900). 73 rooms, pool. AE, MC, V. *Kaupunginhotelli* (E), Hämeenkatu 11 (931-21 380). 71 rooms. AE, MC, V. *Maisa* (E-M), Maisansalo (931-84 141). 50 rooms, extensive sports facilities, part of recent tourist center. 12 km. (8 miles) from city. *Tampere* (E-M), Hämeenkatu 1 (931-21 980). 260 rooms, pool. AE, DC, MC, V. *Domus* (M-I), Pellervonkatu 9 (931-550 000). 200 rooms, pool, disco, summer only. MC, V. *Otavala* (M), Rautatienkatu 22 (931-38 400). 20 rooms, unlicensed cafeteria. MC, V. *Victoria* (M), Itsenäisyydenkatu 1 (931-30 640). 100 rooms, pool, disco. AE, MC, V. *Härmälä* (I), Nuolialantie 50 (931-650 400). 65 rooms, boating, summer only. *Rasti* (I), Itsenäisyydenkatu 1 (931-30 640). 94 rooms without bath, disco, summer only.

Restaurants. *Cabare Oscar* (E), Kirkkokatu 10 (931-21 810). Dancing. MC, V. *Hämeensilta* (E), Hämeenkatu 13 (931-27 207). Dancing. AE, DC, MC, V. *Laterna* (E), Puutarhakatu 11 (931-24 005). Russian style, dancing. MC. *Näsinneula* (E), Särkanniemi. Revolving restaurant on top of great tower. AE, DC, MC, V. *Rustholli* (E-M), Aitolahti. AE, MC, V. On lakeside 8 km. (5 miles) from center, excellent cold table with regional specialties. *Sorsapuiston Grilli* (E), Sorsapuisto 1 (931-556 550). Excellent food including Baltic herring specialties, in pleasant atmosphere. AE, MC. *Tüliholvi* (E), Kauppakatu 10 (931-21 220). MC. *Kaijakka* (M), Laukontori (931-23 494). Dancing. *Merirosvo* (M), Särkänniemi (931-24 697). Splendid Baltic herring dishes. MC, V. *Ohranjyvä* (M), Näsilinnankatu 15 (931-27 217). Intimate atmosphere. DC, MC, V. *Pirkanhovi* (M), Sukkavartaankatu 9 (931-22 960). Dancing. *Antika* (I), Väinölänkatu 1 (931-111 282). MC, V. *Uintikeskuksen ravintola* (I), by swimming hall 3 km. (2 miles) from center, home-made food, good value.

Camping. *Maisansalo-Camping,* Teisko (931-84 141), open June 1 through mid-Aug. *Tampere-Camping,* Härmälä (931-651 250), open June 1 through Aug. 31. *Taulaniemi camping,* Taulaniemi, Teisko (931-83 753), open May 15 through Sept. 30.

Youth Hostels. *YWCA's Youth Hostel,* Tuomiokirkonkatu 12A (931-35 900). *Uimahallinmaja,* Pirkankatu 10-12 (931-29 460).

VARKAUS. Industrial and lake-side town. *Keskus-Hotelli* (E), Ahlströminkatu 18 (972-22 501). 56 rooms, pool, tennis. AE, MC, V. *Taipale* (E), Kanavakatu 1 (972-27 561). 45 rooms, pool, disco. AE, MC, V.

Restaurants. *Kaupunginkellari* (E), Ahlströminkatu 18 (972-22 820). *Onni-Manni* (M), Kauppakatu 62 (972-24 904). *Oskar's Pub* (M), Kauppatori 1 (972-22 539). MC, V.

Camping. *Kankunharju,* open June 1 through late Aug.

Youth Hostel. *Varkaus Youth Hostel* (972-162 882).

VIITASAARI. Forest and lake center, central Finland. *Pihkuri* (E) (946-21 440). 24 rooms, disco, on lakeshore, boating. AE, MC, V. *Rantasipi Ruuponsaari* (E), Ruuponsaari, 15 km. (9 miles) from village, in lovely lake-side location. 55 rooms, pool, disco. AE, DC, MC, V.

HOW TO GET AROUND. By air. There are regular flights serving Joensuu, Jyväskylä, Kajaani, Kuopio, Lappeenranta, Mikkeli, Savonlinna, Tampere and Varkaus.

By train. You can reach all main towns and resorts by train, though some routes are inevitably made devious by the lake-strewn nature of the region. There are car-carrying trains from Helsinki to Oulu. By fast train, it takes nearly four hours to Jyväskylä, five hours to Kuopio and nearly six hours to Savonlinna.

By bus. Services reach to the remotest corners of the region, with express routes to all main centers.

By boat. The greatest concentration of traffic is on the fabulous labyrinthine waters of Saimaa in the east. The only regular schedule on Saimaa nowadays is Kuopio–Savonlinna–Kuopio, taking about 12 hours each way, but there are any number of local and longer cruises from all the main lake resorts, such as Joensuu, Kuopio, Lappeenranta, Savonlinna, lasting from a few hours to several days. Of special interest are the one-day Monastery cruises to Uusi Valamo and Lintula. Local tourist offices can advise. The longest are six–day cruises operated by Roll–Ships Ltd., Passenger Harbor, Kuopio (971-126 744).

Elsewhere regular schedules include: *Western Lakeland,* the Silverline route Hämeenlinna–Tampere; Poet's Way route Tampere–Virrat; Tampere–Maisansalo. *Central Lakeland* on the Päijänne lake system Lahti–Jyväskylä; Lahti–Heinola. *North Karelia* in the Lake Pielinen region, Joensuu–Nurmes via Koli; Lieksa–Koli.

Most services operate from early or mid–June to mid– or late August. Local cruises are also arranged from most of these centers. On the Päijänne and Saimaa lake systems, evening disco or dance cruises are regularly featured.

By bike. Planned cycling routes are arranged from various centers, such as Imatra, Jyväskylä, Kajaani and Lappeenranta.

TOURS. City tours are organized in summer in Joensuu, Jyväskylä, Kajaani, Kuopio, Lahti, Lappeenranta and Tampere (not always daily); elsewhere by arrangement. Bus tours to places of scenic or historic interest in the surroundings are available from several centers. See also *By boat* above. A wide variety of tours throughout the region are arranged ex-Helsinki by a number of Finnish travel agencies.

PLACES TO VISIT. This is the most watery part of the country, and the permutations on the theme of lake and forest, island and ridge, peninsula and bay, offer endless fascination. Historic sights are concentrated in a few main centers, but there are splendid examples of modern architecture almost anywhere in the region. The following is a selection of principal sights. Opening times apply to the peak season.

HÄMEENLINNA. Aulanko Tower. View point in Aulanko National Park. Open June and July daily 10–8, Aug. daily 10–6.

Castle. Dating from medieval times. Open daily 10–6.

Hattula Church. 14th century stone church with splendid interior frescoes from early 16th century. Open daily 10–6.

Sibelius' Home. The composer's childhood home. Open Mon. to Sat. 10–3, Sun. 12–4.

HYVINKÄÄ. Hyvinkää Church. Designed by A. Ruusuvuori, 1961.

Railway Museum. Hyvinkäänkatu 9; locomotive shed and yard from the 1870s, exhibits include Imperial carriages used by Russian czar—a "must" for railway buffs. Open Tues. 12–3, Wed. 6–8, Thurs. to Sun. 12–3.

IMATRA. Church of the Three Crosses. Designed by Alvar Aalto.

Imatrankoski Rapids. A magnificent sight when the harnessed waters are released on selected Sundays in summer.

Karelian Farmhouse. Openair museum. Open 10–6; closed Mon.

JOENSUU. Handicrafts Exhibition. Rantakatu 2.

Karelia House (Karjalan Talo). Ilosaari, including museum of Karelian culture.

THE CENTRAL PROVINCES

Town Hall. Designed by Eliel Saarinen, 1914.

JYVÄSKYLÄ. Alvar Aalto Museum. Focussing on this renowned Finnish architect. Open Tues. 12–8, Wed. to Sun. 12–6; closed Mon.
Aviation Museum of Central Finland. 20 km. (12 miles) north of city. Open daily 10–8.
City Theater. Designed by Alvar Aalto.
Handicrafts Museum. Open Tues. to Sun. 12–7; closed Mon.
Museum of Central Finland. With handicraft workers' cottages. Open Tues. to Sun. 12–7; closed Mon.
Muuramme Sauna Village. 15 km. (nine miles) south of city; over 200 years of Finnish sauna tradition.
Savutuvan Apaja. Haapaniemi; a smoke cabin and other old buildings from central Finland. Open daily.
University of Jyväskylä. Designed by Alvar Aalto.

KAJAANI. Czar's Stable. Paltaniemi, from a visit by Alexander I.
Hövelö. Paltaniemi, birthplace of poet Eino Leino.
Kajaani Castle. Ruins from 1604.
Kainuu Museum. Asemakatu 4.
Paltaniemi Church. Built in 1726.
Town Hall. Designed by C.L. Engel, 1831.

KUOPIO. Cathedral. Completed in 1815. Open daily 10–5.
Market Square. Lively openair market in center of town.
Orthodox Church Museum. Karjalankatu 1, collections from Orthodox Karelia, unique in Western Europe. Open Tues. to Sun. 10–4; closed Mon.
Puijo Tower. Offering superb panorama. Open June and July 8–10, Aug. 8–8.

LAHTI. Art Gallery. Vesijärvenkatu 11, permanent and special exhibitions. Open daily 11–7.
Ethnographic Museum. Lahden Kartano. Open Tues. to Sun. 12–4, Tues. also 6–8.
Hollola Church and Museum. 16 km. (ten miles) from city; dating from the 14th century. Open daily.
Market Place. Openair market on weekdays, special market day first Wed. of month.
Ristin Kirkko (Church of Cross). Designed by Alvar Aalto. Open daily 10–3.
Ski-ing Stadium. Sightseeing platform on top of 90 meter (295 feet) ski jump. Open Mon. to Fri. 11–6, Sat. and Sun. 10–5.
Town Hall. Designed by Eliel Saarinen.

LAPPEENRANTA. Linnoitus (Fortress). The oldest part of town and features many of the principal sights including: **Papilan kahvila** (Vicarage Café) with Orthodox interior and atmosphere, open Tues. to Sun. 11–6; **South Karelian Museum**, open Tues. to Fri. 10–6, Sat. and Sun. 11–5, closed Mon.; **Virgin Mary Church**, built 1785, the oldest Orthodox church in Finland, open Tues. to Fri. and Sun. 12–2, 2–6.
Lappee Church. Central Park. Open daily 12–5.
Lauritsala Church. Lauritsala, designed by Korhonen and Laapotti, 1969. Open daily 12–5.
Market Place. Openair market Mon. to Sat. 7–1, summer also Mon. to Fri. 3–7.
Saimaa Canal. Built in 1856, restored in 1968, about 50 km. (31 miles) long, linking Lake Saimaa to Gulf of Finland through Soviet territory. Finnish section visited on sightseeing cruises.
Town Hall. Wooden building from 1829, still in use.

MIKKELI. Headquarters Museum. Paamajankatu 1–3. Open daily 11–5.
Infantry Museum. Jääkärinkatu 6–8. Open Tues. to Sun. 11–6.

194 **FINLAND**

Provincial Suur-Savo Museum. Otavankatu. Open daily 11-3, Wed. also 6-8; closed Mon.
Provincial Government House. 1842, by C.L. Engel.

SAVONLINNA. Kerimäki Church. 24 km. (15 miles) to the east. Largest wooden church in the world, built in 1847.

Olavinlinna. Magnificent medieval castle, best in Finland. Open daily 8.30-6.30.
Salama Museum Ship. Schooner from 1874, with exhibits illustrating history of Saimaa lake traffic. Open daily 9-8.
Suruton. In restored villa on Kasinosaari, illustrated history of Savonlinna Opera Festival. Open daily.

TAMPERE. Aquarium. See *Särkänniemi*.

Art Museum of Tampere. Puutarhakatu 34, major Finnish collection.
Cathedral (Tuomiokirkko). Designed by Lars Sonck, built 1902-1907; contains works by famous Finnish artists Magnus Enckell and Hugo Simberg. Open daily 10-6.
Children's Zoo. See *Särkkänniemi*.
Haihara Doll Museum. Kaukajärvi, about nine km. (six miles) from city center; enchanting collection from different parts of the world. Open daily 11-5.
Häme Museum. Näsilinna, major collection featuring exceptional hand-woven rugs and tapestries and "chimneyless cottage". Open Tues. to Sun. 12-6; closed Mon.
Kaleva Church. Striking modern design by Raili and Reima Pietilä. Open daily 10-6.
Lenin Museum. Hallituskatu 19. Open Tues. to Sat. 11-3, Sun. 11-4; closed Mon.
Messukylä Church. Five km. (three miles) from city center, beautiful 15th-century stone church. Open daily 10-5.
Näsineula Observation Tower and **Planetarium.** See *Särkänniemi*.
Pyynikki Park. With observation tower, open daily 9-6, and Summer Theater with revolving auditorium.
Sara Hilden Art Museum. Foreign and Finnish 20th-century art. Open daily 11-7.
Särkänniemi Tourist Center. With Aquarium, Planetarium, Näsineula Observation Tower, Children's Zoo and Amusement Park. Open daily 11-8.

SPORTS. Boating. Rowing boats and canoes are available at all lake resorts; motor boats at many of them. Many canoe tours are organized through the lake systems of the region; check with local tourist offices. Sailing boats can be rented in Kuopio and Lappeenranta. Particularly idyllic are the flotilla sailing safaris in well-equipped yachts arranged on Saimaa, between Kuopio and Savonlinna, lasting one or two weeks; details from Nautic Center, Karhusaari, 02100 Espoo 10, near Helsinki; tel. 90-455 2400.

Golf. Tampere has an 18-hole course. There are nine-hole courses at Aulanko near Hämeenlinna, Lahti, Lappeenranta and Mikkeli.
Riding. Facilities are available at Hämeenlinna, Hyvinkää, Imatra, Joensuu, Jyväskylä, Kajaani, Kuopio, Lahti, Mikkeli, Savonlinna, Sotkamo, Tampere and Varkaus.
Swimming. Almost anywhere! You'll have no problem in finding a secluded spot, or even an island to yourself. Much of the bathing is off smooth granite, which is also excellent for sunbathing—a favorite Finnish pastime.
Windsurfing. Facilities are available at Hämeenlinna, Imatra, Joensuu, Jyväskylä, Kuopio, Lappeenranta, Mikkeli, Savonlinna, Sotkamo, Tampere and Varkaus.
Winter sports. You'll find marked trails for cross-country skiing in almost every Finnish community. Centers with the best facilities in this region—usually including one or more ski lifts, ski school and organized ski excursions—are Hyvinkää, Jyväskylä, Koli, Lahti and Sotkamo.

OSTROBOTHNIA

Rural Plains to Forested Ravines

The flatlands of Ostrobothnia are the least visited by tourists, with some reason since they lack that primeval wilderness quality with which so much of the rest of Finland is endowed. Yet there is quite a lot of interest, especially if you want to get to grips with Finnish history and, not least, if you have a taste for huge sandy beaches that you can enjoy with very little interference from other humanity. The coastal towns vary from charming backwaters to busy bustling places, but most of them have played their part in one way or another in shaping Finland's destiny at some time. The land itself, by the way, has noticeably risen over the centuries so that quite a few harbors are now some miles from the modern nucleus of the towns.

Much of the hinterland is agricultural and nearly all of it flat with one notable exception. That is the north-eastern part of the region, close by the Soviet border, where there is as wild and rugged an area as you could wish to meet in the vicinity of Kuusamo.

As many of the coastal towns have a substantially Swedish-speaking population, the Swedish name is also given where appropriate in this section. It is, incidentally, from this province that so many Finns have emigrated to the United States.

Coast and Plains

You may find yourself entering Ostrobothnia either from Turku to the south or from Tampere and the neighboring province of Häme to the southeast. Almost due west of Tampere on the coast is Pori, the biggest industrial town and harbor on the Gulf of Bothnia, and famous for its annual Jazz Festival. This is one of the places where the retreat of the sea is most noticeable. About 19 km. (12 miles) away, the long beach at Yyteri is a favorite summer resort—the sands are really superb and there are all kinds of sports facilities as well as a splendid hotel there. The old fishing communities of Reposaari, an island accessible by road, are other points of interest about 32 km. (20 miles) away. Two charming coastal towns are worth mentioning to the south of Pori, though strictly speaking they are outside Ostrobothnia's boundaries. These are Rauma and Uusikaupunki in both of which some fine old wooden buildings have managed to survive the hazards of fire.

Or you may come into Ostrobothnia further north, taking in on the way Finland's first wild-life park at Ähteri, due north of Tampere and on the boundary of the two provinces. Your first major coastal town then is likely to be Vaasa (Vasa) and, on the way, you will observe how the country begins to flatten out and finally becomes a succession of rolling plains. There is open country in northern Finland too, but nowhere the cultivation that can be seen here. The whole landscape takes on a new aspect, one unlike any in the other regions of Finland: even the houses are different, generally two-storied.

Vaasa is an important port, with regular passenger services across to Swedish ports. After the disastrous fire of 1852 (a few interesting buildings of Old Vaasa can still be seen) the town was moved nearer the sea and given a Russian name. During the 1918 war of independence Vaasa became the capital of "White" Finland, the country's official government having moved there from "Red" Helsinki, and to commemorate the event the city was allowed to include Finland's Cross of Liberty in its coat of arms. In fact, South Ostrobothnia seems to have taken a prominent part in Finnish politics on several occasions. Besides being the site of a Russian defeat in 1808–9, the parish of Lapua is the place where the anti-Communist Lapua Movement originated in 1930. Spreading quickly all over the country, it reached a climax in the so-called Peasants' March, when 12,000 men from all over the country gathered in the capital and forced Parliament to declare Communism illegal.

The plains of Ostrobothnia are strewn with the battlefields of one or another of the numerous wars that the Finns have fought, first against the Swedes, then against the Russians, and for a brief while even among themselves. The coastal scenery is lovely, and there is good sailing in the Gulf of Bothnia. Apart from Vaasa, there are only two other cities of any size in the province: Kokkola (Gamlakarleby) and Pietarsaari (Jakobstad), lying on the coast to the north of Vaasa. Pietarsaari is an attractive place with strong associations with the national poet Runeberg and has an active, modern trade center. Among the smaller coastal towns, Kristiinankaupunki and Uusikaarlepyy are both charming, with a good crop of ancient wooden houses. For beaches, go to Kalajoki

OSTROBOTHNIA

where the sands are truly glorious and there are good amenities in the way of accommodations and sports facilities, set amidst the dunes.

Kokkola has one sight of particular interest to English visitors. On the banks of the small stream which runs through town is the English Park, and here in a small building is an English pinnace captured during the Crimean War when a landing was attempted near here in 1854. One British officer and eight seamen fell in the engagement, and they are buried in the Maaria Cemetery just outside the city. A memorial to this small battle stands on Halkokari Point in the old harbor.

Bothnian Gulf to Bear Country

Towards the top of the Gulf of Bothnia is the lively northern university town of Oulu. Originally a fur- and salmon-trading port, it became one of the major tar export harbors of the world in the last century and is today a busy industrial center. You can find out about the historic tar trade at the fascinating Turkansaari outdoor museum and try out regional specialties at the museum's cafe. Oulu's excellent modern buildings include a fine theater facing ancient warehouses by the harbor, and there are pleasant parks, a colorful market and plenty of cultural activities.

For complete contrasts with the rest of Ostrobothnia, you must turn northeast to the rugged ravines and forested hills that lie just north of Kuusamo, including the fell district of Rukatunturi and Oulanka National Park. It's an area of gorge-like valleys where you have the opportunity to experience the thrills of shooting the rapids. The fishing is particularly good in these parts, and so is the walking, with marked trails to follow such as the 80 km. (50 mile) long Bear's Tour. It's quite appropriately named, too, though these denizens of the wild are rarely to be seen.

PRACTICAL INFORMATION FOR OSTROBOTHNIA

TOURIST INFORMATION. Kalajoki. Bus Station (983 –60 505). **Kokkola** (Karleby). Pitkänsillankatu 39 (968– 11 902). **Kuusamo.** Kaiterantie 22 (989–11 951). **Oulu.** (City) Kirkkokatu 2 (981–15 121); (Region) Koulukatu 15 (981–226 744). **Pietarsaari** (Jakobstad). Rådhusgatan 5 (967–11 796). **Pori.** (Town) Antinkatu 5 (939–15 780); (Region) Pohjoiskauppatori 1 C 29 (939–13 708). **Rauma.** Eteläkatu 7 (938–16 975). **Seinäjoki.** Kauppakatu 17 (964–141 344). **Uusikaupunki.** Levysepänkatu 4 A (922–21 511). **Vaasa.** (City) Town Hall (961–113 853); (Region) Hovioikeudenpuistikko 11 (961–114 441).

TELEPHONE CODES. We have given telephone codes for all the towns and villages in the hotel and restaurant lists that follow. These codes need only be used when calling from outside the town or village concerned.

FINLAND

HOTELS AND RESTAURANTS. Unless otherwise stated, all the hotels listed below have all or some rooms with bath or shower, licensed restaurants, and are open all the year. Where two names are given in this section, the second is the Swedish name, and indicates that there is a substantial Swedish-speaking population in the area.

ÄHTÄRI. Finland's first wild-life park. *Mesikämmen* (E) (965-30 791). 103 rooms, disco, pool, sports facilities. MC, V.

KALAJOKI. Small bathing resort with superb sandy beaches. *Kalajoki* (E-M), Hiekkasärkät (983-60 283). 35 rooms, disco, extensive sports facilities, by beach. MC, V. *Rantakalla* (M), Hiekkasärkät (983-60 442). 34 rooms, pool, extensive sports facilities. MC, V.
Camping. *Hiekkasärkät,* near beach (983-60 301), open late May through Aug. 31.

KAUSTINEN. Small village best known for its annual folk festival. *Marjaana* (E-M), Teerijärventie 1 (968-611 211). 11 rooms, disco, pool, tennis. MC, V.
Camping. *Tastula* (968-614 118), open June 1 through Aug. 10.

KOKKOLA. Town near shores of Gulf of Bothnia. *Vaakuna* (L-E), Rantakatu 16 (968-15 411). 71 rooms, nightclub, pool. AE, MC, V. *Milton* (E), Rautatienkatu 6 (968-14 044). 44 rooms, disco, sports facilities. MC, V. *Seurahuone* (E-M), Torikatu 24 (968-12 811). 73 rooms. AE, MC, V. *Grand Hotel* (M), Pitkänsillankatu 20 B (968-13 411). 40 rooms, unlicensed restaurant, sports facilities. MC, V.
Camping. *Suntisuu,* two km. (one mile) north of rail station (968-14 006), open June 1 through Aug. 31.
Youth Hostel. *Tankkari,* Pengerkatu 2 (968-18 274).

KUUSAMO. Small town near wild fell and forest country not far from Arctic Circle; summer hiking and winter sports center. *Kuusamo* (E-M), Kirkkotie 23 (989-2021). 112 rooms, nightclub, disco, pool. AE, DC, MC, V. *Rantasipi Rukahovi* (E-M), Rukatunturi (989-3131). In splendid fell and forest country about 25 km. (16 miles) north. 76 rooms, disco, pool, excursions into surrounding wilderness landscapes including shooting rapids. AE, DC, MC, V. *Otsola* (M), Ouluntie 3 (989-2051). 40 rooms, disco. MC, V.
Camping. More than a dozen camp sites in the area. Open year-round are: *Juuma,* (989-45 112); *Teeriranta* (989-62 141); and *Petäjälampi* (989-2364).

OULU. Important northern port on Gulf of Bothnia, industrial and university city. *Vaakuna* (L-E), Hallituskatu 1 (981-224 666). 218 rooms, nightclub, disco, pool, boating. AE, DC, MC, V. *Arina* (E), Pakkahuoneenkatu 16 (981-14 221). 63 rooms. AE, DC, MC, V. *Cumulus* (E), Kajaaninkatu 17 (981-220 222). 207 rooms, pool. MC, V. *Oulun Kauppahotelli* (E-M), Asemakatu 7 (981-227 711). 68 rooms. AE, MC, V. *Tulli-Hotelli* (E-M), Rautatienkatu 11 (981-224 522). 30 rooms, disco. *Hospiz* (M), Asemakatu 31 (981-224 344). 27 rooms, unlicensed restaurant. AE, MC, V. *Otokylä* (I), Haapanatie 2 (981-332 672). 88 rooms without bath or shower, disco, summer only. *Välkkylä* (I), Kajaanintie 36 (981-227 707). 120 rooms, disco, pool, summer only. AE, MC, V.
Restaurants. *Hovinarri* (E), Isokatu 35 (981-222 497). MC, V. *Zivago* (E), Saaristonkatu 12 (981-223 886). *Haarikka* (M), Pakkahuoneenkatu 30 (981-220 840). *Merikulma* (M), Merikoskenkatu 2 (981-349 330). *Reidar* (M), Välkkylä, Kajaanintie 36 (981-13 321).
Camping. *Nallikari,* Hietassari (981-343 516); open early May through Sept. 30.
Youth Hostel. *Pohjankaleva,* Tirolintie 2 C (981-345 588).

OSTROBOTHNIA

PIETARSAARI (Jakobstad). Attractive small coastal town and birthplace of national poet Runeberg. *Kaupunginhotelli* (L–E), Alholminkatu 1 (967–10 366). 51 rooms. MC, V. *Pool* (E), Alholmintie (967–13 222). 40 rooms, pool, sports facilities. AE, DC, MC, V.
Restaurants. *Grevinnan Ebba* (M), Amerikagatan 2 (967–18 211). *Källare Terrazzo* (M), Radhusgatan 17 (967–10 355). DC, MC, V.
Camping. *Joutsen* (967–10 660), open May 15 through Aug. 31.
Youth Hostel. *Joutsen* (967–10 660).

PORI. Major port on Gulf of Bothnia, industrial center near excellent beaches. *Cumulus* (E), Itsenäisyydenkatu 37 (939–16 461). 56 rooms, pool. AE, MC, V. *Juhana Herttua* (E), Itäpuisto 1 (939–11 841). 58 rooms. AE, DC, MC, V. *Rantasipi Yyteri* (E), Yyteri (939–443 777). About 20 km. (12 miles) away by the splendid sandy beaches of Yyteri. 113 rooms, nightclub, pool, extensive sports facilities. AE, DC, MC, V. *Satakunta* (E), Gallen-Kallelankatu 7 (939–11 451). 139 rooms. AE, DC, MC, V. *Karhun Kruunu* (M), Rautatienpuistokatu 2 (939–18 041). 54 rooms. AE, DC, MC. *Mantyluodon Hotelli* (M–I) (939–443 270). 8 rooms without bath or shower. MC, V.
Restaurants. *Itäpuisto* (E), Itäpuisto 8 (939–12 164). MC, V. *Monttu* (E), Antinkatu 15 (939–19 093). AE, MC, V. *Punapaula* (M), Isolinnankatu 19 (939–11 486). *Selkämeri* (M), Eteläpuisto 9 (939–13 461). *Jussikka* (I), Yrjönkatu 10 (939–15 361), beer and wine only. MC, V. *Sarkka* (I), Uusikoivistontie 40 (939–23 874), beer and wine only.
Camping. *Isomäki,* Isomäki Sports Center (939–410 620), open mid-June through mid-Aug. *Siikaranta,* Reposaari (939–84 120), open May 30 through mid-Aug. *Yyteri,* by Yyteri beach 20 km. (12 miles) from town (939–443 778); open May 30 through Aug. 30.
Youth Hostel. *Retkeilymaja,* Korventie 52 (939–28 125).

RAUMA. Coastal town with attractive old districts. *Cumulus* (E), Aittakarinkatu 9 (938–221 122). 104 rooms, pool. AE, MC, V. *Raumanlinna* (E–M), Valtakatu 5 (938–221 111). 74 rooms, disco, pool. AE, DC, MC, V. *Rauma* (M), Kanavakatu 45 (938–11 109). 96 rooms, unlicensed cafeteria.
Camping. *Poroholma,* open May 15 through Aug. 31. *Reksaari,* on island with daily waterbus connections.
Youth Hostel. *Retkeilymaja,* Merkuriuksenkatu 7 (938–641 471).

RUKATUNTURI. See *Kuusamo.*

SEINÄJOKI. Inland town, east of Vaasa. *Aapo* (E), Kalevankatu 2 (964–142 111). 49 rooms. AE, MC, V. *Cumulus* (E), Kauppakatu 10 (964–64 141). 71 rooms, pool. AE, MC, V. *Rantasipi Sorsanpesä* (E), Törnäväntie 27 (964–120 100). 90 rooms, disco, pool. AE, DC, MC, V. *Lakeuden Seurahuone* (M), Keskuskatu 12 (964–21 944). 12 rooms without bath or shower, disco.
Camping. *Törnävä,* three km. (two miles) from center (964–120 784), open June 1 through Aug. 31.
Youth Hostels. *Seinäjoki Youth Hostel,* Törnäväntie 28 (964–120 407). *Amec,* Sahalankatu 11 (964–142 662).

UUSIKAUPUNKI. Attractive small coastal town. *Uusikaupunki* (E–M), Levysepänkatu 1 (922–22 636). 22 rooms, pool. *Panketti* (M), Ylinenkatu 21 (922–24 022). 8 rooms.
Camping. *Santtionranta* (922–3862), open June 1 through late Aug.

VAASA. Major west coast port and historic town. *Waskia* (L–E), Lemmenpolku (961–121 444). 184 rooms, nightclub, pool, sports facilities. AE, DC, MC, V. *Central* (E), Hovioikeudenpuistikko 21 (961–111 211). 145 rooms, pool. AE, MC, V. *Coronet* (E), Ylätori D (961–121 044). 53 rooms. AE, DC, MC, V. *Fenno* (E), Niemeläntie (961–121 055). 101 rooms, sports facilities. AE, MC, V. *Wasa* (E), Hovioikeudenpuistikko 18 (961–123 353). 150 rooms, disco, pool. AE. *Astor*

(M–I), Asemakatu 4 (961–114 383). 26 rooms. *Villitys* (M), Pitkäkatu 21 (961–122 581). 64 rooms, unlicensed cafeteria, summer only. MC, V. *Tekla* (I), Palosaarentie 58 (961–117 788). 58 rooms, unlicensed restaurant, tennis.

Restaurants. *Birra* (E–M), Kauppapuistikko 16 (961–112 461). MC, V. *Centrum* (E–M), Vaasanpuistikko 22 (961–115 245). *Fondis* (E), Hovioikeudenpuistikko 15 (961–111 018). AE, MC, V. *Elite* (M), Kauppapuistikko 8 (961–112 970). *Sekstantti* (M), Kauppapuistikko 40 (961–112 429). *Koti* (I), Raastuvankatu 15 (961–113 039), beer and wine only.

Camping. *Vaskiluoto* (961–113 582), open June 1 through Aug. 31.

Youth Hostel. *Tekla,* Palosaarentie 58 (961–117 788).

HOW TO GET AROUND. By air. Regular flights serve Kokkola/Pietarsaari, Kuusamo, Oulu, Pori and Vaasa. **By train.** Main train routes are to Pori, Vaasa and to Oulu (via Kokkola), including car-carrying trains Helsinki–Oulu. Journey time Helsinki–Oulu by fast train is seven hours. There are no train routes along the coast.

By bus. Services reach to every corner of the region, with express routes to main centers. This is the principal means of transport linking coastal communities.

By bike. Planned cycling routes are organized from Kokkola and Kuusamo.

TOURS. During the summer, sightseeing tours are arranged in Pietarsaari, Seiäjoki and Vaasa. There are also archipelago cruises which are available from Rauma, Uusikaupunki and Vaasa.

PLACES TO VISIT. The main scenic features of the region are its sandy beaches (the best in Finland), small island groups that lie just off the coast and, in the northeast, the magnificently wild fell and forest landscapes just south of the Arctic Circle. Some of the coastal communities have a very long trading tradition, and some have played a major part in Finland's more recent history.

KOKKOLA. English Boathouse. Containing a landing craft captured from the British in the Crimean War.

Kaarlela Church. Two km. (one mile) from town, built in 1460.

Renlund Art Gallery. Pitkänsillankatu 39.

OULU. Botanical Gardens. In attractive Hupisaaret park area at mouth of Oulujoki river.

Cathedral (Tuomiokirkko). Designed by C.L. Engel in early 19th century. Open daily 10–7.

Market Place. With lively openair market, near ancient salt storehouses on waterfront.

Museum of North Ostrobothnia. Ainola Park. Re-opening summer 1985.

Turkansaari. Church and openair museum on island in Oulujoki river 13 km. (eight miles) east of town. Open daily 11–9.

PIETARSAARI (Jakobstad). **Jakobstad Rural District Church.** Kyrkostrand, on southern outskirts of town; founded in 13th century. Open by appointment.

Runeberg's Cottage. Home of national poet J.L. Runeberg. Open daily 12–4.

Runeberg's Fishing Hut. Four km. (two miles) north of town, near camp site Joutsen. Open daily 9–9.

Strengberg Tobacco Museum. Strengbergsgatan 1. Open by appointment.

Viexpo. Strengbergsgatan, permanent exhibition of export goods. Open Mon. to Fri. 8–4, Sat. and Sun. 11–2.

OSTROBOTHNIA

PORI. Central Pori Church. Between bridges over Kokemäenjoki river. Neo-Gothic, built in 1863, with altarpiece by Ekman and stained glass windows by Magnus Enckell.

Juselius Mausoleum. In Käppärä cemetery; erected by a businessman in memory of his young daughter with paintings by Pekka Halonen and frescoes by Gallen-Kallela. Open 12–3, Sat. 10–12; closed Mon.

Town Hall. Formerly Junnelius Palace, Hallituskatu 12; built in Venetian style in 1895. Open by arrangement.

RAUMA. Kirsti. Craftsman's home from the 18th century. Lace–making in summer.

Marela Museum. A ship owner's house from the 19th century.

Pyhän Kolminaisuuden Kirkko (Church of the Holy Trinity). Ruins from the 14th century.

Pyhän Ristin Kirkko (Church of the Holy Cross). Founded in the 15th century, with Renaissance ceiling paintings and wooden sculptures.

Vanhakaupunki (Old Town). Old district south of the canal, with wooden houses based on city plan from 16th century.

SEINÄJOKI. Cultural and Administrative Center. By Alvar Aalto.

Museum of Southern Ostrobothnia. Including Gunpowder, Agricultural, Pharmacy and Openair Museums.

UUSIKAUPUNKI. Cultural Museum. Including maritime section with exhibits from the era of sail.

Lokalahti Church. Wooden church from 1763.

Old Church. From 1629.

Myllymäki Park. With four old windmills.

Pyhämaan Uhrikirkko (Sacrificial Church of Pyhämaa). Wooden church from the 16th century.

VAASA. Art Hall (Taidehalli). Changing Finnish and foreign exhibitions.

Brage Openair Museum. Hietalahti; seal hunting and folk museum. Open Mon. to Sat. 4–7, Sun. 12–4.

Mustasaari Church. Old Vassa. Open daily 9–4.

Orthodox Church. Kasarmintori; includes items from Valamo Monastery. Open Tues. to Sun. 10–3.

Ostrobothnian Museum. Museokatu 3; gentry and folk museum. Open Mon. to Fri. 12–8, Sat. and Sun. 1–6.

St. Mary's Church. Ruins in Old Vaasa.

Stundars Handicraft Village. Solf. Open daily 12–7.

Vaasa Church. From 19th century with altar–piece by A. Edelfelt. Open Tues. to Fri. 10–3 and 6–8, Sat. 10–2.

Vaasa Court of Appeal. With fine portrait collection.

Wasastjerna–House Museum. Special section of Ostrobothnian Museum in Old Vaasa. Open daily 12–6; closed Mon.

SPORTS. Boating. Rowing boats are available at Kokkola, Oulu, Pietarsaari, Rauma, Uusikaupunki, Vaasa; sailing boats at Oulu and Uusikaupunki.

Golf. There are 9-hole courses at Kokkola, Oulu and Vaasa.

Riding. Facilities at Kalajoki, Kokkola, Oulu, Pietarsaari, Pori, Rauma, Seinäjoki, Uusikaupunki and Vaasa.

Swimming. Finland's finest sandy beaches are to be found on the west coast, some stretching for miles. Kalajoki and Yteri, near Pori, have excellent tourist facilities.

Windsurfing. Facilities at Kalajoki, Kokkola, Kuusamo, Oulu, Pietarsaari, Pori, Rauma, Seinäjoki and Vaasa.

FINLAND

Winter sports. Top center of the region is Rukatunturi, near Kuusamo, with ski trails, ski lifts, ski school and all kinds of excursions organized. Winter fishing through the ice is also arranged.

FINNISH LAPLAND

Adventure among Forest Wilds

Lapland is a twofold miracle, a product of man and nature working in close harmony. Nature fashioned a wilderness of endless forests and great silences. Man set out to make it habitable and bend the land to his will. So often the human footstep has obliterated all that came before, but here man has walked gently and left the virgin solitude of this country almost unspoiled. Now easily accessible by plane, train or bus, this Arctic outpost offers comfortable hotels and modern amenities, yet you won't have to go very far to find yourself in an almost primordial solitude. Small wonder that this country has so many romantic traditions.

Exploring Finnish Lapland

The oldest traces of human habitation in Finland have been found in Lapland, and hoards of Danish, English and even Arabian coins indicate trade activities many centuries ago. The origins of the Lapps themselves are lost in the mists of history. There are only some 2,500 pure Lapps still living here; the remainder of the provinces' population of some 220,000 are Finns. Until the 1930s, Lapland was still largely unexploited, still a region where any trip was an expedition of exploration. Then the Canadian-owned Petsamo Nickel Company (now in Soviet hands) completed the great road which connects Rovaniemi with the Arctic Sea. Building activities increased along this route (later to be known as the Arctic Highway), the land was turned and sown, and a few hotels were built to cater to the increasing numbers of visitors.

Next came World War II with the Soviet Union still the enemy. In September, 1944, in conformity with the terms of the Armistice Treaty with their foe, the Finns started to drive out the considerable number of German troops then stationed in Lapland. Methodical to the last, they retreated destroying all they could. The capital Rovaniemi was levelled; almost every farmhouse, cottage and cattle-shed was burned down or blown up.

Barely giving the ruins time to cease smoking, the Finns started back again in a few weeks to create modern communities out of the desolation. Certain areas of Lapland had to be ceded to the Soviet Union (the Arctic coastline, Petsamo, and part of the Salla district on the east frontier), but their inhabitants were settled within the new boundaries. They included some 250 Skolt Lapps, a unique Lapp tribe, who were settled at Sevettijärvi on the northern shores of Lake Inari.

Along the Arctic Highway

To get down to rather more practical details for the intending visitor, let us find a base in Lapland itself from which we can explore the country. The southernmost town of the province, Kemi, is somewhat south of the Arctic Circle on the coast of the Gulf of Bothnia. But practically on the Arctic Circle is the "Gateway to Lapland," Rovaniemi, the administrative hub and communications center of the province where the Ounas and Kemi rivers meet.

In the process of post-World War II rebuilding, Rovaniemi's population shot up from 8,000 to its present 30,000, so don't expect to arrive in a backwoods shanty town. This modern city on the edge of the wilderness comes as a surprise to most people with its excellent architecture and amenities—quite a lot of it, including the layout of the town, the work of Alvar Aalto. Note especially Lappia Hall, the concert and congress center which also houses the Lapland Provincial Museum, the world's northernmost professional theater, and the Library, both beautifully designed by Aalto.

Quite a lot of light industry has come to Rovaniemi, too, and with all the varied amenities it has to offer, it attracts visitors from all over the province on business or pleasure, for health or further education, or simply because it has the best selection of shops of anywhere on or north of the Arctic Circle. Among other places to visit here are the modern church with its impressive mural, and various museum collections devoted to the region and its different features.

Local sightseeing also includes summer trips on the Kemi river and year-round ones to Pohtimolampi (28 km./17 miles) where the Sports and Excursions Center features the world's only reindeer-driving school.

But interesting though it is, Rovaniemi is by no means typical of Lapland and to explore the province you have two main alternatives. The first is to fly or take the Arctic Highway from Rovaniemi to Ivalo, the main artery of central and northern Lapland and, like other roads in the region, an important post-bus route. Eight km. (five miles) from

FINNISH LAPLAND

Rovaniemi, on the Arctic Circle, is a shop and café where mail is postmarked with a special Arctic Circle stamp. At Sodankylä is an ancient wooden church under which mysterious mummies were discovered. The nearby fells have been developed into a holiday area; and at Vuotso, further north, you can even try your hand at goldwashing for an hour, a day or several days under expert guidance at Tankavaara, about ½ km. (¼ mile) east of the Highway; there is now an interesting Gold Museum here, with a restaurant and self-catering accommodation.

Goldwashing is also practised on remoter parts of the Ivalojoki river to the northwest where a goldwashing station, built as long ago as 1870 at Kultala, still stands. Most of the Ivalojoki passes through remote landscapes, but from just south of Ivalo township it flows alongside the Arctic Highway for a while. It's an excellent canoeing river and there are now arrangements for renting canoes to paddle down to lake Inari, returning by bus to holiday centers such as Saariselkä.

The latter lies a little north of Tankavaara and is an expanding complex in a fine setting, with a varied range of accommodations from which to embark on lone or guided trips into the true wilderness. Over 2,500 square km. (965 square miles) of this magnificent area has recently been named the Urho Kekkonen National Park after Finland's former president. Further north, the sprawling small township of Ivalo is a main center for northern Lapland with a top class hotel and all the amenities of a modern community.

The huge island-studded expanses of Lake Inari, north of Ivalo, offer endless possibilities for wilderness exploration, and the village of Inari on its southwest shore is a good center from which to radiate in almost any direction. It has a charming modern church and sightseeing cruises on the lake are arranged in summer. West of it lies the Lemmenjoki (River of Love) where there is a small holiday village from which wilderness treks or boat trips are organized, including into a remote goldwashing district where a few hardy souls are still trying their luck.

In recent years, a growing number of small holiday villages have blossomed on or near the Arctic Highway near Inari and to the north of it, usually with a small restaurant and shop attached. Amenities are simple, but the situations are often magnificent and bring you very close to the true pulse of Lapland. Usually there will be a boat at your disposal, fishing possibilities and the experience of preparing your own sauna. From Kaamanen, north of Inari, a side road leads to Sevettijärvi, home of the Skolt Lapps, and eventually into Norway.

Further north still is Utsjoki, a most straggling village on the Norwegian border. This is the country's northernmost parish in which you can travel by boat on the Teno river—famed for its salmon waters and called Finland's most beautiful river. Should you wish to take a trip into Norway, you can drive over the border at Nuorgam northeast of Utsjoki, or from Karigasniemi over the Norwegian Arctic Highway, eventually returning into Finland at Kilpisjärvi in the far northwest, though this is a very long detour. However, Utsjoki and Karigasniemi are now also linked by a minor road following the Teno river, a road which continues further south still along the border with Norway to Angell from which you can return east to Inari, so that there are now several round-trip possibilities of various lengths.

To the Three Countries Boundary

The other alternative from Rovaniemi is to head via Kittilä or Pello and the Tornio valley into western Lapland, reaching right up to the meeting point with Norway and Sweden near Kilpisjärvi. The fells are higher and the scenery more impressive on this side of Lapland, and the fell group of Pallastunturi and the villages of Enontekiö and Kilpisjärvi are particularly recommended. A superb wilderness trail, about 96 km. (60 miles) long, links Pallastunturi and Enontekiö across the fells, with unattended huts along the way in which to overnight. To the east of the fells, a relatively recent minor road passes through Raattama and a number of hamlets whose remoteness at that time protected them from war devastation so that a number of farm buildings survive from quite ancient times. Enontekiö straggles along a lake shore and from it a road leads to Kautokeino in Norway, eventually linking up with the rest of the Norwegian road network. The road from Muonio to Kilpisjärvi, paralleling the Swedish border, is known as the Way of the Four Winds (after the four points of the male Lapp headgear). Along this route, Karesuvanto is well placed for excursions into the wilderness and trips over into Sweden. From Kilpisjärvi itself, a popular excursion is to the simple granite Stone of the Three Countries, marking the boundary of Sweden, Norway and Finland. There are marvelous views for those with energy to climb Saana fell, looming over Kilpisjärvi and, to the northwest, rise more fells including the highest in Finland, Haltia at over 1,220 meters (4,000 feet).

The Wild and Not-so-Wild

But what are those special features that draw some people back to Lapland again and again? It is difficult to put your finger on them for they are made up of many factors as intangible as the Northern Lights that send their flickering veils of color weaving across the winter sky. If you can take the intense but dry cold, winter is a fascinating time in Lapland, not only for the Northern Lights, but for experiences such as the unique reindeer round-ups.

Depending how far north of the Arctic Circle you go, the sun doesn't rise for anything up to several weeks around mid-winter. Don't imagine it is pitch dark, though. There is reflected light from the invisible sun below the horizon during the middle hours of the day, and a luminosity drawn from the ever-present snow.

From December to March, reindeer owners round up their herds all over the Lapland map, and collect them in their thousands into huge corrals. Sometimes dressed in their colorful costumes, the Lapps and also many Finns lasso the reindeer in true Wild West fashion, recognizing their own animals by brand marks on the ear. Once sorted into individual herds, they are counted, some selected for slaughter and the rest go free again. The round-ups are also attended by many buyers, for reindeer meat is considered quite a delicacy not only for eating locally, but for "export" to the south and even abroad.

To get to some of the remoter round-ups you may have to travel by taxi plane, though other corrals are near the road, especially around Ivalo, Inari and Enontekiö. Most Lapps and northern Finns get there

FINNISH LAPLAND

on skis or by one of those motorized sledges which rather sadly have almost entirely replaced the much more attractive (and silent) reindeer-drawn *pulkka* (a kind of boat-shaped sleigh on one runner). In southern Lapland especially, an increasing number of round-ups occur in the fall. Finding out exactly when and where a round-up is taking place is not easy, for much depends on the whims of the weather and the reindeer, so you must check locally. The information offices in Rovaniemi, however, will be able to give some guidance.

A few words should be said about the Lapps—a proud, sensitive and intelligent people some of whom, with justification, resent the attitude of those visitors who regard them as a tourist attraction put there for their benefit. The word for Lapp in their language is *Same* (pronounced Saa-me) and this is how they prefer to be known. Remember this is their country and they have an ancient culture, language and customs of their own. Modern influences (and intermarriage) have rather regrettably changed many aspects of their traditional way of life; for example, the attractive costumes are less frequently seen, except on festive occasions. The young especially have been affected by the changes and many of them are far more interested in becoming teachers, lawyers or engineers than breeding reindeer or hunting from their remote homesteads. Yet others have found profit from selling souvenirs to the tourists. But most prefer to go about their daily life minding their own business. The Lady Day Church Festival in Enontekiö in March and Easter Church Festival in Inari are particularly colorful events, attended by many Lapps in their most brilliant costumes, and usually featuring reindeer racing or lassoing competitions.

Of other winter attractions such as skiing, reindeer safaris and dog sledge tours, more has been said under *Winter Sports* at the end of this section. Summer has the blessing of daylight up to 24 hours long, and often beautiful weather to go with it, but beware of the mosquitoes. In the fall—usually early September—the colors are quite fabulous.

So the new and the old intermingle in this remote northern corner of Europe. The new Lapland is a place of modern techniques in which careful management is gradually driving back the wilderness and creating cornfields beyond the Arctic Circle. The forests are being exploited and managed with expert care, and light industry and hydro-electric projects have added their mark to the Lapland map. Yet goldwashers still wash the gravel of the Lemmenjoki river, cut off from the world except for occasional visitors and the aircraft that swoop down with their mail and provisions, and the rhythm of the seasons still governs the life of all those connected with reindeer. And the experienced traveler who would like to roam through the wilds for days on end without meeting a fellow human being can still do so without any problem at all. Be warned, however, that climatic conditions change rapidly and often unpredictably, especially on those lonely Arctic fells. Always seek and heed local advice, and tell your hotel or friends where you are heading and how long you intend to be away. An attractive alternative is provided by organized canoeing trips with nights in huts or tents in the wilderness.

Details of the many facilities and types of holiday in the region are given in the annually revised brochure *Finnish Lapland* produced by Lapland Travel in Rovaniemi and available from Finnish Tourist Board offices.

PRACTICAL INFORMATION FOR FINNISH LAPLAND

TOURIST INFORMATION. Ivalo. Bus Station, Piiskuntie 5 (997–12 521). **Kemi.** Town Hall, Valtakatu 26 (980–299 450). **Rovaniemi.** (Town) Aallonkatu 2 (991–299 279); (Region) Lapland Travel (Lapin Matkailu), Pohjanpuistikko 2 (991–16 052). **Tornio.** Välikatu 3 (980–42 831).

TELEPHONE CODES. We have given telephone codes for all the towns and villages in the hotel and restaurant lists that follow. These codes need only be used when calling from outside the town or village concerned.

HOTELS AND RESTAURANTS. Unless otherwise stated, all the hotels listed below have all or some rooms with bath or shower, licensed restaurants, and are open all year.

ENONTEKIÖ. Lakeside village in western fell district. *Hetta* (E) (996–51 361). 39 rooms, pool, boating. *Hetta Touristhotel* (M) (996–51 071). 16 rooms, boating, lovely location overlooking lake. AE, MC, V. *Jussan Tupa* (M) (996–51 101). 34 rooms, pool, boating.
  Camping. *Hetta* (996–51 008), open year round. *Kotakieva* (996–51 063), open June 1 through Sept. 30. *Galdotieva* (996–58 064), near Palojärvi on the road to Kautokeino (Norway), best facilities, open year round.
  Youth Hostel. *Hetan Retkeilymaja* (996–51 016).

INARI. Pleasant village by huge lake of same name in northern Lapland. *Inari Touristhotel* (M) (997–51 221). 22 rooms, only one with private bath, boating, attractive riverside location. AE, MC, V. The area to the north offers several small, simple holiday villages including: *Kaamasen Kievari,* simple huts, restaurant serving excellent local specialties; *Muotkan Ruoktu,* cafeteria; *Neljän tuulentupa,* accommodations in 3- or 4-bed rooms in main buildings, pleasant café and restaurant; *Kiellatupa,* modern, 3- or 4-bed rooms in main buildings. West of Inari is *Lemmenjoen Lomamajat* in a fine riverside wilderness setting up the Lemmenjoki river, cafeteria, shop, fishing.
  Camping. There are about ten camp sites in the area, including at or near all the holiday villages mentioned above. *Lomakylä Inari* (997–51 108), has the best facilities, open June 1 through late Sept.
  Youth Hostel. *Retkeilymaja Kukkula* (997–51 244).

IVALO. Main village and communication center in northern Lapland. *Ivalo* (E), Ivalontie 24 (997–11 911). 62 rooms, pool, boating, on banks of river. AE, MC, V. *Ivalo Touristhotel* (M), Petsamontie 1 (997–11 901). 37 rooms without bath, unlicensed restaurant, boating, overlooking river. AE, MC, V. *Kuiri* (I), Petsamontie 14 (997–11 106). 22 rooms without bath, cafeteria only, boating.
  Camping. *Näverniemi* (997–11 621), open year round.

KARESUVANTO. Village near Swedish border, northwest Lapland. *Ratkin* (M) (996–52 101). 26 rooms, attractive local style, boating. MC.

KEMI. Port and industrial center on far north of Gulf of Bothnia. *Merihovi* (L–E), Keskuspuistokatu 6–8 (980–23 431). 52 rooms. AE, DC, MC, V. *Cumu-*

FINNISH LAPLAND

lus (E), Hahtisaarenkatu 3 (980–20 931). 119 rooms, pool. *Kemi* (M), Meripuistokatu 9 (980–23 951). 22 rooms. *Palomies* (M), Valtakatu 12 (980–23 322). 23 rooms without bath or shower, unlicensed restaurant.

Restaurants. *Kippari* (E), Meripuistokatu 16 (980–23 421). MC, V. *Kaleva* (M), Valtakatu 3 (980–15 624). *Reimari* (M), Keskuspuistokatu 15 (980–23 335). *Roma* (I), Valtakatu 1 (980–16 812), beer and wine only.

Camping. *Kemi* (980–32 005), three km. (two miles) from city, open mid-June through late Aug.

KILPISJÄRVI. Beautiful situation by lake and beneath fells in far northwest. *Kilpisjärvi Tourist Hotel* (E–M) (996–77 761). 39 rooms, boating, beautiful setting. AE, MC, V. *Saananmaja* (M) (996–77 746). 15 rooms, unlicensed restaurant.

Camping. *Kilpisjärvi* (996–77 771), open mid-June through mid-Sept.

Youth Hostel. *Retkeilykeskus* (996–77 771), good facilities.

KITTILÄ. Main village at road junction in west central Lapland. *Kittilä* (E), Valtatie 49 (994–13 201). 37 rooms, pool. *Levitunturi* (E) (994–81 301). 82 rooms, boating, winter and summer sports facilities in nearby fells.

Camping. *Kittilä* (994–13 221), open June 1 through Aug. 31.

Youth Hostel. *Retkeilymaja* (994–13 221).

MUONIO. Main village near western fell districts on Swedish border. *Muonio* (M) (996–2200). 13 rooms. *Olostunturi* (M) (996–2208). 35 rooms, pool, a little outside village at foot of fell.

Camping. *Harriniva* (996–2491), open year round. *Olostunturi* (996–1200), open June 15 through Aug. 15.

PALLASTUNTURI. Splendid group of western fells near Muonio. *Pallastunturi Tourist Hotel* (996–2441). 49 rooms, in magnificent lone location. AE, MC, V.

PYHÄTUNTURI. Fine group of southern fells north of Kemijärvi. *Kultakero* (E–M) (992–12 081). 48 rooms, pool, varied sports facilities.

Camping. *Pyhätunturi Kotakylä* (992–52 120), open mid-June through mid-Sept. and mid-Feb. through end May.

ROVANIEMI. Modern capital of Lapland province; winter sports center. *City–Hotelli* (E), Pekankatu 9 (991–14 501). 66 rooms, beer and wine only, sports facilities. AE, MC, V. *Lapinportti* (E–M), Kairatie 2 (991–22 555). 19 rooms, pool, sports facilities. AE, MC, V. *Ounasvaara* (E) (991–23 371). 39 rooms, lovely hilltop position on outskirts of town. AE, DC, MC, V. *Polar* (E), Valtakatu 23 (991–23 751). 53 rooms, nightclub, pool. AE, DC, MC, V. *Rantasipi Pohjanhovi* (E), Pohjanpuistikko 2 (991–13 731). 214 rooms, disco, pool. AE, DC, MC, V. *Oppipoika* (M), Korkalonkatu 33 (991–20 321). 15 rooms, pool. MC, V. *Rova–Motelli* (M–I), Kemintie (991–81 063). 35 rooms. *Domus Arctica* (I), Ratakatu 8 (991–2981). 130 rooms, beer and wine only, summer only. *Rovaniemen Ammattikoulun Kesähotelli* (I), Kairatie 75 (991–192 651). 36 rooms, cafeteria only, summer only.

Restaurants. *Hartsuherra* (E), Kansankatu 8 (991–12 041), modern, attractive. *Lapinpoika* (M), Ruokasenkatu 2 (991–16 890), excellent cold table, intimate atmosphere. *Iisakki* (M), Valtakatu 19 (991–10 272). *Haarikka* (I), Morkalonkatu 27 (991–3277). *Kesäpaikka–Summerplace* (I), Jäämerentie 9 (991–10 181). Bythe river, light meals.

Camping. *Ounaskoski*, Jäämerentie 1 (991–15 304), open June 1 through Aug. 31, by the river. *Ounasvaara*, at the skiing stadium (991–60 606).

Youth Hostel. *Kaupungin Retkeilymaja*, Hallituskatu 16 (991–10 644).

SAARISELKÄ. Expanding tourist and walking center with modern facilities near virgin wilderness area east of the Arctic Highway; guided hiking trips and gold-panning excursions to old gold workings in the area. *Kelohovi* (E–M) (997–81 891). 12 rooms, beer and wine only, sports facilities. *Lapin Maja* (E–M), Saariseläntie 25 (997–81 826). 60 rooms. *Riekonkieppi* (E–M), Raitopolku 2 (997–81 711). 103 rooms. MC, V. *Saariselkä Recreation Center* (E–M), Saariseläntie 25 (997–81 826). 59 rooms. MC, V. *Laanihovi* (M) (997–81 816). 20 rooms without bath or shower. MC, V. Several well–equipped holiday villages in the area include *Kelohovi* and *Kakslauttanen*.

Youth Hostel. *Kiilopään Eräkeskus* (997–87 101).

SODANKYLÄ. Main village on major route north. *Kantakievari* (E), Unarintie 15 (993–11 926). 53 rooms, pool. MC. *Kantakievari Luosto* (E) (993–44 214). 22 rooms, in nearby Luostotunturi fell district. MC, V. *Summer Hotel* (I), Ammattikoulu (993–11 744). 112 rooms without bath, boating, unlicensed cafeteria, summer only.

Camping. *Nilimella* (993–12 181), open mid–June through late Aug. *Orakoski* (993–11 965), open late May through mid–Sept.

Youth Hostel. *Retkeilymaja,* Lapinopisto (993–11 960).

SUOMUTUNTURI. Fell district on the Arctic Circle, near Kemijärvi. *Suommu* (E–M) (992–12 951). 61 rooms, disco, pool, boating. AE, MC, V.

TANKAVAARA. Goldwashing center near Arctic Highway. Simple self–catering accommodations, attractive restaurant (993–461 58).

TORNIO. On Swedish border at northern tip of Gulf of Bothnia. *Kaupunginhotelli* (L–E), Itäranta 4 (980–42 921). 76 rooms, disco, pool. AE, MC, V. *Tornio* (M), Keskikatu 11 (980–42 401). 14 rooms, disco, boating. MC, V.

Restaurants. *Aarninholvi* (M), Aarnintie 1 (980–445 219). *Dar Menga,* Kauppakatu 12–14 (980–42 353). MC, V. *Pizzeria,* beer and wine only.

Camping. *Aittaniemi* (980–42 011), open June 15 through Aug. 31. *Kallioputaa* (980–445 945), open June 1 through Aug. 31.

Youth Hostel. *Kivirannan Retkeilymaja* (980–40 146). *Suensaari,* Kirkkotie 1 (980–41 682).

UTSJOKI. Village in northernmost fell district by Norwegian border. *Utsjoki Tourist Hotel* (E–M) (997–71 121). 32 rooms, boating. AE, MC, V.

Camping. *Ailigas* (997–71 229), open June 15 through Aug. 30. *Kenestupa* (997–72 531), open mid–June through mid–Aug., some distance south of village. *Kevon Lomakeskus* (997–72 506), open mid–June through mid–Aug., some distance south of village. *Nuorgam* (997–74 312), open year round, some distance northeast of village by road to Nuorgam.

HOW TO GET AROUND. By air. Regular flights serve Ivalo, Kittilä and Rovaniemi. **By train.** There are excellent services to Rovaniemi from the south, including car–carrying trains. Rail routes end at Kemijärvi a little north of the Arctic Circle.

By bus. This is the main form of surface transport throughout the province and extending into northern Norway.

By boat. Sightseeing excursions are arranged on Lake Inari from Inari.

TOURS. City sightseeing tours are arranged in summer in Rovaniemi; also excursions to Pohtimolampi Sports Center (and reindeer driving school). A variety of special interest tours to various parts of Finnish Lapland are organized by Lapland Travel, Pohjanpuistikko 2, Rovaniemi. These feature fishing, canoeing, sailing, trekking and gold panning in summer; skiing, skidoo tours and reindeer safaris in winter. Lapland tours, some extending into northern Norway, are also available ex–Helsinki or ex–Rovaniemi through a number of Finnish travel agencies.

FINNISH LAPLAND

PLACES TO VISIT. The magnificent wilderness scenery of the province is its top attraction at any season. Major winter features are the magical Northern Lights and the thrilling spectacle offered by reindeer round-ups. Fall colors (usually September) are of outstanding beauty. Historic monuments are few and far between, but there is some splendid modern architecture and fascinating museums devoted to this unique region, including the culture of the Same (Lapp) people.

INARI. Lapp Museum. Openair museum displaying Lapp dwellings and traditional way of life.
Pielppäjärvi Church. About 7 km. (four miles) east of village; some 200 years old, wood-built.

ROVANIEMI. Arctic Circle Tourist Lodge. Eight km.(five miles) from city. Open year round.
Ethnographic Museum. Pöykkölä, on the outskirts of town in one of Rovaniemi's few old buildings.
Forestry Museum. Pöykkölä. Open Tues. to Sun. 12–6.
Lapland Provincial Museum. Lappia House (Lapland Collection) and Poromiehentie 1A (birds and minerals). Open Tues. to Sun. 10–6.
Lappia House. Hallituskatu 11; modern theater, concert and congress center designed by Alvar Aalto. Guided tours Mon. to Fri. 10, 1 and 4.
Library. Hallituskatu 9, designed by Alvar Aalto, features art exhibition.
Lutheran Church. Kirkkotie 1, with important altar fresco *Source of Life* by Lennart Segerstråle. Open daily 9–8.

SODANKYLÄ. Church. Wood-built, nearly 300 years old.

TANKAVAARA. Gold Museum. Illustrating history of goldwashing since 19th century, including openair section. Open daily 9–6.

TORNIO. Church. Dating from 1686.
Kukkolankoski Rapids. 16 km. (ten miles) north of town.
Tornio Valley Museum.

SPORTS. Boating. Rowing boats or canoes are available in Inari, Kemi, Kemijärvi, Rovaniemi, Sodankylä, Tornio and from many small tourist centers. Sailing is arranged on some lakes by Lapland Travel (see *Tours* above).
Riding. Facilities exist in Kemi, Kemijärvi, Rovaniemi, Sodankylä and Tornio.
Swimming. Secluded spots are legion and settings almost invariably superb, but don't expect the temperature of the water to be anything much above chilly!
Windsurfing. There are facilities in Inari, Kemi, Kemijärvi, Rovaniemi, Sodankylä.
Winter sports. The long treeless slopes of the Lapland fells offer excellent terrain, though in many cases you will have to climb to the top of them first in order to ski down. However, there is now a good selection of centers provided with a ski lift or two, a ski school and the possibility of hiring equipment. From any of them, you can also practise cross-country skiing (it doesn't have to be far!), which is the best way of all of experiencing these far northern landscapes. All offer marked trails of varying lengths, usually with one or more illuminated to compensate for the shorter winter days, though by March there are already 12 hours of daylight and, by April, 16. The following is a selection of the best-equipped centers, all of them—with the exception of Rovaniemi—consisting either of a lone hotel or a small scattered group of establishments, invariably in a glorious setting: Pallastunturi, Pyhätunturi, Rovaniemi, Saariselkä, and

Suomutunturi. In addition, the villages of Enontekiö, Inari and Kilpisjärvi are excellent centers for cross-country skiing with good accommodations.

Other winter activities include the possibility to test your skill at the world's only reindeer-driving school, at Pohtimolampi, near Rovaniemi. In quite a few centers, rides by reindeer-drawn sleigh are arranged and in a few places, notably Rovaniemi, skidoos can be rented. Reindeer safaris provide an unforgettable experience but are expensive. Ice fishing (through a hole in the ice of a frozen lake) is another popular feature.

ICELAND

214 ICELAND

FACTS AT YOUR FINGERTIPS

ICELAND—FACTS AT YOUR FINGERTIPS

NATIONAL TOURIST OFFICE. The Iceland Tourist Bureau publish a number of pamphlets on all aspects of tourism within the country, and they will be able to supply information on a wide range of travel topics. Their addresses are:

In the U.S.: 75 Rockefeller Plaza, New York, N.Y. 10020 (212–582–2802) 908 17th St., N.W., Washington, D.C. 20036 (202–293–2820).
In Canada: Contact the above New York address.
In the U.K.: 73 Grosvenor St., London W.1 (01–499 9971/72).

Within Iceland, the two tourist bureaus in Reykjavik will be well able to provide more information, and these accept personal callers as well. Their addresses are: Reykjanesbraut 6 (25855), and the Information Tower on Laekjartog (25855).

CURRENCY. In 1981 Iceland adjusted its currency to New Krona (Nkr.), where 1 new krona equals 100 old kronur; new bank notes and coins were also introduced. All banks have foreign exchange departments which handle both hard currency and travellers cheques. The latter can also be cashed at hotels, major travel bureaus, and many restaurants. Note that many goods are priced in dollars and can be bought with that currency or with most credit cards. We give most prices in this chapter in U.S. dollars. At the time of writing (mid-1984), the exchange rate was 29 Nkr. to the U.S. dollar, 42 Nkr. to the pound sterling.

COSTS IN ICELAND. There is no such thing as a cheap trip to Iceland at the present time, as very high rates of inflation and the necessity to import most consumer items have brought the cost of living to a very high level. On top of which, do keep in mind when calculating your daily budget that most Icelandic hotels and restaurants add in to the final bill an astronomical sales tax of 23.5%, in addition to a 15% service charge. Certain items are relatively inexpensive however, those being cinema tickets, public transport, petrol, tobacco, and coffee.

A typical moderate day in Iceland might cost two people:

Hotel (Moderate) with bath and breakfast	$76
Lunch, excluding drinks	15
Dinner, with beer	40
4 bus trips	2
1 taxi ride (5 km., 3 miles)	5
	$138

Sample costs. A cinema seat for one, $2.60; theater seat, $7; cup of coffee, $1.20; glass of beer, 90¢; bottle of house wine in restaurant, $10.50; coke, $1.20; visit to a museum, usually free of charge; moderate taxi ride in Reykjavik, $4.80; average bus ride in Reykjavik, 45¢.

SEASONAL EVENTS. Icelanders celebrate as many holidays as they possibly can! Christmas Eve marks the start of the main midwinter celebrations, which last until *Threttándi* (The Thirteenth—January 6). December 24th is the family celebration, the 25th the religious one, and December 31st and January 6th are the main evenings for social events. In April (in 1985 on the 25th) they greet the First Day of Summer. May 1st and Whitmonday (May 27) are other days when tourists might find some offices are closed.

Iceland has a small population, and large-scale festivals are only rarely undertaken. However, every second year in Reykjavik there is a major International Arts Festival, in early June (the next one will be in 1986). The Westman Islanders also celebrate a National Day of their own, and this is treated as a sports and social festival which is held each year on the first weekend in August.

National Holidays. Jan 1 (New Year's Day); Apr. 4, 5, 8 (Easter); Apr. 25 (First Day of Summer); May 1 (Labor Day); May 16 (Ascension); May 27 (Whitmonday); June 17 (National Day); Aug. 5 (Shop and Office Workers' Official Hol.); Dec. 25, 26, (Christmas); Dec. 31 (New Year's Eve).

LANGUAGE. Icelandic is a Germanic tongue first brought to the island by settlers from Norway. The modern language has changed so little from the Old Norse of ancient times that Icelandic children can understand the Sagas as easily as if they had been written only yesterday, though these works date from the 12th to the 14th centuries!

However, it is a difficult language to master thanks to an extremely difficult set of pronunciation rules, and many tourists (most, in fact) will find it nigh on impossible, what with words and constructions like this: "haestaréttarmálaflutnigsmannsskrifstofustúlkuútidyralykill," meaning "a latch key belonging to a girl working in a lawyer's office." Fear not though, as any Icelander you meet will almost certainly speak fairly good English, probably excellent Danish and German, and possibly some French as well.

CUSTOMS. Visitors to Iceland are allowed to import the following items duty-free: 200 cigarettes or 250 grams of tobacco products; plus, 1 liter of alcoholic beverage, and 1 liter wine less than 21% alcoholic content, or 12 bottles of beer (note that only those over 20 years of age can import alcohol, over 16 for tobacco products). Prescription drugs for personal use are also permitted. No limit is put on the amount of foreign currency which may be imported or exported, but no more than Ikr. 2,100 may be exported.

HOTELS. Icelandic hotels are simple if not quite austere, apart from some of the more expensive places within the capital itself. On the whole, they are clean and comfortable, but travelers should note that breakfast is not included in the cost. Also, there is a high service charge imposed, as well as a hefty state tax and this has been added into the figures we list below. Somewhat less expensive accommodation is available in private homes within Reykjavik, which usually run about $26 a night for a single room, $36 for a double. Check with the Iceland Tourist Bureau for lists of homes participating in this scheme.

Prices. We have divided the hotels we list into three categories: Expensive (E), Moderate (M), and Inexpensive (I). These gradings are determined solely by price. The prices behind these gradings vary between hotels within Reykjavik and those elsewhere in the country.

Two people in a double room can expect to pay (in U.S. dollars):

	Reykjavik	Elsewhere
Expensive	$65–$105	$50–$65
Moderate	$45–$65	$35–$50
Inexpensive	$29–$45	$20–$35

These prices include service charges and tax.

Icelandic villages are very small, so for the most part hotels there do not have any addresses as such—you simply enter the village and the hotel will probably be the first thing you see. All of the "Edda" hotels we list are boarding schools throughout the winter, and it's only during the summer tourist season that they are turned into hotels. These are often built out in the middle of nowhere, the location being usually by a hot spring, which explains the numerous swimming pools and saunas that Edda hotels offer.

FARM VACATIONS. Besides being one of the least expensive means of accommodation, farm holidays are an excellent way of meeting the natives to gain an insight into their way of life, and are ideal for those who would happily spend a week or two berry-picking, fishing, rambling, hiking, and pony-trekking. *Samvinn-Travel,* Austurstraeti 12, Reykjavik (27077), are just one of the many agents which book farm holidays; contact the Tourist Bureau for more information.

CAMPING. Over a score of camp sites have been created in Iceland, and a list of these, with their amenities, can be obtained from the Tourist Bureau. Most of them are fairly basic, but usually provide camp toilets and running water, in a few cases hot water and electrical outlets. The site at Reykjavik is well placed next to the swimming pool and sports stadium; in Akureyri, it is adjacent to an open air swimming pool near the town center. Charges are about $2 per night or less.

The best equipped camping grounds are found in Reykjavik, Húsafell, Ísafjördur, Varmahlid, Akureyri, Mývatn, Egilsstadir, Laugavatn, Thingvellir, Jökulsárgljúfur, and Skaftafell. Where there is no site, tents may be pitched in any suitable spot, though campers should request permission (which is usually granted) of the local farmer to camp on any cultivated ground or fenced-in areas.

Where camping is prohibited, such as in parts of a national park, signs are displayed reading *Tjaldstaedi bönnud.* In other places areas have been marked out for camping, frequently marked *Tjaldstaedi,* and no special permission is then necessary. In some areas international signs are posted.

As no firewood or other fuel is to be found in Iceland, and it is forbidden by law to use the scant scrub found in some areas, campers should bring along paraffin or gas stoves for cooking and heating. Supplies of paraffin are available at gas stations and a few stores in Reykjavik, and at gas stations in Keflavik, Hafnarfjördur, Akureyri and Husavik. Propane gas is sold at Shell gas stations in Reykjavik and at the larger Shell gas stations throughout the country. Butane gas and Camping Gaz are available in Reykjavik (at Solvholsgata 1), and at most co-operative stores throughout the country.

Camping equipment can be rented only in Reykjavik and advance reservations are advisable. For rates see the Reykjavik *Camping* section below.

YOUTH HOSTELS. There are hostels located countrywide, though the Y.H.A. headquarters are at Laufásveg 41, Reykjavik (24950); they will supply all details. In Akureyri, the Youth Hostel is at Stórholt 1 (96–23657). *Ferdafélag Íslands* (Touring Club of Iceland), Öldugata 3, Reykjavik (19533 and 11798), oversee a number of huts in somewhat less inhabited areas where travelers can stay overnight, provided they bring their own sleeping bags and food. Groups which are traveling with the Club have priority over others.

For those who travel independently by car, we suggest you buy the *Iceland Road Guide,* an excellent book which marks hostels, sleeping bag cabins, and Edda hotels throughout the country.

RESTAURANTS. Icelandic restaurants have improved a great deal over the past 20 years. Now many good eating places suitable for all budgets are found in Reykjavik and Akureyri, as well as in many of the suburban areas. Down-market, the snack bars usually found adjacent to gas stations are good and reasonably priced, plus you can re-fill your coffee cup free! Budgeteers should note that while restaurant prices will most likely be comparable with what you're used to paying, wine is fiendishly expensive as it is imported, so keep this in mind as you order your magnum! We particularly recommend the fish dishes, since Icelandic fish is always fresh and tasty.

Some of the more expensive Reykjavik and Akureyri restaurants have dancing, particularly at weekends, with singing and modest cabaret shows.

Prices. We have divided the restaurants in our listings into three categories—Expensive (E), Moderate (M), and Inexpensive (I). These gradings are determined solely by price and usually include both tax and service charges, though do check.

Prices, per person, excluding drinks, in U.S. dollars:

	Reykjavik	Elsewhere
Expensive	$20 and up	$14–$20
Moderate	$12–$20	$8–$14
Inexpensive	$7–$12	$4–$8

FOOD AND DRINK. Iceland has to import most of her goods, so prices are quite high. Supermarkets are stocked with a good variety of food, but tinned food is especially expensive. Best to go for local foods which are fresher and cheaper. Milk is excellent, and *skyr*, which is made from milk and tastes a little like yogurt, is delicious with fresh blueberries, served in late summer. Another specialty is *hardfiskur* (dried fish), best in small bits spread with butter. The fish, usually haddock, is dressed, cleaned, and washed, then hung up in airy sheds where it dries until becoming hard and brittle. It is almost as common a sight in Iceland to see row upon row of drying fish as it is in Greece to see the grapes picked and laid out to dry.

An unusual Icelandic dish is cured shark meat, known locally as *hákarl*. Fresh shark meat is not edible and has to be cured before being eaten. The shark is cut into strips which are placed on a clean gravel bed and covered with stones. After several weeks, it is removed, washed, and hung up to dry. The curing process is difficult and only those with experience can turn out a first-class product. Shark meat has a rather pungent odour; it has been said that when eating it, the most ticklish operation is to get it past your nose! To obtain maximum gastronomical enjoyment, it should be washed down liberally with ice-cold Icelandic *brennivin*.

Of the meat dishes, lamb is especially recommended. Smoked lamb, called *hangikjöt*, is used on festive occasions and as a traditional main course for Christmas dinner.

Icelandic cuisine has improved immensely over the past two decades, and fish, in particular, is fresh and delicious. The following dishes are recommended: *Íslenzkur kaviar* (Icelandic caviar), *sherry síld* (marinated herring in sherry), *smokkfiskur Lisbon* (cuttlefish Lisbon), *graflax* (raw pickled salmon, a national dish), and *lambalundir* (tenderloin of lamb). For dessert, try *Íslenzkar pönnukökur* (Icelandic pancakes).

As mentioned before, wine is expensive since it, too, must be imported. The local beers are good, though not as high in alcoholic content as American beers or English lagers.

TIPPING. Hotels and restaurants usually include in the bill both a service charge of 15% plus a sales tax of 23.5%. Extra tipping is not expected, and can, in some cases, even be resented. Taxi drivers, hairdressers, and washroom attendants are not tipped. There is a small charge for leaving coats in cloakrooms, though no more than 50¢. A cover charge is added to the bill in some licensed restaurants.

MAIL. Rates for postcards are 6 Ikr. to the U.K., 6.50 to the U.S.; letters cost 7.50 Ikr. to the U.K., 13.50 to the U.S. Mail boxes are red. The main post office in Reykjavik is on the corner of Austurstraeti and Posthusstraeti; open weekdays 9–5, Saturday 9–12.

FACTS AT YOUR FINGERTIPS

TELEPHONES. An efficient telephone and telegraph service is available throughout the country, both for inter-Iceland and overseas calls; the latter can be booked day and night. You can dial direct almost anywhere in Europe, otherwise telephone "09" for assistance on overseas calls, "02" for local calls. The operator will speak English and will connect you with the required number.

CLOSING TIMES. Shops are open on weekdays from 9 A.M.–6 P.M.; some remain open on Friday evenings till 8 or 9 P.M. Candy stores and flower shops do not shut until 11 P.M. On Saturdays, shops are open from 9 A.M. –12 noon, though some shops close on Saturdays during the summer. Banks are open for business Mon. to Fri. from 9.15 A.M.–4 P.M. On Thursdays, most banks remain open until till 5 or 6 P.M.; note that banks are closed Saturdays. Offices are open 9 A.M.–5 P.M. weekdays, and close on weekends.

SPORTS. Hiking through the extensive uninhabited interior and **mountaineering** are two of the favorite pastimes. A leaflet *Climbing and Skiing in Iceland,* obtainable from the Iceland Tourist Board, gives excellent guidance on some of the best areas and advice on equipment and guides. There are ramblers' clubs in main towns which organize both day and weekend outings; for more details, contact *Ferdafélag Íslands,* Öldugata 3, Reykjavik (19533).

Iceland offers some of the best salmon and trout **fishing** in all Europe, while sea angling for cod, haddock, etc., at Grindavik, and halibut fishing in Breidafjördur is also good. Reindeer **hunting** in Aug. and Sept., and wild goose shooting from Aug. 20–Nov. 20.

Icelandic ponies can be hired in most places for those who want to get in a spot of **riding**. These sturdy steeds are direct descendants of those brought over by the Vikings and are ideally suited to the rough terrain. Riding possibilities range from a few hours to much longer treks with a guide, staying at hotels, hostels or camping. Check the Tourist Bureau's pamphlet entitled The *Viking Horse* for more details.

Swimming is considered the national sport, and excellent facilities are available countrywide.

There is enough snow most winters for **skiing**, and most of the population gets out into it. There are a few skiing centers, notably near Akureyri in the north and, in summer, in the Kerlingarfjöll mountains in remote south central Iceland, about 125 miles from Reykjavik. The latter are best explored from the little valley of Askard where weekly courses are arranged (hostel and camping facilities).

GETTING AROUND ICELAND. By air. *Icelandair* (Flugleidir) flies the domestic routes which link about a dozen of the country's main towns and villages, as well as the Westmann Islands. *Arnaflug Eagle Air* also has services across the country; contact their head office at Lagmula 7, 105 Reykjavik, for further information.

By bus. There is no train service in Iceland, but the country has a comprehensive network of bus services reaching to all but the most isolated communities. Though the road may often seem rough, the routes take you through some incredible and quite unforgettable scenery. There are a number of special runabout tickets available, such as the *Full Circle Passport,* which is good for travel on the main ring route around Iceland. There is no time limit and you can stop-over along the route as often as you like; cost at presstime was $115. The *Omnibus Passport* gives unlimited travel on all scheduled coach routes, main roads, and secondary roads; cost at presstime was $125 for 1 week, $164 for 2 weeks, $202 for 3 weeks, and $235 for a month. Children's discounts available.

Air-Bus Rover tickets—fly one way, bus the other—are also very popular and economical, as well as being conveniently time-saving.

By car. Apart from the asphalt roads through and around the towns, the highway between Keflavik and Reykjavik and a fairly good road to Selfoss, motoring can be a hazardous exercise, often along lava track or dirt and gravel surfaces. The ring route around Iceland is now completed, but it can hardly be called a highway. One motors—and arrives—eventually, and seldom without some minor excitement en route, such as the disappearance of a road under a small river, which wasn't there the day before—but it is a fascinating exercise. On the whole, you must be prepared to handle small repairs and maintenance yourself though there are a few small garages. Fuel service stations are few and far between; at presstime, 1 liter of petrol *(bensín)* was about 77¢. You drive on the right. An international driving license is necessary.

See the *Useful Addresses* section, page 232, for the names of some car hire firms within Reykjavik.

By boat. There is a boat service from Reykjavik to almost all of Iceland's harbour towns; contact *Ríkisskip, Skipaútgerd Ríkisins,* Hafnarhúsi v/Tryggvabraut 101, Reykjavik (28822), for detailed information on fares and schedules.

By bike. On the whole, Icelandic country roads are not suitable for bicycling, though many visitors find it enjoyable to explore some of the cities and towns by bike. Details of rental fees and bike hire establishments are available from both tourist offices and youth hostels.

On foot. As mentioned in the *Sports* section earlier, hiking is very popular and a marvelous opportunity to experience Iceland's rugged landscape. However, we stress that no expedition should be undertaken lightly, certainly never without advising local people where you are going, and in many cases you should consider taking a guide.

PRELUDE TO ICELAND

Land of Ice and Fire

When the Vikings landed in Iceland, they thought they had discovered the entrance to the Netherworld. Centuries later, the cone-shaped Snaefellsjökull glacier was made famous by Jules Verne in his *Journey to the Center of the Earth*. In Iceland you are on the edge of the world—and it feels that way too. This is a land of eerie icescapes and petrified lava fields, steaming thermal springs and spectacular glaciers. It is estimated that over the last 500 years a third of the volcanic lava to have reached the surface of the earth emerged in Iceland. Such is the pressure beneath the surface that the Giant Geysir, which gave its name to geysers all over the world, can spout boiling water and steam over 150 feet in the air. By contrast, the largest glacier here, Vatnajökull, occupies an area equal to all the other glaciers in Europe put together.

Iceland has always been different—and in many different ways. There is hardly a tree to be seen throughout the island. There are no frogs, snakes or reptiles (though there was once a unique breed of man-sized penguins, which disappeared when their nesting grounds literally blew up in an eruption). When the Vikings arrived, foxes were the only indigenous mammals. Since then, man has imported a wide range of animal inhabitants, including inadvertently-introduced mice and rats. Remnants of the reindeer imported by earlier settlers now roam in wild herds in the central highlands.

Mod-Cons Nature's Way

Despite all this, Iceland is a modern Scandinavian country—though it is 500 miles from the nearest landfall (northern Scotland) and nearly 1,000 miles from Copenhagen, which used to be its administrative capital. Nowadays the population is around 235,000—the same as the city of Derby in Britain, or just over half the size of Omaha, Nebraska. Half the Icelanders live in the capital Reykjavik, while over 80% of the rest of the island's 40,000 square miles remains uninhabited.

As its name suggests, Iceland is a chilly country. Though the Gulf Stream may keep its winters slightly warmer than those of New York, in summer a temperature of 70°F has them all swooning. But the summers here have one great advantage—it practically never becomes dark. And even in spring and fall there are long, long twilit evenings. But despite the tempting blue sea washing the weird black volcanic sand of the beaches, the sea is always too cold for swimming.

By contrast, Iceland has a flourishing horticultural industry, producing vegetables to meet the domestic demand, flowers for export, fruit—even bananas! This is all achieved by harnessing the abundant geothermal energy, which is put to a wide variety of use. For instance, most of the houses in Reykjavik are heated by naturally-produced near-boiling water. This is carried by two ten-mile-long, heavily insulated pipelines from the nearby hot springs. The heat lost while the water is running from the undergound streams to the kitchen tap is less than 2°F, enabling the Icelanders to keep their houses at around 70°–75°F both winter and summer. However, you may sometimes notice a rather odd sulfur smell in the bathrooms.

If you happen to visit in winter, you'll find that it's dark for all but a few hours, partially explaining why the Icelanders are such good chess players. The real wizards come from the island of Grimsey, 30 miles off the northern shore on the Arctic Circle, where in mid-winter they only have a few hours of twilight every day. These long nights also explain why, per capita, more books are written, printed, bought and read in Iceland than anywhere else in the world.

However, before you set out for Iceland, there's one vital point you should know. Iceland is an expensive country. Inflation is at present running around 45% and prices are high—though the falling value of the krona does mean that your pounds and dollars go that bit further. The main cause of inflation is that despite its small population, the island is anything but self-sufficient. Only just over 1% of the land is under permanent cultivation (hardly surprising when you realise that Reykjavik is on the same latitude as Archangel in Russia, and the Yukon in Alaska). This lack of land development means that a high proportion of foodstuff has to be imported—and at a considerable expense owing to the distances involved. Indeed, Iceland's whole economy is based upon its sole major industry—fishing.

Despite these drawbacks, Iceland attracts a wide range of visitors, including many biologists, geologists, bird-watchers and photographers: all attracted by the unique colorfulness of the landscape—with its black lava, red sulfur, blue hotsprings, grey and white rivers with spectacular waterfalls creating high arching rainbows, and green, green valleys (unlike Greenland, which, paradoxically, is covered in ice).

PRELUDE TO ICELAND

However, as you trek the wilderness you must be prepared for temperamental weather. Here you can have all four seasons in one day. Even so, when you step inside off the tundra, you enter Scandinavian-style living quarters: this is a land where primeval landscapes and modern comforts exist side by side.

Iceland may not be to everyone's taste—but there's no denying that it's different.

History and Development

The first people to arrive in Iceland were Irish monks. However, their time here was neither long or happy and they were either enslaved, or driven out, by the first recorded settlers, the Norsemen, who arrived in the year 874. The Norsemen were led by Ingólfur Arnarson, who was fleeing from the tyranny of Harold Fairhair in Norway. When Arnarson first saw Iceland rising out of the sea before his longboat, he threw overboard a pair of high seat pillars carved with images of the heathen gods. He swore that he would make his home wherever the wooden pillars landed. Some time later they were found washed up in a mysterious smoke-shrouded bay. The smoke was caused by the steam from the nearby hot springs. The Icelandic word for smoke is "reykur," and for bay is "vík"—and that is how the capital of Iceland, Reykjavik, got its name.

To begin with the new colony prospered, attracting many Norsemen who had already settled in parts of Ireland, Scotland and the Faroe Islands. These new settlers brought with them their wives and slaves, which accounts for the preponderance of Celtic blood in the Icelandic population. Even to this day many of the natives have the appearance and temperament of Irish people.

In 930 the settlers established their first parliament—the Althing. Thus they created the first republic north of the Alps. The Althing still operates today, and is now the world's oldest surviving national legislature.

With prosperity, the forests melted before the axe, the sod was turned with primitive ploughs, imported sheep grazed the uplands, fish thronged the rivers, lakes and bays, and the skalds sang eulogies to the pagan gods. But with prosperity came rivalry and power-struggles. The Icelandic chieftan Eric the Red was forced to flee from his enemies (and in so doing discovered Greenland, founding an Icelandic settlement there). When Eric's son Leif fled, he discovered a land called Vinland—now widely believed to have been the northern shores of America. It was this era which gave birth to the famous Icelandic sagas. These sagas describe the life of the early powerful Viking settlers, their heroic deeds at home and overseas, their vicious blood-feuds, and their great love stories.

Meanwhile, the country continued to be rent by quarrels, feuds and power-struggles. By the beginning of the 13th century there was general civil war. Fratricidal strife continued for more than 50 years, periodically stirred up by the Norwegian kings who hoped to claim Iceland as their own. Their hopes were realized in 1264, when the Norwegian king stepped in as "arbiter" and sovereign. However, in 1380, both Iceland and Norway came under the Danish crown. The islanders then had to cope with the encroachment of Danish officials as well as natural calamities caused by volcanic eruptions. Their problems were further increased in the mid-16th century when the Reformation was imposed by the Danish king, and the last Catholic bishop, Jon Arason, was beheaded without trial. The king confiscated the property of the monasteries and churches, consolidating still more his grip on the country. At the same time, Spanish, Moorish and English pirates also raided the country. Then came famine, smallpox, leprosy, the Black Death, and worst of all, the imposition by the Danish king of a trade monopoly.

Iceland's unhappy story continued until the early 19th century when Icelandic nationalism began slowly to emerge in opposition to the oppressive Danish trade monopolies. But the movement thereafter gained popular momentum rapidly. Partial Home Rule came in 1904, and full sovereignty under the Danish King in 1918. When Denmark was invaded by Germany in 1940, Britain occupied undefended Iceland to keep it from falling into the hands of the Axis. A year later American forces replaced the British (and built Keflavik Airport); and on June 17th 1944, Iceland severed its remaining ties with Copenhagen to become a republic once more. The Icelanders then elected their first president. And in 1980, the Icelanders elected Vigdís Finnbogadóttir as president—the first woman to be elected a president in Europe.

Sagas, Song and Seafaring—Iceland Today

Alone among the world's myriad tongues, modern Icelandic has changed so little since early pagan times that reading the ancient sagas presents no more of a problem to the present-day Icelander than do Shakespeare's works to the average educated Englishman or American. Swedish, Danish and Norwegian all developed from the same stem, of course, but Icelandic bears about the same relationship to them as Anglo-Saxon does to English, and it's an exceptional Scandinavian who can make his way through Icelandic literature without the aid of dictionary and grammar. Even at this late date, Icelandic retains two peculiar letters of the alphabet which long ago disappeared from the other northern languages. One letter looks like a *b* combined with a *p*, and is pronounced like the *th* in *thin;* the other, pronounced like *th* in *leather* resembles a lazy *d* with a horizontal line drawn through the stem. Both look formidable on first acquaintance but yield to a little persistent lisping and buzzing.

In addition to its literary achievements, Icelandic has had a novel effect on matrimony and the position of women. In Iceland the custom persists of giving children the *first* instead of the *last* name of their father. Thus Magnus, the son of Svein, becomes Magnus Sveinsson, while Gudrun, the daughter of Einar, is known as Gudrun Einarsdottir. What's more, Gudrun keeps her maiden name even after she marries, though her children will bear her husband's name.

Another custom is preserved amongst the older women. Many still wear the graceful national costume, which consists of a long, full black skirt and a black bodice, embroidered in gold and laced with gold cord over a colored blouse. An apron, worn as an ornamental panel, is usually of the same material as the blouse. Their hair is done up in two long braids which are looped up behind, and on their heads they wear small black velvet caps, with long black tassels, which are bound by two- or three-inch rings of gold or silver. Many of the younger women treasure the beautiful embroidered costumes worn by their mothers or grandmothers, though they do not wear them except on gala occasions.

Besides chess and books, singing has long been a favourite pastime to while away the long winter evenings. Even today the influence of medieval church music is revealed by the use of harmonies long ago superceded elsewhere. Choral groups are numerous and active—again there are more per capita than in any other country—and part of the explanation seems to be that until relatively recently musical instruments were comparatively unknown. Singing developed naturally from ballad and saga recitals, and the tradition persists.

But fishing is really what Iceland is all about. The fishing industry and its by-products dominate the national economy. The main commodity available for export is fish, and about 75% of Iceland's trade is based in fish products. Per fisherman, the annual catch amounts to a staggering 290 tons, another world record.

Several years ago, over-fishing began to have a serious effect on Iceland's traditional fishing grounds. In consequence, Iceland extended her territorial limit to 200 miles, in a desperate effort to preserve stocks. More than this, it was also designed to protect the jobs of the more than one-in-seven of Iceland's workforce who are employed in the fishing industry. This action by Iceland led to a dispute with Britain—the so-called "Cod War"—which is now, fortunately, a thing of the past. A compromise was reached, and the rich harvest of the Arctic seas remains protected.

EXPLORING ICELAND

Volcanos, Hot Springs and Glaciers

Iceland is the second largest island in Europe (only Great Britain is larger.) It has approximately the same land area as England, or Kentucky, and for many yeaars its strategic position in the north Atlantic made it an important staging post on trans-Atlantic flights. Nowadays, practically all flights go direct between Europe and America—though advantageous rates apply for those willing to make a short stop-over at Keflavik, Iceland's international airport, which is just 29 miles from Reykjavik.

Iceland's Capital

At the turn of the century, Reykjavik was a sleepy fishing village of just 6,000 people. Though it's now 20 times this size, its expansion has been carefully planned. The new apartment blocks are earthquake-proof, and the city is completely smokeless as all its heating is provided by the nearby hot springs. However, some considered that this mania for planning had gone too far when in 1971 it was decided to enforce an earlier law forbidding dogs within the city limits. Controversy over this law still rages—and respectable matrons can be observed furtively ferrying their illegal dogs by car out to the countryside for walks.

Set in its fjord, overlooked by snow-capped mountains, Reykjayik presents a colorful sight—with its concrete houses painted in light

EXPLORING ICELAND

REYKJAVIK (NOT ALL STREETS SHOWN)

1. Althing (Parliament)
2. Arbaer (Folk Mus.)
3. Arnagardur (Manuscript Mus.)
4. Asgrimur Jonsson Art Gallery
5. Asmundur Sveinsson Gallery
6. Campsite
7. City Bus Terminal
8. Einar Jonsson Museum
9. Hallgrim's Church (Leif Eriksson Statue)
10. Idnó Theater
11. Íslenzka Dýrasafnid (Mus. of Icelandic Animals)
12. Kjarvalsstadir (City Art Gallery)
13. Long Distance Bus Terminal
14. National Theater
15. Náttúrugripasafnid (Natural History Museum)
16. Norraena Húsid (Nordic House)
17. President's and Prime Minister's Offices
18. Thjódminjasafnid (National Mus.)
19. University
□ Tourist Information Offices

colours, and their striking red, blue and green roofs. Among the more important buildings are the Parliament or Althing, and the National Theater (both close to the harbor), and the University and the National Museum on Sudurgata beyond Mela Torg. Hallgrim's Church, with its famous statue of Leif Eriksson, dominates a rocky plateau overlooking the harbor by Laugavegur.

Reykjavik's streets are ideal for window-shopping, but you'll find everything very expensive. Bargains are few and far between. Even so, an Icelandic sweater is a must. You'll find them all over town, but the best selection is in the Icelandic Handcrafts Center at Hafnarstraeti 3, down by the harbor near the City Bus Terminal. Good sweaters start at around 200 krona.

Besides being the island's center of government, Reykjavik is also its cultural center. Largely owing to those long dark winter evenings, the arts thrive here. Despite its comparatively small population, the city has its own symphony orchestra, two professional theaters, several museums and art galleries, and numerous cinemas and bookstores. The more popular arts also exist here. Though Reykjavik is hardly known for its night life, there are some good discos. But a word of warning here: drinks in such places cost the earth.

Excursions from Reykjavik

Reykjavik makes a good base for exploring other parts of the country. About 56 km. (35 miles) east of the capital stretches the broad lava plain of Thingvellir, site of the first parliament and now a national park. A placid lake, Thingvallavatn, the biggest in Iceland, lends a deceptively idyllic air, for it was here that chieftains and citizens from every village and farm met each summer to make the law. Here the decision was taken around the year A.D. 1000 to lay aside pagan ways and adopt the tenets of Christianity. The speaker's rock and the hollowed-out seats reserved for the most important men can still be seen, together with the ancient fairgrounds where wrestling matches took place, weddings were contracted, and witches drowned. Nowadays Thingvellir is a favorite place for holiday-makers, and the modern campers' tents in the summer do, in a sense, carry on the tradition of the great meeting place, but in a much more gentle form. Do not miss a stroll along the Almannagja chasm, and the magnificent view from its upper rim.

A little further out from Reykjavik, the Great Geysir, which gave its name to hot springs around the world, bubbles away oblivious of the expectant crowds which gather there daily in hopes of some excitement. Geysir is getting old these days and cannot be relied upon to perform, but a junior geyser, Strokkur, seldom fails, throwing up boiling water to considerable heights at five-minute intervals. In the same area there are small boreholes from which steam arises, as well as beautiful pools of blue water.

Twenty km. (12 miles) away there is more thunder, this time in the form of the deafening Gullfoss waterfall. The river Hvita plunges down a series of steps before throwing itself 30 meters (95 ft.) into a narrow canyon. The noise—and the spray—are on a heroic scale, and towards afternoon the sun illuminates the moist air, making it in fact, as well as name, the Golden Falls. Twentynine km. (18 miles) from Geysir is Skalholt, a hallowed spot in Icelandic history. There has been a Chris-

EXPLORING ICELAND

tian church on this spot for nine centuries, and the present exquisitely simple building is the eleventh in its line. Jon Arason, last Catholic bishop in Iceland, and martyr to the Reformation, was beheaded without trial at Skalholt in 1550. A plaque marks the spot.

To ascend 1,615 meter (5,000 ft.) volcanic Mount Hekla requires two full days, although by road it's only 120 km. (75 miles) from the capital. Getting up and down the mountain is a ten hour undertaking in itself, but the view into the crater, as well as out from the crater's edge, fully justifies the strenuous climb to the top. Hekla has erupted several times in recent years, and the new lava fields stretch for some miles around the crater. For those who dislike trudging, a four-hour plane trip combines a good look at Hekla with a glimpse of the glacier Vatnajökull, and a flight north to the Arctic Circle.

West Iceland

It's a long, sometimes monotonous drive to the Snaefellsnes peninsula. But you call always break it on the way by calling in at the whaling station at the head of Hvalfjördur. If you arrive at the same time as a whale, be prepared for a pungent and bloody experience. Further north, turn inland to visit Reykholt, where you can see the small hot pool which belonged to Snorri Sturluson, Iceland's famous poet, who recorded the sagas. After crossing moorlands where only ponies and sheep graze, you finally arrive below the snout of Snaefellsjökull at the end of the peninsula. This is the glacier where Jules Verne set the starting point for the *Journey to the Center of the Earth.* It is a wild beautiful place, where the main attractions are the hosts of seabirds nesting along the basalt cliffs, and the seals who pop up to gaze curiously at intruders.

On the other side of the peninsula there are weirdly shaped rock castles which are reached by crossing a grey lavafield. Continue along the northern side of the peninsula and you come to Stykkisholmur. The town is popular with many sea-sports fishermen who come for the halibut in Breidafjördur. It is a pleasant little place with a modern hospital run by Belgian nuns. Behind the town is a hill known as Helgafjell. According to local superstition, anyone who climbs Helgafjell for the first time will be granted three wishes—provided he doesn't look back or talk on the way up.

There are several islands in the large bay of Breidafjördur. A few are inhabited, and all have large colonies of birds and seals. A local ferry passing close to some of these islands takes you across the bay to Brjánslaekur Farm, on the remote Vestfirdir, the isolated region of the Western Fjords.

East Iceland

Not until 1974, when the final bridge was completed across the treacherous glacier waters pouring from the tongues of Vatnajökul glacier, was this area accessible by car from Reykjavik. It is still a long journey, but you can watch the miniature icebergs sliding towards the sea while the great Skua gulls swoop overhead and across the black sands.

Following the southern road, you come to Skogar, a tiny settlement beside the impressive Skogafoss. Here you can lunch at the Edda hotel by prior arrangement, then visit the small museum consisting of turf houses brought from elsewhere in the district and re-erected. The locals used to fish this treacherous coast in small boats, and the last of these boats rests in the little museum together with many other interesting mementos from a tough and primitive way of life which persisted until comparatively recent times.

Press on eastward and you come to the Skaftafjell reserve. This contains the famous Svartifoss waterfall, dropping thinly over a cliff whose sides resemble the pipes of a great organ. It's possible to walk on the glacier tongues here, but this should not be attempted without expert guidance or correct equipment. Höfn on the east coast is developing as a popular center from which to explore the extraordinary landscapes created by the outlying glaciers of Vatnajökull and the wild coastline. From here excursions are arranged to these, as well as to Skaftafjell National Park.

On the very eastern tip of Iceland, you come to Borgarfjördur Eystri (a village and fjord with the same name). This is renowned as one of the most beautiful spots in the country. It takes its name from Álfaborg, a hillock just outside the village, reputed to be the legendary home of elves. Iceland's famous painter, Kjarval, lived here for a time. The village has a small hotel and restaurant.

South Iceland, Westmann Islands and Surtsey

The remote Westmann Islands are off the southwest coast of Iceland, and amongst them only Heimaey is inhabited. In 1973, after lying dormant for nearly 5,000 years the Helgafjell (Holy Mountain) on Heimaey erupted, and the entire population of 5,000 was immediately evacuated by local fishing boats to the mainland. This was a disaster for the Westmanners. Their main industry was fishing, and they were dependent on the safe harbour at Heimaey as well as upon the fish processing plants there. However, with the grit and determination of people long used to living with the forces of nature, the Westmanners started to dig themselves out long before the eruption had ceased, removing tons of black lava dust from their buried houses and streets. Now the streets are cleared, the houses rebuilt and repainted, and fishing and processing working normally, though some of the plants were seriously damaged. However, the island now has 600 meters (1,900 ft.) of lava on the approaches to the harbor, and many of the houses which were closest to the eruption were buried for ever. It's a strange sensation, as one scrambles across the volcanic ash, to realize that one is in fact walking over the roofs of buried houses.

The islands are rich in sea birds, especially puffins, which are used in large quantities for food. The puffins were not too greatly affected by the eruption, but a considerable number of sea birds were lost and this has affected the task of egg-pickers, who estimate that it will take several more years before the colonies fully establish themselves again. Egg-picking is hazardous work. Dangling from ropes, the men swing from ledge to ledge down sheer volcanic cliffs to collect eggs from the nests, often attacked fiercely by the birds. Primitive winches haul the men back up with their fragile loads. Throughout the years there have been 18 fatal accidents, and legend has it that when the 19th man falls to his death the volcano Katla on the mainland opposite will erupt. (Its next eruption is in fact long overdue.)

A highlight of the Icelandic calendar is the festival held each August near Heimaey. It is well worth taking time to visit the Westmann Islands, despite the fact that the round-trip flight might be canceled by bad weather and you'll face a 10-hour sea journey instead. But if you really cannot spare more than a few hours, you can always take a shorter sightseeing tour from Reykjavik. A few miles west of the Westmann Islands is the new volcanic island of Surtsey, which was thrown up out of the sea by a submarine volcanic eruption in 1963. Already it is several hundred feet high. Scientists work there recording the progress of nature, but lesser folk are not allowed ashore. Sightseeing trips usually include a sail around the island and also to the multicolored sea cave Kafhellir, on the island of Haena nearby.

Akureyri and the North

The north of Iceland was created by the interplay of fire and ice. The largest lava fields on earth are to be found here, some with plants and mosses, others barren and bare. The country is not all forbidding, and the valleys sheltered by the mountains are lush with vegetation and rich in color. There are also many rivers with good salmon and trout fishing, magnificent waterfalls and strange formations of basalt rock columns.

Iceland's second largest town, Akureyri, is an hour from Reykjavik by plane. Ranged up and down a series of irregular hills on the western side of Eyjafjördur, the town is dominated by a simple ultra-modern Lutheran church whose twin spires accent the barren and treeless landscape. Some of the surrounding mountains reach a height of 1,400 meters (4,500 ft.) and offer fine climbs and ski runs.

Beside the Edda summer hotel there is an interesting statue. In bygone times, if a man transgressed the laws of the community, he was often banished, along with his family, to the lava fields. This was virtually a death sentence, for nothing could sustain life in those regions. This poignant statue, called the *Outlaw*, is by Einar Jonsson and depicts a man carrying his wife and child and accompanied by his dog, walking into outlawry.

From Akureyri you can get a boat to Grimsey, a particularly interesting spot for sea bird enthusiasts. This island is over 32 km. (20 miles) from the mainland and actually straddles the Arctic Circle. From Akureyri you can also take a long jolting bus ride over the weird volcanic plateaux to the magnificent waterfall of Godafoss, where the local chieftain threw his pagan household gods into its foaming depths when he was converted to Christianity in A.D. 1000. In the adjoining district is Glerardalur, a valley where petrified wood is found. The bus continues to Lake Myvatn, a birdwatchers' paradise, where vast numbers of waterfowl make their homes. One can get a guide to some of the more remote nesting areas.

Myvatn also has an especially tasty breed of trout, which feeds on the midges that give the lake its name. Here there are all kinds of exotic phenomena, including Dimmuborgir (the black castles) where the fantastic landscape is said to resemble the lunar surface more closely than anywhere else on earth; Storagja and Grotagja, two pools of natural hot water in underground caves, where one can enjoy wonderful bathing; and Namaskard, where the purple sulfur boils like a witches' cauldron in the strange red and yellow valleys.

When the volcano Askja erupted here two centuries ago, the lava ran directly towards the lake and the small settlement which lay beside it. But in the path of the lava stood the settlement's tiny church, and the molten mass came to a halt within inches of its walls. There is a new church now, but the remains of the old one can still be seen, surrounded on three sides by solidified lava. Farther afield are Dettifoss, Europe's largest waterfall, and the fascinating lush national park of Asbyrgi with the curious echoing rocks of Hljodaklettar. From here you can continue to Husavik, an attractive port on the north coast, and thence back to Akureyri.

Central Iceland

The interior of Iceland is virtually uninhabited apart from the occasional isolated meteorological or scientific station. Though the Icelanders may get rather tired of having it likened to the Moon, the landscape really is strangely reminiscent of some science fiction vision—with its great stony deserts, extravagantly contorted lava fields, and towering glaciers from which crystal clear streams and green rivers drain across the land. The colors are superb, and there is a feeling of timelessness that few other places in the world can match.

This is *not* an area where you go exploring on your own. But there are excellent overland tours escorted by experienced guides. You don't have to be young and hearty or tremendously energetic to enjoy these, but you do need to be an outdoor enthusiast and prepared to camp. Transport is in specially constructed buses, and tents and all necessary equipment are provided; you are usually expected to be in charge of your tent during the trip, but meals are provided for you. Since this kind of tour tends to attract those who are interested in birds or flowers or geology, it's usually a fine meeting ground for like-minded souls of all ages and many nationalities. Over-night stops may be made near a small community or in the heart of a rugged uninhabited wilderness, perhaps on the edge of a lava field or at the foot of some craggy white glacier. There are opportunities to bathe in clear, naturally hot spring-water under the open sky, peer into volcanic craters, walk among wild lansdcapes, and experience a stillness that has barely been disturbed by human presence since time began.

These, then, are the distinctive features of Iceland, a land which beguiles all who have once stood on its grey shores, and felt the rock tremble beneath them with the subterranean forces of an unseen world.

PRACTICAL INFORMATION FOR REYKJAVIK

GETTING TO TOWN FROM THE AIRPORT. For arrivals at Keflavik International Airport, a bus service is stationed outside the terminal entrance which will provide transportation into Reykjavik. Fare at time of

EXPLORING ICELAND

writing is $4.50. Taxis are also available, though as driving time to Reykjavik is approximately 45 minutes, cost will be quite high.

From the town terminal there are bus connections and taxis on hand, night and day, to other parts of the city.

TOURIST INFORMATION. There are five main centers for tourist information in Reykjavik: The Information Tower at Laekjartorg (10044); the nearby *Gimli,* Laekjargata 3 (28025); *Útsýn,* Austurstraeti 17 (26611); and the Iceland Tourist Bureaus at Reykjanesbraut (27488) and in Hotel Loftleidir at Reykjavik Airport (22322). There is also a branch office at Keflavik Airport Terminal. All these bureaus will be able to supply information on the city as well as for the rest of Iceland. Information can also be had concerning local and not-so-local accommodations, as well as special discount fares on city and country-wide bus services.

USEFUL ADDRESSES. Travel Agents. *Gudmundur Jonasson Tours,* Borgartuni 34 (83222). *Samvinn-Travel,* Austurstraeti 12 (27077). *Ulfar Jacobsen Tourist Bureau,* Austurstraeti 9 (13499).

Embassies. *U.S. Embassy,* 21 Laufasvegi (29100). *Canadian Embassy,* Skulagata 20 (25355). *British Embassy,* 49 Laufasvegi (15883).

Car Hire. *ALP Car Rental,* Hladbrekka 2 Kopavogi (42837). *Geysir,* Borgartun 24 (11015). *Icelandair Car Rental.*

Police. Headquarters at Hverfisgata 113, and at Hlemmtorg, tel. 11166.

Medical Services. Emergency telephone no. is 81200. From 8 A.M.–9 P.M., *Landspitalinn,* tel. 21230 and 29000. *Drugstore* (Apótek), tel. 18888.

TELEPHONE CODES. The telephone code for Reykjavik is 91. To call any number in this chapter, unless specified, this prefix must be used. Within the city, however, no prefix is required. For all establishments outside Reykjavik, we have listed the necessary prefix immediately before the telephone number.

HOTELS. Apart from the top hotels in Reykjavik, Iceland's hotels are modest and simple. Breakfast is not included in the hotel price, and there is a high service charge and a state tax. Somewhat less expensive accommodations are available in private homes; check with the Tourist Bureau for a list of homes participating. Students and other adventurous travelers who want to tour the countryside can usually obtain a night's lodging from $5, provided they supply their own sleeping bags. The summer hotels known as "Edda" hotels (university and school hostels used for tourists during the summer vacation) are moderately priced, but demand for rooms is high so book in advance if possible.

Expensive

Hotel Borg. Posthusstraeti 11 (11440). A traditional and comfortable hotel with 46 rooms. Very central. AE, DC, MC, V.

Hotel Esja. Sudurlandsbraut 2 (82200). Situated in the new business center of the city, quite near the indoor sports arena, main swimming pool, and football stadium. All rooms with bath or shower; TV on request. An attractive penthouse bar provides tremendous views of the bay and Mount Esja. All amenities. AE, DC, MC, V.

Hotel Holt. Bergstadastraeti 37 (25700). One of Reykjavik's finest. All rooms with bath or shower; TV on request. Excellent restaurant whose decor features works of Icelandic art. AE, DC, MC, V.

Hotel Loftleidir. Reykjavik Airport (22322). 227 rooms with bath or shower. Very central, with all amenities, including its own theater, sauna, massage facilities, and solarium. AE, DC, MC, V.

ICELAND

Hotel Saga. Hagatorg (29900). 106 rooms, including 7 suites, all with bath or shower. Close to the airport as well as shops and museums. Good restaurant with music and dancing at weekends, plus rooftop grill and no less than six bars. AE, DC, MC, V.

Moderate

City Hotel. Ránargata 4A (18650). 31 rooms, very pleasant, and situated close to the city center. AE, MC, V.

Gardur. Hringbraut (15918). 44 rooms without private bath. Belongs to the University and is therefore open summer only. Quite close to the swimming pool.

Hotel Hof. Raudarárstíg 18 (28866). Very comfortable and in a quiet location. V.

Inexpensive

Guesthouse. Brautarholti 22 (20986). 24 rooms. Open summer only.

Guesthouse. Snorrabraut 52 (16522). 18 rooms, and very comfortable.

Salvation Army Guesthouse. Kirkjustraeti 2 (13203). 24 rooms. Situated right in the heart of the city.

Víking Guesthouse. Ráragata 12 (19367). 11 rooms. Very popular, and quite close to the city center.

Camping

Reykjavik has only one campsite, and a pleasant one at that, conveniently located on Sundlaugarvegur, next to the largest swimming pool and near the sports stadium. Note that fires are not allowed, and all garbage must be collected and disposed of properly. All details from the Iceland Tourist Bureau.

Tjaldaleigan Rent-a-Tent, at Hringbraut v/Umferdarmidstodina 101 (13072), rents out all sorts of camping equipment, from cars with tent-trailers to camping kits including tent, sleeping bag, mattress, gas stove, and even a set of pots and pans. Prices run about $21 per person per week for the kit.

YOUTH HOSTELS

There are several hostels in Reykjavik; full details are available from the Youth Hostels Association (Farfugladeild Reykjavikur), Laufasveg 41 (24950). These hostels are well-equipped and very popular during the holiday season, so it's best to book beforehand. The Y.H.A. will also be able to give addresses of other inexpensive sleeping accommodations for those who have their own sleeping bags; cost usually as little as $6.

HOW TO GET AROUND. By bus. The major form of city transport is by bus which bear the letters S.V.R.— Straetisvaganar Reykjavikur (Reykjavik Buses). The two main stopping points are at Hlemmtorg in the eastern part of town, and the terminal at Laekjartog in the city center. These buses run fairly frequently, while most services start at 7 A.M. and finish at midnight. At weekends, the last buses finish at 1 A.M.

There are usually no ticket conductors on Icelandic buses. Tickets are bought directly from the driver (either individually or in sheets, which is cheaper), and then placed in a receptacle close to the driver's seat. Smoking is not allowed. If you want to get off, just press one of the buttons placed intermittently throughout the bus.

By taxi. Taxis are expensive, though you aren't expected to tip the driver anything over the metered amount. There are taxi stands in many parts of the city, and they also pick up en route. The sign *Laus* means that the cab is available for hire.

EXPLORING ICELAND

TOURS. An excellent way of getting acquainted with Reykjavik is to take one of the city's guided bus tours. Usually lasting around 2½ hours, these tours introduce the capital's past and present, and include a visit to the Museum and Art Gallery. Departures daily at 10 A.M. and 2 P.M., May through Sept.; cost approximately $12.

A varied itinerary of day excursions is also available to and around the surrounding countryside. These day-tours include pony trekking on the Icelandic hills; the starkly dramatic lava arena of Thingvellir, where the ancient Viking parliament met for centuries; the famous Great Geysir, a seething area of erupting hot springs, mud pools, and geysirs, of which Strokkur, the world's most active geysir, is likely to spurt several times up to a height of 100 ft.; Reykholt, home of the famous Saga historian, Snorri Sturluson; and even an aerial tour for an eagle's-eye view of the rugged lavafields, volcanoes, and glaciers of southern Iceland.

All cost and departure details from the Icelandic Tourist Board; day excursion information can also be had from *Reykjavik Excursions* at Hotel Loftleidir at the airport (22322), or from *Gimli,* Laekjargata 3 (28025).

MUSEUMS. Being a small nation, Iceland cannot offer museums on the scale of the Louvre, the Prado, or the Metropolitan Museum of Art. She has, however, produced some very fine artists, many of whom have bequeathed their houses to the nation upon their death and whose works are displayed therein. These museums are normally open from 1.30–4 P.M., closed Mon. Admission is generally free, but occasionally there is a nominal charge.

Árbaer (Folk Museum). On the city outskirts. An interesting collection of old buildings, depicting rural life in the past.

Árnagardur (Árni Magnússon Manuscript Museum). Interesting collection of ancient manuscripts.

Ásigrímur Jónsson Art Gallery. Bergstadastraeti 74. An excellent collection of watercolors and oils by this well-beloved Icelandic painter.

Ásmundur Sveinsson Gallery. Kirkjumýrarbletti 10, Sigtún. An unusual dome-like house built by the artist himself, where you can see his creations throughout both house and garden.

Einar Jónsson Museum. Beside Eiríksgata, in the older part of the city. Most of the sculptures are displayed in the garden.

Galerie Súm. Vatnstigur, just off of Laugavegur. Shows exhibitions of younger Icelandic painters.

Kjarvalsstadir (City Art Gallery). Miklatún. Dedicated to the memory of the great Icelandic painter Johannes S. Kjarval, many of whose works are displayed here, along with those of other Icelandic and foreign artists.

Nattúrugripasafnid (Natural History Museum). At the junction of Laugavegur and Hverfisgate, in Hlemmtorg. Contains a small, but interesting, collection of fauna, especially birds, and minerals.

Norraena Húsid (Nordic House). Close to the University. A cultural center rather than just a museum, with exhibitions, lectures, and concerts.

Thjódminjasafnid (National Museum). On Hringbraut, close to the University. Viking artifacts, plus national costumes and silver work. Also displays of weaving and woodcarving, an ancient craft which has revived in recent years, and some unusual whalebone carvings.

PARKS AND GARDENS. Great efforts are being made to beautify Iceland's cities and towns by planting trees, flowers, and shrubs in parks and gardens, though the persistent wind prevents them blooming until June or even July. Tjarnargardar (Lakeside Gardens) are spread around Lake Tjörnin within Reykjavik's city center. The small but pretty garden behind the Parliament building is called Althingishússgardur. Overlooking the harbour and close to the National Theater is Arnarhóll, a grassy hill crowned by a statue of Ingólfur Arnarson, the first settler. Near the sports stadium and main swimming pool blooms Laugardalsgardur, a lovely botanical garden.

ICELAND

SPORTS. Swimming. Every Icelandic primary school registers swimming as a compulsory subject, and it has become the national sport, somewhat like football to the Americans and cricket to the British. Most travelers will enjoy the marvelous swimming pools, and Reykjavik has many which are open year round. It is particularly invigorating in winter months to dive from a snow-laden poolside into the warm waters of an openair pool. All bathers are required to take a shower both before and after swimming.

Following are some Reykjavik pools and their addresses: *Sundlaugar Reykjavikur,* Laugardal (34039); *Sundlaug Vesturbaejar,* Hofsvallagata (15004); *Sundlaug Kopavogs,* Borgarholtsbraut (41299); *Sundlaug Breidagerdisskola,* Breidagerdi (85860); *Sundholl Reykjavikur,* Baronsstig (14059); and *Sundholl Hafnarfjardar,* Herjolfsgata 10 (50088).

Golf. The city has a number of golf clubs, though most boast only nine holes, except for the main club, *Golfklubbur Reykjavikur,* tel. 84735, which is about 8 km. (5 miles) east of the city center and has 18 holes. Another smaller golf club is at *Seltjarnarnes,* in the western part of the city. Clubs are open daily from May to Nov., and play continues as long as the daylight lasts (it's scarcely necessary to stop at all during June!).

Gliding. Gliding enthusiasts should contact *Flugmálafélag Íslands* (the Icelandic Gliding Club), tel. 24354.

Fishing. Many foreign anglers return year after year for the excellent fishing opportunities that Iceland offers, Prince Charles among them. Trout and salmon are especially good, and sea angling is also possible. Check with the Tourist Office for more details. Remember that not only is a permit necessary, but the angler must also pay for each fish taken.

Hiking. For information on day and weekend outings, contact *Ferdafélag Íslands,* Ölgudata 3 (19533).

Winter Sports. Skating is popular; Lake Tjörnin in particular, in the heart of the capital, is a bustling spot for skaters.

Skiing is practised on the slopes between Reykjavik and Selfoss.

The Sports Stadium in Laugardal (83377), next to the large swimming pool, has excellent facilities, both indoor and outdoor, including **badminton** and **tennis.**

Details of all sports and facilities from the Tourist Office.

MUSIC, MOVIES, AND THEATERS. Music. Reykjavik has an active symphony orchestra, with several well-known Icelandic and foreign guest conductors. An opera, operetta, or musical is staged at least once a year at the National Theater. Some Icelandic opera singers are internationally known. As in other Scandinavian countries, there are several male-voice choirs and some mixed ones. Brass bands are very popular.

Movies. There are several cinemas in Reykjavik and its suburbs. Most films shown are British or American with Icelandic subtitles. Now, however, some new Icelandic films are coming onto the circuit which usually portray life from the Saga Times. Icelandic nature and volcano films are shown daily in the *Osvaldur Knudsen Film Studio,* near the Hotel Holt.

Theaters. Reykjavik's *National Theater,* opened in 1950, is a splendid building at Hverfisgata (tel. 11200), close to the city center. The Theater performs both classical and modern works, but be warned that these are in Icelandic and will therefore be somewhat impenetrable to most (though the spectacle itself is still enjoyable). Ballet is also performed here, and though not as advanced as drama productions, some good programs can be seen, usually during the winter months. Another smaller theater is the *Idnó* in Vonarstraeti by the lake (tel. 16620). Both the National Theater and the Idnó close during Aug.

Light Nights is a small, English-speaking company which performs regularly during the summer tourist season at Tjarnarbió, near the lake. Performances start at 9 P.M., Thurs. through Sun.

EXPLORING ICELAND 237

SHOPPING. Iceland does not exactly qualify as a shopper's paradise, but locally-made sweaters and scarves of undyed Icelandic wool are beautiful and extremely soft and warm. Also worth considering are the sheepskins, lava ceramics, and silver items. Some of the best buys are to be had from the duty-free shop at Keflavik Airport. The following shops are also recommended: *Álafoss Store,* Vesturgata 2, *Framtidin,* Laugavegur 45, *Galleri Langbrók,* Amtmannstigur 1, *The Handknitting Association of Iceland,* Skólavördustig 19, *Hilda,* Borgartún 22, *The Icelandic Handicrafts' Center,* Hafnarstraeti 3, *Kúnst,* Laugavegur 40, and *Rammagerdin,* Hafnarstraeti 19.

In food stores you can buy specially packed samples of Icelandic food to take home yourself or to mail to your friends. The smoked salmon, herring, and shrimps are all excellent.

RESTAURANTS. Reykjavik and the surrounding suburbs have seen some welcome additions recently as far as restaurants go, and there is now an attractive selection of eating places catering for all pocketbooks. Note that all of the expensive hotels mentioned earlier in this chapter have excellent restaurants; we would recommend in particular that of the Hotel Holt.

Expensive

Arnarhóll. Hverfisgata 8–10 (18833). Exclusive and central restaurant where seafood is the specialty. MC, V.

Leikhúskjallarinn. In the National Theater at Hverfisgata (19636). Convenient location for theater-goers, with dancing in the evenings. DC.

Naust. Vesturgata 8 (17759). Top class restaurant, one of Reykjavik's finest, with an attractive nautical atmosphere and excellent cuisine. Dancing occasionally. AE, DC, MC, V.

Moderate

Drekinn. Laugavegur 22 (13628). Reasonable Chinese cuisine. V.

Gullni Haninn. Laugavegur 178 (34780). Small but friendly bistro. V.

Hlidarendi. Brautarholt 22 (11690). Good food in a pleasant setting. AE.

Laekjarbrekka. Bankastraeti 2 (14430). Attractive restaurant in a restored timberhouse in old Reykjavik. Icelandic meat and fish specialties, including smoked lamb with mustard sauce for a real treat. V.

Náttúran. Laugavegur 20B (28410). For a taste of Icelandic vegetarianism.

Potturinn og Pannan. Brautarholti 22 (11690). American salads, fish and lamb dishes. V.

Torfan. Amtmannsstígur 1 (13303). Charming yester-year atmosphere. Serving authentic Icelandic cuisine. AE, MC, V.

Inexpensive

Hornid Restaurant. Hafnarstraeti 15 (20366). Icelandic seafood, pizza, expresso. AE, MC, V.

Hressingarskálinn. Austurstraeti 20 (14353). Right in the city center. Friendly.

Kaffivagninn. Grandagardi 10 (15932). Bustling site on the fish wharf, so understandably serves some of the freshest fish around, plus some meat dishes.

Kokk-Húsid. Laekjargate 8 (10340). Central and reasonably priced.

Lauga-ás. Laugarásveg 1 (31620). Near the campsite and close to the city's biggest swimming pool. Popular. V.

NIGHTLIFE. As your grandmother probably used to say, a word to the wise is sufficient: Iceland doesn't have what you would call a red-hot after-hours scene, and some tourists might find it unbearably tame or quaint. But following is a list of the more popular Reykjavik discos, one of which may take your fancy: *Broadway,* Álfabakka 8, Breidholti (77500); *Glaesibaer,* Álfheimar 74 (86220); *Hollywood,* Ármúli 5 (83715); *Klúbburinn,* Borgartún 32 (35355); and *Ódal,* Austurvollur (11322, 11630).

BARS

All the major hotels in Reykjavik listed earlier in this chapter have licensed bars. It's important to note that the term "bar" to the Icelander refers to snack-bars selling fast foods and soft drinks, so don't get confused. Icelandic law prohibits the sale of strong beers, but low alcohol beers are readily available.

PRACTICAL INFORMATION FOR THE REST OF ICELAND

TOURIST INFORMATION. Akureyri. Ferdaskrifstofan Akureyri, Rádhústorg 3 (96–25000). **Westman Islands.** Ferdaskrifstofan Útsýn, Holgata 6 (98–1515).

TELEPHONE CODES. We have given telephone codes for all the towns and villages in the hotel and restaurant lists that follow. These codes need only be used when calling from outside the town or village concerned.

HOTELS AND RESTAURANTS. It's important to note that although Iceland is a large island, the total population is only around 235,000, so it's not overflowing with huge, sprawling urban areas by any means. Given which, we haven't been able to provide many addresses for hotels and restaurants outside of those in Reykjavik and Akureyri; often there aren't any street names, let alone address numbers! Not to worry, though, as when you drive into the village, the hotel will most likely be the first thing you see.

In the following sections, we have divided Iceland into four areas—North, South, East, and West—and list all hotels and restaurants under the appropriate town or village name. In most of the smaller places, there are no other restaurants except for those in the hotels, but these are usually quite adequate.

The hotels and restaurants listed below fall into three catagories: Expensive (E), Moderate (M), and Inexpensive (I). We give approximate prices for these gradings in the *Facts at Your Fingertips* section on pages 215 and 217 respectively.

NORTH ICELAND

AKUREYRI. *Hotel K.E.A.* (E), Hafnarstraeti 89 (96–22200). 28 rooms, all with bath or shower. First-class hotel with a friendly atmosphere; several bars, a restaurant and cafeteria. AE, MC, V. *Hotel Akureyri* (M), Hafnarstraeti 98 (96–22525). Comfortable hotel in the town center. V. *Hotel Vardborg* (M), Geislagata 7 (96–22600). 24 rooms. Very close to the center, with personal service and a good restaurant. AE, MC. *Skídahotel Hlídarfjall* (M), 96–22930. A ski-hotel in the hills about 2 miles above the town; open Jan. through May. Four chair-lifts, and floodlit ski-trails. *Dalakofinn* (I), Lyngholt 20 (96–23035). Very small (4 guest maximum), with bath, private entrance, and breakfast available on request. Good cooking facilities. *Edda* (I), (96–24055). 68 rooms without bath. Summer only. V. *Guesthouse Árgerdi* (I), Túngusída 2 (96–24849). Bed and breakfast for one to four persons. Swimming pool and sauna. Buses nos. 3, 4, and 5 all days from central square.

Restaurants. *Bautinn* (E), Hafnarstraeti 92 (96–21818). First-class restaurant near the town center. MC, V. *Sjallinn* (M), Geislagata 12 (96–22770). Popular restaurant serving all sorts of seafood. Disco and band from Thurs. to Sun. V. *Smidjan* (M), adjacent to Bautinn (96–21818). Try the spiced lamb

EXPLORING ICELAND

chop. MC, V. *H. 100* (I), Hafnarstraeti 100 (96-25500). Combination restaurant and disco.

Camping. The camping site is at Thórunnarstraeti, just south of the swimming pool (96-23379). Toilet facilities, and hot and cold water available.

Youth Hostel. Stórholt 1 (96-23657).

BLÖNDUÓS. *Edda* (M), (95-4126). 30 rooms, all with bath or shower. V.

DALVÍK. *Hotel Vikurröst* (M), (96-61354). 20 rooms. Swimming pool and restaurant. Also allows sleeping bag stays. MC.

HRÚTAFJÖRDUR. *Edda Reykir* (M), (95-1003). 28 rooms. Swimming pool and steam bath. Summer only. V. *Stadarskáli* (M), (95-1150). Motel with good restaurant. MC.

HÚNAVELLIR. *Edda Svínavatn* (M), (95-4370). 23 rooms. Very comfortable hotel in a picturesque setting near Lake Svínavatn. Swimming pool and sauna. V.

HÚSAVIK. *Hotel Húsavik* (M), Ketilsbraut (96-41220). 34 rooms with bath or shower. AE, V.

KÓPASKER. *Guesthouse* (I), (96-52121). 3 rooms.

LAUGAR. *Hotel Laugar S. Thingeyjarsýsla* (M), (96-43120). 70 rooms; summer only.

MÝVATN. *Reykjahlíd* (M), (96-441412). 12 rooms without bath; summer only. *Reynihlíd* (M), (96-44170). 44 rooms, swimming pool. U.S. astronauts were trained in the lunar-like atmosphere of the surrounding area. AE, MC, V.

RAUFARHÖFN. *Hotel Nordurljós* (M), (96-51223). 30 rooms; summer only.

SAUDÁRKRÓKUR. *Hotel Maelifell* (M), Adalgata 7 (95-5265). 7 rooms. MC.

SIGLUFJÖRDUR. *Hotel Höfn* (M), Laekjargata 10 (96-71514). 14 rooms, none with private bath. MC, V.

SKAGAFJÖRDUR. *Hotel Varmahlíd* (I), (95-6170). 17 rooms, none with private bath.

STORUTJARNIR. Alongside Lake Ljósavatn. *Edda* (M), 96-43221. Comfortable, with 24 rooms. On route from Akureyri to Husavik. Not far from the magnificent waterfall of Godafoss. Summer only.

SOUTH ICELAND

FLÚDIR. *Summerhotel Flúdir* (M), (99-6630). 27 rooms; summer only. *Motel Skjólborg* (I), (99-6624). 8 rooms.

GRINDAVIK. *Guesthouse Bláa Lónid Svartsengi* (M), (92-8650). 10 rooms.

HELLA. *Guesthouse Mosfell* (I), (99-5928). 20 rooms without private bath.

HVERAGERDI. *Hotel Hveragerdi* (M), Breidamörk 25 (99-4231). 12 rooms; summer only. MC.

HVOLSVÖLLUR. *Hotel Hvolsvöllur* (M), (99-8187). 20 rooms, some with bath.

KIRKJUBAEJARKLAUSTUR. *Hotel Edda* (M), (99-7626). 32 rooms, some with bath or shower. Open all year. V.

LUAGARVATN. *Hotel New Edda* (M), (99-6154). 27 rooms; summer only. *Edda Hotel* (I), (99-6118). 88 rooms, all with bath or shower. Swimming pool and steam baths; situated close by a lake. V.

SELFOSS. *Thóristún* (M), (99-1633). 17 rooms.

SKÁLHOLT. *Guesthouse Skálholt* (M), (99-6870). 10 rooms with bath; summer only.

SKÓGAR. *Hotel Edda* (I), (99-8870). 34 rooms without bath; summer only. V.

THINGVELLIR. *Valhöll* (M), Lyngas 4 (99-4080). 37 rooms; summer only. AE, DC, MC.

VÍK MÝRDAL. *Hotel K.S.* (I), (99-7193). 10 rooms.

WESTMANN ISLANDS. *Hotel Gestgjafinn* (M), (98-2577). 14 rooms, all with bath or shower. V. *Guesthouse Heimir* (I), (98-1515). 22 rooms, none with bath.

EAST ICELAND

BREIDALSVÍK. *Hotel Bláfell* (M), (97-5770). 8 rooms, none with private bath. *Hotel Edda Stadarborg* (M), (96-5683). 9 rooms; summer only.

DJÚPIVOGUR. *Hotel Framtid* (I), (97-8887). 9 rooms.

EGILSSTADIR. *Hotel Valaskjálf* (M), (97-1500). 24 rooms, all with bath. V. *Hotel Egilstadir* (I), (97-1114). 15 rooms with bath; summer only.

EIDAR. *Hotel Edda* (I), (97-3803). 60 rooms, none with bath. Summer only. V.

ESKIFJÖRDUR. *Hotel Askja* (I), (97-6261). 7 rooms.

HALLORMSSTADIR. *Hotel Edda* (I), (97-1683). 22 rooms, none with private bath. Summer only. V.

HORNAFJÖRDUR. *Hotel Höfn* (E), (97-8240). 40 rooms, all with bath or shower. DC, V. *Hotel Edda Nesjaskoli* (I), (97-8470). 30 rooms, none with bath. Summer only. V.

REYDARFJÖRDUR. *Guesthouse K.B.H.* (I), (97-4200). 3 rooms without bath.

VOPNAFJÖRDUR. *Guesthouse Tangi* (M), (97-3224). 12 rooms without bath.

WEST ICELAND

AKRANES. *Hotel Akranes Bárugata* (M), (93-2020). 11 rooms, none with bath.

BORGARFJÖRDUR. *Hotel Bifröst* (M), (93-5000). 31 rooms; summer only.

BORGARNES. *Hotel Borgarnes* (M), Egilsgötu (93-7119). 35 rooms, all with bath or shower. MC, V.

BÚDARDALUR. *Hotel Bjarg* (I), (93-4161). 7 rooms.

ISAFJÖRDUR. *Hotel Isafjördur* (E), (94-4111). 31 rooms, all with bath or shower. V. *Hotel Hamrabaer* (M), (94-3777). 8 rooms. *Guesthouse Isafjördur* (I), (94-3043). 17 rooms.

KRÓKSFJÖRDUR. *Hotel Edda Bjarkalundur* (M), (94-4762). 12 rooms; summer only.

ÓLAFSVIK. *Hotel Nes* (M), (93-6300). 38 rooms, none with bath.

REYKHOLT. *Hotel Edda* (M), (93-5260). Summer only. V.

SAELINSDALUR. *Hotel Laugar* (M), (93-4111). 27 rooms, none with bath. Summer only.

SNAEFELLSNES. *Hotel Búdir* (M), (93-8111). 20 rooms, none with bath. Summer only.

STYKKISHÓLMUR. *Hotel Stykkishólmur* (E), (93-8330). 26 rooms, all with bath or shower. MC, V.

THINGEYRI. *Guesthouse Höfn* (I), (94-8151). 3 rooms.

VATNSFJÖRDUR. *Hotel Edda Flókalundur* (M), (94-2011). 14 rooms, all with bath or shower. Summer only. V.

NORWAY

NORWAY

FACTS AT YOUR FINGERTIPS

NORWAY—FACTS AT YOUR FINGERTIPS

NATIONAL TOURIST OFFICE. In the U.S.: 75 Rockefeller Plaza, New York, N.Y. 10019 (212–582 2802).
In the U.K.: 20 Pall Mall, London S.W.1 (01–839 6255)

Within Norway, there are numerous local tourist offices, all identified by the international "i" sign. Many are only open during the summer, but all the major offices are open year round. As well as providing information on their own regions, they will also help in finding accommodations and making reservations for trains, boats, buses and ferries. We list all the major tourist offices at the beginning of each *Practical Information* section.

CURRENCY. The unit of currency in Norway is the *krone*, written as Nok. and divided into 100 øre. The rate of exchange at the time of writing (mid-1984) was Nok. 7.86 to the U.S. dollar and Nok. 11 to the pound sterling. These rates will certainly change before and during 1985, so check them carefully both when planning your trip and during it.

COSTS IN NORWAY. As a result of both its North Sea oil boom and the natural industriousness of its hard working people, Norway has an extremely high standard of living. Costs, for the most part, are therefore naturally very high. In fact certain items, in particular food but above all alcohol, are extremely expensive and above average even by Scandinavian standards.

The Norwegians are conscious of their high-price-tag reputation, however, and have made significant efforts to keep down costs for visitors. We give details of the many hotel, restaurant and travel bargains to be had in the relevant sections below. But at the same time, you should be prepared for some fairly high costs.

A typical day in Oslo might cost two people:

Hotel (Moderate) with bath and breakfast	Nok. 300
Lunch, in Moderate restaurant, no beer or wine	160
Dinner, in Moderate restaurant, with beer	200
Transportation (2 buses, 1 taxi)	50
	Nok. 710

Sample costs. A cinema seat for one, Nok. 30; visit to a museum, Nok. 5 to 10; beer (per bottle), Nok. 30; house wine—by the glass in a cafe, Nok. 20, by the bottle in a restaurant, Nok. 160; a coke, Nok. 12 to 15; a moderate taxi ride in Oslo, Nok. 30; an average bus ride in Oslo, Nok. 9.

SEASONAL EVENTS. Like all the Scandinavian countries, the majority of Norway's special and seasonal events take place in the summer, especially in June. However, as is only appropriate in the country that claims to be the home of winter sports, there are also a large number of winter sports events.

The Norwegian Tourist Board publishes an annual list of all Norway's major festivals, but among the more important are:

January. The Monolith Ski Race, for both men and women, is held in Oslo's Frogner Park at the beginning of the month, while a week or so later Lillehammer holds its ski festival.

February sees the Norwegian Ski Jumping championships—an event long dominated by the Scandinavians—also at Lillehammer.

March is similarly full of winter sports competitions, of which the most important by far is the Holmenkollen Ski Festival in Oslo. But there's also the Mjøsløpene marathon ski race—114 miles, in fact—on Lake Mjøsa outside Lillehammer at the start of the month, while mid-March sees a whole host of other gruelling cross-country ski races, including the Norway–Sweden race at Engerdal. At the end of the month, there is a Winter Festival up beyond the Arctic Circle at Narvik, with skating and skiing competitions and much other wintery celebrating.

April sees a winter festival with a difference, also up beyond the Arctic Circle: reindeer races at Karasjok and Kautokeino.

May gets under way with another gruelling sporting event, the Ancient Marathon at Fredrikstad, a 24-mile hike along a route containing numerous historical and archeological landmarks. May also has two major celebrations: May Day itself, on the 1st, and May 17, Constitution Day, when the whole country celebrates both the end of the long winter and liberation from the Nazis at the end of World War II. Two cultural festivals held now are the International Church Festival at Kristiansand, and the Bergen International Festival, with music, theater and ballet.

June has a host of special events. There's the Greig Festival in Lofthus, commemorating the birth of Norway's most celebrated composer; the Stor Mart'n, a traditional Fair at Nidaroshallen, Trondheim; the North Norway Festival at Harstad, when exhibitions, folklore and an historical play at the openair theater near the ancient Trondenes church are presented; and the Kongsberg International Jazz Festival. June is also packed with sporting events, of which perhaps the most unusual is the Midnight Cup golf tournament at Trondheim, when play continues throughout the night. But there's also the North Sea Fishing Festival, for both individuals and teams, at Haugesund. Finally, June is probably most famous for the myriad celebrations that take place on Midsummer Night: bonfires, fireworks and revelery go on all night long throughout the country.

July. American Independence Day is celebrated in Frogner Park, Oslo. Molde hosts an international Jazz Festival, while at the end of the month there is an historical openair play at Stiklestad, the Olsokspelet.

August. The Tananger International Sea Fishing Festival at Stavanger, again for both individuals and teams, starts off the month. On a more cultural note, Elverum hosts a Music Festival, also at the beginning of the month, while in the church ruins at Maridalen in Oslo, the Maridalspillet, an historical drama, is presented.

September sees the last of the summer's festivities, the Dølajazz festival in Lillehammer.

December is most notable for the presentation of the Nobel Peace Prize at the Aula in Oslo's university. Christmas is celebrated with gusto throughout Norway.

NATIONAL HOLIDAYS. April 4, 5, 8 (Easter); May 1 (Labor Day); May 17 (Constitution Day); December 25. Note that New Year's Day is not a national holiday in Norway.

LANGUAGE. Many Norwegians, especially younger people and those in cities and larger centers, speak English, generally to a very high standard. Certainly in tourist offices, hotels, restaurants, bars, museums and so forth, you will have no difficulties. In rural areas, however, regional dialects abound, sometimes changing from valley to valley. And at the same time, fewer people speak English. Nonetheless, you will be hard put to it to find no one who does speak English.

FACTS AT YOUR FINTERTIPS

CUSTOMS. Residents of non-European countries may import duty-free into Norway: 400 cigarettes or 50 grams of cigars or tobacco and 200 leaves of cigarette papers (except those under 15); plus, 2 liters of spirits or 2 liters of wine and 2 liters of beer; plus, 50 grams of perfume and ½ liter of eau de Cologne; plus, other goods to the value of Nok. 3,500.

Residents of European countries may import duty-free into Norway: 200 cigarettes or 250 grams of cigars or tobacco and 200 leaves of cigarette papers (except those under 15); plus, 1 liter of spirits and 2 liters of wine or 2 liters of wine and 2 liters of beer (except those under 21); plus, a small quantity of perfume and/or eau de Cologne (in opened bottles); plus, other goods to the value of Nok. 700.

Note that alcoholic beverages over 60° (120° proof) may not be imported.

You may also bring in any amount of foreign and Norwegian currency but must declare it on arrival. You may export no more than the equivalent of Nok. 10,000 in foreign currency. No more than Nok. 2,000 may be exported.

HOTELS. The Norwegians are strict about hotels, as indeed they are about many things, and any establishment calling itself a hotel must match up to certain minimum legal standards. As a result, you can be sure that any Norwegian "hotel" will be spotlessly clean, comfortable and very well run. In addition, many are still family-owned and run and offer a degree of personal service and hospitality only rarely found elsewhere. Similarly, for the most part, and with the exception only of the likes of Oslo and Stavanger, the majority of Norwegian hotels are neither especially expensive or particularly cheap, tending instead to be moderately-priced—by Norwegian standards anyway—and perhaps a little unspectacular and staid. But anyone in search of quiet and good service is likely to feel very much at home.

We give basic prices below, but note that almost all hotels, especially in resort areas, will charge "en pension" rates for stays longer than five, or sometimes three, days; that is, charges will be reduced for anyone staying longer than these minimum periods. Note also that resort hotels offering superior accommodations are called "tourist" hotels. You might also discover a breed of hotel known as a "mountain" or *Höyfjellshotel;* to qualify, they must be located at least 2,500 ft. above sea level.

The Norwegian Tourist Board produces an annually updated list of hotels, available free of charge.

In addition to the discounts mentioned above, a number of other special offers are also available. The Norwegian Tourist Board or your travel agent can supply up-to-date information, but among those currently on offer are the following.

The Scandinavia Bonus Pass, costing approximately $20 and valid also in Denmark, Finland and Sweden, gives average discounts of 25% in many leading Norwegian hotels from June 1 to September 1. In addition, children under 15 stay in their parents' room at no extra charge. This scheme is particularly useful for anyone planning to tour more than one Scandinavian country by car. For full details, write *Inter Nor Hotels,* Kronprinsensgt. 5, Oslo 2, Norway.

The Fjord Pass works on a similar basis. It costs approximately $10 for two and is valid at more than 150 Norwegian hotels. Large discounts are given between May 15 and September 15, and again children under 15 stay free in their parents' room.

Summer Hotels consist of student accommodations that are opened to the public during the summer at very low rates. Though housed in modern and cheerful buildings, they necessarily lack something in the way of finesse, but are in other respects more than adequate. Young people in particular will find them useful.

Prices. We have divded all the hotels we list into four categories—Deluxe (L), Expensive (E), Moderate (M) and Inexpensive (I). These grades are determined solely by price.

Two people in a double room in Oslo can expect to pay (prices in Nok.):

Deluxe	600 and up
Expensive	400—600
Moderate	300—400
Inexpensive	200—400

These prices include breakfast and taxes. Outside Oslo, you can expect to pay considerably less, especially in rural districts.

SELF-CATERING. This is probably the most popular kind of vacation in Norway. A chalet holiday is a Norwegian way of life, an escape from the daily routine, a chance to live in close contact with nature. Bear in mind that facilities vary considerably, from well-equipped chalets with electric cooking, heating and frigidaire to cabins with no running water and outdoor sanitation only. Prices vary accordingly. Full details are available from the Norwegian Tourist Board and many travel agents.

The most inexpensive self-catering vacation is to be had by renting a *rorbu*, a fisherman's dwelling. These are available to visitors during the summer and are located in the Lofoten isles and on the South Coast.

Farm vacations are available in several regions, but the most popular area is the Gudbrandsdal valley along the Dovre railroad. These holidays are offered by working farms, and either self-catering or full board with the farmer's family is available. Best contact Lillehammer Tourist Office, Storgaten 56, Lillehammer, or the Norwegian Tourist Board or a good travel agent.

CAMPING. There are over 1,400 authorized campsites in Norway. The Norwegians are great believers in camping, one reason for the high standards encountered almost everywhere.

Several campsites provide log cabins or wooden huts at reasonable rates. Bogstad Camping in Oslo—Norway's largest campsite with space for over 1,000 tents—also offers 20 furnished and well-equipped log cabins, each with four to five beds. The Royal Norwegian Automobile Club (KNA) owns a number of tourist huts, which are available to members of AAA and AA at bargain rates.

A useful folder on campsites and youth hostels in Norway is available from the Norwegian Tourist Board. Campsites are listed with 1, 2 or 3 stars according to their facilities. The cost per night for car and tent ranges from Nok. 20 to 35. Camping huts—where available—can be rented at a cost of Nok. 70 to 220 per night.

YOUTH HOSTELS. There are some 100 youth hostels spread all over Norway. Some are built especially for the purpose and are among the best in Europe. Sleeping bags are obligatory, so bring your own or hire one at the hostel. If you are not a member of YHA in your country, you can buy an international membership card at most youth hostels. There is no age limit. The charge for a bed is generally Nok. 65 per night in the best hostels, or Nok. 35 to 45 in more modest hostels. A useful list is available from the *Norwegian Youth Hostels Association,* Dronningensgate 26, Oslo 1.

RESTAURANTS. Eating out in Norway is expensive, especially if you have even a glass of wine, let alone a bottle, with your meal. And unfortunately, it is also true that with the exception of a few rather more sophisticated and international spots in Oslo and the oil-boom towns, most Norwegian restaurants serve generally dull food. It's always fresh and plentiful—hearty is perhaps the best word—but the fact remains that *haute cuisine* it is not. You'll also find that away from towns and cities nearly all restaurants are in hotels.

However, all is not gloom and despondency. A great many hotels and restaurants offer fixed-price menus or *table d'hote* menus, suggested menus that is, both of which are good value, even if they do not offer a great deal in the way

FACTS AT YOUR FINTERTIPS 249

of choice. Keep an eye open too for the *ferie meny*, or vacation menu, where a main course with coffee costs around Nok. 29 to 43 (children 15).

Most larger centers also have good-value pizza and Chinese restaurants, and even occasionally the odd Greek spot, which while not perhaps introducing you to the delights of Norwegian cuisine, are nonetheless inexpensive and a good budget bet. Similarly fast food chains are commonplace.

Prices. We have divided the restaurants in our listings into three categories—Expensive (E), Moderate (M) and Inexpensive (I). These grades are determined solely by price.

Prices, per person, excluding drinks (in Nok.)

Expensive	130 and up
Moderate	80—130
Inexpensive	50—80

Outside Oslo, prices are often considerably lower. These prices also include service charges.

FOOD AND DRINK. Breakfasts are often enormous with a variety of fish, meats and cheese, and fine bread served from the cold buffet along with coffee and boiled or fried eggs. A national institution is the *koldtbord* (cold table) which will often be in evidence at lunch time, featuring smoked salmon, fresh lobster, shrimp and other products of the sea, also assorted meats, salads, cheese, desserts and hot dishes. The sandwiches are a meal in their own right, single-decker meat, cheese, fish or salad concoctions as open and friendly as the Norwegians themselves. They are called *smörbröd*. Equally appreciated by Norwegians and their visitors are the roast venison, ptarmigan in cream sauce, wild cranberries and a special berry called *multer* with a flavor all its own. If you have a strong palate and really want to go Norwegian, try *lutefisk*, a highly flavored codfish that tastes as though it had been preserved in a potash lye. After that even the fiery Norwegian schnaps, *aquavit*, seems cool by comparison

As well as the very high taxes on alcohol, Norway has strict licensing laws governing its sale. Spirits may not be served on Sundays, national holidays and after midnight. Similarly barmen may not serve you more than one drink at a time, to prevent people from stocking up drinks as midnight and the switch from spirits to beer and wine approaches. Outside restaurants and bars, alcohol can otherwise only be bought at the state-run Vin Monopol liquor stores. Note that these are not open over the weekend. Finally, avoid imported spirits—a bottle of scotch will cost upwards of $30.

TIPPING. The Norwegians do not generally expect tips. Taxes and service are always added to your bill in hotels and restaurants, so only exceptional service should warrant a tip. If you do feel your waiter deserves a tip, round up the bill to the nearest krona; this is generally considered adequate. Similarly, taxi drivers do not expect tips

MAIL. Postal rates for airmail letters to the U.S. are Nok. 3.50, to the U.K. Nok. 2.70. Postcards to the U.S. cost Nok. 3.50, to the U.K. Nok. 2.70. These prices may change during 1985.

CLOSING TIMES. Shops open from 8.30 to 5 (4 in summer). On Saturdays they may close as early as 2, especially in summer. Banking hours are 9.30 to 3.30, Monday through Friday, but closed on Saturdays. Museums are usually open until 7 during the summer season, but consult the local guide for details.

NORWAY

SPORTS. Although spectator sports exist, they do not satisfy the Norwegian individualist. He must have his own skis, his own skates, and his own boat, and these he uses whenever he can and whatever his age or walk of life. The Norwegians are, to put it mildly, *very* fond of the outdoor life.

The south coast and the region around Oslo have several seaside spots where the weather is reliable and the facilities for swimming and other water sports are plentiful. Mandal, on the west coast, has fine sandy beaches. Sailing is enjoyed in Norway all around the coast from Trondheim to Oslo. The capital itself, situated at the head of the picturesque island-studded Oslo Fjord, is the most important yachting center.

Norway's mountain districts are easily reached from all parts of the country. In a few hours' walk from road or railway you can reach beautiful country off the beaten track. The great mountain ranges are ideal for hiking and offer excellent holiday facilities. Although most—but not all—have been climbed, there is still scope for further exploratory mountaineering. All the popular rock climbs are well marked, thus making these ideal for parties of some experience wishing to learn guideless climbing.

Over 200 rivers provide salmon and sea-trout fishing. The season extends from June to September. It is no exaggeration to say that some of the best salmon fishing in the world can be had in these Norwegian rivers. In addition, Norway is honeycombed with several thousand lakes scattered all over the country. There is trout in practically every lake and river, even high up among the mountain ranges.

The Norwegian Tourist Board's inexpensive guide book *Mountain Touring in Norway* is indispensable for hikers, and anglers should get their invaluable guide *Angling in Norway*.

Salmon fishing is offered by *Fly-spesialisten,* Kronprinsesse Märthas plass 1, Oslo 1, while hunting trips are organised by *Trönderreiser,* Kongensgate 30, N-7000 Trondheim.

WINTER SPORTS. In Norway, the home of skiing, the whole country is a vast skiing area, with terrains to fit the abilities of expert and novice, the tastes of ski tourer and downhill runner. Ski lifts are available at all the major centers, and skis may be hired for a small fee. Prices and fares are reduced in January, when the snow also is at its best. However, there is ample snow from Christmas until the end of April, with plenty of warm sunshine and dry, inland air. The cross-country ski craze hit America a few years back and package tours from the U.S. and Canada are very popular to such traditional touring centers as Lillehammer, Voss or Geilo. Check with a travel agent or the Norwegian Tourist Board.

Norway is so mountainous that you can ski almost anywhere. Nevertheless, there are regions where more people congregate for this purpose than elsewhere and which, consequently, offer more facilities to visitors. Oslo—with the wooded hills of Nordmarka—is the biggest winter sports center of east Norway. Other resorts within easy reach of the capital are Kongsberg and Norefjell.

Woodland settings characterize the Telemark resorts of Bolkesjö, Morgedal, Vrådal and Vråliosen, whereas more mountainous country is found at Rjukan, Rauland and Tuddal. West Norway has developed skiing resorts at Kvamskog and Seljestad. Along the Bergen railway are such well-known resorts as Voss, Mjölfjell, and Vatnahalsen in alpine terrain; Finse, surrounded by glorious mountains; while Ustaoset and Geilo (the biggest and most popular resort), Ål, Gol, and Nesbyen, are set in more rolling country.

The top winter sports center on the Dovre railway in the Gudbrandsdal country is Lillehammer. Similar undulating terrain is found at Tretten, Espedal, Harpefoss, Vinstra, and Dombås. Oppdal offers more rugged country, Hamar is set in typical wooded terrain. The hotels in the Jotunheimen mountains—Bygdin, Tyin and Spiterstulen are all situated in alpine terrain. Valdres offers a great variety of skiing country: typical woodland skiing down in the valleys, and mountainous terrain at Beitostølen, Grindaheim, Nystova, Nøsen and Maristova.

FACTS AT YOUR FINTERTIPS

Although skiing is the big sport, there is curling and tobogganing as well, and many resorts have excellent skating rinks. You may even indulge in a week or two of dogsled touring on skis if the fancy strikes you. This is not for novices, but you needn't be an expert skier either.

GETTING AROUND NORWAY. By air. Being so vast and inhospitable a country, Norway has need of, and happily enough possesses, an excellent internal air network. *SAS,* Braathens *SAFE* and *Widerøe's* are the principal carriers. Fares are on the high side, but discounts for family and youth travel—details from the Norwegian Tourist Board and travel agents—help keep costs manageable.

By train. Though the rail network is by no means comprehensive, with most routes fanning out from Oslo thereby leaving much of the coast (except the southeast coast) and practically all of the north with no rail services, train travel in Norway is generally to recommended. Almost all trains pass through beautiful countryside—a number of express trains have special viewing coaches—and are generally punctual, clean and comfortable, if not always especially fast. All principal trains carry both first- and second-class carriages and have either dining or buffet cars. Sleeping cars are available on overnight services, for which a supplement is payable, but there are no couchettes, however. Reservations are required on all Express *(Ekspresstog)* and some Fast *(Hurtigtog)* services.

Generally speaking, the longer your journey, the less expensive proportionately it becomes. However, a number of good-value discounts for family groups, young people and senior citizens are also on offer. Details from travel agents, the Norwegian Tourist Board and local tourist offices.

In addition to these exclusively Norwegian discounts, the *Nordturist* (or Scanrail card), the *Inter-Rail* card, the *Eurailpass* and *Eurail Youthpass, Rail Europ Senior Card* and the *Inter-Rail Senior Card* are all valid within Denmark. See "Getting Around Scandinavia by Rail" in *Planning Your Trip* for further details.

By car. Motoring in Norway is very different from most other European countries. There is never a long and tedious journey to reach your destination, because you are there all the time. The scenery is constantly changing in all its breath-taking beauty. Many roads are outstanding tourist attractions on their own merit—particularly in the Fjord Country—with hair-pin bends and mountain passes, smiling lakes and thundering waterfalls. There are good hotels along every major tourist route. Roads are often narrow, so you should plan to cover no more than 250 km. (155 miles) per day. As filling stations may be far apart, particularly in the north and on the mountain roads, stock up.

The ideal starting point for any motoring vacation in Scandinavia is Bergen on the west coast, reached by direct flights from New York or London. Visitors should first explore the Fjord Country, then drive across the mountain ranges to Oslo and onwards to Stockholm and Copenhagen.

Starting from Bergen, there is a choice of four major routes to Oslo, each of such great scenic beauty that it is difficult to choose among them. All take in the fantastic Tokagjel canyon east of Bergen and the giant Hardanger fjord with stunning vistas of the huge Folgefonn glacier, but here they part. One route goes through the Telemark region to Oslo (538 km. or 334 miles), and another across the Hardanger mountain plateau via Geilo to Oslo (489 km. or 303 miles).

Two other routes from Bergen continue via Voss and the stupendous zig-zag road through Stalheim canyon to Gudvangen on the narrow Naerøy fjord—a branch of the Sogne fjord, longest and deepest in Norway. One route goes by ferry to Revsnes and then via the Tyin mountain road to Oslo (565 km. or 350 miles), whereas the other route goes by ferry to Kaupanger and then along Sogne fjord and across Sognefjell mountain pass—highest in Norway at 1,440 meters or 4,690 ft.—down to Otta and Oslo (735 km. or 456 miles).

Any of these four routes could be covered in two days, but there is great scope for excursions en route, so you could easily spend three or four days on the trip. The Telemark route is open throughout the year, because two mountain passes are now bypassed by tunnels. The other routes are blocked by snow from November to May. See the *Fjord Country* chapter for many other tours of the western fjords. Remember that any combination of two eastern valleys with one or more western fjords invariably makes a perfect itinerary.

Ambitious motoring buffs may like to drive all the way from Oslo to North Cape—a distance of 2,233 km. or 1,383 miles, including three ferry crossings and several mountain passes. You drive through Trondheim, Bodø, Narvik and Tromsø, but in between every town you will experience all the scenic delights that Nature's Wonderland can offer you—fjords, rivers, waterfalls, mountains, glaciers and even Lapps with their reindeer herds.

By boat/cruises. Norway's immense, fjord-indented coast has an intricate network of ferries and larger passenger ships serving it, in many places providing an essential means of transport. A wide choice of services is available, from simple hops across fjords (saving many miles of driving) and delightful one-day excursions among the thousands of islands to luxury cruises. Every local tourist office can supply full details of services and excursions in their region. We also give general information on sailings in the *Practical Information* sections at the end of every chapter.

In addition, Norway also boasts the world-famous coastal express service from Bergen in the southwest to Kirknes in the far north, beyond the North Cape. There's at least one sailing daily from Bergen throughout the summer, and the round-trip takes 11 days calling in at 35 harbors—where side trips are easily arranged—en route. The boats sail along one of the most dramatic coastlines in the world, guaranteeing spectacular views almost the whole way. It is, however, extremely popular, and you should book at least six months in advance. Any travel agent can supply details, as can the Norwegian Tourist Board who also produce an excellent book, *2,500 Miles on the Coastal Express.*

By bus. The country is well covered by bus services. Several of the long-distances buses are of great interest to the tourist. For example the North Norway bus service starting at Fauske (on the railway to Bodø) goes right up to Kirkenes on the Russian–Norwegian border covering some 1,000 km. (625 miles) in four days. There are also long-distance international buses linking the Nordic countries, for example from Trondheim (Norway) to Stockholm (Sweden), Mo i Rana (Norway) to Umeå (Sweden), Bodø (Norway) to Skellefteå (Sweden) and Tromsø to Rovaniemi (Finland). Detailed planning information for Bus/Rail Ferry services is available in the *Tourist Timetable for Norway,* available from the Norwegian Tourist Board and published annually in April.

PRELUDE TO NORWAY

Something New Under the Midnight Sun

by
ANDREW BROWN

Every Norwegian, so the joke goes, can speak four languages, and three of these are Norwegian. There is a reasonable explanation for this, as there is for almost everything in Norway; but it does suggest the extent to which the country consists of different pockets of civilization, cut off from each other by mountains and vast distances, and joined together by water, and, nowadays, television. The name of the country confirms this: Denmark, Sweden, and Finland all derive their names from their inhabitants. "Norway" meant originally "The Way Northwards": instead of giving their name to a place, the Norwegians took their name from the route on which they lived.

It is a very long route: if you set out from Oslo in the south to Alta or Kirkenes in the far north, you are attempting a journey as long as from Oslo to Sicily. To get from Oslo to Sicily, you would pass through some of the most densely-inhabited areas of Europe, but there are only four-and-a-half million people in the whole of Norway, so it is not surprising that their towns and villages have preserved a great deal of the individuality that other parts of Europe have lost.

A Constantly Changing Delight

This diversity makes Norway the most rewarding of all the Scandinavian countries to travel through, and the most difficult to describe. Wherever you go, you can hope to find something peculiar, different, and diverting in the next valley. The scaly wooden stave churches in the south of the country—a number dating from late-Viking times—are the best-known examples of this. None of them looks like a church nearly so much as they look like frozen dinosaurs or trolls. Similarly, it is easy enough to drive from A to B in Sweden and Finland, even if they are 500 miles apart (if you drive even 200 miles in any direction in Denmark, you will end up either in Germany or in the sea). But though it is easy to drive long distances through these other Scandinavian countries, it is not very rewarding. The countryside looks like A for 200 miles, then it looks like B for another 200, then you have arrived. It is beautiful if you stop and examine it closely, as an animal would; it is beautiful if you look to the horizon, as a bird might; but only Norway is rewarding on a human scale too, though it is most famous for the spectacular, inhuman beauty of the fjords. Norway is a marvelous country to drive through, and a constantly changing delight to see. The only snag is that such a plan involves driving on Norwegian roads.

Winter retreats through Scandinavia like a Russian army, devastating the country that it must leave behind. It is the awful months of March, April, and, further north, May, that are intolerable to live through, not the proper winter. The constant and, it seems, unending sequence of thaws and refreezings, sleet and rain, ice and slush, when dirty brown snow lies like scabs on the dead grey earth, and it seems that nothing will ever live anywhere again—these, not the sparkling winter, explain the Scandinavian longing for the sun.

And what these months do to people, they do to roads as well. There are probably more potholes than cars in Norway. The main roads, though narrow, are promptly repaired each spring. But any road too small to be marked on a map of the whole country is likely to be rougher than you would have thought possible. There is nothing to be done about this except to relax (bounce) enjoy the view (bone-jarring crunch) and plan your (bump) itinerary accordingly. The most beautiful view I ever saw from a car in Norway I saw from behind a herd of cows.

This may give the impression that Norway is a primitive country. It is not. Even before the discovery of oil in the North Sea, Norway was one of the most prosperous countries in the world. Now it is one of the very richest (and most expensive) but there is so much of the country, and there are so few people in it, that it is impossible to keep all the roads in order.

But the characteristic view of Norway is one of habitation. Sweden and Finland are mostly forest; Denmark is all meadow and parkland; Norway looks as if people live there. The valleys are astonishingly fertile, almost as rich, in fact, as the sea. Even the Alta valley at the foot of the North Cape, which looks as desolate as any place on earth, supports nearly 1,000 fishermen and small farmers.

Dambusters and Dynamite

Alta is quite a good town from which to consider the rest of Norway. It lies at the mouth of the Alta river, which runs north across the bleak plateaux of Finnmark, 200 miles above the Arctic Circle. The river is—or was—one of the best salmon rivers in the world. Norway is famous for its salmon rivers, but the Alta was extraordinary even by Norwegian standards. The average weight of the fish there was 25 pounds, and in good years 20 tons of fish would be caught by rods alone, and far more than that netted in the fjord outside.

The government in Oslo proposed to dam the river. Finnmark needed the electricity. In some ways, this dam is a symbol of everything admirable about modern Norway. It is an astonishing feat to build anything in Finnmark in winter, when the temperature can drop to 50 below in a cold snap, and the sun sets for a fortnight around Christmas. And winter lasts a long time up there. (There are firms that will fly you out for fishing through the ice of lakes still frozen at midsummer).

Yet the dam was not welcomed by the inhabitants of Alta, and it was hated by the Lapps who live in the bleak hills around the headwaters of the river. One Lapp lost an arm in an accident with explosives when he was attempting to sabotage a bridge necessary to the construction of it. Others went on hunger strikes outside the Parliament building in Oslo. When Parliament decided for the third time that work on the dam must start in 1981, the passive resistance of demonstrators who had come from all over the country demanded enormous resources to overcome. Every traffic policeman in the country was taken from his duties and quartered on a converted passenger ferry moored in Alta harbor.

Helicopters, snow-scooters, snow-cats: every resource of modern technology was deployed against the demonstrators; but just when everyone was expecting a tremendous dust-up, resistance was broken by the imposition of very heavy fines on any unauthorized people found within 10 miles of the construction site. Now the affair is almost forgotten in southern Norway; yet the story is an illuminating one. It contains all the essential elements of modern Norway: vast distances; great wealth and impressive technology; the slightly giddying profusion of riches from the sea; and the whole thing administered by a stubborn people never afraid to pick a good fight for their rights.

Illusion or Idyll?

This last is not obvious about the Norwegians: they tend to strike the visitor as remote and placid beings, like the Eloi in H.G.Wells's novel *The Time Machine*. The hero of this book mounts a Victorian time machine, the first in literature, that resembles nothing so much as a brass-bound bicycle and pedals away from suburbia into the future. After 30,000 years he reaches a country that seems like paradise. The inhabitants, known as the Eloi, are pale and delicate. They live like children, and appear to know nothing of sin. The only things to frighten them are the mysterious towers that stud the parkland where they live. Eventually the hero descends through one of these towers to an under-world where gnarled and dark creatures—the Morlocks—work unremittingly to sustain the Eloi in their carefree existence up above. The hero finally precipitates a revolution and then pedals back home again.

There are no Morlocks beneath Norway. They represent a nightmare of industrialism, and the Norwegians, like all the Scandinavians, were able, when they had their industrial revolution, to benefit from the experience of the countries that had gone through it before. The Scandinavians are among the richest people in Europe now partly because they were among the poorest 100 years ago. The lessons of the 19th century reached Scandinavia at the same time as the technology, whereas the rest of us got the technology first and the lessons second, the hard way. And it is the Norwegians who most closely approximate to the 19th-century idea of the future as expressed by the lives of the Eloi.

This is not simply a matter of material wealth. The Norwegians have a gloss of health about them. Their teeth are perfect, their cheeks are ruddy; everyone seems to ski or skate or walk in the mountains whenever they get the chance.

In fact the Norwegians can easily seem too good to be true; an impression that Norwegian writers and artists have done their best to dispel. The very best of these—Ibsen, Knut Hamsun, Edward Munch—have been as good as any in the world, but for that very reason they are not particularly illuminating about specifically Norwegian traits, any more than Shakespeare provides a reliable guide to the English character. Two lesser figures, though, are very illuminating. Aksel Sandomose was a writer who promulgated the ten commandments of village life in the 1930s. The most memorable of these laws were: You must not think that you are worth anything; you must not think yourself better than anyone else; you must not think yourself capable of anything worthwhile; and you must not think that you are in any way exceptional.

The life of small communities is not always that claustrophobic, but Sandemose certainly touched a nerve. His commandments, known as the *Jaentelagen,* have passed into Scandinavian folklore, and when the book came out, he received letters from all over the peninsular to thank him for saying so clearly what so many had felt and suffered from. Norway's seemingly idyllic state does not mean that it is noticeably more fun to live in than anywhere else is. The fun comes in making it so, in creating the illusion.

The most impressive illustration of this is the sculpture park in Oslo, where a man named Gustav Vigeland spent World War II in seculsion, supported by the city council and protected by a fence, to produce an enormous mass of statuary. The result was unexpected: Evelyn Waugh called it more awful than the ruins of Hiroshima. The centerpiece is a tangled Joycean nightmare—a sort of *Finnegans Wake* done in stone—representing a struggle for air and life. Or so it is said to represent: unkind critics have taken it as an allegory of the artist's struggle for intelligibility. Either way, it is an extraordinary monument, representing nothing but itself, and as such well worth seeing.

But Oslo really misses the point of Norway. It is a pleasant town, but it is the least pretentious capital in the world. This is not because it is small, which it is, or shabby, which it isn't; but because newsworthy politics seem alien to the Norwegian character. Oslo is dominated architecturally by the City Hall, which stands above the Royal Palace

PRELUDE TO NORWAY

and the Parliament building like a hippopotamus watching a pair of chihuahuas. This disproportion seems to say that only local politics are real and worth bothering about. The rest is just a stage set, to be used on high days and holy days, but not to be worried about otherwise.

This is the fundamental difference between the Norwegians and the Swedes, who are entranced by the idea of themselves as a nation. Norwegians tend to think of themselves as inhabitants of a particular town or valley, rather than as Norwegians. This is not internationalism but self-absorption. When a foreigner is someone who lives up the next fjord and speaks a different dialect, who needs to worry about the rest of the world?

Of Fish and Fjords

But the rest of the world can profit greatly from Norway. This is most obviously true of fishermen. I should doubt that there is anywhere in the world outside Alaska that combines, as Norway does, enormous numbers of fish with very small numbers of fishermen. Even the most famous and hard-fished rivers like the upper Glomma are not at all crowded by American standards; while anyone prepared to walk a little can find a private paradise with very little trouble.

And then there is the sea. I don't suppose that anyone would seriously fish there—it's too easy. But a boat-ride up the Norwegian coast is marvelous. The fjords are about the only tourist sight in Scandinavia that is as wonderful as its reputation. They're not by any means the only things worth seeing. The point about them is that no amount of anticipation—and no photographs—can ever prepare the traveler for the real thing.

The Norwegian landscape, at its most spectacular, can make you feel that you have been unwrapped: the cling-film memories and expectations that keeps us from really seeing anything new and wholly unexpected is here peeled away. There is something new under the midnight sun.

OSLO

The Countryside Capital

The bright, breezy and outdoorsy capital of Norway is an hospitable city of some 500,000 people located at the head of the long, low Oslo fjord. Here is a world capital with nature at its very doorstep, a perfect place to adjust from the frenetic, over-civilized existence of some Western countries to the simpler, more wholesome values of Norwegian life.

Oslo is not a city of great architecture, sweeping boulevards and imposing buildings, yet in the somewhat haphazard arrangement of the streets there is a certain charm. And if you really go looking, you will certainly find buildings both old and modern of distinction. But, as every Oslonian says, "The surroundings!" Yes, they are magnificent, and the view of the town from any of the easily-reached heights that surround it is superb. But do not jump to the conclusion that the first thing to do is to rush out of town. That's only part of the program—there is plenty to do in Oslo before you head for the hills.

But hills, forests, fjords and farms, mountains and meadows there are aplenty, all encompassed within the nominal city limits of Oslo. The city is in fact the fourth-largest in the world in total area, but this statistic is really no more than a bureaucratic convenience. The built-up area of Oslo is small and in no way compares even with Stockholm and Copenhagen, let alone the likes of London, Paris or Rome. Thus the presence of a fairly rumbustious Nature close at hand is more than any other the most distinctive feature of this little capital.

So be warned. Anyone coming to Oslo in pursuit of sophisticated urban high-living is liable to be somewhat disappointed. Indeed, it should also be added that the rather puritanical Norwegians actively frown on anything that might be considered high living, principally by imposing stinging taxes and strict regulations on the sale of alcohol. However, those in search of gentle relaxation, with the accent on the great outdoors, though perhaps with just a dash of sophistication to spice up the mixture, will find the Norwegian capital very much to their liking.

By Way of Background

Oslo is an ancient city, founded in 1050 by King Harald Hardvaarda (or Hard Counsel), yet in contrast to most European capitals, very little remains that is more than a couple of hundred years old at most. The reasons for this apparently paradoxical state of affairs are not so hard to find, however.

Despite its antiquity and despite having been capital of Norway since the middle ages, for much of its history Oslo has really been no more than a bit-part player on the European stage, and an unfortunate one at that. With Norway falling under the influence and rule of first Sweden and then Denmark, Oslo was little more than a pawn, intermittently besieged, conquered, traded-off and reconquered. The city, or more exactly the Akershus Fortress that was its strategic heart, was attacked first by Duke Erik of Sweden in 1310—no more than 10 years after it had been completed by Haakon V. It was subsequently besieged (successfully) by Christian II of Denmark in 1531-2 and by the Swedes again in 1537 and 1716, who on both occasions were attempting to wrest it from the Danes. As if this was not enough, the old wooden city was also periodically ravaged by fire, culminating in the disastrous fire of 1624 when practically the whole town was burned to the ground. Thus in contrast to Stockholm, for example, which has rarely been seriously attacked, Oslo's tempestuous past has seen the repeated destruction of much of the city, explaining the relative scarcity of older buildings today.

1624 in fact marks the beginning of the development of the modern city. Following this second fire, Christian IV, Danish ruler of Norway, decided to rebuild the town about a mile to the west of its original location so as to bring it closer to the protecting walls of the Akershus Fortress. He also decreed the houses be built of stone or brick and that the streets be a certain width. As a final flourish, he then renamed the city Christiania.

For the next two hundred years or so the little capital enjoyed a reasonable degree of prosperity, though also suffered further severe fires in 1686 and 1708. But its growth was never more than steady and was in any case punctuated by regular political and economic setbacks, chiefly the result of Norway's continued domination by Denmark. During the Napoleonic Wars, for example, Norway was forced by the Danes to commit herself to the French cause, despite the close ties that by that point existed between Norway and Great Britain. The inevitable result was a British blockade of Norwegian ports with grave consequences for Norwegian trade.

However, it was only after 1814, when Norway finally achieved her independence from the Danes (though at the cost of renewed domination by Sweden) that the little city began to grow significantly. And it is from the middle years of the 19th century that the majority of Oslo's principal buildings date: The Royal Palace, the Stortinget (or Parliament) and the University were all constructed between about 1820 and 1860, while Karl Johans Gate, still the principal thoroughfare, was laid out between 1818 and 1848. The 19th century also witnessed a considerable increase in both trade and population (in 1855 Oslo's population was still less than 40,000, by 1900 it was 150,000; similarly, by the same date Oslo had overtaken Bergen as Norway's principal port). The growth of the city also gave rise to a considerable housing shortage, with the result that many small wooden houses were built, outside the then city limits, by workers flooding into Oslo from elsewhere in Norway. A number of these little buildings can still be seen in areas such as Valerengen, Kampen and Rødeløkka.

Following Norway's emergence into total independence in 1905, the city continued to grow (and, on January 1 1925, reverted to its original medieval name of Oslo), but it was the immediate post-war period that witnessed the greatest period of expansion. The striking and monumental City Hall, completed in 1950, is the most obvious symbol of this growth and the spurt of building that accompanied it. Similarly, much of suburban Oslo dates from this period. Today, though still something of a toy town, Oslo is an harmonious, stable and civilized capital, that has put its troubled history behind it.

Exploring Oslo

The heart of Oslo is Karl Johans Gate, a spacious street (much of it now for pedestrians only) about a mile long that runs east to west from the Central Station to the Slottet (Royal Palace). About half-way along is a little park, the Studenterlunden, which for the sake of argument we'll use as the starting point for our exploration of Oslo. The most obvious feature here is the late-19th-century Nationalteatret (National Theater), an attractive classical building at one end of the little park. It's one of the focal points of the capital's cultural life and, appropriately, twin statues of Henrik Ibsen and Björnstjerne Björnson, Norway's most distinguished men of letters, flank the entrance. The theater is currently undergoing major renovation following a backstage fire in 1982, but should be open again in 1985. No performances, however, are given in the summer. (On either side of the theater, by the way, are the city's principal bus stops and the entrance to the electric tram that runs up to Holmenkollen).

Immediately to the north of the National Theater is the handsome neo-Classical facade of the University of Oslo, built from 1811. In fact, most of the University's departments have long since been moved to more spacious quarters in the north of the city. But the building remains the administrative center of the University and examinations are still conducted here in the *Aula,* or Central Hall, which is famous also for the murals of Edvard Munch that cover its walls. The Aula is also the venue for the presentation of the Nobel Peace Prize.

The forecourt of the University is the scene every fall of the inmatriculation of new students to the University every year. But it's also an excellent vantage point from which to watch the procession on May 17, Constitution Day, of thousands of schoolchildren, marching behind brass bands and banners, as they wend their way along Karl Johans Gate before climbing the hill to the Royal Palace to greet the King and his family.

From the University, in fact, it's no more than a few hundred yards up to the Palace, standing in its fine park (which unfortunately is very much less salubrious at night). The Palace is not open to the public, but you can watch the changing of the guard every day at 1.30 when the King is in residence (all year round except mid-May to October when he moves out to his country home at Bygdøy). The statue on the parade in front of the Palace is of King Karl Johan, a Swedish king of Norway after whom the city's main street is named. To the west is another statue, this time of Queen Maud, daughter of Edward VII, King of England, and mother of the present king, Olav. Across the road is a third statue. This is Haakon VII, who was Norway's king from 1905 to 1957 and presided over his country's independence in 1905. He is still regarded with great affection by the Norwegians, not least for keeping alive the hopes of his beleaguered people during World War II when Norway labored under the Nazi occupation. His son Olav today enjoys the same deep hold on the affection of his people.

Again using the park by the National Theater as a base, this time head east away from the Palace and towards the Stortinget, Norway's Parliament. It's quite a striking building, heavy and sturdy, in parts more like a cathedral than a Government building. Inside, it has been richly decorated by modern Norwegian artists. Leave the Storting to the right and continue up Karl Johans Gate, here paved over and a bustling shopping center, towards the Domkirken, the Cathedral. Just before you reach the Cathedral, you pass through Stortorget, a busy flower market in the spring and summer. Though small, the Cathedral is an attractive church, if a little dour from the exterior. It was consecrated in 1697 and contains a fine carved wooden pulpit dating from 1699. However, it has since been substantially remodeled, notably in 1849–50 and just after the war, when the striking ceiling frescos, illustrating the perpetual battle between the forces of light and darkness, and the stained glass windows, designed by Emanuel Vigeland, brother of the more famous Gustav, were executed.

In the arcades behind the Cathedral, where there has been a market since the middle ages, you will today find the Arts and Crafts Center. It's a good place to potter around for an unusual souvenir. In front of the Cathedral there's another statue, this one of Christian IV, King of Norway and Denmark, who moved the site of Oslo nearer to the Akershus Fortress after the disastrous fire of 1624.

The National Gallery

The third and final exploration of the center of Oslo is to the cluster of museums behind and to the north of the University. Here you will find the Nasjongalleriet (National Gallery), the Historisk Museum (Historical Museum) and the Kunstindustrimuseet (Museum of Applied Art).

The National Gallery, established originally in 1836, is Norway's foremost art collection, containing some 3,000 paintings by Norwegian

OSLO

1. Akershus Fortress;
   Forsuarsmuseet (Defence Mus.);
   Norsk Hjemmefrontmuseum
   (Resistance Mus.)
2. Bislett Stadium
3. Central Post Office
4. Central Station
5. Domkirken
6. Fram Huset; Norsk Sjøfartsmuseum;
   Kon-Tiki Museet
7. Geologisk Museum
8. Historisk Museum
9. Kunstindustrimuseet (Mus. of Applied Art)
10. Majorstua Station
11. Munch Museet
12. Nasjonalgalleriet
13. Nationaltheatret
14. Norsk Folkemuseum
15. Rådhuset (City Hall); Tourist Information
16. Slottet (Royal Palace)
17. Stortinget (Parliament)
18. Universitetet
19. Vigelandmuseet
20. Vikingshiphuset
21. West Station

OSLO 263

artists and about 1,000 by other artists. In addition, there are large collections of engravings, drawings, prints and water colors, the whole amounting to a very creditable 40,000 catalogued works. Though the emphasis is perhaps not surprisingly on Norwegian works from 1800 onwards, there are also many works dating from the Renaissance to the 19th century by both Norwegian and foreign artists. However, perhaps the highlight of the collection are the paintings by Edvard Munch, by some way Norway's most famous and influential painter. In spite of its all round excellence, however, the National Gallery, in common with many leading museums around the world, is severely handicapped by a lack of display space. The modern collections in particular have long been crammed into inadequate galleries. But plans are now afoot to move the gallery's modern works to a new home in the Bank of Norway's old building by the end of 1986, which by a happy coincidence is also the gallery's 150th anniversary.

Back to back with the National Gallery is the Historical Museum, containing the University's collection of antiquities. Of particular interest is the fine display of Viking artefacts, especially jewelry. And a visit here is a useful supplement to one to the Viking ships at Bygdøy (of which more later) on the other side of the harbor.

Finally, continue up St. Olavs Gate, which runs diagonally away from the entrance to the Historical Museum, to the fascinating Museum of Applied Art, or Kunstindustrimuseum. Here you'll find furniture, silver, china, clothes—in short all the bric a brac and clutter that help bring the past alive—from the middle ages to the present, displayed against an imaginative background of music from each period. The emphasis is on Norwegian artefacts, but there are also sizeable collections from other lands, including the Far East.

Toward the Harbor

Having by now explored much of the center of the city, head down toward the harbor and the Akershus Fortress, Oslo's most ancient and historic building. The long, low bulk of the Fortress was built by King Haakon V in the early-14th century and has seen much violent military activity during its troubled life. It's an impressive building, by turns gloomy and romantic, with many spires and unexpected jutting roofs. As befits its military status, the Nazis used it as their headquarters during their occupation of Oslo in the war, and appropriately the Fortress today houses the excellent Hjemmefrontmuseum (Resistance Museum) which graphically and imaginatively charts the progress of the "Long Years," as the Norwegians know the war, and the heroic efforts of Norway's Resistance. The fortress also contains a stone monument honoring the memory of those Norwegians who were executed by the Nazis.

Visit the State Apartments here—tours, in English, by guides dressed in period costume—or take in one of the Sunday lunch-time concerts in the chapel. Alternatively, you may just like to wander around the attractive grounds and along the ramparts, from where there is a magnificent view over the harbor and the city. Just outside, and to the east of the Fortress is the Armed Forces Museum, latest addition to Oslo's museums. It too is well worth a visit for those with a military turn of mind.

From Akerhus, it is no more than a few minutes' walk, past the martial figure pointing out to sea (an impressive statue of one Peter Wessel Tordenskiold, Admiral of the Danish/Norwegian fleet from 1715–20) to the red-brick Rådhuset (City Hall), its twin blunt towers looming over Rådhusplass. Outside, on the harbor side, you'll find another statue, F.D.R. in fact, holding a copy of the Atlantic Charter. The statue was unveiled by his wife Eleanor in 1950.

The main entrance to the City Hall is on the opposite side of the building, away from the harbor. But there's a second entrance on this, the harbor side which leads to the Tourist Information office. (Similarly, city sightseeing buses leave from this side, as do the sightseeing boats from the quays just across the road). But walk around to the principal entrance on the city side. It's well worth having a look inside at the massive central hall and the other rooms—the council chamber, the anterooms and the Munch room—open to the public. The whole of the interior is commandingly impressive, but by far and away the most eye-catching features are the murals, some 2,000 square feet in all, illustrating aspects of life in and around the city. They were produced shortly after the building was finished in 1950—work on the City Hall actually began in 1930 but had to be suspended during the war—and not suprisingly many of them, notably that on the left hand wall of the central hall, also deal with the Nazi occupation. Some may find them gaudy and rather wooden, as well as being perhaps a little dated, but they are undeniably impressive for all that. For those who wish, there are guides on hand to show you around.

The Environs of Oslo

To some extent, one can fairly claim that the principal attractions outside Oslo proper are, quite simply, the hills, forests and fjords that encroach so closely on the city and are so distinct a feature of life here. But there are also five specific places of interest outside the city, none of which should be missed by anyone intent on doing justice to a visit here. These are: the Frogner Park, northwest of the city; Bygdøy, just across the fjord from the harbor; Holmenkollen, north of the city; and two museums, the Henie-Onstad Art Center, overlooking the Oslo fjord at Høvikodden, and the Munch Museum to the northeast.

Frogner, or Vigeland, Park (easily reached by tram—no. two—from the National Theater) contains perhaps the most startling sight in Oslo. This is the 60-foot high monolith, carved from a single block of stone weighing in at 200 tons, by the sculptor Gustav Vigeland (1869–1943) depicting the *Cycle of Life*. But as well as the monolith, the park, which was also designed by Vigeland, contains a further 650 statues by the sculptor which took him a total of 40 years to complete and which combine to illustrate and illuminate Vigeland's central theme: the cycle of life. Thus the entire park and its accompanying statues chart man's birth, growth and inevitable decay, the whole climaxed by the giant monolith. As you walk around the park, starting at the imposing bronze gates, you follow the progress of man's life, beginning naturally with birth and progressing through childhood, adolescence, maturity, old age and death. In addition, there is a massive fountain supported by six monumental figures symbolizing man's burden. Further evidence of Vigeland's prolific output is provided by the adjoining Vigeland Museum. (There is a good openair restaurant here to revive those whose spirits may have flagged after confronting Vigeland's work in the raw). The museum contains 1,650 sculptures, 11,000 sketches and 3,700 woodcuts, all the work of the indefatigable artist.

Opinions have long been divided as to the artistic merit of Vigeland's work. Evelyn Waugh, for example, called the Park "more horrible than the ruins of Hiroshima." Certainly, it is hard to see Vigeland's output as part of any wider European movements or schools, or to think of Vigeland as more than an obsessive eccentric single-mindedly pursuing his own vision. Nonetheless the Park as a whole can have an overwhelmingly powerful impact and many visitors have commented that it provided the high point of their stay here. See it for yourself and make up your own mind.

The museums at Bygdøy, however, present no such problems. They're easily reached by ferry from in front of the City Hall in summer, or by half-hourly bus (no. 30) from the side of the National Theater. The most conspicuous of the buildings at Bygdøy is not actually a museum at all; rather, it's a huge tent-like structure—known as the Framhuset—housing the sturdy little polar ship *Fram*. Actually, "little" is possibly a misleading term—the *Fram* is by no means a large vessel, even by the standards of her day (she was built in 1892), but housed in her permanent enclosed dry dock she appears positively massive. She was built for Fritjof Nansen, earliest of the many remarkable Norwegian polar explorers of the late-19th and early-20th centuries, for his three-year drift across the permanently frozen waters of the North Pole. She was subsequently used by Otto Sverdrup on his journey to map the west coast of Greenland, and then to take Roald Amundsen on the first leg of his successful journey to the South Pole in 1911. She has been beautifully preserved and the visitor can clamber all over this most famous of polar vessels. Outside, you will find another famous Norwegian polar ship, even smaller than the *Fram*. This is the *Gjøa*, built originally as a fishing boat, and subsequently used by Amundsen on his discovery of the Northwest Passage (1903–6). Like the *Fram*, the *Gjøa* spent over three years gripped in the ice of the Arctic making her slow way across the roof of the world, eloquent proof of the skills of Norwegian shipwrights. Visitors are not, unfortunately, allowed on board.

A harpoon's throw from the *Fram* building is Oslo's new Sjøfartsmuseum, or Maritime Museum. It's excellently laid out and graphically charts Norway's illustrious seafaring traditions and triumphs from the Vikings to the present day. The museum contains a veritable treasure chest of models, pictures, nautical bric-a-brac, even the interior of a passenger ship from the early years of this century. It's a must for anyone who has felt the urge to go down to the sea. An interesting annex contains a number of actual vessels, from early fishing boats to a beautifully built and finished Olympic sailing dinghy. There's a good restaurant and cafeteria in the museum (in summer the cafeteria moves outside).

Opposite the Maritime Museum is the third in this trio of nautical haunts, the Kon-Tiki Museum, home of Thor Heyerdahl's famous balsa wood raft of the same name in which he caught the imagination of the world by sailing 4,300 miles from Peru to Polynesia in 1947. The raft, never presumably too sturdy at the best of times, is showing its age somewhat these days, but is still an impressive sight. Underneath it there's an interesting and convincing mock up of the many different types of fish that congregated under its frail balsa wood timbers during the crossing, including a splendid whale shark, almost as long as the raft itself. The museum also houses *Ra II*, the papyrus boat in which Heyerdahl sailed from Morocco to Barbados in 1970, again in an attempt to prove that ancient man undertook long ocean crossings.

A little inland from the three museums is an equally impressive museum celebrating Norway's maritime exploits, though of a very much earlier period—the Vikingshiphuset or Viking Ship Museum. The museum is some 15 minutes' walk from Bygdøy proper, but well sign posted and easy to find. Opened in 1936, it houses three remarkable and very beautiful Viking ships dating from A.D. 800–900, all discovered only this century. Almost as interesting as the vessels themselves are the various artefacts which were found on board, for these were burial ships, buried with Viking chieftains and intended to serve them in the next world as they had in this. Thus the ships were piled high with the goods and chattels of the chieftains, all of which have helped to build our remarkably complete picture of Viking life.

Finally, visit the immense Norsk Folkemuseum, the Norwegian Folk Museum, located just up the road from the Viking ships. Principally an outdoor museum (though no more than a couple of miles from the city center, the museum is practically in the country), it contains some 150 original wooden farmhouses and other buildings from all over Norway, many dating from the middle ages, that have been transported and reassembled here. The chief treasure is one of Norway's unique stave churches, its roofs piled high like a pagoda, dating from the 12th century.

The museum was founded originally in 1894 and moved to Bygdøy in 1902 under the patronage of King Oscar II when the king's collection, which included the stave church, was added. Over the years, collections from other museums have also been transferred here. As well as the buildings themselves, the museum has an extensive collection of interiors, notably Ibsen's study, preserved exactly as it was when he lived in Oslo. There are goings-on galore at the museum in summer, especially on Sundays when there are displays of folk dancing, puppet shows, movies, handicraft demonstrations and lectures. *Oslo This Week* will tell you what's on and when. The museum also has a good restaurant and cafeteria.

Up the Holmenkollen

The next excursion out of Oslo will take you in a completely different direction, northwest out of the city in fact and up into the hills to Holmenkollen and the Tryvannshøgda TV tower. Take the electric train from the station by the National Theater for the climb up to Frognerseter station—it takes about 30 minutes—and then walk up the hill to the TV tower. The walk will take you about 15 minutes, and is well worth it for the spectacular view over the city and the fjord. From the tower you can easily walk down the hill again—for about 20 minutes—to the Holmenkollen ski jump. Norway is generally regarded as the home of modern skiing and no single place played a more significant role in its development than Holmenkollen. Indeed, to many

Norwegians, Holmenkollen possesses a near-mystic significance and is regarded almost as a symbol of Norway. This reverence reaches a peak during the annual Holmenkollen championships, normally held in March. They have been held every year since the beginning of the century—except during World War II—and grip the attention of the entire nation. The King—no mean ski jumper himself in his youth—is one of the staunchest supporters. For the visitor, however, the principal attraction of Holmenkollen is the ski jump itself, a towering ramp stretching skywards down which the intrepid jumpers (once you've seen the jump, you may not think "intrepid" quite strong enough an adjective) hurtle before hurling themselves into space. If you've got a head for heights, take the elevator to the top of the tower—the view is predictably sensational.

Blasted into the rock by the side of the jump is the little ski museum —there's a statue of Nansen outside—which illustrates the development of skiing in Norway. Highlights of the museum are a ski over 2,500 years old and a display of polar equipment used by Nansen and Amundsen on their journeys to the North and South Poles respectively (including a phlegmatic stuffed dog taken—before it was stuffed—to the South Pole).

Finally, walk down the hill again from the jump to the Holmenkollen Park Hotel, a matter of 200 yards or so, to have a look at this marvelous late 19th-century building. It's been substantially renovated and a brand new annex added, but the original wooden building, with its multitude of projecting balconies, gables and overlapping roofs, has been lovingly preserved. The hotel has a variety of cafes and restaurants, though all are pricey. Less expensive refreshments are available at the Holmenkollen restaurant a little further down the hill, where you can sit on the terrace and enjoy the view in rather more comfort than from the top of the ski jump. The tram station for the ride back into town is located just below the restaurant.

Our final two excursions—to the Munch Museum and the Henie-Onstad Senteret, the Henie-Onstad Art Center—will not take you far from the city center, but are nonetheless well outside the downtown area.

The Munch Museum lies to the northeast of the city and can be reached by subway from Jernbanetorget to Tøyen (any train) or by bus (no. 29) from the National Theater, again to Tøyen. Edvard Munch (1863–1944) is the only Norwegian painter who can be claimed to have exercised a decisive influence on the wider European stage, and his work—tormented and expressionist—remains hugely popular today. The museum, opened in 1963, the centenary of the artist's birth, is thus a fitting memorial to Norway's most famous painter. It includes all those works—some 22,000 in all—in the artist's possession at the time of his death, all of which he left to the city. Needless to say, it is not possible to display anything more than a small fraction of this vast collection at any one time, so the exhibits are changed regularly, making repeated visits here a pleasure (though the most important works are generally on view at all times). But as well as Munch's work, the museum also holds regular exhibitions of works by other artists and presents lectures, concerts and films. Guided tours in English are available.

OSLO

Across the street from the Museum are the Geologisk Museum (Natural History Museum) and the Botanical Gardens, the latter an oasis on a hot summer's day.

Finally, visit the Henie-Onstad Art Center, 20 minutes from the National Theater by bus (no. 32) overlooking the fjord at Høvikodden. It's a modern art center in the widest sense. At the heart of the complex is the collection of 20th-century paintings donated by ice skater Sonja Henie and Niels Onstad. But the center also puts on concerts, film shows, theater, ballet, lectures and the like. A good cafeteria and restaurant complete the picture.

PRACTICAL INFORMATION FOR OSLO

GETTING TO TOWN FROM THE AIRPORT. There is a regular bus service from Oslo airport (Fornebu) stopping at the Scandinavia Hotel (opposite the Royal Palace) and at the Central Station; cost is approximately 20 Nok. and journey time is around 25 minutes. There are also city buses from the airport which cost around 12 Nok. A taxi from the airport to the city center will run about 55 Nok. to 65 Nok.

TOURIST INFORMATION. The city tourist office is located in the City Hall, Oslo 1 (427 170). They can supply information on all aspects of the city from sightseeing trips to renting bicycles. In addition, they publish annually the *Oslo Guide,* which gives details of hotels in the city, and *Oslo This Week,* which lists all current activities in the city. The excellent-value *Oslo Card* is also available from the tourist office. Valid for one, two or three days and costing 50, 75 and 100 Nok. respectively, the card gives unlimited free travel on all public transport within the city and free entry to all museums, as well as discounts on many sightseeing buses and boats and car hire, and special rates in some restaurants. (The Oslo Card is also available from travel agents, larger stores and branches of the Akershus Savings Bank).

The tourist office also run an accommodations office at the Central Station; for details see *Hotels* below.

The tourist office is open daily 8.30–3.30; the Central Station office 8.30 A.M. –11 P.M. (Sundays 8.30 A.M.–11 A.M. and 6.30 P.M.–11 P.M.).

USEFUL ADDRESSES. Travel Agents. *American Express,* Karl Johans Gate 33 (205 050). *Tjaerborg Reiser,* Lille Grensen 7 (411 300). *Vest Reisebureau,* Drammensveien 126 (555 795).

Embassies. *U.S. Embassy,* Drammensveien 18 (448 550). *Canadian Embassy,* Oscarsgate 20 (466 955). *British Embassy,* Ths Heftyesgate 8 (563 890).

Car Hire. *Avis,* Munkedamsveien 27 (410 060). *Europcar,* Fredensborgveien 33 (202 150). *Hertz,* Wergelandsvn 1 (200 121).

All the leading car hire companies also have desks at Fornebu airport.

TELEPHONE CODES. The telephone code for Oslo is 02. To call any number in this chapter, unless otherwise specified, this prefix must be used. Within the city, no prefix is required.

NORWAY

HOTELS. Oslo is well supplied with hotels in all price ranges, many offering excellent-value special deals at all times of year. For example, from the end of June to early August, 23 Oslo hotels give substantial discounts and this offer is also valid at weekends all year round. Similarly, two children under 15 can stay in their parents' room at no extra charge. Full details of all Oslo hotels are given in the tourist office's *Oslo Guide.*

The tourist office also runs an accommodations office at the Central Station for hotels, pensions and rooms in private rooms. You must, however, apply in person at the office and no advance bookings will be taken. There is a fee of 9 Nok. plus 10% of the room rate. This will be refunded when you check in.

Deluxe

Bristol. Kristian IV's Gate (415 840). 156 rooms, most with bath. Quietly located on a side street, the Bristol has an excellent restaurant, the *Bristol Grill,* while *El Toro* is a Spanish restaurant with dancing and floor shows. There is also the *Leopard* grill, plus a nightclub and disco on the second floor. The *Trafalgar* bar, the *Library* bar and the *Winter Garden* complete the picture. AE, MC, V.

Continental. Stortinsgate 24/26 (419 060). 189 rooms, all with bath. Opposite the National Theater and with view of the Royal Palace. Its *Annen Etagen* restaurant is one of the most elegant in Oslo; the *Loftet* is a beer and wine restaurant with billiards and disco. There is also the *Tivoli* grill, a modern and inexpensive restaurant, and the *Continental* bar near the lobby. However, of outstanding interest is the *Theatercafeen* on the ground floor, an elegant and hardly changed late-19th-century meeting place much frequented by Oslo high society. AE, DC, MC, V.

Grand. Karl Johansgate 31 (334 870). 350 rooms, most with bath or shower and all with color T.V. On Oslo's main street and opposite Parliament and city park. Indoor pool, sauna and solarium. The *Speilen* restaurant is Oslo's most exclusive and has dancing; but the hotel's other restaurants include the *Etoile,* the *Palmen,* a sandwich buffet, and the *Fritzner* grill, a top-grade spot. The *Grand Cafe* is a famous Oslo rendezvous, with murals depicting life in late-19th-century Oslo; the *Bonanza* is a restaurant and nightclub with a Western theme. AE, DC, MC, V.

Holmenkollen Park. Kongevein 26 (146 090). 200 rooms, all with bath and most with balconies. Magnificent old Norse–style building overlooking the city and located by the Holmenkollen ski jump. Luxurious annex added in 1981 but the original part of the building remains the chief attraction. Facilities include gourmet restaurant, coffee shop, bar and nightclub, indoor pool, whirl pool, sauna, gym, squash court, curling rink and parking for 90 cars. AE, DC, MC, V.

Scandinavia. Holbergsgate 30 (113 000). 476 rooms, all with bath. Norway's largest hotel and tallest building. The restaurants include a first class gourmet grill, the *Cafe Royal,* which offers a spectacular smørgasbord for lunch, and the *Hetland Juballong,* a nightclub with disco and live music. There are also two bars, an indoor pool, and a shopping center; plus round the clock room service. The Scandinavia also doubles as the city air terminal. AE, DC, MC, V.

Expensive

Ambassadeur. Camilla Collettsvei 15 (441 835). 54 beds. Near Royal Palace, with indoor pool and sauna. AE, DC, MC, V.

Astoria. Akersgaten 21 (336 700). 136 beds. Near Parliament building, with popular restaurant. MC, V.

Carlton Rica. Parkveien 78 (563 090). 86 beds. In quiet street west of city center; its *Rica* restaurant is famous for fine food. AE, DC, MC, V.

KNA. Parkveien 68 (562 690). 226 beds, most rooms with bath or shower. In same quiet street as the Carlton Rica and run by the Royal Norwegian Automobile Club. Intimate restaurant and bar, and good bistro. AE, DC, MC, V.

Müllerhotell West. Skovveien 15 (562 995). 59 beds, most rooms with bath. Behind the Royal Palace. The *Coq d'Or* grill is a popular eating place; also has bar. AE, DC, MC, V.

OSLO

Nobel. Karl Johansgate 33 (337 190). 104 beds, most rooms with bath or shower. On Oslo's main street, with bistro and bar. Has seen better days. AE, DC, MC, V.

Sara. Gunnerusgate 11/13 (336 470). 343 rooms, 100 with bath. Opposite the Central rail station. *Crystal Garden* restaurant has both Scandinavian and international menu. *Glåmrik* pub has Viking style decor; coffee shop. DC, MC, V.

SAS Globetrotter. Fornebu park (120 220). 273 beds, all rooms with bath or shower. Located near the airport. Has *Globetrotter Grill* and good bar; ample parking space. AE, DC, MC, V.

Moderate

Esso. Ramstadsletta 12/14, Høvik (121 740). 115 beds, all rooms with bath or shower. At Høvik, 6 km. (4 miles) west of city on the E18. Restaurant, cafeteria, sauna, parking. AE, MC, V.

Europa. St. Olavsgate 31 (209 990). 300 beds, all rooms with bath and color T.V. Centrally located and modern hotel. Special reductions for parents with children. DC, MC, V.

Forbunds. Holbergs pass 1 (208 855). 137 beds. Near the Scandinavia Hotel, with cafeteria (no alcohol). AE, MC, V.

Norum. Bygdøy Alle 53 (447 990). 90 beds, most rooms with bath. In residential area to west of city center; bistro with good food. AE, DC, MC, V.

Sara. Universitetsgate 11 (202 655). 97 beds. Near the National Gallery; with restaurant. AE, DC, MC, V.

Stefan. Rosenkrantzgate 1 (336 290). 200 beds, most rooms with bath or shower. Centrally located, with popular restaurant (no alcohol). AE, MC, V.

Inexpensive

Anker. Storgata 55 (114 005). 426 beds, many rooms with 4 beds; open June to Aug. only. Centrally located, with cooking facilities, supermarket, cafeteria and restaurant. AE, MC, V.

Gyldenløve. Bogstadvei 20 (601 090). 330 beds. Bed and breakfast only, no alcohol. No credit cards.

Norrøna. Grensen 19 (336 085). 61 beds. With cafeteria, but no alcohol. AE, DC, MC, V.

Ritz. Fr. Stangsgate 3 (443 960). 68 beds. Hotel and pension; with restaurant. AE, DC, MC, V.

Standard. Pilestredet 27 (203 555). 72 beds. With restaurant. MC, V.

Youth Hostels

Haraldsheim Youth Hostel, Haraldsheim 4 (218 359). 4 km. from city center, with 270 beds, family rooms, restaurant, lounge, TV. Take tram 1 from National Theater to Sinsen.

Camping

Bogstad Camp, (507 680). Open all year. Take tram 41 to Bogstad.

Ekeberg Camping, (198 568). 3 km. from city center. Open June 20 to Aug. 20. Bus 24 from Jernbanetorget or 74 from Parliament.

Stubljan Camping, (286 235). Bus 75 to Ingierstrand from Oslo S.

HOW TO GET AROUND. By bus and tram. The bus and tram network is generally good. The heart of the network is by the National Theater in the city center. All stops here give details of schedules, but details are also available from the tourist office. There is a flat fare of 8 Nok. for all journeys, but a number of good-value discount tickets are available. Best of all is the Oslo Card (available from the tourist office) which gives unlimited free travel on all public transport for one, two or three days at a cost of 50, 75 and 100 Nok. respectively (children half price). Alternatively, there is a Tourist Ticket, again available from the tourist office, which gives 24 hours' unlimited travel for 30 Nok. (children half price). There are also two multi-journey tickets called

Flerreisekort. The first, costing 60 Nok., gives you 10 coupons, each entitling you to one hour's travel with unlimited transfers. The second, costing 24 Nok., contains four coupons. Both are half price for children.

By metro. The Oslo metro, currently divided into eastern and western sectors—the western sector radiating from the National Theater and the eastern sector from the Sentrum station—is due to be linked by 1985. A single ticket, valid for one hour and allowing one transfer, costs 8 Nok. But the Oslo Card is also good for metro travel. The most important line for most visitors is that from the National Theater to the Frognerseter station on the Holmenkollen high above the city. But the metro services, some supplemented by electric trains, also extend into the suburbs.

By taxi. Cabs are expensive but numerous. They can be hailed in the street if the light on the roof is on, but there are also cab stands at the Central and West rail stations. Otherwise, call 348, though you may have to wait for up to 30 minutes. There is an additional charge for more than two passengers and at night. Tip around 10% of the fare.

By bicycle. The tourist office can supply lists of all places where bikes can be rented. No deposit is generally required; instead, you may be asked to surrender your passport. Oslo, not least because of its small scale, is a delightful city to cycle around, though hilly in parts, and rides out into the country are easy to make.

On foot. The city is easily explored on foot and the tourist office can supply lists of suggested walks.

TOURS. Regular city tours offered include: (a) Morning sightseeing by bus, starting from City Hall and including the Cathedral, Munch Museum, Vigeland Park and Holmenkollen, 3 hours. (b) Afternoon sightseeing by bus including the Folk Museum, Viking Ships, *Fram,* and *Kon-Tiki,* 3 hours. (c) Sightseeing launch around the harbor leaving every hour in front of City Hall, 50 mins. There is also a 2½-hour tour 4 times daily. (d) All-day sightseeing by boat and bus. Start at Pier C.

Other excursions include a sea tour which starts out from Pipervika, behind the City Hall. Modern and comfortable sightseeing boats with English-speaking guides depart regularly from this point. If you're allergic to crowds, you'll get a more authentic picture of life in Oslo's seaside suburbs by taking one of the regular passenger ships that ply between the city and Nesodden. Travel by return boat, or get off at Nesodden to explore, and return by a later boat.

Or you can take the bus (starts from Grønlandstorg, but best entered outside the University), to Sundvollen, final destination Hønefoss. For the next hour you will see some of the most magnificent scenery to be found in the Oslo region as you wind and climb your way around the precipitous edges of the crystal blue Tyri Fjord. At Sundvollen you can walk up Dronningveien, or go by car, to the top of Krokkleiva with famous views from Kongens Utsikt (the King's View), one of the most beautiful in Norway. The walk is quite stiff (takes about 3 hours altogether). Alternatively, take the 36 bus to Javnaker, where you can visit the Hadeland Glass Works, the largest of its kind in Scandinavia. Founded in 1762, the work is still performed by craftsmen and visitors may see glassblowing, cutting and etching of crystal.

English language guides are available from tourist office. All guides are licensed.

MUSEUMS. Most cities in the world have museums of the traditional kind, and Oslo has its share—but in addition, Oslo has a series of unique museums, particularly its "one man" and "one ship" museums. Opening times quoted below are for *summer only,* and are changed according to season, so always consult the current *Oslo Guide.*

Forsuarsmuseet (The Norwegian Defence Museum). Situated in the old arsenal building in the lower grounds of Akershus fortress. It is still under construction, but when complete it will cover the history of Norwegian defence from late in the Middle Ages to contemporary times. Open Tues. to Sun. 11–3; closed Mon. Admission free.

Framhuset (The Polar Exploration Ship). *Fram* was built by the well-known designer Colin Archer for Nansen's Polar expedition 1893–96. It was also used by Otto Sverdrup 1889–1902, and later Roald Amundsen used it on his expedition to the South Pole 1910–12. Open Mon. to Sat. 10–6, Sun. 11–6; closed in winter. Admission Nok. 5.

Geologisk Museum (Natural History Museum). Sarsgata 1. Botanical garden and conservatories, mineralogical and geological museum, paleontological museum with fossil plants and animals, and zoological museum. Open Tues. to Sun. 12–3; closed Mon. Admission free.

Henie-Onstad Senteret (The Sonja Henie-Niels Onstad Arts Center). At Høvikodden, 11 km. (seven miles) from Oslo. The Center was opened in 1968 and contains a permanent collection of 20th–century art, donated by Sonja Henie and her husband Niels Onstad. Current trends and ideas in literature, film, dance, music, architecture and applied arts are displayed in changing exhibitions and other events. Buses leave regularly from the city center. Open Mon. to Sat. 9 A.M.–10 P.M., Sun. 11 A.M.–10 P.M. Admission Nok. 15.

Historisk Museum (The Historical Museum). Frederiksgate 2. Contains the University's Ethnographical Museum, Numismatic Collection and its Collection of Antiquities. The collection from the Middle Ages is Oslo's richest art collection from that period. Open Tues. to Sun. 11–3; closed Mon. Admission free.

Kon–Tiki Museet (The Kon–Tiki Museum). At Bygdøynes, the museum contains the raft on which Thor Heyerdahl and five companions drifted nearly 8,000 km. (5,000 miles) across the Pacific from Peru to Polynesia. It also houses the 14–meter (46–foot) reed boat *Ra II* and items belonging with it from Heyerdahl's 1970 expedition across the Atlantic Ocean. Open daily 10–6. Admission Nok. 5.

Kunstindustrimuseet (The Museum of Applied Arts). St. Olavsgate 1. Collections of both Norwegian and foreign applied arts from the Middle Ages through to the 20th century. Displayed are furniture, silver, glass, ceramics and textiles. Of note is the Baldishol tapestry, woven in Hedmark in the 1180s, one of the five tapestries which have been preserved from the Romanesque era. Open Tues. to Sun. 11–3; closed Mon. Admission free.

Kunstnerforbundet (Artists Association). Kjeld Stubsgate 3. Contemporary Norwegian art, also handicrafts. Open Mon. to Fri. 10–4, Sat. 10–2; closed Sun. Admission free.

Kunstnernes Hus (Artists' Center). Wergelandsveien 17. Changing exhibitions of Norwegian and foreign paintings, sculpture and prints. Open Tues. to Sat. 10–6, Sun. 12–6; closed Mon. Admission free.

Munch-Museet (The Munch Museum). Tøyengaten 53. In 1940 Edvard Munch bequeathed the City of Oslo many of his works; paintings, drawings, water colours, prints and sculptures, books, letters and private papers. The collection has been increased by gifts from individuals. Lectures and concerts. Guided tours available. Open Tues. to Sat. 10–8, Sun. 12–8; closed Mon. Admission free.

Nasjonalgalleriet (The National Gallery). Universitetsgaten 13. Norway's largest public collection, with emphasis on Norwegian painting, sculpture and lithographs. Also has a collection of French and modern European paintings. Open Mon. to Fri. 10–4, Sat. 10–3, Sun. 12–3. Admission free.

Norsk Arkitektmuseum (Norwegian Architecture Museum). Josefinesgt. 32. Alternating exhibitions. Library. Open Mon. to Fri. 9–2; closed Sat. and Sun. Admission free.

Norsk Folkemuseum (The Norwegian Folk Museum). Museumsveien, Bygdøy. Outdoor collection of 170 buildings, including 12th–century stave church. Indoor collection designed to illustrate Norway's urban and rural culture. Henrik Ibsen's study, a Lapp collection and a Pharmacy museum are also to be seen here. In summer: restaurant, folk dancing, concerts. Open Mon. to Sat. 10–6, Sun. 11–6. Admission Nok. 5.

Norsk Hjemmefrontmuseum (Norway's Resistance Museum). Situated in an old building in the grounds of Akershus Fortress, close to the monument to patriots who gave their lives in World War II. Attempts to give a true picture

NORWAY

of major events in Norway during the German occupation. Lecture hall, library, war publication archives. Open Mon. to Sat. 10–4, Sun. 11–4. Admission Nok. 5.

Norsk Sjøfartsmuseum (The Norwegian Maritime Museum). Bygdøynes. Contains a collection of boats used along the Norwegian coast, models of sailing ships and a model shipyard. Ocean navigation is presented through models, paintings and objects. Slide projectors, radar instruments, library, restaurants, cafeteria. Open daily 10–8. Admission Nok. 5.

Norsk Teknisk Museum (Norwegian Science and Industry Museum). Fyrstikkalleen 1, Etterstad. Technical development in Norway, model railroad, oil rig, working model of atomic plant. Closed for rebuilding. (Phone 675 195 for details).

Oslo Bymuseum (The City Museum). Frognerveien 67. Situated in Frogner Hovedgård (Frogner Manor), built around 1790. Contains maps, portrait gallery, views of Oslo, rooms furnished as in former days. The collection covers the period 1600–1850. Open Mon. to Fri. 11–5, Sat. 11–4, Sun. 12–5. Admission free.

Oslo Kunstforening (Oslo Art Association). Radhusgate 19. Situated in residence dating from 1626; exhibitions of paintings, sculpture, prints and etchings. Open Tues. to Sat. 11–4, Sun. 12–4; closed Mon. Admission free.

Postmuseet (Post Museum). Dronningensgt. 15. Contains displays of stamps, postal accessories, and the development of communications over three centuries. Open Mon. to Fri. 10–3, Sat. 10–1; closed Sun. Admission free.

Skimuseet (The Ski Museum). Collections of skis, including the 2,500 year old Øvrebø ski and part of Nansen's and Amundsen's polar equipment. A lift gives access to the 55–meter (180–foot) tower, which has a magnificent view. Open daily 9–9. Admission Nok. 8.

Teatermuseet (Theater Museum). Nedre Slottsgt. 1. New museum, showing the development of Oslo's theater from the beginning of the 19th century up to 1950. It is situated in one of the oldest buildings in Oslo, built around 1600. Open Wed. 11–3, Sun. 12–4. Admission Nok. 5.

Vigelandmuseet (The Vigeland Museum). Nobelsgate 32. Formerly Gustav Vigeland's studio and residence. It contains 1,650 sculptures, 3,700 woodcuts, 423 plates for woodcuts and around 11,000 sketches. Concerts in summer. Guided tours. Open Tues. to Sun. 1–7; closed Mon. Admission free.

Vikingskiphuset (The Viking Ships and Archeological Finds). Huk Aveny 35, Bygdøy. Remarkable relics of the Viking Age, all found near the Oslo fjord. Open daily 10–6. Admission Nok. 5.

PARKS, ZOOS AND GARDENS. Botanisk Hage (Botanical Garden and Museum). Trondheimsveien 23. Hot houses, geological and zoological collections. Open Tues. to Sun. 12–3; closed Mon.

Dyre Parken (Zoo). Animals, funfair, minigolf, cafeteria. Open daily 10–8.

Frogner Parken (The Vigeland Sculptures in Frogner Park). Gustav Vigeland's most gigantic work—a world of people carved in granite, iron and bronze. Openair swimming pool, cafeteria, sports arena, tennis courts, restaurants. Always open. Admission free.

Gamlebyen Ruiner (Ruin–Park). Park with archeological excavations, part of the center of ecclesiastical affairs in medieval Oslo. Open summer only. Admission free.

Sørenga Ruiner (Ruin park, Sørenga). Ruins of the earliest buildings in Oslo: The Royal Palace and the Maria Church from approx. 1050. This was the king's center of power. Open summer only. Admission free.

HISTORIC BUILDINGS AND SITES. Akershus Slott Og Festning (Akershus Castle). One of Oslo's most attractive buildings, first built by Haakon V around 1300. It was then rebuilt by Christian IV around 1620 and has subsequently been restored and redecorated. It contains the royal mausoleums, the World War II Resistance museum, and the defence museum. Open Mon. to Sat. 10–4, Sun. 12.30–4. Admission Nok. 3.

OSLO

Basarhalene (Bazaar Arcade). Behind Oslo Cathedral, a center for applied art. Open all year.

Bogstad Gård (Bogstad Manor). Sørkedalen. Patrician manor built around 1760, once owned by prime minister Peder Anker. Landscaped garden and art treasures. Open Thurs. 6–7, Sun. 12–6. Admission free.

Damstredet. Charming suburban village from the beginning of the 19th century.

Domkirken (Oslo Cathedral). At Stortorvet. Built between 1694 and 1699, the exterior was restored in 1849–50. The interior was restored in 1949–50. Altar piece and pulpit from 1699. Concerts. Open Mon. to Fri. 10–2, Sat. 10–1; closed Sun. except divine service 11 and 7.30. Admission free.

Gamle Aker Kirke (Old Aker Church). Akersbakken 26. Built around 1100, this is the oldest stone church in Scandinavia still in use as parish church. Tues. and Thurs. 12.30–2, Sun. service 11. Admission free.

Hovedøya Klosterruiner (Monastery Ruins). Constructed by Cistercian Monks, who arrived from Kirkstead in England in 1147. Ferry from Vippetangen. Admission free.

Konserthuset (Concert Hall). Johan Svendsens plass. Inaugurated 1977, designed by Gösta Åbergh. Facade covered with polished light Tolga granite. Concert hall and chamber music hall. Concerts of all kinds. Open only in connection with arrangements. See daily press and *Oslo This Week*.

Ladegården (Oslo Ladegård). Oslogate 13. Medieval Bishop's residence. The ecclesiastic center of ancient Oslo, together with the St. Hallvard Church. Later the Mayor's residence then pleasure residence. The present Baroque building dates from the 17th century, with vaults from the Middle Ages. Restored by the City of Oslo 1957–68. Open Wed. 10–6, Sun. 12–1. Admission free.

Oscarshall. Bygdøy. Pleasure palace built in 1847–52 by King Oscar I of Norway and Sweden. Open Sun. 11–4. Admission Nok.1.

Rådhuset (Oslo City Hall). Foundation stone laid in 1931, inaugurated in 1950 for the celebration of Oslo's 900th anniversary. Lavishly decorated by Norway's leading painters and sculptors during the 1930s and 40s. Open Mon. to Fri. 10–2; closed Sat. and Sun. Admission free.

Slottet (Royal Palace). Drammensveien 1. Constructed 1825–48. Residence of King Olav V, King of Norway. Public admitted to the park only. Changing of the guard takes place at 1.30 P.M. When the King is in residence the band of the Royal Guard play Mon. to Fri.

Stortinget (Parliament). Karl Johansgt. Built 1861–66. Richly decorated by Norwegian artists. Open Mon. to Sat. 12–2; closed Sun. Admission free. Guided tours during parliamentary recess (June through mid-Sept.).

Tryvannstårnet (Tryvann Observation Tower). The largest observation tower in the north, with an optical horizon covering about 30,044 sq. km. (11,600 sq. miles). It is situated on the Tryvann hill on the outskirts of Oslo. Lift, binoculars, refreshments, souvenirs. Reached by Holmenkollen Railway from the National Theater to Frognerseteren, then a 25-minute walk.

Universitetet (Oslo University). Karl Johansgt. 47. The Aula of the University with murals by Edvard Munch. Open summer only, or on request. (Tel. 330 070 ext. 756).

SPORTS. Swimming. There are excellent bathing beaches on both sides of the fjord, all easily reached by bus from the City Hall. On the east side you'll find: Ingierstrand, Katten, Hvervenbukta, Ljanskollen and Bestemorstrand, all reached by bus 75. On the west side, Rolfstangen, near Fornebu airport, is reached by bus 31. Also good are the two adjoining islands of Langøyene, owned by the city and with good sandy beaches; take the ferry from pier 4. Water temperatures in July and August average about 68° F (20° C). There are a number of very popular swimming pools dotted around the city, of which the most popular is by the Vigeland sculpture park.

Tennis. Courts are available at Frogner Stadium near Vigeland Park.

Fishing. Good trout fishing can be had in many places around the city. Permits are necessary but may be bought at the many sports shops in Oslo and

NORWAY

in the fishing chalets of Kobberhaughytta, Kikutstua and Lövliseter, where fishermen can also stay overnight.

Golf. The Bogstad golf course is 10 km. (6 miles) from the city center and enjoys unrivalled surroundings and offers excellent golf from May to October.

Winter Sports. The season runs from Christmas to the end of March. There is fine skiing country in the hills around the city, though the emphasis is naturally on cross country rather than downhill skiing. All the trails and runs around the city can easily be reached from the center of town, and many are also floodlit. In addition, there are a number of skating and curling rinks and tobogganing trails. Details of all from the tourist office.

MUSIC, MOVIES AND THEATERS. Music. The musical life of the Norwegian capital is impressive, to say the least. The Oslo Philharmonic is the city's principal orchestra, and has frequent visits from soloists and conductors of international fame. Concerts are normally held in the *Konserthuset,* the Oslo Concert Hall, at Ruseløkkveien, a modern and lavish building completed in 1977. As well as the main auditorium there is also a smaller hall for chamber music.

In addition to the orchestra, the city has a thriving opera and ballet company, whose season generally lasts from September to June. Performances are most usually given at the *Den Norske Opera,* Storgaten 21. But there are also some performances at the *Henie-Onstad Art Center* at Høvikodden. For details of performances, see *Oslo This Week.*

Movies. There are numerous movie theaters around town. See the daily press or ask at the tourist office to see what's playing and when. A wide range of American and British movies are shown, nearly always with Norwegian subtitles, but check to make sure performances are in English. Smoking is not permitted in Norwegian cinemas.

Theaters. Oslo's principal theater is the *Nationalteatret* at Stortingsgaten 15 in the heart of the city. The theater has been closed for a year or so following a backstage fire and major renovation, but it is due to reopen in 1985. Note, however, that it is not open during the summer. Performances are in Norwegian, naturally enough, making their appeal somewhat limited as far as American or British visitors are concerned. But a production of Ibsen for example can still be a thrilling experience here. In the same building is the little *Amfiscenen,* used for both classical drama and more experimental work.

Among Oslo's other leading theaters are the *ABC Teatret,* St. Olavs plass; *Det Norske Teatret,* Stortingsgate 16, which presents works in *Nynorsk* or "new" Norwegian; the *Oslo Nye Teater,* Rosenkrantzgt. 10, which presents predominantly foreign plays, though again principally in Norwegian; the *Dukketeatret* in the City Museum, the Bymuseet, at Frognerveien 67, a puppet theater and an excellent place for families and children.; the *Centralteateret,* Akersgaten 38, presents plays for children and young people. For details of all performances, check *Oslo This Week.*

Finally, there are demonstrations of folk dancing throughout the year. The best and most colorful are held on Sundays at the *Folk Museum* at Bygdøy, but there are also displays, which you can join in if the spirit so moves you, at *Bygdelagssamskipnaden,* Nordahl Brunsgate 22, in the winter.

SHOPPING. In Norway, as in the other Scandinavian countries, you will find continuity with the peasant heritage in handicraft—ceramics and textile weaving, wood carving and decorative painting. It is easy to see why strong individualistic traditions developed in isolated areas where the people observed the beautiful color and form of their natural surroundings. Self expression was so strongly reinforced by resourcefulness that the subsequent foreign influxes were reinterpreted and absorbed into the native creative culture. You may find it has all the more distinctive appeal, and certainly flavor, for its unselfconscious strength and simplicity.

Arts and Crafts. *Forum,* Rosenkrantzgate 7 (opposite the Bristol Hotel), is a good place to start, especially if your time is limited. It is a permanent sales exhibition of contemporary Norwegian arts and crafts. Each item on display must first be accepted by a jury.

A similar establishment is *Norway Designs,* Stortingsgate 28 (entrance from Roald Amundsengate), the capital's largest center for the exhibition and sale of top quality Norwegian applied art, with special facilities for export.

For the most indigenous Norwegian handicraft try *Husfliden* (Norwegian Association for Home Arts and Crafts), Möllergate 4, near the cathedral and just behind the *Glasmagasin* department store. A non-profit organization for preserving and continuing the traditions of Norwegian handicrafts and rustic culture, it offers a wide range of home industry products including the well-known knitted sweaters, woven tapestries, dolls in national costumes, woodcarvings, ceramics etc.

Pewter, Ceramics and Crystal. A great Norwegian specialty is its pewterware: sugar bowls and creamers, all sizes of trays and bowls, candlesticks and pitchers. With a light-finish technique, Gunnar Havstad has created the best contemporary works, whereas the Groseth pewter bears the marks of the heavy sandstone presses that formed them after the old English manner.

Tinnboden, Tordenskioldsgate 7, has a good selection, as well as a splendid array of dolls in colorful regional dresses. Also *Småkunst,* Tordenskioldsgate 6.

These ceramics are perhaps more primitive than those you have found in Denmark and Sweden—the plates and bowls often thicker and embellished with peasant figures and symbols of the life they know. Norway's best known porcelain factory is Porsgrund. Also outstanding are the pottery works at Egersund and Stavanger, and the Hadelands glass company. Since their production, though of top quality, cannot incorporate all the vigorous ideas of young creative innovators, the works of individual craftsmen are equally numerous. Originality and taste are the rule in even the most common art glass, ceramics, and porcelain.

Arts and Crafts Center in Basarhallene, behind the cathedral, is worth looking into for all of the above.

For the very best in crystal and glass etching be sure to go by *Christiania Glasmagasin,* Stortorget 10. In the glass department here you will find distinguished modern glassware, amusing cocktail glasses, and exquisite art glass in a range of delectable colors.

Knitwear. All department stores have good stocks of traditional Norwegian sweaters, but certain specialist shops also have particularly fine designs. Among them are:

Heimen, Kristian Augustsgate 14, with handknitted sweaters and mittens. They can also make up authentic Norwegian costumes—each valley has its own—to order.

The *Oslo Sweater Shop* is in the arcade under the Hotel Scandinavia; *Maurta,* Fridjof Nansensplass, opposite the City Hall, has a wide range of knitwear and textiles; *Trønderstna,* Vikaterrace, also has textiles and knitwear and a good selection of wool and patterns.

Sports Shops. In Oslo the sports lover comes into his own. *Gresvig Sports Shop,* Storgata 20 and Haakon VII gate, also *Christiania Glasmagasin* at Stortorget 10, are probably the best in town and, in this sportsman's paradise, that means a lot. The Norwegian packsacks mentioned previously, flies for your fishing rod—or the rod itself—skis, any kind of sports equipment for use during your trek through the countryside or for shipment home (which *Gresvig's* will happily and efficiently handle for you) are featured here.

Norway's famous ski jumper, *Sigmund Ruud,* has a shop at Kirkeveien 57.

RESTAURANTS. Oslo is singularly blessed with great numbers of excellent restaurants, particularly at the top end of the scale. Similarly, many of the more expensive hotels also have first-class restaurants, details of which are given in the Hotel listings above. But bear in mind that expensive restaurants here are very expensive, even by Scandinavian standards, while even a quick bite at one of the fast food spots, of which there are many, will also cost significantly more than in the U.S. Alcohol, especially wine, is also extremely pricey in all restaurants, with a humble bottle of table wine costing upwards of $35. Be careful!

For fast food, try the city center, which has any number of pizza and hamburger joints. Likewise, both the *Steen & Strøm* and *Glasmagasin* department stores have several restaurants ranging from the inexpensive and simple to something a little more elaborate.

Expensive

Bagatelle. Bygdøy Alle 3 (446 397). Sophisticated and elegant French spot to the west of the Royal Palace much frequented by Oslo high society and with excellent food. AE, DC, MC, V.

Blom. Karl Johansgate 41 (330 956). Fine food in Bohemian atmosphere; popular with artists and journalists. MC, V.

Caravelle. Fornebu Airport (122 929). International restaurant overlooking the runways with excellent salad bar. Also has less expensive *Caravelle Cabin* (M), for pizzas, steaks and sandwiches, and *Caravelle Cafeteria* (M). AE, MC, V.

Frascati. Stortinsgaten 20 (416 876). French rotisserie with first class menu; next to the National Theater. AE, DC, MC, V.

Frognerseteren. Voksenkollen (143 736). By the Holmenkollen ski jump with spectacular views over the city. Old timber building in traditional Norse style with open hearth and Norwegian specialties. A must. MC, DC, V.

Holmenkollen. Holmenkollveien 119 (146 226). Also up on the hill by the ski jump and with the same wonderful views. AE, DC, MC, V.

King George Steakhouse. Torggaten 11 (336 019). On pedestrian street in the city center and located in an old stable—horsemeat steaks a specialty. AE, DC, MC, V.

La Petite Cuisine. Solligaten 2 (444 575). Grill restaurant with French atmosphere and cuisine in the west of the city. Fine wines. AE, DC, MC, V.

Mølla. Sagvn 21 (376 519). Charmingly-renovated old spot in one-time weaving factory on the Aker river; fish and game a specialty. AE, DC, V.

Najaden. Bygdøynesveien 37 (554 490). Excellent spot in the Maritime Museum across the fjord from the city center; attractive and atmospheric and with good lunch buffet. AE, DC, MC, V.

Regnbuen. Klingenberggate 4 (423 980). Centrally-located and enormous hall with dancing to internationally known bands; with floor show, bar and nightclub and excellent food. MC.

Tostrupkjelleren. Karl Johansgate 25 (333 605). Intimate cellar restaurant opposite the Storting and next to the Grand Hotel. One of the oldest restaurants in the city, dating from 1897, with open hearth and candle light setting the tone. International cuisine. AE, DC, MC, V.

Tre Kokker. Drammensveien 30 (442 650). Norwegian-style charcoal grill with outstanding food near the Royal Palace; run by Norway's top gourmet. Dancing in bar. AE, MC. V.

Moderate

Bajazzo Rica. Bygdøy Alle 5 (562 571). To the west of the Royal Palace; restaurant during the day, disco at night; pub in the cellar. AE.

La Brochette. Dronning Mandsgate 1-3 (416 733). Select your own steak in this fine French spot; distinctive millieu and personal attention. AE, MC, V.

Cheese Inn. Ruseløkkveien 3 (419 679). Small and intimate restaurant south of the Royal Palace specializing in cheese dishes, naturally. DC, MC, V.

Cossack. Kongensgate 6 (423 357). Russian food the specialty here; with bar, dancing and disco. AE, MC, DC, V.

Ekeberg. Kongsveien 15 (194 414). Magnificent views of the harbor, city and fjord. AE.

Gallagher's Steak House. Karljohansgate 10 (336 346). Restaurant with pub and pizza parlor on Oslo's main street; steaks and pancakes, music in the evenings. AE.

Herregårdskroen. Frogner Park (553 424). Small inn in the City Museum with openair restaurant in summer; adjoins the Vigeland scuplture park.

The Scotsman. Karl Johansgate 17 (428 953). Pub and steakhouse with Scottish atmosphere on Oslo's main street; entertainment in the evenings.

OSLO

Wessels Kro. Stortingsgate 6 (412 251). Cozy inn opposite the Storting in a replica of the Copenhagen street where famous Norwegian satirist, Johann Herman Wessel, used to stroll; fish specialties and traditional Norwegian dishes.

Inexpensive

Bella Napoli. Storgt. 26 (410 052). Italian dishes and pizza. Friendly, informal atmosphere. Popular with young people. AE, MC, V.

Den Lille Fondue. President Harbitzgate 18 (441 960). Oslo's only fondue restaurant; small and intimate; music. MC, V.

Kaffistova. Recommended chain of coffee shops with generous helpings; check the *Oslo Guide* for locations.

Kurbadets Vegetarrestaurant. Akersgaten 74 (206 414). Vegetarian dishes only; no alcohol and no smoking.

Pinocchio Rica. Bogstadvn 53 (607 786). Just by Colosseum cinema. Cheap and good. AE, MC, V.

NIGHTLIFE. A combination of high prices and puritanism have long conspired to render Norwegian nightlife a somewhat low key, not to say dormant affair. However, despite still strict licensing laws—no spirits can be served after midnight and not at all on Sundays and national holidays, and a bottle of scotch in a nightclub will certainly cost in excess of $50—the oil boom and its attendant influx of big spending oil men, coupled with Norway's high standard of living, have resulted in a gradual hotting up of the nighttime tempo over the last few years.

A number of the larger and more expensive hotels have cabarets and dancing —either discos or to bands. Similarly, some, though by no means all, restaurants have entertainment of one sort or another. See our *Hotel* and *Restaurant* listings for details. In addition there are also a growing number of regular night spots, though their ranks are still thin. Most, not least as a result of their scarcity, tend to get very crowded, especially at weekends. The city also boasts a thriving jazz scene, not perhaps to be compared to Copenhagen's but lively enough nonetheless.

Among the recommended spots are:

Amalienborg Jazzhouse, Arbeidergate 2 (423 024). Unpretentious but frequently excellent.

Ben Joseph. Solligate 2 (444 575). Grill restaurant and nightclub in one.

Club 7. Munkedams 15 (423 060). Definitely for the younger and more adventurous jazz lover; top international stars perform regularly.

Down Town Key Club. Universitetsgate 26 (202 089). Jazz bands every night.

Guldfisken. Raadhusgate 2 (411 489). Good spot for trad. jazz.

Hot House. Pilestredet 15 (203 989). Definitely for swingers; lots of jazz.

Jazz Alive. Observatoriegate 2 (440 745). Live bands every night; one of the top jazz spots.

P 17. Pilestredet 17 (112 757). One of the few genuinely late night spots; popular with Oslonian sophisticates.

THE OSLO FJORD DISTRICT

Vikings, Whalers and Twisting Valleys

Östfold is that section of Norway lying between the Oslo Fjord and the Swedish border. A part of the greater Oslo region, its major towns of Moss, Fredrikstad, Sarpsborg, and Halden are all points on the main rail line to the capital. At the same time Östfold also belongs economically to the forest and lumber district of eastern Norway and to the great valley of Österdal, whose river Glomma flows through Sarpsborg to empty into the fjord just beyond Fredrikstad. It is a small section of the country, rich in history and modern industry. On the west side of the Oslo Fjord is located another small district, the opposite number of Östfold, quite logically called Vestfold.

Exploring the Oslo Fjord District

By leaving Oslo's Central Station some morning on a southbound express you will reach Moss in about an hour (if the wind's right, you'll know it by the smell!). Formerly known for its tremendous distillery, the town has now both paper and pulp and other types of industries. It is also the eastern terminus of the cross-fjord Horten-Moss ferry which links Östfold and Vestfold. Unless you intend to cross on this ferry, stay aboard the train another half-hour, then descend at Fredrikstad. Here is a thriving industrial town which converts animal and vegetable oil into many useful products, cans first-class anchovies,

THE OSLO FJORD DISTRICT

exports lumber, etc., yet is at the same time filled with historical monuments. Across the Glomma river in the New Town there is a super-cafeteria, part of Scandinavia's biggest food center—"Stabburet."

The fortified Old Town, with its earthen and stone ramparts, built in the 17th century as a protection against the Swedes, is fully worth wandering about, both on top of the walls and down among the ancient buildings. Particularly fascinating is the great stone fortress of Kongsten standing alone beyond the ramparts as an outpost to meet the first waves of attackers.

In Old Town, is the arts and crafts center—"PLUS." Many of its workshops are open for demonstrations and sales. You will find PLUS represented in many of the leading stores and centers for good Norwegian design.

East of Fredrikstad, road 110 runs in the direction of Halden. This road—also known as the Antiquity Road—is only 16 km. (ten miles) long but takes visitors back 3,000 years. Along it can be seen some of Norway's finest prehistoric finds, notably rock carvings and grave mounds, very clearly marked.

Home of the internationally-known Borregaard Paper Mills, Sarpsborg has had a long and checkered history since its founding in 1016 by St. Olav. Like Fredrikstad, it was burned many times during the conflicts with Sweden, but with the expansion of its paper industry in recent decades Sarpsborg is now a thriving and stable industrial town. Sarpsborg's great attraction is the waterfall which the Glomma River forms in the middle of the town. This 20-meter (64-foot) waterfall is always impressive and simply marvellous at flood periods. Visitors interested in history might browse around the grounds of the Borgarsyssel Museum, where the ruins of St. Nikolas Church are found, or if it happens to be a Sunday, visit the charming Hafslund Manor, impressive as any castle.

Stay overnight at Halden and devote the next morning to visiting the Fredriksten Fortress, constructed on a steep hill in the town. The views over the border country and the tales told by the guide about sieges and sorties during the 17th and 18th centuries will amply reward one for the effort expended.

Vestfold, Home of the Vikings

Even smaller than its eastern twin, Vestfold has many links with the Oslo region as well as a thriving industrial life of its own which included until 1968 that unique occupation, Antarctic whaling. Historically Vestfold, like southern Norway, has had more contacts with Denmark than with Sweden, but what will stir the imagination most of all are the traces of Viking kings and seafarers to be found there. This district has no clear-cut boundary such as the Swedish border provides for Östfold, but merges into the mountain district of Telemark.

The first half hour of the journey takes one as far as Drammen on the same main line that leads to Kristiansand and Stavanger.

The scenery is interesting but not spectacular; and it demonstrates, moreover, how quickly one gets from Oslo to the land of farms, forests and bare rock. And if you are wondering why more Norwegian railroads haven't been laid down in duplicate, the answer is easily seen on this 48-km. (30-mile) stretch to Drammen which has just been made doubletrack at staggering costs. Here you can see some of the difficulties that Norwegian railroad engineers encounter all over the country: steep up and down grades, cuts through solid rocks and tunnels . . . tunnels. In fact the Norwegian State Railways on the Oslo-Drammen run has blasted Norway's longest tunnel (11 km./seven miles) through the mountains to open the double track. The sisyphean job was completed in 1973. After the tunnel is passed there is a view over the valley and across Drams Fjord to the lumber, paper and shipping town of Drammen, sixth largest city in Norway. Located at the mouth of the large timber-floating river, Drammen has the same strategic location as Fredrikstad on the other side of the Oslo Fjord, albeit without any walled town or fortress. The "Corkscrew Road" tunnelled through the mountain to the top of the Bragernes Hill is a unique attraction.

The Vestfold express branches off here and inside an hour we pass through long, narrow Holmestrand, squeezed in between fjord and hillside, and Skoppum, from where the bus runs to the former naval base (also car-ferry) town of Horten. A short ride beyond brings Tönsberg which the inhabitants proudly claim as Norway's oldest town, founded in the year 870. The hill rising steeply beside the railway station demands a visit even though all that is left of the extensive fortress, castle and abbey which once crowned it are some ruined foundations. The outlook tower on top is of modern construction, erected in 1870 to commemorate the 1,000th anniversary of Tönsberg's founding, and it offers a panorama comparable in sweep to that from Frognerseteren is Oslo.

Because of the passages both to the Oslo Fjord eastwards and to the open sea southwards you can see at once why Tönsberg was a strategic place, not only for the old Viking chieftains and raiders but also for shipping. From the sailing ships of the 18th and 19th centuries there has been a steady peaceful development to today's fleet of cargo liners and oil tankers which has won Tönsberg fourth place among shipping ports in Norway.

Looking back north along the railway from the Millenium Tower, one can almost locate Borre, site of many ancient Viking burial mounds; while much nearer Tönsberg is another famous site: Oseberg, where one of the Viking ships now at Bygdøy was found. You should really have a guide or Norwegian friend along to point out other historic spots, such as Ramnes, where rival pretenders to the throne fought decisive battles in the 12th century, and the old manor house at Jarlsberg, the seat of Norway's last family of nobility. Hereditary titles were abolished by parliament early in the 19th century, but Count Wedel Jarlsberg was permitted to keep his distinction until he died in 1893.

Don't forget to look southwards also, for in that direction you can see the start of famous recreational territory: the islands of Nötteröy, Tjöme, and Hvasser, which are the holiday haunts of thousands of Oslo-ites each summer. The tip of the island of Tjöme is the "End of the World" (Verdens Ende), facing the waves of the Skagerrak.

Sandefjord and the World's Largest Mammal

Next stop is the picturesque town of Sandefjord, which was once the main base for the Norwegian whaling fleet. Sven Foyn, a native of

Tönsberg, invented the explosive harpoon, but it was the skippers from Sandefjord who developed the business of Antarctic whaling to its recent level. The sight of the huge floating factories—up to 25,000 tonnes—and of their dozens of attending whale-catchers, tiny 200-tonners, used to be a fascinating and instructive sight. The great era of Antarctic whaling, nevertheless, has come to an end. With Japanese and Russian whalers joining the Norwegians after the last war, the whales are becoming fewer and fewer, and Sandefjord has withdrawn from the great hunt. However, in compensation, Sandefjord has acquired Norway's fifth largest merchant fleet. By all means visit the Whaling Museum given to the town by the local "whale king", Consul Lars Christensen.

An interesting side-trip by taxi from Sandefjord is to Gokstad Mound where another of the Viking ships at Bygdøy was found in 1880. Only a grass-covered mound can be seen there now, but it will give some idea of the magnitude and pomp of medieval Viking burials.

Larvik is another of Vestfold's busy ports but it combines this with important lumbering activities, lying as it does at the mouth of another great timber-floating river: the Lågen from Numedal Valley. Walk up to the little park on the height near the harbor for a splendid view. Larvik is also important for motorists, since the car-ferry plies from here to Frederikshavn, Denmark. Other claims to fame are having one of Norway's very rare beech forests and being the home of the well-known Farris mineral water springs.

PRACTICAL INFORMATION FOR THE OSLO FJORD DISTRICT

TOURIST INFORMATION. Tourist Information Offices are located in the following places: **Fredrikstad** (032-20 330). **Halden,** Kongens Brygge (031-82 487). **Moss,** Christiesgt 3 (032-55 451). **Sandefjord,** in the Town Hall. **Sarpsborg,** St. Mariegt 96 (031-54 855). **Tønsberg,** Storgt 55 (033-14 819).

TELEPHONE CODES. We have given telephone codes for all the towns and villages in the hotel and restaurant lists that follow. These codes need only be used when calling from outside the town or village concerned.

HOTELS AND RESTAURANTS. The only resort hotel of international standing is the *Hankö,* the rest are modest family hotels. But in this district, as in other places, it is perfectly feasible to stay in modern town hotels and enjoy swimming on the neighboring beaches. The town hotels are mostly unpretentious, but the *Grand* at Larvik, the *Klubben* at Tönsberg, and the *Park* at Sandefjord are among the best in Norway. Some of the seaside resort hotels offer reduced terms before and after the peak season.

DRAMMEN (Buskerud). *Park* (M), Gamle Kirkeplass 3 (03-838 280). 202 beds, most rooms with facilities, restaurant. MC. V. *Central Hotel* (M), Kon-

nerudgt (03-831 590). 40 beds. *Victoria Hotel* (M), Konnerudgt (03-831 890). 30 beds.
Restaurant. *Skansen Restaurant.* At the top of the Spiral, a tunnel hewn out of the rock, running in six convolutions to a superb viewpoint at Skansen.
Youth Hostel. *Drammen Youth Hostel* (I), Korsvegen 62. 140 beds.

FREDRIKSTAD (Østfold). *City Hotel* (M), Nygaardsgt 44-46 (032-17 750). 208 beds, 50 rooms with bath, restaurant. AE, DC, MC, V. *Victoria Hotel* (M), Turngt 3 (032-11 165). 82 beds, most rooms with facilities. AE, DC, MC, V. *Fredrikstad Motel* (I), (032-20 315). 140 beds, swimming.
Restaurants. *Hawk Club A/S,* Storgt 20 (032-11 035). *Løwendals Galei,* Storgt 4 (032-16 944). *Peppe's Pizza,* Torvgt 57 (032-22 202). *Restaurant Tamburen,* Faergeportgt 78 (032-23 313). *Tordenskiol Danserest,* Storgt 4 (032-16 944).

HALDEN (Østfold). *Park* (M), Marcus Thranesgt 30 (031-84 044). 84 beds, restaurant. MC, V.
Restaurants. *Cafena,* Storgt 18 (031-81 340). *Dickens,* Storgt 8 (031-83 503). *Fredriksten Kro,* Fredriksten Festning (031-85 425).
Youth Hostel. *Halden Youth Hostel* (I), 40 beds.

HANKØ (Østfold). Famous yachting center, summer only. *Hankø New Fjord Hotel* (M), 1620 Gresvik (032-32 105). 140 beds, most rooms with facilities, restaurant. *Hankø Seilerkro* (I) (032-32 350). 14 beds.

LARVIK (Vestfold). *Grand* (M), Storgaten 38-40 (034-83 800). Overlooking fjord, 222 beds in 117 rooms, most with facilities, restaurant. AE, MC, V. *Holms Motel* (I), Amundrød (034-92 796). 144 beds, cafeteria. AE, DC, MC.
Restaurants. *Hansemann,* Kongensgt 33 (034-86 148). *Jahren Gård & Feriested,* (034-99 030). *Selma,* Tatjanas Kjeller (034-98 311). *Skipperstua,* Stavern (034-99 215). *Vertshuset Sydvesten,* Helgeroa. *Victoria Mat og Vinhus,* Storgt 26 (034-82 830).

MOSS (Østfold). *Moss Hotel* (M), Dronningensgt 21 (032-55 080). 96 beds, outstanding restaurant. MC, V. *Refsnes Gods* (M), Godset 5 (032-70 411). On Jeløy island, 90 beds, 30 rooms with bath, charming. AE, MC.
Restaurants. *Møllhausen A/S,* Dronningens 1 (032-53 898). *Queen's Rotisserie,* Dronningensgt 14 (032-53 127). *Taverna Kafeteria,* Kongensgt 43 (032-54 372).
Youth Hostel. *Moss Youth Hostel* (I), 64 beds.

SANDEFJORD (Vestfold). *Park* (E), Strandprom 9 (034-65 550). Overlooking harbor, one of Norway's best hotels, 273 beds, all rooms with facilities, restaurant, bar, swimming, saunas. AE, DC, MC, V. *Atlantic* (M), Jernbanealléen 31 (034-63 105). 60 beds, some rooms with bath. AE, DC, V.

SARPSBORG (Østfold). Industrial town with spectacular waterfall. *Saga* (M), Sannesundvn 1 (031-56 080). 120 beds, all rooms with facilities. AE, DC, MC, V. *St Olav* (M), St Olav's Plass (031-52 055). 143 beds, 25 rooms with bath. AE, DC, MC, V.
Restaurant. *Dickens A/S,* St. Mariegt 109 (031-52 892).
Youth Hostel. *Tuneheimen Youth Hostel* (I), 63 beds.

TØNSBERG (Vestfold). *Klubben* (E), Nedre Langgt 49 (033-15 111). 175 beds, all rooms with facilities, restaurant. AE, DC, MC. *Grand* (M), Øvre Langgt 96 (033-12 203). 80 beds, some rooms with facilities.
Restaurants. *Bonanza,* Møllegt (033-12 606). *Fregatten,* Storgt 17 (033-14 776). *Håndverkeren,* Kammegt 6 (033-12 388). *Le-Ni Swing Steak House,* Torvet (033-11 892). *Penguin Pub,* Rådhusgt 2 (033-15 837). *Pizzanini,* Munkegt 10 (033-11 915). *Speilen,* Møllegt (033-12 203).

THE OSLO FJORD DISTRICT

Youth Hostel. *Tønsberg Youth Hostel* (I), 48 beds.

Camping

There are good campsites in the vicinity of most towns on both sides of the Oslo Fjord, particularly along the main road in Østfold from Sweden to Oslo.

HOW TO GET AROUND. There are good train services from Oslo down both sides of the Oslo fjord—on the west side to Drammen, Tønsberg, Sandefjord and Larvik, and on the east side to Moss, Fredrikstad, Sarpsborg and Halden. It is possible to do a one-day round trip to either of these areas, allowing an hour or two in any one of the towns. There is a 40 minutes ferry crossing by car ferry between Moss and Horten.

TOURS. For information on suggested touring routes, guided tours, boat trips and car ferries, visit the local Tourist Information Offices, listed under "Tourist Information" at the beginning of this *Practical Information* section.

PLACES TO VISIT. The Oslo Fjord District has many churches and cathedrals of historical interest. The area also has its share of galleries and museums for the tourist to enjoy. Some of these places are listed below.

DRAMMEN. Drammen Museum. Outdoor museum, with Marienlyst Manor from the 1770s. At Bragernesåsen.
Rock carvings. On Skogerveien road, these carvings are 6,000 years old.

FREDRIKSTAD. Fredrikstad Domkirke. The cathedral is richly decorated by Norwegian artists. One of the largest and best organs in Norway.
Fredrikstad Museum. At the Gamle Slaveri. Open daily 10–4.
Gamelbyen (The Old Town). Scandinavia's oldest preserved fortress town, dating back to 1663.
Glemmen Church. Built in stone around 1100, with a Roman font. Crucifix and apostle sculpture from Lubeck, around 1450.
Kongsten Fort. Dates back to 1685. Now the property of the Town of Fredrikstad.
Oldtidsveien (Highway of the Ancients). The most concentrated collection of archaeological monuments in the country is to be found along Highway No. 110, between Fredrikstad and Skjeberg.

HALDEN. Fredristen Festning. Mountain Fortress from the end of 1600s, empire style buildings. War and cultural history museum in the old prisons.
Larvik Bymuseum. A manor house from 1673; the town museum.
Larvik Maritime Museum. In the old customs house (1714).

SARPSBORG. Borgarsyssel Museum. County museum for Østfold with cultural history collections and old buildings.

TØNSBERG. Haugar. In the center of town, with old burial mounds. Site of local assembly in olden times.
Memorial Park. With sculptures by Gustav Vigeland and glass mosaics by Per Vigeland.
Slottsfjelle. Contains one of the largest collections of medieval ruins in Northern Europe.
St. Olav's Church. The largest circular church in the North. There has been a monastery in Tønsberg since the 1190s.

Tønsberg Cathedral. Erected in 1858 on the site of the old Lavran Church.
Vestfold County Museum. Includes outdoor museum, whaling and shipping sections. Viking ship from 800.

SPORTS. Swimming everywhere outside the Dröbak Narrows is pleasant in crystal-clear and surprisingly warm water (averaging 68°F. throughout the season). The bathing beaches at Ula are particularly good.

Sailing and boating are in evidence everywhere; the waters of the outer Oslo Fjord, with the mixture of open stretches and sheltered channels, are ideal for this activity. A sailing school with first-class instructors is run by the Hankö Hotel. **Fishing** from a boat—or with a spinning-rod from the rocks—is a popular sport, best early (May) and late (September) in the season.

TELEMARK AND THE SOUTH COAST

A Land Fit for Heroes

The Telemark district, whose name has become a part of the skier's lore, is among Norway's most beautiful and most interesting. Winding valleys, precipitous gorges, silvery lakes, snow-covered mountains, pastoral farmlands with their ancient stave churches—all present an unforgettable picture of contrasts and surprises. Dotting the islands and inlets of the South Coast—aptly called Norway's "Summer Smile"—are delightful resorts forming a holiday paradise, ideal for exploring or just basking in the sun. Telemark is well served by public transport—as described below—but the best way of seeing this remarkable area is to go by car.

Exploring Telemark and the South Coast

The Vestfold express takes you from Oslo via Larvik to the end of the line at Skien. Besides serving as terminus, Skien is also the beginning of another rail line to Oslo via Kongsberg and Drammen if you want to return to the capital by another route. Even more important, however, is Skien's position as a main gateway to Telemark, for no eager tourist should leave Norway without at least a glimpse of that ruggedly charming mountain district.

First, though, look at the city from Brekke Park on the inevitable high ridge back of Höyer's Hotel, where not only a fine outdoor Folk Museum is located but also an excellent collection of Ibseniana. For Henrik Ibsen was born in Skien in 1828 and grew up on Venstöp farm (now an Ibsen memorial), five km. (three miles) from the town center, and in Snipetorget 27.

The classic approach to Telemark from Skien is the Bandak Canal. The charming old ship *Victoria* makes the journey from Skien to Dalen in one day, by lock and lake through the province of Telemark.

Leaving Skien at 8:30 sharp you have got a glorious 108 km. (65 miles) in front of you, out of which 100 (60) stay quiet, the rest are streams, canals and locks. *Victoria* is in no particular hurry to get you to Dalen. There is too much to show: the park-like lower Telemark, manor houses and timber industry at Ulefoss, winding streams, locks and narrows between Lake Norsjø and Lake Kviteseidvatn and wild Lake Bandak with precipitous mountain sides. While the boat is negotiating the locks you may stroll along the canal path, visit the local shop, chat with the locals—in fact imbibe the peaceful charm which is the very essence of this water excursion.

If this does not appeal, you may board a morning bus from Skien and skirt Lake Norsjø, passing through Ulefoss, with its manor houses on the hills and timber industry along the river en route to Bö, one of the famous districts of Telemark. We might well make the Lifjell Hotel, in the hills above the station, our first stay, for the view from there is probably Telemark's most panoramic, which is saying quite a lot. Bö is the traffic hub of central Telemark. Travelers direct from Oslo alight from the express trains at this junction and board the buses of the efficient West Telemark Bus Company for a ride along the silvery bank of Lake Seljord to the village of Seljord, with its medieval church and wealth of local tradition, thereafter continuing to Brunkeberg crossroads. The main bus line continues straight west from Brunkeberg, heading for the Hardanger Fjord. En route it passes through the steep valley of Morgedal, famous as the cradle of modern skiing. The Bjåland Museum in Morgedal contains an interesting collection of Antarctic items, as well as old skis.

But our aim is to ramble about a bit in Telemark, in the general direction of Dalen. Thus we catch an afternoon bus from Brunkeberg (a study of timetables is important when dealing with criss-cross Telemark), and wind down a "vistaful" road to Kviteseid and across the hills to Vrådal. This resort is located at an altitude of about 300 meters (1,000 feet), and anyone wanting a quiet stay, with fishing and rowing, on a beautiful mountain-fringed lake, should stop here for a few days.

You can proceed southward by bus from Vrådal along Lake Nisser to Nelaug, and reach Arendal on the South Coast by train from there. But that's another trip. Our route takes us along another beautiful lake, the Vråvatn, to Vråliosen and across the mountains, but if traveling by car make a short detour to Skafså to visit Anne Grimsdalen's sculpture museum, before hairpinning down to Dalen, with a breathtaking view of Lake Bandak. Dalen, formerly the tourist pivot of Telemark, is today the center of the gigantic Tokke hydro-electric scheme which involves

TELEMARK AND THE SOUTH COAST

great areas of Telemark; the power station of Dalen (Tokke I) yields 400,000 kilowatts, and has few competitors in Europe.

If you decide to explore Dalen more closely, you should take a taxi up the north wall of Lake Bankad the eight km. (five miles) to Eidsborg for a most impressive hairpin climb from the water's edge up to the mountains. Here is a small but ancient stave church. Visit the old building close to it, which has been turned into a local museum and boasts the oldest washing-machine in the world, invented a couple of centuries ago by an imaginative Telemark farmer. From Dalen you can also go by taxi to another of the wonders of Telemark, the Ravnejuvet ravine, dropping some 300 meters (1,000 feet) into the valley of Tokke and having peculiar air currents that bring papers—and even such heavier objects as bushes—thrown down into it back over the brink. Throw in your banknotes and they will return to you.

From Dalen we travel along the Tokke Valley to Åmot, where the beautiful Hyllandsfoss Falls disappeared into the Tokke project, and head for the village of Rauland.

Culture and Sabotage

Located 1,000 meters (3,300 feet) above sea level, the Rauland Hotel is your best base of operations to combine fishing, hunting, or hiking with a study of the genuine rural culture of Telemark. From the hilltop near the hotel one can see far across Lake Mösvatn into the wild Hardanger plateau and, in the opposite direction, many of the mountain summits of Telemark. Southeast lies Lake Totak and Rauland village—15 minutes by car—with a concentration of more *stabburs,* farm buildings, etc., than can be found anywhere except in the Oslo Folk Museum. But here they have the added charm of completely natural surroundings and are still in use. Beyond Lake Totak the horizon is formed by a long row of peaks running north-south: the mountains guarding the approach to Setesdal valley.

Rauland was the home of the late Dyre Vaa, the sculptor who designed the Swans Fountain in the courtyard of the Oslo Rådhus. A collection of his work is open during the summer season. (Some of his later efforts in "modern painting" are displayed on the walls of the hotel salons.) One of the most famous country fiddlers in Norway, Myllargutten (The Miller Boy), lived at the west end of Totak, and either the hotel manager or local guides can tell you any number of stories and legends about him and the "old days" in Rauland.

Whatever the complications in choosing your route to Rauland, there is one best way out: the bus trip along the edge of Lake Mösvatn and down to Rjukan. As you cut across this southeast corner of the Hardanger plateau you are again on historic ground. In a solitary hut not far from the mountain hotel, the Norwegian leader of the famous Linge Company of saboteurs, Major Leif Tronstad, was killed in early 1945. And during the winter of 1943 this whole area was the scene of dramatic actions by the Norwegian underground against the Vemork Plant of Norsk Hydro where "heavy water" was produced by the Nazis for their atomic bomb experiments in Germany. Thus, when the bus halts at the Skinnerbu stop on Lake Mösvatn near the big dam, you may have time to buy postcards at the mountain chalet run by one of the saboteurs.

Beyond the dam the road enters a canyon which grows steadily deeper and with more precipitous walls until, in a hairpin swing, it brings you right opposite Vemork, scene of the daring coup now so widely known through the film reconstruction, *Heroes of Telemark*. In spite of the thousands of Nazi soldiers guarding the entire valley, Norwegian saboteurs climbed down into this steep-sided, snow-filled gulch on a bright moonlit night to set off dynamite charges that destroyed the heavy-water plant.

Cable Car Views of Rjukan

Still further down the canyon is the electric power and industrial town of Rjukan, squeezed in between the river and cliffs, while overhead towers the great peak of Mount Gausta, almost 1,850 meters (6,000 feet) high. Small wonder that the sun does not shine at the bottom for five months of the year. However, the inhabitants of Rjukan can quickly get up into the sunshine on the northern rim of the canyon by means of a cable car that rises over 500 meters (1,600 feet) in a trajectory of 1,000 meters (3,000 feet). Don't miss taking a ride on this *Krossobane:* there are magnificent views down the narrow valley and of Mount Gausta.

From Rjukan you have two glorious ways of leaving Telemark, each with its particular attractions. One is by bus around the head of Lake Tinnsjö and across more mountains with farms and *stabburs* to Bolkesjö and then to Kongsberg. An important junction on the main Oslo-Stavanger railway, Kongsberg, an old silver mining town and still the seat of the Royal Norwegian Mint, is today famous for its remarkable 18th-century church, its Mining Museum and the miniature train taking visitors down into the old mines, 350 meters (1,140 feet) below the surface.

The other way out is by bus from Rjukan to Mel, and by train-ferry down nearly the entire length of Lake Tinnsjö: a wild, roadless district much like Bandak. At Tinnoset the train takes to dry land once again, pauses briefly at the industrial town of Notodden and then joins the main railway at Hjuksebö Junction below Kongsberg. For an appropriate leave-taking of Telemark, stop over at Notodden long enough to take a bus or taxi the few miles to Heddal and see that largest of Norwegian stave churches.

Exploring the South Coast

The south coast railroad from Oslo to Kristiansand and onwards to Stavanger, forces its way through crevasses and along lakes and rivers as far as Kristiansand; then there is no alternative but to go right through the mountains, bridging the rivers in vast spans of concrete and steel. Thus you will become acquainted with some of Europe's largest rail tunnels and airiest bridges, and a wild and desolate interior, but the south coast itself will still escape you—unless you take the sidetracks to Kragerø, Arendal and Flekkefjord.

Therefore our suggestion is that you should go by bus, (or car), starting in Porsgrunn (which we presume you have reached via Oslo). However, by bus it is a question of detours if you wish to imbibe the atmosphere of Kragerø and Risør, resuming travel by a later bus.

Anybody might be tempted to stay over in Kragerø until the next day, for here is a picturesqueness that has inspired generations of painters to haunt the little town and its many islands. In any case, reserve a few hours to wander through the narrow and winding streets in the old part of Kragerø. The Berg-Kragerø Museum is housed in a period building of great beauty, and contains collections illustrating the life and history of the coastal population.

Risør is even more romantic than Kragerø, with its stately patrician houses from the early 19th century lining the harbor. Don't worry about the winding streets of little Tvedestrand, your bus will take you right into them. We suggest you "jump ship" in Tvedestrand, leave the through-service bus to find its own way to Arendal, and enter the coastal bus which will take you to Arendal via Flosta.

Once known as "Little Venice," Arendal's canals have been turned into wide streets, but it still retains its beautiful harbor. The town is a center for holiday-makers and offers interesting boat trips among the skerries and on the delta of the River Nid.

Despite nature's charm on the south coast and despite the bustle of modern industry and communications there is a slight atmosphere of sadness about Sörlandet (the "south land"), a hint of bygone and better days. For all of these small towns and hamlets had their heyday when sailing ships were the masters of the sea. These were the times that brought the small white cottages and the large white mansion houses into being—the times described in Jonas Lie's novels, when skippers and pilots were the heroes and their wives the heroines.

You can recapture a bit of this spirit, if you stay in Arendal, by taking a trip to the large island of Tromøy and visiting the old church of the same name: and by crossing over to little Merdøy Island, where a typical skipper's home has been taken over unchanged, forming a part of the Aust-Agder Museum, and kept exactly as it was in its owner's day.

Between Arendal and Grimstad you may be tempted to step off the bus in Fevik and entrust yourself to the Strand Hotel there, facing the Skagerak from a bathing beach position. Grimstad brings back the history of both sailing ships and Ibsen, for it was here that the great dramatist served as a druggist's apprentice and began writing his first lyrics.

Lillesand, further on, will delight your eye not only by its fine mansion houses, but also by its location behind a complicated maze of channels and skerries. This is where you should finally abandon your bus—if the weather is fine—and lodge at the intimate Hotel Norge, because we suggest you investigate those skerries which are the essence of the south coast.

Kristiansand, Capital of Sörlandet

You can take the south coast railway for a dramatic but comfortable and quick ride to Stavanger, or continue to rough it along the highroad. One bus service links up with the other, and there is no doubt about it, you will reach Stavanger in the end, especially if you have been provident enough to supply yourself with the latest Norwegian timetable *(Rutebok for Norge)*. Moreover, you will have had a marvellous time, if you are the type of adventurer and Norway-lover that we suspect. You will probably fall in love with Mandal's narrow streets which are lined with 18th- and 19th-century houses. You will be thrilled by the view of Kvinesdal and the Fedafjord, almost scared by the wildness of Jøssingfjord, and amazed at the number of fishing vessels in the harbor of Egersund. Your last surprise on the journey will probably be that mountainous Norway contains a stretch of flat farming land the size of Jaeren, south of Stavanger.

But now let's assume that, having decided to make the journey to Stavanger another time, you have stayed overnight in Kristiansand. Formerly the arch-enemy of the other southern towns, because of its founding by the Danish king in 1641 and special royal privileges, Kristiansand has now made peace with them and is a respected industrial leader.

Kristiansand is the capital of Sörlandet, and offers good shopping facilities. Take a stroll through the old-world Kvadratur area, the checker-board plan of streets between the harbor on two sides and the Otra River on the third, the old fortress of Christiansholm, the cathedral. An exceedingly visible but non-cultural landmark is the tall chimney of the nickel-refining plant on the east side of the harbor approach, claimed to be the highest stack in Europe. Despite the regularity of the old part of the city, there are many delightful houses of typical southern Norway style and neatness, but most of them are jammed so tightly against each other that there is no place for the little garden in front. Apparently Kristiansand has always been crowded, for Gabriel Scott quotes a visitor in 1799 as having said that if a man absent-mindedly smoked his pipe by his own open window, he might easily happen to spit into a neighbor's parlor. At Kristiansand you also find Norway's largest animal and amusement park, covering more than 40 hectares (100 acres). In the district you also find excellent possibilities for swimming and sunbathing.

The Otra River, which flows into the sea at Kristiansand, provides the clue for our next move: namely, to follow it upstream about 160 km. (100 miles) through Setesdal to its source. The charming narrow-gauged Setesdal Railway runs no more, except as a hobby train along a five-km. (three-mile) track on summer week-ends. Therefore, we enter a morning bus at Kristiansand in the direction of Setesdalen. The first two hours are uneventful. Whereas the old railway criss-crossed the foaming Otra and clung to it like a stamp, the Setesdal highway, to begin with, roams about the provinces miles away from the lively river. At Haegeland, river contact is once more established and we advise you to discontinue your morning nap. At Evje a wide flat area suddenly appears and, sure enough, here is Evje-*moen,* or the military training ground, for there are not too many places in upland Norway where naturally level drilling grounds are available.

Byglandsfjord, former terminus of the Setesdal Line, is reached in 2½ hours. The Otra is quite logically called Byglandsfjord at this point, for it's now a lake two km. (one mile) wide in places and at least 40 km. (25 miles) in rambling length. We are now entering the real Setesdal, that formerly most isolated and inaccessible of all Norwegian valleys, and the one which still bears many traces of its erstwhile quaint manners and culture.

Cliffs and Cutthroats of Setesdal

In olden days its inhabitants were not the most peaceful and lawabiding of citizens—witness the "Robbers' Hole" (Tjuvehola) in the mountain side just beyond the hamlet of Byglandsfjord, where thieves used to waylay farmers returning from town and relieve them of their purchases and leftover cash. And not far beyond there, we have the most dramatic evidence conceivable of how natural barriers for ages cut off Setesdal, not only from the outside world, but from itself. Just above the water's edge the road runs through a 550-meter (600-yard) tunnel blasted out of a cliff which, before the highway engineers came along, rose perpendicularly from the lake without offering even enough foothold for a mountain climber.

Byglandsfjord is the undisputed central point in lower Setesdal, as well as a convenient stopping place for tourists. However, another couple of hours will bring you to Valle which, in our opinion, is the most rewarding part of all Setesdal. Spend a day or two in Valle, trying trout fishing in the river (permission must be obtained), and go walking among the remarkable old farms that line the lower, moderately sloping hillsides. This will enable you to see more closely the unusual outfit that a few older men still wear while working in the fields. It consists of a white shirt and black trousers that give a remarkably dressed up appearance to men pitching hay; an appearance partly comprised, however, by the very battered and narrowrimmed black felt hat which completes the costume. Some elderly women may also be seen in the fields raking hay and hanging it up to dry on racks in their distinctive attire: black woolen stockings, white woolen skirt with black edgings, white blouse, black bolero or red jacket; while the older ones also wear a curious scarf-like headgear which shades their eyes like a bonnet in front and hangs down at back like a pigtail.

Yet these working clothes in Setesdal are nothing compared to the Sunday and festive costumes. The women put on black skirts and blouses over the white ones for church-going, while for weddings they add a bright red skirt, also over the previous foundation. The men change to black trousers with a heavy piece of leather reinforcing the seat and with gaily colored cuffs, and wear a heavy pullover with decorations in front and at the wrists to match the trouser cuffs. But again all this pales in contrast to what the bride and groom must don for their wedding! To the basic festive outfit are added embroideries, silver, ornaments and a bridal crown, said to be worth at least a thousand dollars. However, everyone can afford it in this valley, for helpful neighbors each lend a certain item, or else the young couple can rent a complete set of finery from the local "Housewives Association" just as one hires a dress suit in a city.

Hikes and Hideouts

The history of Setesdal is as interesting as its costumes, yet one would need to be something of a hiker to appreciate it at first hand. At Valle begins the old "Skin Trail", so called because it took the peasants westward over the mountains to the nearest tax-collector's office where they paid in skins, a 2-day journey that was extremely unpopular with the inhabitants. East from Valle the energetic tourist can take a 2-hour hike along the road leading to the mountain farms or *seters* where the cattle graze in summer and where *seter*-maidens make cheese. Or he can follow the "Bishop's Trail" into Telemark, along which church officials made their way in olden times on their not too frequent visits to the "stubborn devils" in Setesdal.

Indeed, the valley's parishioners were so averse to change in the early days of the Reformation that they killed or drove out more than one of the new Lutheran priests. Tax-collectors and sheriffs were equally disliked, and some natives carried on feuds with the royal officials which remind one of the encounters between American hillbillies and revenue officers.

Such a famous local character was "Bad Aasmund", and you should not miss a visit to his hideout four km. (six miles) up the valley from Valle. He tangled with the law four centuries ago, fled to Holland, returned after many years but just in time—according to the legends—to abduct his former fiancée as she was about to be married to a persistent farmer she didn't like. Again outlawed, "Bad Aasmund" lived with his bride in the farm at Rygnestad, taking refuge in a stoutly fortified *stabbur* or *loft* whenever the sheriff was so rash as to put in a decidedly apprehensive appearance.

However, the gentleman apparently didn't call very often, for Aasmund was as handy with a bow and arrow as Robin Hood, and the massive logs of his *loft* still stand there today as impregnable as ever. But strangely enough, after all the glamorous days of adventure and rebellion, the bad man settled down, and in later life became a sheriff and tax-collector himself.

The bus ride north from Valle to Bykle and Hovden is perhaps the most exciting part of the trip. The road climbs steeply, now running close to the rushing torrent Otra, now hugging the valley walls. Like all other mountain highways in Norway, this one has its share of curves with the customary steep slope or even precipice on the outside edge. Low cement parapets or large stones are set up along this edge as guard-rails and there is usually room for two vehicles to pass. Nevertheless, the tourist driving his own car should exercise particular caution at such points and make his presence known by sounding the horn before entering a blind curve.

Near Bykle you will see another dramatic reminder of former hardships in communication: the Byklestigen or Bykle-ladder. This is a narrow path cut across the face of a cliff, which used to be the only way people could get from the lower valley to Bykle. Supplies had to be carried on their own backs, for not even pack-horses were able to negotiate Byklestigen. A full-width roadway has been carved out at the bottom of the rock wall along the river, so the distance which formerly took hours of toil is now made in a few minutes.

An hour later you are at Hovden, where there is easy access to both mountain lakes and rivers, in case you are a fisherman. (By the way, the source of the Otra River lies up in one of these lakes.) Hovden is also the end of the Setesdal bus line and here we change to another bus whose ultimate destination is Odda on the Sör Fjord.

You may think that you've seen everything in the way of wild scenery by this time but there is still much more in store, thanks to our *northbound* route. The great advantage of traveling up-stream through

TELEMARK AND THE SOUTH COAST

Setesdal rather than down is that one can thus enjoy the natural crescendo of change from miniature Sörlandet up through the ever-higher, ever-shifting Setesdal to something even more magnificent but as yet unknown, which you sense lies right ahead.

And sure enough, just beyond Hovden comes another climax. There's a long straight piece of road ahead bordered on either side by a forest of dwarf birches which grow smaller and sparser for each kilometer. Beyond and above them on all sides rises a vast mountain plateau with snow patches here and there on the heights. This is the great central massif of the Hardangervidda: thousands of square kilometers of heath, lakes and mountain peaks.

The bus follows this road for many minutes but then, just as you think you are reaching these highlands, a deep, broad valley appears 300 meters (1,000 feet) below with the familiar pattern of cultivated fields and green meadows with golden hay drying on the racks. This is Haukeligrend village, an important road junction. If the purpose has been only to discover Telemark and the South Coast, this is where we turn east and take a bus that will bring us through the winding valleys of Telemark to Bö, and from there by train to Oslo. If you wish to wander farther afield, the direction to follow is westward across the mountain passes to Hardanger. Magnificent scenery and stupendous hairpin curves await you along this route—the high mountains around Haukeliseter, the steep and winding ascent into Röldal with its pilgrim stave church, the unsurpassed view of Lake Röldal from the mountain road to Seljestad, the Seljestad Gorge and the view of the Folgefonn Glacier. Without a doubt, this can be an immensely impressive journey.

PRACTICAL INFORMATION FOR TELEMARK AND THE SOUTH COAST

TELEPHONE CODES. We have given telephone codes for all the towns and villages in the hotel and restaurant lists that follow. These codes need only be used when calling from outside the town or village concerned.

HOTELS AND RESTAURANTS. The majority of Telemark hostelries are in the moderate price category. Since they are for the most part "tourist" or "mountain" hotels, you can rest assured that they will automatically reach the high standards of equipment, service and food required by law.

ARENDAL (Aust Agder). *Phønix* (E), Tyholmen (041–25 160). 150 beds, restaurant, dancing, bar, disco. DC, MC, V. *Central* (M), Vestregt 11 (041–22 020). 70 beds, restaurant. DC, MC, V.
Restaurants. *Breidablikk Vertshus,* Faervik, Tromøy (041–85 127). *El Paso Western Saloon,* Havnegt 8 (041–21 805). *Grand Restaurant,* Langbryggen 19 (041–25 160). *Teje Vigen Cafe,* Langbryggen 3 (041–21 972).

BØ (Telemark). *Bø Hotel* (M), (036–60 111). 150 beds. AE, MC. *Lifjell* (E), (036–60 011). Situated below Mt Lifjell, 120 beds. AE, MC, V. *Lifjellstua* (I), (036–60 236). 140 beds.
Restaurant. *Vertshuset Bø* (036–61 099).

NORWAY

Youth Hostel. *Grivi Youth Hostel* (I), 134 beds.

BOLKESJØ (Telemark). *Bolkesjø* (E), (036–18 600). Built in 1881, rebuilt and enlarged, old interiors preserved, fine views of Telemark, 450 beds, all rooms with bath or shower, restaurant. MC, V. *Gran* (M), (036–18 640). 60 beds. MC, V.

BYGLANDSFJORD (Aust Agder). *Revsnes* (M), (043–34 105). 84 beds, most rooms with facilities. DC.

DALEN (Telemark). *Bandak* (M), (036–77–100–8). 24 rooms, 3 with bath. MC.
Youth Hostel. *Dalen Youth Hostel* (I), (036–77–100–9). 70 beds.

FARSUND (Vest–Agder). *Farsund Fjord Hotel* (E), Floridaodden (043–91 022). 108 beds, all rooms with bath/shower. AE, DC, MC.
Restaurants. *Henrich og Pernille,* Nytorvet 1 (043–91 443). *Kaperstuen,* Listerv. 6 (043–91 502). *La Mer Restaurant,* Vanse (043–93 622). *Travellers Inn,* Meierigården Vanse (043–93 382).

FEVIK (Aust Agder). *Strand* (E), (041–47 322). 86 beds, most rooms with bath, restaurant, sea view, sandy beach. AE, DC, MC, V.

FLEKKEFJORD (Vest–Agder). *Maritim* (E), Sundegt (043–23 333). 96 beds, all rooms with bath/shower. AE, DC, MC, V. *Grand* (M), (043–22 355). 33 beds, most with bath/shower. *Bondeheimen* (I), (043–22 171). 19 beds.

GRIMSTAD (Aust Agder). *Müllerhotell Helmershus* (M), Vesterled 23 (041–41 022). 70 beds, all rooms with bath or shower. DC, MC, V.
Restaurants. *Furuly Cafeteria,* Øvre Fevik (041–47 109). *La Pepita Pizza,* Juskerstr. 4 (041–41 641). *Spisekrogen,* Juskerstr. 2 (041–40 300). *Villa Ernst,* Arendalsvn 19 (041–40 300).
Youth Hostel. *Grimstad Youth Hostel* (I), (041–41 410). 21 beds.

HOVDEN (Aust Agder). *Hovden Apartment Hotel* (E), (043–39 606). Weekly rental, 300 beds. DC, MC, V. *Hovden Mountain Hotel* (M), (043–39 600). 180 beds, all rooms with bath or shower. AE, DC, MC, V. *Hovdestøylen* (M), (043–39 552). 41 rooms plus 20 cabins, all with shower and bath. AE, DC, MC, V.

KONGSBERG (Buskerud). *Grand* (M), Christian Augustgt 2 (03–732 029). 166 beds, 64 rooms with bath. DC, MC, V. *Gyldenløve* (M), Herm Foss Gate 1 (03–731 744). 150 beds, 12 rooms with bath. AE, DC, MC, V.
Restaurants. *Cafena,* Storgt 12 (03–732 758). *Ernst's Kafeteria,* Drammensvn 87 (03–733 530).
Youth Hostel. *Kongsberg Youth Hostel* (I), (03–732 024). 90 beds.

KRAGERØ (Telemark). *Victoria* (M), (036–81 066). 22 rooms, 6 with bath. DC, MC, V.
Restaurants. *Bucholmen Cafe,* Hovedbyen 13 (036–80 123). *El Paso Western Saloon,* Hovedbyen 12 (036–81 532).
Youth Hostel. *Kragerø Youth Hostel* (I), (036–81 866). 100 beds.

KRISTIANSAND (Vest–Agder). *Caledonien* (E), Vestre Strandgt 7 (042–29 100). 400 beds, all rooms with facilities, restaurants. AE, DC, MC, V. *Christian Quart* (E), Markensgate 39 (042–22 210). 230 beds, all rooms with facilities, restaurant. AE, DC, MC, V. *Ernst* (E), Rådhusgate 2 (042–21 400). 120 beds, many rooms with bath, restaurant. AE, DC, MC, V. *Fregatten Rica* (M),

TELEMARK AND THE SOUTH COAST

Dronningensgate 66 (042-21 500). 110 beds, most rooms with bath, restaurant. AE, DC, MC, V.
Hamresanden Apartment (M), (042-46 098). 22 units, all with facilities, restaurant. *Metropole* (M), Dronningensgate 8 (042-21 465). 21 beds. MC, V. *Norge* (M), Dronningensgate 5 (042-23 320). 140 beds, all rooms with bath/shower, restaurant. AE, DC, MC, V. *Vestre Rooms* (M), Vestre Strandgate 28 (042-24 525). 32 beds, no meals. *Bondeheimen* (I), Kirkegate 15 (042-24 440). 64 beds.

Restaurants. *Baldakin Kafeteria,* Markensgt 42 (042-29 606). *Bowlers Steakhouse,* Kirkegt 7 (042-29 009). *Bølgen Grill,* Elvegt 1 (042-25 838). *Cafe Louise,* Markensgt 6 (042-25 255). *Holmenfoss Kro,* Holmenfoss Søgne (042-69 853). *Peppes Pizza,* Gyldenløvesgt 7 (042-25 715). *Ravnedalens Friluftscafe* (042-10 347). *Skipperhuset,* Skippergt 21 (042-29 075).

Youth Hostel. *Roligheden Youth Hostel* (I), (042-94 947). 135 beds.

KVINESDAL (Vest-Agder). *Utsikten* (M), (043-50 444). 78 beds, all rooms with bath/shower. MC, V. *Alfarheim* (I), (043-55 285). 20 beds.

MANDAL (Vest-Agder). Adjoining popular Sjøsanden sandy beach. *Solborg* (M), Neseveien 1 (043-61 311). 102 beds, 40 rooms with facilities, restaurant, swimming, sauna, sightseeing boat. AE, DC, MC, V. *Bondeheimen* (I), (043-61 422). 30 beds, some with shower.

Restaurants. *Cafe Clubben Store,* Elvegt 59 (043-62 660). *Sjøstjerne Kro,* Sjøsandvn 2 (043-63 005). *Vic Kafeteria,* Marnavn 35 (043-62 288).

Youth Hostel. *Mandal Youth Hostel* (I), (043-61 501). 48 beds.

MORGEDAL (Telemark). *Morgedal* (M), (036-54 144). 130 beds in 70 rooms, all with bath/shower. AE, DC, MC, V.

RAULAND (Telemark). 1,000 meters (3,300 feet). *Rauland Mountain Hotel* (M), (036-73 222). 70 rooms, 23 with bath. AE, DC, MC, V. *Rauland Fjellstoge* (M), (036-73 425). 75 beds. DC, MC.

RJUKAN (Telemark). *Rjukan Hotel* (M), (036-90 288). 60 beds, all rooms with bath/shower. MC, V. *Skinnarbu* (M), (036-95 461). 110 beds. *Rjukan Fjellstue* (I), (036-95 162). 140 beds. MC, V.

The Gaustablikk holiday center is situated 15 km. (nine miles) southwest of Rjukan, access by road throughout the year, 970 meters (3180 feet), views of Mt. Gausta. *Gaustablikk Mountain Hotel* (M), (036-91 422). 165 beds, all rooms with shower or toilet. DC, MC, V. *Kvitåvatn Fjellstoge* (I), (036-91 174). 108 beds in family rooms.

Restaurant. *Kinokafeen,* Storstulsgt 1 (036-91 265).

Youth Hostel. *Rjukan Youth Hostel* (I), (036-90 527). 88 beds.

SKIEN (Telemark). *Ibsen Hotel* (E), Kverndalen 10 (035-24 990). 238 beds, all rooms with bath/shower, restaurants, swimming. AE, DC, MC, V. *Høyer* (M), Kongensgt 6 (035-20 540). 130 beds, 35 rooms with bath. DC, MC, V. *Skien Sportell* (M), (035-96 311). 52 beds, all rooms with shower.

Restaurants. *Brekke Parkkafe,* Brekkeparken (035-23 873). *Cafe Henrik Ibsenhuset* (035-23 670). *El Bravo Western Saloon,* Torggt 18 (035-21 222). *Gregorious Restaurant,* Torggt 10 (035-27 398).

VALLE (Aust Agder). *Valle Motel* (M), (043-37 127). 160 beds, all rooms with shower. DC. *Bergtun* (M), (043-36 270). 23 beds.

Restaurants. *Noreheim Kafe* (043-36 629). *Setesdalsstoga Kro* (043-36 832).

VRÅDAL (Telemark). *Straand* (M), (036-56 100). 130 beds, most rooms with facilities, dining room, cafeteria, swimming, sauna. DC, MC, V. *Vrådal* (M), (036-56 127). 58 rooms, 30 with bath. MC, V.

VRÅLIOSEN (Telemark). *Vråliosen* (M), (036-55 111). 56 beds, 2 rooms with bath. MC, V.

HOW TO GET AROUND. From Oslo, Sørlandsbanen railroads runs through Kongsberg, Kristiansand and Egersund to Stavanger, with branches to Arendal and Flekkefjord. In addition, connecting bus services go from the main line to other towns and villages, both on the coast and inland, generally connecting with the trains. Fastest trains to Kristiansand take between 4½ and 5 hours. Several services daily to Kristiansand with the majority running through to Stavanger or with good connections.

TOURS. There are many excursions offered by boat and ferry, throughout Telemark and the South Coast. One of particular interest is at Skien, where the passenger vessel *Victoria* cruises Telemark's Inland Waterway. The Waterway is a system of canals and locks linking lakes and rivers, and it stretches from the Skagerak to Dalen, 130 km. (80 miles) inland. Information on these cruises from the Tourist Information Center (Turisttrafikk) in Skien (035-22 212).

PLACES TO VISIT. The highlights of Telemark include the lakes of Bandak, Fyresvatn, and Tinnsjö; the views from Lifjell, Nutheim (across Flatdal), Brunkeberg, and Bolkesjö; the majestic Mount Gausta and the stupendous Vestfjord valley at Rjukan; the old farms at Rauland and the stave churches of Heddal and Eidsborg.

No such inventory can be made up for the South Coast, where the charm is everywhere—in the white-painted towns and fishing villages, and the tang of sea and tar.

As well as the natural beauties of the area, there are also museums, preserved houses, and churches and other buildings of historical interest. Some of these are listed below.

ARENDAL. Aust–Agder Museum. At Langsae Manor.
City Hall and Old Town on Tyholmen. The City Hall, in Empire style from 1813, is one of the largest wooden buildings in Norway.
Merdøgård Museum. A sailing-ship captain's home from 1700s, beaches, boat from Langbryggen pier in town.

FARSUND. Farsund Museum. Laid out as a South Coast skipper's house.

GRIMSTAD. Burial grounds. From the Iron Age with mounds, monoliths and stone circles.
Town Museum. In the old pharmacy where Henrik Ibsen was an assistant.

KONGSBERG. Kongsberg Church (1761). With Baroque interiors.
Lågdals Openair Museum. With many fine lofthouses and cottages.
Mining Museum. In the old melting hut. Displays the history of the silver works.

KRAGERØ. Berg-Kragerø Museum. Four km. (two miles) from the town center, in a summer residence dating from around 1800. Open May through Sept. 12–7; Tues., Thurs., Sat. 5–7.

KRISTIANSAND. Arne Vigeland Collections. 130 works of art, primarily sculptures cast in gypsum and bronze.
Christiansholm Fortress. Built 1674 by Fredrik III.
Oddernes Church. Built 1040. Baroque pulpit from 1704. Runed stone.

TELEMARK AND THE SOUTH COAST

The Setesdal Railway. Grovane-Vennesla. Steam train from 1894. Reopened as veteran railway on a 5 km.-long narrow track.

Vest-Agder County Museum. 28 old buildings originally from Setesdal and Kristiansand. Church furnishings/urban and rural furniture textiles etc.

MANDAL. Mandal Church. Norway's largest wooden church in empire style. Built 1821.

MORGEDAL. Olav Bjåland's Museum. Shows the development of skis. Open July 1 through Aug. 20.

Sondre Norheimstogo. The cotter's farm where the ski pioneer S. Norheim (1825–97) was born.

SKIEN. Ibsen House. Skien's community center, opened in 1973. Library, art-exhibitions, concerts, theater performances and cinema.

Ibsen's Venstop. The farm where Henrik Ibsen spent his childhood, now a museum north of the town center.

Gjerpen Church. Is built around a Romanesque stone church erected before 1200. Rebuilt and restored several times.

Kapitelberget. Is the ruin of a medieval crypt church believed to have been built during the 1100s.

Maehlum Church. Timber-constructed from 1728. Altarpiece from 1618. Restored in 1968.

Rock Carvings. At Norde Maele, Fossum and Løberhaugen.

SPORTS. In summer there is quite good **fishing** in the mountains of western Telemark, very good on the Hardanger Plateau. **Hiking** from chalet to chalet on the Hardanger Plateau is another attraction. The South Coast offers **swimming** from the cliffs or lovely beaches (best are Sjösanden near Mandal, Hamresanden near Kristiansand, and the beach at Fevik), **boating** among the skerries, and **fishing** in the sounds. The mountain lakes of Setesdal hold plenty of sleek trout.

Telemark, the cradle of **skiing,** is today one of Norway's most popular winter sports areas. The principal resorts are Bø/Lifjell, Bolkesjø, Morgedal, Rauland, Rjukan, Vrådal and Gautefall. The season extends from Christmas until after Easter. Most hotels have ski lifts of various types, employ their own ski instructors, and have ski equipment for hire.

THE FJORD COUNTRY

Wonders and Waterfalls

Norway's Fjord Country provides one of the world's unique travel experiences. The fjords tell different things to different people, with their awesome power and majesty, their changing moods. More likely than not, however, the visitor will recall something more, something of the atmosphere of quiet beauty. Whether it might be on the banks of one of the fjord's famous salmon or trout streams, or rowing in the shadow of a 300-meter (1,000-foot) rock face, or relaxing with a pot of good coffee and pleasant company on some fjord farm, there will always be that element of tranquil calm. There's a peace in these parts which will give one the satisfaction that comes only to those who have found what they are seeking.

Exploring the Fjord Country

Conspicuously located in downtown Stavanger, only a stone's throw from the busy wharves with their hundreds of larger and smaller craft, is a monument to Alexander L. Kielland, the city's literary light and chronicler. With a good view from his pedestal, he stands there somewhat critically appraising the scene before him. Today it's certainly not the same town which he so vividly described some 80 or 90 years ago. But neither has it acquired the impersonal self-absorbed air which one might expect in the fishcanning capital of the world as well as one of the headquarters of Norway's North Sea oil fleet.

The new Stavanger of modern buildings, bustling traffic and great waterfront factories has emerged from the familiar, flat sardine can; and the man who turned the key bringing about this change was the former broom peddler, Christian Bjelland. Bjelland was the founder of Stavanger's canning industry, which each year probably exports more canned foods than any other city on the globe. It's an interesting spot in which to spend some time. With a population of over 92,000, Stavanger is the fourth largest city in Norway, and the oldest in this part of the country. It was founded in 1100, and boasts a stately Anglo-Norman cathedral well over 800 years old.

Every visitor to Stavanger should walk around the older quarters with their picturesque alleyways, old style wooden structures and cobblestone streets. The venerable Kongsgaard school, as well as Ledaal—the old Kielland estate which is now public property—and the royal residence in Stavanger, should also be seen. Like so many Norwegian cities, Stavanger appears to be in a period of transition when the old must adjust itself to the demands of the times, while the new, in turn, must temper its urge to tear down and modernize. Stavanger has often been called the city with the many churches and has long enjoyed an active highly individualist spiritual life. One of its streets, Berglandsgate, is lined practically solid on both sides with a spectrum of churches, chapels and missions representing a large number of dissenting faiths and groups.

The Ryfylke fjords north and east of Stavanger form the southernmost part of the Fjord Country. Stavanger is well suited for its part as port of entry to this district, because the "White Fleet", consisting of low-slung, speedy craft known as "sea buses", provides swift and comfortable transport for both passengers and cars to the surrounding fjords. You may stay in Stavanger's fine hotels and make daily excursions on the ships of the "White Fleet" even to the most distant fjords of Ryfylke and return to your base in the afternoon. Stavanger is also the western terminus for the South Norway Railway, which skirts the whole of the southern coast.

The visitor should also make it a point to visit the Lyse Fjord. This trip should be made if for no other reason than to see the fjord's "cliff-dweller" communities, where farms cling to narrow ledges hundreds of meters above the sea.

Though Stavanger has been primarily oriented towards the sea, it has more recently recognized its role as the gate to what has become one of Norway's leading agricultural counties. Stretching southward along the coast is a huge glacial moraine known as Jaeren. Flat and stony, it is probably the largest expanse of level ground to be found in all of Norway. But it is practically without harbors, nor is there much fishing. The inhabitants were therefore forced to turn to farming at an early date, and the district's hundreds of kilometers of stone fences stand today as monuments to centuries of back-breaking labor.

Once freed from stones, however, the soil was capable of growing crops of all kinds. There is little if any snow here, the climate is mild and the growing season long. Today, Jaeren is the country's leading producer of eggs and wool. For the vacationer, the district's wide sandy beaches and mild sunny weather provide just the antidote for overwrought city nerves. Stavanger is also Norway's new "oil city", serving as a base for the oil rigs in the North Sea. Many American oil experts are now residents of Stavanger, which even has an American school.

The "Discovery Route"

The "Discovery Route" is the classic route through the Ryfylke fjords to Hardanger and Bergen, with traditions dating back to the days of the pony cart. Thanks to the "White Fleet" and modern buses, this time-honored route has become popular lately.

The fjord boat leaves Stavanger early in the morning for Jelsa at the entrance to the Sand Fjord, where your bus is waiting. It takes you via Sand, along the famous Suldalslågen salmon river to Solheimsvik, where a ferry will bring you across Lake Suldal to Nesflaten. The journey then leads through the narrow and rugged Bratlandsdal Valley, where the road is hewn from the steep mountainside. At Breifonn you join the main Telemark road from Oslo to Bergen. Years ago it was blocked by snow every winter, but by means of huge tunnels, the road now goes straight through the impeding mountains.

At Breifonn you change to another bus, which takes the zig-zag road to the Seljestad mountain pass (now bypassed in tunnel) with fine views of Lake Røldal and the Breifonn Glacier. Descending on the Seljestad side, the bus will make a short stop at the Låtefoss waterfall, tumbling down the mountainside in a double avalanche and gently spraying the road. The Discovery Route terminates in Odda, the industrial center at the very head of the Sør Fjord—a branch of the mighty Hardanger Fjord.

Of all the popular spots in Hardanger, most of the visitor's enthusiasm is probably reserved for the Sör Fjord. This fjord arm extends from Utne, almost due south to Odda, its east shore a continuous sweep of orchards—in springtime an undulating sea of white and pink blossoms. This setting, with its old farms, orchards, green plots and eternal mountains, has provided inspiration for great works of art, literature and music during the resurgence of national romanticism in the last century. Paintings of Adolf Tidemand and Hans Gude, songs like Ole Bull's *Seter Maiden's Sunday,* and many of Grieg's melodies had their origin in this part of the Hardanger Fjord. Visitors to Sör Fjord should not fail to see the old farm community at Aga on the west shore. The old buildings preserved here in their natural setting have retained an air of antiquity which no outdoor museum can match. A rather narrow road on the left of Sör Fjord leads through Aga to the charming resort of Utne.

Out of the Sör Fjord and continuing almost due east, the Eid Fjord comprises the eastern extremity of the Hardanger Fjord, pushing inland almost to the very base of the Hardangerjöklen, a high-lying glacier. Eidfjord village, at the head of this fjord arm, has for centuries been a junction point between eastern and western Norway. From the earliest times, travelers on foot, horseback or on skis have followed this natural declivity down from the Hardanger plateau. Today, one of the main east-west highways follows this route through the magnificent Måbödal valley, passing by the well-known waterfall, the Vöringfoss.

It is time now to look around for some of those renowned Hardanger beauty spots in which to relax. We have already passed the peaceful

THE FJORD COUNTRY

villages of Röldal and Seljestad, and on the eastern shore of the Sör Fjord there is the district of Ullensvang, with more fruit trees than any other Norwegian community, with a medieval church on a romantic point in the fjord, waterfalls draping the cliffs, the Folgefonn glacier capping the mountains across the fjord, and Edvard Grieg's studio hut. Exuding the same charm is lovely Utne on the point between the main fjord and Sör Fjord, Ulvik nestling at the head of its own little fjord and with terraced farms climbing the steep hills. Granvin, terminal of the Hardanger Railway (a branch of the Bergen Line) is also an unforgettable resort.

Continuing from Odda along Sør Fjord, we ferry across the Hardanger Fjord from Kinsarvik to Kvanndal, and ride along the northern shores of the mighty main fjord. The highroad takes us across the Fyksesund bridge, spanning the 230-meter (755-foot) gap of that imposing offshoot of the Hardanger Fjord, and along it we ride into the charming villages of Öystese and Norheimsund, both famous Hardanger resorts.

From Norheimsund we have the choice of two roads to Bergen. The main route takes us through another of those wild canyons—the Tokagjel Gorge—and across the mountain moors of Kvamskogen to the "Capital of the Fjords". The other route, narrower but no less interesting, continues along the Hardanger Fjord to the smiling district of Strandebarm, another flourishing Hardanger resort, and via Mundheim westwards to Bergen.

Waterways to Haugesund

Hydrofoil boats have been introduced between Stavanger and Bergen making the trip to Haugesund in 75 minutes and Bergen in less than four hours. However, the more leisurely way of going by ferry to Kopervik and bus to Haugesund fits in better with most itineraries. Haugesund, built, it is said, on a foundation of herring bones, is a major shipping center.

Just north of the city is King Harald's Column, a monument raised on the burial mound where the Viking King Harald the Fairhaired is believed to lie. The column was dedicated in 1872, presumably 1,000 years after the battle of Hafrs Fjord, when Norway was united into a single kingdom. This historic battleground is located a short distance southwest of Stavanger.

Across the channel from Haugesund is the level, treeless island of Karmöy, the site of one of King Harald's favorite estates. A wealth of archeological finds have verified the island's importance during Viking times, when its strategic position controlled an important section of the country's coastal waterways.

Northward by boat or northeast from Haugesund via Highway E76 the destination is the same. By highway, one enters the back door, by boat the wide-open front door of Hardanger, loveliest of the fjords. Going by road a dilemma arises. By following Highway E76 all the way we travel along one of the finest fjordside roads hewn into the vertical wall of the Åkrafjord. By branching left at Håland, however, we include such gems as the villages of Skånevik and Rosendal, with modern hotels. Rosendal estate, which became a barony in 1678, has a history going right back to the days of the ancient Norse king, Håkon

Håkonsson. The main building dates from the 1650s and is one of the most beautiful in all Norway, while the Rosendal Gardens are a sight long to be remembered. Estate and gardens were deeded to the University of Oslo in 1927 and the property is now being operated as an experimental farm.

While Hardanger is a tourist's paradise from early spring to late fall, one is in the habit of thinking of this fjord in terms of blossomtime. For Hardanger is the richest orchard district in Norway, with fruit trees often forming a seemingly endless border between fjord edge and the snow-capped mountains.

Northward to Sogne Fjord

Sailing northward from Bergen, we keep pretty well within the island fringe that provides a good sheltered waterway along much of the Norwegian coast. Inland the mountains rise range upon range, but along the coast the land is scraped and bare—nothing but smooth rounded stones with an occasional farm wherever a handful of soil made it possible. These weathered, rocky islands were evidently former mountain tops, and even farther inland the mountains seem rounded and worn. In fact only a few peaks in these parts protruded above the vast ice field that covered this whole fjord district in the Ice Age. When this huge blanket began to slip from east to west, it ground off the mountain tops and chiseled a series of deep valleys extending westward to the sea.

Then followed a period of indecision while the coastline rose and fell, finally sinking until the tops of former peaks had been turned into islands, and long fingers of sea water had been sent probing into the innermost recesses of the valleys—in the case of the Sogne Fjord, a good 200 km. (125 miles). In the latter, the present sea level is halfway up the former valley wall, and the water is 1,128 meters (3,700 feet) deep at one point. Here in the fjord country people are now living five or six hundred meters above what was the valley floor some millions of years ago. Hence the fjords, and so much for a second-hand geography lesson.

Bypassing a little spot called Eivindvik, about three quarters of the way up the coast between Bergen and the mouth of the Sogne Fjord, you may notice two old stone crosses on the shore. It seems that these fjord districts were popular spots with the chieftains and clan leaders, most of whom preferred the rough, bald coastal tracts to the more protected and fertile inner fjords, a preference based on tactical rather than personal considerations. By establishing himself at a strategic point on the island-protected waterway which extends along a good length of the Norwegian coast, a chief who used foresight could secure himself a little Norwegian Gibraltar. Back in those early days, the landed peasants, clansmen and chieftains from the fjord districts used to meet somewhere in this section for their Gula Parliament, the laws of which have served as a model for the parliament of Iceland. Its location, as well as the stone crosses, suggest that Eivindvik was the site of this ancient legislative body.

Rounding the corner and swinging eastward into the Sogne Fjord, some interesting changes take place. As you push deeper into the fjord, the strip of land between the water's edge and the mountain wall

THE FJORD COUNTRY

becomes broader and greener. There are more farms, and the bald, naked rocks of the outer coast disappear. By the time Lavik is passed, you can begin to get an insight into the true fjord country.

Lavik sits just inside the outer Sogne Fjord, where the main highway leading northward to Sunn Fjord and Nord Fjord connects with a side road leading to the aluminum center of Höyanger. Thanks to quantities of cheap hydro-electric power, bauxite can be shipped in and processed into aluminum more cheaply here than in any other part of the world. The same is being done at Årdal, all the way at the end of the fjord. Höyanger itself is one of the best planned industrial towns on the globe. High, and near the top of one of the two peaks between which the town nestles, fumes pour out of a hole in the mountain top through a tunnel which functions as a gigantic smokestack. Here mountain breezes carry it away so that none of it ever reaches the town.

About halfway up the fjord at Balestrand begins the true fjord country. For generations this has been the most famous tourist region in Sogne. Here the harsh and bare landscape of the coast and outer fjord has gradually been building up to something surprising and exciting. By the time you push as far inland as Balestrand the world is new, and the inner Sogne lies before you. Here it's the magnitude that impresses. Towering snowcapped mountains drop 1,200 meters (4,000 feet) into the fjord often no wider than a city block. Against a background like this, a tourist steamer can look as insignificant as a water bug. In many places there's no shore at all; the perpendicular mountain faces continue right down beneath the water for hundreds, thousands of meters, and even the largest boats can slip along these rock walls at hand-shaking distance without worrying about where the bottom is.

From Balestrand, the long, narrow Fjaerlands Fjord probes northward towards Jostedalsbreen, Norway's mighty glacier. A short distance inland from Fjaerland, at the fjord's head, are the Suphelle and Böyum glaciers. Resembling a massive waterfall, the slow forward movement of the glacier pushes ice over the precipice and adds to the glittering blue-white wall along one side of the valley.

Second only to the magnitude of Norway's longest and mightiest fjord, it is the color and the ordered neatness of man's contribution to the scene that makes inner Sogne an event of discovery. Although the mountains are sheer and push to the very heavens, rivers and streams have built up sizeable deltas between mountain and sea. There are green, well-kept fields, separated by fences of a million stones plucked from the land, and orchards of fruit trees turning a whole fjord rim into a single great orchard. It is easy to see why farming is the major source of livelihood here.

Like many of the innermost fjord communities on the Norwegian coast, this district enjoys an inland climate even though it is located on salt water. Moisture-laden clouds sweeping in from the ocean are deflected skyward by the mountains farther out towards the coast and drop their rain there. Here there are clear skies, sunshine, and often enough dryness to necessitate irrigation. Fjord-ends and narrow valleys cuddled between these huge bastions of sheer rock are actually natural greenhouses. Rock walls absorb the heat from the sun during the daylight hours and radiate it after sundown. Crops are heavy, the fruit is the finest in Norway and even tobacco may be grown.

Four Fingers of the Sogne Fjord

About two-thirds of the way along its length the Sogne Fjord becomes undecided, and before it makes up its mind has branched off in four different directions. The southernmost finger worms due south past Aurland and finally lodges fast between two mountain peaks at Flåm. From that point an electric spur line carries visitors up 1,000 meters (3,000 feet) in 45 minutes to Myrdal on the Oslo-Bergen railway. The next, and shortest, of these fingers comes to rest at Laerdal, near which is the famed Borgund Stave Church. This is one of the most interesting and best preserved of these early medieval edifices. Constructed of hewn timber and roofed and sided with long round-tipped shingles, the church dates from the middle 12th century and presents an amazing insight into the period when Norway was newly Christianized. Crosses vie with dragons, reflecting a charming indecision on the part of the builders as to just what would do proper justice to their new-found faith. Standing there on the earth floor of that gloomy interior, with the scent of century-old wood smoke and tar in his nostrils, the visitor can't help but hear gruff and probably faltering voices intoning the strange new chants to the Church of Rome. Notice the worn round hole in one wall; this was the lepers' hole, through which the afflicted who stood outside could hear the priest.

Continuing northward, the third of these four fjord fingers was once probably longer than it is now. Millenniums ago a huge glacial dump was deposited about midway up this fjord valley, forming what is now a large fresh-water lake. Here at Årdal is one of Norway's largest aluminum factories based on hydro-electric power from Tyin Lake, some 1,000 meters (3,000 feet) above the plant, and the Jotunheim Mountains. The water drops that full distance through underground conduits to a turbine-generator room blasted out of solid rock deep in the mountain. From outside, there is little in the diminutive tunnel entrance to suggest that you are looking at one of Norway's mightiest power plants.

The fourth and longest of these fingers of the Sogne Fjord, known as the Luster Fjord, extends almost due north, terminating between the Jotunheim range to the east and the Jostedal Glacier to the west. What this scenery may lack in wild gradeur it makes up for in pastoral beauty and neatness, but if you sidetrack to Nigard glacier (a "tongue" of the massive Jostedal) you'll find all the spectacle you could wish for. Guides wait at the ice tip which is reached by boat across the glacier lake, twice a day in summer. Remember to wear sensible clothing. The Urnes Stave Church dating from 1070 and probably the oldest of its kind in Norway, is an easier excursion from Sogndal via Solvorn, across Luster Fjord. From Fortun, at the end of this fjord, a highway climbs over Jotunheimen to Lom in Ottadal.

Going to the Sogne Fjord by boat is only one of the methods—though certainly one of the best—to probe its wonders. Another way of approach from Bergen is by railway to Myrdal and down the stupendous Flåm Line, one of the most remarkable pieces of railway engineering in the world. From Flåm a tourist steamer plies daily to Balestrand and Fjaerland on the northern shores.

THE FJORD COUNTRY

Another star-spangled route (because of Nature's beauty and Americans' predilection) is the one from Voss by bus via Stalheim—a true eyrie overlooking the Naeröydal valley with rainbow-dancing waterfalls and sugarloaf mountains—and out to the finest piece of fjord scenery belonging to Sogne, the Naeröyfjord, often not more than 500 meters (1,650 feet) across, with mountains towering to 1,000 meters (3,000 feet) and more on both sides, and sprinkled with waterfalls. By an ingenious system of connections (boarding one boat from another in mid-fjord) not only Laerdal but Balestrand and other important places on the northern shore are reached.

The straightest approach to the Sogne Fjord is a variation of this latter route, branching off at Vinje from the main road, and crossing the mountain plateau before gently unwinding itself down to the village of Vik, with its characteristic stave church. From Vangsnes, where Emperor Wilhelm II of Germany saw fit to erect a Viking monument of gigantic dimensions, there is a ferry across the fjord to Balestrand, the central point.

The Nord Fjord and the Geiranger Fjord

Exploring the Nord Fjord can again be done by fjord steamer from Bergen or by choosing one of the scenic overland routes from the Sogne Fjord area, such as the one from Lavik via beautiful Lake Jölster, which at Moskog is joined by the route across the Gaularfjell Mountains from Balestrand. The most impressive of these routes, however, is the Sognefjell road, which climbs in magnificent curves from the head of the Luster Fjord to the high mountains of Jotunheimen and Norway's highest mountain pass 1,430 meters (4,690 feet) to descend into the romantic Böverdal valley. At the village of Lom you turn westward again, climbing to the mountain plateau at Grotli. Here there is a choice of two routes, the one heading northwest to Geiranger, and the other one southwest to Nord Fjord. By choosing the second, you will more or less complete a circuit around the mightiest glacier of the European continent, Jostedalsbreen.

By steamer, you continue on from Sogne Fjord to Måöy and Nordfjordeid. As at Årdal, a glacial moraine has filled in the natural fjord valley, separating Nordfjordeid from Hornindal Lake by a barrier of land about two km. (one mile) wide. Much of this is cultivated, but these lush fields represent generations of work.

At Loen you may follow the Loen valley up to a long, narrow lake where blue-white glaciers overhang the valley walls. It is here that subterranean rumblings have twice preceded natural catastrophes when a part of the mountain has crashed down into the lake. From the road, you will notice Loen Lake practically filled in at one point; whole communities have simply disappeared here in the course of minutes. At the extreme end of the valley the road peters out amid a moraine at the foot of cliffs whose walls are laced with glacial brooks.

There are many who regard Nord Fjord as the most beautiful of Norway's fjord districts. It is more gentle, probably a bit more willing and every bit as colorful, but at the same time just a little more secretive and reserved than the other districts we explored. There seems to linger something of the old days of trolls and giants and a strain of that mystery which in Grieg's music belittles the man who believes only what he sees.

In Geiranger the mountain tower upward for thousands of meters straight out of a channel so narrow that the boat seems barely to squeeze through. Yet here, high on what appears to be a notch on the mountain face, people actually lived and farmed a generation ago on the few hundred square meters of soil that Nature has scattered in this niche.

The road to Geiranger from Nordfjord worms its way upward via a series of switchbacks to a height of over 1,000 meters (3,000 feet). After some 20 bends there is a stop at Videseter to enjoy the view of one of the world's wildest valleys—the Hjelledal. As you progress upward, you enter a strange, new world—the roof of Norway, a vastness of snowcapped peaks, lakes, stone and more stone. From Djupvasshytta a private toll road leads upwards another 450 meters (1,500 feet) to the top of Mount Dalsnibba, from whose peak it is possible to see for more than 150 km.

The spectacular "Eagle Road" with its unforgettable view of the Seven Sisters waterfalls, zigzags from Geiranger to Eidsdal. Stop at the "Eagle's Turn" to take in one of the outstanding views of the fjord country. From the village of Eidsdal there is a ferry across the fjord to Linge, where the road leads on to Valldal. Here you may notice the zig-zag stripe in the mountain wall—this was the sea monster that Norway's holy king, St. Olav, smashed against that cliff when it tried to oppose his landing in Valldal some 900 years ago. The "Trolls' Path" (Trollstigveien), between Valldal and Åndalsnes, is a giant among Norway's serpentine roads, coming down the vertical clif-face in 11 unbelievably audacious bends, among majestic mountains—the "King", the "Queen", and the "Bishop" (all of which challenge the rock climber)—with the 150-km. (500-foot) Stigfoss fall and fantastic views thrown into the bargain.

Another wonderful route runs north from Geiranger. You go by ferry on the Geiranger Fjord past the Seven Sisters waterfalls to Hellesylt, where you take a bus for a breathtaking ride high above the Sunnylvs Fjord, via Stranda and Sykkylven to Ålesund.

"Top of the Fjord Country"

Thus we have arrived at the "Top of the Fjord Country", a title aptly applied to the northernmost fjords of Vestlandet as it indicates both their geographical position and their striking character. It is doubtful whether there are many areas of this size where Nature has concentrated such an abundance of magnificent scenery as in the county of Möre and Romsdal. It comprises such fjords as the Geiranger Fjord—the very quintessence of fjords—the Hjörund Fjord, magnificent nave of a Gothic Cathedral, the Romsdal Fjord surrounded by alpine peaks, and the Sunndalsfjord, a water-filled canyon among towering cliffs. There are valleys of almost supernatural grandeur and beauty—the Innerdal, Eikesdal, and Norangsdal; waterfalls among the world's highest, such as the Mardalsfoss of Eikesdal, with an uninterrupted fall of 297 meters (975 feet), followed by one of 220 meters (722 feet), the total measuring 656 meters (2,150 feet) and appearing from the valley in spring as one unbroken whole; mountains like the wild formations of Trollheimen,

THE FJORD COUNTRY

the vertical cliffs of Sunndal, the unruly sea of alpine peaks in Sunmöre, and the "troll" pinnacles of Romsdal. Åndalsnes and Geiranger are the main resorts, second come Ørsta, Hellesylt, Stranda and Øye.

The three towns of the "Top of the Fjord Country" are tourist attractions in their own right. The *klipp*-fish town of Kristiansund, built out on islands facing the sea, connected by bridges and ferry boats, and almost totally rebuilt in colorful architecture after World War II, is extremely pleasing to the modern eye. In the ocean outside lies the island of Grip, Norway's smallest community, until it was incorporated into Kristiansund, clustering round an old stave church. The sea has taken its toll of the Grip people; after the catastrophes of 1640 and 1802 only the church remained. No wonder that the surrounding skerries have such names as "Devils", "Man Killer", and "Hard Skull". As late as 1897, Grip was without both franchise and taxation.

The residential town of Molde is known for its panorama that takes in the 87 snow-crowned peaks of the Romsdal mountains. This is a typical resort town, offering a host of interesting excursions, fishing in sea and lake, mountaineering and other activities and an annual and highly popular jazz festival.

The biggest town of Möre and Romsdal, Ålesund, has its own "Acropolis" with no temple but with a restaurant and a stadium on top and a view of ocean, fjords, and mountains that rivals the view from Flöyen, Bergen. The fjord flights starting from Oslo offered by the Braathen SAFE Airline are something very much out of the ordinary walks of life and travel. Just south of Ålesund is the island of Runde, Norway's southernmost bird sanctuary, with 700,000 inhabitants, including some very rare species, sea-grottos and needle-shaped cliffs. About five km. (three miles) to the east of Ålesund, at Borgund, is the openair Sunmöre Museum comprising 30 old timber dwellings, a medieval church and the excavated sites of a Viking town.

PRACTICAL INFORMATION FOR THE FJORD COUNTRY

TELEPHONE CODES. We have given telephone codes for all the towns and villages in the hotel and restaurant lists that follow. These codes need only be used when calling from outside the town or village concerned.

HOTELS AND RESTAURANTS. The Fjord Country has been popular for nearly a century so it has an impressive array of small attractive resorts and a high assortment of hotels. Most of those listed below are licensed but the smaller pensions *(gjestgiveri)* and farm-pensions sometimes are not; if it's important to you, check first. Many hotels offer reduced rates before June 15 and after August 25. For easier reference, localities are listed under the districts in which they are situated.

Stavanger District

BRYNE (Rogaland). *Jaeren Rica* (M), Arne Garborgsvei (04–482 488). 110 beds, 51 rooms with facilities, restaurant, swimming, sauna. AE, DC, MC, V.

Restaurants. *Guddy's Bu,* Meierigt 28 (04–482 472). *Mølledammen Kafé,* Torget 1 (04–482 274).

HAUGESUND (Rogaland). *Saga Hotel* (E), Skippergt. 11 (047–14 044). 140 beds. AE, DC, MC, V. *Touring Motor Hotel* (E), Ystadvn 1 (047–27 673). 175 beds. AE. *Haugaland* (M), Karmsundgt 215 (047–13 466). 37 beds. MC, V. *IMI* (M), Strandgt 192 (047–23 699). 40 beds, mission hotel, unlicenced. *Saga Maritim* (M), Åsbygt 3 (047–11 100). 92 beds. AE, DC, MC, V.

Restaurants. *Amtmandstuen,* Haradlsgt 133 (047–25 069). *Cafena,* Haraldsgt 139 (047–14 767). *Captains Cabin,* Skjoldavn 1 (047–21 440). *The Shakespeare,* Haraldsgt 169 (047–23 222). *Williams Grill,* Haraldsgt 70 (047–24 108).

Youth Hostel. *Skeisvang Youth Hostel* (I), (047–12 146). 60 beds.

SANDNES (Rogaland). *Holiday Motel* (M), Ganddal (04–674 811). 74 beds, 25 rooms with bath/shower. MC, V. *Sandnes Motor Hotel* (M), Lura (04–663 088). 100 beds, all rooms with bath/shower. AE, DC, MC, V.

Restaurants. *Cafena,* Solavn 3 (04–665 910). *Kalles Kafteria,* Industrigt 2 (04–662 829). *Nille Café,* Erl Skjalgssonsgt 1 (04–661 111). *Sandnes Kafteria,* Vågsgt 34 (04–661 502).

SAUDA (Rogaland). *Grand* (M), (047–92 148). 36 beds. DC. *Kløver* (M), (047–92 633). 38 beds, all rooms with bath/shower. *Sauda Fjord Hotel* (M), at Saudasjøen (047–93 208). 60 beds, good restaurant. DC, MC, V.

Restaurants. *Kro Maxim,* Rådhusgt (047–92 151). *Kroa Brugaten* (047–92 057).

STAVANGER (Rogaland). *Alstor Hotel* (E), Tjensvollvn 31 (04–527 020). 140 beds, all with facilities. AE, DC, MC, V. *KNA* (E), Lagardsvei 61 (04–528 500). 210 beds, 120 rooms with bath/shower, restaurant, grill, bar. AE, DC, MC, V. *SAS Royal Atlantic* (E), Jernbanevei 1 (04–527 520). Best hotel in town, 438 beds, 280 rooms with facilities, several restaurants and bars, dancing. AE, DC, MC, V. *Scandic Hotel* (E), Eiganesvei 181 (04–526 500). 270 beds, 153 rooms with facilities, restaurant, grill, bar. DC, MC, V. *Victoria* (E), Skansegaten 1 (04–520 526). On quay, 160 beds, 97 rooms with bath/shower, restaurant, bar. AE, DC, MC, V. *St Svithun* (M), Klubbgate 3 (04–533 020). 110 beds, 70 rooms with bath/shower, cafeteria, temperance hotel. AE, DC, MC, V.

Pensions. *Bergeland Hospits* (M), Vikedalsgate 1a (04–528 485). 100 beds. *City Hospits* (M), Madlaveien 18–20 (04–520 437). 27 beds. *Commandør* (M), Valbergsgate 9 (04–528 000). 92 beds, 48 rooms with bath. AE, DC, MC, V. *Øglaend Hospits* (M), Jens Zetlitzgate 25 (04–520 832). 15 beds. *Rex Hospits* (M), Wesselsgate 11 (04–524 570). 20 beds. *Rogalandsheimen* (M), Musegate 18 (04–520 188). 20 beds.

Restaurants. *Angus House,* Østervåg (04–531 636). Chinese. *Elisabeth Restaurant,* Kongsgt 41 (04–532 967). *Jan's Mat og Vinhus,* Pedersbakken 1 (04–524 502). *La Gondola,* Nytorget 8 (04–534 235). *Peking Cuisine,* Skagenkaien 10 (04–533 350). *Pernille,* Kirkegt 36 (04–521 287). *Skagen,* Skagenkaien (04–526 190). *Viking Restaurant,* Jernbanen (04–528 747).

Youth Hostel. *Mosvangen Youth Hostel* (I), Tjenstvoll (04–532 976). 200 beds.

Bergen District and Hardanger Fjord

GODØYSUND (Hordaland). A cluster of small islands, famous yachting center. *Godøysund Fjord Hotel* (M), (054–31 100 no.36). 100 beds, 45 rooms with facilities, restaurant. DC, MC, V.

GRANVIN (Hardanger fjord). *Lilletun Guest House* (M), (055–25 208). 24 beds, some rooms with bath.

THE FJORD COUNTRY

KINSARVIK (Hardanger fjord). Busiest ferry point in Hardanger, fine views of fjord and glacier. *Kinsarvik Fjord Hotel* (M), (054–63 100). 140 beds, 28 rooms with bath/shower. AE, MC, V.
Restaurants. *Harding Hage–Kro* (054–63 182). *Kinsarvik Kafé* (054–63 103).

KVAMSKOG (Hordaland). Skiing center, 370 meters (1,200 feet). *Ungdomsheimen* (I), (055–58 947). Kvernavollen, popular youth center, 101 beds, cafeteria.
Restaurant. *Vegkroa* (055–58 960).
Youth Hostel. *Kvamskog Youth Hostel* (I), (055–58 940). Kvernavollen, 40 beds.

LEIRVIK (Hordaland). Village on Stord island, bathing, boating, fishing, riding. *Grand* (M), (054–10 233). 150 beds, 50 rooms with facilities. *Stord Motor Hotel* (M), (054–10 544). 130 beds, all rooms with bath/shower.
Youth Hostel. *Lillebø Youth Hostel* (I), (054–14 310). 45 beds.

LOFTHUS (Hardanger fjord). Famous resort in fruit growing district, facing Sør fjord and Folgefonn glacier. *Ullensvang* (E), (054–61 100). Outstanding, 250 beds, most rooms with facilities, Edvard Grieg's composing cabin in garden. AE, DC, MC, V.

NORHEIMSUND (Hardanger fjord). Resort. *Norheimsund Fjord Hotel* (M), (055–51 522). Facing fjord, 80 beds, all rooms with bath/shower. AE, DC, MC, V. *Sandven* (M), (055–51 911). Facing fjord, 75 beds, 20 rooms with bath/shower, large restaurant used in many package tours. AE, MC, V.
Restaurants. *Fossatun Kafe* (055–51 677). *Grillkroa* (055–51 215). *Sjøbotn Kafeteria* (055–51 215).

ODDA (Hardanger fjord). At head of Sør fjord, industrial center with outstanding surroundings. *Hardanger* (M), Eitremvn 13 (054–42 133). 82 beds, 32 rooms with bath. DC, MC, V. *Sørfjordheimen Pension* (M), (054–41 411). 63 beds, 10 rooms with bath.
Restaurants. *Hjørna Kro* (054–41 356). *Iris Cafe* (054–41 105). *Sporstkafeen* (054–42 278). *Vasstun Cafe* (054–41 505).
Youth Hostel. *Odda Youth Hostel* (I), (054–42 005). 125 beds.

OS (Hordaland). *Solstrand* (E), (05–300 099). Facing fjord, one of finest hotels on west coast, 200 beds, all rooms with facilities, restaurant, swimming, sauna. AE, DC, MC, V.

ØYSTESE (Hardanger fjord). *Hardangerfjord* (E), (055–55 333). 170 beds, most rooms with facilities. AE, DC, MC. *Øystese Fjord Hotel* (M), (055–55 600). 49 beds, 8 rooms with bath. *Øystese Pension* (I), (055–55 305). 15 beds.
Restaurants. *Øystese Kafe* (055–55 305). *Sjøbua and Nøring Spisested* (055–55 523).
Youth Hostel. *Øystese Youth Hostel* (I), 20 beds.

ROSENDAL (Hordaland). Ancient manor, medieval stone church. *Rosendal Fjord Hotel* (M), (054–81 511). 90 beds, all rooms with facilities. AE, DC, MC, V. *Rosendal Gjestgiveri* (I), (054–88 340). Old but well–run inn, 40 beds.

SELJESTAD (Hordaland). 300 meters (980 feet), fine views of Folgefonn glacier, ski center with lifts and instructors. *Solfonn* (E), (054–45 122). 150 beds, 64 rooms with facilities. AE, DC, V. *Seljestad* (M), 5763 Skarde (054–45 155). 121 beds, 43 rooms with facilities. DC, MC, V.

SKÅNEVIK (Hordaland). *Skånevik Fjord Hotel* (M), (047–65 255). 110 beds, all rooms with facilities, salmon and trout fishing. DC, MC.

NORWAY

STRANDEBARM (Hardanger fjord). *Strandebarm Vegetarhotell* (M), (055-59 150). 63 beds, vegetarian food. MC.

ULVIK (Hardanger fjord). Fashionable resort at head of narrow Ulvik fjord. *Müllerhotell Brakanes* (E), (055-26 105). Outstanding, 200 beds, most rooms with facilities, restaurant, boats. AE, DC, MC, V. *Bjotveit* (M), (055-26 300). 60 beds, 4 rooms with bath, sun terrace, boats. *Strand* (M), (055-26 305). 94 beds, 30 rooms with bath. AE, MC, V. *Ulvik Tourist Hotel* (M), (055-26 200). 120 beds, 27 rooms with bath. AE, DC, MC, V.

UTNE (Hardanger fjord). Idyllic village, orchards, views of Folgefonn glacier. *Utne* (M), (055-66 983). Traditional style, 46 beds, 7 rooms with bath. AE, DC, MC.

Sogne Fjord

BALESTRAND. One of Norway's oldest tourist centers. *Kringsjå* (M), (056-91 303). 55 beds, 17 rooms with bath, private ketch for fjord trips. *Kvikne* (M), (056-91 101). 400 beds, 79 rooms with facilities. AE, DC, MC, V.
Youth Hostel. *Balestrand Youth Hostel* (I), (056-91 378). 90 beds.

FJAERLAND. Secluded fjord village, access by boat only, excursions to glaciers. *Mundal* (M), (056-93 101). Good family hotel, 75 beds, 30 rooms with bath. AE. *Fjaerland Pension* (I), (056-93 161). 45 beds, 6 rooms with bath.
Restaurant. *Flatbrehytta* (056-93 118).

FLÅM. Terminal of railroad, descending 866 meters (2,840 feet) from Myrdal through a string of tunnels. *Fretheim* (M), (056-32 200). 140 beds, all rooms with facilities, salmon and sea trout fishing, boats. *Heimly Lodge* (I), (056-32 241). 65 beds.

HERMANSVERK. *Sognefjord* (M), (056-53 444). 80 beds, all rooms with facilities. AE, DC, MC, V.
Restaurants. *Elvegard Cafe* (056-53 224). *K-senteret Kafe* (056-53 422).

LAERDAL. Fjord village on famous Laerdal salmon river. *Lindstrøm* (E), (056-66 202). 152 beds, 70 rooms with bath/shower. *Offerdal Pension and Youth Hostel* (I), (056-66 101). 90 beds.

LEIKANGER. *Leikanger Fjord Hotel* (M), (056-53 622). 85 beds, 33 rooms with bath. MC.
Restaurant. *Sogn Samvirkelang Kafe* (056-53 700).

MARIFJØRA. Village on Luster fjord. *Tørvis Fjord Hotel* (M), (056-87 200). 90 beds, 20 rooms with bath. AE.

SKJOLDEN. Fjord village in fruit-growing district. *Skjolden* (M), (056-86 606). 95 beds, 56 rooms with bath.
Youth Hostel. *Skjolden Youth Hostel* (I), (056-86 615). 48 beds.

SOGNDAL. Village with orchards, salmon fishing. *Hofslund* (M), (056-71 022). 90 beds, 87 rooms with bath. *Sogndal* (M), (056-72 311). 190 beds, 85 rooms with bath. AE, DC, MC, V. *Loftesnes Pension* (I), (056-71 577). 15 beds.
Youth Hostel. *Sogndal Youth Hostel* (I), (056-71 061). 90 beds.

TURTAGRØ. 990 meters (3,250 feet), ideal starting point for walks into Jotunheimen mountain ranges. *Turtagrø* (M), (Skjolden 6616). 85 beds, 5 rooms with bath.

THE FJORD COUNTRY 313

VIK. Old churches. *Hopstock* (M), (056-95 102). 70 beds, all rooms with bath/shower. DC, MC, V.
Restaurant. *Sogn Viking Cafeteria* (056-95 321).

Sunn Fjord and Nord Fjord

FLORØ (Sunn fjord). Norway's most westerly town, sheltered by numerous islands. *Victoria* (M), Markegt 43 (057-41 033). 150 beds, 42 rooms with bath. AE, DC, MC, V.

FØRDE (Sunn fjord). At head of Førde fjord. *Sunnfjord* (E), (057-21 622). 330 beds, most rooms with facilities, salmon and trout fishing, angling school. AE, DC, MC, V. *Førde* (M), Hafstadvegen 26 (057-21 411). 120 beds, 50 rooms with bath. AE, DC, MC, V.
Restaurants. *Firdatun Kafe,* Storehagen (057-21 832). *Muri Center,* Honnesveien 36 (057-21 454).

JØLSTER (Sunn fjord). *Skei* (M), (057-28 101). On lake Jølster, 102 beds, 33 rooms with bath, good trout fishing in lake, rowing boats. DC, V.

LOEN (Nord fjord). A fine resort, excursions to Jostedal glacier. *Alexandra* (E), (057-77 660). Outstanding family hotel, 360 beds, all rooms with facilities, folk dancing. AE, DC, MC, V. *Richards* (M), (057-77 661). 43 beds, all rooms with facilities. AE, DC, MC. *Loen Pension* (I), (057-77 624). 50 beds. MC, V.

MÅLØY (Nord fjord). On island connected with mainland by 1,224-meter (4,016 feet) long bridge. *Hagens* (M), (057-51 800). 100 beds, 30 rooms with facilities. MC.
Restaurant. *Kannestein Kro* (057-51 699).

NORDFJORDEID (Nord fjord). *Nordfjord* (M), (057-60 433). 110 beds, all rooms with facilities. DC, MC, V.
Restaurants. *Eid Cafeteria* (057-60 464). *Sjøsanden Kro* (057-60 060).

OLDEN (Nord fjord). Excursions to Jostedal glacier. *Olden Fjord Hotel* (M), (057-73 235). 77 beds, 36 rooms with bath. AE, DC, MC. *Yris* (M), (057-73 240). 170 beds, 59 rooms with bath. DC, MC. *Olden Krotell* (I), (057-73 296). 30 beds, all rooms with bath/shower. AE, MC.
Restaurant. *Briksdalsbre Fjellstove* (057-73 811).

SANDANE (Nord fjord). Folk museum, church. *Sivertsen* (M), (057-65 333). 80 beds, 26 rooms with bath/shower. *Heimen Pension* (I), (057-66 177). 34 beds, 17 rooms with shower.

STRYN (Nord fjord). Traffic junction for regional bus services. Several inexpensive pensions.
Youth Hostel. *Stryn Youth Hostel* (I), (057-71 106). 88 beds.

VIDESETER (Nord fjord). 600 meters (1,970 feet), magnificent views down Hjelledal valley, glacier skiing in summer. *Videseter Mountain Hotel* (M), (057-75 242). 57 beds, 19 rooms with facilities. AE.

Møre and Romsdal

ÅLESUND (Sunnmøre). *Noreg* (E), Kongensgate 27 (071-22 938). 181 beds, 44 rooms with bath. AE, DC, MC, V. *Parken* (E), Storgaten 16 (071-25 050). 248 beds, 138 rooms, all with facilities, large restaurant, bar, grill, sauna, whirl pool. DC, MC, V. *Scandinavie* (E), Løvenvoldgate 8 (071-23 131). 90 beds in

NORWAY

63 rooms, all with facilities, restaurants. AE, DC, MC, V. *Havly Pension* (I), Rønnebergsgate 4 (071–24 960). 95 beds, 10 rooms with facilities. DC, MC.

Restaurants. *Astoria Mat og Vinhus,* Røysegt 15 (071–25 980). *Fregatten Mat og Vinhus* (071–27 024). *Maritim Restaurant,* Kongensgt 27 (071–22 324). *Saga Restaurant,* Kongengt 27 (071–22 923). *Skateflue Kafeteria,* Skaregt 1 (071–24 259). *Sula Kafe,* Langevåg (071–92 707).

ÅNDALSNES (Romsdal). *Grand Bellevue* (M), (072–21 011). 100 beds, 35 rooms with bath. MC, V. *Rauma Pension* (M), (072–21 233). 20 beds.

Restaurants. *Go'bitn Kafe,* Måndalen (072–23 580). *N-Kafe,* Jernbanegt 1. *Vengetind Kafe,* Vollan 5.

Youth Hostel. *Setnes Youth Hostel* (I), (072–21 382). 75 beds.

GEIRANGER (Sunnmøre). Fjord boat trips. *Union* (E), (071–63 000). 240 beds, 68 rooms with bath, swimming, sauna. AE, DC, MC, V. *Geiranger Hotel* (M), (071–63 005). 151 beds, 70 rooms with bath, swimming. AE, DC, MC, V. *Meroks Fjord Hotel* (M), (071–63 002). 105 beds, 33 rooms with bath. AE, DC, MC, V.

KRISTIANSUND (Nordmøre). *Grand* (E), Bernstorffstredet 1 (073–73 011). 225 beds, 33 rooms with bath. AE, DC, MC, V. *Fosna* (M), Hauggt 16 (073–74 011). 85 beds, 14 rooms with bath. AE, DC, MC, V.

Restaurants. *Cafe Maritim,* Storgt 34 (073–72 002). *Nordmørskafeen,* Fosnagt 3 (073–74 547). *Utsyn,* Kongens plass 4 (073–72 414). *Vetshuset,* Skolegt 2 (073–71 966).

Youth Hostel. *Atlanten Youth Hostel* (I), (073–71 040). 32 beds.

MOLDE (Romsdal). *Alexandra* (E), Storgt 1–7 (072–51 133). Magnificent views of fjord and mountains, 207 beds, most rooms with facilities, swimming, sauna, sun terrace. AE, DC, MC, V. *Nobel* (M), Amtm Kroghsgt 5 (072–51 555). 48 beds, 6 rooms with bath. AE, DC, MC, V. *Romsdalsheimen* (M), Storgt 19 (072–51 711). 50 beds, 4 rooms with bath. MC, V.

Restaurants. *Gimle,* Hamnegt 35 (072–54 122). *Kaffistova,* Storgt 19 (072–51 711). *Najaden Mat og Vinhus,* Romsdalsgt 20 (072–56 965). *Naust-Gryta,* Hamnegt 47 (072–51 030).

Youth Hostel. *Studentheimen* (I), (072–54 330). 232 beds, summer.

ØSTA (Sunnmøre). *Viking Fjord Hotel* (E), (071–66 800). 82 beds, 44 rooms with bath, salmon fishing, deer shooting. MC.

SUNNDALSØRA (Nordmøre). At head of Sunndal fjord. *Müllerhotell Sunndalen* (M), (073–91 655). 115 beds, 30 rooms with bath. MC, V.

Youth Hostel. *Sunndalsøra Youth Hostel* (I), (073–91 301). 30 beds.

SURNADAL (Nordmøre). *Surnadal Hotel* (M), (073–61 544). 150 beds, 17 rooms with bath. DC, MC.

VOLDA (Sunnmøre). *Svendsen* (M), (071–76 034). 20 beds, 3 rooms with bath. *Volda Tourist Hotel* (M), (071–77 050). 48 beds, some rooms with bath. AE, DC, MC, V.

Restaurants. *Porse Kafeteria* (070–77 057). *Viking Kafe,* Hamnegt 6 (070–76 268).

HOW TO GET AROUND. If coming from Oslo you can travel by train to Stavanger (about 8 hours), to Bergen (6–8 hours) and to Åndalsnes (7–8 hours) with both day and overnight services. These places are connected by air with the capital either directly, or via nearby airports with onward bus

THE FJORD COUNTRY

connections. And the internal air services go to a number of other small towns in the region.

Getting about in this large area is a matter of judicious combination of ferries, buses and trains, allowing you to reach even the smallest community. There are express coastal boat services from Bergen to the Sognefjord as well as the daily "trunk route" ship service to the Far North. Coastal ferries to the south link Bergen with Haugesund and Stavanger (plus other places en route) with both express and local services. Both hydrofoils and catamarans are used on some of these. As the whole system is somewhat complicated, you should enquire locally about those routes of particular interest. Apart from one of two summer "specials," they all operate through the year.

By car. The coastal road from Oslo to Stavanger and many mountain roads (among which the Haukeli, Valdres-Fillefjell, Romsdal, and Sunndal roads are open all year) run into the Fjord Country. Bergen is an excellent starting point for a circuit north to Kristiansund (via Voss-Gudvangen-Balestrand, lake Jölster and the Geirangerfjord, returning by Nordfjord and the Vadheim-Bergen ferry: about 1,220 km., 757 miles) or south to Stavanger along the "Discovery Route" (via Röldal and Sand, returning via Haugesund). Motoring in the fjord country is by nature a leisurely affair, interrupted by spectacular trips across blue fjords. Along these winding roads and in such scenic surroundings there is little sense in covering more than 150–200 km. (100–125 miles) a day.

TOURS. As is appropriate to the Fjord Country, there are many, many boat excursions available throughout the area. There are fjord cruises, trips out to the islands, fishing trips and visits to local beauty spots. There are also plenty of road tours, walking routes and even seaplane and helicopter excursions. The local Tourist Information Offices will have details of guided tours, and suggestions for those who prefer to explore on their own.

PLACES TO VISIT. Glaciers and waterfalls are a particular feature of this beautiful region, and every district has its share of natural wonders that shouldn't be missed. The local Tourist Information Offices will have maps and suggestions as to which ones you should see. There are also a number of museums, and farm and church buildings of interest. Some of these places, both natural and man-made, are listed below.

Stavanger District

HAUGESUND. The City Hall with Haugesund Museum.

The Five Foolish Virgins. Monoliths from around A.D. 300, by Karmsund bridge.

Haraldshaugen. Where tradition claims Norway's first king, Harald Hårfagre, is buried. The stone cross on Krosshaugen nearby is from the very early Christian era.

SANDNES. Høyland Openair Museum. At Austråt farm.

STAVANGER. Old Stavanger is not a museum, but a living part of the town between Øvre and Nedre Strandgate, with some 130 lived-in white wooden houses from 1800s.

Stavanger Domkirke (Stavanger Cathedral). Norway's best preserved medieval church. Anglo-Norman style, construction probably started around 1125.

Stavanger Museum. Musegt 16. Archeological, cultural and natural history collections. Stavanger Maritime Museum in the same building.

Ullandhaug Farm. A reconstructed farm from the migration period on an archeological site with burial mounds from the Bronze and Iron ages.

Utstein Cloister. Augustinian cloister from the second half of the 13th century. Restored 1965; the only preserved cloister in Norway.

Bergen District and Hardanger Fjord

KINSARVIK. Bu Museum. The Bu Museum is a branch of the Hardanger Folk Museum. It occupies an open site to the left of highway 7 from Kinsarvik to Eidfjord, 15 km. (nine miles) from Kinsarvik. There are three old houses containing furniture and domestic and craft equipment and the basement of a farmhouse stocked with an immense variety of relics from the stone age to modern times.

Skredhaugen Museum. About 6 km. (four miles) from Kinsarvik on highway 47 to Odda a minor road forks left and provides an alternative route to Lofthus. A few hundred meters from the fork is the Skredhaugen branch of the Hardanger Folk Museum, a collection of seven timber houses gathered from the area and furnished and equipped in the period.

LOFTHUS. Edvard Grieg's cabin. Where he composed some of his famous works, in the hotel garden.

ROSENDAL. Kvinnherad Church from mid–1200.
Rosendal Barony. A Renaissance castle from 1600s, surrounded by a garden and park.

Sogne Fjord

FLÅM. Flåm Church from 1600 with stone age graves nearby.

LAERDAL. Borgund stave church from 1150.
Leikanger Church. Erected in 1250. Restored to its form of the 17th century. Altar and pulpit from 1606.

SOGNDAL. Kaupanger Stave Church. Largest in the area, from 1200. Alterations made in 1862. Today restored to its original form and decor.
Sogn Museum "The Heiberg Collection". The most comprehensive museum in Western Norway particularly strong on Norwegian agricultural history.
Stedje Church (1867). The third church on the same site. The first was built when King Olav christened Norway.

VIK. Hopperstad Stave Church from 1130, a fine example of medieval building style.
Hove Stone Church. The oldest stone building in Sogn, from medieval times.

Sunn Fjord and Nord Fjord

FLORØ. Kinn Church. Romanesque stone church from 1100 on the island of Kinn, one hour by boat from Florø.

Møre and Romsdal

ÅLESUND. Ålesund Aquarium. With coastal, North Sea and Norwegian Sea species.
Ålesund Museum. Including fishery section with old boats.

MOLDE. The Fishery Museum. Built as a small fishing village, on Hjertøya island (boat from Torgkaien).
Romsdalsmuseet. The Romsdall Museum with 27 old houses in farmyards.

ØRSTA. Ørsta Church (1864). With a Flemish altarpiece from 1520.
Iron Age area. With burial mounds, cairns and stone circles at Løken.

THE FJORD COUNTRY

Sunndal Openair Museum. On Leikvin farm which in the 1860s belonged to Lady Arbuthnott, an English lady known as Sunndal's uncrowned queen.

SPORTS. Angling is a time-honored sport in the fjord country. For generations fine salmon rivers, such as the Sand, Laerdal, Åröy, Flåm, Rauma, and Sunndal have attracted sportsmen from all over the world. Oslo travel agencies *Mytravel,* N. Vollgate 19, and *Flyspesialisten,* Kronprinsesse Märthasplass 1, offer first rate salmon fishing in the fjord country. Deep sea fishing jaunts, run on the principle "no catch—no cash" on board the *Sea Queen* are a Stavanger must. *Mountaineering* is another specialty of this land of fjords and mountains. Expert **rock climbing** can be done from such centers as Turtagrø in Sogne; Öye, Åndalsnes, Sunndalsöra, and Innerdalen in Möre and Romsdal; and ordinary "Sunday climbing" almost everywhere. The fells of Ryfylke, the Hardangervidda mountain plateau, the Finse-Aurland-Fillefjell district, the Jotunheimen-Jostedal area, the mountains south and north of the Rauma Railway, and the Trollheimen mountains all have well-marked paths with pleasant and fully staffed chalets among them. Thus it is perfectly feasible to walk carrying a light rucksack through the Fjord Country or parts of it. **Swimming** in the fjords at the height of summer is extensively done; **waterskiing** is practised at Ulvik and Balestrand; fine beaches and bathing resorts are found near Stavanger. The honeymoon island of Godöysund, south of Bergen, is ideal for **boating** (hotel has boats). A number of centers have sprung up in the Hardanger area, and in the superb **skiing** country along the Bergen Railway. As at other Norwegian winter sports resorts, skiing and skating equipment may be hired for a small fee. It is well to remember, too, that winter sports equipment is not very different in price from other countries, but the quality is very high. There are well-stocked sports shops in such Bergen Railway area resorts as Ål, Geilo, and Voss.

CENTRAL MOUNTAINS, EASTERN VALLEYS

Cradle of Liberty—Home of Giants

As each area of Norway unfolds, chapter by chapter, so the scenery that we describe becomes more and more spectacular. This chapter is no exception, and has a variety of territory to cover which will offer even more of interest when actually seen, rather than read about. In fact, the area which this chapter describes contains some scenery which can compete even with the northern parts of Norway for breathtaking things to see. In the eastern valleys holidaymakers will find a wealth of beautiful countryside, dappled with lakes, swift-flowing streams, and silent forests, while the Jotunheimen—"Home of the Giants"—mountain range is a paradise for nature lovers and hikers.

Exploring the Central Mountains and Eastern Valleys

First we shall follow the great valley of Østerdal, which runs southward parallel to the Swedish border for about 320 km. (200 miles). From Trondheim we follow the bends of the Gauldal until, at 600 meters (2,000 feet) above sea level, we reach Röros, once the center of Norway's coppermining region.

CENTRAL MOUNTAINS, EASTERN VALLEYS

With its heaps of slag and its many unpainted timber houses, Röros looks like a mining town, and it has had such a character since its founding three centuries ago. A dominating landmark is the town's main building in stone, the late 18th-century church, one of Norway's best examples of baroque architecture. The countryside around is nearly bare of trees; for most of the forests were cut down years ago when charcoal was the chief fuel for the smelting ovens.

Don't be frightened away by the drab side, however; Röros has many attractions. And there is the great plateau, Rörosvidda, stretching north and east to the Swedish border and inhabited by Lapps with herds of reindeer. The Röros plateau is crisscrossed by marked trails and dotted with tourist-huts, mountain farm *(seter)* quarters, etc., so it is quite possible—given good feet and some ambition—to walk from Lake Aursunden near Röros all the way to the Trondheim-Sweden railway, about 95 km. (60 miles) north. Röros also had its great writer, Johan Falkberget, who died in 1967. His novels about past and present life in this mining district have become literary classics.

Norway's longest river, the 595-km. (370-mile) Glomma, rises just north of Röros and meanders the entire length of the vast eastern forests to empty into the outer Oslo Fjord beyond Fredrikstad. The train from Trondheim parallels the Glomma for about half the distance, or for six hours. This river's chief task is to float logs downstream to the sawmills and paper factories, and the traveler also might as well follow the current. In this way you can watch the Glomma start as a mountain stream in the copper mining district, and finally develop into the mighty timber conveyor that sweeps through Elverum and Kongsvinger.

Elverum serves as junction point for the railway west to Hamar and for a main road leading east to Sweden. It is famous for the final meeting of the Norwegian Parliament in April, 1940, just before the town was destroyed by bombing. It gave King Håkon power to carry on the war outside Norway.

You are now in the region of the great forests which some writers have described as the "ocean of east Norway". Vast, undulating expanses of pine trees whose sounds and whose silence have shaped the lives of people just as the sea has on the west coast, or the long winter nights and long summer days have in Finnmark. Here are persistent influences, reflected not only in literature but in the folk customs, superstitions and tales of trolls, huldra, and other supernatural forest creatures which have been handed down for untold generations.

Gudbrandsdal

If in possession of a good walking outfit, you start out from Oslo's Central Station for the central mountains by way of Lake Mjösa and that greatest of Norwegian valleys, Gudbrandsdal, which is 200 km. (124 miles) long. The area is rich in traditional Norwegian arts, and folk music and dancing are both popular. Wood carving and painting are also held in high esteem.

Eidsvoll, on the south end of Mjösa, is perhaps the most resounding name in Norwegian history, for it was here that the Norwegian Constitution was framed and adopted in mid-May of the year 1814. This event marked Norway's emancipation from Danish rule and gave her that now-famous Independence Day, the 17th of May, as widely and enthusiastically celebrated as the American 4th of July. However, the main feature of the Norse celebration—as you will discover if you are in any town in May—is not shooting off fire-crackers but the huge and colorful parades of school children.

While the Eidsvoll "Cradle of Liberty" is well worth a visit for its own sake and for the excellent collection of contemporary furniture, engravings, etc., you will not be able to combine it on the same day with the absolute *must* for travelers in this area: the boat trip on Lake Mjösa. The Eidsvoll Building lies about three km. from the station, and since the early morning train from Oslo which connects with the steamer gives you only ten minutes' leeway, you'll have to board her right away.

By Steamer to Lillehammer

This steamer, the old side-wheeler *Skibladner,* will probably remind you of Mark Twain and the old days on the Mississippi, for in 1976 she celebrated 120 years of service. She takes almost six hours to reach Lillehammer at the head of Mjösa, but dinner is served on board, and on a warm day it's a fine trip. You stop briefly at Hamar on the eastern shore, and have, both when approaching and leaving, excellent views of its hinterland of fertile farms. Hamar has the ruins of what was once an impressive stone cathedral.

From Hamar you cross the widest part of the lake, passing near Helgöy or Saints' Island, where many leading Norwegian churchmen were interned during the war because of anti-Nazi activities, and call at Gjövik on the west side. Gjövik is an active industrial town, the terminus of a railway that connects with the Valdres-bane at Eina. Side-wheeling northwards from Gjövik, you see that both shores are more rugged and forest-covered and come closer together until, just above Lillehammer, Lake Mjösa narrows into a non-navigable river, the Lågen. Here is the entrance to Gudbrandsdal.

Lillehammer is well aware of being a tourist center. Everything is available for visitors, except perhaps some of the genuine and unspoiled atmosphere that one still finds in Telemark and Setesdal. Nevertheless, Lillehammer is also a cultural center, thanks to the famous Sandvig Collection at Maihaugen, an openair museum much like the Folk Museum in Oslo, but specializing in farm buildings, *stabburs,* water-wheels, etc., of Gudbrandsdal. There is also the museum of Norwegian historical vehicles in Lillehammer, which features vintage cars, the country's largest miniature railway, bicycles and motorcycles.

The town is also famous as having been the residence for many years of the well-known author and Nobel prize winner Sigrid Undset; while the Nansen School, Norway's only "academy of humanism", was founded here in 1939. And at Aulestad, a few miles northwest of Lillehammer, in Östre Gausdal Valley, stands the former home of the great 19th-century poet, Björnstjerne Björnson, author of the Norwegian national anthem. Hunderfossen "Playland" offers various activities for children and adults.

Throughout most of this stretch the valley of Gudbrandsdal has nearly the same topographical pattern: fertile fields on the level ground on either side of the river, patches of cleared farmlands on the wide sloping hillsides, sometimes way up to the first shoulders, but intermin-

CENTRAL MOUNTAINS, EASTERN VALLEYS

gled with wooded patches. Beyond the forests on top begin those *seter* highlands and mountains so prized by skiers in winter and hikers in summer. The district of Vinstra is associated with Henrik Ibsen's famous drama "Peer Gynt".

Across Dovrefjell and from Otta to Vågå and Lom

If you are making the journey between Trondheim and Oslo by car, you will be certain to travel over the impressive Dovrefjell plateau and, sooner or later, arrive at Dovregubbens Hall, a delightful place at which to stop and have coffee. Take a look at the quaint, but entirely natural trolls formed by the trees. Legend has it that every stone, every tree in Norway has its own troll or fairy and who are we to argue?

Just beyond Otta, you skirt the Rondane Mountains and adjacent hiking areas that extend clear to Österdalen. At Dombås, the railway divides in two lines: the Rauma-bane to Åndalsnes, and the Dovrebane which crosses over the Dovre Mountains to Trondheim. In between the forking rail lines and beyond are the trails and huts of three other upland Norwegian playgrounds: the Romsdal Alps, Trollheimen, and Dovre.

For our purposes, however, it's best to leave the train at Otta, an hour and a half above Lillehammer, and change to a westbound bus. This vehicle will soon bring you to Lake Vågå and the village of Vågå in the midst of a district as interesting as Telemark and with an abundance of grass-roofed timber houses and *stabburs*. It is also a region abounding in legends and folklore, for the surrounding mountains have sheltered many a strange monster or giant.

A tale is told, for example, about Johannes Blessom, a native of Vågå, who had to spend considerable time in Copenhagen because of a lawsuit, but who kept pining away for his native hills. He was walking the streets in the Danish capital on Christmas Eve when a stranger driving a horse and sleigh accosted him and asked if he wanted to go home. Blessom said yes, and in an instant he was whirled through the air and shortly afterwards deposited on the ground just outside his own farm in Norway. The stranger then drove full speed into a mountainside which opened in a blaze of light to let him enter, for he was, of course, the Jutul or Vågå-giant.

There is an interesting stave church at Vågå, and another at Lom, half an hour further west, at both of which you can take a quick look while the bus has a rest-stop. At Lom two possibilities open up: to continue westwards to Grotli and the notorious zig-zag descent to Geiranger (or the new year-round road to Stryn), or to branch off southwest on the Sognefjell highway which crosses part of Jotunheimen. This time suppose you take the latter road up Böverdal Valley as far as Elvesaeter.

Aerial Vistas over the Jotunheimen

Next morning step aboard the bus that makes the daily ascent from Böverdal to a tourist hut called Juvass-hytta. The rough ride up a very rocky trail will certainly lead you to suspect that altitude is being gained—but you will be thoroughly amazed to learn that Juvass-hytta is over 1,675 meters (5,500 feet) above the sea. Stay overnight to get acclimatized and then join the forenoon promenade of roped-together guests and guide across Styggebreen Glacier and up to the summit of Galdhöpiggen, Norway's highest rock peak at 2,495 meters (8,181 feet).

Once on top, and with good visibility, you will agree that this is the place to look at Jotunheimen. On every hand there stretches an overwhelming ocean of cliffs and deep valleys, peaks and glaciers: a sight as spectacular as anything to be seen in Norway.

From Galdhöpiggen you can make the same sort of survey of this part of the world as you did of the Oslo region from Kolsås. Your compass and the detailed maps of Jotunheimen will show you, for example, the location of Mount Glittertind, whose thick snowcovering on top gives it a 12-meter (40-foot) margin over your vantage point; or of the many other peaks on all sides. When you tire of mountain identification, turn to the N.T.C.'s general map of trails and huts and plan what to do next.

There's the three-hour descent to Spiterstulen in the valley between the two rival peaks and from there a long walk to Gjendebu on Lake Gjende; seven hours by land or eight if you choose the route over Memuru Glacier. Or you can do it the really hard way by toiling from Spiterstulen up over Glittertind and down to the hut at Glitterheim (seven hours) and then—preferably another day—cross the eastern edge of Memuru Glacier to reach Memurubu (nine hours). Either way you arrive in one of the most famous parts of Giant-Land.

This is the Gjende country, haunt of both historical and legendary characters. For instance, Jo Gjende himself, the mighty reindeer hunter and mountain philosopher who served as guide to many visiting sportsmen and alpinists during the last century, and whose exploits are part of the modern saga of Jotunheimen. Then, of course, there is the Peer Gynt of folklore and the one in Ibsen's great drama, both of whom were well acquainted with these hills.

By all means take the hike from Memurubu to Gjendesheim, allegedly a five-hour jaunt, via the famous Besseggen or Edge of Bess. This brings you along that scenic but narrow pinnacle path where you can look down on one side to Lake Bess and 610 meters (2,000 feet) on the other to Lake Gjende. But there's plenty of room for your feet, and if dizzy, just think of Peer Gynt, who claimed to have ridden this path one night at top speed on the back of a reindeer.

Safely down at Gjendesheim, you will find many alternatives lying in wait. The trail east to Sikkilsdalseter (four hours) and the bus down to Vinstra in Gudbrandsdal; or the trail or bus southwards to Bygdin and Beitostølen Tourist Center, whence you can continue all the way by bus to Fagernes. From there the Valdres Railway can take you either to its junction with the Bergens-bane at Roa, or all the way to Oslo.

If this Besseggen excursion sounds too strenuous, a boat plies from Memurubu to both Gjendesheim and Gjendebu at opposite ends of the lake. From the latter hut you can elect the two-day trip to Leirvassbu and Skogadalsböen, which in turn provides possibilities too numerous to describe here. Suffice it to say that from Skogadalsböen you can proceed to the Sogne Fjord either west via Turtagrø and by bus on the cross-mountain highway from Lom, or south all the way by foot through Vetti (275-meter (900-foot) Vettisfoss waterfall) to Upper

Årdal. Inveterate alpinists, who naturally snort at such tame hiking, may seek their thrills by climbing about in the Hurrungene Range, that chaos of pinnacles and precipices which lies between the Vetti trail and the road to Sogne Fjord. Upper Årdal is the site of one of Norway's newest aluminum processing plants.

But in planning your route through the Home of the Giants, keep two points in mind. First, that at least 20 per cent must be added to the times given in the trail maps for the various journeys from hut to hut; and even more if you intend to proceed at a leisurely pace, take photographs, etc. Second, that ropes and guides are necessary when crossing glaciers as on many of the longer routes. That boaster, Peer Gynt, may have performed reckless deeds in his imagination, but real mountaineers like Jo Gjende never took foolhardy chances.

Valdres and Hallingdal

Let's say that after criss-crossing Jotunheimen we have decided to end up in Årdal, ferry to Revsnes (Laerdal), and wind our way back to Oslo via Valdres. The first part of our bus ride is as wild as they come, up through the canyon-like Laerdal valley to the village of Borgund, where the best-preserved of Norway's stave churches is in perfect keeping with the stern surroundings; and across the high fells of Fillefjell, where the hostels (now modern resorts) date back to medieval times.

The first part of Valdres to greet us, Lake Vangsmjösi, is surrounded by fierce mountains, making it reminiscent of the West Country we have just left. But hardly is the lake left before the smiling, open, farm-dotted Valdres landscape—lakes, silvery rivers, ancient farms on sloping hillsides—arrives to keep us company all the way down to the railhead at Fagernes. The Valdres Express—as it proudly used to call itself in posters all over Norway during the late '20s—is not exactly flying along. It is more of a "Berg und Thalbahn", which climbs painstakingly to the top of a pass to rattle triumphantly down into the following valley, repeating this process on diminishing scales time and again before reaching Oslo. But all the charm of Norway's railways is here to feel and enjoy for those who are not speed maniacs; the open hospitality and friendliness of the conductors, the somewhat inexplicable halts; the breathtaking scenery, the peace that follows from gentle travel through generous landscapes in good company.

From Fagernes, instead of returning by the Valdres Railway, we might have entered a bus that would have brought us to an even more scenic line—the Bergen Railway—at Gol in the Hallingdal. The most spectacular part of that railway lies west of Gol—that part which leads across the high mountains to the fjord country. If one includes the Flåm Railway into the bargain, it is indeed doubtful whether there is anything in the way of railroads to match it in Europe. East of Gol the railway follows impulsive Hallingdal valley, where abrupt changes of scenery and the funniest mountains crop up at every swerve and squiggle of the snake-like train. Now put these east and west parts of the Bergen Railway together, and the whole magnificent Oslo-Bergen run is complete, giving a cross-section of Norway that is hard to beat. Sixty busy years in the business of hauling tourists across the mountains have in no way diminished the spell of this spectacular line.

PRACTICAL INFORMATION FOR CENTRAL MOUNTAINS AND EASTERN VALLEYS

HOTELS. This area, particularly in the mountains lining the Gudbrandsdal valley, boasts the finest group of resort hotels in Norway. Resorts are so numerous that we list only the best known. Some open only for the summer and winter seasons, others all the year.

BEITOSTØLEN (Oppland). 905 meters (2,970 feet), ski touring area, ski lifts, ski school. *Beito Mountain Hotel* (E), (061–41 050). 400 beds, all rooms with facilities. AE, DC, MC, V. *Beitostølen Mountain Hotel* (M), (061–41 028). 175 beds, 80 rooms, all with shower and toilet. AE, DC, MC, V. *Bithorn Mountain Lodge* (M), (061–41 033). 126 beds. *Bergo Mountain Lodge* (M), (061–41 045). 70 beds.

BØVERDALEN (Oppland). Romantic entrance to Jotunheimen, good skiing area. *Elveseter* (M), (062–12 000). 698 meters (2,290 feet), 170 beds, 47 rooms with bath/shower. *Spiterstulen Lodge* (M), (062–11 480). 1,100 meters (3,610 feet), situated between the two highest peaks in Norway, Galdhøpiggen and Glittertind, 120 beds, some rooms with bath. *Leirvassbu Fjellstue* (I), (062–12 932). 1,491 meters (4,890 feet), access by jeep from Elveseter, 195 beds, many rooms with shower.
Youth Hostel. *Bøverdalen Youth Hostel* (I), (062–12 064). 40 beds.

BYGDIN (Oppland). 1,064 meters (3,490 feet). *Bygdin Mountain Hotel* (M), (061–53 813). 56 rooms, 14 with bath.

DOMBÅS (Oppland). 659 meters (2,160 feet), good ski touring. *Dombås* (M), (062–41 001). 271 beds, many rooms with bath. AE, MC, V. *Dovrefjell* (M), (062–41 005). 165 beds, most rooms with bath or shower. MC, V.
Youth Hostel. *Dombås Youth Hostel* (I), (062–41 045). 85 beds.

ELVERUM (Hedmark). *Elgstua Pension* (M), (064–10 122). 45 beds. *Dano Kro* (I), (064–26 294), 32 beds.

ESPEDALEN (Oppland). 300 to 930 meters (985 to 3,050 feet), popular for ski touring. *Dalseter Mountain Hotel* (M), (062–99 910). 154 beds, most rooms with facilities. *Espedalen Fjellstue* (M), (062–99 912). 70 beds. *Ruten Fjellstue* (M), 60 beds. *Strand Fjellstue* (M), (062–26 123). 43 beds.

FAGERNES (Oppland). 360 meters (1,180 feet), ski touring. *Fagernes Tourist Hotel* (M), (061–31 100). 240 beds, all rooms with facilities, swimming. AE, DC, MC, V. *Fagerlund Hotel* (M), (061–30 600). 50 beds. AE, DC, MC, V.

GJØVIK (Oppland). Facing lake Mjøsa. *Strand Rica* (E), Strandgate 15 (061–72 120). 150 beds, most rooms with facilities, swimming, sauna. AE, DC, MC, V. *Grand* (M), Jernbanegate 5 (061–72 180). 90 beds, some rooms with bath. DC, V. *Trandberg Guest House* (M), (061–72 950). 103 beds. *Park Inn* (I), Strandgate 28 (061–71 237). 70 beds. DC.
Youth Hostel. *Hovdetun Youth Hostel* (I), (061–71 011). 156 beds.

CENTRAL MOUNTAINS, EASTERN VALLEYS

GRINDAHEIM (Oppland). *Grindaheim Hotel* (M), (061–37 005). 90 beds, 38 rooms with bath/shower. AE, MC, V. *Mjøsvang Pension and Motel* (M), (061–37 077).

HAMAR (Hedmark). *Victoria* (E), Strandgaten 21 (065–30 500). 200 beds, all rooms with facilities, sauna. AE, MC, V. *Astoria* (M), Torggt 23 (065–21 690). 125 beds, all rooms with facilities. DC, MC, V. *Olrud* (M), (065–50 100). 360 beds, all rooms with bath/shower. DC, MC, V.
  Youth Hostel. *Hamar Youth Hostel* (I), (065–23 641). 97 beds.

HARPEFOSS (Oppland). 222 to 930 meters (730 to 3,050 feet), popular skiing area. *Golå Mountain Hotel* (M), (062–98 109). 80 beds, all rooms with facilities, sauna. *Wadahl Mountain Hotel* (M), (062–98 300). 170 beds, 90 rooms with facilities, swimming, sauna. AE, MC, V. *Grøntuva Gjestgiveri* (I), (062–98 147). 40 beds.

HØVRINGEN (Oppland). 952 meters (3,120 feet), ideal terrain for ski touring. *Høvringen Hotel* (M), (062–33 722). 100 beds, 31 rooms with bath. DC. *Brekkeseter Fjellstue* (I), (062–33 711). 65 beds. *Haukliseter Fjellstue* (I), (062–33 717). 54 beds. AE. *Høvringen Fjellstue* (I), 70 beds.

LILLEHAMMER (Oppland). 180 meters (590 feet), probably Norway's largest tourist resort, on hillside overlooking lake Mjøsa, grand terrain for ski touring, many ski lifts, ski school, marked trails, skating rink. *Lillehammer Hotel* (E), (062–54 800). 330 beds, most rooms with facilities, swimming, sauna. AE, MC. *Rica Victoria* (E), Storgt 82–84 (062–50 049). 180 beds, 93 rooms with facilities. AE, DC, MC, V. *Breiseth* (M), (062–50 060). 80 beds, some rooms with bath. *Kronen* (M), Storgaten 87–89 (062–51 600). 130 beds, all rooms with bath/shower, sauna. AE, MC. *Lillehammer Turistheim Motel* (M), 300 beds, all rooms with shower, summer only (June to Aug.). MC. *Oppland* (M), Hamarvn 2 (062–51 528). 160 beds, many rooms with bath, swimming, sauna. AE, DC, MC, V. *Bellevue Sportell* (I), (062–50 400). 140 beds. *Dølaheimen* (I), (062–50 430). 40 beds, all rooms with shower.
  Youth Hostel. *Birkebeiner Youth Hostel* (I), (062–51 994). 88 beds.

LOM (Oppland). 381 meters (1,250 feet). *Fossheim* (M), (062–11 005). Traditional Norse style, 140 beds, 54 rooms with bath/shower. AE, DC, MC, V.

MARISTOVA (Oppland). 836 meters (2,740 feet). *Maristuen Mountain Center* (E), (056–68 712). Original 1790 inn now a museum, 20 apartments, each for 4–5 persons, restaurant, supermarket, swimming, ski school, marked trails for ski touring. MC.

NOREFJELL (Buskerud). 836 meters (2,740 feet), Oslo's nearest mountain resort, wonderful view of lake Krøderen. *Fjellhvil* (M), (067–46 174). 98 beds, many rooms with bath, sauna.

NYSTOVA (Oppland). 1,009 meters (3,309 feet), popular for ski touring. *Nystuen Mountain Hotel* (M), (061–37 710). 115 beds, all rooms with facilities. AE, MC, V.

OTTA (Oppland). 290 meters (950 feet). *Müllerhotell* (M), (062–30 033). 189 beds, all rooms with facilities, swimming, sauna. AE, DC, MC, V. *Rapham Mountain Hotel* (M), (062–30 266). 98 beds. *Rondane Mountain Hotel* (M), (062–33 910). 140 beds, 35 rooms with bath/shower, swimming, sauna. AE, DC.

TRETTEN (Oppland). Fine skiing terrain, 805 meters (2,640 feet). *Guasdal* (E), (062–28 500). 250 beds, 55 rooms with bath, swimming, sauna. *Austlid*

NORWAY

Feriesenter (M), (062–28 513). 375 beds. MC. *Skeikampen* (M), (062–28 505). 113 beds, 45 rooms with bath, swimming, sauna.

VÅGÅMO (Oppland). Mountain village, stave church, old farms. *Villa* (M), (062–37 071). 120 beds, all rooms with facilities, sauna. AE, DC, MC, V.

VINSTRA (Oppland). Fine views. *Amundsen Guest House* (M), (062–90 045). 42 beds. *Fefor* (M), (062–90 099). 930 meters (3,050 feet), 221 beds, 45 rooms with bath, sauna, swimming, ski lift. AE, DC, MC, V. *Gudbrandslia* (I), (062–90 411). 50 beds. AE, MC. *Sødorp* (I), (062–91 000). 90 beds. AE, DC, MC.

HOW TO GET AROUND. By train. Getting about is fairly simple as the main valleys are served efficiently by railways. The Röros Railway runs through the entire length of forestclad Österdal; the Dovre Railway covers the Gudbrandsdal both with express and express special trains and night trains; the same services are effected by the Bergen Railway through the Hallingdal; the Valdres Railway charmingly deals with that province, and even the Numedal has its little railway running between Kongsberg and Rödberg. If you want to get from one valley across to the next one, have a look at the map, pick out the connecting roads, and at those junctions of roads and railway you will find buses waiting to perform exactly the service you desire.

MOTORING. By car. The combination of beautiful scenery, excellent accommodation, and varied excursion possibilities, makes touring this area by car especially rewarding. Note that some of the smaller roads are fairly bumpy.

SPORTS. Sports play an important part in the holiday life of this region. **Fishing** comes first. The lakes and rivers are too many to be mentioned. The best fishing in lakes and rivers above 1,500 feet is available after June 15, and above 2,500 feet after July 15. Mountain **hiking** comes second. The Jotunheimen mountain ranges are the finest in northern Europe, with more than 200 peaks above 6,500 feet, glaciers, wild valleys, and mountain lakes of great beauty. The other famous mountain area is the Rondane mountains. Both Jotunheimen and Rondane are perfectly organized from the hiker's point of view, with cairned routes between the staffed chalets. The chalets open at the end of June. (Remember to get a copy of the Norway Travel Association guide book "Mountain Touring in Norway".) The best period for walking would be in July and August. The many first class resort hotels of the Eastern Valleys offer good **tennis**, **boating** and **bathing** in pools or nearby lakes. Some offer **riding** also.

WINTER SPORTS. This is excellent *skiing* country, with plenty of snow and terrain to suit every degree of skill—nursery slopes for beginners, downhill and slalom runs for experts, and ski touring. Skis can be hired at most of the resorts. Many resorts have their own skating rinks which are floodlit at night, and *sleigh* rides by the light of pitchpine torches are an added feature.

BERGEN, CAPITAL OF WEST LAND

City of Quays and Grieg

Walking along the quay of Olav Kyrre's old town at night, you will see the thousands of lights that mark the houses, streets and highways as they follow the valleys and shores, now concentrated in narrow belts, now spreading out widely. Meanwhile, out in the fjords, heading north and south and west, are other lights. Those are the fishing boats, cargo liners, and passenger ships to which Bergen mainly owes its position as Norway's second city and capital of Vestlandet.

Bergensers do not suffer from any inferiority complex and particularly not as far as the capital of Norway is concerned. They point out that Bergen was an important commercial and military center when Oslo was still a village, and further, that until as late as the 1830s their town had the larger population. (Today Oslo has just over twice as many people as Bergen.) But they are especially proud of their cultural achievements and point to the great playwright Ludvig Holberg, the National Theater founder in 1859 (which they claim to be the first in Norway), their symphony orchestra, organized way back in 1765, and their annual International Festival.

Exploring Bergen

The steepest 300-meter mountain in the world is surely Bergen's own Flöyen. A visitor once made this remark about the most renowned of the seven hills among which Bergen has grown up. But he must have been inspired by a native, for the words reflect perfectly the pride, independence and not-too-carefully-hidden superiority complex which mark the true Bergenser. In any case, let's jump on the funicular which leaves the head of Vetrlids-almenning every 30 minutes, ride up those lofty 300 meters (1,000 feet), and have a bird's-eye view of this westernmost city in Norway.

Flöyen is a perfect place from which to plan our sightseeing, since the whole city is spread out below like a relief-map. (But bring a conventional map along for reference.) We see how Bergen stretches out in an elongated form running roughly from north to south, bounded for the most part by the fjord on one side and steep mountain slopes on the other. Sandviken, with its old warehouses at the seashore and contrasting new villa sections, is the most northern part, Paradis and Fjösanger the most southern; while farthest to the west are the industrial sections of Laksevåg and others along the Pudde Fjord. The central part in between is of most interest to us, and we shall descend for a look. Almost underfoot, and near the octagonal but somewhat lopsided lake called Lille Lungegårdsvann, lies the railway station.

Continuing our round-up from the air, we turn to the right bank of the central harbor, where the original town was founded by Olav Kyrre in 1070. There is the age-old fish market and, farther inland, Maria Church, which dates from about 1100, easily recognizable by its square twin steeples. Near the waterfront are the old warehouses of Hanseatic times, while beyond medieval Håkon's Hall, a long pier juts out into the fjord. That is Skoltegrunds-quay, where the Newcastle steamers dock. Directly opposite, on the southwest side of Vågen as the inner harbor is called, we see the park on Nordnes Point and back towards town, more of that complex pattern of wharves, warehouses, cottages, office buildings, narrow lanes and wide fire-prevention avenues or *almenninger,* which is the unmistakable trademark of Bergen.

Now the funicular lowers us swiftly down the inclined railway, which is so steep that one involuntarily shivers a bit. There's no reason for alarm, since every existing safety device is installed on the car, and the trackgripping brakes work automatically in case of emergency. We reach the bottom in a few minutes and walk down the Vetrlids-almenning into the midst of history.

First, a pause at the well-known fish market—Torget—at the inner end of Vågen, to observe or photograph the thousand-year-old scene of thrifty housewives negotiating for their daily supply of fish with the men who caught them a few hours ago. Then we pass by two short blocks of modern buildings and arrive at that world-famous monument to medieval life and trade, the old warehouses of the Hanseatic period in the 14th and 15th centuries.

Bryggen

"Yes, it used to be called Tyskebryggen, or the German Quay," admits the cicerone, "but by unanimous vote at the first meeting of the city council after the liberation, we decided to call it Bryggen, or The Quay." And, as if by way of further explanation, he looks down the waterfront towards the restored Bergenhus Fortress and Håkon's Hall, Bergen's most prized examples of 13th-century architecture.

The old wooden warehouses, long and narrow, jammed so closely against each other that air and daylight can enter only through tiny slits, are both the acme of picturesqueness and a working model of life in bygone times. They are still used for storage and for offices, and wares are still hauled up by hand pulleys from the narrow planked alleyways to the lofts above. The Hanseatic Museum and the old Schötstuene, in nearby Engelsgaarden, complete the medieval picture with their collections of ancient documents, coins, furniture, etc.

Nevertheless, this quarter is not equally reverenced by all Bergensers. Our friend can tell us that a good-sized fraction of the public, including a few town-planners, look on it more as a rat-ridden firetrap than as a sacred memorial. Others say that these buildings are unpleasant reminders of a previous period of national downfall and of occupation by an enemy, so why preserve them? And they frankly bemoan the fact that a north gale was blowing that night in January, 1916, when the central town was burned down; an east wind would perhaps have taken care of Tyskebryggen as well. This school of thought had no regrets when, in July of 1955, part of the Quay was devastated by fire.

Fire has been the greatest enemy of Bergen and has harried it far longer than the Hansa ever did. As in old Oslo, fate seemed to decree that some careless person would let his house catch fire every 50 or 100 years, with the result that whole areas would be destroyed. But whereas Oslo was simply abandoned after the fire of 1624 and rebuilt on a new site, the citizens of Bergen had to rebuild on the old foundations. As they learned from each catastrophe, the town planning became more safety-conscious, until after 1916 the present series of broad streets was developed in addition to the old crosstown *almenninger* at regular intervals. Today, it is said that in the main business section streets occupy almost as much area as the buildings.

Ferry and Fortress

We take the little ferry which plies from near the Rosenkrantz Tower across to the middle of Nordnes, and walk out to the point. Here there is much of interest: another old fortress called Frederiksberg, a beautiful park, the Nordnes bathing establishment, and a fascinating Aquarium. From the south side of the point we have a good view down Pudde Fjord to Laksevåg and the other modern industrial suburbs which have spread out along the narrow stretch between shore and steep mountainside. Just north of Laksevåg the Naval Academy is located at Gravdal.

On top of Sydnes Hill is the former Bergens Museum, where Fridtjof Nansen worked as an assistant before making his astounding trip across Greenland on skis, and where the meteorologist Vilhelm Bjerknes first worked out his now internationally known methods of weather-forecasting. The museum is at present part of the new University of Bergen, which was created in 1948. The Graduate School of Business Administration is very appropriately located in Bergen, for this is the city with the longest and strongest traditions in commerce and trade, yet also one of the most progressive business centers in Norway. It has its new and monumental headquarters at Helleveien in the northern outskirts of Bergen.

Famous Sons

If you bring up the subject of Vigeland and the sculpture-park in Oslo, our man from Bergen admits that there is nothing like it here, "not even in the Fish Market!" But he says it with such a glint in his eye that it's hard to know whether he's bragging or complaining. At least until he starts to point out how many well-placed statues there are in Bergen. In the City Park is Edvard Grieg, for example; and on the steps of the National Theater, Björnstjerne Björnson, who was its director for a time. This statue, by the way, is the work of Vigeland. But our guide's favorite is obviously sculptor Stephen Sinding's highly original likeness in bronze of Ole Bull. For here is the giant violinist standing on some rocks beside a waterfall, right in the heart of Norwegian nature, yet transplanted to the center of Bergen.

Many famous men have come from Bergen, like the painter I. C. Dahl, and the statesman Christian Michelsen, who was Prime Minister in 1905 when Norway finally succeeded in breaking out of the union with Sweden. But unquestionably the greatest is that trio: Ludvig Holberg, Ole Bull and Edvard Grieg. And while Holberg lived his adult life in Copenhagen, both the violinist and the composer not only claimed Bergen as home but actually lived there even after they had achieved fame. Consequently, we can visit their homes. Ole Bull's at Lysöya, and Grieg's Troldhaugen, which has now become a museum. Situated in a beautiful natural part of Hop, five miles from Bergen, Troldhaugen (whose name means "hill of trolls") has become a Norwegian national shrine. Grieg's studio, his piano, his notes, are all to be seen.

No mention of famous sons can omit those who in every generation have taken the initiative in maintaining or improving Bergen's economy. Such pillars of society range from the untold numbers of fishermen and skippers, like those in Revold's murals in the Stock Exchange, to scores of organizers of great shipping, canning and manufacturing concerns. It was they who created Bergen when the town was almost entirely dependent on sea communications with the rest of Norway; that is until the railway to Oslo was cut through the barricade of mountains and opened for traffic in 1909. And today the sea is still the only connection with many parts of Vestlandet, though since the Flesland airport, 19 km. (12 miles) away, was opened Bergen has been on both domestic and international air routes communicating with places as widely diverse as Bangkok and Vancouver. It is this mixture of remoteness and integration into the modern world which gives Norway its peculiar fascination.

BERGEN

PRACTICAL INFORMATION FOR BERGEN

GETTING TO TOWN FROM THE AIRPORT. There is a frequent bus service running between the airport and the Bergen Bus Station. For departure times, inquire at the airlines, or at the Tourist Information Center.

TOURIST INFORMATION. Bergen Tourist Board run a special Tourist Information Center, Torgalmenning (321 480). They publish information of various kinds and also provide assistance in obtaining accommodations and in changing currency after banking hours. The Center sells tickets for city sightseeing by bus or boat and tickets for fjord tours of one or more days. They can also give advice and information on events taking place in Bergen and on tours that are available.

During the summer the Center is open Mon. to Sat. 8.30 A.M.–10 P.M., Sun. 9.30 A.M.–10 P.M. During the winter it is closed on Sundays, and open for shorter hours during the week.

USEFUL ADDRESSES. Travel Agents. *Bennett Reisebureau A/S,* 9–11 Ole Bulls plass (323 010). *Myrtravel International,* 3 Torgalm (318 095). *Norwegian State Railways,* Bergen Railway Station (319 615). *Winge Travel Bureau Ltd.,* 1–3 Chr. Michelsensgt. (321 080).

Car hire. *Avis,* Lars Hillesgt. 15 (320 130). *Hertz,* Lars Hillesgt. 18 (327 920). *Europcar,* Markevien 8–10 (327 048).

TELEPHONE CODES. The telephone code for Bergen is 05. To call any number in this chapter, unless otherwise specified, this prefix must be used. Within the city, no prefix is required. In the final section *Hotels Along the Bergen Railroad,* we have given telephone codes for each town or village. These codes need only be used when calling from outside the town or village concerned.

HOTELS. The overcrowding that has plagued the Bergen hotel scene has eased, and there is space for visitors all year round. However, it is always wise to make reservations ahead, especially at festival times.

Deluxe

Norge. Ole Bulls plass 4 (233 000). 498 beds, all rooms with facilities incl. piped music/radio, 15 suites, several restaurants and bars. Garden room with nightly dancing June/Aug. AE, DC, MC, V.

SAS Royal. Bryggen (318 000). Opened in Feb. 1982 on site of old warehouses ravaged by fire nine times since 1170. The houses were rebuilt each time in the same style and SAS has incorporated this ancient architecture in the hotel, which makes it one of the most interesting in Europe. 500 beds in 265 rooms, all with facilities incl. piped music/radio, swimming, exhibition of Hanseatic artifacts unearthed during construction. AE, DC, MC, V.

Expensive

Neptun. Walckendorffsgate 8 (326 000). 195 beds, all rooms with facilities. AE, DC, MC, V.

Orion. Bradbenken 3 (318 080). 250 beds, 110 rooms with facilities, dining room, disco bar. AE, DC, MC, V.

Rosenkrantz. Rosenkrantzgate 7 (315 000). 155 beds, 88 rooms with bath, restaurant. AE, DC, MC, V.

Terminus. Kong Oscarsgate 71 (311 655). 225 beds, 116 rooms with bath, temperance hotel, restaurant. AE, DC, MC, V.

Moderate

Bergen Apartment. Haakonsgate 2 (233 962). Two km. from station; 59 beds, all rooms with facilities. MC.

Bergen Center (formerly Bristol). Markevei 2 (232 300). On city square, 100 beds, 65 rooms; bed and breakfast hotel. AE, DC, MC, V.

Esso Motor Hotel. Kokstad (227 150). Near Flesland airport, new in 1982; 300 beds in 175 rooms, all with facilities, restaurant, taverna, indoor pool, sauna, ample parking. DC, MC, V.

Gjestehuset Rica. Vestre Torggate 20a (219 666). Central location, 36 beds. MC, V.

Hotel Hanseaten. Sandbrogate 3 (316 155). One km. from station; 57 beds, 21 rooms with bath/shower, restaurant, grill. No credit cards.

Strand. Strandkaien 2–4 (310 815). Facing harbor; 100 beds, 15 rooms with bath, dining room. AE, DC, MC, V.

Toms. C Sundtsgate 52 (232 335). Near the station; 78 beds, all rooms with facilities inc. refrigerator; dining room. AE, DC, MC, V.

Camping

Bergenshallens Camping. 24 Vilh. Bjerknesvei (282 840). Ten minutes from city center, bus no. 3. Open June 20 through Aug. 15. All facilities.

Bratland Camping. Haukeland, on road E68.

Grimen Camping. Helldal (100 615). On road E68. Camping huts open from May to end Oct. Rooms with access to kitchen and bath open all year.

Lone Camping. (240 820). Main camping site for the Bergen area, 19 km. (12 miles) from town on main road E68. All modern conveniences. Service shop and hostel with 128 beds. TV room. Lakeside position. Open all year. Resident watchman.

Midttun Camping. (136 036, 101 269, 101 095). On the main road E68, 11 km. (seven miles) south of Bergen; 12 camping huts, 23 rooms, 127 beds. Most rooms with toilet, shower and mini-kitchen. All modern conveniences. Sauna, laundry. Open all year.

Youth Hostels

Montana Youth Hostel. Johan Blydtsv. 30 (292 900). Wonderful view of the town and surroundings. 250 beds in five–bedded rooms, all with H&C water. Family rooms. Showers in corridors. Ample parking. Inexpensive. Apply to IYHA information office at Strandgaten 4 (326 880). Open from May 15 through Sept. 20.

HOW TO GET AROUND. By bus. The central bus station is at 8 Strømgaten (326 780). It is the terminal for all buses serving the environs of Bergen and the Hardanger area. There are luggage deposits, shops, a cafeteria and a restaurant there.

All buses are marked with destination and route number. Special tourist tickets for unlimited travel within 48 hours are available from the Tourist Information Office and at Bergens Sporveis Office. The cost is Nok. 25

By train. There are day and night trains from Oslo and en route stations. The railway station (319 640) has luggage deposits and a cafeteria.

By taxi. To order a taxi, phone 322 222.

By ferry. Across the harbor, Mon. to Fri. 6.30 A.M.–5 P.M., Sat. 10 A.M.–2 P.M.; no ferries Sun. Fare Nok.3.50, children Nok. 2.

From Nøstekaien there are frequent ferries to the island Askøy (20 mins.).

On foot. The mountains surrounding Bergen offer a wide range of walks in mountainous and wooded country. Information about walking routes, and maps

BERGEN

for walkers are available at Bergen Turlag, 3C Sundtsgate. Maps are also available from booksellers.

By fjord and coastal steamer. Coastal steamers for North Norway leave daily from Skoltegrunnskaien. There are hydrofoil boats to Stavanger and Haugesund. Steamers for Hardanger fjord and Sunnhordland leave from Holbergkaien. Steamers for Sognefjord, Nordfjord and Sunnfjord leave from Nykirkekaien, with express steamers from Strandkaien. Local steamers serving the islands and fjords immediately north and south of Bergen, dock at the inner harbor on both sides of the fish market.

TOURS. The Tourist Information Center, Torgalmenning (321 480) can give advice and information on tours that are available. They also sell maps, including maps for walkers.

MUSEUMS. Bergen Billedgalleri (Municipal Art Museum). (311 130). Notable collection of Norwegian paintings covering the last 150 years. Also fine examples of European art. Open mid–May through mid–Sept., Mon. to Sat. 11–4, Sun. 12–3. Off season, Tues. to Sun. 12–3; closed Mon.

Bryggen Museum. (316 710). Erling Dekke Naess Institute for Medieval Archaeology. A cultural history museum based on extensive excavations of Bryggen. Displays of artefacts illustrate commerce, shipping, handicrafts, daily life and cultural activities in the Middle Ages. Open mid–May through mid–Sept., Mon., Wed., Fri. 10–4, Tues. and Thurs. 10–8, Sat. and Sun. 11–3; mid–Sept through mid–May, Mon. to Fri. 11–3, Sat. and Sun. 12–3. Admission Nok. 5, children free.

Buekorps Museum. A collection of pictures and other items showing the activities over 125 years of the Buekorps, a kind of boys' brigade found only in Bergen and best known for their drill, usually with crossbows. Information on opening hours from the Tourist Office. Admission free.

Hanseatic Museum. Bryggen (314 189). One of the oldest and best preserved wooden buildings in Bergen, furnished in 16th-century style. Open June through Aug., daily 10–4; May and Sept., daily 11–2; Oct. through Apr., Sun., Mon., Wed., Fri. 11–2. Admission Nok. 6, children Nok. 3.

Historical Museum. Sydneshaugen (213 050). Fine collections showing West Norwegian culture from prehistoric and medieval times to about 1850, as well as good ethnographical collections. Open Sat. to Thurs. 11–2; closed Fri. Admission free.

Hilmar Rekstens Art Collection. 7 Stamerbakken, Fjøsanger (272 420). Permanent exhibition of pictorial art, oriental carpets and old English silver. During the Festival period, guided tours daily at noon. Admission Nok. 35. The rest of the year, open on appointment.

Hordamuseet. Stend (117 130). Folkmuseum for agriculture and fishing. Open daily 12–3; closed Mon. and Sat. Admission Nok. 5, children Nok. 1.

Kunstforeningen (Bergen Fine Arts Society). (321 460). Alternating exhibitions of contemporary art. Open Tues. to Fri. 12–4, Thurs. also 6–8, Sat. and Sun. 12–3; closed Mon. Admission Nok. 7, students Nok. 3, artists, art students and children free.

Langegaarden–Fjøsanger Hovedgård. Manor farm, with art gallery and handicraft center, surrounded by beautiful woodlands. Six km. (four miles) from city center.

Leprosy Museum—St. George's Hospital. 59 Kong Oscarsgate. The Bergen Collections of the History of Medicine. In the Middle Ages a hospital for lepers. The buildings of today date back to the beginning of the 18th century. Open mid–May through late Aug., daily 11–3. Audiovisual programmes in English, French, German and Spanish. Admission Nok. 7, children Nok. 1.

Maritime Museum. Sydneshaugen (327 980). A modern museum of great interest to those who wish to follow the development of shipping from the Old Norse period up to the present day. Open Sun. to Fri. 11–2. Admission Nok. 1, children Nok 0.50.

NORWAY

Museum of Natural History. Muséplass 3 (213 050). Displays of botany, geology and zoology. Open Fri. to Wed. 11–2; closed Thurs. Admission free.

Old Bergen. Elsesro, Sandviken (256 307). An openair museum with about 35 wooden houses representative of Bergen architecture in the 18th and 19th century, with interiors from the 18th, 19th and 20th centuries. Guided tours every hour. Restaurant with hot and cold meals (257 034). Open May 6 through June 16, daily 11–6; June 17 through Aug. 26, daily 11–7; Aug. 27 through Sept. 16, 11–6. Admission Nok. 8, children, students, pensioners Nok. 4.

Permanenten (Fishery Museum). (318 984). A cross-section of Norwegian fisheries and their natural foundation. Has served as a model for similar collections abroad. Open May 15 through Aug. 31, Mon. to Sat. 10–3, Sun. 12–3; off season, Wed. and Sun. 12–3. Admission Nok. 4, children Nok. 2.

Rasmus Meyer's Collection. (311 130). Fine collection of Norwegian paintings, including many works by Edvard Munch. Open May 15 through Sept. 15, Mon. to Sat. 11–4, Sun. 12–3. Off season, Wed. to Mon. 12–3; closed Tues.

Schøtstuene. 50 Øvregaten (316 020). Old assembly rooms, which vividly illustrate social life among the Hanseatic merchants in Bergen. Open during summer daily 10–4; May and Sept., daily 11–2; off season, Sun., Tues., Thurs. and Sat. 11–2. Admission Nok. 6, children Nok. 3.

Seter Museum (Hill Farm Museum). (117 130 Hordamuseet). Recently erected on Fanafjell near Bergen, showing features of early Norwegian farming.

Stenersen's Collection. (311 130). 250 works by well-known modern artists (Munch, Picasso, Klee). Open May 15 through Sept. 15, Mon. to Sat. 11–4, Sun. 12–3; off season Tues. to Sun. 12–3; closed Mon.

Theta Room. Enhjørningsgården Bryggen. Museum of resistance. For opening hours, check with the Information Center.

Vestlandske Kunstindustrimuseum (West Norway Museum of Applied Art). (325 108). Collections of European arts and crafts, antique Bergen silver, contemporary Norwegian and foreign ceramics, glass, furnitures, metalwork and Chinese art. Open May 15 through Aug. 31, Mon. to Sat. 10–3, Sun. 12–3; Sept. 1 through May 14, Tues. to Sun. 12–3; closed Mon. Admission Nok. 5, children Nok. 2.50.

PARKS, ZOOS AND GARDENS. Milde Arboretum (The Norwegian Arboretum). (226 972). The arboretum was founded in 1971 and only a few of its 50 hectares have been planted. In spite of this, a lot of trees and shrubs from different parts of the world may be found. The area is very attractive with hills, rocky gorges, a small lake and a shoreline of several kilometers length. Bus from Bergen Bus Station to Mildevågen, then a 15 minute walk. Open daily. Admission free.

HISTORIC BUILDINGS AND SITES. Alvøen Main Building. The discontinued Alvøen paper-factory is located 18 km. (11 miles) west of Bergen city. It opened as a museum in 1983. The main building, dating from 1797, contains a collection of old furniture, silver, East-Indian porcelain and pictures. Open May 15 through Sept. 1, details in the daily press. Admission free.

Bryggen. Wooden buildings with characteristic pointed gables facing the harbor. A unique example of Norwegian medieval architecture. Today it is a growing center for arts and crafts, where painters, weavers and craftsmen have their workshops, some of them open to the public.

Fana Folklore. An evening spent in true Norwegian tradition with old farm customs, traditional Norwegian food, lively dances and folk music. For details phone Fana Folklore (117 240).

Fantoft Stave Church. A fine example of a Norwegian stave church. Built in the early-12th century in the Sognefjord area, it was later moved to its present site. Open May 15 through Sept. 1, Sun., Tues., Thurs., Sat. 10–1 and daily 3–6; July, also daily 10–1. Admission Nok. 5, children Nok. 2.50

BERGEN

Gamlehaugen. Fjøsanger (220 222). Residence of the King when visiting Bergen. Open June 1 through Sept. 1, Mon. to Fri. 12–2. Garden open at all times. Admission Nok. 4, children Nok. 2.

Håkonshallen. (316 067). King Håkon's hall was built in the mid–13th century. It was badly damaged by an explosion and fire in 1944 and restored 1957–61. Open May 15 through Sept. 14, daily 10–4; off season Fri. to Wed. 12–2, Thurs. 3–6. Admission Nok. 4, children Nok. 2.

The Island Lysøen, and Ole Bull's villa. This distinctive villa and concert hall were built in 1872 by the world–famous violin virtuoso Ole Bull, as a summer residence and meeting place for his many friends. The villa is largely unchanged since Bull's death there in 1880.

Ole Bull built a network of walking paths all over the island, with a total length of some 13 km. (eight miles). These paths provide pleasant rural walking for the visitor.

For information on access and guided tours contact the Information Office.

Rosenkrantz Tower. (314 380). Erected by the feudal lord of Bergenhus in the 1560s as a fortified official residence, the tower was badly damaged by an explosion in 1944. It was restored 1945–65. Open May 15 through Sept. 14, daily 10–4; off season, Sun. 12–3. Admission Nok. 4, children Nok. 2.

Troldhaugen. Hop (135 438). Edvard Grieg's home for 22 years, situated beside the Nordås lake. Grieg composed many of his best–known works here, and he and his wife are buried here. Open May 2 through Oct. 1, daily 11–2 and 3–6. Open only in the afternoon during the Festival period. Admission Nok. 6, children Nok. 3.

Wall Gate. Built in 1562 by the feudal lord of Bergenhus. On the ground floor, trade has been carried out in much the same way for 400 years.

SPORTS. Swimming. The *Nordnes sjøbad,* an outdoor heated swimming pool, is situated near the Aquarium and Helleneset. South of Bergen there are swimming places at *Grønevika* near the Arboretum at Milde; *Austrevågen,* Krokeide; *Mjølkevika,* Stend; and *Os.* North of Bergen there are swimming areas at *Tømmervågen; Våganeset,* Åstveit; and *Vollane,* Eidsvåg.

MUSIC, MOVIES AND THEATERS. The most important event of the Bergen cultural year is the *Bergen International Festival,* which takes place over 15 days in late-May and early-June, with a splendid programme of music, drama, ballet, folklore, arts and entertainment. Details of the great variety of events are published in a separate festival brochure. Tickets are available from the Festival Office, Grieg Hall (tel. 313 104 or 320 406).

Music. The music of Edvard Grieg is often featured in Bergen. During the summer there are daily recitals of his work at the *Rasmus Meyer Art Collection,* 7 Rasmus Meyer's Alle. These recitals are for one hour, beginning at 4 P.M. Tickets at the entrance. There are also recitals of Grieg's music at *Troldhaugen,* his home, every Wednesday during the summer, and daily during the festival period.

A special feature is the *Grieg Hall,* Bergen's new concert hall, with its unusual architecture.

The city Brass Band play in the *City Park* many evenings in summer, and sometimes at lunchtime if the weather is good. They also play at the entrance to King Haakon's Hall on Thursdays from 12–1, during summer.

Movies. All movies shown in the cinemas of Bergen are in the original language with subtitles in Norwegian. Performances from 11 A.M.–11 P.M.

Theaters. A permanent theater was founded in 1838, the oldest in the country—*Den Nationale Scene.* Note that it is closed in July and August. They perform Norwegian plays alternating with musicals and light entertainment.

NORWAY

SHOPPING. If you are going to Bergen you might wish to hold back on furs till you have been to *Motepels,* the shop which is perhaps among the best in Norway for serving the overseas visitor. Prices for export are reasonable, though your own customs man may not be when you return home, so check with your consulate before making a large purchase.

We must also mention the handwrought silver of *Theodor Olsen,* to be found here in his own shop. *Prydkunst Hjertholm,* Torgalmenning 8, has a good assortment of pewter and textiles. *Husfliden,* Vagsalmenning, and Østre Skostredet, is best for authentic homemade arts and crafts.

RESTAURANTS. Bergen's "vista-vision" restaurants, *Bellevue* and *Fløyen,* provide magnificent views of the city and fjord beyond. In town are a number of fashionable restaurants, particularly in the two luxury hotels *(Norge* and *SAS Royal).* The following restaurants can also be recommended.

Expensive

Bellevue. Bellevuebakken 9 (310 240). On hillside overlooking city and fjord, in charming 17th century manor, silver, crystal, good food and personalized service. AE, DC, MC, V.

Moderate

Bryggen Tracteursted. Bryggestredet (314 046). In Hanseatic surroundings. You may buy live fish from the fish market and ask the chef to prepare it any way you want it! DC.

Bryggestuen Restaurant. Bryggen 6 (310 630). Popular for morning coffee and light lunch. AE, DC, MC, V.

Chianti. Strømgaten 8 (326 430). At central bus station, speciality spaghetti and fish, dancing daily except Mon. MC.

Excellent. Torvgaten 1a (327 735). Grill, speciality sea food. Show Boat dancing every night. AE, DC, MC, V.

Fløyen Restaurant. Fløyen, at top of funicular, famous view of city and fjord, grill, openair restaurant in summer, dancing.

Grand Cafe. Olav Kyrresgate 11 (317 732). Opposite Norge Hotel, speciality Chinese food and—in season—boiled cod; pavement cafe in summer.

Holbergstuen. Torvalmenning 6 (318 015). Will serve fish any way you want it, popular meeting place.

Holms Discosteak House. Kong Oscarsgate 45 (315 930). Grill, dancing on weekdays. DC.

Villa Amorini. Rasmus Meyer's Allé 5 (310 039) New, good food. AE, DC, MC, V.

Wesselstuen. Engen 14 (322 900). Pot luck and fish, much frequented any time of day, favorite haunt of the Bergensers.

NIGHTLIFE. There are not many nightclubs in Bergen, but several of the restaurants provide some sort of entertainment, often with music and dancing until the small hours of the morning. The two big hotels *(Norge* and *SAS Royal)* both have night spots, with dancing until 3 A.M. every night. There is also *Christian,* in Chr. Michelsensgate (320 262), which remains popular.

Hotels Along the Bergen Railroad

ÅL (Buskerud). 436 to 1,100 meters (1,430 to 3,610 feet). *Bergsjø* (M), (067-84 630). 25 km. (15 miles) by bus from station, 140 beds, most rooms with facilities, swimming, sauna, solarium, trout fishing, ptarmigan shooting (Sept.), fine skiing terrain, ski lift, ski school. MC, V. *Sundre* (I), 48 beds, some rooms with bath/shower. MC.

BERGEN

FINSE (Hordaland). 1,223 meters (4,010 feet), magnificent surroundings of mountains and glaciers. This is where Captain Scott trained for his South Pole expedition of 1910–11; and later both *Scott of the Antarctic* and *The Empire Strikes Back* were shot here. The skiing season lasts until May, but you can ascend the glacier on skis in mid-summer! *Finse Hotel* (M), (055-26 733). 19 rooms, all with facilities, swimming. MC, V. *Finse 1222* (I), (055-26 711). 90 rooms, restaurant, disco, sauna.

GEILO (Buskerud). 800 meters (2,625 feet), renowned tourist center and ski resort, varied terrain, ski lifts, ski school, skating rink. *Bardøla* (E), (067-85 008). 180 beds, 95 rooms with facilities, swimming, sauna, resident orchestra. AE, DC, MC, V. *Holms* (E), (067-85 622). One of the most famous resort hotels in Norway, 140 beds, all rooms with facilities. AE, DC, MC, V. *Vestlia* (E), (067-85 611). 146 beds, all rooms with facilities, swimming. AE, DC, MC, V. *Geilo Apartment Hotel* (M), (067-85 005). 240 beds, 30 apartments, each for 4 persons. *Geilo Hotel* (M), (067-85 511). 145 beds, all rooms with bath/shower. DC, MC, V. *Highland* (M), (067-85 600). 174 beds, most rooms with facilities. AE, DC, MC, V. *Ustedalen* (M), (067-85 111). 100 beds, all rooms with facilities. DC, MC, V.

Youth Hostel. *Geilo Youth Hostel* (I), (067-85 300). 200 beds, comfortable.

GOL (Buskerud). 207 meters (680 feet), ski center, lift, marked trails. *Eidsgaard* (M), (067-74 955). 60 rooms. AE, DC, MC, V. *Pers* (M), (067-74 500). 270 beds, all rooms with facilities, swimming. AE, MC, V. *Gol Camping/ Apartment* (I), (067-74 023). 170 beds.

MJØLFJELL (Hordaland). 714 meters (2,340 feet), grand area for ski touring.

Youth Hostel. *Mjølfjell Youth Hostel* (I), (055-18 111). Six km. (four miles) from station, 140 beds, sauna, all meals, popular.

OPPHEIM (Hordaland). 26 km. (16 miles) by bus from Voss, 332 meters (1,090 feet), good skiing country, chairlift. *Oppheim* (M), (055-22 500). 94 beds, some rooms with bath. AE, DC, MC, V. *Vossestølen* (I), 48 beds, 13 rooms with bath.

STALHEIM (Hordaland). 35 km. (22 miles) by bus from Voss, overlooking the Nerøy valley. Zig-zag road now bypassed by giant tunnel, opened 1980, but hairpin bends still there in summer for venturesome motorists. *Stalheim* (E), (055-22 122). Outstanding, 212 beds, all rooms with facilities, souvenir shop with local arts and crafts, museum. MC, V.

USTAOSET (Buskerud). 991 meters (3,250 feet), views of Mt Hallingskarvet, good ski touring. *Ustaoset Mountain Hotel* (M), (067-87 161). 147 beds, all rooms with facilities. AE, DC, MC, V. *Ustaoset Motel* (I), (067-87 123). 50 beds.

VATNAHALSEN (Sogn). On Flåm railroad, 850 meters (2,790 feet), good skiing terrain. *Vatnahalsen* (M), (055-18 722). 80 beds, many rooms with bath.

VOSS (Hordaland). 55 meters (180 feet), large village facing lake Vang, educational center of the province. St Olav stone cross from 1023. Finneloftet, built around 1250, Norway's oldest nonecclesiastical timber building. Voss Folk Museum, ancient farmhouses at Mølster and Nesheim. Voss church, completed 1277 with two–meter (seven–foot) thick walls. Cablecar to mountain top with panoramic restaurant. *Fleischer* (M), (055-11 155). 122 beds, all rooms with facilities, swimming, sauna. AE, DC, MC, V. *Jarl* (M), (055-11 933). 130 beds, 35 rooms with facilities, sauna. AE, DC, MC, V. *Kringsjå Pension* (M), (055-11 627). 34 beds, all rooms with facilities. MC, V. *Park* (M), (055-11 322). 96 beds, all rooms with facilities. AE, DC, MC, V. *Vossevangen* (M), (055-12 144). 130

beds, 45 rooms with bath/shower. DC. *Nøring Pension* (I), (055–11 211). 45 beds. *Rondo Pension* (I), (055–11 980). 45 beds, 10 rooms with bath. MC.

Youth Hostel. *Voss Youth Hostel* (I), (055–12 017). Facing lake Vang, special facilities for handicapped, 220 beds, cafeteria.

ANCIENT TRONDHEIM AND DISTRICT

Stronghold of Crown and Church

A glance at the map will show you that Trondheim is situated more or less where Norway's long tadpole-like tail joins the rounded body which is usually described as South Norway, and it is not surprising that the Viking kings should have chosen this site for their first capital. From the sheltered waters of the land-locked Trondheim Fjord their longboats would sail out on raids that carried them west to the coast of America and east to the shores of the Byzantine Empire.

Norwegian towns have a disconcerting habit of reverting to their former names, but you may rest assured that Trondheim has now made up its mind as to what it wants to be called. This city was once the capital of Norway under the name of Nidaros, and when the Norwegian people were seized 40 years ago with a burning desire to toss aside newfangled names of a mere 300 years' standing, the authorities in Oslo (then Christiania) decided to change Trondheim back to Nidaros. However, they were reckoning without the proverbial obstinacy of the Trönder, and Trondheim it remains to this day.

Exploring Trondheim and District

Trondheim is a delightful city, possibly the only one in Norway with a genuine air of the medieval about it. King Olav Tryggvason founded the town in the 10th century on the southern shores of the fjord of the same name, where the Nid River runs into the sea. Just before the river pours its waters into the fjord, it makes an abrupt loop, so that the triangle of land on which Trondheim stands is surrounded on two sides by the river and on one side by the sea, and is thus a sort of peninsula connected to the mainland by a narrow strip. A number of bridges cross the Nid River to modern suburbs, but the essential Trondheim is to be found north and west of the Nid.

The cathedral occupies an imposing position to the south. From it a broad avenue runs straight through the central part of the old town to the statue of King Olav in the marketplace.

Sitting at home, you may imagine that a visit to Trondheim would resemble one of Amundsen's polar explorations, but the climate is essentially continental, with surprisingly warm summers. Furthermore, Trondheim is not only a cultural and industrial center, but the hub of a large agricultural district which in some years actually exports hay to the British Isles. Trondheim is also an excellent winter sports center, and it is not surprising that in recent years local skiers and skaters have created almost a monopoly of championships in Norwegian winter sports.

Cathedral, Capital and Court

In the Middle Ages Trondheim enjoyed a European reputation when the great Nidaros Cathedral was raised as a shrine to Saint Olav, King of Norway and one of the greatest figures from the Saga Age. King Olav's shrine was visited by pilgrims from every Christian land in the world, and a chain of inns or hostels was built all the way from Oslo in the south, through the broad-bosomed Gudbrandsdal, over the mighty back of Mount Dovre and down to the Gothic cathedral by the banks of the Nid River. This cathedral, now almost completely restored, still stands in all its pristine glory, and it is not only the pride of the citizens, but Trondheim's chief claim to fame. The architecture bears clear marks of the influence of the English Gothic style and it is probable that English masons assisted in its erection.

When the cathedral was built, Trondheim was the undisputed capital of Norway: here the king had his court and here the ecclesiastical dignitaries had their seat. On the little island of Munkholmen, which lies like a cruiser at anchor in the bay, you can still see the ruins of an old monastery, bringing to mind Longfellow's own description of the island in his poem *The Saga of King Olav,* where he says, "At Nidarholm the priests are all singing."

King Haakon VII of Norway was crowned here in 1906, but formal coronations are no longer a part of the ceremonies of state in Norway. Still, it is interesting to know that it was here that all Norway's kings—including Canute, King of Denmark, Norway and England—were elected by the old Norse *tings,* the 10th-century forerunners of the modern Norwegian Storting, or Parliament.

Like most Norwegian towns, Trondheim has from time to time suffered devastating fires, but in one respect Trondheim was more fortunate than either Oslo or Bergen. In the 17th century, after most of the residential quarters had been razed to the ground, a town planning scheme was carried out by Johan Cicignon, a Norwegian of French extraction, who replaced many of the narrow twisting streets with broad avenues. To this canny "foreigner" the people of Trondheim owe the spacious layout of their town. Some people may consider it a little too spacious for its size, though the narrow streets which survived the first contrast charmingly with the well-planned, orderly alleys and streets of Cicignon.

Other Notable Buildings

The Stiftsgården, or royal residence, used by the King whenever he visits Trondheim, is a magnificent structure in late baroque style dating from 1775. Incidentally, this is the second largest wooden building in Scandinavia, and doubtless provides the local firemen with an oversize headache. The largest, Singsaker Studenthjem, also belongs to Trondheim. The Bishop's Palace, only a stone's throw from the cathedral, is another interesting relic of the medieval days when Trondheim had some 16 churches and two monasteries. From the nearby market place the statue of King Olav Tryggvason, Carlyle's "wildly beautifullest" king, surveys the town he founded in the year 997.

In the Folk Museum you will find an excellent collection of buildings, customs and implements illustrating the life in Trondheim and surrounding districts in medieval times. The Kunstforeningen Art Gallery, with a fine collection of paintings by representative Norwegian artists, and the Fortress of Kristianstein, which in the old heroic days guarded Trondheim from the landward side, are also both worth a visit. The latter is situated on a rocky eminence to the east of the city, where it commands a magnificent view of the fjord and of Munkholmen.

On another rise overlooking Trondheim Fjord is Ringve. The estate dates from the 1600s but was given to the city, as a music center, by the will of the last owner, who was responsible for acquiring many of the fine and rare instruments including a magnificent harpsichord once housed at Versailles.

Trondheim, in common with Bergen, has older cultural traditions than Oslo, which both cities regard as somewhat of an interloper, or at best an upstart. While Bergen glories in a Philharmonic Orchestra which is the third oldest in the world, antedating its counterpart in Vienna by a good 70 years, Trondheim has a number of societies which make their opposite numbers in Oslo mere striplings by comparison. Chief among these is the Videnskapsselskapet, or Academy of Sciences, which has been running ever since the 18th century.

Trondheim is also the site of Norway's Tekniske Hågskole, where Norway's architects and engineers receive their training. This institute is now part of the university, and in the course of time a student milieu has grown up in the town unlike that of any other Norwegian city. The University of Bergen, founded in 1948, is as yet only an infant in arms, while the students at the University of Oslo tend to be swallowed up in the capital and have little chance of giving it the stamp of a university town. Not so Trondheim, where the students have their own special societies, clubs and restaurants, and put on a musical revue every other year that is not only traditional, but a box-office success as well.

The Tröndelag Provinces

Few parts of Norway are so varied in their scenery as the twin counties of North Tröndelag and South Tröndelag, of which Trondheim is the capital. Apart from the agricultural districts, there are vast forests, rivers and waterfalls, fjords and mountains.

These provinces are also unusually rich in historical mementos, including such sights as the old ting-place at Frosta, where representatives from eight counties met regularly to pass laws and mete out justice from A.D. 940 right up to the 16th century. No place in Norwegian history is better known than the battlefield of Stiklestad, where St. Olav met his death in A.D. 1030, and where the church was built, on the very spot he was slain, a hundred years after the battle. The Reformation proved a stirring time for Tröndelag, the citadel of Roman Catholicism in the north. Olav Engelbriktsson, last archbishop of Norway, held out in his fortified castle of Steinvikholm (interesting ruins) before fleeing the country. Austråt Castle, at the mouth of the Trondheim Fjord, has been described as the most original building of the Norwegian Renaissance, and in the 17th century the copper-mining town of Röros was founded. Röros is a favorite excursion from Trondheim by rail or road, as this remarkable little town, immortalized in the great novels of Johan Falkberget, has retained its original appearance right down to the present. The old mines were closed in 1978, but have now been re-opened as a unique museum. There are guided tours throughout the year to the Olav mine.

The other great resort of Tröndelag is the mountain village of Oppdal on the Dovre Railway. At Oppdal, some of Norway's longest lifts whisk the visitor up to the Troll Eye Restaurant, 1,037 meters (3,400 feet) above sea level, from where there is a superb panorama of the surrounding mountains.

If you have a sense of the macabre, you might go to Hell—quite literally. Hell in this case is not a roaring inferno where sinister-looking gentlemen will chase you around with pitchforks, but a charming little railway station not more than half an hour by train from Trondheim. You will have the satisfaction of being able to buy a round-trip ticket, and you should not miss the opportunity of mailing a letter or two and taking advantage of the unique postmark.

PRACTICAL INFORMATION FOR TRONDHEIM AND DISTRICT

TOURIST INFORMATION. *Trondheim Travel Association*, Kongensgate 7, 7000 Trondheim (07–511 466). Accommodations service, guides, sightseeing, brochures, etc. Open Mon. to Sat. 9–6, Sun. 10–5.

ANCIENT TRONDHEIM AND DISTRICT

USEFUL ADDRESSES. Travel Agents. *Bennett Reisebureau A/S*, Dronningensgt 12 (07-520 620). *Universitetenes Reisebyrå*, NTH Gløshaugen (07-593 277) and Avd. Dragvoll (07-596 759). *Winge Reisebureau A/S*, O. Tryggvasonsgt. 30 (07-533 000).
Consulates. Great Britain, Sluppenvn. 10 (07-968 211).

TELEPHONE CODES. We have given telephone codes for all the towns and villages in the hotel and restaurant lists that follow. These codes need only be used when calling from outside the town or village concerned.

HOTELS AND RESTAURANTS. Though by no means as large or as well-known as its more famous rivals, Bergen and Oslo, Trondheim is nonetheless well provided with both hotels and restaurants in most price ranges.

LEVANGER (Nord-Trøndelag). Area rich in archeological finds. *Backlund* (M), Kirkegt 41 (076-81 600). 120 beds, most rooms with bath. DC, MC. *IMI* (I), bed and breakfast only, 75 beds, mission hotel.
Youth Hostel. *Levanger Youth Hostel* (I), (076-81 638). 58 beds.

MERÅKER (Nord-Trøndelag). Folk museum, old copper mines, skiing, chairlift. *Meråker Inn* (M), 85 beds, some rooms with bath. *Teveltunet* (M), (07-813 611). 100 beds in cabins and main building, most rooms with shower/toilet. Fishing, riding.

NAMSOS (Nord-Trøndelag). Small mountain in center of town, Namdal folk museum. *Grand Hotel Bondeheimen* (M), (077-73 155). 77 beds, 10 rooms with bath. *Namsen Motel* (M), (077-76 100). 101 beds, all rooms with bath/shower.

OPPDAL (Sør-Trøndelag). 537 meters (1,790 feet), popular ski resort with all facilities, curling, skating. *Hovd Inn Sportell* (M), (074-21 911). 94 beds, all rooms with facilities, swimming, sauna. AE, DC, MC, V. *Mullerhotel* (M), (074-21 611). 62 rooms, all with shower/toilet. Dancing, bar, restaurant. DC, V. *Oppdal Turisthotel* (M), (074-21 111). 90 rooms, most with shower/toilet. Swimming, sauna, dancing, bar, good restaurant. DC, MC, V.
Youth Hostel. *Turistheimen* (I), (074-21 330). 48 beds, cafeteria.

ORKANGER (Sør-Trøndelag). *Bårdshaug Herregård* (E), (074-81 055). Converted manor, 117 beds, many rooms with bath, swimming, sauna. MC, V.

RØROS (Sør-Trøndelag). *Bergstadens Tourist Hotel* (E), Osloveien 2 (074-11 111). 130 beds, all rooms with facilities, swimming, sauna. AE, DC, MC. *Røros Tourist Hotel* (M), (074-11 011). 226 beds, all rooms with facilities, swimming, sauna. MC.
Youth Hostel. *Røros Youth Hostel* (I), (074-11 089). 120 beds.

STEINKJER (Nord-Trøndelag). Fold museum, burial mounds, salmon fishing. *Grand* (E), Kongensgt 37 (077-64 700). 180 beds, most rooms with facilities, sauna, restaurant. DC, MC, V.

TRONDHEIM. *Ambassadeur* (E), Elvegate 18 (07-527 050). 85 beds, all rooms with facilities, roof terrace. AE, DC, MC, V. *Astoria* (E), Nordregate 24 (07-529 550). 103 beds, most rooms with facilities, restaurant, bistro, dancing, bar. DC, MC, V. *Britannia* (E), Dronningensgate 5 (07-530 040). 180 beds, all rooms with facilities, excellent Palm Garden restaurant, breakfast/lunch restaurant, bar. AE, DC, MC, V. *Larssens* (E), Ths Angellsgate 10 (07-528 851). 45 beds, most rooms with facilities, restaurant. AE, MC, V.

Nye Sentrum (E), Olav Tryggvasonsgate 5 (07-520 524). 98 beds, most rooms with facilities, restaurant and cafeteria. DC, MC, V. *Prinsen* (E), Kongensgate 30 (07-530 650). 110 beds, 70 rooms with facilities, excellent Coq d'Or restaurant, bistro, cafeteria, grill, wine lodge, beer garden. AE, DC, MC, V. *Residence Hotell* (E), Torget (07-528 380). 150 beds, most rooms with facilities, bar, restaurant, openair restaurant in summer. DC, MC, V. *Royal Garden Hotel* (E), Kjøpmannsgt. 73 (07-534 010). 600 beds, top standard, opened 1984, indoor pool, gymnasium, solarium, sauna. MC, V.

Esso Motor Hotel (M), Brøsetveien 186 (07-939 500). 300 beds, all rooms with facilities, sauna, restaurant, bar. AE, DC, MC, V. *Gildevangen* (M), Søndregate 22b (07-528 340). 71 beds, some rooms with bath/shower, dining rooms and cafeteria, unlicenced. AE, DC, MC, V. *IMI* (M), Kongensgate 26 (07-528 348). Mission hotel, 120 beds, dining room, unlicenced. AE, DC, MC, V. *Neptun* (M), Ths Angellsgate 10b (07-512 133). 60 beds with facilities, bistro. AE, MC, V. *Norrøna Misjonshospits* (M), Ths Angellsgate 20 (07-532 020). Mission hotel, 35 beds, cafeteria, unlicenced. *Trønderheimen* (M), Kongensgate 15 (07-527 030). 85 beds, some rooms with bath/shower, dining room, cafeteria. AE, MC.

Singsaker Sommerhotell (I), Rogersgate 1 (07-520 092). Summer only (June 15 through Aug. 15), 200 beds, some rooms with bath/shower, sauna, restaurant. AE, MC, V.

Restaurants. The most elegant restaurants in Trondheim are found in the leading hotels, such as *Britannia* and *Prinsen* described above, but in addition the following restaurants can be recommended. *Bajazzo Rica* (M), Søndregate 15 (07-525 760). Grill, dancing, disco, billiards, nightclub. AE, DC, MC, V. *Benito* (M), Vår Fruegate 4 (07-26 422). Italian food, wine lodge. AE, V. *Braseriet* (M), Nordregate 11. Pizzeria, disco, openair cafe in summer. *Cavalero* (M), Kongensgate 3 (07-523 303). Restaurant, grill, bar. MC. *China House* (M), Søndregate 17 (07-525 220). Chinese food, closed Mon. MC, V. *Daniel* (M), Tinghusplass 1. Steakhouse and grill. *Erichsen* (M), Nordregt 8 (07-521 960). Lunch and dinner, bar. AE, MC. *Grenaderen* (M), Kongsgården (07-522 006). Music, openair restaurant in summer. AE, DC, MC, V. *Krovertens Hus* (M), Nordregate 23 (07-534 815). Three different restaurants, dancing. AE, MC, V. *Kunstnerkroen* (M), Prinsensgate 38 (07-521 880). Intimate, artistic restaurant with music, dancing, bar. DC, MC. *Landlord Pub* (M), Prinsensgate 40 (07-522 515). English pub. MC. *Munken Kro, Pizzeria Frati* (M), Munkegt 25. Italian food and pizza. *Naustloftet* (M), Prinsensgate 42 (07-521 880). Seafood restaurant, bar. DC, MC. *Peppe's Pizza Pub* (M), Kjøpmannsgate 25. American pizza parlor in old warehouse. *Zia Teresa, Pizzeria* (M), Vår Frue Strete.

Youth Hostel. *Trondheim Youth Hostel* (I), Weidemannsvei 41 (07-530 490). 200 beds, cafeteria.

Camping. *Flak Camping.* Flak ferry harbor, highway 715, 11 km. (seven miles) west. (07-835 108). 2 cabins, 60 caravans. *Sandmoen Camping.* Heimdal, 11 km. (seven miles) south. (07-886 135). 27 cabins, 14 rooms, minigolf. *Storsand Gård, Motell and Camping.* Malvik (07-976 360). 40 cabins, tents and caravans, minigolf, openair bathing.

HOW TO GET AROUND. By bus. The bus station in Trondheim is situated at Sverresgt. 3 (07-527 322). The staff can be contacted for information on itineraries and prices for services throughout the district. The bus station also has a separate office dealing with longer trips. Motor coaches can be booked through travel agents.

By steamship. The coastal express steamer Bergen—Kirkenes northbound and southbound calls daily at Trondheim. For reservations and timetables inquire at any travel agent. There are also express steamer services from Trondheim to Vanvikan (190 passengers, frequent departures daily) and from Trondheim, via Brekstad, Hitra, and Frøya to Sula (140 passengers, at least two departures daily).

ANCIENT TRONDHEIM AND DISTRICT 345

By car ferry. The most important are: Flakk (Trondheim)—Rørvik (Fosen); Valset (Agdenes)—Brekstad (Ørland); Sunde (Snillfjord)—Sandstad (Hitra); and Kjerringvåg (Hitra)—Flatval (Frøya). All have frequent departures all year round, and the crossings take 20–25 minutes. Tickets can be bought at travel agents or *Fosen Trafikklag,* Fosenkaia, Post Box 512, N-7001 Trondheim (07-525 540). Advance bookings cannot be accepted.

By train. The Nordland Railway goes through the entire length of North Tröndelag, and the Dovre and Röros Railways go through South Tröndelag. There is also the Meråker–Sweden Railway, which goes through to Stockholm once daily.

By taxi. In Trondheim, to call a taxi day or night, phone 07–527 600. There are taxi stands at Torget (Market Place), Søndregt., Nordregt., and Studentersamfunnet.

TOURS. There are many interesting tours of one to four days, that can be made around the Trondheim district, either by car or by bus. The Trondheim Travel Association should be contacted for details and further suggestions. Some examples are: the Atlantic tour to Hitra and Frøya, a three-day round trip from Trondheim, through Orkanger, Sunde and on to Sandstad (Hitra); a fishing trip to Åfjord, for which a stay of at least two days is recommended, for deep sea fishing, salmon fishing in rivers, and brown trout fishing in lakes and streams; and a trip around the Trollheimen (a "see–Norway–in–a–nutshell" tour) going Trondheim—Oppdal—Sunndalsøra—Orkanger—Trondheim.

There are also short tours around Trondheim itself, by bus, tram or even on foot. Ask the local Tourist Office for details.

PLACES TO VISIT. The principal sights of the district include: *Röros,* with its old copper mines; *Oppdal,* with its alpine character; *Austråt Castle* at the mouth of the Trondheim Fjord; the battlefield and church at *Stiklestad;* the Frosta *ting*-place; the village of *Hell;* and the rock drawings at *Hegra.* Trondheim itself has quite a number of museums, art galleries and places of historic interest. The Tourist Office will have further details; however, among the more interesting places are: the *Folkemuseet* (Folk Museum) at Sverresborg, which is Trøndelag's museum of urban and rural culture. Buildings have been brought to the site from all over the country and reassembled to provide an authentic cross–section of life and architecture of the past; the island of *Munkholmen,* which in pagan times was a place of execution. In early Christian times an abbey was built there, probably the first in Norway. After the Reformation it was converted into a fortress. Today the island is a public bathing resort; the *Nidaros Cathedral,* Scandinavia's largest medieval building, erected on the shrine of St. Olav. The cathedral (built around 1150) is the center of the annual festivals that commemorate the traditions that surround the name and person of St. Olav; and the *Ringve Gods* (Ringve Museum of Musical History), which is at Ringve Manor, Lade. Visits are based exclusively on conducted tours run by the museum's own guides. Each tour (in Norwegian, English or German) lasts about 80 minutes and includes demonstrations of musical instruments.

PARKS. Not far from the Ringve Music Museum is the Ringve Botanical Garden, at the University of Trondheim, Lade Allé (07–914 620). The garden is open all year and admission is free. Conducted tours of the openair exhibitions are available by appointment.

SPORTS. Outdoor life is the chief attraction. **Swimming** in the Trondheim Fjord may be chilly, but is popular with the Trönders themselves. Excellent trout and salmon **fishing** is within reach; in the Namsen, Gaula, Nea, Orkla, and Stjördal rivers. The mountains of Snasa and Namdal in the north, and Sylene in the south, also provide good angling. Elk **hunting** in the Snåsa forests is the best in Norway, and the coastal islands, especially Hitra, are the haunt of red deer. Ptarmigan, a game bird similar to grouse, can be shot during September and October.

Mountaineering and **hiking** in the Trollheimen and Sylene districts, where there are trails and charming chalets.

Trondheim is one of the few towns to boast a **golf course** (9 holes), which is situated at an elevation of 215 meters (700 feet), overlooking the cathedral city and the fjord. Famous for its annual Midnight Sun Golf Tournament. On the outskirts of town, Trondheim, much the same as Oslo, has its own private stretch of **skiing** country, Bymarka. Easily reached from the center of town by bus or train (20 minutes), it is a sportsman's paradise. **Skistua,** opposite the Gråkallen ski jump, is the center. Ski lift and ski trails in all directions.

Other centers include Meråker, Oppdal and Røros, as described above.

WAY TO THE NORTH

Folklore, Finnmark and the Midnight Sun

Norway's main problem was how to care for tourists, not how to attract them. This is still true of northern Norway. From Steinkjer at latitude 64° on up towards the Arctic Ocean, it's just one feast of scenic beauty after another, and the whole, incredible northern outdoors is lit up by both the noonday and the midnight sun. From the moment you pull away from the quay and head out of the Trondheim Fjord, you know that a new kind of adventure has begun.

Exploring North Norway

The great charm of the express steamer trip is seeing the sights when they appear, no matter how awkward the hour. The 240-meter (800-foot) stone mountain, Torghatten, for example, is passed about 1 A.M., and there's enough light to observe the famous hole clear through the rock about halfway up and a good 150 meters (500 feet) long. Geologists talk about the action of waves washing out this tunnel when the shoreline was much higher, but local folklore has a far more colorful explanation which we'll come to shortly. At 4 A.M. you pass the Seven Sisters—seven snow-covered peaks, each more jagged than the last.

If you're breakfasting around eight, you'll have to stop and run out on deck when the approach to Hestmannen or The Horseman is announced. Not just because the silhouette of this rocky island, from a certain point, looks remarkably like a horse and rider, but because he is the clue to Torghatten. It seems that Hestmannen, quite some time ago, was enamored of the Leka-Maiden near Rörvik, but she paid no attention to him. Whereupon the enraged Horseman shot a long-distance arrow at her, only to have it intercepted by Torg who threw his hat in the way; hence the great hole. To top things off, when the sun rose, everyone involved in the affair was turned into stone, including the Seven Sisters, who fled with the Leka-Maiden.

At the north end of the petrified Hestmannen you encounter something far more stimulating to the imagination than folklore, though quite invisible. This is the imaginary parallel of 66° 32′ North of the Arctic Circle, and once it is crossed, you are in that much-advertised, much-described Land of the Midnight Sun. The coastal express boat calls at the little village of Ørnes, and overland excursions are arranged by bus via the Saltstraumen *maelstrom* (or whirlpool) to Bodø.

After a forenoon among the ever-present islands you dock at Bodø where you stay for a couple of hours.

By engaging a cab, you may even have time to combine looking across the Salt Fjord south of Bodø towards the spot where the notorious Salstraumen churns and eddies during each change of tide, with a quick trip to the Rønvik Restaurant three km. (two miles) north of town. From here there's a panorama of rock masses, islands, valleys and fjords that will open the eyes of the most scenery-satiated traveler.

There would also be a fine view of the Midnight Sun from Rønvik if you stayed there long enough, but by midnight the *hurtig-rute* is steaming through Raft Sound in the Lofoten Islands. In fact, by supper time you are close upon the "Lofot-Wall", as the Norwegians so aptly describe the jagged series of mountain peaks of this island-chain.

Catch as Catch Can

First it's Stamsund at 7 P.M., one of the largest of the many fishing ports and shipping centers in the Lofotens, where the scenery consists of boats, warehouses, rocky shores covered with wooden racks for drying codfish, and steep snow-covered mountains in the not-distant background. About two hours later it's Svolvaer, largest town of the islands and with the same sights, only more of them.

Svolvaer is also the fishing capital of the north during the cod season each winter in February and March. Furthermore, it is already something of a tourist center at that time, since many hardy travelers each winter take advantage of special excursions by boat to witness this fantastic spectacle. Thousands of craft of all kinds engage in fishing with all kinds of gear. But there's plenty of fish for everyone, no matter what his apparatus, and all return loaded to the gunwales. On shore the activity is equally hectic, for all these tons of cod must be cleaned and processed; fillets are sent away for deep-freezing, livers for stewing, roe for canning and the split cod is hung up to dry into *törr-fisk*.

"But some places they don't bother with such drying contrivances," says the friendly captain. "Near Kristiansund, for example, the cod are just spread out on the bare rocks along the shore. We've got plenty of those, you know. That's why around there, they're called *klipp-fisk*, for *klipp* means cliff."

WAY TO THE NORTH

"Where's that Midnight Sun?" you'll sooner or later ask. The answer will be disappointing. Throughout June and most of July there is plenty of twilight, or rather a combined sunset and sunrise effect, but there are too many islands and mountain walls for you to see the sun when it approaches the horizon at midnight. So, after looking at the wildest parts of the Lofot Wall—Digermulen Mountain and the narrow Raft Sound which you sail through after leaving Svolvaer—you may as well turn in for some much-needed sleep. Of course, if you are troubled with insomnia you'll find plenty to look at all night while the steamer winds among the Vesterålen Islands, which in contrast to the Lofotens, are amazingly flat.

Before breakfast the second full day from Trondheim, you can go ashore in Harstad for an hour and a half. Not only is this an important fish-canning and shipping town, but it can show, a couple of miles north, the curious fortified church of Trondenes. Built in the 13th century, this edifice has stone walls two and a half meters thick and is one of the very few church-fortresses in Norway. Harstad is one of the few ports where the coastal steamers call simultaneously on their daily sailings southwards and northwards. Harstad, with some 22,000 inhabitants, is today a modern center of the region comprising southern parts of Troms county and northern parts of Nordland county.

Senja island, between Harstad and Tromsø, is the second largest island in Norway, with interesting small fishing and farming communities; there is a link with the mainland via Finnsnes. Fjords and mountains there are aplenty—visit Tranøy, Berg and Torsken.

Approaching Tromsø you pass the Rystraumen whirlpool, which can move dramatically fast. On the Rya island, in the middle of Rystraumen, a colony of 15 musk oxen live and thrive.

At Tromsö, the capital of Troms Province and the largest city above the Arctic Circle, the Midnight Sun is still elusive because of those ever-present mountains to the north. In any case, you can get a good night's rest and look at the sights next day. These include the longest bridge in Northern Europe spanning the Tromsö Sound, the gondola lift to Storsteinen, the Tromsdalen Church, the Observatory for Northern Lights—which devotes the long Arctic night to studying the Aurora Borealis—and another well-known scientific institution, the Tromsö Arctic Museum.

If you don't want to go on an expedition for your polar bear, you can meet one in the street in Tromsö itself, but stuffed into immobility. You'll find others, the alive kind, at the zoo, together with seals and otters. But don't wander too far, at 6 P.M. that next *hurtig-rute* leaves with you on board, according to our plan. And this night is your first real chance for a look at the sun, weather permitting, for here's an open space northward between the two islands of Vannöy and Arnöy which the steamer should cross around midnight.

At about 4.30 A.M., the steamer reaches Hammerfest. Again there's an hour for sightseeing, and this time you are in the northernmost city in the world. (By the way, Hammerfest was also the first town in Norway to install electric lights: in 1891). Climb the 100-meter hill just behind the town for a good look at this plucky little community and its not-too-friendly natural environment. Not only was it completely razed in late 1944 by the retreating Nazis, who applied scorched earth destruction to almost all of Finnmark Province, but it has also been damaged repeatedly by avalanches. Yet in spite of all handicaps the town was rebuilt, and one of its most impressive sights is the church with its tall tower shaped like an elongated Lapp tent or *kåta*.

Fish export is the main industry of Hammerfest, together with tourist trade in normal times, and here you will see another of the deep-freezing plants which have revolutionized the processing of fish in these parts. Fresh frozen fillets are rapidly replacing the age-old dried *klipp-fisk* and *stokk-fisk* as export items, and are bringing a correspondingly new year-round prosperity to communities which formerly suffered much from seasonal unemployment.

The North Cape

On leaving Hammerfest, you have only 24 hours left of the four-day cruise from Trondheim, but most of them will be spent on the very top of Norway. The steamer crosses several stretches of water that open directly north of the Arctic Ocean, and on approaching the big island of Mageröy, it may be that you'll head into this "Ice-Sea" as the natives call it.

There's not much to see except a cliff of blackish granite, either from the water or on top, but if your life ambition has been to follow the example of King Oscar II of Norway and Sweden, who climbed this northernmost piece of Europe in 1873, you can do so. The ships call at Honningsvåg, from where buses are run to North Cape to save a really steep 300-meter (1,000-foot) climb. Perhaps the best idea is to step off the ship at Honningsvåg and take an evening bus to North Cape across arctic Mageröy (literally Meager Island). The North Cape Hall will greet you upon arrival with a panorama window offering a sweeping view, and perhaps the Midnight Sun hanging above the Arctic Ocean for good measure.

The road itself was opened by King Olav (then Crown Prince) in 1956. It offers magnificent views of the Cape itself. Honningsvåg is connected by an auto-ferry with Kåfjord, the nearest point on the mainland.

The steamer now crosses the mouths of three vast fjords—Porsanger, Lakse, and Tana—all of which cut far south into the mainland, and call at some fishing villages. But the main event after the North Cape is passing the enormous bird-rock of Svaerholtklubben on the tip of the peninsula between Porsanger Fjord and Lakse Fjord. Midnight will again find you with an unobstructed view to the north so, weather permitting, you'll have another chance to watch the sun toy with the horizon as it passes without interruption from setting to rising.

There'll be an opportunity to walk around the historic fortress of Vardöhus at Vardö, the easternmost town in Norway. The most ancient part of the stronghold, now long disappeared, was constructed in the early 1300s, while the present ramparts, shaped like an eight-pointed star, date from the 1730s.

Depending on which day of the week it is, the express steamer may or may not call at Vadsö, the administrative capital of Finnmark. This town is located on the upper edge of the wide Varanger Fjord which, unlike the previous three, cuts westward instead of south. In any case, early in the morning next day, you will reach the end station of the North Norway *hurtig-rute:* the important mining town of Kirkenes.

WAY TO THE NORTH

Between Allied bombing raids and Nazi earth-scorching, both Kirkenes and the Syd-Varanger iron mines were almost totally wrecked at the end of World War II. Today, the huge plant in Kirkenes produces by magnetic separation about 1 million tonnes of iron-ore concentrate annually.

Many interesting side-trips can be made from Kirkenes. First of all, a visit to the iron mines a few kilometers from town which, being open-pit affairs, can be seen just by looking at them from the road. Then there's the road south along the Pasvik River which forms most of the boundary between Norway and Soviet Russia. The 64-km. (40-mile) drive to Skogfoss, for example, will provide a good view of the friendly scenery—birch trees, green fields and rolling hills—which is astonishingly different from the stern rockiness of the North Cape country. And you can also have a glimpse of the land on the other shore, behind the Iron Curtain. Incidentally, it's forbidden to carry cameras into this area near the border, a regulation strictly enforced by Norwegian guards.

From Kirkenes you have two new ways of returning to Trondheim: swiftly and spectacularly by plane with landings at Lakselv, Alta, Bardufoss and Bodø; or slowly and fascinatingly by bus or car, "slowly" meaning in this case exactly three days to either Tromsö or Narvik, with two overnight stops. And while the plane trip presents a wonderful bird's-eye view of the top of Norway, the slower route overland is more rewarding.

Finnmark by Bus

You leave Kirkenes after early breakfast and drive along the lower side of Varanger Fjord to Tana bridge. Then the new road runs alongside the River Tana into Lapp country. The Tana is a long and interesting river, famous for heavy salmon. It also forms the border between Norway and Finland over a long distance. The road leaves Tana river at Karasjok, one of the largest Lapp villages on the Finnmark mountain plateau, and the day's journey ends at Lakselv on the Lakse Fjord.

Of the many things which impress you on this tour, probably the most remarkable is the tremendous difference between the rocky bareness of the Arctic coast, and the mildness and fertility of inland Finnmark. Here are farms with pastures as green as any you saw in western Norway, with healthy-looking cows, goats and sheep. True enough, little grain will ripen in this far north, even with 24 hours of sunshine during part of the summer, but potatoes and other root crops give a good yield.

Another striking characteristic is that everything up here is new: houses, barns, boats, piers, even the telegraph poles. All is new for the simple reason that the Nazis burned everything in 1944; hence any manmade structure dates from 1946 or later. But in between the villages, one can drive for scores of kilometers without seeing a habitation and sometimes without even meeting another vehicle.

Next morning you leave Lakselv for another day of scenic beauty. At Skaidi, you may make a detour to Hammerfest, but the main road continues southwards along Repparfjord salmon river to Alta on the Alta Fjord. The Alta River is one of the world's best salmon waters, and millionaires have been competing throughout the last century for fishing rights.

From Alta a highway runs about 129 km. (80 miles) south to Kautokeino, a village chiefly inhabited by Lapps. This is a side-trip which can be made the year round and will let you see the semi-nomads in their own setting rather than as a tourist attraction on the side of the road. There are a number of souvenir shops in the village, as well as the atelier of Regine and Frank Juhls whose design jewelry has become famous outside Norway too. There are designs based on traditional Lappish jewelry as well as modern ones. Even if you don't intend buying any jewelry go and visit Juhls' atelier.

The Arctic Highway continues along several fjords, also across the Kvenangen peninsula, on the Sørkjosen in Troms county, where you spend the night.

Troms by Bus

The third day you have a pleasant change in routine by riding the ferry straight across Lyngen Fjord instead of following around its shores, or you may go by the new road along the eastern side of the fjord. This may also be your introduction to the custom in North Norway of allowing bus-passengers to help support the ferry company, even though they have already paid for their through ticket by bus. (It seems that this arrangement simplifies bookkeeping for the bus companies.)

Soon you are speeding nearly south along the west shore of Lyngen Fjord to Nordkjosbotn, at the south end of still another fjord, this time an old acquaintance called Bals Fjord, which stretches more or less north for 64 km. (40 miles) to Tromsö.

Olsborg is a hamlet consisting of a small inn, a service station and a few houses, in the picturesque district bordering the Målselv River. This part of Troms Province was colonized 150 years ago by pioneers from the eastern valleys in lower Norway, and today is a thriving agricultural district with solid houses and barns, and, in good years, a harvest of grain beyond the needs of the inhabitants.

In the afternoon the bus passes the sprawling Bardufoss Airport and climbs over a 425-meter (1,400-foot) pass. Here there is a good view out to sea, or rather towards the Vågs Fjord through which you sailed after leaving Harstad. Then it's down to sea level again at Bjerkvik in the midst of both spectacular and historic country, for here are many scenes of battle from World War II. Within an hour you will have crossed the magnificent new bridge across Rombaken Fjord and entered Narvik in Nordland county.

Nordland by Bus and Train

Narvik is a name that awakes a response in most travelers, whether from the Continent or from English-speaking lands. For here occurred the great naval engagement in the Ofot Fjord in April, 1940, when the Germans seized Narvik, and the ensuing campaign in which Norwegian troops, aided by British, French and Polish detachments, inflicted the first defeat of World War II upon the Nazi military machine by recapturing the town, so General Fleischer of Norway was the first field commander to defeat Hitler in battle. Narvik was, of course, a much sought-after prize because of its importance as the shipping port for the

WAY TO THE NORTH

valuable iron ore from the Swedish mines located a short way over the border at Kiruna. The town has been rebuilt and is a pleasant place. While you are there, take a look at the small museum which commemorates the action with a model reconstruction.

Besides the economic importance of Narvik, it can well stand on its own feet as a tourist center in competition with any part of Norway for its panorama of fjords with rows of snow-topped peaks in the background. During the Midnight Sun season, the combination sunset-sunrises enhance the scene with those incredible color and light effects you have now seen so many times. However, for a really breathtaking view of all this the cable railway (Fjellheisen) will carry you from the town to the Fagerness mountain plateau—well, go and look for yourself.

Ore-Train Route

The best way to combine economic studies with sightseeing is to ride the ore-carrying railway up to the mines and back, or at least as far as Björnefjell on the Norwegian-Swedish border. You can ride the regular passenger trains up and back, about one hour each way, returning in time to have dinner in Narvik and spend the evening looking around the town. As at Kirkenes there is great activity in Narvik. Ore trains run day and night, unloading their valuable contents at the tremendous quay installations where several freighters are always tied up having their holds filled, while out in the fjord are others waiting their turn. Along the streets at night and in the cafés you'll see and hear the sailors of a dozen nationalities; all of which adds to the impression of a busy cosmopolitan port.

Motorists should note that a new main road between Narvik and Kiruna was opened in September 1984.

The fourth and final day of the bus journey provides even more scenic variation and grandeur than before. Now begins a really amphibious part of the journey which we'll summarize as follows: first, a mixed run of 80 km. (50 miles) on dry land and a 40-minute cruise across a genuine fjord, Tys Fjord. Again there's a pleasant 32-km. (20-mile) dry run to Innhavet. Here you can look out over the Sag Fjord towards Svolvaer and the Lofoten Islands. But your day has only begun; moreover, you find that the stages are now getting longer. Thus it's 71 km. (44 miles) over rising and falling land to Bonåsjöen, a 15-minute sail across Leirfjord, and then a mere 48 km. (30 miles) to Fauske. At this far-inland port town you must make up your mind whether to return to Bodø—due west of here on the Skjerstad Fjord—for a closer look at the Saltstraumen *maelstrom* or to continue southward.

Fauske is your junction for the Nordlandsbane to Trondheim or Bodø, if that is your destination. Hardy travelers may want to take the night express that same evening to Trondheim. But a better plan is to take this train to Lönsdal only, spend a night or a couple of days there in magnificent mountain scenery, with a Lapp encampment, excellent trout fishing, and the wildly luxurious Junkerdal valley close at hand, and continue by day train. Whatever you do, about a half-hour from Lönsdal there will be a long blast on the locomotive's whistle. Nothing to cause alarm—it merely marks the crossing of the Arctic Circle.

Mo-i-Rana is only a brief stop for the summer expresses, but it's a fascinating place for anyone wishing to combine hiking, glacier-exploration, etc., with the study of the Norwegian kind of industrialization based on abundant hydro-electric power. The largest electric-process steel mill in Scandinavia was built by the Norwegian Government, partly financed by American contributions to the European Recovery Program which released Norwegian capital for this project.

The afternoon brings you down the long narrow handle of Norway, with stops every half-hour or so at the most important places. There's Grong, junction for the side-line to Namsos, and Steinkjer, scene of crushing air attacks upon the British Expeditionary Force which, in 1940, was trying to make its way south from Namsos.

You are now in sight of the upper end of the Trondheim Fjord, and back in North Tröndelag province. The express next stops at Verdal, where it's possible for those who are historically inclined to alight and make the brief side-trip by bus or taxi to Stiklestad, catching a local train afterwards to Trondheim.

Spitsbergen

Although it's highly unlikely you'll spend any time on the inhospitable archipelago which comprises Spitsbergen, a number of cruise ships do call in at Longyear, its administrative center. Since the treaty of 1920, Spitsbergen has been recognized as Norwegian territory but Russia still mines coal there and there is a sizeable Russian community. For the visitor, however, it's the sheer magnificence of the icy wastes which provide the attraction, especially in good weather. The icefloes provide a glimpse of a world far removed from everyday surroundings. Walking trips of 4 or 11 days were introduced in 1982. Programs are available from the Norwegian Tourist Board.

PRACTICAL INFORMATION FOR THE NORTH

TOURIST INFORMATION. Tourist information offices are located in the following places: **Bodø**, Storgt. 16 (081–21 240); **Fauske**, Salten (081–43 303). **Hammerfest**, Rådhusplassen 2 (084–12 185). **Harstad**, Torvet 7 (082–63 235). **Honningsvåg**, Holmen (084–72 894). **Karasjok** (084–66 446). **Kautokeino** (084–56 524); **Kirkenes**, Parkveien (085–92 294). **Mo I Rana** (087–50 421). **Mosjøen** (087–71 321). **Narvik**, Kongensgt. 66 (082–43 309). **Stamsund** (088–89 394). **Tromsø** (083–84 776).

TELEPHONE CODES. We have given telephone codes for all the towns and villages in the hotel and restaurant lists that follow. These codes need only be used when calling from outside the town or village concerned.

WAY TO THE NORTH

HOTELS AND RESTAURANTS. It is advisable to plan any trip north of Trondheim well in advance in view of the limited accommodations. Generally speaking, the best hotels in North Norway are found in the towns, which are in themselves sufficiently small and picturesque to provide a resort atmosphere. In Finnmark there are several inns along the Arctic Highway, which cater to the in-transit tourist. The best known of these inns are located in Alta, Karasjok, Levajok, Skaidi and Lakselv. The best inns and hotels along the Arctic Highway in Troms are found in Kvaenangsfjell, Sørkjosen, Olderdalen, Nordkjosbotn, Skibotn, Setermoen and Øse. Fine inns along the Arctic Highway in Nordland at Innhavet, Rognan and Majavatn.

The best restaurants are generally found in the hotels and other accommodations listed.

ALTA (Finnmark). Salmon fishing in river Alta. *Alta Hotel* (M), (084-35 311). 105 beds, all rooms with bath/shower. AE, DC, MC, V. *Altafjord Vertshus* (M), (084-34 055). 127 beds, many rooms with shower, sauna. AE, DC, MC, V.
Restaurants. *Alta Gjestesture* (I), Bossekop (084-35 290). *Alta Snackbar* (I), Bossekop (084-35 291)
Youth Hostel. *Alta Youth Hostel* (I), (084-34 409). 52 beds.

BARDU (Troms). *Bardu Motor Hotel* (M), (089-81 022). 78 beds, all rooms with facilities. AE, DC, MC, V. *Bardu Gjestgiveri* (I), (089-81 133). 50 beds, some rooms with bath/shower. MC.
Restaurants. *Altevann Cafe and Camping* (I), (089-84 601). *Setermoen Camping and Holiday Center* (I), (089-81 558).

BODØ (Nordland). Excursion to Saltstraumen maelstrom, 33 km. (20 miles) from town. *SAS Royal* (E), Storgaten 2 (081-24 100). 290 beds, all rooms with facilities. AE, DC, MC, V. *Grand* (M), Storgaten 3 (081-20 000). 91 rooms, many with bath/shower. AE, MC, V. *SAS Norrøna* (M), Storgaten 4 (081-24 100). 200 beds, most rooms with facilities. AE, DC.
Restaurants. *Rønvikfjell Restaurant* (M), outstanding views of ocean and mountains. *Løvold's Kafeteira* (I), Tollbugt 9 (081-24 080). Cafeteria in the center of Bodø overlooking the harbor.
Youth Hostel. *Flatvold Youth Hostel* (I), Rønvikkrysset (081-21 240). 132 beds.

FAUSKE (Nordland). *Fauske Hotel* (M), Storgt. 82 (081-43 833). 150 beds. DC, MC, V.
Restaurants. *N-café* (I), (081-43 905). At the railway station. *Ritz Kafeteira* (I), (081-43 621). *Tom's Gatekjøkken* (Kiosk), (081-44 442). *Tuva Leirsted* (I), (081-45 927).
Youth Hostel. *Fauske Youth Hostel* (I), (081-43 822). 114 beds.

HAMMERFEST (Finnmark). *Brassica Pension* (M), Storgaten 9-11 (084-11 822). 30 beds. DC, V. *Finnmarksbo Pension* (M), (084-11 622). 32 beds. *Grand Rica* (M), Sørøygt 15 (084-11 333). 120 beds, many rooms with bath/shower. AE, DC, MC. *Hammerfest Motel* (M), (084-11 126). 180 beds.

HARSTAD (Troms). *Grand* (E), Strandgate 9 (082-62 170). 130 beds, most rooms with facilities. DC, MC, V. *Viking Nordic* (M), Fjordgate 2 (082-64 080). 160 beds, all rooms with facilities, swimming, sauna. AE, DC, MC, V.
Youth Hostel. *Stangnes Youth Hostel* (I), Plassenvei 27 (082-73 820). 90 beds.

HONNINGSVÅG (Finnmark). Small town on Magerøy island, situated 2,110 km. (1,308 miles) from North Pole. *Nordkappmuseet* (E), Nordkappgt 4 (084-72 333). Special sightseeing trips by fishing vessel to bird sanctuaries at Svaer-

holtklubben. 250 beds, all rooms with facilities, restaurant, cafeteria. DC, MC, V. *Havly Pension* (M), (084–72 966). 57 beds, some rooms with shower.
  Restaurants. *Dagunen Restaurant and Cabins Disco* (M), (084–72 702). *Cafe Corner* (I), (084–72 701). *Cafe Ritz* (I), (084–72 711).
  Youth Hostel. *NAF Nordkapp Youth Hostel* (I), (084–75 113). At North Cape, 34 km. (21 miles) from town, 40 beds.

KARASJOK (Finnmark). Lapp village, 30,000 reindeer, Lapp museum, Karasjok library has world's greatest collection of literature on Lapps. *Karasjok SAS Turisthotell* (M), (084–66 203). 76 beds. AE, DC, MC, V. *Karasjok Tourist Center* (I), (084–66 446). 65 beds, sauna, camping huts and youth hostel.

KAUTOKEINO (Finnmark). Lapp village on Finnmark mountain plateau, famous Easter race by Lapps and reindeer on ice-bound river. *Kautokeino Tourist Hotel* (M), (084–56 205). 116 beds, all rooms with facilities, sauna. AE, DC, MC, V.
  Youth Hostel. *Kautokeino Youth Hostel* (I), (084–56 016). 35 beds, modern.

KIRKENES (Finnmark). 50 km. (31 miles) from Soviet frontier, large iron ore mines at Bjørnevatn, 11 km. (seven miles) from Kirkenes. *Kirkenes Rica Tourist Hotel* (E), Pasvikvn 63 (085–91 491). 117 beds, many rooms with facilities, sauna. AE, DC, MC, V.
  Restaurants. *Cockpit Grill and Dancing,* Storgt 1 (085–92 175). *Grillstua,* Dr. Wesselsgt 18 (085–91 287).

LØNSDAL (Nordland). 509 meters (1,670 feet), situated near "Arctic Circle" on Saltfjell mountain plateau, good ski touring. *Polarsirkelen Rica Mountain Hotel* (M), (081–94 122). 90 beds, most rooms with facilities, sauna. DC, MC, V.

MÅLSELV (Troms). *Målselvfossen Tourist Center* (M), Bakkehaug (089–35 213). 50 beds. *Rundhaug Hotel* (M), Bakkehaug (089–37 311). 46 beds.
  Restaurants. *Målselv Kro* (089–33 403). At Heggelia. *Reiersaeter Sportel,* Møllerhaugen (089–35 686).

MO I RANA (Nordland). *Holmen* (M), Sørlandsveien 62 (087–51 444). 80 beds, all rooms with bath/shower, grill, cafeteria, swimming. AE, DC, MC, V. *Meyergården* (M), (087–50 555). 250 beds, most rooms with facilities. AE, DC, MC, V.
  Youth Hostel. *Fageråsen Youth Hostel* (I), (087–50 963). 64 beds.

MOSJØEN (Nordland). Salmon fishing in river Vefsna, folk museum. *Fru Haugans* (M), (087–70 477). 131 beds, 38 rooms with bath/shower. MC, V. *Lyngengården* (M), (087–70 622). 50 beds, 17 rooms with bath/shower. MC.
  Youth Hostel. *Mosjøen Youth Hostel* (I), (087–87 843). In Sandvik folk high school, 80 beds, swimming, sauna.

NARVIK (Nordland). Major export harbor for iron ore from Sweden, chairlift to top of Fagernesfjell at 600 meters (1,970 feet), grand skiing terrain. *Grand Royal Hotel* (E), Kongensgate 64 (082–41 500). 230 beds, 118 rooms with bath/shower and radio, restaurant, bars. AE, DC, MC, V. *Nordstjernen Pension* (M), Kongensgate 26 (082–44 120). 55 beds, some rooms with bath/shower. *Breidablikk Gjestgiveri* (I), Tore Hundsgate 41 (082–41 418). 48 beds. *Malm Pension* (I), Frydenlundsgate 28 (082–42 383). 50 beds, some rooms with bath/shower.
  Youth Hostel. *Nordkalotten Youth Hostel* (I), Havnegate 3 (082–42 598). 110 beds, modern and popular.

WAY TO THE NORTH

NORDKJOSBOTN (Troms). Road E6/E78. *Vollan Gjestestue* (M), 30 beds.

NORTH CAPE (Finnmark). Northernmost point in Europe at 71 10′ 21″, on mountain plateau with 309 meters (1,013 feet) sheer precipice into Arctic Ocean, Midnight Sun from May 14 to July 30.
Restaurant. *Nordkapphallen,* restaurant and cafeteria with post office, expensive car park, no camping.

SKAIDI (Finnmark). Salmon fishing in Repparfjord and Skaidi rivers. *Repparfjord Tourist Hotel* (M), (084–16 121). 104 beds, most rooms with bath/shower, sauna. V. *Repparfjord Youth Center* (I), Kvalsund (084–16 165). 39 beds. *Skaidi Gjesthus* (I), (084–16 120). 95 beds.

SØRKJOSEN (Troms). *Sørkjos Hotel* (M), (083–65 277). 100 beds, some rooms with bath/shower, swimming, sauna.

SORTLAND (Nordland). On Langøy island in Vesterålen. *Sortland Nordic Hotel* (E), Vesterålsgaten 59 (088–21 833). 120 beds, most rooms with facilities. AE, DC, MC, V.

STAMSUND (Nordland). On Vestågøy island in the Lofotens. *Stamsund Lofoten Hotel* (M), (088–89 300). 56 beds, most rooms with facilities, swimming, sauna. AE, DC, MC.
Youth Hostel. *Justad Rorbu Youth Hostel* (I), (088–89 166). In fishermen's dwelling, 50 beds, primitive.

SVOLVAER (Nordland). On Austvågøy island in the Lofotens. *Lofoten Nordic Hotel* (M), (088–71 200). 98 beds, all rooms with facilities. AE, DC, MC, V. *Vita–Nova Motel* (M), (088–70 544). 110 beds, some rooms with bath/shower.
Youth Hostel. *Svolvaer Youth Hostel* (I), (088–70 316). 88 beds.

TROMSØ (Troms). On island in a narrow sound, hemmed in by mountains, connected with mainland by 1,036 meter (3,398 feet) long bridge. Arctic museum, aquarium, Northern Lights observatory, whaling station at Skjelnan, chairlift to top of Storsteinen. *Grand Nordic Hotel* (E), Storgate 44 (083–85 500). 300 beds, all rooms with facilities. AE, DC, MC, V. *SAS Royal Hotel* (E), Sjøgate 10 (083–56 000). 370 beds, all rooms with facilities. AE, DC, MC, V. *Saga Hotel* (M), Rich Withs Plass 2 (083–81 180). 100 beds, all rooms with facilities. AE, DC, MC, V. *Tromsdalen Guest House* (M), (083–35 944). 64 beds, most rooms with facilities.
Youth Hostel. *Tromsø Youth Hostel* (I), Øvre Breivang (083–85 319). 64 beds.

VADSØ (Finnmark). On Varanger fjord, town museum, Esbensen manor is only remaining patrician building left in Finnmark, airship tower used by Amundsen's "Norge" in 1926 and Nobile's "Italia" in 1928. *Vadsø Hotel* (M), (085–51 681). 103 beds, most rooms with facilities. AE, DC, MC, V.

VARDØ (Finnmark). On an island; now connected with the mainland by a new 2,800 meter (9,240 feet) tunnel, completed in 1982. Vardøhus octagonal fortress built in 1737, Vardø museum, Reinøya island with large bird sanctuaries. *Vardø City Hotel* (E), (085–87 761). 86 beds, all rooms with facilities, sauna. MC, V.

NORWAY

HOW TO GET AROUND. The enormous distances of North Norway demand time. Chief means of transport is the daily year-round service maintained by the fine **coastal express steamers,** sailing from Bergen to Kirkenes and back in 11 days and calling at important coastal places en route.

From Trondheim, the **North Norway Railway** (Nordlandsbanen) will take you to Fauske and Bodø north of the Arctic Circle in a day. On top of that comes a one day bus ride to Narvik, two days to Tromsö, and four days to reach Kirkenes on this longest **bus** line in Europe, called Nord-Norge-Bussen.

Narvik can be reached **by train** from Stockholm (25 hours), and Narvik is an excellent place to enter the North Cape Bus for a ride to Kirkenes. Return by coastal steamer or plane, as time and purse allow.

By air. One can go from Oslo to Bodø (1½ hrs), Tromsö (1¾ hrs) and Bardufoss (3 hrs), Alta (3 hrs), Lakselv (4 hrs), and Kirkenes (4 hrs).

By car. Norway's Number One highway—E6—will take you from Oslo and right across the Arctic Circle to Kirkenes near the Soviet Russian frontier. It is also the gateway to North Cape, but since the road distance from Oslo to North Cape is 2233 km. or 1383 miles, there are few people who can afford the time to do it. Many prefer to travel by air to one of the northernmost towns and rent a car there. The distance from North Cape to Tromsø is 484 km. (299 miles), Narvik 750 (464) and Bodø 925 (572). The return trip can be made via Finland or Sweden or by coastal steamer—but in the latter case it is essential to have reservations long in advance.

TOURS. There are tours available throughout the region, with the emphasis on the water. There are many boating excursions—river boats, steamers, catamarans and ferries. Most areas also offer fishing trips, on river, sea or lake.

In some areas there are helicopter or plane tours, and at Narvik and Tromsø there are cable cars going up into the mountains.

For those who prefer to keep their feet on solid ground, there are plenty of conventional road tours to places of great natural beauty and interest. For example there are trips from Karasjok to a gold diggers' camp; from both Karasjok and Kautokeino to visit reindeer herds; from Kirkenes to the Soviet border; and from Tromsø to see the rock carvings at Kvaløy.

Details of all tours are available from the local Tourist Information offices, the addresses of which are listed under "Tourist Information" at the beginning of this *Practical Information* section.

PLACES TO VISIT. The North abounds with places of scenic beauty, but there are also many museums, and buildings of historic and architectural interest, for the tourist to visit. Some of these places, both natural and man-made, are listed below.

ALTA. Alta Church. One of only two buildings left after the last war, the other being Kåfjord Church.

Alta Museum. Komsa School. Open all year Wed. 6–8. Additional opening times published locally.

Kåfjord Church. Typical English "village church," constructed in 1837. Gift from the English owners of the coppermine in Kåfjord.

BARDU. Bardu Church at Setermoen, octagonal all-timber structure, built in 1829 and a perfect replica of the Tynset Church.

Bardustua, at Eggen Farm near Bardujord. This building was erected by settlers newly arrived in the valley. Exhibition of tools, implements etc. owned and used by these immigrants.

BODØ. Bodin Church, a medieval stone church built about 1200; has an altar panel of rich Baroque design from 1670.

WAY TO THE NORTH

Bodø Cathedral. Modern three-nave basilica with separate clock–tower.
Nordland County Museum, has a particularly interesting fisheries section.
Saltstraumen. 34 km. (21 miles) from Bodø, the world's strongest whirlpool.

FAUSKE. Røsvik Manor. A trading center from 1760. Picturesque collection of houses around a courtyard. Main building (built 1832) is in Bergen style.
Sulitjelma Mining Center. 30 km. (19 miles) east of the Fauske center. Mining Museum.

HAMMERFEST. Meridianstøotten. The Meridian Stone was erected to commemorate the first international measurement of the world's size—1816-1852.

HARSTAD. Grytøy Bygdetun. At Lundenes. An ancient building, parts of which date back to 1770. Some 2,000 items on show, also an old boathouse with a number of boats, including a Nordland boat fully equipped for sailing.
Trondenes Church. Built in 1250, the world's northernmost medieval stone church. Open daily.

HONNINGSVÅG. The North Cape Museum, Havnegata. In addition to the local collections, the museum has specialized in fishing– and coast–culture.

KARASJOK. Karasjok Churches. One built in 1807, the oldest in Finnmark; the other consecrated in 1974.
Karasjok Smithy and **Isak Strømeng's Knife Workshop** at Badenjarg.
The Samic Collections. Norway's only specialist museum of Samic culture.

KAUTOKEINO. Lapp Traditional Crafts. Silversmiths, with Lapp collections.

KIRKENES. King Oscar II's Chapel. At Grense Jacobselv, 61 km. (38 miles) from Kirkenes, this is a stone building with the U.S.S.R. and the Arctic Ocean as its nearest neighbours. It was erected as a spiritual watchtower in 1869.

MÅLSELV. Fossmustua Regional Museum. Near Bardufoss.
Konglistua Bygdetun. Farmstead and buildings from 1840, situated near lake Rostavatn.

MO I RANA. Grønligrotten. Stalactite cave with underground waterfall.
Stenneset. Openair museum at the restored parsonage.

MOSJØEN. Dolstad Church. Norway's oldest octagonal church; dates from 1732.
Vefsn Museum. Local openair museum. Ancient farm buildings. Most comprehensive of its kind.

NARVIK. Rock Carvings. In the Brennholtet Park.
The War Museum. Near Torghallene; uniforms and weapons from World War II.

SVOLVÆR. Lofoten Aquarium and Fishery Museum. At Kabelvåg.
Vågan Church. The Lofoten Cathedral built in 1898 is the largest timber church north of Trondheim.

TROMSØ. The Arctic Ocean Cathedral. Tromsdal church, a modern masterpiece in glass and concrete. Large stained glass painting.
Polar Museum. Opened in 1978.
Tromsø Cathedral. One of the largest wooden churches in Norway.

Tromsø Museum. Established in 1872, the largest in North Norway; central research institute and interesting range of collections.

SPORTS. Fishing is *the* pastime in North Norway. The salmon rivers are famous, particularly those in Finnmark, where you may fish for a trifling fee: star attractions are the world famous Alta River in Finnmark and the Malangsfoss in Troms, where salmon is a certainty. The trout fishing on the Finnmark mountain plateau is fabulous, but includes a bit of walking.

The mountains of Lyngen, Lofoten, and the Narvik district lend themselves to strenuous **rock climbing.** Here there is still scope for exploring new routes. **Hiking** in the mountains of North Norway is only for the experienced, as the trails are seldom marked and staffed huts are few and far between.

Boats can be rented for trips on the Reisa, Karasjokka, Kautokeino, and Tana rivers. There's excellent **skiing** in March, preferably around Narvik (Narvik and Gratangen 300 meters), and Lönsdal (500 meters), south of Bodø.

Lofoten Islands Shanty Hire. Fishermen's shanties, built on the waterside, can be rented from about Nok. 80–150 per night (2–4 bunks). Accommodation is basic and meant for the adventurous who seek the world's best sea-fishing off Europe's wildest coastal scenery. Visitors must bring camping type equipment, sleeping bags, etc.; only bunks and mattresses, primitive furniture is provided. Boats can be hired.

SWEDEN

SWEDEN

FACTS AT YOUR FINGERTIPS

SWEDEN—FACTS AT YOUR FINGERTIPS

NATIONAL TOURIST OFFICE. In the U.S.: Swedish Tourist Board, 75 Rockefeller Plaza, New York, N.Y. 10019 (212–582 2802).

In the U.K.: Swedish National Tourist Office, 3 Cork St., London W.1 (01–432 5816).

Within Sweden, there are around 250 local tourist offices, about 100 of which are open all year round. Lists are available from the Swedish Tourist Board, but we also give addresses and telephone numbers of all the major tourist offices at the beginning of each *Practical Information* section. Local tourist offices are usually located in the center of towns and can be identified by a green "i" symbol.

CURRENCY. The unit of currency in Sweden is the *krona* (plural, *kronor*), or crown. It is divided into 100 *öre* and written as SEK. There are coins (all silver) of 10, 25 and 50 öre and of 1 and 5 SEK; notes come in denominations of 10, 50, 100, 500 and 10,000 SEK. The rate of exchange at the time of writing (mid-1984) was 8.20 SEK to the U.S. dollar and 11 SEK to the pound sterling. However, these rates will certainly change both before and during 1985, so check them carefully when planning your trip and on it.

You can change money or traveler's checks in banks and exchange offices. Some hotels will also change money for you, but their rate is likely to be much less favorable.

COSTS IN SWEDEN. Sweden is a country with a high standard of living and many costs are correspondingly high. Some items—liquor especially, particularly the imported variety—are very expensive, while most are perhaps no more than 10–15% expensive than their equivalents in the U.S.

However, a relatively low rate of inflation, estimated at 7% for 1985, plus vigorous efforts by the Swedes, who are only too conscious of their high-price-tag reputation, mean that for most visitors it should be possible to keep most expenses within reasonable bounds. Many hotels for example have special low summer rates and also cut costs during weekends in winter (though you would admittedly need to have a pretty good reason for coming to Sweden in the winter). Similarly, both hotels and restaurants offer tourist menus in the summer. There are likewise many discounts available for train, plane and bus travel, and most larger cities also have inexpensive tourist cards giving free travel on public transport and free entry into many museums. We give details of all these schemes in the sections that follow. The Swedish Tourist Board also have full details; alternatively, ask your travel agent.

A typical day in Stockholm might cost two people:

Hotel (Moderate) with bath and breakfast	SEK 500
Lunch, no drinks	100
Dinner, in moderate restaurant, including wine	300
Transportation (2 buses, 1 taxi)	65
	SEK 965

Sample costs. A cinema seat for one, SEK 35; visit to a museum, SEK 10; coffee, SEK 6; glass of beer, SEK 8–20 depending on strength; bottle of wine, SEK 65–100; coke, SEK 7; a moderate taxi ride, SEK 35; an average bus or subway ride, SEK 8.

SEASONAL EVENTS. Summer sees the bulk of Sweden's seasonal events and the Swedish Tourist Board and local tourist offices will be able to advise what's happening where. But the following are some of the major events.

February sees the Great Lapp Winter Fair in Jokkmokk in the far north of Sweden.

March sees a more modern winter event, the 55-mile cross-country ski race from Sälen to Mora; over 10,000 people take part.

April 30 is Walpurgis Night, when the end of the winter is celebrated; fires are lit throughout the country.

May sees the Svenska Mässan International Trade Fair in Gothenburg, normally in the second half of the month.

June 6 is Swedish National Day, with celebrations the length and breadth of the country. Stockholm's Skansen Park is the site of the most dramatic festivities. Midsummer Day is celebrated with equal gusto, especially in the provinces of Dalarna and Hälsingland.

July sees the Visby Festival, held in the ruins of the medieval cathedral there. The Swedish Derby is also held now, at Jägersro in Mälmo.

August has a series of Swedish-American days, notably at Skansen Park in Stockholm and at Vaxjo in southern Sweden.

September sees the International Consumer Goods Fair at Gothenburg, incorporating the "Household of Today" exhibition.

December has many events celebrating the imminent arrival of Christmas, notably St. Lucia's Day on the 13th, celebrated throughout Sweden (you'll also find a picture of St. Lucia in every hotel). The Nobel Prize awards also take place in December in Stockholm's Old Town.

NATIONAL HOLIDAYS. January 1 (New Year's Day); January 6 (Epiphany); April 5, 7, 8 (Easter); May 1 (Labor Day); May 16 (Ascension); May 27 (Whitsun); June 6 (Swedish National Day); November 6 (All Saint's Day); December 24–26.

LANGUAGE. The Swedes are great linguists. Most speak excellent English, and a good number also manage more than just a smattering of French and German. Most films and many TV programs are also in English with Swedish subtitles.

CUSTOMS. Residents of non-European countries may bring duty-free into Sweden 400 cigarettes or 200 cigarillos or 100 cigars or 500 grams of tobacco; plus, 1 liter of spirits and 1 liter of wine *or* 2 liters of beer; plus a reasonable amount of perfume; plus, goods to the value of SEK 600.

Residents of European countries may bring duty-free into Sweden, if they are 15 or over, 200 cigarettes or 100 cigarillos or 50 cigars or 250 grams of tobacco; plus, for visitors aged 20 or more, 1 liter of spirits, 1 liter of wine and 2 liters of beer; plus, a reasonable amount of perfume; plus, goods to the value of SEK 600.

Alcoholic beverages over 60° (120°) may not be imported.

There is no limit to the amount of foreign currency that may be imported or exported, but no more than SEK 6,000 may be imported or exported.

HOTELS. Hotel standards in Sweden are generally very high, even in the lowest price categories. As well as the larger and more expensive establishments—in almost every town you will find a "Grand Hotel," "Stadshotellet," or "Stora Hotellet"—the country is well provided with inexpensive guesthouses and pensions. In addition, all cities and most towns have a centrally-located hotel booking office *(Hotellcentral* or *Rumsförmedling),* usually operated by the local tourist office. Nonetheless, advance reservations, par-

FACTS AT YOUR FINGERTIPS

ticularly in larger towns, are recommended during the high season (May 15 to Sept. 30).

Though prices can be high, many hotels and hotel chains also offer special low rates during the summer and at weekends in the winter. Other cost-cutting bargains include the Swedish Hotel Check and the Scandic Hotel Check. Both schemes operate as hotel vouchers—only available in advance—giving substantial reductions at all participating hotels. The Swedish Hotel Check comes in two varieties: the first, known as the Quality Check, costs SEK 180 for two people per night; the second, the Budget Check, costs SEK 125 for two people per night. Only your first night can be reserved in advance, but thereafter any hotel participating in the scheme will make reservations for you, free of chrage, at any other member hotel. Ask your travel agent or the Swedish Tourist Board for details, or contact *Holiday Tours of America,* 40 East 49 St., New York, N.Y. 10017 (800–223 0567).

The Scandic Hotel Check is valid at more than 60 hotels in Sweden, Norway and Denmark. This too comes in two forms: the Summer Check, priced at SEK 160 for two per night and valid June 1 to September 15; and the Weekend Check, priced at SEK 140 and valid Sept. 16 to May 31.

Alternatively, a Biltur-Logi pass is good for even more inexpensive accommodations at 300 hotels in Sweden. The pass, available in both shops and all participating hotels, costs SEK 30 and qualifies you for bed-and-breakfast accommodations in any of the member hotels. Reservations can only be made one day in advance. Contact *Biltur-Logi,* Siljansgården, S-79 303 Tällberg for details.

Prices We have divided all the hotels we list into four categories—Deluxe (L), Expensive (E), Moderate (M) and Inexpensive (I). These grades are determined solely by price.

Two people in a double room can expect to pay (prices in SEK)

Deluxe	800 and up
Expensive	600—800
Moderate	400—600
Inexpensive	200—400

These prices include breakfast and a 15% service charge.

CAMPING. Sweden boasts more than 600 camp sites, about 140 of which are open all year round. Most, however, are open from mid-May to late September. All camp sites are inspected and classified—from one to three stars—by the Swedish Tourist Board and all authorized sites display a green sign with a white "C" against a black tent. Most sites are located by the sea or on a lake and facilities such as mini-golf, windsurfing, riding and tennis are common.

Charges range from SEK 30 to 50 per tent. An international camping carnet is required for all sites; alternatively, buy a Swedish Camping Card at any site. The Swedish Tourist Board's *Camping in Sweden* leaflet, listing all sites, is available from all tourist offices.

For those who fancy the simple life but draw the line at being under canvas, some 250 sites also have "camping cottages" for hire. These have between two and four beds. Top prices are around SEK 175 per night. Sheets and blankets can be rented at camp sites; alternatively, bring your own.

YOUTH HOSTELS. There are around 250 youth hostels in Sweden, all operated by the Swedish Touring Club (STF). Hostels range from simple, student-type accommodations to restored manor houses and, in the case of the *af Chapman* in Stockholm, a restored sailing ship. Some can provide lunch and dinner, as well as breakfast, and a number also have hot and cold running water in every room. Linen may be rented in all hostels.

Members of the International Youth Hostels Federation are entitled to special low rates, but hostels in Sweden are otherwise open to all, regardless of age. It is generally advisable to make reservations in advance. Prices per night range from SEK 30 to 40. For further details, contact the Swedish Tourist Board or the *Swedish Touring Club,* PO Box 25, S-101, 20 Stockholm (08–22 72 00).

RESTAURANTS. Swedish restaurants, especially in more cosmopolitan centers, are varied both in style and price. At the top end of the spectrum, especially in Stockholm, you will find restaurants the equal of those anywhere in the world, while lower down the scale restaurants are generally of a high standard if somewhat more expensive than in the U.S.

Fast food of every variety is now available everywhere. Similarly, Chinese and Greek restaurants—all generally inexpensive—abound. Alternatively, anywhere calling itself a Bar will also provide self-service food but not, confusingly, alcohol.

Away from larger centers, the majority of restaurants are in hotels, though you will still find the occasional regular spot. Most hotels—and a good number of restaurants too—will provide a tourist menu in the summer. These are filling and very good value, but are normally not served after 7 P.M. Similarly, many restaurants also provide "office menus," or *dragens rätt;* these normally cost around SEK 35 and include a main dish, salad, beer or milk, bread and butter, coffee and service.

Alcohol is generally very expensive in all restaurants.

Prices. We have divided the restaurants in our listings into three categories—Expensive (E), Moderate (M) and Inexpensive (I). These grades are determined solely by price.

Prices, per person, excluding drinks (in SEK)

Expensive	75 and up
Moderate	50—75
Inexpensive	35—50

All prices are inclusive of service.

FOOD AND DRINK. The Swedish *smörgåsbord,* someone once said, is often abused in spelling, pronunciation and preparation. *Smörgåsbordet* is a large table usually placed in the middle of the dining room and easily accessible to all guests. It is piled high with a large number of delicacies to which you help yourself as often as you like. To appreciate it properly, however, the various dishes should be eaten in proper succession and not helter-skelter. Traditionally, the order goes something like this: pickled herring (possibly more than one kind) with a boiled potato; a couple more fish courses, probably cold smoked salmon, fried Baltic Sea herring, and sardines in oil; the meats, liver paste, boiled ham, sliced beef, not uncommonly smoked reindeer; a salad, fruit and/or vegetable; and finally the cheeses. Bread and butter is served throughout.

Many of the items that appear in the *smörgåsbord* may be familiar to you. Some of the appetizers which you may not have tasted, and which are recommended, are herring on ice with chives and sour cream sauce, fried Baltic Sea herring, smoked eel (delicious, really), smoked reindeer (likewise), and the Swedish Chantilly-type cheese, milder and firmer than its French cousin.

And finally you end up with a dessert such as fruit salad or pastry. A main dish after the *smörgåsbord* is optional (you are unlikely to need one!) and costs extra. Sadly, however, *smörgåsbord* is not so common as it once was. But ask at your hotel for the best place to go.

Other national dishes are crayfish, in season from August to September and the occasion for a rash of informal parties, preferably outdoors; pea soup and pork, followed by pancakes, traditional Thursday supper from autumn through spring; and in November, particularly in southern Sweden, goose.

FACTS AT YOUR FINGERTIPS

Generally, the Swedes do better with fish than they do with meat. If you like good, tender beef, stick to the *à la carte* menu.

Practically everything in the way of wines and liquors is regularly available at the better restaurants and bars, even the latest cocktail, although any kind of mixed drink seems somehow out of place in this land where liquor is traditionally drunk straight (neat) with no nonsense, thank you.

Quite another matter is the question of drinking hours. Before noon (1 P.M. on Sundays) you're doomed to soft drinks (not even wine or beer), unless you buy your own bottle at one of the state-owned liquor shops, known as Systembolag. These, however, are closed on Saturdays and Sundays and are by no means thick on the ground. At midnight everything is put away again except at those nightspots with licenses to stay open to 2 or 3 A.M.

Anyhow, if you're going to eat Swedish, order snaps and beer or table water with the *smörgåsbord*. *Snaps* is the collective name for *aquavit* or *brännvin*, Swedish liquor made under a variety of brand names and with flavors varying from practically tasteless to sweetly spiced. Recommended brands: Skåne, Herrgårds, and O. P. Andersson. Swedish beers are good—made in a variety of light and dark qualities and strengths.

But do remember that almost all alcohol is expensive in Sweden—even a beer can cost upwards of $2.

TIPPING. Tipping in hotels, restaurants and bars is not generally necessary in Sweden as the service charge is always included in your check. However, exceptional service may warrant a tip. Similarly, many round up restaurant bills to the nearest 5 or 10 krona. There are only two exceptions to the no-tipping rule. Taxi drivers—who pay tax on tips whether they get them or not—should always be given 15%. And give coat check attendants in restaurants around SEK 4.

Otherwise, bear in mind that tipping is the exception rather than the rule.

MAIL. Post offices are open from 9 to 6 Monday to Friday and 9 to 1 on Saturdays. During the summer, some do not open on Saturdays. Aside from post offices, you can also buy stamps from the machines outside post offices, in department stores and hotels. These take 1 and 5 krona coins. Similarly, some shops selling postcards also sell stamps. Mail boxes are painted a distinctive yellow.

Postal rates for airmail letters to the U.S. are SEK 3.20, and SEK 2.40 to Europe; postcards to the U.S. are SEK 2.40, and to Europe SEK 2.

CLOSING TIMES. Shops are generally open from 9 to 6; on Saturdays they close around 3 or 4. However, in larger cities you will normally be able to find supermarkets that stay open late. Banks are open from 9.30 to 6, but are closed on Saturdays. In addition they generally close around 1 the day before official holidays. Stockholm's Arlanda airport has a bank that is open every day between 7 A.M. and 10 P.M.

TAX-FREE SHOPPING. Over 6,000 Swedish shops—900 in Stockholm alone—participate in a tax-free shopping scheme for visitors enabling you to save around 15% on all buys exported within one week of purchase. Take your passport with you to shops and ask for the special tax-free receipt. All airports and ports have repayment offices which will refund in cash—deducting a 5% service charge—the tax paid. Even credit card purchases qualify for this rebate.

For further details, contact the Swedish Tourist Board, or call (0420) 19560 or (0760) 92080 once in Sweden.

SWEDEN

GETTING AROUND SWEDEN. By air. Sweden has a good internal air network, with *SAS* and *LIN* (Linjeflyg) the main carriers. To give a rough idea of flying times, Stockholm to Kiruna, north of the Arctic Circle, takes around 90 minutes, while Stockholm to Gothenburg, down in the south of the country, takes around 50 minutes.

Outside peak times, there are many fare bargains to be had. All off-peak or "red" period fares are some 30% below peak or "black" period fares for one-way trips. Similarly, senior citizens pay only SEK 200 on all one-way fares in red periods.

Anyone planning to stay away for more than two nights or over one Saturday night is entitled to a "Minipris" fare. This gives a 50% discount, and in addition your wife or husband and young people between 15 and 25 traveling with you pay only SEK 200 each. The demand for Minipris tickets is very great, however, especially in the summer, so be sure to book well in advance. Those under 26 are also entitled to special fares of only SEK 150 on all one-way trips, subject to availability.

Finally, both airlines operate good-value fly-drive schemes over the summer and at weekends throughout the year. But you must book your car at the same time as you reserve your seat.

By train. Swedish trains are comfortable, clean and reliable with efficient express services linking all main cities. First and second class carriages and dining or self-service cars are carried on most trains. Sleeping cars—costing approximately SEK 100 in addition to the normal fare—and couchettes—costing approximately SEK 55—are also available on all overnight runs. No smoking signs must be strictly observed. Note also that the letter "R" in timetables means that seat reservations—SEK 10—are required.

Fares are generally quite low, but a host of budget deals make them even more accessible. The best buy is the discount card, available for around SEK 125 and valid for one year. It entitles you to a reduction of up to 45% on all second-class rail travel except suburban trains. But note that it is not valid on Fridays and Sundays. Even one trip, especially a long distance ride, will justify the price of the card. But needless to say, the more you use it, the better value it is.

Senior citizens are entitled to a 40% fare reduction on all trains, but proof of age must be provided. At the opposite end of the age spectrum, all children between four and 11 pay only half fare on all trains. A family of three or more traveling together also qualifies for a 45% discount on all trains.

In addition to these exclusively Swedish discounts, the *Nordturist* (or Scandrail card), the *Inter-Rail* card, the *Eurailpass* and *Eurail Youthpass*, *Rail Europ Senior Card* and the *Inter-Rail Senior Card* are all valid within Sweden. See "Getting Around Scandinavia by Rail" in *Planning Your Trip* for further details.

By car. Given its vast size and the excellence of the air and rail network, car travel in Sweden may seem a less than ideal means of getting around, especially as only main roads, particularly in the north of the country, are paved, all others being gravel. Having said this, however, roads are very well engineered, and the small population also means that there is generally very little traffic. Similarly, there are no toll roads anywhere, and even car ferries are free.

There are strict speed limits, however, even outside built-up areas. These are 110, 90 or 70 km.p.h. (68, 56 or 43 m.p.h.). In built up areas the speed limit is always 50 km.p.h. (31 m.p.h.), and 30 km.p.h. (19 m.p.h.) outside schools. Speed limits are always well sign-posted. Towing a trailer with brakes, the limit is 70 km.p.h. (43 m.p.h.); without brakes, it is 40 km.p.h. (25 m.p.h.).

Note also that seat belts are compulsory for drivers and front seat passengers and that you must *always* use dipped headlights, both at night and during the day. U.S. drivers' licenses are valid in Sweden.

Gas stations, nearly all self service, are common in most regions, but can be few and far between in the north. They generally close around 6 outside cities, but a good many now have automatic machines that accept 10 and 100 krona notes.

Parking restrictions are strictly observed. You should always park only in designated areas. Parking meters accept one krona coins. Wrongly-parked cars will be towed away.

FACTS AT YOUR FINGERTIPS

The best people to try in the event of a breakdown are the police or "Larmtjänst," a 24-hour service. They are listed in the phone book. English is always spoken.

Finally, it is very important to observe the extremely strict (and equally strictly-enforced) drink/drive regulations. Anything in excess of two bottles of beer will be enough for a conviction, and tests are made frequently. Fines are very heavy and imprisonment by no means rare. On the whole, the smart thing is simply not to drink if you're driving.

By bus. Swedish buses are run by the national rail network and a small number of private companies. Prices are very low, but services relatively slow. In more remote parts of the country, however, a reasonable Post Bus service knits the scattered communities together.

By bicycle. Bikes can be rented throughout Sweden. For a complete list of rental companies, write *Cykelfrämjåndet,* P.O. Box 30 70, S-103 61, Stockholm. The *Swedish Touring Club,* P.O. Box 25, S-101, 20 Stockholm, can also provide details of organized bike tours in practically every province. Prices are very reasonable.

Many buses and trains will also carry bikes free of charge; inquire at tourist offices or write *Svenska Cykelsällskapet,* P.O. Box 6006, S-163 06, Spånga, for details.

PRELUDE TO SWEDEN

Dolls' Houses in the Wilderness

by
ANDREW BROWN

Because Sweden is the largest and the richest of the Scandinavian countries, it is also the most typical: any idea of what is "Scandinavian" is informed by Sweden. If the other countries differ from the Swedish model, this tends to suggest that they are not truly "Scandinavian."

The word suggests a combination of gloom and cleanliness; efficiency combined with joyless affluence, conjuring up a vision of somewhere very impressive, but not really suited to human life. Elks and mosquitoes thrive; other lifeforms do not.

It is easy enough to find parts of Sweden that correspond to this stereotype—and they are almost certainly the first parts that the tourist will see. But the tension and the interest of Swedish life comes from the fact that the Swedes themselves could no more stand to live as they seem to do than anybody else could. If the foreigner recoils from certain aspects of Swedish life, so do the Swedes themselves. The result can be extremely confusing, but it is both more interesting and a great deal more pleasant than the rather inhuman front presented to the world would suggest. The moral, for anyone who wants to enjoy Sweden—and there is much here to enjoy—is 'Get off the Main Street'.

The Minor Arts of Peace

A perfect example of this is provided by Uddevalla, a town on the west coast that looks from the main road like every other town in Sweden. Admittedly, there is nowhere in Europe but Stockholm where you will find towns that look good from a four-lane highway, but the drabness of Uddevalla is remarked upon even by guidebooks.

Between the main road and the sea is a low-lying area that floods after westerly gales every year. One of the traditional sights of the Swedish fall is that on the television news of the octagonal tourist office in Uddevalla surrounded by water, and accessible only to those tourists who have had the foresight to pack canoes or waders.

On the other side of the road, the town itself is concealed by a line of modern developments: car lots and demolition sites, and large grey concrete buildings that look like overgrown Lego models without either the color or the imagination of the originals.

Seeing all this, the average traveler gets away down the highway as quickly as possible. He may admire the engineering that has made the highway possible, but if he thinks anything at all about the town, it is only that Uddevalla is one of those places that Nature meant to be bypassed. But the wise man turns off the main road into the town, and gets lost in the one-way system. The belt of nastiness is only one block deep. The buildings behind are not particularly beautiful, but they are not inhuman. One conceals a rocky garden, where you can sit on terraces drinking beer all through the summer twilight, moving occasionally to keep within the shade of trees. The streets are crowded with people, not with cars. There is an openair market. A little more exploration discovers a comfortable cafe, and a shop that sells foreign newspapers. An indoor market sells fish so fresh their eyes and flanks still gleam. Much more surprisingly, it sells kippers, that you can only otherwise buy in Scotland. These are the minor arts of peace. They may not be spectacular, but they're important; and very well done throughout Scandinavia, but to find them in Sweden you must go behind the facade of grey modernity.

In a Meadow by a Lake

The town of Uddevalla, however, is still public Sweden. Even after you have learned to find and enjoy the shops and cafes, the houses on the hills around remain closed and mysterious. The less privacy people have, the more closely they guard it. To discover what makes Swedes tick, you must go still further from the main road, perhaps to a house that stands some miles south of Uddevalla. It's not a tourist attraction: in fact it is a private house, though people are encouraged to visit the lakes and the woods around it. And those with a taste for the outdoor life can spend a night in the cabin across the meadow.

The house is not far from the main road, but you must travel for some time to get there. The branch road starts at a modern gas station on a highway, leads past a couple of supermarkets and then a much older general store. When it climbs into the hills there is no metalled surface. In the space of a mile you have traveled back 30 years. Five miles of gravel road lead to a track through the forest that only a tractor could get down.

The woods around are typical of Southern Sweden. They seem untamed—elk hairs lie in clumps along the tracks—but they are not oppressive. The lack of undergrowth makes the forest seem extraordinarily spacious, and though the trees are almost all conifers, they're not monotonous. No one who has not seen a Scandinavian forest in early summer can imagine how many shades of green there are in the world, each one distinct and bright and clear. The elements of the view are limited, but they are never quite the same; which keeps the forest beautiful however far you walk, but makes it very easy to get lost in. So be a little careful.

The house stands at the end of this track, in a meadow by a lake. It was built 50 years ago by two Finnish lumberjacks, who lived what must have been a life of monotony remarkable even by the standards of immigrant Finnish lumberjacks. In winter they worked in the forests; in summer they netted pike out of the lake and sold what they could not eat. Eventually they moved away. The house fell into disrepair. This is an old pattern. You *can* live off the land in Sweden, but few would choose to do so. (In the 19th century, Sweden was so poor that a quarter of all the descendants of Swedes living then are now Americans). Walking through the woods in the south of the country you will often come across the remains of cabins from this time, their stone foundations worn down like old teeth.

Even the lake where the lumberjacks had netted their pike died, poisoned by acid rain. The prevailing winds from England and Germany are loaded with sulphur dioxide from factories and car exhausts. This turns to weak sulphuric acid and falls on Sweden, where the peat and granite cannot buffer it as English soil can. The snow that looks so pure in winter is actually weak sulphuric acid, frozen, fluffy, and deadly. When it melts each spring, four months' worth of acid runs into the lakes and rivers in a week, killing fish fry and eggs, most forms of algae, and most insects too. The lakes are neatly sterilized. Of the thousand or so lakes in Bohuslan, only a handful can now support any lifeform higher than the water-louse.

So far this story has dealt with the effects of the country on the people who live there. The point, however, is how they have changed the country. In the early 70s the house and the lake were taken over by a group of local fishermen. They filled the lakes with trout—each one of which had to be carried down the track in rucksacks full of water—and arranged to have lime spread on the ice each spring to counteract the acid rain. All this is paid for by selling fishing permits for the lakes, but by this time catching fish had become a secondary consideration for the fishermen. Their treasure was the house.

It has been lovingly restored, with stripped and polished pine floors, prints and ornamental driftwood on the walls. It seems that the attraction is that they can get away from all respectable life here. They can drink all night and not worry about driving in the morning; they can chop wood and cover themselves with paint; they chew tobacco and spit into an open fire. It is a small boys' paradise, and irresistible to anyone over the age of 15.

But these small boys in their 30s and 40s turn into old maids in the morning. They tiptoe around in their socks, brushing and sweeping;

PRELUDE TO SWEDEN

they agonize over the exact placement of a hat-stand; they would, if they could, reintroduce the death penalty for littering. The wilderness camp is turned into a dolls' house.

It is this clearing up that is the point of the whole thing. This is Sweden in microcosm. The fishermen do not go into the woods to get away from it all, but to extend it all: to build a perfect, private society together in the middle of nowhere. All Swedish life is best understood as conducted in dolls' houses in the wilderness, and it demands of its participants the same passion and concentration as a children's game.

Just as heroism is the Polish vice, sincerity is the curse of the Swedes. They can believe anything—and they do—but this belief is almost always a communal activity. Swedes in discussion are like a shoal of fish. They all point in the same direction, and if they change direction, all do so at once. Sometimes they split into competing shoals, but within each group the discipline remains. What's rare in Sweden, and always seems slightly ridiculous, are self-sufficient individuals, or, if you like, lone fish.

How to Move a Mountain

These attitudes are easily misunderstood. Because belief—sincerity—comes so naturally to the Swedes, they may seem to outsiders insincere, just as the girl who can't say "No" seems incapable of loving because she falls in love so easily. But this is unfair. If the sceptical British, for example, strike ridiculous attitudes, they are being hypocritical. If the Swedish do the same, this is not hypocrisy, but wholly sincere self-deception. And they could easily justify this quirk of character if they ever felt the need to justify something that is to them so self-evident. Faith *has* moved mountains in Sweden, most obviously in the iron-mining town of Kiruna, above the Arctic Circle.

But there is no need to go as far as Kiruna to see this, even though it is one of the most remarkable towns in the world. Stockholm itself is best enjoyed as the most beautiful dolls' house in the world. The most famous sights of the city all have this quality of toys: there is the restored 17th-century warship, the *Vasa;* the royal palace, for show rather than for living in; the openair museum at Skansen, where houses, churches, and workshops from all over Sweden have been re-erected on the slopes around a zoo. In the workshops there are real craftsmen playing at being real craftsmen; in the zoo there are wolverines and seals playing in beautifully landscaped enclosures.

The modern center of the city is extremely ugly, but this, too, is the result of a communal fantasy. This was the dream of the American '50s (and the Swedish '60s) that with enough money and enough cars, everyone would be happy if there were no buildings in sight more than five years old to remind them of what they had lost. The tourist office in Sweden House marks the furthest outpost of this dream. Beyond it lies a park—the Kungsträdgården—and when the city council proposed to ruin that, too, for the sake of a new subway station, mass demonstrations stopped the plan. Respectable Swedes, who would tell you even then that they were the most buttoned-up and formal people in the world, climbed the trees that were to be cut down, and clung to the branches with the workmen poised below, axes at the ready, until the city council gave way, as they were forced to do. Opposition broke the spell; when communal belief was no longer possible, the ideas that had laid waste the city center lost all their power.

This is not to say that all modern Swedish architecture is ugly; odd bits of it are extremely beautiful, though nowhere as lovely as in Finland. But again, this beauty is to be found in hidden places, not in public ones. The beautiful public buildings of Stockholm are all old, and almost all of them are built at the edge of islands which greatly increase their beauty.

Angst and Elks

Of course, one of the things the visitor to Stockholm expects to see is porn. This is most odd for anyone who lives in Sweden—we cannot imagine how the legend of "Swedish Sin" arose. There was admittedly a period in the late '60s when the Swedes decided that since pornography is unavoidable, it must be good for you. That decision later came to seem foolish. Now they are just confused, but not very worried. The guilt, fear, and anguish that Anglo-Saxons lavish on sex are devoted by the Swedes to alcohol.

The Swedish attitude to drink is one of the things that most intensely irritates the foreigner. Drink is not so much difficult as inconvenient to obtain; in those few restaurants that serve it, it is extremely expensive. An elaborate network of law and tabu has almost eliminated drunken driving, except for those drivers too drunk to remember the consequences. This may have kept death off the roads (elks cause more car crashes every year in Sweden than ever humans do) but it has also eliminated social drinking, except in large towns. No amount of pleasure is worth the risk of losing your license in a country where cars are as common and as vital as they are in Sweden. In the countryside there is no-one who can afford to drink with strangers except the town drunk, and who would want to drink with him?

It sometimes seems that the Swedes cannot enjoy a drink unless they are convinced that it is harming them. The windows of the state liquor stores are lined with anti-alcohol posters displayed behind ramparts of a purplish fluid called *Schloss Boosenburg,* an "alcohol-free wine." But things are loosening up nowadays, largely as a result of the introduction of real wine, which women can drink and enjoy with men. The old Swedish tabus on drink had a partially sexual underpinning: men drank; women picked up the pieces, and resented having to do so. This was clearly unsatisfactory, though it did produce one marvellous recipe: Put a small silver coin in the bottom of a cup; add sweetened black coffee till you can no longer see the coin; then pour in vodka until the coin becomes visible again. This is not a drink for those who wish to remain gentlemen in their cups.

It's worth dwelling on this subject because the tabus of a country are more informative even than the local newspapers. The superstitious horror with which the Swedes regarded drink is really a result of the facts that drunks quarrel. They forget the rules of the communal game, and stumble through the dolls' house, breaking things and shouting, interrupting everybody else. No wonder their fellows turn on them with the ferocity of children. For a children's game has power only when all the players believe in it. Otherwise the dolls have no life, and will quickly be broken.

PRELUDE TO SWEDEN

This need not worry the visitor. The Swedes treat foreigners with great courtesy and kindness. Almost all of them speak English, and all are delighted to show you their splendid game. They will perhaps complain that theirs is the most regulated and tightly controlled society in the Western world; and in a sense they are right. For the last 12 years, the Swedish parliament has been passing laws and regulations at a rate of one every eight hours of the day and night, or more than 1,000 a year. But for the most part the citizens treat this activity as lightly as do the parliamentarians themselves. The system has reached such a pitch of complication that no-one takes very much notice of it any more. The Swedes obey such rules as they feel are sensible, and ignore the others. They feel entitled to do so because it is, after all, their game. This sense of belonging makes them a very restful people to be among; nor can anyone who has known a Swedish summer feel that there is anywhere in the world that is more beautiful in the months of May and June.

STOCKHOLM

Open Nature and City Planning

Stockholm, Sweden's capital, has been called the most beautiful city in the world. This is open to debate, but few will deny that it is a handsome and civilized capital with a natural setting that would be hard to beat anywhere. When it was founded as a fortress on a little stone island where Lake Mälar reaches the Baltic, nobody cared much about natural beauty. It was protection the founders were after, military defense. But around the year 1250, the fortress became a town, and the town, spreading to nearby islands and finally to the mainland, became a city. And, though Nature remained the same, men's opinion of it changed, and Stockholm delights the tourist today with its openness, its space, its vistas over a great expanse of water. Of course it's been called the "Venice of the North," but that happens sooner or later to any northern city with more water than can be supplied by a fire hydrant.

Stockholm's beauty has been jealously guarded by the city fathers. The town is full of parks, tree-lined squares and boulevards, playgrounds, wading pools and other amenities of urban life, and the building codes are extremely strict. Nature and city planning have thus combined to create a pleasing metropolis, and it is hard to realize as you gaze out over the water from a table on the Strömparterren terrace that you are in the heart of a bustling metropolis, a town that has grown from less than 100,000 inhabitants to over a million in the space of a century.

Nowhere is the striking modernity of much of Stockholm more obvious than in the brand new streets and squares around Sergels Torg, a startling glass and steel tower in the heart of the new city, and the rail station, where multi-lane highways, skyscrapers and underground shopping malls have all sprung up in the space of a few years. Yet no more than five minutes' walk will bring you to the medieval heart of the city on the islands of Gamla Stan (Old Town), where narrow twisting streets huddle around the bulk of the imposing Royal Palace, the Cathedral and the Riksdag, the Parliament.

June, July and August are the best months to visit this capital. Then you have the best weather and the greatest variety of sight-seeing facilities. Bring a reasonably warm coat along. What most people would call a mild summer day is apt to be announced in the Stockholm papers as a heat wave. In May or October the weather is brisker, but so is the normal life of Stockholm.

History and Growth

The earliest origins of Stockholm are largely unknown. Perhaps the first somewhat reliable report is a Viking saga, which, as all Viking sagas should, ends in violence. It seems that Agne, a warrior king of the Ynglinga dynasty, had been off on a visit to Finland. There, among other treasures, he had acquired a chieftain's daughter named Skjalf, by the effective if crude device of cutting down her father. Coming home, he stopped on the shore of an island which is now a part of Stockholm, to drink the health of his new bride and a proper toast to his late father-in-law. The mead flowed freely, Agne slept, Skjalf freed her fellow Finnish prisoners, and they hanged Agne. Then the Finns safely sailed home. The place was subsequently called Agnefit, or Agne Strand.

The first written mention of Stockholm in preserved chronicles gives the date 1252. Tradition—and some historical evidence—has it that a powerful regent named Birger Jarl here founded a fortified castle and city, locking off the entrance to Lake Mälar and the region around it. At all events, it is known that a castle of substance was built in the 13th century, and during the same period the Great Church was begun (dedicated to St. Nicholas, patron saint of shipping) and the first monasteries.

From these dim beginnings the history of the city can be divided into four fairly distinct epochs: the erratic, confused first centuries; the arrival of King Gustav Vasa, who made Stockholm a capital beginning in 1523; King Gustavus Adolphus, who made it the heart of an empire a century later; and the modern era.

After the time of Birger Jarl the Swedish nation, still unorganized, groped its way forward. Up to this time Stockholm had not been the capital; the latest city to enjoy the favor had been Sigtuna. The real physical heart of Sweden remained uncertain. Nevertheless, Magnus Eriksson, a king of some importance, was crowned here in 1336. Toward the end of the century Sweden, Norway, and Denmark were united under one ruler. A period of confusion and revolt followed.

Stockholm continued to be a commercial center, with monopoly trading rights for much of the territory around.

On Midsummer's Eve, 1523, when King Gustav Vasa returned from his victorious uprising for Swedish independence from the union (and from a Danish king), the real history of Stockholm began. Vasa was a powerful figure, sometimes called the George Washington of Sweden, and, although he moved from castle to castle throughout the country, his treasure chamber was in the old Stockholm Royal Palace. Succeeding kings tended in the same direction, making Stockholm more and more important.

Under Gustavus Adolphus, a great organizer as well as a military leader, who reigned from 1611 to 1632, the city became a capital in fact as well as name. Sweden had already begun to engage in political machinations and wars on the Continent and in Russia. It was partly his need to keep his military forces at top efficiency, his need for tax money, for supplies and for men that led Gustavus to concentrate the administration of the country in Stockholm. When he died on the battlefield of Lützen in 1632, Protestantism had been saved, Sweden had become an empire and Stockholm was its capital.

Prosperity and population grew accordingly. Gustavus himself, in a farewell address of 1630, had told the citizens of Sweden's cities that he hoped "your small cottages may become large stone houses". Many of them did. From a population of perhaps 3,000 when Gustav Vasa came home victorious, the number of inhabitants had grown to some 9,000 by the time Gustavus Adolphus fell, and rose to perhaps 35,000 by 1660. Meanwhile, the wars continued. Fortunately for Stockholm, they were fought on foreign soil. This did not, however, diminish the importance of the city, for it functioned as the capital even during the long absence of hero King Charles XII, who spent almost his entire reign in the field—losing much of what Gustavus Adolphus had won.

Rulers came and went, political battles were fought, won, and lost. But the building of Stockholm went on, sometimes in the hands of eminent architects like Nicodemus Tessin and his son, who are responsible for both the Royal Palace and Drottningholm Palace, as well as many other buildings which still stand. In the 18th century, Stockholm began to attract scientists and scholars, to share the spotlight with Lund and Uppsala as a center of learning. Gustav III (assassinated in 1792), a dilettante who could put on steel gauntlets when required, did much to make Stockholm a cultural, musical, and dramatic capital.

In 1850 Stockholm was still a quiet town. It had many of the stately buildings which even now give it its characteristic profile, but it numbered less than 100,000 people—a peaceful administrative center, perhaps dreaming of past glories. The first municipal cleaning department was established in 1859, the first waterworks in 1861, and gaslights had arrived but a few years earlier. As late as 1860, Drottninggatan, the most prominent commercial street, had no sidewalks. But the same year the first train arrived from Södertälje, 25 miles away. Modern communications had been born. The new era had begun.

Modern Development

The last 100 years of Stockholm's history are the story of a peaceful revolution, of industrialization, and of the remaking of a government

STOCKHOLM

from a monarchy with four estates in the parliament—nobles, clergy, farmers, as well as burghers—into a full parliamentary democracy with a king at its head. As the country has progressed and grown, Stockholm has progressed and grown with it. You will see the physical evidence wherever you go—the squat Parliament House on the site of one-time royal stables; the City Hall, a splendidly quirky and lavish brick creation overlooking the waters of Lake Mälar; the extensive and striking developments in the center of the city; and two huge satellite suburbs to the west and east of the city.

Exploring Stockholm

If Stockholm's island geography poses communication problems, it has the advantage of dividing the city neatly into sections and of making it possible to know easily where you are.

Gamla Stan. The Old Town, site of the Royal Palace and center of the city and nation, and the adjoining islands, Riddarholmen (The Isle of Knights), and Helgeandsholmen (Island of the Holy Spirit).

Södermalm. As the name implies, this is the southern section, across the bridge leading from the Old Town.

Norrmalm. North of the Old Town, the financial and business heart of the city. The new building construction from Hötorget to Klarabergsgatan, which forms the new commercial center of Stockholm, constitutes the most important part of the redevelopment of Nedre Norrmalm (Lower Norrmalm).

Kungsholmen. A large island west of Norrmalm, site of the Town Hall, and most of the offices of the city government.

Östermalm. East of Norrmalm, largely residential, many embassies and consulates.

Djurgården. The huge island which is mostly park, projecting east toward the Baltic Sea in the channels between Östermalm and Södermalm. Here are concentrated museums, including Skansen, the openair museum, amusement parks, restaurants.

Regardless of how long you intend to stay and how thoroughly you expect to see the city, begin by one or more boat excursions. Nothing else can give you a quick idea of the unique nature of Stockholm.

Let's take as a starting point the south of the large downtown park known as the Royal Gardens (Kungsträdgården), just across the rushing channel from the Royal Palace. It's an unmistakable point, easy to find. Immediately beside you is the striking profile of the statue of King Charles XII, arm raised and pointing east; behind him stretches the long park; to his right the unmistakable solid stone of the Royal Opera House, a block or so to his left the familiar façade of the Grand Hotel; and across the water the dominating walls of the palace. Furthermore, just at the water's edge at both sides of the bridge there are kiosks that serve as starting points for some of the boat and bus excursions which show you the city.

The best way to see the city is by boat—there is practically no major place of interest in and around Stockholm that isn't within easy reach of the many little boats that ply around the busy harbor. But you'll find it equally easy to explore the city on foot. Most of the principal sights are concentrated in the center of Stockholm and are relatively close to one another. If you feel like venturing further afield, use the excellent

SWEDEN

STOCKHOLM

1. Cathedral (Great Church)
2. Kaknäs Tower
3. Museum of Far Eastern Antiquities
4. Museum of Modern Art
5. National Museum
6. National Museum of Antiquities; Royal Cabinet of Coins
7. Nordiska Museum
8. Rail Station
9. Riddarholm Church
10. Riddarhuset (House of Nobility); Supreme Court
11. Riksdag (Parliament); Bank of Sweden
12. Royal Opera House
13. Royal Palace
14. Sergels Torg
15. Skansen
16. Stock Exchange
17. Tourist Information Office
18. Town Hall
19. Waldemarsudda
20. Wasa

STOCKHOLM 381

Gamla Stan

The best place to begin your exploration of the city is the Old Town, Gamla Stan, situated on three little islands. From the statue of Charles XII at the foot of the Kungsträdgården, there are two bridges leading to the Old Town, both no more than a couple of minutes' walk away. The more interesting, however, is the second, the Norrbro, leading directly to the imposing bulk of the Royal Palace. As you cross the bridge, you'll also see the Parliament building, a ponderous stone structure dating from the turn of the century, on your right. And just behind and to one side of the Parliament building is the one-time building of the Bank of Sweden, the oldest existing bank in the world, founded in 1656. Today the building is used as offices for members of parliament.

The Royal Palace is not old, as palaces go, but the site is. It was here that Stockholm was born. The original palace, the Three Crowns, burned down one night in 1697, with the exception of the northern wing of today's palace. A new palace on the old site was ordered immediately. Three generations of Sweden's most famous architectural dynasty had an important part in its creation—Nicodemus Tessin the Elder planned the exterior and began the interior decoration, which was continued by his son, Tessin the Younger, and grandson, Carl Gustav Tessin. The whole project took more than 60 years, and was not completed until 1760. The building consists basically of a perfect square—enclosing a large court—with two wings sticking out on the east side and another on the west.

A number of interiors are open to the public. You may be interested in the Hall of State, which contains the king's silver throne. The Chapel Royal in the same wing has, among other impressive historical and artistic treasures, pews saved from the old palace. If you have time, look in on the Apartments of State, the Apartments of King Oscar II and Queen Sophie, and the Guest Apartments, notable for the furnishings and extremely fine Gobelin tapestries. There's also a palace museum, with bits of the previous palace, other historical finds, and the collection of classical sculpture brought from Italy by King Gustav III in the 1780's. The Royal Treasury, in the old vaults, can now be visited.

Diagonally across the street from the south side of the palace, and intimately associated with it, is the Great Church, the Stockholm cathedral and, in a sense, the national church. You would hardly guess from the well-kept exterior that it is believed to be the oldest building in the city, dating from about 1250. Many Swedish kings have been crowned here (until Gustav V gave up the custom when he ascended the throne in 1907), and it is still used for solemn celebrations attended by the king. There are a number of art treasures, of which perhaps the oldest, best known, and most distinguished is the statue carved in wood of St. George and the Dragon by Bernt Notke of Lübeck, which was presented to the church in 1489 to commemorate a Swedish victory over the Danes some 18 years earlier. A sound and light show is performed here for a few weeks during summer.

You are in the heart of the Old Town now and there are several ways of continuing your look about. Here are two good suggestions immedi-

STOCKHOLM

ately at hand. The first is to walk downhill on the lane called Storkyrkobrinken, to the right of the main entrance of the Great Church as you come out. This lane, like practically all those of the Old Town, follows the same route it did in the Middle Ages. Everywhere around you are buildings centuries old, living history. At the base of the hill you step out in a little square called Riddarhustorget. The two dominating buildings, across the square from where you enter, both date from the 17th century. One is Riddarhuset, House of the Nobility, in which you will find the crests of Swedish noble families. The white palace to its right was once a private possession, became the city courthouse in the 18th century, and is now occupied by the Supreme Court.

From here you will see the weathered red brick and openwork spire of Riddarholm Church. This is the Swedish Pantheon, burial place of Swedish kings for about four centuries. The most famous figures buried here are King Gustavus Adolphus, hero of the Thirty Years' War, and Charles XII (in Swedish, Karl XII), who is renowned for his signal victories over the Russian and Continental armies, with inferior forces, until the tide turned against him and he fell in Norway in 1718. Two medieval kings, Magnus Ladulås, who died in 1290, and Karl Knutson Bonde, some 180 years later, are also buried here. The latest king to be put to rest was Gustav V, on November 9, 1950. Except for the funeral of a king, the church has not been used for services for a long time. The sarcophagi of the various rulers, usually embellished with their monograms, are clearly visible in the small chapels given over to the various dynasties. The church building itself is interesting as the second oldest structure in Stockholm. It is a former monastery church completed about 1290, with many additions since.

Take five minutes to continue past the church down to the quay on Lake Mälar. It's well worth it. You get a fine view of the lake, the magnificent arches of the West Bridge in the distance, the southern heights, and above all the imposing profile of the Town Hall, which appears to be almost floating on the water. At the quay you may see one of the Göta Canal ships.

The second alternative to continuing your stroll from the Great Church is to turn left as you come out of the main entrance and walk up Trångsund to a little square called Stortorget, the oldest square in Stockholm. The dominating building, on the north side, is the Stock Exchange. This is also the headquarters of the Swedish Academy, which awards the Nobel Prize in literature. The other buildings are also old; note the tall, narrow, red merchant house and its sculptured portal from the 17th century.

The Old Town is the perfect kind of place to wander around without any decided aim, looking at the old portals, poking about in crowded antique shops, savoring the Bohemian atmosphere and the sense of age, peeking into doll-sized courtyards, making your way through curving, narrow lanes. There is little auto traffic, and the passages are too narrow to provide both streets and sidewalks. Go along Skomakaregatan to the German Church (Tyska Kyrkan), turn right for a few meters, then left again on Prästgatan. Keep your eyes open as you near the end of Prästgatan, on the right you will see one of the narrowest thoroughfares in the world. It is called Mårten Trotzigs Gränd (*gränd* means lane), and leads down to Västerlånggatan. It is scarcely a meter wide, half of it is a stairway, yet it is a public thoroughfare maintained and lighted by the city.

It's only a couple of short blocks from here to the south end of the Old Town. You should really stroll on to that point. Above you are the southern heights, connected with the Old Town by an intricate cloverleaf of bridges and streets at about four levels, called Slussen. Katarina elevator—you see it poking up all by itself on the other side of the channel—takes you up to a platform with a fine view of Stockholm.

Though the Old Town is, of course, the most ancient and historic part of the city, you will have noticed by now that it is by no means lacking in modern chic. In fact it is very definitely the trendiest area of the city, both for shopping and eating, with a veritable surfeit of expensive and glamorous restaurants and shops: there are some 300 restaurants alone.

Skansen

After the sophistication and history of the Old Town, the openair amusement park of Skansen, founded in 1891, provides a striking contrast. It is situated on the large island of Djurgården, located to the west of the city. The park contains a museum, a zoo, numerous restaurants and cafes, a circus, an aquarium, a theater, a concert hall and much else besides, all combining to make it one of the enduring highlights of the city. One of its principal delights are the buildings—farm houses, windmills, barns, whole estates almost—that have been brought here from all parts of the country, giving even the most casual visitor a taste of traditional rural Sweden. There is even an 18th-century church that is still used for divine services and weddings. But many of the other buildings are in use too. Geese cackle near the entrance to the farm houses from southern Sweden; glass blowers blow glass—you can help blow it if you want to—in the old-time glass blower's hut.

Here also are moose, wolves, foxes and other Nordic animals; Sweden's largest aquarium with Cuban crocodiles; and nocturnal bushbabies, pygmy kangaroos and other strange animals in the Moonlight Hall. Many activities designed especially for children include a children's zoo.

You can walk to Skansen from the statue of Charles XII in about 30 minutes. It is a long walk, but it will take you through much of Stockholm's most gracious and substantial waterfront areas, past elegant apartment blocks and smart shops, with yachts and ferry boats ever-present, particularly on the broad expanse of Strandvägen.

Djurgården is also home to three outstanding museums: the Nordiska Museum, the Waldemarsudde and the *Wasa*. The *Wasa* is the most popular of the three, and for good reasons. The museum, distinguished by a blocky cantilevered exterior, contains one of the most remarkable maritime exhibits in the world—the 17th-century warship *Wasa*, once the pride of the Swedish navy, built at vast expense and the most powerful fighting ship of her day in the Baltic. Launched amid great pomp, she set out on her maiden voyage on August 10, 1628 in full view of the population of Stockholm, including of course the King himself. She had sailed less than a mile when a gust caught her, and she heeled over and unceremoniously sank—the *Titanic* of her day. Her precious guns were immediately savalged, but with the passage of time the *Wasa* faded from memory.

However, in 1956 her positon was rediscovered and it was found that, remarkably, the briny waters of the harbor had all but preserved her intact. A complex and difficult salvage operation was begun and in May 1961 the *Wasa* was raised to the surface and moved to her present location. Painstaking restoration has returned the ship almost to her original condition, providing the visitor with an unparalled experience of life afloat in a great warship of the past: regular guided tours, an interesting film (with English sub-titles) and a small attached museum help bring the ship to vibrant life. There are plans to move the ship to a new site a few hundred meters away, but even in her present cramped home she provides a magnificent experience.

The Nordiska Museum (the Nordic Museum), housed in a splendid late-Victorian pile, is located just by the Djurgårdsbron, the bridge leading to Djurgården. It contains a vast collection of exhibits that chart Sweden's progress from 1500. Of particular interest are some magnificent fabrics, costumes and rugs, a lovely collection of bridal gowns and the charming gold and silver coronets traditionally worn by Swedish brides.

Finally, visit Prince Eugen's "Waldemarsudde," the former home of "the Painter Prince," brother of the late King Gustav V, which was bequeathed to the people on the prince's death. The many paintings, some by Eugen himself, constitute a fine collection of Swedish art, and the mansion, art gallery, and beautiful grounds are well worth seeing.

Treasures of the Town Hall

The Stockholm Town Hall, one of the great architectural works of the 20th century, is another appropriate excursion that you can manage in a couple of hours—more if you like. Starting at the statue of Charles XII, turn to the right and merely follow the waterfront until you arrive at its massive portal. The distance is less than a couple of kilometers.

Superlatives have not been lacking in describing the structure. It has sometimes been called "the most beautiful building of this century in Europe." This opinion is not unanimous, of course; some people have reacted violently against it, but even this sharp reaction is a measure of the strength of the total impression. The building was completed and dedicated in 1923, and has become a symbol of the city. It is the seat of the city council and central administration.

The building is certainly unusual—a massive square tower rising from the corner of a graceful central block, the whole built of dark and delicately worked brick and topped by pale-green roofs with spires, domes and minarets abounding. It successfully synthesizes elements of traditional Swedish architecture, notably in the tower, which is derived from the massive castles of 16th-century Sweden, with classical elements, the resulting mixture spiced by Oriental and Byzantine windows and spires. It is difficult to decide finally whether the end-product is beautiful or kitsch—it is undoubtedly impressive.

You can go inside and look around. Among the highlights are the Golden Hall, whose walls are decorated lavishly with mosaics; the Blue Hall, confusingly named perhaps, as the only blue visible is the sky glimpsed through the windows ranged around the top of the walls; and the Prince's Gallery, with large murals by Prince Eugene. You can also go up the 106-meter (348-foot) tower (don't worry, there's an elevator) for a predictably spectacular view. At noon and 6 P.M. the carillon plays the medieval war song of the Swedes that helped gird their loins at the Battle of Brunkeberg in 1471. The adjoining Maiden Tower is surmounted by a bronze St. George and the Dragon. Finally, visit the Terrace, a formal garden on the banks of Lake Mälar with wonderful views of the Old Town and the southern heights rising beyond it.

Other Sights

Depending on the amount of time you have available and your special interests, there are many other places and institutions well worth a visit. Among the dozens of museums, these are particularly recommended: The National Museum, just a few doors down the quay from the Grand Hotel, which is home to the largest collection of paintings and sculptures, by both Swedish and foreign artists, in the country.

A few minutes walk from here on the island of Skeppesholmen are the Museum of Modern Art and the Museum of Far Eastern Antiquities, both with fine collections, the latter a pleasing spot to explore or simply from which to admire the view of the Old Town.

The National Museum of Antiquities and Royal Cabinet of Coins, located to the east of the city on the spacious boulevard of Narvavägen, contains a veritable mass of historical finds dating back well into the Stone Age.

Although not a museum, there is a further attraction on Djurgården—the 155-meter (508-foot) high Kaknäs Tower, Stockholm's latest tourist attraction. The fastest elevators in Europe hurtle you up to the observation deck, from where an unparalleled view of the city and the Stockholm Archipelago stretches before you.

Music and Markets

The Concert Hall, at Hörtorget, is the center of Stockholm's musical life. The building, designed by Ivar Tengbom, was completed in 1926. In front is Carl Milles' huge sculptured group of Orpheus calling up the spirits. It is in this hall that the awarding of the Nobel Prizes takes place.

It's well worth your while to get to one of the market squares fairly early in the day—9:00 A.M. will do—which are masses of color whatever the season of the year. One is just in front of the Concert House, another on Östermalm. Flowers, fresh fruits and vegetables are the principal stock in trade. Look in at the indoor markets which adjoin these squares—there you can fill your whole grocery basket from the little shops of independent dealers, and have a snack in one of the small restaurants. This is a unique aspect of Stockholm life. Incidentally, the outdoor markets operate right through the winter.

Excursions from Stockholm

Immediately outside the city limits of Stockholm proper are a number of popular attractions which you can reach within an hour by public transportation, or half an hour by car.

The sculptor Carl Milles, who was perhaps better known as an inhabitant of Cranbrook, Michigan, had his permanent home on the island of Lidingö, a Stockholm suburb, where he collected not only some of his own best works but other outstanding pieces from several eras and countries. It was here that he died in September 1955, still hard at work at the age of 80.

The royal palace of Drottningholm is located on a little island in Lake Mälar—the name means "Queen's Island"—a few kilometers from Stockholm. The trip is a pleasant experience, particularly by boat. If you have seen Versailles, you will be reminded of it at once when you arrive at Drottningholm, for it was clearly inspired by the French style. The palace was built by Nicodemus Tessin the Elder, and his son, Tessin the Younger, completed the gardens in the style of Le Nôtre.

Drottningholm is one of the most delightful of European palaces, embracing, as it does, all that was best in the art of living practiced by mid-18th-century royalty. In the grounds, a kind of Trianon, is the China Palace, conceived in Chinoiserie terms, a lovely little palace, hidden in the trees, where the royal family could relax and entertain their friends. Also in the grounds is the Theater. This fascinating building slumbered like the Sleeping Beauty undisturbed for well over a century, the settings and stage machinery of the 18th century in perfect condition and working order. It now houses a theater museum and delightful productions of baroque opera are once again staged in the auditorium that saw the efforts of Gustavus III to create a Swedish Golden Age. The Royal Family occupies one wing at the palace.

Haga Palace, formerly the home of the late Crown Prince Gustav Adolf, is located only a few minutes from downtown, right on the city limits of Stockholm. A more interesting building located on the same grounds is Haga Pavilion. It is a miniature summer palace built by Gustav III (late 18th century), exquisitely furnished.

The resort of Saltsjöbaden is a residential suburb the year round. During the summer it is a rendezvous for yachtsmen and motorboat enthusiasts, and the harbor is excellent. In winter there is skating, skate-sailing, iceboating, and skiing. The modern Stockholm observatory is located here. You can reach Saltsjöbaden from Slussen on an electric train. In the same general direction, but to the north, is Gustavsberg, where the noted ceramics works may be visited in groups by previous appointment.

PRACTICAL INFORMATION FOR STOCKHOLM

GETTING TO TOWN FROM THE AIRPORT. Buses from Arlanda Airport to the city, a distance of 45 km. (28 miles) are frequent. The trip takes about 45 minutes and the bus stops at the Scandic Hotel on request and at the Haga Air Terminal. The final stop is at the Central Station, which, as the name suggests, is in the center of town. The Sheraton, Royal Viking, Terminus and Continental hotels are all within two minutes' walk. The fare is approximately SEK 30, payable to the driver. You can also buy a ticket at special ticket offices at the airport and the air terminal. A scheduled bus service to Brommaplan from the airport is also available, with stops at Kista and Sundbyberg subway stations.

A taxi to the city from the airport will cost you about SEK 300. However, a share-a-taxi service is available, which takes you direct to your address or hotel for about SEK 125 per person; the reservation desk at the airport is clearly marked. For the return journey, ask the hotel to book for you.

TOURIST INFORMATION. The Tourist Center is located in the middle of the city in Sverigehuset (Sweden House), opposite the large department store *Nordiska Kompaniet*, or *N.K.*, in Kungsträdgården (789 20 00). There you will find information about interesting sights and events, one-day tours and so on. They also sell maps, postcards, books and souvenirs. The Tourist Center is open every day.

A useful publication is *This Week in Stockholm* which you can get from most hotels and all tourist centers. From a kiosk on Norrmalmstorg you can buy last-minute tickets at reduced prices to concerts and theaters.

USEFUL ADDRESSES. Embassies. *American Embassy,* Strandvägen 101 (63 05 20). *British Embassy,* Skarpögatan 6–8 (67 01 40). *Canadian Embassy,* Tegelbacken 4 (near the Sheraton) (23 79 20).

Travel Agents. *American Express,* Sturegatan 8 (22 88 60). *Cooks,* Vasagatan 22 (762 58 37).

Car-Hire. *Avis,* Linnegatan 9–11 (63 07 15), and Sheraton Hotel, Vasagatan 4 (20 20 60). *Hertz,* Odengatan 32 (16 00 95). *Europcar,* Birger Jarlsgatan 59 (23 10 70). All the major car-hire companies also have desks at Arlanda airport.

TELEPHONE CODES. The telephone code for Stockholm is 08. To call any number in this chapter, unless otherwise specified, this prefix must be used. Within the city, no prefix is required.

HOTELS. It is recommended that you reserve hotel rooms well in advance, especially from September to November. If you arrive in Stockholm without a reservation, consult the Hotellcentralen in the underground Central Station. This room booking-service is open Mon. to Fri. 8 A.M.–9 P.M., Sat. 8 A.M.–5 P.M., Sun. 1 P.M.–9 P.M., June to September. During the rest of the year it is open on weekdays from 8.30 A.M.–4.45 P.M., Sun. 2–11 P.M. A charge is made for each room reserved. Most hotels have smoke-free rooms and rooms for the handicapped. Breakfast is usually included in the room rate. In general, Stockholm hotels are comfortable, but prices are high.

For information about low-priced packages at weekends and during the summer months, write to *Destination Stockholm,* Stora Hoparegränd 5, S-11130 Stockholm. This company offers Stockholm packages which include low hotel

STOCKHOLM

rates, free transportation within the city and free or reduced entry to museums. Travelers with caravans can make arrangements to park them at some schools in the city during the summer months. Enquire at tourist offices.

Deluxe

Amaranten. Kungsholmsgatan 31 (54 10 60). 363 rooms. Contains the *Amaryllis* restaurant, the *Travellers'* piano bar and a nightclub called *Cindy*. It also boasts a Japanese-style recreation area and an "executive tower" with a roof garden and luxurious accommodation. Subway stop in the building. AE, DC, MC, V.

Boatel Mälardrottningen (Queen of Lake Mälar). Riddarholmen (24 36 00). 59 cabins on what was formerly American heiress—and wife of Cary Grant—Barbara Hutton's luxury yacht (built 1924). All cabins are furnished to deluxe hotel standards and the yacht has an attractive permanent berth at Riddarholmskajen, close to the Old Town. It has a restaurant and a bar on the bridge. Quiet location. AE, DC, MC, V.

Grand. Blasieshamnen 8 (22 10 20). 352 rooms; front rooms face the Royal Palace and the waterfront. A distinguished European deluxe hotel. SAS office, splendid ballroom, famous restaurant. *Thé dansant* on Sun. AE, DC, MC, V.

Grand Hotel Saltsjöbaden. Saltsjöbaden (717 00 20). 100 rooms in a suburban resort setting, 30 minutes by train from Slussen. Castle-like building in landscaped grounds fronting on to the water, with a marina. Elegant turn-of-the-century interior. Restaurant with a wonderful view. Sauna. AE, DC, MC, V.

Park Hotel. Karlavägen 43 (22 96 20). 205 rooms. Quiet, central location next to Humlegården Park, within walking distance of the city center. Restaurant, garden café, garage. AE, DC, MC, V.

Reisen. Skeppsbron 12–14 (22 32 60). 125 rooms. A SARA hotel built behind the facade of three 17th-century houses. Has the *Quarter Deck* restaurant and the best piano bar in town. Saunas, pool, garage. AE, DC, MC, V.

Royal Viking. Vasagatan 1 (14 10 00). 400 rooms. The newest hotel of high international standard. Within walking distance of the city center and shopping. Has a "skybar" overlooking the Town Hall and Old Town, a relaxation center with saunas (private saunas also available) and a wintergarden, the *Royal Atrium*, with a 36-meter-high (120-ft.) ceiling. Airport bus, trains and subway just outside the door. AE, DC, MC, V.

Sergel Plaza. Brunkebergstorg 31 (24 40 20). 425 rooms, very central. Features trees and waterfalls in the glass-roofed lobby. Opened in 1984, it has a restaurant, the *Café des Artistes*, saunas, solarium, bubblepool. AE, DC, MC, V.

Sheraton-Stockholm. Tegelbacken 6 (14 26 00). 476 rooms. Next to the air terminal and railway station with a view of the Old Town and the Town Hall. The restaurant, *Le Bistro*, is open until 2.30 A.M. Piano bar, boutiques, garage. AE, DC, MC, V.

Strand. Nybrokajen 9 (22 29 00). 135 rooms. Central location opposite the *Royal Dramatic Theater*. The building dates from 1912 and was completely renovated in 1984. Wintergarden with a ceiling seven stories high and an outstanding gourmet restaurant. AE, DC, MC, V.

Expensive

Anglais. Humlegårdsgatan 23 (24 99 00). 212 rooms. One of the leading hotels in Stockholm, conveniently situated near shopping districts and the subway. Popular restaurant, own video channel, garage. AE, DC, MC, V.

Continental. Vasagatan (24 99 00). 250 rooms. Opposite the railway station and the air terminal (RESO). *Nike* restaurant, *Bistro Chez Charles, Cafetaria Concorde*. AE, DC, MC, V.

Diplomat. Strandvägen 7C (63 58 00). 132 rooms. On the waterfront, within walking distance of Djurgården Park and Skansen as well as the city center. Turn-of-the-century atmosphere. Popular tea-house. AE, DC, MC, V.

Lady Hamilton. Storkyrkobrinken 5 (23 46 80). 35 rooms. A gem of a hotel. Built in 1470 and converted to an hotel in 1980. A large collection of antiques including one of George Romney's portrait of Lady Hamilton. The Storkyrkan (the cathedral) and the Royal Palace are neighbors. Cafeteria. AE, DC, MC, V.

Lord Nelson. Västerlånggatan 5 (23 23 90). 31 small rooms. Small hotel right in the middle of the Old Town and twinned, naturally enough, with the nearby Lady Hamilton. Atmosphere throughout is decidedly nautical, even down to the cabin-sized rooms. However, standards of comfort and service are high. Sauna; no restaurant. Cafeteria. AE, DC, MC, V.

SAS Arlandia. At Arlanda Airport (0760-618 00). 307 rooms. Five minutes by bus from the airport. Restaurant, bar, nightclub, cinema, sauna, indoor pool, tennis. Close to golf and bathing. AE, DC, MC, V.

Terminus. Vasagatan 20 (22 26 20). 155 rooms. Handy down-town location, if possibly noisy, opposite Central Station and close to airport buses. Popular restaurant, *Kasper.* AE, DC, MC, V.

Moderate

Adlon. Vasagatan 42 (24 54 00). 58 rooms, 38 with bath. Central. AE, MC, V.

Alexandra. Magnus Ladulåsgatan 42 (84 03 20). 90 rooms. In the heart of Södermalm (south of Slussen). Five minutes to the city by the nearby subway. No restaurant. AE, DC, MC, V.

Aston. Mariatorget 3 (44 06 90). 68 rooms. Near the subway, a short walk to Skinnarviksbergen, with an enchanting panorama of the city. A well-run hotel. Popular dance restaurant. AE, DC, MC, V.

August Strindberg. Tegnérlunden 38 (32 50 06). 19 rooms in a building dating from 1890. Near a park, quiet, central. No elevator. AE, MC, V.

Birger Jarl. Tulegatan 8 (15 10 20). 251 rooms. Unlicensed. Quiet location within walking distance of Stureplan and the city center. Connected with neighboring church; has weekly services in English. Keep-fit area with a sauna and pool. Cafeteria. AE, DC, MC, V.

Brooma. Brommaplan (25 29 20). 140 rooms. Ten minutes by subway downtown, ten minutes by bus to Drottningholm Palace. Direct bus to Arlanda Airport. Restaurant, garage, small garden (RESO). AE, MC, V.

City. Slöjdgatan 7 (22 20 40). 300 rooms. Central. Close to the Hötorget market. Many smoke-free rooms; seven rooms specially equipped for the handicapped. Run by the Salvation Army. Unlicensed. Elegant restaurant. Magnificent indoor wintergarden. AE, DC, MC, V.

Eden. Sturegatan 10 (22 31 60). 60 rooms, some with balconies. On two top floors of an office building. Breakfast room with a summer terrace overlooking Humlegården Park. Central. AE, DC, MC, V.

Esplanade. Strandvägen 7A (63 07 40). Within walking distance of Djurgården, Skansen and the city center. A turn-of-the-century atmosphere. Breakfast only. Closed in July. AE, DC, MC, V.

Flamingo. Centralvägen 20, Solna (83 08 00). 129 rooms. Ten minutes by subway from the city. Restaurant, dancing, grillroom. Solna has a large shopping center. AE, DC, MC, V.

Flyghotellet. Brommaplan (26 26 20). 68 rooms. By subway, ten minutes from the city; by bus, ten minutes to Drottningholm Palace. Direct airport bus. AE, DC, MC, V.

Gamla Stan. Lilla Nygatan 25 (24 44 50). 62 rooms, 20 with baths. In the Old Town. Run by the Salvation Army. Cafeteria. AE, MC, V.

Karelia. Birger Jarlsgatan 35 (24 76 60). 87 rooms. A few minutes walk from Stureplan. Finnish sauna and pool. Restaurant with Finnish and Russian specialities, dancing, nightclub. A bit of Finland in the heart of Stockholm. AE, DC, MC, V.

KOM. Döbelnsgatan 17 (23 56 30). 63 rooms. Central, quiet. Kitchenette with refrigerator in all rooms. Breakfast only. Near the subway. AE, DC, MC, V.

Mornington. Nybrogatan 53 (24 36 00). 123 rooms. Near the indoor market at Östermalmstorg, within walking distance of theaters and shopping. Elegant fish restaurant. AE, DC, MC, V.

Palace. St. Eriksgatan 115 (24 12 20). 215 rooms. Near the Haga Air Terminal. Sauna, garage. AE, DC, MC, V.

STOCKHOLM

Scandic Hotel. Järva Krog, Uppsalavägen, Solna (85 03 60). 215 rooms, of which 79 are smoke-free. North of the city on E 4. The airport bus stops here on request, and there's a regular bus service to the city. The *Rotisserie Musketör* on the 11th floor has a fine view of Brunnsviken Lake. AE, DC, MC, V.

Stockholm. Norrmalmstorg 1 (22 13 20). 101 rooms, 64 with baths. The hotel is on the top floor of an office building with Kungsträdgården Park and the *N.K.* department store just around the corner. Breakfast only. AE, MC, V.

Inexpensive

Anno 1647. Mariagränd 3 (44 04 80). 40 rooms, 16 with baths. Also some higher priced and elegant rooms. Located in a centuries-old building close to Slussen. Historic surroundings. A few steps from the subway and the ferry to Skansen. Breakfast only. No restaurant. AE, DC, MC, V.

Domus. Körsbärsvägen 1 (16 01 95). 78 rooms. Near subway. Family apartments with pantry available. Restaurant. AE, DC, MC, V.

Jerum. Studentbacken 2 (15 50 90 and June through Aug. 63 53 80). 120 rooms, all with showers. This student hostel is only open June, July and August. Close to Gärdet subway station, five minutes to the city. Cafeteria. AE, DC, MC, V.

Kristineberg. Hjalmar Söderbergsväg 10 (13 03 00). 143 rooms, 12 with baths. Near a subway station, seven minutes from the city. Free sauna. Popular restaurant suitable for motorists. AE, DC, MC, V.

Regent. Drottninggatan 10, 3rd floor (20 90 04). 16 rooms without baths. Central. No credit cards.

Savoy. Bryggargaran 12 (22 12 80). 53 rooms. By the main post office. No restaurant. AE, MC, V.

Zinken. Pipmakargränd 2 (58 50 11). 25 rooms. The hotel consists of a number of pavilions near Zinkensdam subway station. Large garden with play area, access to washing machine and kitchen. Also youth hostel. No credit cards.

Camping

Bredäng Camping. (A4) Skärholmen (97 70 71). A 3-star camping site at Ålgrytevägen in Sätra, ten km. (six miles) south of Stockholm. Follow the signs from E4. 500 meters (about 500 yards) to the subway, bathing, canoe rentals and so on. Rates approximately SEK 60 per night. Open all year.

Ängby Camping. (A3) Bromma (37 04 20). West of Stockholm at Södra Ängby. A 2-star camping site. Beach at Lake Mälar. Rates approximately SEK 45 per night. Summer only.

Youth Hostels

af Chapman. Skeppsholmen (10 37 15). 130 beds. A 100-year-old sailing ship with the same view as the Grand Hotel in the historic heart of the city. Open all year. Stays are limited to five nights.

Skeppsholmen Hostel. (20 25 06). Behind af Chapman. 132 beds. Open all year.

Columbus Hostel. Tjärhovsgatan 1 (44 17 17). 120 beds. Open all year.

Gustaf af Klint. A ship at quay-berth 153, at Stadsgården near Slussen (40 40 77). 51 beds. Open all night and all year.

Zinken. Pipmakargränd 2 (68 57 86). 268 beds. Near Zinkensdamm subway station. Garden. Open all year.

Karlsholmen. Norra Stavsudda (0766-65 090). 17 beds. In the archipelago. Open June through Aug.

There are also hostels at Gällnö, Möja, Arholma and Fjärdlång—all in the archipelago.

HOW TO GET AROUND. By subway and bus. The transport system is divided into zones. Tickets may be bought as coupons from ticket counters or from drivers. The basic fare is SEK 3 for journeys within one zone. Your ticket entitles you to unlimited transfers within one hour of the time your ticket was punched. Additional fares are paid for trips to the suburbs and an average trip would cost SEK 6. Senior citizens and youths under 18 can travel for half fare.

A discount card with 20 coupons is available at SEK 35. However, if you plan to use the transportation system frequently, it's a good idea to buy a monthly card at SEK 140—you'll need a photo for this one. A one-day tourist card giving unlimited travel costs SEK 16 and a card for three days SEK 55. Again, children pay half fare. Discount tickets and tourist cards are sold at *Pressbyrån* kiosks at the stations.

New stations are added to the subway system every three years or so, as the new lines become ready. At many of the newer stations, there are interesting works of art on display—the T-banan must be the world's deepest and longest art gallery. Just to get a brief look, take the subway from T-Centralen to Fridhemsplan via Rådhuset and return via Odenplan, where you will find an old horse-drawn carriage on the platform. A pamphlet in English is available from the T-Centralen Station (exit Drottninggatan).

By taxi. For a taxi ring 15 00 00. English-speaking drivers are available on request if you want to go sightseeing by taxi or on a special excursion. Ask for a "tourist taxi." You can also hail a taxi on the street—the sign *Ledig* indicates that the cab is for hire. Taxis are expensive in Stockholm, and more so at night. Tip about 15% in all taxis.

By boat. For information about boats to the archipelago call at the kiosk outside the Grand Hotel.

TOURS. A number of sightseeing tours around Stockholm are available, of which perhaps the most interesting are the numerous boat trips to and around the archipelago. The majority of these leave from in front of the Grand Hotel—normally at 8 A.M.—and can provide meals. There is an information office here, but details are also available from the tourist office. In addition, there are walking tours around the Old Town every evening from the end of May to mid-September. Authorized city guides may also be hired through the tourist office; call 789 20 00, but book well in advance.

For excursions further afield, try Sandhamn, a yachting center reached by boat from Stavsnäs, where races are held during July and August. A one-hour boat trip from Strömkajen in Stockholm will take you to Vaxholm, where an ancient fortress which is now a military museum guards the channel into Stockholm. A trip by boat or bus to the Gustavsberg porcelain factory might be worthwhile for reduced-price bargains. The porcelain museum is open weekdays only. A fascinating trip on Lake Mälar can be made on the classic steamer S/S *Mariefred* (daily; approximately SEK 100). Also of interest is the university town of Uppsala, an hour north of Stockholm by train. The cathedral here is the seat of the Archbishop of Sweden. Every Sunday in July and August there is a "Viking Tour" starting in Uppsala at 1 P.M., which includes breaks for "mead" at Odinsborg and for coffee at Vendel (SEK 100).

MUSEUMS. The visitor to Stockholm has a wide choice of museums to see. The entrance fee is from SEK 5 to SEK 10, with children at half price or less. Many museums are closed on Monday; they also tend to close earlier on Saturday and Sunday.

Armemuseum (Royal Army Museum). Located behind the Royal Dramatic Theater at Riddargatan 13. Exhibits from crossbows to automatic rifles and missiles. Equipment of the Swedish Army from many centuries. Open daily 11–4.

STOCKHOLM

Biologiska Museet (Biological Museum). Next to Skansen. An old museum showing Nordic animals against panoramic natural backgrounds. Open daily 10–4.

Etnografiska Museet (Ethnographical Museum). Djurgårdsbrunnsvägen 34. Famous collections from Third-World cultures. A newly-built museum. Bus 69. Open Mon. to Fri. 11–4, Sat. and Sun. 12–4; closed Mon.

Hallwyl Museum. Hamngatan 4, near Norrmalmstorg (10 21 66). A palatial building dating from around 1900. Fine collections of painting, sculpture, furniture, ceramics, arms etc. Guided tours only, at 12 A.M., 1, 2 and 3 P.M., with no more than ten people in every group. July through Aug., daily tours at 2 P.M. in English. Musical entertainments on summer evenings. Closed Mon.

Historiska Museet (Museum of National Antiquities). Narvavägen 13–17. Treasures of the Vikings and their ancestors. In same building as the **Royal Cabinet of Coin**, which includes the world's largest coin. Bus 44 and 47. Open daily 11–4; closed Mon.

Liljevalchs Konsthall (Liljevalch Art Gallery). On Djurgården. Temporary exhibitions, mostly of Swedish contemporary art. Café Blå Porten. Bus 47. Open Tues. to Sun. 11–5, also Tues. and Thurs. 5–9; closed Mon.

Livrustkammaren (Royal Armory). In the cellars of the Royal Palace with entrance at Slottsbacken. Swedish State collections of historical objects, such as costumes, arms and armory of Swedish royalty from 16th century on. Gilded parade coaches. Light and sound effects. Open Mon. to Fri. 10–4, Sat. and Sun. 11–4.

Medelhavsmuseett (Mediterranean Museum). Fredsgatan 2 at Gustav Adolfs Torg. 2,500 year-old terracotta sculptures of Cypriot warriors. Also a large Egyptian collection and an exhibition from the Islamic countries. Open Tues. to Sun. 11–4; closed Mon.

Millesgården. Lidingö. Former residence of Swedish-American sculptor Carl Milles. He had his home at Lidingö in later years, where he collected not only some of his own work, but also other outstanding pieces from several eras. He died here in 1955 at the age of 80, still at work. Sparkling fountains and monuments with a view of Stockholm as a background. (The Orpheus Fountain outside the Concert House was made by Milles in 1936). Subway to Ropsten and then by bus. Open daily 11–4; closed in winter.

Moderna Museet (Museum of Modern Art and Photography). On Skeppsholmen, behind the sailing ship youth hostel *af Chapman*. Paintings by Scandinavian artists and Picasso, Dali, Matisse, Warhol and many more. Temporary exhibitions. Restaurant. Open Tues. to Fri. 11–9, Sat. and Sun. 11–5; closed Mon.

Nationalmuseet (National Art Gallery). A few steps from the Grand Hotel. Great masters from 1500 to 1900. Also prints, drawings and applied art from the Renaissance to the present day. Cafeteria and good shop. Open Tues. 10–9, Wed. to Sun. 10–4; closed Mon.

Nordiska Museet (Nordic Museum). Djurgården. Largest collection of objects showing the progress of civilization in Sweden since 1500. Magnificent specimens of rural art. Lovely collection of bridal crowns and much more. Bus 47. Open Tues. to Fri. 10–4, Sat. and Sun. 12–5; closed Mon.

Sjöhistoriska Museet (National Maritime Museum). Djurgårdsvägen 24. Collections illustrating history of Swedish navy and merchant marine. Unique ship models. The original stern of a royal schooner with the king's cabin. Bus 69. Open daily 11–5.

Stockholms Leksaksmuseum (Toy Museum). Mariatorget 1C. Thousands of toys, dolls, dollshouses, tin soldiers etc. on four floors. Two large model railways are usually demonstrated on weekends. Subway Mariatorget. Open Tues. to Fri. 10–4, Sat. and Sun. 12–4; closed Mon.

Stockholms Stadsmuseum (City Museum). At Slussen subway station. The history of Stockholm, illustrated by many archeological finds. Models of the former palaces "Tre Kronor" (Three Crowns) and "Non Pareil." Pleasant cafeteria. Open Tues. to Thurs. 11–9, Fri. to Mon. 11–5.

Tekniska Museet (Science and Technology Museum). Museivägen, on the way to the Kaknäs Tower. Models of machines illustrating developments in technical engineering and industry. Vintage aeroplanes, cars' engines; comput-

394 **SWEDEN**

ers, telecommunications. A mine with shafts etc. Cafeteria. Bus 69 from Karlaplan. Open Mon. to Fri. 10–4, Sat. and Sun. 12–4.

Thielska Galleriet (Thiel Art Gallery). Djurgården near Blockhusudden. Private collection of Scandinavian and French art from around 1900. Beautiful surroundings. Bus 69 from Karlaplan. Open daily 12–4.

Waldemarsudde. Djurgården. Former home of Prince Eugen, a great-grand uncle to the present King. He was a well-known painter and many of the Prince's own works are displayed here. Also Nordic collections. The turn-of-the-century house is surrounded by a beautiful garden on the shores of the Baltic. Cafeteria. Bus 47. Open Tues. to Sun. 11–4; closed Mon.

Wasavarvet (Wasa Museum). On Djurgården, on the way to Skansen just below the Liljevalchs Konsthall. The salvaged 17th-century man-of-war, *Wasa*. She sank in Stockholm harbor on her maiden voyage in 1628. Rediscovered in 1956, she was raised and drydocked in 1961. The restoration is now almost complete. This is the oldest preserved warship in the world. A film of the *Wasa* rebirth is shown every hour. Guided tours in English. Cafeteria, souvenir shop. Bus 47. Open daily 10–5.

PARKS, ZOOS AND GARDENS. Djurgården (Royal Deer Park) and Skansen. A beautiful island covered in pathways, meadows and trees. Also a marina, many museums, Gröna Lund amusement park, Skansen and its zoo, aquarium, openair theater and various displays, and much more. Rent a bike near the bridge or take a leisurely stroll. You can also rent canoes. In summer most of the roads are closed to cars. Bus 47 or ferry from Slussen or Nybroplan (summer only).

Fjällgatan. To get a good view of the Old Town and the harbor, take the subway to Slussen and walk up on Katarina Bangatan to Fjällgatan. Most sight-seeing buses stop here for a short time.

Kungsträdgården (King's Garden). Easy to find, just across the rushing water from the Royal Palace. It contains the striking statue of King Charles XII (Karl den tolfte) with his arm raised pointing east. On the right is the Royal Opera House, and behind that the elm trees, once threatened to make way for a new subway station, but saved by city-wide protests in 1971. The station was built elsewhere. Have a sandwich under the elms at the teahouse. The fountain in the park, built in 1873, features pictures of Nordic mythology. There are many activities in the park in summer. You can listen to music, learn to dance the Swedish *Hambo* or play chess; in winter you can skate. A meeting place for tourists and others.

Långholmsparken. Below Västerbron on the south side. Take the path to the top for the view. Some former prison buildings are still here—debate continues over the possibility of using them for a youth hostel or hotel. The little cottage is open for coffee when the flag is up. Subway Hornstull.

Skinnarviksparken. Beautiful panorama from this park. Nearest subway is Zinkensdamm. Walk towards the lake and up the mountain past some newly restored historic buildings.

HISTORIC BUILDINGS AND SITES. Drottningholm Palace. On an island in Lake Mälar, a few kilometers from Stockholm. Reminiscent of Versailles, a magnificent 17th-century French-style building. Also in the grounds are the lovely Chinese Palace and the original court theater, with its 18th-century settings and stage machinery in perfect working order. Theater museum. Subway to Brommaplan and bus. The Palace, Court Theater and Chinese Palace are open daily May through Sept. The latter also Apr. and Oct.

Gamla Stan (Old Town). Follow a lane called Storkyrkobrinken from the Great Church, past buildings that are centuries old, to a square at the base of the hill called Riddarhustorget. The two dominating buildings in the square, Riddarhuset (House of Nobility) and the white palace to its right, both date from the 17th century. The latter now houses the Supreme Court.

Haga Palace and Haga Pavilion. On the city limits of Stockholm, in Haga Park near Brunnsviken. Former home of the late Crown Prince Gustav Adolf.

STOCKHOLM

The Pavilion is the more interesting building—a miniature summer palace built by Gustav III in the late-18th century. Bus 52 to Haga Air Terminal. Guided tours every hour. Open May through Aug., Tues. to Sun. 12–3; Sept., Tues. to Sun. 1–3.

Kaknästornet (Kaknäs Tower). Djurgården. T.V. tower, 155 meters (508 ft.) high. Indoor and outdoor platforms with breathtaking view. Cafeteria and restaurant, tourist bureau and souvenir shop. Bus 69. Open Oct. through Mar., daily 9–6; Apr. and Sept., daily 9–10; May and Aug., daily 9–12 midnight.

Kunglia Slottet (Royal Palace). Completed 1760. Hall of State (contains the King's silver throne), the Chapel Royal (Sunday service open to the public), the Apartments of State and of King Oscar and Queen Sophie, as well as the Guest Apartments are all open to the public daily. Also the Palace Museum (classical sculptures and antiquities), the Royal Treasury, with its collection of Crown Jewels, and the Royal Armory. All or part of the palace may be closed when state visits, royal dinners etc. are held. Changing of the guard, June through Aug., Mon. to Fri. at 12.10 P.M., Sun. at 1.10 P.M. Jan. through May, Wed., Sat. and Sun.; Sept. through Dec., Wed. and Sun. There is no band playing in the winter.

Mårten Trotzigs Gränd (Yard-wide Lane). In the Old Town, at the end of Prästgatan, leading down to Västerlånggatan. One of the narrowest thoroughfares in the world, scarcely a yard (a meter) wide.

Riddarholm Church. On Riddarholm Island. This is the Swedish Pantheon; burial place of 17 Swedish kings over about four centuries. Subway Gamla Stan. Open May through Aug., daily.

Stadshuset (Town Hall). Completed 1923, it is the symbol of Stockholm and of considerable architectural interest. The tower, with a magnificent view, is open May through Sept., daily 11–3. Guided tours of the Town Hall, Mon. to Sat. at 10 A.M.; Sun. and holidays at 10 and 12 A.M.

Storkyrkan (Great Church). Across the street from the south side of the Royal Palace. Believed to be the oldest building in the city, dating from about 1250. Contains Ehienstrahl's *Last Judgement*, one of the world's largest paintings, and other art treasures. As Stockholm's cathedral, this is a living church with a congregation and sightseeing during services is not allowed. Occasionally there are sound and light performances.

Swedish Academy. North side of Stortorget, near the Royal Palace. Historic building, the headquarters of the Swedish Academy, which awards the Nobel Prize in literature.

SPORTS. Tennis. There are a number of indoor tennis courts as well as outdoor courts at: Hjorthagen, in Jägmästargatan; Smedslätten, in Gustav Adolfs Park; South Ängby, in Färjestadsvägen; Enskede, Mälarhöjden, and Älvsjö sports grounds.

Golf. Golfing enthusiasts have a choice of 14 18-hole courses. Among the best are: Stockholm Golf Club, Kevinge, train from Östra Station or bus from Jarlaplan; Djursholms Golf Club, Eddavägen Station, train from Östra Station; Drottningholm Golf Club, bus from St. Eriksgatan; Lidingö Golf Club, Sticklinge, underground to Ropsten thence bus; Saltsjöbaden Golf Club, Tattby Station, train from Saltsjöbanan Station, Slussen (change at Igelboda); on Värmdö, at Hemmestavik (bus from Borgmästaregatan) where Sweden's first Country Club recently opened.

Swimming. Långholmsparken or Mariebergsbadet. It's quite something to be able to swim in the center of a big city these days.

Fishing. You may fish free of charge from the bridges of Stockholm; the water is cleaner today than 50 years ago and salmon have been caught just in front of the Royal Palace. *Fritidsfiskarna* (19 78 20) can arrange to rent you tackle, if you give them a few days' notice. For deep-water fishing, call 51 51 14. The boats leave from Dalarö. Take the train to Handen and then bus 839 to the pier. Tackle for rent on board. Cost is approximately SEK 100 for a day's excursion.

Winter sports. There are a number of ski trails in the vicinity of Stockholm and in the Södertörn and Roslagen areas. The track at Nacka is floodlit for night skiing. Both Fiskartorpet and Hammarby have slalom runs, lifts and ski jumps.

For ice skating, there are the Stadium, Östermalm Sports Ground, Tennis Stadium and Johanneshov Rink at Sandstuvägen; many parks, including central Kungsträdgården, have winter rinks.

You can rent downhill skiing equipment and cross-country skis at Skidmarknaden, Sturegatan 20 (67 75 75).

Spectator sports. If you want to be a spectator, call 22 18 40 and Miss Frida will tell you about the sporting events of the day in a taperecorded message.

Biking and canoeing. Bikes and canoes are available for rent at Djurgården bridge.

MUSIC, MOVIES AND THEATERS. Music. Stockholm's two musical centers are the *Royal Opera House* and the *Stockholm Concert House.* The Royal Opera, located just across the bridge from the Royal Palace, has a season running from mid-August until about June 10. The Ballet Festival is in the first week of June.

The concert season lasts from about the middle of September to about the middle of May. The Stockholm Concert Association Orchestra is in regular service at the Concert House and is fully up to international standards. But of even greater interest perhaps is the veritable parade of top international virtuosos and guest conductors, representing the cream of European, British and American talent.

Every day during the summer, concerts and other kinds of entertainment are held in the openair at *Skansen.* Also, the *Gröna Lund* amusement park, open May through September, has daily open-air performances with Swedish and foreign artists. Between June 15 and the end of August, there are free concerts in the city's many parks. In the *Kungsträdgården* there are daily recorded concerts and, three evenings a week at least, free entertainment on the outdoor stage, often featuring leading variety artists.

A unique experience is to attend a concert at the *National Museum* (Art Gallery), held four times during August. Occasionally there are also concerts in the *Royal Palace.*

For information about concerts and theaters, call at the kiosk on Norrmalmstorg where you can also buy reduced price tickets for same-day performances.

Movies. English and American movies dominate. They are shown with Swedish sub-titles and are often released at the same time as they appear in London or New York. See the evening papers for programs. The advertisements usually mention the English as well as the Swedish title.

Theaters. Several theaters specialize in light opera—playing classics and modern musicals. It's great fun hearing and seeing a familiar perennial in a strange theater and a strange language (though many may find the language barrier insuperable). Season: Sept. to mid-June.

The *Royal Dramatic Theater*—scene of the debuts of Greta Garbo and Ingrid Bergman—actually consists of two theaters, one for major performances and a smaller one for those of more limited public interest. A number of the plays presented here and at other Stockholm theaters are hits still running in New York or London. Season: Sept. through May.

Particularly recommended is the *Court Theater* of Drottningholm Palace, a few minutes to a half-hour from downtown Stockholm by car or bus (or 50 minutes by boat). This is an 18th-century theater which was somehow lost sight of, closed up for years, and when reopened a few decades ago was found to be in its original condition. The repertoire consists almost entirely of operas and ballets contemporary with the theater: in other words, of works written for that kind of stage. Seeing a performance there is a unique theater event. Performances during May, June, July, August and September, two to four evenings a week. Again, call at the kiosk on Norrmalmstorg for information and tickets.

STOCKHOLM

SHOPPING. Shopping in Stockholm tends to be expensive, but you can be sure of the quality. You can also take advantage of the Scandinavian Taxfree scheme, under which a part of your sales tax will be refunded at the airport. Ask for details at the shop; you need special receipts to present at the airport, harbor or on board ship. See also "Shopping" in *Facts at Your Fingertips*. When you see the word REA, it means there's a sale in progress. The best REAs are after Christmas and mid-summer.

First shopping stop in Stockholm should be the *Nordiska Kompaniet*, known as N.K., at Hamngatan 18–20. This store is a sort of combination Neiman-Marcus and Harrods, with a few specialities of its own thrown in; you can find almost anything you might want to buy here. Opposite the N.K. is the *Gallerian shopping arcade*, where you can find shoes, clothing, books, antiques, perfume, cameras and much more. On the other side of the fountain is *Åhléns*, a huge department store near Sergels Torg, Drottninggatan and Hötorget. And here also is the *P.U.B.* department store, in buildings on both sides of Drottninggatan with a tunnel connection. The P.U.B. also has an extensive range, but is less luxurious and lower-priced. It faces on to Hötorget and the Concert Hall, in an area where shops of all kinds can be found.

In Gamla Stan many speciality shops can be found on Västerlånggatan. If you walk towards Slussen and to the right on Hornsgatan, you come to a hill called Puckeln, where many small and interesting art galleries are to be found. Handicrafts are on sale at *Svensk Hemslöjd*, Sveavägen 44, the *Stockholm Handicraft Shop* at Drottninggatan 18 and at *Handarbetets Vänner* (Friends of Needlework) at Djurgårdsslätten 82.

There are shopping malls in suburbs such as Vällingby, Kista and Skärholmen, where you can also find the huge furniture store *IKEA*, and an indoor flea market which is open on Saturdays and Sundays.

RESTAURANTS. Since restaurants play such an important part in Stockholm life, a fairly extensive list is given here. Most have liquor licenses, though do remember that alcohol is very expensive. Some of the downtown establishments close for three or four weeks during the summer. As in all big citys, there are many types of restaurant in Stockholm, such as Greek, Japanese, Chinese, Korean. All the main hotels have their own restaurants. If you are on a budget, look for bargains such as Sunday Specials, happy hours, tourist menus etc. You'll find details in the newspapers.

Expensive

Aurora. Munkbron 15 (21 93 59). Located in a beautiful 300-year-old house in the Old Town with pleasant small rooms in vaults. Excellent food and service. AE, DC, MC, V.

Bacchi Wapen. Järntorgsgatan 5 (11 66 71). In a medieval lane in the Old Town near Slussen with cozy cellar vaults. International cuisine; good steaks. Music, dancing, nightclub. AE, DC, MC, V.

Coq Blanc. Regeringsgatan 111 (11 61 53). Was once a theater; stage and stalls intact. Excellent food. AE, DC, MC, V.

Coq Roti. Sturegatan 19 (10 25 67). A gourmet restaurant run by professionals; very fine food in sophisticated setting. AE, DC, MC, V.

Den Gyldene Freden. Österlånggatan 51 (10 12 59). Old Town. Medieval cellars with historical traditions and atmosphere. Lute singers some evenings. Oldest restaurant in Sweden. AE, DC, MC, V.

Djurgårdsbrunns Värdshus. (67 90 95). A few minutes from downtown by taxi or bus in the direction of the Kaknäs Tower. A charming 17th-century inn overlooking a meadow and a canal, with a constant flow of pleasure boats during summer. AE, DC, MC, V.

Erik. On quay-berth 17, Strandvägen (60 60 60). This former sand barge has been converted into a *de luxe* restaurant. In summer enjoy the view from the dock. Choose your own fish. AE, DC, MC, V.

Fem Små Hus. Nygränd 10 (10 04 82). In the Old Town. Its name means "five small houses." Many small rooms in vaults. Very good food. AE, DC, MC, V.

Garbo. Blekingegatan 32 (40 12 07). It was here that Greta Garbo was born in 1905. Naturally enough, the atmosphere is very movie oriented. AE, DC, MC, V.

Gourmet. Tegnérgatan 10 (31 43 98). Lives up to its name: one of the best French restaurants in town. Nice atmosphere. AE, DC, MC, V.

Grand Hotel. S. Blasieholmsh 8 (22 10 20). Excellent restaurant (terrace outside in the summer) with marvellous views of the Royal Palace and the Old Town. This is the place for *Smörgåsbord* in relaxed and sophisticated surroundings. AE, DC, MC, V.

K.B. or Konstnärshuset. Smålandsgatan 7, near Norrmalmstorg (11 02 32). Eat and drink in intimate surroundings in the heart of town. Murals by Swedish artists who paid for their drinks with paintings. AE, DC, MC, V.

Latona. Västerlånggatan 79 (11 32 60). Cavernous cellar-restaurant in the heart of the Old Town, by Järntorget. Scores for atmosphere, service and excellent food. AE, DC, MC, V.

Maxim. Drottninggatan 81 (11 00 90). Popular restaurant also featuring dancing, a pub and a nightclub. Call for reservations. AE, DC, MC, V.

Operakällaren. In the Opera House facing Kungsträdgården, the waterfront and the Royal Palace (11 11 25). World-famous for the food and the atmosphere. There is also a snack-bar, the *Bakfickan,* for quick meals and the *Café Opera* for night people. AE, DC, MC, V.

Östergök. Kommendörsgatan 46 (61 15 07). Specializes in fish, but there's also a steakhouse and a pizzeria here. Popular. AE, DC, MC, V.

Riche and Teatergrillen. Birger Jarlsgatan 4 (10 70 22). The *Riche* side has a veranda on the street. Fine paintings create an elegant ambience. Roast beef—not perhaps one of the most obvious things to expect in Stockholm—is served from a silver trolley every day. The *Teatergrillen,* or *Theater Grill,* is more intimate and lives up to its name in attracting some of the theater crowd. Good for a quiet dinner. The grill is closed in July. AE, DC, MC, V.

Solliden. Skansen (60 10 55). On the heights at Stockholm's favorite pleasure grounds, ten minutes from the center of town. Wonderful view of the city and harbor. Also self-service on the ground floor and a big outdoor restaurant in summer. AE, DC, MC, V.

Stallmästargården. Norrtull, near the Haga Air Terminal (24 39 10). Historic inn with view of Brunnsviken Lake. Coffee in the courtyard, with a lovely garden, after a good meal on a summer evening is a delightful experience. AE, DC, MC, V.

Stortorgskällaren. Stortorget 7 (10 53 33). Charming medieval cellar in the Old Town near the Cathedral and the Royal Palace. Adjoining a fish restaurant with the same management. AE, DC, MC, V.

Ulriksdals Värdshus. In a fine park near Ulriksdal Palace (85 50 81). 15 minutes by car or bus 540 from Humlegården Park. Old Swedish inn with famed *Smörgåsbord.* AE, DC, MC, V.

Victoria. Kungsträdgården (10 10 85). Friendly restaurant conveniently open until 3 A.M. Mixed crowd. AE, DC, MC, V.

Moderate

Bäckahästen. Hamngatan 2 (20 01 36). Modern décor; openair service on pavement in summer. Good food and large portions. AE, DC, MC, V.

Brända Tomten. Stureplan 13 (11 49 59). Period décor. Reasonable prices. Quick lunches served in the cellar. Some tables outside in summer. AE, DC, MC, V.

Cattelin. Stora Gråmunkegränd 8, in Old Town (120 18 18). Seafood a specialty, but there's also a bistro. Members of Parliament meet here. AE, DC, MC, V.

Colibri. Corner Drottninggatan and Adolf Fredriks Kyrkogatan (10 81 20). Plank steak.

Daily News Café. Kungsträdgården in Sverigehuset (21 56 55). Good food. Swedish and foreign newspapers to hand (but not on the menu). AE, DC, MC, V.

STOCKHOLM

Gondolen. (40 22 22). Suspended under the gangway of the Katarina elevator at Slussen. View of the harbor and the Old Town. AE, DC, MC, V.

N.K. Department Store. Opposite Sverigehuset. A shoppers' favorite, with a restaurant, salad bar and coffee shop. In summer there is an open-air terrace for lunch. Enjoy the view and get a suntan. AE, DC, MC, V.

Rodolfino. Stora Nygatan 1 (11 84 97). Italian specialties, though not exclusively, in small, chic spot in the Old Town, by the Riddarhuset. Popular with the younger crowd; good food and service. AE, MC, V.

Sturehof. Stureplan (14 27 50). A fairly large, unpretentious restaurant, which makes fish its business. Pub in old English style. Quieter in the back of the restaurant. Just in the middle of town. AE, MC, V.

Inexpensive

Gröna Linjen. Mäster Samuelsgatan 10, third floor (11 27 90). Good for lunch. Vegetarian. No credit cards.

Panorama. Fifth floor of Kulturhuset at Sergelstorg. Self-service; lunch only. Fine view of city center. Closed Mondays. No credit cards.

Tehuset (the tea house). Under the elms in Kungsträdgården Park. Lively and chic outdoor place. Have a hot sandwich there at noon and watch the Royal Guard march by. Summer only. No credit cards.

Zum Franziskaner. Skeppsbron 44 (11 83 30). German-style restaurant on the waterfront in the Old Town. Food is reasonable and service very friendly. Popular. AE, MC, V.

In the **Gallerian shopping arcade** there are several good places to eat, including *Glada Laxen* (M), a café specializing in fish, but often with lines waiting at lunchtime. Also the *Pizzeria* (I), with a salad table and other dishes besides pizza. On the balcony, you can find *Edelweiss,* with a choice of salads and cakes.

The indoor market at *Östermalmshallen* has many food shops. At this 100-year-old indoor market visit *Gerdas and Lisa Elmquist's* fish shop, where you can get an excellent lunch at a reasonable price in unusual and noisy surroundings. In the same building, on the second floor, you can find the biggest salad table in town. It's called *Örtagården* (the Herb Garden) (I) (67 17 00). Closes at 7 P.M.

NIGHTLIFE. Stockholm has a wide range of nightspots to choose from, the names and ownership of which change fairly frequently. See the last page in the daily papers for what's on and where. There are no real nightlife bargains and you should expect a supper in one of these nightspots to cost you around SEK 200 or 300. When there is a show it could cost you more. It's also a good idea to book in advance.

Entry to a pub with live music would be about SEK 20–40. Also many restaurants have dancing a few nights a week.

Atlantic. Teatergatan 2 (21 89 07). Mixed, elegant crowd.

Bacchi Wapen. Järntorgsgatan 5 (11 66 71). As well as the restaurant, there's a piano bar and café.

Börsen. Jacobsgatan 6 (24 92 10). Stockholm's biggest "show restaurant," with international artists.

Club Alexandra. Stockholm Plaza Hotel (11 47 47). Most famous nightspot in Stockholm.

Club Cindy. Amaranten Hotel (54 10 75).

Cabaret. Barnhusgatan 12 (11 06 08). A show restaurant seating 450 people. Also at the same address, *Aladdin* (10 09 32). Oriental décor. Big dance floor.

Engelen. Kornhamnstorg 59 (10 07 22). In an old pharmacy in the Old Town. Long lines and mixed crowd, but more for the younger set.

Gamlingen. Stora Gråmunkegränd (20 57 93). Again, for the younger set.

Kaos. Stora Nygatan 21 (20 58 80). In the Old Town. Wide range of music. Young, mixed crowd.

King Creole. Kungsgatan 18 (24 47 00). Some evenings features "old-time" dancing.

Stampen. Stora Gråmunkegränd (20 57 93). Old Town. A pub with "trad" jazz music.

Bars

There are piano bars at the Hotel Sheraton, Amaranten, Reisen, Continental and Malmen.

If you want something to eat after midnight, there are a few places near Norrmalmstorg such as **Collage,** Smålandsgatan 2 (10 01 95), **Café Éclair,** Hamngatan 6 (20 87 00) and **Monte Carlo,** Sveavägen 23 (11 00 25).

STOCKHOLM ENVIRONS AND GOTLAND

The Capital as an Excursion Center

Stockholm is, in a literal sense, two-faced. It turns at one and the same time to two diametrically opposed worlds which have really only one thing in common—water. To the east the world is harsh, rough, rugged, primeval and its water is the treacherous salt water of the sea. To the west the world is friendly, civilized, the cradle of an ancient culture, and its water is the sweet water shed by farmland and forest. The former is the Stockholm Archipelago, the latter the valley of the sprawling, multi-armed Lake Mälar.

The Swedes have given the archipelago a name which is both romantic and descriptive, Skärgården, or Garden of Skerries. There are thousands of them, large and small, some wooded, some rocky, some even cultivated, separated by broad and narrow channels, indented by bays —in short, a unique seascape. The archipelago has supported a small and hardy farming and fishing population for centuries, living out quiet lives almost unnoticed until a few decades ago. Now the skerries are also a summer playground. And one of the great joys is convenience: you can get well out into the archipelago and back in a few hours.

Exploring the Stockholm Environs

Here are some of the principal summer resorts and sights, of which several are only an hour or so from Stockholm.

Sandhamn. Yachting center at the extreme eastern edge of the skerries, on the open Baltic Sea. Sandhamn's original importance was as a pilot station, but it is now also a popular summer resort because of its sandy beaches and good sailing facilities. The Royal Swedish Yacht Club has a clubhouse here and arranges a number of international races in the July-August regatta season. Daily boat connections from Stockholm.

Vaxholm. Characterized by an ancient fortress guarding the channel into Stockholm. (The German Field-Marshal von Moltke is said to have laughed on only two occasions in his life—one of them was at the sight of Vaxholm Fortress.) The fortress is now open as a museum showing the military defense of Stockholm over the centuries. Vaxholm is a small but progressive town with good tennis courts and bathing.

Tyresö Castle. An ancient estate southeast of Stockholm, only 40 minutes from Ringvägen, (bus No. 10). The estate has belonged to some of Sweden's outstanding noble families since the Middle Ages. Its last owner willed it to the Nordiska Museum in 1930. Interesting art, including 18th-century French paintings.

Nynäshamn. A seaside town. Good beaches. Port of departure for steamers to the Baltic Sea island of Gotland.

Here is an important note: *Some parts of the archipelago are defense zones, closed to foreigners.* To avoid possible inconvenience, check before starting. If you put ashore at a strange point, look for the presence of a sign which might indicate that it is a prohibited area. They are posted in several languages, including English. If, for any reason, you wish to enter one of the zones—it may be quite possible that some Swedish friend or acquaintance of yours has a summer cottage within one—you can apply to the "Kustartilleri-stationen" in Vaxholm. The regulations are fairly strict, and there is no guarantee that such an application will always be approved.

Sigtuna, Skokloster and Gripsholm Castles

Sigtuna was founded about the year 1000 by Sweden's first Christian king, Olof Skötkonung, and for a time it was the chief political and religious center of the country. Sigtuna is located north of Stockholm, a little more than half way to Uppsala. It is not on the main railway line; you change to a bus in Märsta. A visit to Sigtuna can suitably be combined with an outing to Uppsala.

The Sigtuna sun rose rapidly and sank rapidly. Bearing witness to its brief age of glory are the ruins of the first stone edifices erected in Sweden, pre-Norman churches dedicated to St. Per, St. Olof, and St. Lars. These were also fortresses, designed as much with an eye to defense as to the glorification of God. They overlooked a thriving community for nearly 200 years, during which the first Swedish coins were minted and Anglo-Saxon missionaries pushed the conversion of the Swedes.

STOCKHOLM ENVIRONS AND GOTLAND

Despite the stone churches, the city was more or less destroyed in 1187 by Vikings from across the Baltic, but lived on, thanks partly to the Dominican Monastery. The Reformation delivered a new blow, the monasteries were closed, and Sigtuna sank into obscurity. In modern times it has begun to flourish again as an educational and religious center.

You will find Sigtuna more idyllic than exciting. Note the charm of its narrow main street—Stora Gatan—which is said to follow its original route of 950 years ago and is known as the oldest street in Sweden. The layers of earth here have furnished the archeologists with a wealth of finds, from which they have reconstructed the life of various centuries. Maria Church, once the Dominican Monastery church was one of the first brick churches in the whole Lake Mälar valley, but only a few ruins remain of the monastery itself. St. Olof's Church gives you a good idea of the military aspects of early church architecture—it dates from about 1050. The construction material was rough granite blocks, the windows are mere loopholes, and the entrance just large enough to admit one person at a time.

On the heights overlooking the city you will find the modern institutions which have given new life to Sigtuna. One is the Sigtuna Foundation, sponsored by the Swedish Church, which includes a continuation college for adults, a chapel, and a guest house—the latter popular among authors as a good place to work. The others are the Sigtuna Academy and the Humanistic Academy, both boarding schools, and the College for Laymen, for instruction in volunteer parish work. Note also the unique little 18th-century Town Hall—supposed to be the smallest in the country—and a number of rune stones. About 16 kilometers (ten miles) northeast of Sigtuna lies Skokloster Castle.

Skokloster has recently been sold to the Swedish State. It has the richest collection of art treasures from the Swedish Imperial Era, and its display of weapons is outstanding.

The castle was built between 1654 and 1679 by Carl Gustaf Wrangel, one of Gustavus Adolphus' best-known field marshals. When he died it went to a relative, Count Nils Brahe, and was passed on from one Brahe to another until the family died out about 20 years ago. It then came into the hands of a related family, the von Essens. For the most part the furniture, paintings, and tapestries antedate the Thirty Years' War. The library contains some 30,000 volumes. A motor museum is the last private owner's contribution to his forefather's collection, and there is now a hotel and vacation center in the grounds.

A pleasant place for a short excursion from Stockholm is Sturehov, 22 kilometers (14 miles) west of the city. This is an old mansion and estate belonging to the city of Stockholm and used for civic entertainment, but it is also open to the public. The mansion is an exceptionally fine example of 18th-century Swedish architecture and interior design, and contains about a dozen porcelain stoves from the famous Marieberg factory, apart from many other treasures.

Gripsholm Castle is an ideal day-excursion by boat from Stockholm. You ride three pleasant hours through the beautiful scenery of Lake Mälar, stop in Gripsholm long enough for an inspection of the old castle and a good lunch, and get back to Stockholm by early evening. As a castle site, Gripsholm dates back to some time in the 1300s but the present towered structure was begun about 1535 on the orders of

King Gustav Vasa. Fully restored, livable and well maintained—after a period as a state prison—Gripsholm today is an outstanding museum, with a large and fine collection of historical portraits.

In the castle, note particularly the little theater. It, like Drottningholm Theater, owes its existence to drama-loving King Gustav III, and has been preserved in its original condition. Although much smaller, in the opinion of many it is vastly more beautiful and full of atmosphere than its counterpart at Drottningholm. Nearby is the prison tower, where the tragic King Erik XIV (whom Strindberg made the central figure of one of his most powerful dramas) was held captive after his dethronement. The collection of portraits was begun by King Gustav Vasa himself in the 16th century, and now numbers nearly 3,000 paintings, with emphasis on Swedish royalty but with a number of royal figures from other lands.

In the courtyards note particularly the rune stones, among the best preserved to be found, and the artfully designed bronze cannons, war booty from the Swedish wars with Russia centuries ago. (Incidentally, the Soviet government has made unsuccessful efforts to get them returned to Russia. The Swedes, however, seem inclined to keep these memories of days when inferior Swedish forces often licked the tar out of the Czar's finest.)

Visby, City of Ruins and Roses

If you choose to visit Visby—the "City of Ruins and Roses" on the storied isle of Gotland in the Baltic Sea—during the off-season, say early November, you will find the short flight from Stockholm unforgettable. The sunset will provide one of those incredible displays of color that are to be found only in this part of the world.

At the Visby airport, you will be amazed to see a bed of red, red roses, in this northern corner of the world, still blooming. According to the inhabitants, roses are sometimes to be seen blooming in even December and January. Whatever the season, the red has a special brilliance resulting from the composition of the soil.

You feel something in the very atmosphere of Visby, a sense of the Middle Ages living on into the 20th century. Looping around the city is the magnificent wall, completely embracing it on all but the sea side. When you enter one of the 13th- or 14th-century gates, you find this special atmosphere among the beautiful buildings. Stepped, gabled houses date back to Visby's era of greatness. And everywhere are buildings centuries old, some of them well preserved, others, particularly the churches, in a gaunt state of disrepair that adds to their charm. Try, if you can, to see the view from the Powder Tower in the moonlight. This tower, serving as one of the main anchors of the wall, near the sea on the north side of town, is perhaps the oldest of the watch towers that rise up at intervals along the medieval wall.

The history of the island of Gotland, and the capital city Visby, goes back thousands of years, and its earth has yielded treasures speaking eloquently of contacts with the Minoan, Greek, and Roman cultures. But the Golden Age arrived in the 12th century, when Visby and Gotland dominated the trade of northern and western Europe and the town could undoubtedly be classed as one of the major cities of the world. Wealth followed wealth, and within the confines of the city wall

STOCKHOLM ENVIRONS AND GOTLAND

alone, itself a magnificent structure from every standpoint, the rich merchants erected no less than 17 churches. Outside of the city, farmer-merchants built parish churches more like small cathedrals than rural houses of worship.

Trade routes shifted. War parties ravaged. The first of a series of major catastrophes took place in 1361, when the island and city fell to Danish King Valdemar Atterdag. The decline had set in with a vengeance. The island was variously occupied by Baltic powers during the succeeding century and more, until 1645, when it was definitely sealed into the Swedish kingdom.

Exploring Gotland

Today, the island is a vacation paradise *par excellence*. There is no lack of sights in the traditional meaning. See the churches and medieval merchant palaces of Visby—St. Nicholas, St. Clemens, the Church of the Holy Spirit, St. Catarina, and a half dozen more—and the wall. *Walk* to see Visby—pick up a map and an English guidebook at the travel bureau in Burmeister House, itself a historic building near the harbor—and wander. Wherever you go, you can't go wrong. Don't miss the museum, Fornsalen, particularly the impressive picture stones, which antedate the Viking rune stones. There are other remarkable finds on display, too—coins and jewelry from many centuries, religious art (note particularly the gentle loveliness of the Öja Madonna, a medieval wood sculpture), and ancient weapons unearthed from the scenes of battles for this once flourishing island.

If you happen to be in Visby at the end of July or in early August don't miss the pageant opera "Petrus de Dacia" performed in the ruin of St. Nicholas Church.

Justice cannot be done to the cultural history of Visby and Gotland in anything smaller than a complete book. The names of the masters who designed and decorated these churches have been lost to history, but scientists have been able to identify and classify a few of them by characteristic features of their styles as they recur in various works. Although Visby is hilly and there are cobbled stones on the streets, you should take the time to walk leisurely around the city. Car traffic is restricted here.

The stalactite caves at Lummelunda are unique in this part of the world and are worth visiting, as is the Krusmyntagarden (herb garden), north of Visby, close to the sea.

Though most tourists rent bicycles for tours of the island, there are cars for rent and there is a good network of buses. The Tourist Office arranges many day tours by bus—call and ask for details. It should be noted that the island of Fårö, to the north of Gotland is restricted for foreigners.

The Local Churches

On the whole island, which measures only about 48 kilometers (30 miles) by 128 kilometers (80 miles), there are approximately 100 churches still intact and in use today, dating from Gotland's great commercial area. Among them are:

Barlingbro, dating from the 13th century, with vault paintings, stained glass windows, remarkable 12th-century font.

Dalhem, one of the 16 largest rural religious edifices, construction begun about 1200 or somewhat earlier, an exquisite example of Gotland church architecture.

Gothem, one of Gotland's most impressive country churches, mainly built during the 13th century, with notable series of paintings of that period.

Grötlingbo, a 14th-century church with stone sculpture and stained glass: note the 12th century reliefs on the façade.

Tingstäde, another of the 16 largest, a puzzle of six building periods from 1169 to 1300 or so. Note the general proportions, the stained-glass windows, and murals from the 14th century.

Roma Cloister Church, the massive ruins from a Cistercian monastery founded in 1164. The ruins are sufficiently well preserved to give a good picture of the architecture and contruction.

Öja, decorated with paintings and containing a famous Holy Rood from the late 13th century.

Island Bird Refuges

There are a number of other sights well worth your time. Among them are curious rock formations along the coasts, including the "Old Man of Hoburgen" at the southern tip of the island; and two island bird refuges off the coast south of Visby, Stora and Lilla Karlsö. The bird population consists to a large extent of guillemots, which look like penguins. Visits to these refuges are permitted only in company with a recognized guide, and the easiest way to see them is to join a conducted tour from Visby.

PRACTICAL INFORMATION FOR GOTLAND

TOURIST INFORMATION. There are tourist offices at: **Klintehamn** (0498-403 08), open June through Aug. **Slite,** Storgatan 15 (0498-209 50), open June through Aug. **Visby,** Burmeisterska Huset (0498-109 82) and the ferry terminal (0498-190 10).

TELEPHONE CODES. We give telephone codes in the hotel and restaurant lists that follow. These codes need only be used when calling from outside the area concerned.

HOTELS AND RESTAURANTS. *Snäck* (E), (0498-600 00). 204 rooms. Between airport and Visby. All rooms face west. Excellent restaurant, nightclub. Beach, pool, sauna, canoes. Airport bus. AE, DC, MC, V. *Visby Hotel* (M), Strandgatan 6 (0495-119 25). 92 rooms. Central, airport bus. Restaurant, *Oskar* nightclub. AE, MC, V. *Solhem* (I), (0495-790 70). 80 rooms. Central. On two floors. Restaurant, dancing. MC. *Toftagården* (I), Tofta (0498-654 00). 60 rooms. 300 meters (about 300 yards) from beach. Restaurant, windsurfing, billiards. MC

STOCKHOLM ENVIRONS AND GOTLAND

Restaurants. *Jacob Dubbe,* Strandgatan 16 (0495-497 22). International menu. In medieval building. Open 22 hours a day. *Rosengården,* Stora Torget (0495-181 90). Close to cloister ruin. Italian and French cuisine. Open-air service in garden. Charming. MC. *Värdshuset* (Inn), Lindgården, Strandgatan 26 (0495-187 00). In old building. Excellent food. MC

Youth Hostels. For information about youth hostels on the island of Gotland, call 0498-254 00. *Visby,* Gråboskolan (0498-169 33). Central. Open June 15 to Aug. 7.

Camping. There are many three-star sites on the island. Try *Kneippbyn* (0498-643 65). On the beach four km. (2½ miles) south of Visby. 24 cottages for rent.

HOW TO GET AROUND. One way, but not the least expensive, to see the archipelago is by chartered cruiser (Taxi-Båt). In summer scheduled water-bus services ply to most points of the archipelago from Stockholm: *embarking* at Klara Strand (near City Hall) for Gripsholm Castle and Drottningholm Castle; at Munkbron (Old Town) for Skokloster Castle; at Strömkajen (near Grand Hotel) for Sandhamn, Husarö, Möja and Vaxholm; at Slussen for Sandhamn (bus with boat connection); from Central Station by train, bus and coach to Utö.

It takes only 40 minutes to fly from Stockholm to Visby—the airport is three km. (about two miles) from the city. There are also day or night trips from the port of Nynäshamn (one hour by train, bus or car from Stockholm). You can leave Stockholm in the evening and return by midnight the next day. The boats on this run carry cars.

Gotland is an ideal island for a bicycling holiday. There are over 4,000 bicycles for rent and the tourist office will sell you complete bike "packages." Gotland has a tourist office at Norrmalstorg in Stockholm.

PLACES TO VISIT. In the archipelago. The castles at Vaxholm and Tyresö. In the valley of Lake Mälar: Gripsholm Castle and its portrait gallery, the 17th-century castle (with its Motor Museum) of Skokloster, Sigtuna, with its rune stones and House of Antiquities.

GOTLAND. Fornsalen (Gotland Historical Museum). At Strandgatan 12. It features graves from the Stone, Bronze and Iron Ages. Also picture stones and hoards from Viking times, ecclesiastical art. Open Tues. to Sun 1–3; closed Mon.; May 15 to Aug 15, daily 11–5.

Krusmyntagården. Herb garden, two km. (1.2 miles) south of Lummelundagrottorna Caves, near the sea. 300 different herbs; also herbs for sale. On Tues. and Thurs. nights, entertainers (from Gotland) and *asado* (barbecue). Open mid-June to Aug., daily 9–6. For information call 0498-701 53.

Lummelundagrottorna. 13 km. (nine miles) north of Visby. 400-year-old limestone caves with stalactites. 300-meter (984-foot) long cave with smaller and larger caves 6–8 meters (19–26 feet) high. Guided tours continuously. Souvenir shop and cafetaria. Open May to Sept., Mon. to Sat. 9–1, Sun. 9–4; July, daily 9–7. For information call 0498-730 50.

SWEDEN'S SOUTHLAND

Breadbasket, Battlefield and Summer Playground

Southern Sweden is a world of its own, clearly distinguished from the rest of Sweden by its geography, culture, and history.

Scania (the Swedish name is Skåne, pronounced "scone-eh"), the southernmost province, is known as the "granary of Sweden." It occupies a more or less rectangular area, including the almost square peninsula that forms the southern tip of the country and supports no less than one-eighth of the whole Swedish population. It is a comparatively small province of beautifully fertile plains, sand beaches, scores of castles and châteaux, thriving farms, medieval churches, and summer resorts.

East of the northern end of Scania is the province of Blekinge, called "Sweden's garden," occupying another southern coastal reach extending to the east coast. North of the western part of Scania, ranging along the west coast of Sweden, is the province of Halland, a rolling country of heaths and ridges rising above the beaches. Halland faces the Kattegat (the southeastern part of the North Sea), and contributed its full share of the Viking forces which once struck terror into the populations of many countries. It still produces its share of modern sea captains.

There is an old tradition that while the Lord was busy making Scania into the fertile garden that it is today, the devil sneaked past him farther

SWEDEN'S SOUTHLAND

north, and made the province of Småland. The result was harsh, unyielding, unfriendly country of stone and woods and more stone. When the Lord caught up with Satan and saw what had happened he said, "All right, it's too late to do anything about the land . . . so I'm going to make the people." He did, and He made them so tough and stubborn and resilient and long-lived that they carved a true civilization out of their sparse heritage. There is still a folk saying that you can deposit a son of the province of Småland on a barren stone island with only an ax in his hands and he'll manage—and have a garden going before long.

Whatever the validity of the legend, it is true that Småland is vastly different from the other three provinces of southern Sweden. It is a good deal larger and is noted particularly for its glass industries, as well as furniture and other wood products, and its great historic region with Kalmar at the center.

Skåne, Blekinge, and Halland (Halland is described in the *West Coast* chapter) also form a natural historical group of provinces; they were actually the last incorporations of territory into what constitutes the present-day Swedish kingdom. The time was 1658. These southern provinces had been part of Denmark for centuries (and thus the medieval architecture is Danish). Sweden and Denmark had been fighting intermittently for generations. Karl X (anglicized as Charles X), a king and general of parts, whatever his faults, was off in Poland on one of the many indecisive Swedish attempts for a reckoning with that country. This looked to the Danes like a perfect opportunity for a reckoning with the Swedes. But when the Danish fleet arrived at Danzig to fall on the Swedish rear, the Swedes were moving overland at top speed toward Denmark. After two bold, unprecedented marches across the ice of the sounds separating the Danish islands, the Swedish army of 12,000 battle-hardened men faced an almost undefended Copenhagen. Although Sweden was also at war with Poland and Russia, Karl X was in a position almost to name his own terms. They were so rough that one of the Danish commissioners, preparing to sign this historic Peace of Roskilde, complained, "If only I didn't know how to write!".

By virtue of that treaty Sweden achieved natural southern boundaries—the coasts of the Baltic Sea—for the first time in its history, and acquired the rich territory which now nurtures one-fourth of the population. But the marks of long association with Denmark and its Continental culture live on in the language, the architecture, the way of life.

Exploring Helsingborg

Let's say that you have arrived in Helsingborg from the Danish side by ferry. In front of you stretches a long, comparatively narrow square, dominated at the far end, on the height, by a medieval tower stronghold known as Kärnan (the Keep). The surviving center tower, built to provide living quarters and defend the medieval castle of Helsingborg, is the most remarkable relic of its kind in the north. The interior, which may be visited, is divided into several floors, containing medieval kitchen fittings, a chapel, etc. From the top you have a magnificent view of the coast, the Sound, and the Danish shore.

A thousand years ago, this city was an important European capital. Today it is a thriving industrial town of some 101,000 inhabitants, the eighth largest city in Sweden. For centuries Helsingborg and its Danish neighbor across the Sound, Elsinore (Helsingør), only about five kilometers (three miles) away, controlled all shipping traffic in and out of the Baltic Sea. There is a train and ferry terminal here for services between Sweden and Denmark, with a boat or ferry every 20 minutes.

In Södra Storgatan are St. Mary's Church, built in the 13th century and rebuilt during the 15th century, with an interesting triptych and magnificent late Renaissance pulpit, and the Town Museum, containing exhibits depicting the early history of Helsingborg. Take time to visit Fredriksdals Friluftmuseum, an 18th-century mansion set in a lovely old park around which old Scanian farmhouses and buildings have been set up to form an open-air museum. During summer there are performances in the attractive open-air theater.

About five kilometers (three miles) north of the city—bus to Pålsjöbaden, then a half-hour walk along the Sound—is Sofiero Castle, summer residence of the King, built in 1865 in Dutch Renaissance style. The grounds are open to the public (enter by northern gate near gardener's lodge).

Golf and Tennis in Båstad

If you proceed north from Helsingborg, you come immediately into a region of summer resorts stretching along a promontory. One of the main resort towns is Mölle, near the end of the peninsula, which looks out upon the south end of the Kattegat. Proceeding back along the north shore of this peninsula, you arrive in Ängelholm, a small and charming city at least 500 years old, which has become a popular summer resort. Here you can see Sweden's oldest local prison—now a museum.

Only some of the main stops can be mentioned here. As you continue north along the coast, the next in line will be Båstad, perhaps the most fashionable of the summer resorts in this region. It is frequented throughout the summer by the international set, and ambassadors and ministers of several countries may sometimes be in residence there at the same time. The principal attractions include the natural beauty of the region (known for its flowers and fruit orchards), 18-hole golf course, and several tennis courts. International tennis tournaments every year at the beginning of July.

Recommended is a visit to the Norrviken Gardens, three kilometers (two miles) northwest of Båstad. They comprise a number of gardens of various styles, agreeably laid out in varied grounds and each one in character with the landscape's lines, perspectives and vistas. Just east of Båstad is Malen, with an interesting sepulchral mound from the 11th century B.C. It has been excavated and restored so that you can enter and study the stones set up in the form of a ship. Also here are a 15th-century church and many old houses in picturesque narrow winding streets.

Don't miss Torekov, a little fishing village on the point of a peninsula about nine kilometers (six miles) due west of Båstad, which has many summer visitors. Despite a too generous influx of summer folks in July and August, many of whom have built or bought their own homes, the community remains an authentic part of this coastal region. There is a tiny but interesting museum—not a few of whose treasures have been gathered from ships wrecked in the treacherous waters off the point. The days here are serene and rhythmical with the pulse of an ancient way of life, a life close to the sea. Just off the coast is an island—Hallands Väderö—a national reserve known for its flora and bird life.

Continuing north from Båstad, you cross almost at once into Halland, another of the provinces acquired by Sweden in the fantastically profitable peace of 1658. By this time you will have noticed the changing nature of the landscape, the way ridges billow up in more pronounced fashion from the coast. In back of them are broad heaths unique to this part of Sweden. This whole coastal province is another section of the long vacation playground of the west coast which starts here and goes all the way up to the Norwegian border.

Malmö—Third Largest City

If you start south from Helsingborg, the first coastal town of any size will be Landskrona, a modern industrial and shipping center with some 35,000 inhabitants. The 17th-century fortifications surrounding Landskrona Castle are reputed to be the best preserved relics of their kind in Europe. The citadel was built in 1549. From Landskrona there are boats to the beautiful island of Ven, between Sweden and Denmark.

Malmö, with a population of 235,000, is the small but opulent capital of a small but opulent province and a sense of well-being strikes you upon arrival. It has the friendly atmosphere normally associated with much smaller places. There are many reminders here of the great trading days of the Hanseatic League. The Rådhuset (Court House) dates back to the 16th century and the Malmöhus Castle, now a museum, to the 16th century. Nearby is the Malmö Technical Museum. The Lilla Torg, an attractive small cobblestoned square, has buildings from the 17th and 18th centuries.

The impressive statue on the central square is that of Karl X—the king who acquired this part of the country for Sweden. Just off the square (look for the steeple and follow your eyes) you will find St. Peter's Church, a brick structure from shortly after 1300. It is the largest Gothic church in south Sweden and the oldest building in Malmö.

In addition to the usual historical sights offered by most Swedish cities, Malmö distinguishes itself by having also a top-flight modern one—the City Theater. It is surprising that this comparatively small city has been able to build and maintain such an imposing stage. It was completed in 1944, seats 1,700 persons (other theaters in Malmö are the Intima, in the same location, and the NYA Theater, Amiralsg 35). If you have a chance to see an operetta or musical comedy here, by all means do so. The Malmö-card gives you free transportation and free or reduced entrance to various attractions, as well as convenient sightseeing. Buy it at the airport, railway station or tourist office.

The University City of Lund

Less than 30 kilometers (19 miles) northeast of Malmö, connected by frequent bus and train services, is Lund. Lund was once the religious capital of a region which stretched from Iceland to Finland, over which the Roman Catholic archbishop resident here held more or less absolute sway in matters of faith. The city was founded almost a thousand years ago by the Danish King Canute the Great, and during its early burst of prosperity could boast a score of churches and a half-dozen monasteries. The Reformation changed all that. But the founding of Lund University in the 1660s, after the province became part of Sweden, brought new intellectual prosperity, and the arrival of the railroads, not quite a century ago, brought industrial prosperity. The population is about 80,000, and enrollment at the university and high schools about 20,000. The most colorful students' events are Walpurgis Eve, April 30, and the carnival in mid-May every four years.

The principal sight is the cathedral, whose construction was begun about 1080, a massive structure and one of the few churches in this part of the world in Romanesque style. There are a number of medieval treasures, of which the most notable is the huge, ornate, intricate astronomical clock that still plays daily at noon. This remarkable instrument, several yards high, will tell you practically everything about the position of the heavenly bodies and time except the date of your own birthday. The intricate mechanism and the beautifully carved figures which go into action when the clock plays make a fascinating sight. Nor should you miss Lund's Museum of Cultural History, the Archive for Decorative Art, and the Art Gallery. The Botanical Gardens have specimens of 7,000 plants from all over the world.

The Chateau Country

Only 32 kilometers (20 miles) from Malmö, on a tiny peninsula projecting out from the very southwest corner of Sweden, are the idyllic little twin cities of Falsterbo and Skanör, both very popular summer resorts.

Continuing on from Malmö, you can make your way to Ystad, a medieval city on the southern coast. If you are driving, you might go by way of Torup Castle, a typical example of the square fortified stronghold, built about 1550. Ystad, perhaps more than any other city on the Swedish mainland, has preserved its medieval character, with winding, narrow streets and hundreds of half-timbered houses from four or five different centuries. Perhaps the principal ancient monument is St. Maria Church, begun shortly after 1200 as a basilica in Romanesque style, but with additions from several centuries. An historical curiosity is a half-timbered house (at Stora Västergatan 6) supposed to have been occupied by King Charles VII during two brief visits in Ystad shortly before and after 1700. Do see the old Franciscan monastery and its museum. Ystad has become a popular summer resort town.

The plains, the gently rolling hills and fields of the province of Skåne are broken every few miles by lovely castles, which have given this part of Sweden the name of the "Chateau Country." Usually they are surrounded by lovely grounds, often by moats, and they add a graceful note to travels through this region. Here, perhaps more than anywhere else in Sweden, these huge estates have remained in the hands of the original families, and they date from many centuries and many architectural periods.

These hundreds of castles, chateaux, and manor houses, of every size, type, and age, constitute the great tourist attraction of Sweden's

SWEDEN'S SOUTHLAND

"Chateau Country." Among the oldest are Glimmingehus and Torup —quadrangular, thick-walled strongholds of the medieval type, built to withstand long sieges. Belonging to the great castle-building age of the 16th century are Vittskövle, Skarhult, Trolle-Ljungby, and Bosjökloster, while others, such as Trolleholm, Wrams-Gunnarstorp, and Knutstorp, bear the distinctive architectural marks of successive post-16th century reconstructions. Thousands come every year as well to visit their lovely formal gardens and parks.

Most of the chateaux are still inhabited and cannot be visited except by special arrangement, often requiring personal contact. The best way to get more than a simple exterior view is to join an organized tour. These guided tours originate in most of the major towns in Skåne during the summer season, but Malmö offers the greatest variety. However, Bosjökloster at Lake Ringsjön, Christinehof in eastern and Svaneholm in southern Skåne, Bäckaskog near Kristianstad, Snogeholm near Sjöbo and Bjärsjölagård near Hörby—with catering facilities—are regularly open to the public. Inquire at any tourist office.

On the coast here in Skåne is Kåseberga or Ales Stenar, a remarkable group of 57 stones. It is thought to be a memorial to a Viking chieftain. Or is it the Stonehenge of Sweden . . . ?

Eastern Skåne

Turning north again, along the east coast of Skåne, you may want to have a look at Simrishamn, a charming village with a pronounced medieval atmosphere, a favorite haunt for painters because of its clear air. Still farther north you find little Kivik, center of an orchard region, boasting an ancient royal grave which the scientists say dates from 1400 B.C. The Kivik grave is a huge, rounded mound of boulders and stones, and the crypt itself contains interesting picture stones. Near Kivik is Stenshuvud, a rock rising imposingly from the Baltic and its sandy beaches. Between Brösarp and Sankt Olof you can find a veteran railway.

In Maglehem, a few kilometers farther on your route north, is to be found one of the most exquisite old churches in the whole region. It's an outstanding example of the architecture which prevailed here during the Danish era, with the massive white walls and stepped gables that you have been seeing everywhere in the province. Most of the interiors had been plastered over through the passage of the centuries, but thanks in great measure to the initiative of the local pastor, Erik Söderberg, who had devoted years to this labor of love, magnificent wall paintings have been brought out from as far back as the 14th century. There are a great many medieval churches in Sweden of which more than 150 are to be found in the province of Scania.

The next main town on this route is Kristianstad, founded in 1614 by Danish King Christian IV as a border fortress against Sweden. The Church, the Holy Trinity, is a typical example of Christian's building style. Not far from here is Bäckaskog Castle, and from here you can proceed to Kalmar by traveling east through the province of Blekinge, then north along the Baltic coast. You can stay overnight at Bäckaskog Castle, which was originally a monastery, dating from the 13th century.

Blekinge—the Garden of Sweden

With attractive seaside resorts, forests and hills and fertile valleys, this province has earned its title as the garden of Sweden. The eastern part of the province has more hours of sunshine than any other part of the country, while the northern part gives a hint of the rocks and woods of Småland across the border. Blekinge, like Skåne and Halland, shares a long association with Denmark.

Sölvesborg, according to legend, was founded in A.D. 700 by a seagoing king named Sölve. Today it is a small port supported also by industry. The principal sights are the old castle, which played an important part in the Swedish-Danish feuds, and the church begun in the 13th century and constructed in Gothic style.

In Listerlandet, near Hällevik, there are several picturesque fishing villages. It also boasts a small fishing museum, with relics of fishing from long ago. The ferry from Nogersund will take you to Hanö, with one of the tallest lighthouses in Northern Europe.

At the Salmon Aquarium at Mörrum you can see salmon and trout in their natural environment. The King and his guests gather at Mörrum around April 1 each year to open the salmon-fishing season. Mörrum's river has a world-wide reputation for salmon fishing. It was here that the world's biggest sea-trout was caught—32.3 lbs. Salmon up to 44 lbs. are not uncommon here.

Karlshamn, a port which accommodates ocean-going vessels, is an idyllic coastal town. The Kastellet, or fortress, overlooking the channel into the harbor, was started by Karl X to defend the province of Blekinge from the Danes, who had just yielded it up to him. The elevators for grains and oilseeds are said to be the largest such concentration in Europe. The emigrants monument "Karl-Oskar and Kristina" commemorates the great Swedish exodus to America. There is a replica of this moving monument in Lindstrom Square, Minnesota. The boat trips to the Kastellet in the harbor, and from Järnavik to the beautiful island of Tjärö are to be recommended.

Ronneby was well known to vacationers of a couple of generations past for its mineral wells. The rebuilt resort hotel is set in an unusually beautiful park. The principal sight is the fortress church, Heliga Korsets Kyrka (Holy Cross Church), dating from the 12th century.

Karlskrona, a city founded in the 17th century, is built on 30 islands. Until recently it was the home port of the Swedish Navy and the naval station still dominates the city. At the Varvsmuseet (Marine Museum), there is an excellent collection of figureheads, model ships and much more. It is one of the finest marine museums in the world. Here in Karlskrona is Sweden's oldest wooden church, Amiralitetskyrkan, with its poor-box, Rosenbom, outside. Two churches here, the Holy Trinity and Fredrik's, were designed by the outstanding architect Nicodemus Tessin. The Kungsholmens Fortress, built around 1680, was erected to protect the harbor. Another fortress dating from the same time, the Drottningskärs Kastell on the island of Aspö, is still intact.

Historic Kalmar

Kalmar has the distinction of a mention on a rune stone from the 11th century. The oldest part of its famous castle dates back to the 12th century. You can see at a glance why Kalmar was once called "the Lock and Key of Sweden," and why it played an historic role in Scandinavian history before the airplane added a third dimension to warfare. The magnificent Renaissance castle—the earliest parts of which date from the 12th century—was also a mighty fortress, dominating the sound which separates the mainland from the island of Öland. When Kalmar began its age of greatness, the southern border of Sweden was only a few kilometers south—on the then Danish province of Blekinge. The long narrow island lying parallel to the mainland and thus forming a narrow channel completed the strategic picture: whoever controlled Kalmar controlled traffic along the coast north to Stockholm.

The importance of Kalmar is reflected in the name Kalmar Union (an agreement signed here in 1397), an ill-starred attempt to unite Scandinavia under one ruler. It limped along for more than a century of intermittent civil wars before it was formally dissolved by Swedish independence under Gustav Vasa in 1523. It was this great king who made Kalmar Castle what it is today—with its courts and battlements, its moat, its round towers. But even this powerful stronghold could not prevent the destruction and ravaging of the city in the recurring Danish-Swedish wars. The city was practically wiped out in the so-called Kalmar War of 1611–13. Fire again destroyed the town in 1647, and, with the Peace of Roskilde, the region lost some of its strategic importance. The decline had begun. Today Kalmar is the commercial and administrative center for southeastern Småland, a port and tourist attraction.

The principal sight is, of course, the castle. (*Note:* it closes at 4 P.M.) You get a good picture of the integrated life of a whole royal establishment as it functioned centuries ago, from the king's bedroom to the huge kitchens. Note especially the Castle Chapel, a charming little place of worship in rococo and Renaissance, which is still used for divine services (Sundays at 10 A.M.). The grim dungeon is a curiosity—it was cunningly placed below the surface level of the nearby sea—thus making attempts to tunnel out impossible. Prisoners sometimes survived for years in this dingy, damp hole. The castle also contains the extensive collections of the Kalmar Museum. One of the major attractions of the Kalmar Museum is the exhibition of the results of the salvage operation, still in progress, on the Swedish man-of-war *Kronan* (the Crown), which sank in battle with the Danish–Dutch fleet in June 1676, off the southeast coast of Öland. The *Kronan* was twice the size of the *Wasa* in Stockholm and fully equipped for war. The ship was blown up and bits and pieces are scattered on the ocean floor.

You will find the city itself rich in atmosphere and structures from the 17th and 18th centuries, when the present city was largely laid out and constructed. In particular see the cathedral (designed by Nicodemus Tessin the Elder and built about 1675). Not far from here is a smaller square (Lilla Torget), with the residence of the provincial governor, originally from 1674. It was the scene of a footnote to history

—the French King Louis XVIII lived here briefly in exile shortly after 1800.

Windmills and Rune Stones on Öland

The island of Öland is reached by a 6,070-meter (about four miles) bridge, the longest in Europe. There are many rune stones here, dating from the Viking era. There are also relics from the Iron Age in the many graves and 16 fortifications on the island.

Gråborg Fortress, probably dating from about A.D. 500, must have been a gigantic establishment at one time, for the walls enclose an area some 229 meters (250 yards) long and 174 meters (190 yards) wide. Now only the massive stone walls, as much as eight meters (25 feet) high and eight meters (25 feet) thick, remain of this onetime stronghold.

Probably the most interesting site is at Eketorp—an excavated fortified village. Here visitors can see what life must have been like in a 5th-century community.

Borgholm Castle ruin is perhaps the biggest and most beautiful ruin of a castle stronghold in Sweden. It originated as a medieval fortress, was rebuilt during the 16th and 17th centuries, and ravaged by fire shortly after 1800. It overlooks the city of Borgholm from a commanding site and is most impressive by moonlight.

Solliden is one of the summer residences of the royal family. The beautiful grounds around the sparkling white mansion are open 12 noon–2 P.M., depending on the time of year and whether the royal family is in residence. Located on the outskirts of Borgholm, within easy walking distance.

The nature of Öland is so different from the mainland that you feel almost as though you had entered another country. This, and a great profusion of old-fashioned, more or less Dutch-type windmills, give the island an unmistakable profile. With luck you may be able to count as many as 54 of the 400 windmills in a couple of hours' auto tour.

Much of Öland is covered by a huge, treeless steppe known as the Alvar, a limestone plateau without counterpart in northern Europe. It gives a sense of peace bordering on quiet desolation. During spring and fall, this is the place to watch the migratory birds. Hundreds of species rest up here from their long flights. On the southern tip of the island, at Ottensjö, is a bird station and an old lighthouse, from which there is a magnificent view.

During the summer, Öland is a tourist mecca. The capital, Borgholm, is a town of 2,700 people, offering many holiday activities during the season.

A Kingdom of Glass

In Kalmar or Växjö you are only an hour or two from some of the finest glass works in the world—Orrefors, Kosta, Boda, Strömbergshyttan. Exquisite pieces by famed designers from these factories are found in exclusive shops almost all over the world. But don't look for something that resembles an industrial region. The plants are scattered in the wooded wilderness of Småland, communities of a few hundred people built around the factory. From these isolated, unprepossessing

SWEDEN'S SOUTHLAND

villages go regular shipments to London and Paris, New York's Fifth Avenue, the cities of South America; special orders start on their way addressed to kings and emperors, presidents and ministers, tycoons and simple lovers of beautiful things. The glassblowers show off their skills every weekday. To be sure of times, enquire at the tourist office in the area.

At well-stocked factory outlets, you can find a huge selection of glass of varying quality at bargain prices. The finished pieces are normally sold through regular retail channels, and you'll have to do your buying at one of the shops to be found in almost every city. Even so, however, you save substantially in comparison with prices in other countries. Conducted tours are arranged round most of the glassworks.

Orrefors is the best-known Swedish glass maker, probably produces the greatest variety, and the quality and design are, of course, unsurpassed. The community of Orrefors is located about an hour west and a little north of Kalmar (train connections). It's so unpretentious you'll pass right through it if you're not looking.

Watching the skilled craftsmen of Orrefors is almost like a slow dance—with the pieces of red hot glass being carried back and forth, passed from hand to hand, as they are blown and shaped by trained, sensitive muscles. The basic procedure and the tools are said not to have changed appreciably in 2,000 years. It seems peculiar, but the glass is actually cut with shears in its molten state—like scissors cutting tough taffy. The designing and engraving processes are also fascinating —and the finished product is the result of unusual teamwork, from the designer to the craftsman to the finisher. (Many of the pieces get no further treatment after leaving the blower and shaper, however.) One of the special attractions of Orrefors is a magnificent display of various pieces made through the years, ranging in value up to thousands of kronor.

Other glassworks are: Johansfors, with a Crystal Museum showing a complete collection from the beginning of this century; Kosta, with a museum and exhibition hall. There are local glass museums at Lindshammar, Pukeberg, Rosdala and Skruf. The largest glass museum in Northern Europe is in Växjö, in the Småland Museum.

Tracing the Emigrants

There are about ten million Americans with Scandinavian blood. Of the Swedes, most came from Småland and the island of Öland. The emigration started in the middle of the last century and continued until the last war. On Öland, for instance, practically every household has someone who has been in America for a couple of years. Many come back, and nearly a fifth of the population, or 5,000 people, have lived and worked in America. Strangely enough, the people never traveled elsewhere to any extent. Some have seen Denmark and England en route to or from the States, others saw something of France, courtesy of the American Army in World War II. The story of some early Swedish emigrants to the U.S. has been masterfully told by a Swedish author, Vilhelm Moberg, in *The Emigrants, Unto a Good Land* and *Last Letter Home,* published, and made into a film, in English. It deals with a family from the mainland, only a few miles from Kalmar, and a look at it will give you an interesting sidelight on the histories of Sweden and America.

In Långasjö there is a small wooden house called Klasatorp open to visitors in the summer months. This was an emigrant's home, and the people here wear the costume of former days and work the farm in the traditional manner. The following tour is suggested for those who wish to see the land of their forefathers: Hovmantorp–Kosta–Ljuder–Algotsboda–Rävemåla–Linnerud–Ingelstad–Växjö. This tour covers a distance of 155 kilometers or 93 miles.

In Växjö the Emigrant Institute has an exhibition telling the story of the "American Dream" and the emigrants. There is also a research center here where the names of most emigrants are kept on file. In August Minnesota Day is celebrated in front of the Emigrant Institute.

PRACTICAL INFORMATION FOR SWEDEN'S SOUTHLAND

TOURIST INFORMATION. The region's tourist offices may be found at the following places: **Ängelholm**, Storgatan 21 (0431-163 50). **Eksjö**, Österlånggatan 31 (0381-133 05). **Helsingborg**, Rådhuset (042-12 03 10). **Jönköping**, V. Storgatan 9 (036-16 90 50). **Kalmar**, Larmgatan 6 (0480-153 50). **Karlskrona**, Ronnebygatan 28 (0455-834 90). **Lund**, St. Petri Kyrkogatan 4 (046-12 45 90). **Malmö**, Hamngatan 1 (040-34 12 70). **Ronneby**, Snäckebacksplan (0457-150 70). **Västervik**, Strömsholem (0490-136 95). **Växjö**, V. Esplandaden 18 (0470-223 25). **Ystad**, St. Knuts Torg (0411-770 00).

The **Malmö card**, costing about SEK 45 for three days and SEK 70 for a week, offers free bus transport in the Malmö area, free entrance to museums, and discounts on such things as restaurants, sightseeing and souvenirs in shops. Children half price.

TELEPHONE CODES. We have given telephone codes for all the towns and villages in the hotel and restaurant lists that follow. These codes need only be used when calling from outside the town or village concerned.

HOTELS AND RESTAURANTS. Because of its many tourist attractions and the popularity of its summer holiday resorts, this region is one of Sweden's best equipped from the point of view of hotel accommodations. Remember, too, that resort hotels have advantageous pension rates for stays of three days or longer. A Malmö hotel package is on offer from June 25 to Aug. 15 at 20 hotels in Malmö. The prices vary from SEK 150 to SEK 200 (double occupancy). The package includes breakfast and the Malmö card (described above). For children under 15, the price is SEK 40, for which they also get breakfast and the Malmö card.

For fine provincial cuisine—salmon and eel dishes are a specialty—in an authentic atmosphere, stop at some of the old country inns for a meal or two. The word for inn is *Gästgivargård*. Here you often find *Smörgåbords* with up to 150 dishes, such as pickled herring, shrimp, patés, home-made pies etc. To finish, ask for *spettekaka*, a delicious cake baked with eggs and plenty of sugar. Apart from those restaurants listed below, most of the region's restaurants will be found in the hotels themselves—see the listings.

SWEDEN'S SOUTHLAND

ÄNGELHOLM. *Continental* (I), Storgatan 23 (0431-127 00). 20 rooms. Central. Restaurant, bar, pub. AE, MC, V.

BÅSTAD. *Hemmeslövs Herrgårspensionat* (Manor House) (I) (0431-700 32). 150 rooms. Pension. Restaurant, dancing. Sauna, heated outdoor pool, tennis, 1.5 km. (a mile) to beach. Open Easter to Dec. 20. AE, V. *Hotel Pension Enehall* (I) (0431-702 12). 75 rooms. Pension. Restaurant, cafeteria. Sauna, outdoor pool nearby, 400 meters (440 yards) to beach. AE, DC, MC, V.

BODA. Youth Hostel. *Boda Glassworks* (0481-242 30). 47 beds. Outdoor pool. Bus from Nybro. Open all year.

BORGHOLM. (On the island of Öland). *Halltorps Gästgiveri* (Inn) (M), nine km. (five miles) south of Borgholm (0485-552 50). 10 rooms. Manor house from 17th century. Pension. Sauna. Known for excellent food. AE, MC, V. *Strand* (M), Villagatan 4 (0485-110 20). 141 rooms. Pension. Sauna, indoor pool, squash, fishing. AE, DC, MC, V.

EKETORP. Youth Hostel. *Eketorp Viking.* Village seven km. (four miles), beach 1.5 km. (1 mile). Near Långe Jan (Long John) lighthouse. Open June through Aug.

EKSJÖ. *Stadshotellet* (I), Stora Torget 5 (0381-130 20). 36 rooms. Central, 500 meters (546 yards) from railway station. Pension, restaurant, dancing. Also vegetarian food. Street with best-preserved 17th-century low wooden houses in the country. AE, DC, MC, V.
Youth Hostel. At Eksjö Museum, Österlånggatan 31 (0381-119 91). 50 beds. Central. Open June through Aug.

HELSINGBORG. *Grand Hotel* (M), Stortorget 8 (042-12 01 70). 130 rooms. Air terminal, 200 meters (218 yards) to railway and ferries to Denmark. Restaurant in English style, cocktail bar, sauna. AE, DC, MC, V. *Högvakten* (the Guardhouse) (I), Stortorget 14 (042-12 03 90). 39 rooms. Restaurant, sauna. AE, DC, MC, V.
Youth Hostel. *Villa Thalassa,* Dag Hammarskjöldsvag (042-11 03 84). 153 beds. Wonderful view of the sea. Closed Dec. 18 to Jan. 7.

HÖÖR. Youth Hostel. *Frostavallen* (0413-220 60). 62 beds. Cafeteria. Solarium. Canoes, bikes for rent. Skånes Zoo with northern animals. Closed Christmas to New Year.

KALMAR. *Witt* (M), S. Långgatan 42 (0480-152 50). 110 rooms. Restaurant, cocktail bar, pub, dancing. Sauna, pool, airport bus. AE, MC, V. *Möre Motel* (I), Motellvägen 1, Söderåkra (0486-214 55). 20 rooms. 40 km. (25 miles) south of Kalmar on E66. Self-service and restaurant. Homely fare from province. Indoor pool. MC. *Slottshotellet* (I), Slottavägen 9 (0480-882 60). 29 rooms. Near the park, 500 meters (546 yards) from town center, view of the bay. Sauna. Breakfast only. No credit cards.

KARLSHAMN. *Scandic* (M), Strömmavägen—E66 (0454-166 60). 100 rooms. Motor hotel. Restaurant, sauna. AE, DC, MC, V.

KARLSKRONA. *Stadshotellet* (M), Ronnebygatan 37 (0455-192 50). Central. Restaurant, nightclub. AE, MC, V.
Restaurants. *Krutviken* (M), Wämö, three km. (two miles) from the town center (0455-115 37). In park with a fine view of sea. Fish menu. In winter open 1–6 P.M. only. In summer open in evenings also. Closed Mon. MC, V. *Skeppet* (the Ship) (M), N. Kungsgatan 1 (0455-103 71). Marine atmosphere overlooking

the main square. Fish dishes a specialty. Has pub section—*Jollen.* Closed Sat. and Sun. MC, V.

KRISTIANSTAD. *Bäckaskog Castle* (I) (044-532 50). 51 rooms. 12 km. (seven miles) from Kristianstad. Castle from 13th century, formerly a monastery. Unique atmosphere. Bus. Rowboats and bikes for rent. AE, DC, MC, V.

LÅNGASJÖ. Youth Hostel. 65 km. (40 miles) from Kalmar, near the glassworks (0477-503 10). Many emigrants to America came from this area. Rowboats and bikes for rent. Open Feb. through Nov.

LUND. *Grand* (M), Bantorget 1 (046-11 70 10). 86 rooms. Central. Restaurant, also vegetarian menu. AE, DC, MC, V. *Sparta* (I), Tunavägen 39 (046-12 40 80). 150 rooms. Pension, restaurant, sauna. Prices from SEK 75 to SEK 350. AE, MC, V.

MALMÖ. *Alexandra* (M), Sallerupsvägen 5 (040-18 09 00). 72 rooms. DC, MC, V. *Garden* (M), Baltzaragatan 20 (040-10 40 00). 174 rooms. Central, in shopping district, close to airport bus. Restaurant *Gustaf.* AE, DC, MC, V. *St. Jörgen* (M), Stora Nygatan 35 (040-773 00). 282 rooms. In the heart of Malmö, five or ten minutes' walk to airport bus, rail station and harbor. Restaurant *Trädgården,* dancing. *Tahonga Bar,* self-service salad bar. MC, V. *Savoy* (M), Norra Vallgatan 62 (040-702 30). 100 rooms. Central. Restaurants, nightclub. AE, DC, MC, V. *Scandinavia* (M), Drottninggatan 1F (040-93 67 00). 220 rooms. Restaurant *Vivel.* Cocktail bar, cafeteria. Billiards, bowling, sauna. AE, DC, MC, V. *Skyline* (M), Stadiongatan at Exhibition Halls (040-803 00). 270 rooms. Luxury accommodation at low cost. Restaurant, sauna. AE, MC.

Astoria (I), Gråbrödersgatan 7 (040-786 60). 26 rooms. In old city, close to railways, airport bus and ferries. A fine family-run hotel. MC, V. *Hembygden* (I), Isak Slaktaregatan 7 (040-10 49 50). 26 rooms. Five-minute walk from rail station and boats to Denmark. Very inexpensive. AE, MC, V. *Jägersro* Motel (I), Jägersrovägen 160 (040-94 34 20). 64 rooms. Near the E4. Taverna. DC, MC, V. *Sjöfartshotellet* (I), Citadellsvägen 4 (040-23 96 05). 75 rooms. Near railway station and harbor. Restaurant. MC. *Strand* (I), Strandgatan 50 (040-16 20 30). 24 rooms. Quiet, near ferry Limhamn to Dragör. Breakfast. AE, MC.

Restaurant. *Översten* (E), Regementsgatan 52A (040-91 91 00). The tallest building in the area—26 stories above Malmö. Fantastic view with the Danish coast on the horizon. Shopping arcade on ground floor. Open Mon. to Fri. 11.30 A.M.–11 P.M. AE, MC, V.

Youth Hostel. *Södergården,* Backavägen 18 (040-822 20). 174 beds. Bus 36 from Central Station to bus stop "Vandrarhemmet." Sauna. Open Feb. through Nov.

MÖRRUM. *Walhalla* (I), Stationsvägen 24 (0454-500 44). 25 rooms. Three km. (two miles) to beach on the Baltic. Pension, restaurant. Salmon fishing. AE, MC, V.

OSKARSHAMN. *Påskallavik Gästgiveri* (Inn) (M), Kustvägen 31 (0491-913 50). Ten km. (six miles) south Oskarsjamn. Old inn, nicely decorated. Gourmet restaurant. Closed Jan. and Mon., except in July. MC, V.

OTTENBY. Youth Hostel. (On the island of Öland.) Near Ås Church on the southern tip of the island, three km. (two miles) from Ottenby Kungsård (0485-620 68). 96 beds.

RONNEBY. *Ronneby Brunn* (M) (0457-127 50). 314 rooms. Pension, restaurant, dancing, nightclub. Sauna, heated outdoor pool in summer, tennis, minigolf. Airport bus. AE, DC, MC, V.

SWEDEN'S SOUTHLAND

SIMRISHAMN. *Svea* (I), Strandvägen 3 (0414-117 20). 27 rooms. View of the Baltic. Picturesque fish harbor and houses. Restaurant, dancing, sauna. AE, DC, MC, V.

VÄXJÖ. *Statt* (M), Kungsgatan 5 (0470-134 00). 132 rooms. Restaurant, dancing, *Gyllene Oxen Pub*, *Lucky Swede Bar*, honoring a goldigger in the Klondike. Whirlpool, sauna, solarium. Airport bus. 200 meters (218 yards) to rail station. AE, DC, MC, V.
  Restaurant. *Teaterkällaren* (M), Nygatan 26 (0470-255 41). Central. Fish is the specialty. MC, V.
  Youth Hostel. *Evedal,* three km. (two miles) from road 23, six km. (four miles) northeast of Växjö (0470-630 70). 55 beds. In summer direct bus to Växjö. Minigolf; canoes, boats and bikes for rent. Open Jan. 15 to Dec. 15.

YSTAD. *Ystad Saltsjöbad* (Salt-Sea Bath) (M) (0411-136 30). 112 rooms. On the beach, one km. (two-thirds of a mile) from city center. Restaurant, dancing. Sauna, tennis, indoor pool; golf nearby. AE, DC, MC, V.

CAMPING

There are 125 camping sites in this area. Some are: **Hörby**, Ringsjöstrand (0415-105 67). 7 cabins. At Lake Ringsjön. Open May to Sept. 16; **Kalmar**, *Stensö Camping,* two km. (1.2 miles) south of Kalmar (0480-207 33). 15 cabins. Open all year. Camping site only June through Aug.; **Kosta**, *Kosta Camping*, 500 meters (546 yards) southeast of Kosta Glassworks (0478-505 17). 4 cabins; **Kristianstad**, *Charlottsborg Camping,* three km. (1.8 miles) west of town center (044-11 07 67). 9 beds. Open all year; **Urshult**, *Urshults Camping,* Rävabacken (0477-202 43). At Lake Åsnen, two km. (1.2 miles) north of Urshult. 9 cabins. Open June through Aug.

HOW TO GET AROUND. By car. If you are driving from Stockholm and Helsingborg is your goal, follow Highway E4 all the way (584 km. or 363 miles). From there, Highway E6 leads into Malmö. A more scenic route to Malmö from Stockholm follows Highway E4 to Norrköping, then swings off on the mainly coastal Highway 15.

By bus and train. From Stockholm, Malmö is six hours by train, and 10¼ hours by bus. Helsingborg is five hours by train and nine hours by bus. There are bus services on all major roads. The express bus from Malmö to Kalmar along scenic Highway E66 takes seven hours. There is a bus service to the airport at Kastrup, Copenhagen over Linhamn–Dragör. It starts at the Central Station in Malmö.

By air. Malmö is a mere 25 minutes by air from Copenhagen (four flights daily). There are daily flights from Stockholm to Malmö (one hour). Local flights run between Malmö and Visby.

By boat. Southern Sweden is linked with Denmark by boat via: Malmö to Copenhagen (1½ hours), Linhamn to Dragör (55 minutes), Landskrona to Tuborg (1¼ hours), Helsingborg to Elsinore (25 minutes), Varberg to Grenå (4½ hours) and Gothenburg to Frederikshavn (3¾ hours). Traffic is heavy on all runs and the ferries carry cars and international trains. A hydrofoil operates between Malmö and Copenhagen, with regular trips taking only 35 minutes. A hovercraft service from Kastrup Airport (Denmark) to the harbor at Malmö is planned for 1985.

By bicycle. Puncture-free bicycles are for rent from the tourist office in Malmö at SEK 30 per day. Or rent a tandem for SEK 50.

SWEDEN

TOURS. There are daily sightseeing tours by bus leaving from Gustav Adolfs Torg in Malmö at 1 P.M. and 2.30 P.M. From June to Aug. Sightseeing by boat can be enjoyed daily from May through Aug. Tours leave from the quay opposite the Central Station in Malmö every hour between 10 A.M. and 5 P.M.

From May through Aug. there are a number of day tours to the castles, manor houses and churches in Skåne. Call at the Malmö tourist office for details.

PLACES TO VISIT. Apart from the castles, chateaux and manor houses of Skåne and Sweden's "Chateau Country," there are many other attractions in this region. When visiting Malmö, remember the **Malmö card**, which offers free bus transport, free admission to the museums and discounts on restaurants, sightseeing, souvenirs etc. It costs about SEK 45 for three days and SEK 70 for a week. Children half price.

HELSINGBORG. Fredriksdals OpenAir Museum and Botanical Garden —18th-century mansion and farmhouses and buildings from Skåne province. Open May through Sept., 10–6.

Kärnan tower (Medieval Keep). View from the ramparts of city and Danish coast. Open May through Aug., daily 9–8.

Rådhuset (Town Hall). Including tourist office.

Stottshagen (Castle Park). Beautiful park within the ramparts. Also the Rosengården with thousands of roses and a fine view of the strait.

Sofiero. A former royal summer residence. Five km. (three miles) north of Helsingborg. Beautiful garden. View of the straits. Open May through Aug., 10–6.

HÖÖR. Frostavallen, 60 km (37 miles) from Malmö or Helsingborg, is a recreation center, hotel, youth hostel, park and zoo with Nordic animals. Also a Stone-Age village where you can stay overnight. Hides and skins are for rent, and you prepare your own Stone-Age meals. Experience how people lived 8,000 years ago. Open all year round (0413-220 60).

KALMAR. Kalmar Castle. Chapel and museum. Museum has archeological finds, weapons, furniture etc. and exhibits from the warship *Krona.* Open May through Sept., Mon. to Sat. 10–4, Sun. 1–4; Dec. through Feb., Sun. only; rest of year, daily 1–5.

KARLSKRONA. Varvsmuseet (Marine Museum). Amiralitetsslätten. Galleon figureheads, ship models. 300 years of marine history. Open daily 12–4.

KRISTIANSTAD. Bäckaskog Castle. 10 km. (six miles) east of Kristianstad. Swedish King Charles XV's summer residence. Chapel, gardens. Open May 15 to Aug., 10–4.

Film Museum. Östra Storgatan 53. Old films (shown on request) and film equipment. Open Tues. to Fri. and Sun. 1–4; closed Mon. and Sat. Admission free.

LANDSKRONA. Ängelholm House. Stora Norregatan 80. Built 1628, the oldest building in Landskrona.

Borstahusen. A genuine village with small houses and alleyways.

Landskrona Museum. At Slottsgatan. European and Swedish art, workshops and shops. Also prehistoric section where you can try out primitive tools. Open daily 1–5. Admission free.

Weilbullsholms flower nurseries. At southern entry to city. Open daily for inspection.

The island of Ven. Half-hour boat trip—flowers, foundations of a castle and a reconstructed observatory called **Stjärneborg** (Star Castle).

SWEDEN'S SOUTHLAND

LUND. Kulturen Museet (Museum of Cultural History). Tegnérsplatsen. Openair museum with 30 buildings from South Sweden. Exhibits of ceramics, glass, textiles, silver, weapons and toys. Open daily 12–6.

MALMÖ. Bosjökloster. 45 km. (28 miles) from Malmö on Lake Ringsjön—founded in 1080 as Benedictine convent. Garden, exhibitions. Open May through Oct., daily 9–5.30 (0413-250 48). Admission free.

Malmö Museum. Malmöhusvägen in the **Malmöhus Castle,** dating from 1542. Museum shows art, natural history, history of Malmö. Outside the castle is the **Kommendanthuset,** the Technical and Marine Museums. Open Tues. to Sun. 12–4; closed Mon.; June through Aug., museum tour by boat, once a week.

ÖLAND. Eketorp—reconstructed fortified village with small museum. 50 km. (31 miles) south of Öland Bridge near Gräsgård. Open May through Sept., 9–5; in July, 9–6. Guided tours; call 0485-620 23 for current times. Regular buses from Färjestaden.

VÄXJÖ. Smålands Museum, behind railway station. Large collection of glass and tools, weapons, coins, 18th- and 19th-century art. Open Mon. to Fri. 9–4, Sat. 11–3, Sun 1–5.

Utvandrarnas Hus (the Emigrant Institute). Adjoining the museum (0470-201 20). Archives, research. Permanent exhibition of "Dream of America"—the emigration of more than one million Swedes to the New World. Open Mon. to Fri. 9–4, Sat. 11–3, Sun. 1–5. Minnesota Day celebrated here each year in Aug.

SPORTS. There are fine sandy beaches at Falsterbo, Mölle, Tylösand, Ängelholm, Malen, Mellbystrand Skrea, Ystad, Åhus, and on the isle of Öland. Most resort hotels have **tennis** courts, and **golf** may be played at several places. 18-hole courses at Båstad, Falsterbo, Helsingborg, Kalmar, Lund and Mölle.

Good salmon **fishing** in the Mörrum River, with the season from April-May until September 30. It is advisable to order fishing cards in advance if you come during April or May. Write Hotel Walhalla, Mörrum. Sea-fishing tours are arranged from Helsingborg.

There's a good **horseracing** track near Malmö, at Jägersro, where the Swedish Derby, usually about mid July, draws a big, international crowd.

There are many **biking** and **hiking** trails in the region.

GOTHENBURG AND THE WEST COAST

Gateway to Northern Europe

It is only proper to approach Gothenburg (or Göteborg) by the sea, for at heart it is a product of the oceans and the ships that sail them. Shipping, shipbuilding and fishing set their stamp on this region long before the age of the Vikings. You never get far from the maritime influence, and the harbor bustles (as does Europe's newest airport here, Landvetter).

A classic example of honesty, modesty and frankness once was found in a shipping company's guide to Gothenburg. "Gothenburg is by no means a Tourist Mecca," it read, "but it has its points." This is to certify that it does have its points, and plenty of them. Actually, Gothenburg is a gateway to the entire world, with regular freight services and frequent passenger connections to all the Seven Seas. If you come to Scandinavia with one of the Danish or Swedish lines—Sessan Torline from Germany, England or with Stena Line from Germany, or Denmark—Gothenburg is your first Scandinavian port of call. And the city is the ideal place to begin a round trip tour of Scandinavia, since it occupies almost the exact center of a triangle of which the capitals of Stockholm, Oslo, and Copenhagen are the points.

Exploring Gothenburg

An intangible air, perceptible enough almost to be held in your hands, distinguishes Gothenburg from Stockholm. Many attribute it to centuries of close relations with Great Britain, birthplace of the Anglo-Saxon tradition of freedom. It has even been called "Little London." The residents are fully conscious of this pronounced attraction westward. Others attribute it to the physical nature of the city, with its broad avenues, its huge, sprawling harbor, its comparatively great geographical area for a city of some 430,000 people. Finally, age has something to do with this sensation. Gothenburg is young, officially born in 1621, when parts of Stockholm's Old Town looked about as they do now. There is something of a friendly rivalry between the cities.

A great Swedish king, Gustavus Adolphus, the "Lion of the North," gave Gothenburg its charter in 1621. He called in Dutch builders, and the canals and architecture will show the strength of their influence. The town soon began to play a part in history. Karl X summoned the parliament to meet there in 1659–60, in Kronhuset, the oldest building extant, and there his son was crowned Karl XI after Karl X's death. Scotsmen and Germans had by this time settled in the town in considerable numbers.

As early as 1699 the British community formed an association for mutual support. The influx of Scots and Englishmen continued through the 18th and 19th centuries, and they and their descendants have had a decisive importance in the commercial and cultural development of the city. Many of the finest old families of Gothenburg have typically English names.

At one time Gothenburg enjoyed a thriving trade with the East Indies, as evidenced by the old factory building in the Norra Hamngatan, which now houses the Ethnographical, Archeological, and Historical museums. However, the city's first great commercial impetus resulted from Napoleon's continental blockade in 1806, when its port became the principal depot of British trade with northern Europe.

The opening of the Trollhätte Canal shortly after 1800, connecting Gothenburg by water with huge Lake Vänern and the rich forest and iron products of the region around the lake, offered a new commercial stimulus. Before the middle of the century the first shipbuilding yard was turning out sailing vessels, and industrializing was under way. Today Gothenburg is the headquarters of many industries, including the world-wide SKF ballbearing empire; AB Volvo, Scandinavia's largest maker of automobiles; three hyper-modern shipyards; and the Hasselblad camera factory. About one third of the population gets its living from industry. Incidentally, Gothenburg is one of the few remaining cities with streetcars.

Landvetter Airport provides West Sweden with access to very large aircraft with direct lines to other countries. This new airport has a capacity that will meet the requirements of the regions for many years. With its location close to Highway 40, the new airport is easy to reach from all the towns in West Sweden. Signposts marked with the airport symbol clearly show the way from the roads in the vicinity.

City Highlights

You must really see the harbor to appreciate it. There are 22 kilometers (14 miles) of quays, 200 cranes that sometimes seem to rise up like steel forests, and the warehouse and customs sheds cover more than 1½ million square feet. Gothenburg is the home port of 40 per cent of the Swedish merchant fleet—better than 4 million tons of shipping—and handles a third of the country's imports and a quarter of the exports. During the summer there are boat tours that take you around the harbor and entrance.

Skandiahamnen is the new port for container and roll-on/roll-off traffic. Here you find the terminals of Tor Line, Atlantic Container Line and other shipping companies.

Gothenburg's Fish Harbor, one of the largest in Scandinavia, opened in 1910. Its early morning fish auction, at which wholesalers publicly bid for cod, catfish, sole, herring, and occasionally even whale, has become something of a tourist attraction.

Trädgårdsföreningen, site of the magnificent gardens of the horticultural society, begins right across the square from the Central Station. The Palm House is an impressive example of what you can grow in a northern climate with the help of heat and glass. Flowers by the acre, beautifully tended lawns.

Götaplatsen is an impressive square which might be described as the cultural heart of Gothenburg. In the center is the famed "Poseidon" fountain by Milles. The columned building which rises up above the broad steps at the end of the square—and dominates it—is the Art Gallery. As you face the art museum, the building on the left is the modern City Theater, the one on the right the Concert Hall. If you climb the steps leading up to the museum, you get a fine view of the wide boulevard Kungsportsavenyen, with the profile of downtown Gothenburg in the distance. This square is notable as an expression of modern architecture, as impressive as older and better-known counterparts elsewhere in Europe.

Liseberg Amusement Park is only a few minutes from downtown by streetcar or taxi, a walk of only 15 minutes or so from the Park Avenue Hotel. This is one of the best, neatest, and best-run amusement parks in existence—partly because of beautiful gardens that you don't ordinarily find in this kind of establishment. There are several restaurants, open-air concerts, variety theater, and wide range of the usual carnival attractions.

Among other sights are the Sailor's Tower, near the Maritime Museum, a tall monument to seamen who lost their lives in World War I, from which you have an excellent view of the harbor and city; Masthugget Church, a striking modern edifice on an impressive site overlooking the city; Guldesheden, a housing development with an unusually pleasant central square; and the huge natural park, Slottsskogen.

There are several good museums with fine, often unique, collections. Anyone interested in shipping should by all means see the Maritime Museum between Karl Johansgatan and route E3.

Gothenburg Environs

In the neighboring industrial town of Mölndal, only a short distance away, is the delightful 18th-century mansion of Gunnebo. It is a good example of architecture and landscaping of a period that combined the best of French and English influence. The house was designed by C. W. Carlberg, who also designed the furniture in 1796. John Hall, a merchant of British origin, was the first owner of Gunnebo. It is now the property of Mölndal community. During the summer visitors are shown around in the early afternoon; there are hourly buses to Mölndal and Gunnebo from Nils Ericsonsplatsen (behind the Central Station).

Särö, a bit farther south, by bus, is known for its thriving foliage and oak trees, which grow right at the edge of the sea. On the route to Särö is the beautifully situated Hovås golf course.

On a day tour to the south of Gothenburg, visit Fjärås Bräcka (32 kilometers or 20 miles), an ice-age sand ridge that divides Lake Lygnern from the sea. From the top there is a splendid view over this coastal area, and on the slopes are Iron Age and Viking graveyards.

Only a few minutes away lies the impressive turn-of-the-century Tjolöholm Palace, now open to the public—hourly tours every day during summer and on weekends in winter—and there is also a "stable" cafeteria, a horse carriage museum, and a park.

A few kilometers east of Tjolöholm is the tiny, picturesque village of Eskhult, now an open-air museum.

To the east of Gothenburg is a large, hilly forest-and-lake area. Visit the 19th-century Nääs manor house on route E3 (32 kilometers or 20 miles from Gothenburg; hourly tours in the summer). In the outbuildings there are stables, restaurant, coffee shop and several exhibition shops selling traditional Swedish products—textiles, wood, furniture, antiques and souvenirs.

Nearby is the medieval Öijared chapel, in the middle of a 45-hole golf course. Further northeast is the Anten-Gräfsnäs Veteran Railway.

The West Coast

The coast north of Gothenburg (Bohuslän province) is the beginning of fjord country, with its dozens of fishing villages and thousands of islands. Forty minutes from Gothenburg by car lies the former fishing village of Stenungsund, today Sweden's busy petrochemical center. Just outside, the mighty Tjörn bridges span the fjord—the breathtaking view will give you a strong incentive to explore.

North and slightly west of Gothenburg stretches the province of Bohuslän, a coastal and island summer playground among the most popular in Sweden—a part of the famed west coast. It was more or less discovered by the royal family. Prince Vilhelm, brother of the late king, wrote with much great feeling about Bohuslän, beginning with a visit there in the '90s with his father, King Gustav V. "So the ocean, the ships, and the rocky islands form the trinity that characterizes Bohuslän," Vilhelm writes. "A name that sounds good to all seafaring folk, for it bespeaks a coast peopled by strong men and sturdy objects, an archipelago formed of gneiss and granite and water which eternally stretches foamy arms after life."

How to Explore the Area

Proceeding north from Gothenburg, you come to Kungälv, which was a commercial center before the year 1000. It is overlooked by a hugh medieval stronghold, Bohus Fortress, built by the Norwegians in 1308. Kungälv is a sea of flowers during apple blossom time.

The island city of Marstrand was also built by the Norwegians, some time during the 13th century. This was the favorite west coast summer resort of King Oskar II, who died in 1907, and the resort hotel emits something of a turn-of-the-century air. It is still a popular summer resort. There is an interesting 17th-century fortress overlooking the city—Karlsten—used as a prison during the 18th and 19th centuries. The church is from the 14th century.

Lysekil is a popular and reasonably typical example of the villages along the west coast which have become Meccas for summer vacationers. It rests on the mouth of a long fjord, protected from sea and wind by cliffs.

On the other side of the fjord is Fiskebäckskil, another popular summering place. Farther inland, roughly northeast, is the city of Uddevalla, the biggest municipality in this region (population, over 46,000). Uddevalla as a city leaves much to be desired in its appeal to the eye, but is a good overnight halt. The principal industries are textiles, paper, wood processing, and shipbuilding.

Along the coast north of Lysekil are a whole row of villages familiar to west coast vacationers and to the painters and sailors who haunt this region in the summer time—Smögen (a singularly picturesque fishing village), Bovallstrand, Fjällbacka, Grebbestad, and many more. At the very north end of the province, just below the border to Norway, is Strömstad, the northern anchor of the Bohuslän vacation region, so to speak. The city has old traditions both as a port and military objective and as a summer resort. In addition, Strömstad offers you interesting excursions. The best from a historical point of view is to Fredriksten Fortress, just over the Norwegian border at Halden, where King Charles XII fell in 1718. This whole region was bitterly contested for centuries in the Scandinavian wars.

Just 45 minutes by boat from Strömstad are the Koster Islands, a holiday paradise for people who like boating, fishing and swimming in a car-free environment.

The west coast area of Sweden actually stretches about 400 kilometers (250 miles) south from the Norwegian border as far as Laholm. Going south from Gothenburg, you reach the town of Kungsbacka, whose square is the site of a colourful market on the first Thursday of every month. Nearby is Fjärås Bräcka, where an ice-age sand ridge divides Lake Lygnern from the sea. From the top there is a splendid view over this coastal area, as well as over the lake, which resembles those of middle or north Sweden. On the slopes are Iron Age and Viking graves. Also to be found in Fjärås are the largest horse-radish plantations in the country!

Only a few minutes away lies the impressive turn-of-the century Tjolöholm Palace, now open to the public—hourly tours every day during summer and on weekends in winter—and there is also a "stable" cafeteria, a horse carriage museum, and a park. A few kilometers east of Tjolöholm is the tiny, picturesque 18th-century village of Äskhult, now an open-air museum.

Also nearby are Lerkil and Gottskär on the Onsala Peninsula, the scene of plenty of activity in the small-craft harbors. You might be able to spot some seals on skerries nearby.

South again is Varberg, an industrial center and holiday resort. It's only five minutes' walk from the city center to the nearest beach here. The old fortress has sections which date from the 13th century and was once the most formidable stronghold in Europe. Today it contains a unique youth hostel and a museum with the world's only known fully dressed medieval body (the Bocksten Man). Daily fishing tours are offered from Varberg with the prospect of catches of dogfish, cod and mackerel. The Getterön Reserve for migratory birds can boast more species than most similar reserves in Sweden.

Further south is the little town of Falkenberg, known for its salmon fishing and popular among vacationers. The outstanding sight is the stately bridge over the Ätran River, which dates from 1756. The Törngrens Pottery, dating from 1789, is also worth a visit.

Halmstad is the center of this tourist region; a provincial capital with some 76,000 inhabitants. The town is about 600 years old and the oldest building is the church, a 14th-century Gothic structure. Miniland, near Halmstad, shows Sweden modelled in miniature (scale 1:25).

Other popular resorts nearby are Tylösand, Laxvik and Steninge.

PRACTICAL INFORMATION FOR GOTHENBURG AND THE WEST COAST

TOURIST INFORMATION. The tourist office in **Gothenburg** has information about Gothenburg and all the attractions on the West Coast as far as the Norwegian border. The address is Kungsportsavenyen 2 (031-13 59 92 or 031-13 60 28). Open daily 10–8. There is also a tourist office in the Nordstan shopping center (031-13 60 28). Open summer, Mon. to Fri. 9.30–6, Sat. 9.30–3; closed Sun.

Other regional tourist offices are at: **Falkenberg,** Sandgatan-Holgersgatan (0346-174 10) **Halmstad,** Kajplan (035-11 15 81) **Kungsbacka,** Storgatan 41 (0300-342 84) **Lysekil,** Rosviktorg (0523-109 07) **Strömstad,** Norra Hamnen (0526-130 30) **Varberg,** Västra Vallgatan 39 (0340-887 70).

USEFUL ADDRESSES. Gothenburg. *British Consulate,* Nordstan shopping center, Götgatan entrance (031-11 13 27). *American Consulate General,* Södra Hamngatan 2 (031-10 05 90).

TELEPHONE CODES. We have given telephone codes for all the towns and villages in the hotel and restaurant lists that follow. These codes need only be used when calling from outside the town or village concerned.

SWEDEN

HOTELS AND RESTAURANTS. Many new hotels have been built in Gothenburg recently, so there should be plenty of choice. If you are without a room, use the room-booking service at the tourist office. A hotel-booking service is also available with 2,700 rooms (031-10 11 40). If you are staying for five to eight days and do not need big lounges and cocktail bars, it would pay to rent a room on a weekly basis at SGS, Utlandagatan 24 (031-81 33 60). The price for a single room is about SEK 700. Special low rates during weekends and in summer can be obtained with the Gothenburg package and card. Enquire at your travel agent or write to the tourist office.

For the rest of the West Coast, accommodations are in general on the modest side. A few towns draw a more or less fashionable trade, but most of the people who come to the region in summer live in cottages or aboard their sailboats. Many resort hotels offer demi-pension rates (breakfast and dinner) and advantageous pension rates for a stay of three days or more.

The West Coast is dotted with camping sites (more than 75)—most are on beaches and all are up to a good standard. Many also have camping cabins or bungalows for rent.

ÅSA. *Motel E6* (I), Åsa, 17 Km. (ten miles) south of Uddevalla (0340-516 66). 20 rooms. Room with breakfast SEK 125. Restaurant with homely fare. MC, V.

FALKENBURG. *Grand* (I), Ågatan 1 (0346-144 50). 54 rooms. Central, 500 meters (546 yards) to railway station. Restaurant, dancing, sauna; three km. (two miles) to outdoor pool. AE, DC, MC, V.

FISKEBÄCKSKIL. Youth Hostel. *Bassholmen,* three km. (two miles) southeast of Fiskebäckskil (0522-513 08). 30 beds. In the archipelago in a nature reserve. Open June 18 to Aug. 21.

GOTHENBURG. *Europa* (L), Köpmangatan 38 (Nordstan) (031-80 12 80). 400 rooms. A few steps from central station and air terminal. 116 shops in big center outside door. Restaurants *Newport, Europa Garden* and *Culinaire. Jonny's* piano bar. Private saunas, pool, nightclub. AE, DC, MC, V. *Park Avenue* (L), Kungsportsplatsen 36–38 (031-17 65 20). 320 rooms. One of Sweden's finest. Double rooms have a balcony. *Panorama* cocktail lounge on top floor. Restaurants *Belle Avenue* and *Harlequin,* as well as *Lorensburg* with dancing and floor show. Sauna, pool. AE, DC, MC, V. *Victor's* (L), Skeppsbroplatsen 1 (031-17 41 80). 38 rooms. Most exclusive. Restaurant. sauna. AE, DC, MC, V.

Carl Johan (E), Karl Johansgatan (031-42 00 20). 153 rooms. Close to ferries to Germany. Restaurant. AE, DC, MC, V. *Ekoxen* (E), N. Hamngatan 38 (Nordstan) (031-80 50 80). 80 rooms. Very central. Oyster bar, whirlpool, sauna. AE, DC, MC, V. *Gothia* (E), Örgrytevägen 4 (031-40 93 00). 300 rooms. New in 1984. View of the city. Near Liseberg and fairground. Restaurant, piano bar on the top floor. Sauna on the 18th floor. Exercise center. Airport bus. AE, DC, MC, V. *Opalen* (E), Engelbrektsgatan 73 (031-81 03 00). 230 rooms. Smoke-free rooms. Close to *Scandinavium,* the Swedish Fairground and Liseberg. *Club Opalen* with dancing. Exotic *Tahonga* bar. Sauna. AE, DC, MC, V.

Restaurants. *Fiskekrogen* (E), Lilla Torget (031-11 21 84). 30 fish dishes to choose from. Excellent for lunch. AE, DC, MC, V. *Gamle Port* (E), Östra Larmgatan 18 (031-11 07 02). Central. Fine atmosphere. Pub, nightclub. AE, DC, MC, V. *Johanna* (E), Södra Hamngatan 47 (031-1 22 60). One of the best restaurants in Sweden; French and Swedish cuisine. Closed Sun. AE, DC, MC, V. *Libretto* (E), Kungsportsavenyen 24 (031-81 08 00). Gourmet restaurant in Hotel Rubinen. AE, DC, MC, V.

Bräutigams (M), Östra Hamngatan-Kungsgatan (031-13 60 46). Traditional café. Home-made pastries, sandwiches, salad bar. Also warm dishes. AE, DC, V. *Räkan* (the Shrimp) (M), Lorensbergsgatan 16, behind Hotel Rubinen (031-16 98 39). Direct your order to your table in small radio-controlled fishing-

GOTHENBURG AND THE WEST COAST

boats. You can also have your snapps arrive by boat . . . fun. Usually dancing in basement. AE, MC, V. *White Corner* (M), Vasagatan 43 (031-81 28 10). Pub in English style. Steakhouse, cafeteria, music. Open late. AE, DC, MC, V.

Annorlunda (I), Lilla Korsgatan 2 (031-13 80 26). The oldest vegetarian restaurant in Gothenburg. Open until 7 P.M. No credit cards.

In the N.K. department store there are three restaurants: the *N.K. Valvet* (M) in 18th-century vaults (031-17 33 00), the self-service bar (I) and the *Tea House* on the fourth floor. Service on terrace in summer. All AE, DC, MC, V. *Riverton* (E), Stora Badhusgatan 26 (031-10 12 00). 212 rooms. New 1985. Restaurant, sauna, near airport bus. AE, DC, MC, V. *Rubinen* (E), Kungsportsavenyen 24 (031-81 08 00). 189 rooms. Central, on an elegant avenue. Restaurant *Librette* and bistro. Cocktail bar and tearoom. AE, DC, MC, V. *Scandanavia* (E), Kustgatan 10 (031-42 70 00). 323 rooms near the Älvsborg bridge with a view of the harbor. Close to the ferry terminal for Germany. Restaurant *Oscar IV*, dancing. Cocktail bar *Langunen*, on poolside. Free garage. AE, DC, MC, V. *Windsor* (E), Kungsportsavenyen 6 (031-17 65 40). 83 rooms. Secluded British atmosphere, best location. Popular cocktail bar, restaurant. SAS office. AE, DC, MC, V.

Lorensberg (M), Berzeligatan 15 (031-18 70 85). 125 rooms. In the heart of the cultural center. Breakfast only. AE, MC, V. *Panorama* (M), Eklandagatan 5 (031-81 08 80). 360 rooms. New 1984. Quiet, central location, airport bus nearby. Restaurant, piano bar. Sauna, pool, free parking. AE, DC, MC, V. *Ritz* (M), Burggrevegatan 25 (031-17 52 60). 110 rooms. Central, no restaurant. Run by Salvation Army. AE, DC, MC, V. *Tre Kronor* (Three Crowns) (M), N. Kustbanegatan 15 (031-80 15 00). 172 rooms. Within walking distance of the shops etc. Restaurant, nightclub, sauna, heated garage. AE, DC, MC, V. *Vasa* (M), Victoriagatan 6 (031-17 36 30). 50 rooms. Central, breakfast only. Buffet, sauna, solarium. AE, DC, MC, V.

ME-Room pension (I), Chalmersgatan 27A (031-20 70 30). 8 rooms, 3 baths. No credit cards. *Pension Kungsport* (I), Karl Gustavsgatan 21 (031-13 52 36). 6 rooms. No credit cards. *Royal* (I), Drottninggatan 67 (031-17 01 00). 78 rooms. Central. The oldest hotel in Gothenburg. Has charm and atmosphere. On shopping street. Breakfast only. AE, MC, V.

Liseberg, the amusement park, has many excellent restaurants. You can dine in the open and watch lighted fountains and outdoor performances of various kinds. Some restaurants are open only from April to September. Those restaurants in Liseberg Park open all year are: *Lisebergs Restaurant* (M), (031-83 62 72). Classical restaurant, dancing. *Wärdshuset* (the Inn) (031-83 62 77). Includes English pub in 18th-century milieu. *Tyrolen* (031-83 62 82). A sing-along place with Tyroler music every night except Mondays.

Youth Hostels. *Kärralund Camping*, Delsjövägen-Olbersgatan (031-25 27 61). 12 four-bed bungalows. Tram 5. SEK 200 per bungalow; open all year. *Ostkupan*, Mejerigatan 2 (031-40 10 50). 219 beds. 3 km. (two miles) from city center. Bus 64 from Central Station or tram 5 to St. Sigfridsplan and then bus 62. Walking distance to Liseberg. SEK 60. Breakfast service, gymnasium, sauna, laundrette, T.V. room. Open all year.

Camping. *Kärralund*, see *Youth Hostels*. Three-star site, open all year round. During the summer months there is a central city camping site at *Valhallabadet*.

HALMSTAD. *Tylösand Havsbad* (M), on the sea eight km. (five miles) from Halmstad (035-30 500). 136 rooms. Restaurant, dancing and nightclub in summer. Sauna, indoor saltwater pool. 200 meters (about 200 yards) to Sweden's most popular golf course (36 holes). Open all year. AE, MC, V. *Grand* (I), Stationsgatan 44 (035-11 91 40). 50 rooms. Near bus and railway station, close to beaches. Restaurant, sauna. AE, MC, V.

Youth Hostel. At Steninge on the coastal road 18 km. (11 miles) northwest of Halmstad (035-520 54). 49 beds. Open June through Aug.

KUNGSBACKA. *Halland* (I), Storgatan 35 (0300-115 30). 65 rooms. Restaurant *Mistral*, dancing, cocktail bar. AE, MC.

Restaurant. *Leksandsgården* (M), Gottskärsvägen, Onsala (0300-607 05). Ten km. (six miles) from Kungsbacka. Rustic old upper-class milieu. Specialty fish dishes. *Smörgåsbord* Sundays. AE, DC, MC, V.

KUNGÄLV. *Fars Hatt* (M) (0303-109 70). 115 rooms. An inn here since 1684. Restaurant, dancing, sauna, heated outdoor pool. AE, DC, MC, V.
Youth Hostel. *Fridhem,* Tvetgatan, 1.5 km. (a mile) from center (0303-129 62). 50 beds. Open June through Aug.

LYSEKIL. *Fridhem* (I), Turistgatan (0523-139 12). 18 rooms. On the sea, 500 meters (546 yards) from center and bus. Breakfast only. MC, V. *Lysekil* (I), Rosviktorget 1 (0523-118 60). 50 rooms. Central, seaview. Restaurant, nightclub *Nautic.* Excursions arranged in summer. AE, DC, MC, V.

MARSTRAND. *Alphyddan* (I), Långgatan 11 (0303-612 00). 35 rooms. Close to everything, 50 meters (164 ft.) to outdoor pool. MC.

SMÖGEN. *Smögenbaden* (I) (0523-310 35). 20 rooms. 50 meters (164 ft.) from the sea with expansive view. Family-run hotel, restaurant, dancing. Open May through Aug. only. AE, DC, MC, V.

STRÖMSTAD. *Stadshotellet* (I), opposite Societetsparken (0526-124 00). 27 rooms. Restaurant, dancing. AE, MC, V.
Youth Hotel. At Norra Kyrkogatan 12 (0526-101 93). 70 beds. Open June through Aug.

TANUMSHEDE. *Tanums Gestgifveri* (Inn) (M), at bus stop 2.5 km. (1.5 miles) east of railway station (0525-290 10). 33 rooms. The inn has been in continuous operation since 1663. Bridal suite with circular bathtub, excellent food. Famous rock carvings nearby. AE, MC, V.

UDDEVALLA. *Bohusgården* (M), on route E6 with panoramic view of the fjord, two km. (1.2 miles) south of Uddevalla (0522-364 20). 47 rooms. Sauna, heated outdoor pool, golf nearby. MC. *Carlia* (M), Norra Drottninggatan 20 (0522-141 40). 64 rooms. Central. Piano bar, dancing. AE, MC, V.
Restaurant. *Gustafsbergs Badrestaurant* (E), 5 km. (three miles) south of Uddevalla (0522-100 38). In a charming building from the last century. Shrimp evenings Tues. and Thurs. Café on the sea. Dancing May through Aug. 15. AE, DC, MC, V.

VARBERG. *Statt* (M), Kungsgatan 24 (0340-161 00). 126 rooms. 500 meters (546 yards) to beach. Restaurant, dancing, sauna. AE, MC, V.
Youth Hostel. In the fortress (0340-887 88). 70 beds. Spend a night in a guaranteed genuine prison environment. . . .

HOW TO GET AROUND. The Gothenburg card is your personal key to the attractions of Gothenburg. It gives you free travel on trams and buses, sightseeing by bus and boat, entrance to all museums and the Liseberg amusement park, free trips in spring and fall to Fredrikshamn, Denmark and much more. The price (in 1984) was SEK 45 for 24 hours, SEK 60 for 48 hours and SEK 90 for 90 hours. Children are cheaper at SEK 25, 40 and 60.

The minimum fare on a tram or bus is SEK 6. Discount coupons are available. A guided tour by bus will cost you SEK 30 for 50 minutes and SEK 55 for a longer trip.

GOTHENBURG AND THE WEST COAST 433

TOURS. You can take a six-hour tour of the West Coast, including lunch, for SEK 185. The tour goes over the Tjörn Bridge to Orust Island and the picturesque fishing village of Mollösund, where lunch is waiting. All tours start from the tourist office at Kungsportsplatsen 2 (031-80 05 18).

There are many passenger boats going along the coast and from the mainland to the islands. There is also a boat package available which will give you an opportunity to get to know the waterways. The cost is approximately SEK 1,000, including accommodations for seven days.

PLACES TO VISIT. GOTHENBURG. All museums in Gothenburg are open Tues. to Sat. 12–4, Sun. and holidays 11–5, Wed. evenings 6–9. The only exceptions are the Fartygmuseet, open Sat. and Sun. only, 11–5; and the Kronhuset, which is not open on Wed. evenings.

Älvsborgs Fästning (Elfsborg Fortress). Historic fortress dating from 1670. Regular boat trips from Lilla Bommen and Stenpiren, including harbor sightseeing. Cafe in fortress.

Botaniska Trädgården (Botanical Garden). South of Slottsskogen Park. Rock garden, herbarium, hot houses. Open 9 A.M. to sunset.

Fartygmuseet (Ship Museum). Lilla Bommen. Openair museum. See an old light-ship, old barges, a canoe hewn from a tree trunk, boats from Viking times etc. Sat. and Sun. only.

Göteborg Museet (Gothenburg Museum). Norra Hamngatan 12, close to Gustav Adolfs Square. In this building you can find three museums: the **Arkeologiska Museet** (Archeological Museum). Prehistoric finds from the west coast of Sweden, such as arrow heads, fossils etc. **Etnografiska Museet** (Ethnographical Museum). Pre-Columbian Peruvian textiles, South American Indian cultural artifacts etc. Also a Lapp section. **Historiska Museet** (the local History Museum). The development of Gothenburg from the earliest times.

Industri Museet (Industrial Museum). Åvägen 24. Articles produced by industrial concerns in and around Gothenberg; imaginative concepts of the future; exhibit of veteran cars. Closed Mon.

Konstmuseet (Art Gallery). Götsplatsen. Excellent collections of Dutch and Italian masters, French Impressionists, Swedish paintings and sculpture from 18th century to the present. Works of Rembrandt, Rubens and Van Gogh. Closed Mon.

Kronhuset (Crown House). A block from the Gothenburg Museum. 17th-century building, cobbled courtyard, shops and cafeteria. A living handicrafts center. Closed Wed. evening.

Röhsska Museet (Röhss Museum of Arts and Crafts). Vasagatan 37–39, off the main avenue. Displays of Swedish and other furniture, glass, textiles, pewter etc. Oriental collection. Temporary exhibitions from around the world. Closed Mon.

Sjöfartsmuseet (Maritime Museum). Stigbergsparken. Devoted to history of merchant shipping, fishing and Swedish Navy. Many unique models. In same building the **Aquarium** shows the aquatic life of Scandinavian coastal waters and lakes. Open daily. Also the **Sjömanstornet** (Sailor's Tower), a monument to Swedish seamen who lost their lives in World War I. From the top you have an excellent view of the harbor and city.

TANUM. Prehistoric rock carvings. At Vitlycke, 1.5 km (about a mile) from Tanum Church on E6. Guided tours three or four times daily, May through Aug. Call the tourist bureau (0525-290 60) for exact times.

VARBERG. Museum at Varberg Castle. Provincial farm culture, textiles, furniture etc. The medieval Bocksten Man, with authentic clothing from that time. Open June 15 to Aug. 15, daily 10–7; rest of year, Mon. to Fri. 10–4, Sat. and Sun. 12–4.

Samfärdselmuseet (Museum of Communications). Also at the castle. A small museum with old wagons, carts, boats and bicycles. Open June 15 to Aug. 15, daily 10–7.

Varberg Castle. Guided tours every hour on the hour June 15 to Aug. 15, daily 10–5. Meet the guide at Mellersta Valvet. A small fee.

GOTHENBURG PARKS. Liseberg Amusement Park, only a few minutes from downtown Gothenburg, with beautiful gardens, several restaurants, variety theater and more, is one of the best of its kind in the country.

Slottsskogen, near the Botanical Garden, is a nature reserve with a small zoo and space observatory. Huge park, cafeteria and restaurant. Open daily.

Trädgårdsföreningen, across the square from the Central Station, has acres of magnificent gardens and lawns. See the Palm House. Outdoor entertainments every week. Restaurant and nightclub.

SPORTS. Swimming. There are more than a dozen swimming spots around Gothenburg and in the environs of Mölndal, Kungälv and Marstrand. Valhallabadet has an indoor pool in summer, also an outdoor pool.

Golf. 18 holes—at the Gothenburg Golf Club links. Hovås, 15 minutes by bus from Linnéplatsen; also at Delsjön, Albatross and at Öijared, with two 18-hole and one 9-hole courses. Four other courses within 30 minutes by car.

Horseracing and trotting. At Åbyfältet, Mölndal, 15 minutes by tram 4.

Football, speedway, skating. At Ullevi, one of the most modern sports stadiums in the world, holding 52,000 spectators.

Athletics. At legendary Slottsskogsvallen, where the Scandinavium stadium, the largest indoor arena in Scandinavia, is located. It can seat 14,000 people. Both Ullevi and Scandinavium are in the center of the city, within walking distance of all hotels.

LAND OF LAKES AND FOLKLORE

Home of the Goths

To the north and east of Gothenburg spreads a broad region known as Sweden's lake district, containing thousands of small lakes, medium-sized lakes, and two of the largest lakes in Europe, Vättern and Vänern. The Göta Canal, a blue ribbon stretching across Sweden, combines some of them with rivers and with manmade channels and locks to create a water route from Gothenburg to Stockholm.

This part of the world, ancient home of the Goths, has been settled for some 4,000 years or more, and has a number of historic sights setting exclamation points to its variegated natural beauty. Each of the region's provinces has its own history and traditions and its own distinct character. The lake district is the cradle of Swedish culture and it is here that most Swedes live.

Västergötland

The name of Västergötland means, literally, "the western land of the Goths"—as contrasted with Östergötland, or the eastern land of the same people. The Swedish Goths apparently originated on the continent of Europe. They were thus at least distant cousins of the barbarians who overran the Roman Empire and made the name Goth a synonym for "one who is rude or uncivilized." Some investigators think this region of Sweden was the first home of the Goths. Others believe that Östergötland should have the dubious honor of having spawned all branches of this people. Certain it is, however, that Västergötland was one of the first regions of Sweden to be settled in the wake of retreating glacial ice. Giant sepulchers have been uncovered from the late Stone Age, about 2500 to 2000 B.C., and so-called gallery graves from the age following.

Geographically, the province is rich in coastline, although it can boast only the small but important piece of the ocean which includes Gothenburg. In the northwest it has some 145 kilometers (90 miles) of the shore of Lake Vänern, the largest fresh-water sea in Western Europe, and to the southeast it has Lake Vättern, not so wide but almost as long. The scenery varies from wooded mountains with rare flora, to the fertile plain around the city of Skara.

Lidköping is a city of some 35,000 people at the inner end of a bay of Lake Vänern, on the southeast shore. It is the oldest city on the lake (its charter was granted in 1446), and is proud of the Rörstrand Porcelain works where 18th-century faience and modern ceramics are made side by side. The principal sight in the city proper is the Old Courthouse, once the hunting lodge of Magnus Gabriel de la Gardie, a powerful politician, noble, and controversial figure from the time of Queen Christina, King Karl X, and his son and successor, Karl XI.

De la Gardie was responsible for an even more impressive structure, however—Läckö Castle. It lies about 24 kilometers (15 miles) north of Lidköping on a beautiful road leading to the end of Kålland peninsula. Actually, the oldest parts of the structure date from 1298, when the building was begun as the residence of the bishop of Skara. De la Gardie—during his brief period of power in the 17th century—made it largely what it is today. Few of the 200-plus rooms are now furnished, but don't miss the chapel, the Hall of Knights, and the guest room prepared for King Karl XI. By one of the ironies of history, it was this king who deprived De la Gardie not only of the Läckö earldom but of most of his other holdings, in a great program of reform reducing the property and power of the nobility. Every summer an exhibition is put on at the castle, which is always worth seeing.

Across the bay to the east from Läckö Castle you see the bold outlines of Kinnekulle, one of the unique "table mountains" of this region. To reach it you will have to retrace your route to Lidköping and move up to Kinnekulle on the eastern side of the bay. Kinnekulle (sounds approximately like "chin-eh-culeh") is notable for two things —the view from its top and the millions of years of geological history it lays open to the naked eye. The process was a complicated one—in brief, Kinnekulle and the other table mountains are masses of subsurface igneous rock which forced themselves up through fissures in the sedimentary rock when this country was still one big sea. When the sea went out and time went to work, the less resistant sedimentary rock was eaten away, but the more durable igneous rock—battered and weather-beaten though it be—still stands. You can study the various layers and get an idea of the whole process at Kinnekulle, besides enjoying the far-flung view.

LAND OF LAKES AND FOLKLORE

Moving south and west from Lidköping, you find yourself, after about 24 kilometers (15 miles) of travel through charming country, in the city of Skara, one of the oldest in the country. It was ravaged by war and burned several times, and the only surviving building of any real age is the cathedral. It was founded about the middle of the 11th century, and is probably the second oldest church in Sweden (oldest— Lund Cathedral). Successive reconstructions and additions have mixed the styles—it was originally Romanesque, changed into Gothic, and its exterior is now largely a product of the last century, in traditional high Gothic style.

Skara became a religious center early in medieval times, and has been an educational center ever since 1641, when one of the first higher institutions of learning in Sweden was established here. Its history goes back to at least 829. If you are a bird watcher, come early in the spring to see the migrating cranes perform their mating dance at Hornborgasjön. Also near Skara is a newly built "sommerland" or playland for children and the young-at heart.

Don't miss Varnhem Abbey Church, 16 kilometers (ten miles) or so east of Skara, perhaps the best preserved monastic building in Sweden. It is, furthermore, the outstanding example of the Cistercian Order's considerable building activities in Sweden (well before the Reformation, of course). The Varnhem Abbey Church, started about 1250, is notable—aside from its age and architecture—as the burial place of four medieval kings, Magnus Gabriel de la Gardie (builder of Läckö Castle), and Birger Jarl, founder of Stockholm.

Östergötland and Lake Vättern

The land of eastern Goths, or Östergötland, is a country between two coasts, as different as an imaginative nature could make them. The western coast is formed by Lake Vättern, a long, narrow inland sea around which nestle some of the nation's most treasured natural and historical sights. The east coast is on the Baltic Sea, comparatively harsh and unyielding, but just as beautiful in a bolder fashion. Between are some of the most fertile farmlands and finest estates in the entire country. Linköping, an ancient religious, administrative, and cultural center, lies in almost the exact middle of this luxuriant plain. Norrköping, sometimes inaccurately called a twin city of Linköping, is a modern industrial center forming the northeast anchor of the province on the Baltic Coast.

This whole area can be divided roughly into two regions for purposes of a visit, the east coast of Lake Vättern, ranging from Jönköping, at the southern tip, north as far as the medieval city of Vadstena, and the Linköping-Norrköping area.

Lake Vättern is the second largest lake in Sweden, and its surface area of about 1,000 square kilomteres (750 square miles) ranks it among the major inland seas in Europe. It stretches almost due north and south for nearly a hundred miles, but its greatest width is less than 40 kilometers (25 miles). Around its shores, particularly on the eastern side, lived an ancient culture.

If you approach Lake Vättern from Gothenburg or from the south, your starting point will be Jönköping, at the very southernmost tip of the lake. Jönköping's greatest claim to fame is perhaps as the central stronghold of the Swedish Match Company, a great international enterprise. It was here, about 100 years ago, that the history of one of our most commonplace daily necessities, the safety match, began to be written. The Swedish Match Company still operates a factory and makes its headquarters in Jönköping. There is a museum in the old factory illustrating the history of manufacturing safety matches.

Jönköping is an important administrative center—besides serving as the residence of the provincial governor, it is the seat of the Göta Court of Appeals for southern Sweden. This is the second oldest appeals court in Sweden, and you can see its distinguished building, from about 1650, on the main square. Several of the other buildings, including nearby Christina Church, are from roughly the same period.

Proceeding now along the lake shore, first east and then north, the first main town is Huskvarna, only 6.4 kilometers (four miles) away. It is comparatively young and owes its existence principally to an arms factory moved there shortly before 1700. The factory is still turning out weapons—in newer quarters, of course—and there are other ultramodern plants turning out sewing machines, sporting rifles, chain saws, moped motors, refrigerators, deep-freezers. Specially trained guides show visitors round the factory.

Gränna and Historic Visingsö Island

The next main point of interest is Gränna and, if you are spending any time in this region, you might make this your headquarters. Stay at the Gyllene Uttern (Golden Otter) Inn, situated about 61 meters (200 feet) above Vättern, with a magnificent view of the lake and surroundings (including the isle of Visingsö).

Gränna is never more beautiful than when the fruit trees blossom. You'll see signs along the road advertising *Polkagrisar*— meaning literally "polka pigs"—a kind of red and white striped peppermint candy for which Gränna is famous in Sweden. Do try them, fresh from the hands of the maker.

This little community is the birthplace of a famous polar explorer, and there are two museums devoted to his memory near the site of the house where he was born. His name was S. A. André—and he tried to reach the North Pole by air in 1897. He and two companions started by balloon from an island near Spitsbergen, and disappeared silently into history. More than three decades later the remains of the ill-fated expedition were discovered on White Island, not far from Spitsbergen, and so well-preserved that not only could the diaries be read but the films could be developed.

André was buried in Stockholm with great honors, but the record of his premature tragic death in the cause of science is to be found in the interesting exhibits of the André and Vitö museums in Gränna. See also the ruins of the castle built by Count Per M. Brahe some 300 years ago on road E4. The view is magnificent.

As you look out upon Lake Vättern from Gränna you see a long, narrow island resting peacefully 6.4 kilometers (four miles) across the water. This island, Visingsö, played a role in history up to about 1725. Today there are about a thousand inhabitants, mostly farmers. There is a regular boat service (several crossings a day) to the island from Gränna, and you can easily arrange transportation on the island to see

LAND OF LAKES AND FOLKLORE

the sights. Join one of the horse-drawn vehicles, which take ten passengers each. The principal sight is the ruins of Visingsborg Castle, built around 1550, and last used as a prison for captives taken in Charles XII's wars with Russia, before it burned shortly after 1700. See also the Brahe Church, the 12th-century Kumlaby Church (with interesting murals), the remains of the tower and walls of the medieval castle on the southern extremity of the island. It won't take you long to get around, the whole island is only about 16 kilometers (ten miles) long.

Proceeding north again from Gränna to Vadstena, you come first to Omberg, a national park containing Mount Omberg. There are interesting caves near the shore, but the principal attraction is the broad view from the crown of Mount Omberg, "eight cities, 30 churches, and four provinces."

Ancient Vadstena

Vadstena, the next stop, has all the natural beauties of this region plus unique historical memories. To a great extent Vadstena is the physical reflection of the long and strange life of St. Birgitta (or Bridget), high-born (shortly after 1300) daughter of the royal Folkunga dynasty, mistress of a great estate and mother of eight children, religious mystic, and founder of the Roman Catholic Birgittine Order for women. Birgitta received her instructions from God in the form of visions, which led to the founding of the order in Vadstena. About 1350 she made the strenuous journey to Rome to get the papal blessing and died there in 1373 after a pilgrimage to Jerusalem. Her remains were returned home for burial in the church she designed for Vadstena.

You can easily visit Vadstena on foot. The church is an architectural jewel, begun shortly after 1350 and requiring some 70 years in the building. Aside from the noble Catholic architecture, note particularly the triumphal crucifix, the so-called Lovely Madonna, the Maria triptych at the high altar, the Birgittine triptych showing St. Birgitta presenting her revelations to two cardinals, and—behind the high altar—the lovely coffin containing the recently authenticated relics of the saint and one of her daughters. Also behind the high altar are the confessional stalls once used by the nuns.

Ironically enough, King Gustav Vasa, whose reformation dealt a death-blow to Catholicism in Sweden, chose Vadstena for one of his great fortified castles. The castle is still framed by its protecting moat, but a massive outer wall has disappeared. Construction was begun by King Gustav Vasa about 1540 and the place was used for some time by him and his descendants, but by about 1700 had ceased to be occupied as a royal seat. Note the wedding room (so-called because Gustav Vasa took his 16-year-old bride here about 1550), the small Hall of State, and the chapel.

If you have time, take a look at the interesting old house of Mårten Skinnare (Martin the Tanner) from about 1550, located not far from the church. Theater lovers will be interested in another nearby building, the theater, opened about 1825. It is said to be the oldest provincial theater in the country, and gives you a good idea of what life on the boards was like over a century ago.

Note: Vadstena has acquired quite a reputation within Sweden for its hand-made laces. It will be worth your while at least to have a look at them in one of the shops. Not far from Vadstena are the ruins of the first monastery in Sweden, Alvastra, founded in 1143. Nearby Skänninge is a community at least 1,000 years old, which is mentioned in the text of a 10th-century rune stone. Its Church of Our Lady dates from the late 13th century.

Linköping and Norrköping

Linköping is smaller than Norrköping but vastly more interesting for a pleasure visit. It is an ancient seat of religion and learning, in the middle of a fertile agricultural region. In recent years, a growing industry (most notably aircraft and the SAAB automobile) has forced the idyllic to give ground. Even the cathedral—unhesitatingly called the most beautiful in Sweden by its highly partisan admirers—harmoniously combines both old and new.

You can't miss the cathedral. It is located a block from the central square, where you ought also to study the Milles fountain. (The sculptor Carl Milles was a well-known Swedish-American artist.) The fountain was erected to the memory of the great Folkunga dynasty of the Middle Ages (Birger Jarl, King Magnus Ladulås, St. Birgitta), and shows the progenitor, Folke Filbyter, searching for his lost grandson on a weary horse. Man and beast have traveled together for so long that the sculptor has protrayed them as one living being. The dynasty originated in this area. The oldest part of the cathedral dates from the 12th century, but was really not completed until shortly after 1500, a building period of more than 300 years. The steeple was added only about 75 years ago. Of particular interest are the truimphal crucifix and the baptismal font of the 14th and 15th centuries, the modern altar painting by Henrik Sörensen, and the modern tapestries behind. They are by Märta Afzelius, on a theme from the Creation.

If you have any interest in museums, you ought by all means to see the Provincial and City Museum in Linköping. Examine it as much for the application of modern architectural and display techniques as for the valuable collections.

11 kilometers (seven miles) from Linköping you will find Vreta Cloister, once a thriving establishment of the Cistercian Order. The cloister church, still preserved, was dedicated about 1290 by no less a personage than King Magnus Ladulås himself. The baptismal font of Gotland stone was fashioned before 1300. Several notables, from medieval times on, are buried here. The nunnery itself has fallen into ruins, but you can see fragments of the old walls. The conducted bus excursions from Linköping include both Vreta and some historic manor houses.

Norrköping, fourth largest city in Sweden with 120,000 inhabitants, is notable principally for its industries—largely textiles and wood products. It is one of the major east coast ports. A comparatively young town, the oldest building, Hedvig's Church, is from about 1675. Incidentally Norrköping and Linköping share a full-time professional theater company of high quality, which is particularly remarkable in terms of the relatively small population of the two municipalities. Norrköping is located on a bay of the Baltic Sea, Bråviken, leading out to the archipelago. At the mouth of the bay is Arkösund, a coastal community popular with summer sailors. Kolmårdens Djurpark, 24 kilometers

LAND OF LAKES AND FOLKLORE

(15 miles) north of Norrköping on Highway E4, is a zoo and recreation ground with camping site, hotel, bathing beach and a swimming pool, cableway. There is a regular boat service from Norrköping to the zoo, and the park is open all year round.

Building the Göta Canal

A bountiful Nature in this country of almost 100,000 lakes and rivers provided much of the route ready-made, but man had to do his full share before it was possible to travel between Stockholm and Gothenburg by water. The builders were not interested in tourists—for them the canal was a straight-out commercial freight proposition, of tremendous importance for the country's future. No less than 65 locks were required, as well as kilometers of channels to connect the lakes and rivers. The result was a waterway which tremendously facilitated the movement of freight within and across the country.

In 1800 the Trollhätte Canal connecting huge Lake Vänern with Gothenburg and the North Sea was completed and soon demonstrated its value. Then, in 1808–9, Baltzar von Platen, a military man and ranking government official, advocated the bold plan of continuing on from Lake Vänern to Lake Vättern and across to the Baltic Sea. It is a tribute to the leaders of the country in an era when the whole outlook for the future of the nation was as dismal as it had ever been, that they boldly appropriated 2,400,000 *dalers* to begin the project. It was a tremendous piece of work, and during the years of building ran into constant obstacles and required some five times the original financial appropriation. A masterful piece of hard-headed Swedish logic was applied to overcome one of them. The farmers of one region had refused to sell their land for the right of way. The representative of the canal company asked, "Did you ever see water run uphill?" Nobody could answer in the affirmative. "Well, then," he said, "when this idiot von Platen fails, too, you'll get the land back." The farmers signed. But von Platen *did* make water "run uphill", and it was been doing so in the Göta Canal ever since. Von Platen was never able to take the trip himself: he died shortly before his great dream was realized and the canal opened to traffic. You will find his grave and a statue of him in the city of Motala, on Lake Vättern, one of the cities along the route.

Some of the high points have already been described: Bohus Fortress, Trolhättan Falls, Läckö Castle, Vadstena. You can take it easy, seeing the various sights as thoroughly or superficially as suits you, enjoying the company of your 50-odd fellow passengers. You come in intimate contact with the countryside—here and there the grass alongside the narrow channel and the overhanging trees actually brush the rails and decks. You also see an almost unlimited variety of drawbridges.

You come out on the island-strewn Baltic Sea just south of Norrköping, and follow the coast north for a way before turning into the Södertälje Canal. The canal carries you into Lake Mälar, which brings you, via the beautiful channel from the west, right to the heart of Stockholm. You tie up at Riddarholmen—rested, full of fresh air, and with a real mental image of the heart of Sweden. There are many day tours available on the canal, such as the trip between Söderköping and Arkösund, between Berg and Motala, and on the canal's western leg from Lake Vättern.

Romantic Värmland

Perhaps no other region of Sweden has been so romanticized as the province of Värmland. Sweden's greatest authoress, Selma Lagerlöf, made it a national legend in *The Saga of Gösta Berling*, and there is a widely sung, melancholy, hauntingly beautiful song titled *Song of Värmland*. It is often an anticlimax to visit a region which has been sung in song and story, Värmland will not disappoint you.

Don't be deceived by the endless woods and the idyllic nature of the landscape. The woods, the rivers, and the iron ore of the ground actually make this a leading industrial region, with ultra-modern factories dotted here and there in pleasant, comparatively small towns. The wood and iron ore industries have centuries-old traditions, and the old semi-rural culture was based to some extent on them.

Karlstad is the provincial capital and seat of the diocese, with some 74,000 inhabitants. The oldest building is the cathedral, built between 1723 and 1730. There is a comparatively large harbor on Lake Vänern which has direct connections with the ocean through the Trolhätte Canal.

The origins of Karlstad are lost in antiquity, but because of destructive fires the city hardly looks old. It has apparently been the capital of this region from the beginning of time and was formerly known as Tingvalla, after the *ting*, or meetings of the legislature, which were held here. When Duke Karl issued it a charter in 1584, he also gave it a name. Karlstad means "the city of Karl".

Värmland is cut by rivers and long narrow lakes, running roughly north to south (with a slight bias of the southern end of the axis to the east). The largest of these, and the best known, is the Fryken chain consisting of three lakes. The most popular sightseeing route is the Fryken Valley. You can rent a raft and enjoy a peaceful trip down the Klaralven River.

A tour along the following lines can be managed easily in one day by car. During the summer season, you will find guided bus tours to the principal points of interest. Take the main road north along the beautiful Klar River (in the spring full of timber being floated down to factories) about 40 kilometers (25 miles) to Ransäter, where you will find a rural museum, a lookout tower, and the home where Erik Gustaf Geijer, a national literary great, was born in 1783. A few kilometers farther on you come to Munkfors, site of one of the major steel plants of the Uddeholm Corporation. It will give you an idea of the highly-developed quality steel industry of this part of the world. Just north of Munkfors, turn off to the right on the road to Sunnemo. It brings you down to the narrow lake called Lidsjön, and a ferry that accommodates two cars. The crossing takes only five minutes or so. The Sunnemo church is a little known exquisite rural parish church, utterly charming in its modest expression in wood of the people's religious feeling. Note the individual carved shingles.

From here you proceed north again along Råda Lake to Uddeholm, a deceivingly peaceful village of 500 souls or so. You'd never know by looking at it, but this is the main headquarters of a huge international corporation. It is truly peaceful. But inside some of the unprepossessing buildings, direct telephone and teletype lines keep Uddeholm in con-

LAND OF LAKES AND FOLKLORE

stant touch with its far-flung empire, with its many plants producing iron and steel, wood products, chemicals, and paper, with its sales organization in two hemispheres. The Uddeholm Corporation descends in a direct line from a 17th-century ironworks, and today it is perhaps the largest private employer in Sweden.

Selma Lagerlöf's Home

Now, your best bet is to continue around the north end of the lake, then turn due south again and make your way back to Munkfors. But here, instead of returning directly to Karlstad, you can cut almost due west (to the right) to Sunne, which brings you into the very heart of the Selma Lagerlöf country. It's only 55 kilometers (34 miles) south of here to Mårbacka, her ancestral home, now a public museum maintained largely as she left it at the time of her death in 1940. You are better advised to go back to Sunne from Mårbacka, cross over to the west side of the Fryken Lakes, and turn south towards Karlstad again. Only a couple of kilometers below Sunne you reach famed Rottneros, the "Ekeby" of the Lagerlöf book, a truly fine example of the old culture of the landed gentry, distinguished by sculptures, flowers and a wonderful view. The buildings themselves are stately, and the grounds, overlooking the lake, are well kept. About 16 kilometers (ten miles) before you reach Karlstad, near Kil, is the Apertin Manor House. It's worth a look, but, since it is privately owned, don't expect to get inside without special arrangements. The same thing applies to Rottneros, although the public is permitted to wander freely through the grounds. There is an entrance fee. While in the area, the more adventurous might like to try an elk safari, arranged some evenings by the Sunne tourist bureau.

The city of Filipstad, about 64 kilometers (40 miles) from Karlstad, has a special interest for Americans. It is the home ground of John Ericsson, whose iron-clad ship, the *Monitor,* meant victory at sea for the North in America's War Between the States. Ericsson's place in history would have been assured had he never seen America, however, for he contributed a number of major inventions to the exploding technological progress of the 19th century. Because of his contribution to American national unity, his body was delivered to Sweden in 1890 by the United States Navy, and buried with great pomp. You will find his tomb, and a memorial statue, in this idyllic little city where he grew up. The population is now something over 7,000, and there is a varied industry. The peaceful appearance of the city belies its industrial and commercial importance, however, and it is perhaps never more beautiful than in the spring, when the high waters of the Skiller River go rushing through the heart of the town, almost on a level with the sidewalks.

Dalsland and Its Canal

The province of Dalsland is for lovers of the outdoors. It is shaped in the form of a huge, irregular wedge, with Bohuslän and Norway forming the western border, Lake Vänern the eastern, and the province of Värmland the northern.

Actually, the most beautiful part of Dalsland is perhaps not the coastal regions but the deep forests and lakes of the western and northern areas. The principal tourist centers are Bengtsfors, the northwest anchor of the lovely Dalsland Canal; Ed, on the road to Norway; and Åmål, the principal city.

The Dalsland Canal, built in 1860 under the direction of Nils Ericsson, brother of John Ericsson of U.S. Civil War fame links up a 272-kilometer (169-mile) waterway with no less than 29 locks. You can travel by boat from Köpmannebro on the shores of Lake Vänern up through the whole of northern Dalsland, over the aqueduct at Håverud, and on by the way of Värmland lakes to the Norwegian border.

The Dalsland Canal is actually a system of lakes and only 9.6 kilometers (six miles) is excavated canal. Most indigenous Swedish mammals can be found in this area, including some rare creatures like the lynx and beaver, which have quite large populations here. This is real canoe country and numerous tours are offered, from one to two days up to three weeks. Many tourists also come to see the aqueduct at Håverud and its busy boat traffic. There is an exhibition there showing what the Dalsland region produces and its major sights and attractions.

Dalarna

Dalarna—the name actually means "the valleys"—was one of the first regions of Sweden to be discovered by vacationers. Here there are deep forests with moose and bear, mountains and wilderness, as well as music and myriad arts festivals. The small villages around Siljan Lake have a maypole up all year, and at mid-summer there is fiddle-playing and dancing in colorful regional costumes. The Vasa Ski Race takes place in March between Sälen and Mora and attracts more than 12,000 participants.

In Mora you can find memorablia of the painter Ander Zorns, and in Rättvik "Gammelgarden" there is an open-air museum. On Sundays, people in Rättvik go to church by longboat.

A trip through Tällberg with its red wooden houses is well worth making, and at Falun the coppermine offers an underground sightseeing trip and an industrial museum.

The "Bergslagen" Region

The name of this region derives from the "bergslag", co-operatives formed by the mining communities holding mineral rights. People first moved to the Örebro and Västmanland counties to work the "öres" in the early middle ages. There are still many traces of blast furnaces, blackened sites of charcoal piles and the homes and other buildings of these early miners. The iron industry is still flourishing in places like Hällefors, Karlskoga and Degerfors. Amateur mineralogists find this a fascinating area to dig.

Near Örebro the Kilsbergen mountain range rises. There is also abundant natural beauty being kept intact for coming generations at Tiveden National Park. At nearby Västerås, one of the biggest industries in Sweden, ASEA, has its base.

LAND OF LAKES AND FOLKLORE

Strömsholms Castle at Lake Mälaren is a popular tourist attraction with its many horses and stables. Refreshments are served in the kitchen of the castle in summer. The Strömsholms Canal was built to transport the iron and ore of the region. These 96.5 kilometers (60 miles) of waterway and 26 locks are a popular route for smaller craft.

At Engelsberg you can see an old smelting house and relics from the Norberg mining area dating from the 14th century. From the middle of the last century until the 1920s, the power transmission system constructed by the Swedish inventor Christopher Polhem was still in use here. You can see the "Polhem Wheel" measuring 15 meters (49 feet) in diameter, well-preserved after so many years. The 400-year-old silver mine at Saka is also open to the public during the summer months. Nearby, the Östa canoe trail can provide all the excitements of a combined length of 180 kilometers (110 miles).

Sörmland

South of Lake Mälaren and bordering Stockholm is Sörmland, a county of manor parks and pastoral beauty. You can take the steamer from Stockholm to Mariefred and then join a narrow-gauge veteran railway. In Mariefred is Gripsholm Castle, one of the best-known Swedish historical monuments. Mariefred also houses the national portrait collection—the largest in Europe. Strängäs and its cathedral is nearby.

Have you ever owned a Swedish pocketknife? If you have, it was manufactured in Eskilstuna. The Rademacher Smithies here are a must to see. There's also a zoo with many rare animals, such as the panda and snow leopard. There are some 50 prehistoric sites near Eskilstuna. The best-known are the Sigurd rock carvings.

Ancient Sweden—one hour from Stockholm

Sweden begins in Gamla Uppsala (Old Uppsala). It is here that the first Swedish kings, Aun, Egils and Adils, are buried. See the tombs and drink real Viking mead from big horns at the Odinsborg.

The magnificent Gothic cathedral in Old Uppsala is 800 years old and the seat of the Archbishop of Sweden. Nearby on a hill is the Castle with the Coronation Hall and dungeons—over 400 years old. Carl Linnaeus or Carl von Linné, the world famous botanist and scientist, had his home here, in Hammarby. In the botannical garden in Uppsala there are still living plants dating from the days of Linnaeus. The university at Uppsala is 500 years old and thus the oldest university in Scandinavia.

This was also a mining district. In the 17th and 18th centuries Österby Bruk and Leufsta were the largest ironworks in the country. The Walloons came here to teach the Swedes how to make iron and were the origin of "Swedish" family names like De Laval, Hubinette and Gille. There are many folk festivals and music weeks at Österby Bruk.

PRACTICAL INFORMATION FOR THE LAND OF LAKES AND FOLKLORE

TOURIST INFORMATION. The most important tourist offices, all open all year round, are at the following places: **Borås**, Rådhuset (033-16 70 84). **Eskilstuna**, Fristadstorget 5 (016-10 22 50). **Falun**, Stora Torget (023-83 638). **Karlstad**, V. Torggatan 26 (054-10 03 45). **Kolmården Zoo**, summer only (011-95 006). **Lidköping**, Gamla Rådhuset, summer only (0510-60 505). **Mariefred**, Rådhuset (0159-10 207). **Norrköping**, Rådhuset (011-18 52 82). **Örebro**, Drottninggatan 9 (019-13 07 60). **Rättvik**, Torget (0248-10 910). **Sunne**, Mejerigatan 2 (0565-10 681). **Uppsala**, Kungsgatan 44 (018-11 75 00). **Fästerås**, Köpmangatan 6 (021-16 18 30.

TELEPHONE CODES. We have given telephone codes for all the towns and villages in the hotel and restaurant lists that follow. These codes need only be used when calling from outside the town or village concerned.

HOTELS AND RESTAURANTS. Accommodations in this region are modest on the whole. Many of the vacationers who come here stay in cottages and on sailboats.

ARVIKA. *Bristol* (M), Kyrkogatan 25 (0570-13 280). 40 rooms. Central, with sauna club. Golf, tennis nearby. Breakfast only. AE, DC, MC, V. *Stadshotellet* (M), Torggatan 9 (0570-131 20). 37 rooms, 10 baths. Breakfast only. AE, DC, MC, V.
Restaurant. *Stavnäsgården "Kvarnen"* (the Mill) (M), Klässbol, 15 km. (nine miles) south of Arvika. Cafeteria with home-baked bread. Beautiful surroundings. Open May 15-Aug., Mon. to Fri. 10–4. AE, MC, V.

BENGTSFORS. *Dalia* (M), Karlbergsvägen 9 (0531-11 650). 50 rooms. 400 meters (437 yards) from Dalsland Canal and near Gammelgården, the homestead museum. Resort hotel, restaurant, cafeteria, sauna, golf, illuminated ski trail, ski lifts. AE, DC, MC, V.

BORÅS. *Vävaren* (M), Allégatan 2 (033-10 00 20). 80 rooms. A well-run family hotel in the city center. Sauna, cafeteria. Golf and tennis in the outskirts. AE, DC, MC, V.

BORLÄNGE. *Gylle Värdshus* (Inn) (M), two km. (1.2 miles) from center of Borlänge (0243-11 900). 32 rooms. Cafeteria. AE, DC, MC, V.

ESKILSTUNA. *Country Hotel* (M), Strängnäsvägen (016-11 04 10). 60 rooms. Built 1983. Restaurant, cocktail bar, dancing, sauna. Close to golf, trotting track and ice hockey. AE, DC, MC, V.
Restaurants. *Sommarrestaurangen* (Summer Restaurant) (M), in the zoo (106-14 73 80). No credit cards. *Jernberghska Gården* (I), at the Rademacher forge museum (016-14 65 05). Also outdoor service. Closes 4 P.M. in winter and 6 P.M. in summer. No credit cards.

FALUN. *Grand* (E), Trotzgatan 9 (023-187 00). 183 rooms. Restaurant *Moriska Gården*, cocktail lounge. Sauna, pool. AE, MC, V. *Bigittagården* (I), Uddnäs, Hosjö (023-321 47). 18 rooms. No credit cards.

LAND OF LAKES AND FOLKLORE

FILIPSTAD. *Hennickehammars Herrgård* (Manor House) (M) (0590-12 565). 63 rooms. 18th-century manor house by Lake Hemtjärn in a wonderful park. Excellent cuisine—restaurant. Sauna, 15 km. (nine miles) to golf, tennis, fishing, ski sports, rowing boats, canoes etc. AE, MC, V.
Restaurants. *Långbans Gästgiveri* (Inn) (E), John Ericsson homestead (0590-221 69). In an old stable at the mineral-rich Långban. Fish and game specialties. *Storhöjden* (E) (0590-103 13). In an old manor house with a view of the city. Outdoor tables. Outlook tower. AE, MC, V.

GRÄNNA. *Gyllene Uttern* (Golden Otter) (M), near E4, south of Gränna (0390-10 800). 53 rooms, many smoke-free, 13 bungalows in summer. Wonderful view of Lake Vättern. Restaurant, cafeteria. Wedding chapel. Built like an old castle. AE, DC, MC, V.
Restaurant. *Värdshuset Hjorten* (the Stag) (I), Torget (0390-106 36). Friendly, old atmosphere. Fish from Lake Vättern is a specialty, also pears from Gränna with whipped "polka cream". AE, MC, V.
Youth Hostel. *Grännastranden* (0390-107 06). 48 beds. Cafeteria. Bus to Jönköping. Rentals of bikes, boats and fishing gear. Open May through Aug.

GRYTHYTTAN. *Grythyttan Gästgifvargård* (Inn) (E) (0591-14 310). 55 rooms. Family-owned inn from 1640. Well-located by old market place. Known for good food and excellent wine cellar. Golf, fishing etc. AE, MC, V.

JÖNKÖPING. *Grand* (I), Hovrättstorget (036-11 96 00). 60 rooms, 23 baths. A fine old hotel, tastefully renovated. A few steps from the shopping area. AE, DC, MC, V. *Ramada* (I), Strandvägen 1 (036-14 24 00). 113 rooms. North of Huskvarna-Jönköping. Most rooms have view of Lake Vättern. Restaurant, cocktail bar. Sauna, pool, golf. AE, DC, MC, V.
Restaurants. *Svarta Börsen* (E), Kyrkogatan 4 (036-11 22 22). Cosy restaurant in the center of town. New French cuisine. Seibling from Lake Vättern; crow! AE, DC, MC, V. *Mäster Gudmunds Källare* (M), Kapellgatan 2 (036-11 26 33). Nice atmosphere in cellar vaults. Smörgåsbord. AE, MC, V. *Warpa Skams* (M), on Lake Vättern and the E4 (036-14 21 00). 50 meters (164 ft.) from Brunstorp Inn, north of Huskvarna. *Smörgåsbord,* country-style. Geared for bus groups. AE, MC, V.

KARLSTAD. *Gösta Berling* (M), Drottninggatan 1 (054-15 01 90). 75 rooms. Genuine Värmland atmosphere in the center of Karlstad. Restaurant, cocktail bar, sauna. AE, DC, MC, V. *Stadshotellet* (M), Kungsgatan 22 (054-11 52 20). 140 rooms. On the Klarälven River, central, centuries of tradition. Restaurants, cocktail bar, nightclub, sauna, pool. AE, MC, V.
Restaurants. *Inn Alstern* (E), Morgonvägen 4 (054-13 49 00). Beautifully situated with a view of Lake Alstern. Gourmet food. AE, MC, V. *Skogen-Terrassen* (E), in Mariebergsskogen (054-15 92 03). Nicely situated in one of the leading openair museums and amusement parks in the country. Specializes in food from the area. MC, V.

KOLMÅRDEN. Youth Hostel. *Kvarsebo* (011-960 46). 35 beds. Coffee, kitchen. Bus to Kolmården Zoo. Open end June to beginning Aug.

LEKSAND. Youth Hostel. *Parkgården,* on route 70, two km. (1.2 miles) south of center (0247-101 86). 85 beds. Sauna, bikes for rent. Bus or train to Tällberg. Open all year.

LIDKÖPING. *Stadt* (M), Gamla Stadenstorg (0510-220 85). 69 rooms. In old town, not far from Lake Vänern. Close to Rörstrand porcelain works and museum. Restaurant. AE, DC, MC, V.

LINKÖPING. *Ekoxen* (M), Klostergatan 68 (013-14 60 70). 117 rooms. Central, beside a park. Restaurant, cocktail bar, sauna, pool. AE, DC, MC, V.

Restaurants. *Wärdshuset Gamla Linköping* (Old Linköping Inn) (M), Gästgivargatan 1 (013-13 31 10). In house from 18th century with beautiful painted ceilings. Self-service in genuine cellar vaults. AE, MC. *Restaurang och Cafe Må Gott* (I), Stora Torget (013-11 06 47). In old Lagerström House. Salads and small dishes. Also outside tables. AE, MC, V.

Youth Hostel. *Centrumgården Ryd* (013-17 64 58). 70 beds. Sauna. Buses to center and railway station. Open June through Aug.

MORA. *Mora Hotel* (M), Strandgatan 12 (0250-117 50). 91 rooms. On the shores of Lake Siljan and opposite the old church. Sauna, pool. AE, DC, MC, V.

Youth Hostel. *Prästholmens Camping* (0250-163 15). 30 beds. Kitchen, cafeteria, food store and indoor pool on grounds. Open middle of May to end Sept.

NORRKÖPING. *Grand* (E), Tyska Torget 2 (011-19 71 00). 242 rooms. Restaurant, piano bar, wintergarden, sauna. AE, DC, MC, V. *Strand* (I), Drottninggatan 2 (011-16 99 00). 24 rooms, 3 baths. Breakfast only. No credit cards.

Restaurants. *Palace* (M), Bråddgatan 13 (011-18 96 00). Gourmet food, with a view of the river. MC, V. *Plalce Café* has chairs outside in summer. Known for plank steak and *Caféflorett* nightclub. Music every night in café. AE, DC, MC, V. *Peter's Steakhouse* (M), Trädgårdsgatan 6B (011-18 31 30). Rustic, paintings, grouped sofas. Closed July; Sun. AE, DC, MC. V.

ÖREBRO. *Grev Rosen* (Count Rosen) (M), Södra Grevrosengatan 2 (019-13 02 40). 74 rooms. Five minutes' walk fom railway station. Cafeteria. Swedish fare at low-price lunch. AE, MC. V.

Restaurants. *Gyllene Drotten* (Golden Ruler) (M), Drottninggatan 15 (019-11 77 82). Central, cellar vaults. AE, MC, V. *Två Krögare* (Two Innkeepers) (M), Rudbecksgatan 18 (019-11 13 67). Central. Good food in pleasant surroundings. AE, MC, V.

SÖDERKÖPING. *Söderköpings Brunn* (Spa) (M), in large wooded park on the Göta Canal (0121-109 00). 109 rooms. Historic spa hotel from 1774. Entertainment in park, dancing, sauna. MC, V.

SUNNE. Youth Hostel. *Sunne Homestead Museum* (0565-107 88). 54 beds. Close to all sights in the Fryken Valley. Open June through Aug.

TÄLLBERG. *Green* (E) (0247-502 50). 89 rooms. Timber building, dating from 1917. Wonderful view of Lake Siljan. Some rooms with open fireplaces. Unique art collection. Staff dressed in folk costumes. Restaurant, cocktail bar. Five saunas, golf, tennis, outdoor and indoor pools, dancing on Sat. AE, DC, MC, V. *Siljansgården* (M) (0247-500 40). 24 rooms and some bungalows. Timber-built on shore of Lake Siljan. Restaurant, not licensed. Sauna, golf, tennis. Sleigh tours. DC, MC, V. *Tällbergsgården* (M) (0247-500 26). 45 rooms. Family atmosphere, fine view of Lake Siljan. Restaurant, cocktail bar, cafeteria. Sauna, golf, tennis, bikes, skiis. Smörgåsbord served every day. Folk fiddlers entertain on Sun. MC, V.

VADSTENA. *Vadstena Klosters Guesthouse* (M) (0143-115 30). 25 rooms. *Birgitta Systrarna* (I), Myntbacken 2 (0143-109 43). 22 rooms. Also pension. No credit cards.

Restaurants. *Munkklostret* (the Monastery) (M) (0143-130 00). Medieval atmosphere. Fish from Lake Vättern is specialty. AE, DC, MC, V. *Värdshuset Kungs Starby* (M), near the south entrance to Vadstena from road 50. 75-year-old building, outdoor service in summer, large park. Smörgåsbord every day; about SEK 85 on Sun. AE, DC, MC, V.

Youth Hostel. *Vadstena Vandrarhem*, Skänningegatan 20 (0143-103 02). 70 beds. Walking distance to sights. Täkern bird sanctuary, eight km. (five miles) away. Bike rental.

LAND OF LAKES AND FOLKLORE

VÄSTERÅS. *Park Hotel* (M), Gunnilbogatan 2 (021-11 01 20). 139 rooms. Restaurant, nightclub, dancing, sauna. AE, DC, MC, V. *Stora Hotellet* (M), Vasagatan 15 (021-13 72 90). 80 rooms. A family-owned hotel. Central, walking distance to restaurants, shopping. Sauna. AE, DC, MC, V.

Restaurants. *Bacchus Källare* (M), (021-11 56 40). In a building dating from 17th century. Near the Svartå River. Central. AE, MC, V. *Johannes* (M), Stora Torget (021-13 06 63). Central. Well-known restaurant with excellent food. Outdoor service in summer. AE, DC, MC, V.

UPPSALA. *Linné* (M), Skolgatan 45 (018-13 92 00). 86 rooms. Central. All rooms face the Linné botanical gardens. Breakfast only. AE, DC, MC, V.

Restaurants. *Slottskällan* (Castle Spring) (E), Sjukhusvägen 3 (018-11 15 10). In house dating from 18th century, below the castle at the swan pond. AE, MC, V. *Domtrappkällaren* (M), St. Eriksgränd 15 (018-13 09 55). In the oldest building near the Cathedral (Domkyrkan). Restaurant established 1939. Good Swedish food, also coffee with home-baked bread, ice cream. AE, DC, MC, V.

Youth Hostels. *Sunnersta Herrgård* (Manor House), about six km. (four miles) south of the center (018-32 42 20). 80 beds. Open May through Aug. *Gläntan*, Norbyvägen 46 (018-10 80 60). 50 beds. 1.6 km. (one mile) from the center. Bus 6 or 7 from Stora Torget (the main square). Kitchen, coffee, sauna. Open from end of June to middle of Aug.

The following places have camping sites with bungalows or rooms for rent. It is advisable to book a few days in advance: **Dals-Långed,** Laxsjön (0531-30 010); **Lidköping,** Framnäs (0510-26 804); **Mora,** Uskavi (0587-30 025); **Norrköping,** Himmelstalund (011-17 11 90); **Rättvik,** Siljansbadet (0248-11 691); **Sunne,** Kolsnäsudden (0565-11 312); **Tärnsjö,** Osta (0292-43 004); **Vadstena,** Vätterviksbadet (0143-12 790).

HOW TO GET AROUND. By car or train. The best way to see a lot of this region is to take the main highway or the train from Gothenburg to Stockholm, or from Stockholm to Karlstad. The section of road between Vadstena and Jönköping is one of the most spectacular, with the road winding along the eastern shore of Lake Vättern.

Karlstad is easily reached by car or train from Gothenburg or Stockholm. If you go from Gothenburg, you will pass the lakes and forest of Dalsland and should plan to stop at Håverud to see the locks of the Dalsland Canal.

Linköping and Norrköping are respectively 217 km. (135 miles) and 145 km. (90 miles) from Stockholm and are close enough for a day excursion. There are daily bus tours to Kolmården Zoo.

By air. The area is well served by air. From Stockholm there are 15 flights a day to Borlänge/Falun, six to Karlstad and Jönköping, and four to Norrköping.

By boat. You can see this region with graceful ease by boat on the Göta Canal, a waterway which is more than 100 years old. Several boats ply the Göta Canal, offering tours of varying length. There are boats that go from Söderköping to Arkösund, from Norsholm to Söderköping, and from Karlsborg to Töreboda. If you are at Trollhättan, you can take the *Strömkarlen* to Vänersborg. For schedules call 0141-100 50 or call at the nearest tourist bureau.

The traditional tour to take on the canal is the three-day trip on the *Diana, Juno* or *Wilhelm Than.* They operate between the middle of May and the beginning of September. You can book this tour through your travel agency before you leave for Sweden. You can also rent your own boat by phoning Rent-a-Boat at 08-717 28 50.

Boats also operate on the big lakes such as Fryken in Värmland, the Siljan in Dalarna and the Vänern and Vättern.

By bicycle. There are many bicycle trails in this region and maps for them are available in book shops or at the tourist bureaus. In particular, look for maps of a marked trail called "Mälardalsleden." There is also a biking or hiking trail along the Göta Canal, where oxen once drew barges.

You can rent bicycles in Söderköping (0121-134 75), Borensberg (0141-400 60), Töreboda (0506-104 96), or in Sjötorp (0501-510 03).

SWEDEN

PLACES TO VISIT. In addition to the veritable inland seas of Lakes Vänern and Vättern and the Göta Canal which wends its scenic way from Stockholm to Gothenburg, there are many other distinctive glimpses of past and present in this region.

ESKILSTUNA. Djurgården Museum and Sörmlandsgården. At Carlavägen-Djurgårdsvägen. Openair museum showing local history. Sörmlandsgården is an early 19th-century farm complete with stables, hay barn etc. Open May through Sept., daily 11–4.
Rademacher Smedjorna. The Rademacher Smithies, built in 1658 and now an openair homestead museum. Demonstrations in the copper and iron smithies; a hatter making hats and tin soldiers being made in the tin foundry. Also an industrial and armory museum nearby (closed Mon.). Daily performances at the Rademacher in Jul. Cafeteria. Open daily 10–4; Jul. through Aug., Mon. to Fri. 10–6, Sat. and Sun. 10–4. Admission free.

GRÄNNA. Andrée Museet. Pictures and memorabilia of S.A. Andrée's unsuccessful attempt to reach the North Pole by balloon in 1897. Open May through Aug., daily 12–5; Sept., daily 12–4; closed rest of year.

JÖNKÖPING. Riddersberg Manor. In Rogberga, 10 km. (six miles) east of Jönköping. Huge wooden sculptures in a park, such as the 103-meter (338-ft.) high *Indian Rope Trick* and the *Bounty* (a ship on land). *The Giant Vist*, another sculpture by the same artist, is visible from the road at Huskvarna. Artist lives on the premises. Open daily 10–6. Admission free.
Tändsticksmuseet (Match Museum). Storgatan 18 (036-10 55 43). Match manufacturing started here in Jönköping in the middle of last century and made the city famous. Here in the original factory are machines and exhibits showing the development of the match industry. 13-minute film *The Match*. Large collection of match-box labels. Open June through Aug., Mon. to Fri. 10–6, Sat. 11–1, Sun. 3–5; Sept. through Dec., Sat. 11–1, Sun. 2–5.

KARLSKOGA. Nobelmuseet. Björkborn. The Alfred Nobel residence, including library, study and laboratory with original equipment. Open June through Aug., daily 1–4. On request at other times. Call 0586-818 94.

KATRINEHOLM. Julita Gård. On Lake Öljar, 25 km. (16 miles) north of Katrineholm. Typical turn-of-the-century manor house with parks and gardens. A homestead museum, dairy museum and the Skansen church. Museums open mid-May to mid-Aug., daily 11–4. Main building, guided tours only. For information call 0150-912 90 or 08-22 41 20.

MALMKÖPING. Museiispårväg. Vintage tramway. 75-year-old tram on which you can take a half-hour trip. Tram museum, road museum. Open mid-June through Aug., daily 11–5; May and Sept. on Sat. and Sun. only.

MARIEFRED. Gripsholm Castle. Castle was begun in 1370's. Among the many interesting things is an 18th-century theater. National portrait collection is here, one of largest in Europe. Modern portraits are in school building nearby. Boats from Stockholm. Open May through Aug., daily 10–4. For times Sept. through Apr., call 0159-101 94.
Östra Sörmlands Järnväg. Veteran railway operating between Mariefred and Läggesta during summer months. Call 0159-110 06 for timetable.

MORA. Zorn Museum. Vasagatan 36. Original paintings, sketches and sculptures of Swedish artist Anders Zorn. Open Mon. to Sat., 10–5, Sun. 1–5.
Zorngården. Adjoining museum. Zorn's home 1896–1920. In unchanged condition with silver collection, art, furniture etc. Guided tours every half-hour. Open June 15 to Aug. 15, Mon. to Sat. 10–5, Sun. 11–5; rest of year, daily 1–5.

LAND OF LAKES AND FOLKLORE 451

ÖREBRO. Wadköping. In Stadsparken, 1.5 km. (a mile) from the center of town. Open-air museum. Old Town of Örebro with old wooden houses, streets and squares, as well as handicrafts, workshops, exhibitions. Cafeteria. Open daily 12–5.

SUNNE. Mårbacka. Östra Ämtervik, 10 km. (six miles) south of Sunne. The home of Nobel prize winner (1909) Selma Lagerlöf, who wrote many of her books in English. Manor house in unchanged condition. Cafeteria. Guided tours—for information call 0565-310 27. Open May to Sept. 15, daily 10–7.
Rottneros Manor. 3 km. (two miles) south of Sunne. One of Sweden's most beautiful gardens with flowers, herb garden, sculptures and a wonderful view of Lake Fryken. Open May 15 to Sept. 10, daily 9–6; July, daily 8–9.

NORRLAND AND LAPLAND

Europe's Last Wilderness

The Swedish highlands, ranging from central Sweden up beyond the Arctic Circle for a distance of 800 kilometers (500 miles) or more, offer you holidays quite unlike any others anywhere; this is truly Europe's last wilderness. The region has been settled for centuries, its natural resources are among the most important in northern Europe, yet it is a country of open spaces, virgin wilderness, and a combination of natural beauties not to be found anywhere else in the world.

Norrland—as the entire region of northern Sweden is called—occupies half of Sweden's territory but holds only 17 per cent of its population. Modern industry already has put its stamp on parts of Norrland, with its vast resources of timber, iron ore, and water power. But the traditional peasant culture of the river valleys and coastal areas, deep-rooted in the Middle Ages, and the ageless civilization of the independent, nomadic Lapps have remained virtually unchanged.

This area has its charm at all seasons of the year and offers a variety of delights to lovers of the outdoors. From Christmas to May skiing predominates. If the winters are long, the summers are brilliant—the countryside bursts into bloom, temperatures of 80–85°F (27–29°C) are not unusual, and the "sunlit nights" merge day into day with only a few hours of twilight between. In the far north, the Midnight Sun sees to it that there is no night at all from May 25 to July 15.

Härjedalen

Sandwiched between Norway in the west, Jämtland in the north, the coastal provinces in the east, and Dalarna in the south, Härjedalen possesses only one center of any size—Sveg, with a little over 4,000 inhabitants. Because of this—or in spite of it—Härjedalen was the first mountain province to attract visitors in the days when both tourism and skiing were in their infancy. One reason for its continued popularity with skiers is the great variety of terrain it offers, from the gentle rounded southern mountains to the originally volcanic Helag Mountains in the north. Fjällnäs, Funäsdalen, Bruksvallarna and Vemdalskalet all offer comfortable lodging and are both summer and winter resorts.

Across the Flatruet plateau in the western part of the province runs the highest road in Sweden (914 meters or 3,000 feet), offering a breathtaking view from its summit. On one of the cliff walls are rock paintings, almost 4,000 years old, depicting animal and human figures. Another curiosity is the "frozen sea" of the Rogen area, with its striated and pitted Ice Age boulders.

Jämtland

Östersund is on the railroad line that crosses the Scandinavian peninsula from Sundsvall, industrial center on the east coast of Sweden, to Trondheim on Norway's Atlantic coast, a fact which accounts for much of its growth in recent years. Despite its northerly clime, however, the region around Storsjön, or the Great Lake, has been settled since heathen times. The ancient capital of this region was Frösön, an island in the lake just off what is now Östersund. It was the site of a heathen sacrificial temple and the place where the *ting,* or popular council, met. The strange Viking alphabet also penetrated here, and the northernmost rune stone in Sweden is to be found on Frösön near the bridge. It was erected there by one Östman Gudfastsson about the year 1050. From the heights of Frösön you have unbelievably distant views —of the lake, the cultivated areas around the shores, and, in the west, the mountains reaching above the timberline.

Today Östersund has taken over Frösön's role as capital of the province, and has grown into a city of 56,000 inhabitants, with several industries. It is a good starting point for motor tours within the province or into Norway—the joint Swedish-Norwegian "Trondheimsleden" highway leads via Enafors and Storlien to Trondheim.

Here are some of the principal resorts in the region stretching west of Östersund:

Åre, site of a former World Ski Championship, and located in the beautiful Åre valley at the foot of Mount Åre, is popular both winter and summer. It is the largest resort in this region and also boasts a church dating from the 12th or 13th century.

There are a dozen or so other resorts or mountain hotels, among them Duved, Undersåker, Hålland, Ånn, Bydalen, and Anjan, all with good terrain. Farther north, in even more isolated country, are Gäddede and Jormlien. You're really in the wilderness here—observe reasonable precautions before taking off from your hotel. There are expert guides. The requirement that you notify the management of your intended route when you go out any distance is a simple precaution for your own safety. Don't laugh at it. Even if you're in perfect safety, which is likely, you'll feel awfully silly if half the population drops its other pursuits to come out looking for you.

Gästrikland and Hälsingland

Going north along the coast you reach the regions of Gästrikland and Hälsingland. The provincial capital is Gävle, a town with a busy harbor on the Baltic. Gävle's "old section" still has the small wooden houses of former times, and a castle built in 1613. Further on, 80 kilometers (50 miles) from Gävle, is the veteran Jädraås-Tallås railway. Here the traveler can enjoy a landscape of forest and lake, and a coastline dotted with bays, inlets and islands.

Hälsingland is known throughout Sweden for the world's largest folk dancing competition, with 1,500 couples competing. It is held in July in Hårga, Bollnäs, Arbrå and Järvsö. A visit to Järvsö should also be relished for the magnificence of its scenery. The manor houses to be seen in this area are generally large and memorable. Characterized by folklore and handicraft products, this country's culinary specialty is smoked Baltic herring, called "böckling."

Medelpad and Ångermanland

Here, in a region also known as Västernorrland, you are right in the middle of Sweden: Flataklacken at Torpshammar is actually the geographical center. You will encounter stretches of coast here that are quite different from the rest of the country. On the Höga Kusten, or High Coast, at Nordingrå, steep hills rise straight out of the sea and the inlets would be better described as fjords.

The rivers are also distinctive features of the landscape, with the Indal and Ångerman Rivers being the most impressive. On the Indal there is a 72-kilometer (45-mile) long channel for canoeing with rustic overnight cabins. There are many hiking trails in this area. An important beaver colony can be found near Ramsele.

Near Sundsvall is Alnön, known for its unusual geological features. From neighbouring Härnösand, a pleasant town with old-world charms, and Örnsköldsvik you can take a boat trip to Trysunda and Ulvön, which is known as the "Pearl of the Baltic." The view from the 350-meter (1,150-foot) high "Skuleberget" is fantastic. A chair lift operates from Docksta.

Västerbotten—the Gateway to Lapland

The road from Umeå is called Blå Vägen, or the Blue Route (E79). This beautiful road goes all the way to the Atlantic. Other parallel routes have names like the Silver Road, the SAGA Road and the Road of the Seven Rivers. The Stekenjokk Road goes from Vilhelmina over bare mountains to the province of Jämtland.

Along the coast at Lövånger are more than a hundred timber cottages dating from the 17th century. They are now renovated and available for tourists to stay in. At Lycksele on the Blue Route there is a

NORRLAND AND LAPLAND

large zoo featuring Nordic animals. Also Gammelplatsen—an outdoor museum—and a pretty 18th-century church.

Lapland

There is nothing more dramatic in all of Scandinavia than this region north of the Arctic Circle. It seems terribly far north, terribly distant, and it is at about the same latitude as northern Alaska. Yet it is a remarkably accessible place. You climb aboard an express train in Stockholm one afternoon, sleep soundly in a comfortable sleeper, eat in the diner, and by noon the next day you have arrived in a strange and wonderful world. (The flight from Stockholm to Kiruna takes 90 minutes.)

These contradictions never fail to fascinate the visitor. The region is huge—the province of Lapland covers about one fourth of Sweden's total area, but is only sparsely settled, of course. And its great beauty as a vacation region is the ease and comfort with which you reach it, without strain, special clothes or equipment, or much traveling time.

If you travel by train, the main line proceeds on or near the eastern coast, along the Gulf of Bothnia, all the way to the city of Boden. You pass through a huge industrial region—largely forest products—and magnificent natural scenery. Since this is a night train you will sleep through most of it, but the coastal cities, such as Gävle, a major port; Sundsvall, a paper and pulp center; Umeå, the cultural capital of northern Sweden; and Luleå, with a museum featuring Lapp collections and a 15th-century church, are of more than passing interest. Outside Luleå there is an archipelago of 300 islands.

The whole of northern Sweden is a region of forests and huge rivers. The rivers cut eastward across country from the mountain range along the Norwegian border to the east coast of Sweden, and are used both to float logs to factories on the Baltic coast and for hydro-electric power. A trip through this region shows you why Sweden is one of the world's great producers of paper, woodpulp, and other wood products —the forests seem endless. At Boden, a northern military and industrial hub, the line makes a junction with the line going diagonally across Norrland, from Luleå on the Swedish coast to Narvik, Norway. It was built around the turn of the century to exploit the huge finds of iron ore (up to 70 per cent pure) at Gällivare and Kiruna. Narvik has become the principal shipping point, and Luleå ranks second. Up to 16,000,000 tons of ore are taken out and shipped annually via this line, and the ore trains run day and night.

The coast at Piteå is called the Riviera of the North; there is a lot of sun here in summer and the water is sometimes as warm as the water in the Mediterranean. This is a favorite vacation spot for Norwegians from northern Norway, since the water in the Atlantic is much colder.

North of the Arctic Circle

Keep your eyes open after you leave Boden. About 97 kilometers (60 miles) north—and a little west—you will see a line of white stones cutting squarely across the railroad tracks and a sign "Arctic Circle" in two or three languages, including English. You're now in the land of the Midnight Sun, near the legendary home of Santa Claus.

The sun never sets from the end of May until the middle of July, and if you have looked at pictures of it making its way across the horizon, let us assure you at once they are misleading. The apparent darkness in the photos, giving more of an impression of moonlight than sunlight, is caused by the filters used when shooting directly at the sun. Actually, the Midnight Sun is as bright as it is anywhere an hour or so before sunset. The whole thing has a mystical, unreal, ethereal quality—you sometimes find yourself feeling almost light headed. But well before the date when the sun actually stays above the horizon all night and well afterwards, the nights are light all night long. So if your visit must take place a week or two before or after the specific dates given, you will still enjoy the "sunlit nights" that give you approximately the same sensation.

64 kilometers (40 miles) north of Boden you arrive in Gällivare, center of a mining region with ore reserves estimated at 400,000,000 tons. The principal mine is Malmberget, about four miles out of town. From here you can take an interesting side trip, the railway to Porjus and then by a new road to Vietas, not far from the Saltoluokta Tourist Station, and from there a motorboat trip in Sjöfallsleden, "Lapland's Blue Ribbon", the source lakes of the Big Lule River. Combined with some 19 kilometers (12 miles) walking you will, by this westbound route, finally reach the Atlantic. At Gällivare you will get the first glimpse of the Lapland mountains. Dundret (Thunder Mountain), 760 meters (2,500 feet), has a convenient chair lift to its summit, and the view is well worth the trip. The midnight sun is visible in this neighborhood from June 1 to July 12.

Kiruna

Another 80 kilometers (50 miles) or so north on the main railway line is Kiruna, the world's biggest city. Kiruna became big enough to accommodate, shall we say, London, New York, and a few dozen other cities by incorporating the whole province within the municipality some years ago. It covers no less than 4,800 square kilometers (3,000 square miles), about the same size as the province of Skåne. The mining town proper had a population of some 21,000, but only picked up an additional 6,000 or so people by this huge extension of its borders. The people, including the Lapps, were quick to react to the knowledge that they were living in the world's biggest city. A man we know was trying to get hold of a Lapp friend of his by telephone to a remote village. He finally succeeded in locating the man's wife, who said her husband wasn't at home: "He's out in the city with the reindeer herd."

Kiruna lies on a slope between two ore-bearing mountains with the jaw-cracking names of Kirunavaara and Luossavaara. The ore reserves are estimated at 500,000,000 tons. Mining operations are going more and more underground, but during the past decades most ore has been taken out by the open-pit method. You should try to see the biggest pit—if possible when blasting is going on. Tons of dynamite go off at one time in a huge manifestation of explosive power. From high points around Kiruna you get beautiful views—on clear days you can see the irregular contours of Kebnekasje, Sweden's highest mountain, about 80 kilometers (50 miles) away. And here in Kiruna you may see the blue and red costumes of the Lapps for the first time.

Meeting the Lapps

For a long time the Lapps were believed to be of Mongolian origin, but the latest theory now supposes they stem from somewhere in central Europe. Presumably they came to northern Scandinavia more than 1,000 years ago. They number about 8,000 in Sweden (of which only 2,000 are nomads deriving a living from the breeding of reindeer), 20,000 in Norway, 2,500 in Finland, and perhaps less than 2,000 in the Soviet Union.

The reindeer is the bone, sinew, and marrow of the economy of the nomadic Lapps of this area. (There are also forest Lapps and fishing Lapps.) Reindeer is the only domestic animal which can feed itself on the meager vegetation here beyond the Arctic Circle. The Lapps are nomads perhaps less from a restless desire to keep on the move than from the necessity of following their reindeer herds from one grazing ground to another. In the winter they move down to the protected forests, east and south of the mountains, but in the spring they travel in the opposite direction for the grazing on the high slopes. The total number of reindeer in the Swedish herds has been estimated at something like 200,000.

The Lapp culture is not as primitive as many have chosen to believe —rather, it is a highly developed culture perfectly adapted to perhaps the only way of life which will mean independent survival in these northern wastes. Take just the matter of languages, for example: practically all of the Lapps are at least bi-lingual and many are fluent in three or four tongues—their own language, Swedish, Norwegian, Finnish, and possibly others. Their handicrafts make use of the horns and skins of reindeer, and their distinctive costumes, largely in red, yellow, and blue, are as functional as they are ornamental. During the war they performed invaluable services to the Allied cause by helping Norwegians and other prisoners of the Nazis escape from Norway through the mountains to Sweden.

The Lapps, as they follow their herds, live in a special type of tepee, or hut, which is called a *kåta*. They eat reindeer meat—some reindeer are milked—and about the only things a Lapp family needs from the outside world are coffee and salt. They, like other people in the North, are devoted to coffee. Some of the larger reindeer owners are wealthy. Many now move to and from the summer camps by helicopter, leaving only the young men to accompany the herds. But don't ask a Lapp how many reindeer he has. It is the measure of his wealth, and is about as rude and nosy a question as asking an acquaintance how much money he has.

The Lapps have equal status with other Swedes under the law, and some special privileges. The government provides special schools for their education, and attendance is compulsory, as it is for all the other groups. There is a special inn for Lapps in Kiruna, and you may see them on the streets. Or you may meet them on the train carrying knapsacks. Don't be patronizing—they're not "simple" people. They have produced at least one great primitive artist and some university professors. But whatever their talents, whatever their education, most of them prefer their own way of life. You may get some idea of the traditional Lapp way of life by visiting the "Lappstaden" at Arvidsjaur, an old village of 70 cone-shaped Lapp huts which are still used for church visits at festival times.

Jukkasjärvi

Almost due east of Kiruna, about 15 to 25 kilometers (ten or 15 miles), is Jukkasjärvi, a little village. This is a sort of semi-permanent Lapp headquarters, with a modern school, an equally modern home for aged Lapps, and an appealing old church. The structure dates from 1726, was built on the site of a previous church (1611) which was the second one in all of Lapland. Note the remarkable architecture. At the times of the great religious holidays, Lapps gather here in huge crowds, and a Lapp wedding may be a tremendous event.

To get to Jukkasjärvi you must cross the mighty Torne River. These rushing waters make a magnificent sight, and beneath the turbulent surface there are fighting game fish—including salmon, trout, and grayling.

At Kaitum, 24 kilometers (15 miles) south of Kiruna is the Kaitum Chapel consecrated in 1964 as an ecclesiastical center for Laplanders but also as a memorial to Dag Hammarskjöld.

Mount Kebnekajse, 2,123 meters (6,965 feet) above sea level, the highest mountain in Sweden, is an excursion point best reached from Kiruna. It is really in the wilderness, about 32 kilometers (20 miles) by bus, 40 (25 miles) by motorboat, and the last 24 (15 miles) on foot. (In the winter it's bus and skis; sometimes sleighs are available.) Here you literally get away from it all, but the trip is recommended only for those who are in good physical condition. From Kebnekajse the sun is visible round the clock from May 23 to July 22.

An hour or so north of Kiruna on the main railway line you approach the southern shore of Lake Torneträsk, a long, narrow body of water which extends for miles almost to the Norwegian border. This is the real wilderness, but modern communications put it right outside your window. The railroad follows the southern shore, and at the eastern end you come to one of the most popular resort regions in Lapland.

The first resort, and the best known, that you reach is Abisko. There are regular motorboat tours on Lake Torneträsk, mountain excursions during the summer season and skiing during the spring. The sun is visible round the clock from June 12 to July 4. Björkliden is a few kilometers farther along, also on the railway line, located near Lake Torneträsk. About eight kilometers (five miles) away is Låktatjåkko.

The very last resort before you cross into Norway is Riksgränsen (the frontier; a road has recently been built from Kiruna to Narvik, however). The little railway station also serves as the customs house. Here you can enjoy skiing by the light of the Midnight Sun, which shines from May 26 to July 18.

PRACTICAL INFORMATION FOR THE NORTH

TOURIST INFORMATION. There are tourist offices in the following places: Åre, Torget (0647- 500 10). Dorotea, Torget (0942-112 06). Fundäsdalen (0684-214 20). Gävle, Stotorget (026-11 49 55). Kiruna, Bus Station (0980-188 80). Luleå, Rådstugatan 9 (0920-937 46). Östersund, Rådhusgatan 44 (063-14 40 01). Skellefteå, Storgatan 46 (0910-772 60). Sollefteå, Storgatan 59 (0620-143 67). Sundsvall, Storgatan 3 (060-11 42 35). Tärnaby, Blå Vägen 30 (0954-103 00). Umeå, Rådhustorget (090-16 16 16).

TELEPHONE CODES. We have given telephone codes for all the towns and villages in the hotel and restaurant lists that follow. These codes need only be used when calling from outside the town or village concerned.

HOTELS AND RESTAURANTS. North, south and west of Östersund, the mountain resorts of Jämtland are concentrated. These are not generally luxury establishments: they are designed principally for people who like the outdoors, and the rates are reasonable. In Lapland, you will find both modest hotels and modern, comfortable tourist hotels.

ÅRE. *Diplomat-Åregården* (M) (0647-502 65), 42 rooms. *Åregården* (I), 110 rooms. 400 meters (1,312 ft.) above sea level. 100 meters (328 ft.) to cable lift and railway station. Sauna, pool, dancing. Sports equipment for rent. Open Dec. through Sept. 15. AE, MC, V. *Sunwing Åre* (I) (0647-504 30). 50 rooms, 102 flats. Restaurant, dancing, nightclub, cafeteria. Sauna, pool, ski lift. AE, DC, MC, V.

BJÖRKLIDEN. *Hotel Fjället* (I) (0980-410 50). 70 rooms, 80 cottages. On railway and road to Swedish border. 500 meters (1,640 ft.) above sea level. Overlooking majestic mountain and Lake Torneträsk. Midnight Sun May 31 to July 16. Pension. Restaurant, dancing. Saunas, ski lifts. Excursions summer and winter. Open Feb. to middle Sept. (bookings 08-24 86 30). AE, MC, V.

BORGAFJÄLL, S. LAPPLAND. *Hotel Borgafjäll* (I) (0942-420 16). 30 chalet-type rooms. 540 meters (1,772 ft.) above sea level. Bus to Dorotea. Restaurant, sauna, slalom, fishing. Also self-service cottages. Open Feb. 15 to Apr. 30 and middle June through Sept. AE, MC, V.

BRUKSVALLARNA, HÄRJEDALEN. *Ramundbergets Fjällgård* (I) (0684-270 10). 58 rooms. Nine km. (five miles) to Bruksvallarna. 750 meters (2,460 ft.) above sea level. Pension. Restaurant, dancing. Sauna, indoor pool, ski lifts, excursions, fishing. Open Dec. to beginning May and July through Sept. MC, V.

DOCKSTA. Youth Hostel. Three km. (two miles) south of Docksta on E4 (High Coast) (0613-130 64). 58 beds. Bikes and canoes for rent. Open June through Aug.

GÄVLE. *Grand Hotel* (M), Nygatan 45 (026-12 90 60). 240 rooms. Central. Restaurants *Trägårn* and *Skeppet* with marine atmosphere. Dancing, nightclub. AE, DC, MC, V.

Restaurants. *Skeppet* (the Ship) (M), Nygatan 45 (026-12 90 60). In 100-year-old cellar vaults. Fresh *strömming* (Baltic herring) in all variations. MC, V. *Strandgården* (M), at Bönan fishing village, 13 km. (eight miles) north of Gävle (026-992 80). View of the sea. Fish, especially *strömming*. MC, V.

HEMAVAN, LAPPLAND. *Hemavan Fjällhotell* (Mountain Resort Hotel) (0954-301 50). 72 rooms. 500 meters (1,640 ft.) above sea level. Pension. Restaurant, sauna. Ski lifts, helicopter lift, marked trails, canoes etc. Open Christmas to beginning June and July through Aug. AE, DC, MC, V.

HÄRNÖSAND. *Statt* (M), Skeppsbron 9 (0611-105 10). 76 rooms. Restaurant, cocktail bar, dancing, sauna. AE, MC, V.
Restaurant. *Gästegiveri Spjutegården* (M), Murberget (0611-110 99). Inn dating from 1801. At the open-air museum, on a mountain with a view of the harbor. Two km. (1.2 miles) from the center of town. MC, V.

JÄRVSÖ. Youth Hostel. At camping site, 300 meters (330 yards) from railway station (0290-701 51). 30 beds. Bike rentals. Open all year.

KIRUNA. *Ferrum* (M), Köpmangatan 1 (0980-186 00). 170 rooms. 510 meters (1,673 ft.) above sea level. Restaurant, cocktail bar, saunas. Also 90 flats at *Ripan*. AE, DC, MC, V.
Youth Hostel. Strandstigen (0980-171 95). 90 beds. 500 meters (546 yards) from bus stop and railway station. Open June 15 through Aug.

LULEÅ. *SAS Globetrotter Hotel* (M), Storgatan 17 (0920-940 00). 214 rooms. SAS office, airport bus. Restaurant *Cooks Krog*, nightclub, sauna, solarium. AE, DC, MC, V. *Scandic* (M), Mjölkudden (0920-283 60). 164 rooms. Restaurant, sauna, solarium, airport bus. AE, DC, MC, V.

ÖSTERSUND. *Winn* (M), Prästgatan 16 (063-12 77 40). 117 rooms. Central, airport bus. Restaurant *Stadshuskällaren,* dancing, sauna. AE, MC, V.
Youth Hostel. Rådhusgatan 106 (063-11 30 78). 100 beds. Open end June to beginning Aug.

SODERHAMN. Restaurants. *Albertina* (M), at Skärsö fishing harbor (0270-320 10). Smoked, fried and fresh fish of all kinds. MC. *Faxe* (M), Kungsgatan 14 (0270-120 14). Central. Old-fashioned restaurant with traditions from the beginning of this century. *Smörgåsbord* is served from a skiff. Specialty trout. MC, V.

SUNDSVALL. *O.K. Motorhotel* (M), Esplanaden 29 (060-17 16 00). 203 rooms. Restaurant, dancing, sauna. AE, DC, MC, V.
Restaurants. *Oskar* (M), Vängåvan (060-12 98 11). Central. French cuisine and Nordic fare. MC, V. *Turistpaviljongen* (I), Norra Stadsberget (060-11 42 22). On a mountain-top with an excellent view of the city. Three km. (two miles) from the center. MC, V.
Youth Hostel. Gaffelbyn (060-11 21 19). 155 beds. 2.5 km. (1.6 miles) from center of town, on hill. Open all year.

TÄNNDALEN, HÄRJEDALEN. *Skavruet Fjällhotell* (Mountain Resort Hotel) (I) (0684-221 11). 32 rooms, 8 flats. 830 meters (2,723 ft.) above sea level, seven km. (4.3 miles) west of Funäsdalen. Pension prices. Ski lifts, sauna, fishing, row boats; golf course nearby. Open March through Apr. and July to middle Sept. MC, V.

TÄRNABY. Youth Hostel. Fritidscenter (0954-104 20). 50 beds. Open June through Aug.

NORRLAND AND LAPLAND

UMEÅ. *Blå Aveny* (M), Rådhusesplanaden 14 (090-13 23 00). 165 rooms. Central. Restaurant, cocktail bar, dancing, pub. Sauna, peaceful atmosphere. AE, DC, MC, V. *Blå Dragonen* (Blue Dragon) (M), Norrlandsgatan 5 (090-13 23 80). 71 rooms. Central. Steakhouse *Ryttmästaren* (Cavalry Captain) and restaurant *Blå Dragonen*. Dancing, sauna, heated outdoor pool, sun terrace. AE, DC, MC, V.

Restaurants. *Sävargården* (E), at the open-air museum Gammlia, five minutes by car from center (090-11 02 22). Dates from 18th century. Headquarters of the Russian General Kamenski for a time during the 1808–9 war. *Smörgåsbord,* with food from Västerbotten. AE, MC, V. *Cajsa Warg* (I), Kungsgatan 52 (090-12 44 22). Central. Steakhouse. Specialties from area. During day self-service, at night table service. AE, MC, V.

Youth Hostel. Åliden (090-12 57 60). 100 beds. Three km. (two miles) from railway station. Bus 8. Open June through August.

Camping

There are over 200 camping sites in this area. Many of them have log cabins and chalets for rent and most of them can be reached by bus or train: **Bollnäs,** Orbaden, Vallsta (0278-455 63). 24 chalets. On Lake Orsjön. Bus 500 meters (546 yards). Near ski lifts. Bike, canoe rentals. Open all year. **Delsbo,** *Delsbo Camping,* west of Delsbo on road 84 (0653-163 03). 4 chalets. On lake, 500 meters (546 yards) from bus stop. Canoes for rent. Open June 15 to Aug. 15. **Haparanda,** Kukkolaforsen (0922-310 00). 20 chalets. On route 99, 15 km. (nine miles) north of Haparanda. Restaurant, fishing, canoe safaris. Open all year. **Hede,** *Hede Camping* (0684-110 20). 15 chalets. On lake, excursions, boats, canoe rentals. Open all year. **Jokkmokk,** Kuossinjarka, Vaihijaur (097-310 13). 50 chalets. Bus stop, 12 km. (7.4 miles) from center. On lake. Bike, boat, canoe rentals. Open June to Aug. **Lycksele,** Ansia (0950-100 83). 38 chalets. On road 90 on east side of Umeå River, 1.5 km. (a mile) from town center. Bus 200 meters (200 yards). Canoe and bike rentals. Open June through Aug. **Luleå,** *Luleå Camping* at Skogsvallen (0920-932 64). 26 chaltes. Central, bus stop, bike and canoe rentals. Open June to Aug. **Nordingrå,** Norrfällsviken, 30 km. (19 miles) from E4 (0613-213 82). 20 chalets. Canoes for rent. Open June 18 through Aug. **Östersund,** Fritidsby, Odenslingan 831, on E75 (063-11 37 06). 112 cabins. Central. Open all year. **Skellefteå,** *Skelleftea Camping,* on E4 (0911-188 55). 34 chalets. 14 km. (8.6 miles) north of town center. Sauna, ski lift; bikes for rent. Open all year. **Storuman,** *Storuman Camping,* 200 meters (200 yards) south of Blue Route (0951-106 96). 22 cabins. On lake. Sauna; boats and canoes for rent. Open June through Aug. **Sundsvall/Härnösand,** Bye Rast, Söråker, on E4 (060-450 55). 20 chalets. 38 km. (24 miles) north of Sundsvall. Canoes and boats for rent. Open all year. **Undersåker,** Ristafallet, on Indal River (0647-311 10). 8 cabins. 400 meters (440 yards) south of E75 and seven km. (4.3 miles) west of Järpen. Waterfall. Open June through Aug.

HOW TO GET AROUND. By car. The most important route to northern Sweden, Highway E4, continues from Stockholm to Haparanda on the Finnish border—1,134 km. (681 miles). The main routes to the interior highlands branch off this highway at Hudiksvall: road 84 via Sveg to Funäsdalen—322 km. (193 miles); Sundsvall: E75 via Östersund to Åre—300 km. (186 miles) and Storlien, so further into Norway to Trondheim; at Umeå: roads 92, 93 and 361—the very scenic Blå Vägen—through Storuman to Tärnaby and Hemavan, and on to Mo i Rana, below the Arctic Circle; at Luleå: roads 97 and 98 via Jokkmokk and Gällivare to Kiruna—381 km. (229 miles).

A road leading into Norway goes from Vilhelmina along the beautiful Lake Vojmsjön to Dikanäs and Kittelfjäll and via the frontier village of Skalmodal to Mosjöen in Norway—400 km. (248 miles).

Note that it is forbidden to take photographs near the defense areas of Sundsvall and Kalix on Highway E4, and Boden on Highway 97.

By train. Two main rail lines traverse Sweden in a south-north direction: from Stockholm near the coast to the Finnish border, and from Dalarna prov-

SWEDEN

ince through the interior to Gällivare; the Sundsvall-Trondheim and Luleå-Narvik lines cross it in an east-west direction. Secondary lines and postal buses, fanning out from the railroad stations, supplement this network and make even remote districts conveniently accessible. From Stockholm it is 7 hours to Östersund by express train, 12 to Storlien, 17 to Luleå, 20 to Kiruna, and 22½ to Abisko.

By bus. Long-distance buses link Stockholm with Funäsdalen and Härnösand, and Sundsvall with Luleå. Swedish State Railways also offer nine-day guided bus tours of the North Cape twice weekly from mid-June to mid-August, starting at Luleå and ending at Narvik in Norway. RESO operates a seven-day North Cape tour starting and ending in Kiruna daily from early June to mid-August.

By air. There are airports at Gävle, Östersund, Sundsvall, Kramfors, Skellefteå, Umeå, Luleå, Gällivare and Kiruna. You can fly from Stockholm to Sundsvall in 45 minutes, to Umeå in 55 minutes, to Luleå and Östersund in just 70 minutes, to Kiruna in 90 minutes. From mid-June to mid-July, SAS/RESO operate round-trip "Midnight Sun" flights from Stockholm to Kiruna.

By ferry. If your preference is for a more leisurely route, there is a car ferry service from Vaasa in Finland to Sundsvall (nine hours) and Umeå (four hours), and from Pietarsaari in Finland to Umeå and Skellefteå.

PLACES TO VISIT. Wilderness, forests and mountains—though plentiful and impressive—are not the whole story. Among the other sights at the far north of Sweden are:

ARJEPLOG. Silvermuseet. Storgatan 20. Large collection of Lapp handicrafts and silver; 600-year-old tools and fireplaces, and much more. Open Mon. to Fri. 11–3, Sat. and Sun. 12–3. In summer, longer opening hours. Admission free.

HÄRNÖSAND. Murberget Homestead Museum. 1.5 km. (a mile) from center of town. Old farmhouses from the area; church, shop, school from 19th century. Tour every day. Demonstrations of spinning, weaving etc. weekly—for information on tours call 0611-232 40. Open June to Aug. 15, daily 10–4. Admission free.

Länsmuseet (Provincial Museum). Near Murberget. Has archeological finds, handicrafts etc. and is open same times as Homestead Museum.

JOKKMOKK. Jokkmokk Museum. Kyrkogatan. Also called the "Arctic Circle Museum." Large collection of Lapp handicrafts and silver." Exhibits showing the frontier life of settlers from the south. Animals of the north. Open Mon. to Fri. 12–3, Sat. and Sun. 1–4; June through Aug., Mon. to Fri. 10–7, Sat. and Sun. 12–6.

JUKKASJÄRVI. Jukkasjärvi Homestead Museum. 17 km. (11 miles) south of Kiruna. Old farm, log cabins and many types of Lapp *kåta* (huts) and sheds. Beautiful altar painting in nearby wooden church. Cafeteria. Tour four times daily—call 0980-211 90 for times. Open June through Aug., daily 10–9.

ÖSTERSUND. Jamtli Open-Air Museum. Centrally placed. 18th-century manor house, Lapp *kåta* (huts), town houses, market place etc. Mid-summer to Aug. there are activities in many of the buildings, daily 10–6. Park open all year. Small admission fee.

Jämtlands Läns Museum. Provincial museum close to Jamtli. Rich collections of folk art, paintings etc. Temporary exhibitions. Open Mon. to Fri. 10–4, Sat. and Sun. 11–5. Admission free.

STORFORSEN. Skogsbruksmuseet (Forestry Museum). At Storforsen River, 40 km. (25 miles) west of Alvsbyn. Permanent exhibition of forestry and

NORRLAND AND LAPLAND

timber-floating through the ages. Charcoal and tar are occasionally made here in the traditional way. Tour three times daily—call 0929-310 91 for times of tours. Open June through Aug., daily 10–4. Admission free.

SUNDSVALL. Norra Berget (North Hill) Homestead Museum. Two km. (1.2 miles) from center of city (uphill). Buildings from the 19th century. Open Mon. to Fri. 10–4, Sat and Sun. 11–4; June through Aug., daily 9–7. Admission free.

Sundsvall Museum. Storgatan 29. Sawmill and city history. Finds from Iron Age, paintings etc. Temporary exhibitions. Open Mon. to Thurs. 11–8, Fri. to Sun. 11–4; summer, daily 11–4. Admission free.

SPORTS. Many well-marked trails for **hiking** and **climbing** criss-cross the entire mountain area. Most spectacular of these is the "King's Trail" leading from Jäckvik through the Sarek district north to Abisko. Kvikkjokk is the starting point for tours up the beautiful Tarra valley and can be conveniently reached from Jokkmokk. From Kiruna you can reach Nikkaluokta at the foot of 2,123-meter (6,965-ft) Mount Kebnekajse, Sweden's highest mountain. An extensive network of mountain huts is maintained by the Swedish Touring Club, and expeditions with guides start regularly from the various tourist stations.

Fine possibilities for trout **fishing** exist throughout the region; also char, redbelly, grayling, and salmon. Among the waterways, try the Dalälven, Ljungan, Indal, Ljusnan, and Torne rivers, and the "Ströms vattudal", nine connecting lakes stretching northwest from Strömsund to Frostviken. Other excellent fishing centers are Saxnäs, Tärnaby, Ammarnäs, and Arvidsjaur. Fishing license fees are low; for fishing in Jämtland waters write to the Tourist Office, Rådhusplan, Östersund, and for fishing in Lapland to Norrbotten Tourist Board, Box 80003, S-95121 Luleå, or to Västerbotten Turistnämnd, Box 317, S-90107 Umeå.

Forests abound in game for the **hunter,** especially moose, particularly plentiful in Jämtland; open season: four days, usually starting the second Monday of September. Special permits are required for the import and export of rifles and ammunition, and expeditions are arranged for hunters from abroad; write to the Tourist Office, Rådhusplan, S-83182 Östersund.

WINTER SPORTS. The northland is **skiing** country—slalom and cross-country. The Swedes are specialists in cross-country, with a string of Olympic titles to prove the point. Härjedalen: Smallest of Sweden's four skiing provinces, also the highest; not quite as accessible as the others but very good skiing facilities, ski lifts in most resorts, and many good hotels; season in Fjällnäs district runs from January to mid-April. Jämtland: Sweden's most frequented winter resort area, thanks to its accessibility, facilities, and fine accommodation along Stockholm-Östersund-Trondheim railway; "snow weasels" are a feature, also torchlight sleigh rides, fishing through the ice, curling; season in Åre-Storlien district from January to mid-April. Lapland: Only distance from the capital and the lateness with which its season starts prevent this area from nosing out Jämtland as Sweden's top skiing region; this is purely skiing country—no ice sports or sleighing parties; the tree line is low, so there are plenty of open slopes; latitude is the greatest asset here and spring skiing the greatest delight—this is where you enjoy the sensation of skiing in the Midnight Sun; season in the Tärna district runs from March to early May, in Abisko district from March through May.

Informality is the keynote of Swedish winter resort life. No ice bars or *apres-ski,* but plenty of good companionship, relaxing before open fires, and the opportunity of acquiring a mid-winter tan. A word of caution with respect to the latter: the late winter-spring sun here has an unsuspected power—take good sun-glasses and be careful generally about over-exposing your face and body. Here is a brief survey of the provinces with their resorts and facilities.

SWEDEN

Härjedalen is sleigh-ride and cross-country skiing territory, with market trails and sleeping huts enticing skiers to two or three-day excursions. Its chief resorts are all clustered together, on a U-shaped road starting on the Norwegian border at *Fjällnäs* (732 meters or 2,400 ft.) and then paralleling the Tännån River southeastward through *Hamrafjället* (732 meters or 2,400 ft.) and *Tänndalen* (695 meters or 2,280 ft.), after which it swings around northeastward, with *Funäsdalen* (663 meters or 2,175 ft.) in the center of the bottom of the U and then turns northwest, with the last of the principal resorts, *Bruksvallarna* (778 meters or 2,550 ft.) falling at about the middle of the upper line of the U. *Vemdalsskalet,* finally, lies a little apart farther eastwards and just on the border to Jämtland province. Ski lifts at Fjällnäs, Hamrafjället, Bruksvallarna, Tänndalen, Tännäs, Funäsdalen, Sveg, Lofsdalen and Vemdalsskalet.

Jämtland offers a bewildering richness of resorts. Its transportation key is *Östersund,* the main station on the Stockholm-Trondheim line, which, while not strictly a resort, can be used as a center from which to sally forth to skiing slopes in the vicinity. It has excellent skating rinks. The most easily accessible resorts are those on this rail line, which, starting from Östersund, are *Hålland* and *Undersåker,* both with ski lifts; *Åre,* the chief winter sports center of Jämtland, with an overhead cable railway, several ski lifts and skating and curling rinks; *Duved* with new chair lift; *Ånn;* and *Storlien,* the second largest resort, which has a jump, ski lifts, slalom runs, one of which drops 235 meters (770 ft.) in a distance of 999 (3,280 ft.), ski instructors and skating rinks.

Another important area hugs the frontier south of Storlien, which gets you into some fairly high altitudes. First comes *Blåhammarstugan* (1,084 meters or 3,559 ft.). Southeast lies *Storulvåstugan* (730 meters or 2,394 ft.), south of that *Sylstugorna* (951 meters or 3,123 ft.), with a ski camp built another 91 meters (300 ft.) above it; and a little more than a few kilometers more to the south is the province's highest peak, *Mount Sylarna* (2,066 meters or 6,779 ft.). Of these resorts, Storulvåstugan has slalom runs and ski instructors on hand.

A few other resorts south of the main railway, between the border and Östersund, are worth mentioning. Farthest west, reached by road from Undersåker (on the rail line) is *Vålådalen,* a small popular resort with slalom and downhill runs, ski lift, a practice jump and a skating rink. Vålådalen is known as a training center for Sweden's Olympic cross-country skiiers. About halfway between here and Östersund, and just about as far south of the railway, is *Bydalen,* with ski lift, and about as much farther south again, *Arådalen.* At *Hammarstrand,* some 97 km. (60 miles) east of Östersund, is a winter sports center with bobsleigh track, slalom run, ski lifts.

Lapland's most popular section is its farthest north, above the Arctic Circle. The entrance to this region is the iron-ore center of *Kiruna,* 200 km. (124 miles) north of the Arctic Circle. Kiruna is not itself a resort, but the nearby mountains provide slopes of all degrees of difficulty within easy reach, and by continuing through it on the Stockholm-Narvik railway, you pass in rapid succession through the three big winter sports centers of northern Lapland, all of which have slalom slopes, lifts, ski instructors and guides for the long excursions.

The first one reached from Kiruna is *Abisko* (310 meters or 1,250 ft.). A chair lift takes you up to the summit of Mount Nuolja with Midnight Sun from May 31 to July 16. Next comes *Björkliden,* which has a ski lift. Last station on the line, practically on the Norwegian border is *Riksgränsen,* also with a ski lift; the great attraction here is not simply sliding downhill from the top of the lift, but making excursions across the spectacular broad snowfields high up in the Riksgränsen mountains under the Midnight Sun.

There is also a winter sports center in southern Lapland around the resorts of Hemavan and Tärnaby. Ski lifts and good accommodation, but a little awkward to reach: direct train with sleepers from Stockholm to Storuman, then by bus.

INDEX

The letter H indicates Hotel and other accommodations. The letter R indicates Restaurants.

GENERAL INFORMATION

(See also Practical Information sections for each country and Practical Information at the end of each chapter.)

Air travel
　from Britain 10
　from N. America 8-9
　in Scandinavia 14
Auto travel
　from Britain 13-14
　in Scandinavia 16-17

Bus travel
　from Britain 13

Climate 3-4
Clothing & packing 4
Conversion tables 17
Credit cards 5
Culture 44-51
Currency 4-5
Customs
　returning home 18-19

Ferry & hydrofoil travel
　in Scandinavia 15-16
Food & drink 52-7

Handicapped travelers 7-8
History 30-43
Independent travel 1-2
Information sources 1
Insurance 6-7
Introduction to
　Scandinavia 20-9

Local time 4

Package tours 1-2
Passports & visas 5-6

Ship travel
　from N. America 10
Student & youth travel 7

Tour operators 2-3
Travel agents 2
Traveler's checks 4-5
Train travel
　from Britain 10-13
　in Scandinavia 14-15

Denmark
Practical Information

Air travel 66
Auto Travel 66-7

Bicycling 67
Bus travel 67

Camping 64
Costs 61

Currency & exchange 61
Customs 62-3

Ferry travel 67
Food & drink 65

History & background 68-72
Hotels 63
Hours of business 66

Information sources 61
Language 62

Mail 66

Map 60

Restaurants 64-5

Seasonal events 61-2
Self-catering holidays 63-4

Tipping 66
Train travel 66

Youth hostels 64

Geographical

Aalborg 124
Åbenrå 119, HR129
AErø 112-3
AErøskøbing 112-3, H114
Åkirkkeby 139, H140, R141
Albertslund H104
Allinge 137
Als 113, 119
Anholt 126, H129
Århus 126-7, HR130
Assens 113-4, H114

Billund 128
Bogø 104
Bornholm 136-40, HR140-1
　information sources 140
　shopping 142
　sightseeing 142
　sports 142
　telephones 140
　transportation 141-2

Central Islands 110-4, HR114-5
　camping 116
　information sources 114
　museums & castles 116-7

telephones 114
tours 116
youth hostels 116
Christiansø 140
Copenhagen 73-84, H85-7, R94-5
　airport transportation 85
　camping 87
　excursions 84
　historic buildings & sites 90-1
　information sources 85
　map 76-7
　museums 89-90
　music 92
　nightlife 96-7
　parks & zoos 90
　shopping 92-3
　sightseeing 74-84, 88-9
　sports 91-2
　telephones 85
　Tivoli Gardens 78, 90
　tours 88-9
　transportation 87-8
　youth hostels 87

Djursland 125-6
Dragør 84
Dyrehaven 84

Ebeltoft 126, HR130
Egeskov 113
Elsinore *see* Helsingør
Esbjerg 121, HR130

Fåborg 113, H114
Falster 103-4
Fanø 121, H130
Fredensborg 100, H104
Frederica 119, H130
Frederiksborg 100
Frederikshavn 123, H130
Funen (island) 110-4

Givskud 128
Glostrup H104
Grenå 125-6, H130
Greve Strande 104
Gudhjem 138, HR141

Haderslev 119, H130
Hammershus 137
Hantsholm H131
Hasle 137, H141
Helsingør 98-9, H105
Herning H131
Hillerød 100
Himmelbjerget 127, H131
Himmerland 124
Hjerl Hede 122

INDEX

Hobro 124
Holbaek 100, H105
Hornbaek H105
Horsens HR131
Hovborg H131
Hvide Sande 122
Hvidsten R131

Jons Kapel 137
Jutland 118-28, HR129-33
  camping 133
  information sources 129
  museums & castles 134-5
  sports 135
  telephones 129
  transportation 133-4
  youth hostels 133
Jyderup H105

Kalundborg 101
Karrebaeksminde R105
Karup H131
Kertminde 111, HR115
Knuthenborg Safari Park 103
Køge 102, HR105
Kolding 119, HR131
Korsør H105

Laesø 123, HR131
Langeland 112
Lolland 103

Mandø 122
Maribo 103, HR105
Marstal 112, H115
Menstrup H105
Middlefart 114, H115
Møgeltønder 120
Mogenstrup H105
Møn 102-4
Mors 123
Mullerup Havn H105

Naestved 103, H105
Nexø 139, HR141
Nordby 128
Nyborg 110, 113, HR115
Nykøbing (Falster) 100, 103, H105
Nykøbing (Sjaelland) H105, R106
Nylars 139
Nymindegab H131
Nyord 104
Nysted 103

Odense 111, HR115
Olsker 138
Øsløs H131
Østerlars 138

Randers 125, HR131
Rebild Bakker 124
Ribe 120-1, H132
Ringsted 101, HR106
Rinkøbing H132
Rø 138
Rold Skov 124, H132
Rømø 122
Rønne 137, HR141

Rønnede H106
Roskilde 101-2, HR106
Rudbøl 120
Rudkøbing 112, HR115

Saeby H132
Samsø 128, H132
Sandvig 137, HR141
Silkeborg 127, HR132
Skagen 123, HR132
Skandeborg 127, H132
Slagelse 101, HR106
Søllerød 100, R106
Sønderborg 119, H132
Sorø 101, H106
Spøttrup 122-3
Stege 104, H106
Svaneke 138-9
Svendborg 112-3, HR115

Tåsinge 112
Thisted H132
Thurø 112
Tisvildeleje 99, H106
Tønder 120, H132
Tranekar H115
Troense 112, H115

Vejle 128, HR133
Viborg 124-5, HR133
Vordinborg 103

Zealand 98-104, HR104-6
  camping 106
  information sources 104
  museums & castles 107-9
  telephones 104
  tours 107
  transportation 106-7
  youth hostels 106

Finland
Practical Information

Air travel 150
Auto travel 151

Bicycling 151
Bus travel 151

Camping 148
Costs 145
Currency & exchange 145
Customs 147

Farm vacations 148
Food & drink 149

Hiking 151
History & background 152-6
Hotels 147
Hours of business 150

Information sources 145

Language 146-7

Mail 150
Map 144

National holidays 146

Restaurants 148-9

Seasonal events 145-6
Self-catering holidays 147-8
Ship travel 151
Sports 150

Telephones 150
Tipping 149
Train travel 150-1

Youth hostels 148

Geographical

Ähtäri 183, H198
Åland Islands 176
Aulanko 182

Central Provinces 181-7, HR187-91
  camping 187-91
  information sources 187
  sightseeing 192-4
  sports 194
  telephones 187
  tours 192
  transportation 191-2
  youth hostels 187-91

Enontekiö 206-7, H208

Hämeenlinna 182, HR187
Hanko 175, HR177
Heinola H187
Helsinki 157-65, H166-7, R170-1
  airport transportation 165
  auto rentals 165
  camping 167
  historic buildings & sites 168-9
  information sources 165
  map 160-1
  museums 168
  music 169
  nightlife 172
  parks & zoos 168
  shopping 169-70
  sightseeing 158-65
  sports 169
  telephones 165
  tours 167
  transportation 167
  youth hostels 167
Hovinsaari 174
Hyvinkää 182, HR188
Hyvitträsk 174

Imatra H188
Inari 205, H208
Ivalo 205, H208

Joensuu 186, HR188
Jyväskylä 184, HR188

Kajaani 187, HR188
Kalajoki 196-7, H198

INDEX

Karesuvanto 206, H208
Kaustinen H198
Kemi 204, H208-9, R209
Kerimäki 185
Kilpisjärvi 206, H209
Kittilä 206, H209
Kokkola 196-7, H198
Koli 186, H189
Kotka 174, HR177
Kuopio 186-7, HR189
Kuusamo 197, H198

Lahti 183-4, HR189
Lapland 203-7, HR208-10
 camping 208-10
 information sources 208
 sightseeing 211
 sports 211-2
 telephones 208
 tours 210
 transportation 210
 youth hostels 208-10
Lappeenranta 186, H189-90, R190
Lemmenjoki 205
Lohja H177
Loviisa 174, H178

Mariehamn 176, HR178
Mikkeli HR190
Muonio 206, H209

Naantali 175, HR178

Ostrobothnia 195-7, HR198-200
 camping 198-200
 information sources 197
 sightseeing 200-1
 sports 201-2
 telephones 197
 transportation 200
 youth hostels 198-200
Oulu 197, HR198

Pallastunturi 206, H209
Pietarsaari 196, HR199
Pori 196, HR199
Porvoo 173, HR178
Punkaharju 185, H190
Pyhätunturi H209

Rauma H199
Rovaniemi 204-5, HR209
Rukatunturi 197, H199

Saariselkä 205, H209-10
Savonlinna 185, HR190
Seinäjoki H199
Sevettijärvi 204
Sodankylä 205, H210
Sotkamo H190
South Coast & Islands 173-6, HR177-9
 camping 177-9
 information sources 177
 museums 179-80
 sports 180
 telephones 177
 tours 179
 transportation 179
 youth hostels 177-9
Suomutunturi H210
Sysmä 184, H191

Tammisaari 174, HR178
Tampere 182-3, HR191
Tankavaara 205, HR210
Turku 175, H178-9, R179

Utsjoki 205, H210
Uusikaupunki H199

Vaasa 196, H199-200, R200
Varkaus HR191
Viitasaari H191

Yteri 196

Iceland
Practical Information

Air travel 219
Auto travel 220

Bicycling 220
Bus travel 219-20

Camping 217, 239
Costs 215
Currency & exchange 215
Customs 216

Farm vacations 217
Food & drink 218

Hiking 220
History & background 221-5
Hotels 216-7
Hours of business 219

Information sources 215, 238

Language 216

Mail 218
Map 214

Restaurants 217-8

Seasonal events 215-6
Ship travel 220
Sports 219

Telephones 219, 238
Tipping 218

Youth hostels 217, 239

Geographical

Akranes H241
Akureyri 231, H238, R238-9

Blönduos H239
Borgarfjörður Eystri 230, H241
Borgarnes H241
Breiðafjörður Bay 229
Breiðalsvík H240

Dalvík H239
Dettifoss Falls 232
Djúpvogur H240

Egilsstaðir H240
Eiðar H240
Eskifjörður H240

Flúðir H239

Glaciers (area) 229-30
Goðafoss Falls 231
Great Geysir 228
Grímsey 231
Grindavík H239
Gullfoss Falls 228

Hallormsstaðir H240
Heimaey 230-1
Hella H239
Höfn 230
Hornafjörður H240
Hrútafjörður H239
Húnavellir H239
Húsavík 232, H239
Hveragerði H240
Hvolsvöllur H240

Ísafjörður H241

Kirkjubæjarklauster H240
Kópasker H239

Laugar H239
Luagarvatn H240

Mývatn 231-2, H239

Raufarhöfn H239
Reykholt 229, H241
Reykjavík 226-8, H233-4, R237
 airport transportation 232-3
 camping 234
 information sources 233
 map 226
 museums 235
 music 236
 nightlife 237-8
 parks & gardens 235
 shopping 237
 sports 236
 telephones 233
 tours 235
 transportation 234
 youth hostels 234

Sauðárkrókur H239
Selfoss H240
Siglufjörður H239
Skaftafjell 230
Skagafjörður H239
Skálholt 228-9, H240
Skógar 230, H240
Snæfellsnes 229, H241
Storutjarnir H239
Stykkishólmur 229, H241
Svartifoss Falls 230

INDEX

Thingvellir 228, H240

Westmann Islands 230-1, H240

Norway
Practical Information

Air travel 251
Auto travel 251-2

Bus travel 252

Camping 248
Costs 245
Currency & exchange 245
Customs 247

Food & drink 249

History & background 253-7
Hotels 247-8
Hours of business 249

Information sources 245

Language 246

Mail 249
Map 244
National holidays 246

Restaurants 248-9

Seasonal events 245-6
Self-catering holidays 248
Ship travel 252
Sports 250-1

Tipping 249
Train travel 251

Youth hostels 248

Geographical

Aga 302
Al H336
Ålesund 309, HR313-4
Alta 351
Åndalsnes 309, HR314
Arendal 291, HR295
Aulestad 320

Balestrand 305, 307, H312
Bandak (canal & lake) 288-9
Bardu HR355
Beitostølen H324
Bergen 327-30, H331-2, R336
 airport transportation 331
 camping 332
 historic building & sites 334-5
 information sources 331
 museums 333-4
 music 335
 nightlife 336

parks, zoos & gardens 334
shopping 336
sports 335
telephones 331
tours 333
transportation 332-3
youth hostels 332
Bjervik 352
Bö 288, HR295
Bodø 348, HR355
Bolkesjø 290, H296
Borgund 306, 309, 323
Bøverdalen H324
Bryne HR309-10
Bygdin 322, H324
Bygdøy 266-7
Byglandsfjord 292-3, H296
Bykle 294

Central Mountains & Eastern Valleys 318-23, HR324-6
sports 326
transportation 326
youth hostels 324-5

Dalen 288-9, H296
Dombås 321, H324
Drammen 281-2, HR283-4,

Eidsborg 289
Eidsvoll 319-20
Elverum 319, H324
Espedalen H324

Fagernes 323, H324
Farsund HR296
Fauske 353, HR355
Fevik 291, H296
Finse H337
Fjaerland 305, HR312
Fjord Country 300-9, HR309-14
 museums & churches 315-74
 sports 317
 telephones 309
 tours 315
 transportation 314-5
 youth hostels 310-4
Flåm 306, H312
Flekkefjord H296
Florø H313
Førde HR313
Fredrikstad 280-1, HR284

Geiranger 307-8, H314
Gjendesheim 322
Gjövik 320, H324
Godøysund H310
Gol 323, H337
Granvin 303, H310
Grimstad 291, HR296
Grindaheim H325

Halden 281, HR284
Hamar 320, H325
Hammerfest 349-50, H355
Hankø H284
Hardanger 302-4

Harpefoss H325
Harstad 349, H355
Haugesund 303, HR310
Heddal 290
Hell 342
Hermansverk HR312
Holmenkollen 267-8
Honningsvåg 350, HR355-6
Hovden 294, H296
Høvringen H325
Höyanger 305

Jaeren 301-2
Jölster 307, H313

Karasjok 351, H356
Karmöy Island 303
Kautokeino 352, H356
Kinsarvik 303, HR311
Kirkenes 350-1, HR356
Kongsberg 290, HR296
Kragerø 290-1, HR296
Kristiansand 291-2, HR296-7
Kristiansund 309, HR314
Kvamskog HR311
Kvinesdal H297

Laerdal 306, H312
Lakselv 351
Larvik 283, HR284
Leikander HR312
Leirvik H311
Levanger H343
Lillehammer 320, H325
Lillesand 291
Loen 307, H313
Lom 307, 321-2, H325
Lönsdal 353, H356

Måløy 307, HR313
Målselv HR356
Mandal 292, HR297
Marifjøra H312
Maristova H325
Meråker H343
Mjølfjell H337
Mo-i-Rana 354, H356
Molde 309, HR314
Morgedal 288, H297
Mosjøen 356
Moss 280-1, HR284
Mösvatn 289

Namsos H343
Narvik 352-3, H356
Nordfjordeid 307, HR313
Nordheimsund 303, HR311
Nordkjosbotn H357
Norefjell H325
North Cape (area) 350-4, HR357
Northern Norway 347-54 HR355-7
 information sources 354
 museums & churches 358-60
 sports 300
 telephones 354

INDEX

transportation 358
youth hostels 355-7
Nystova H325

Odda HR311
Olden HR313
Olsborg 352
Oppdal 342, H343
Oppheim H337
Orkanger H343
Os H311
Oslo 258-65, H270-1, R277-9
  airport transportation 269
  auto rentals 269
  camping 271
  excursions 265-9
  historic buildings & sites 274-5
  history 259-60
  information sources 269
  map 262-3
  museums 272-4 environs 268-9
  music 276
  nightlife 279
  parks, zoos & gardens 274
  shopping 276-7
  sightseeing 260-5
  sports 275-6
  telephones 269
  tours 272
  transportation 271-2
  youth hostels 271
Oslo Fjord District 280-3, HR283-4
  camping 285
  information sources 283
  museums & sites 285-6
  sports 286
  telephones 283
  tours 285
  transportation 285
  youth hostels 284-5
Østa H314
Otta 321, H325
Øystese 303, HR311

Rauland 289, H297
Ravnejuvit 289
Risør 291
Rjukan 290, HR297
Rønvik 348
Røros 318-9, 342, H343
Rosendal 303-4, H311
Runde Island 309

Sandane H313
Sandefjord 282-3, HR284
Sandnes HR310
Sarpsborg 281, HR284
Sauda HR310
Seljestad 302-3, H311
Seljord 288
Senja Island 349
Setesdal 292-4
Skaidi H357
Skånevik 303, H311
Skien 287-8, HR297
Skjolden H312

Skogadalbően 322
Skogfoss 351
Sogndal H312
Sørkjosen 357
Sortland H357
Spitsbergen 354
Stalheim 307, H337
Stamsund 348, H357
Stavanger 300-2, HR310
Steinkjer 347, H343
Strandebarm 303, H312
Stryn H313
Sunndalsøra H314
Surnadal H314
Svolvaer 348, H357

Telemark & South Coast 287-95, HR295-8
  museums, churches & sites 298-9
  sports 299
  telephones 295
  tours 298
  transportation 298
  youth hostels 296-7
Tönsberg 282, HR284
Tretten H325-6
Tromsö 349, H357
Trondenes 349
Trondheim 339-42, HR343-4
Trondheim & District 339-42, HR343-4
  information sources 342-3
  parks 345
  sightseeing 345
  sports 345-6
  telephones 343
  tours 345
  transportation 344-5
  youth hostels 343-4
Turtagrø H312

Ullensvang 303
Ulvik 303, H312
Ustaoset H337
Utne 302-3, H312

Vadsö 350, H357
Vågå 321
Vågåmo H326
Valdres 323
Valle 293, HR297
Vardø H357
Vatnahalsen H337
Videseter 308, H313
Vigeland (Frogner) Park 265-6
Vik 307, HR313
Vinstra 321-2, H326
Volda HR314
Voss 307, H337-8
Vrådal 288, H297
Vråliosen 288, H298

**Sweden
Practical Information**

Air travel 368
Auto travel 368-9

Bicycling 369
Bus travel 369

Camping 365
Costs 363
Currency & exchange 363
Customs 364

Food & drink 366-7

History & background 370-5
Hotels 364-5
Hours of business 367

Information sources 364

Language 364

Mail 367
Map 362

National holidays 364
National Tourist Offices 363

Restaurants 366

Seasonal events 364
Shopping (tax-free) 367

Tipping 367

Youth hostels 365-6

Geographical

Abisko 458
Åmål 444
Ängelholm 410, H419
Åre 453, H459
Arvidsjaur 457-8
Arvika HR446
Åsa H430
Askhult 429

Båstad 410, H418
Bengtsfors H446
Björkliden 458, H459
Boden 455
Borås H446
Borgafjäll H459
Borgholm 416, H419
Borlänge H446
Bruksvallarna H459

Dalsland Canal 443-4
Drottingham Palace 387

Eketorp 416
Eksjö H419
Eskhult 427
Eskilstuna 445, HR446

Falun H446
Filipstad 443, HR447
Fjärås Bräcka 427-8
Frösön 453

Gällivare 456
Gävle 454-5, H459, R460

INDEX

Göta Canal 441
Gothenburg 424-6, H430, R430-1
Gothenburg & West Coast 424-9, HR430-2
 camping 431
 information sources 429
 museums & castles 433-4
 parks & gardens 434
 sports 434
 telephones 429
 tours 433
 transportation 432
 youth hostels 431-2
Gotland 404-6
Gränna 438-9, HR447
Gripsholm Castle 403-4, 445
Grythyttan H477

Haga 387
Halmstad 429, H431
Härnosänd 454, H460
Helsinborg 409-10, H419
Hemavan H460
Huskvarna 438

Järvsö 454
Jönköping 437-8, HR447
Jukkasjärvi 458

Kalmar 415-6, H419
Karlshamn 414
Karlskrona 414, HR419-20
Karlstad 442-3, HR447
Kiruna 456, H460
Kivik 413
Koster Islands 428
Kristianstad 413, H420
Kungälv 428, H432
Kungsbacka 428, H431, R432

Lake District 435-45, HR446-9
 information sources 446
 museums & castles 450-1
 telephones 446
 transportation 449
 youth hostels 447-8
Låktatjåkko 458
Landskrona 411
Lidingö Island 387
Lidköping 436, H447
Linköping 440, H447, R448
Lövånger 454
Luleå 455, H460
Lund 411-2, H420
Lycksele 454-5

Lysekil 428, H432

Maglehem 413
Malen 410
Malmö 411, HR420
Mariefred 445
Marstrand 428, H432
Mölle 410
Mölndal 427
Mora 444, H448
Mörrum 414, H420

Norrköping 440-1, HR448
Norrland & Lapland 452-8, HR459-61
 camping 461
 museums 462-3
 sports 463-4
 transportation 461-2
 youth hostels 459-61
Nynäshamn 402

Öland Island 416
Omberg 439
Örebro HR448
Oskarshamn H420
Östersund 453, H460

Piteå 455

Ransäter 442
Rättvik 444
Riksgränsen 458
Ronneby 414, H420

Sälen 444
Saltsjöbaden 387
Sandhamn 402
Särö 427
Sigtuna 402-3
Simrishamn 413, H421
Skara 437
Skokloster Castle 403
Smögen 428, H432
Söderhamn R460
Söderköping H448
Sölvesborg 414
Southern Sweden 408-18, HR418-21
 camping 421
 information sources 418
 museums & castles 422-3
 sports 423
 telephones 418
 tours 422
 transportation 421
 youth hostels 419-21
Stenungsund 427
Stockholm 376-86, H388-91, R397-9

airport transportation 388
 auto rentals 388
 camping 391
 excursions 387
 historic buildings & sites 394-5
 information sources 388
 map 380-1
 museums 392-4
 music 396
 nightlife 399-400
 parks, zoos & gardens 394
 shopping 397
 sightseeing 379-86, 392
 sports 395-6
 telephones 388
 tours 392
 transportation 392
 youth hostels 391
Stockholm environs & Gotland 401-6, H406, R407
 camping 407
 information sources 406
 museums 407
 telephones 406
 transportation 407
 youth hostels 407
Strömsholms Castle & Canalk 445
Strömstad 428, H432
Sturehov 403
Sundsvall 454-5, HR460
Sunne 443
Sunnemo 442
Sveg 453

Tällberg 444, H448
Tänndalen H460
Tanumshede H432
Tjolöholm Palace 427-8
Torekov 410-1
Tyresö Castle 402

Uddeholm 442-3
Uddevalla 428, HR432
Umeå 455, HR461
Uppsala 445, HR449

Vadstena 439-40, HR448
Varberg 429, H432
Varnhem 437
Västerås HR449
Vaxholm 402
Växjö 417-8, HR421
Visby 404-5, H406, R407
Visingö Island 438-9

Ystad 412, H421